BRINGING CHILDREN & YOUTH INTO CANADIAN HISTORY

BRINGING CHILDREN & YOUTH INTO CANADIAN HISTORY

The Difference Kids Make

Edited by **Mona Gleason** and **Tamara Myers**

OXFORD

UNIVERSITY PRESS

OXFORD
UNIVERSITY PRESS

Oxford University Press is a department of the University of Oxford.
It furthers the University's objective of excellence in research, scholarship,
and education by publishing worldwide. Oxford is a registered trade mark of
Oxford University Press in the UK and in certain other countries.

Published in Canada by
Oxford University Press
8 Sampson Mews, Suite 204,
Don Mills, Ontario M3C 0H5 Canada

www.oupcanada.com

Library and Archives Canada Cataloguing in Publication

Bringing children and youth into Canadian history : the difference kids
make / edited by Mona Gleason and Tamara Myers.

Includes index.
ISBN 978-0-19-902448-3 (paperback)

1. Children—Canada—History—Textbooks. 2. Children—Canada—Social
conditions—Textbooks. 3. Canada—History—Textbooks. I. Gleason, Mona,
1964–, editor II. Myers, Tamara, 1964–, editor

HQ792.C3B7 2016   305.230971   C2016-905043-2

Cover image: Joan Latchford

CONTENTS

Chapter 4   Gender and Childhood   141

Chapter 5   Endangered and Dangerous Children and Youth   171

Chapter 6   Children and War   210

Chapter 7   Regulation and Children's Embodiment   249

Chapter 8   Challenging "Normal"   286

Chapter 9   Residential Schooling Reconsidered   327

We are fortunate to stand on the shoulders of two exceptional scholars of childhood, Neil Sutherland and Veronica Strong-Boag, and it is to them that we dedicate this book.

A NOTE TO STUDENTS: HOW TO GET THE MOST FROM THIS READER

This reader is intended to help you, the student, engage with the past, regardless of your level of history knowledge. Not only will you get a good sense of the major themes in the history of children and youth, you will be able to try your hand at thinking historically, and doing historical research. Each chapter presents a different issue related to growing up in Canada that will introduce you to a time period and how young people's actions, status, or symbolic meaning were understood. The primary documents that accompany each essay provide examples of the kinds of sources historians work with. We encourage you to consider how the history you read about in the chapters is reflected (or not) in the accompanying primary sources.

Recognizing that studying history is not always easy or straightforward, we've designed this book with several features to help you become more engaged as you read through the essays.

- **Timeline.** At the beginning of the book, we include a timeline to help you understand when some of the major events in the history of children and youth in Canada happened. When you are reading the thematic chapters, you can plot the history you are reading about along this broader timeline.
- **Chapter Introductions.** Each thematic chapter has an editors' introduction written specifically with students in mind. These help place the individual essays into a broader historical context and they provide a brief overview of the main points made by the authors. We wrote the chapter introductions with an important question in mind: "Why are these essays important in the history of children and youth"?
- **Primary Documents.** Each essay has an accompanying primary document chosen by the essay's author(s). The documents allow students to get a sense of the range of materials available to those writing young people's history. Think about how historians interpret—or use—sources in their historical sleuthing.
- **Study Questions.** Our study questions encourage students to read deeply and to develop their critical thinking skills. They indicate what is important about each essay and allow you to focus on key issues and concepts. Some questions include ideas about other related resources, like films or websites, that you might find useful.
- **Selected Bibliography.** Historical knowledge about children and youth in Canada is a growing field and we wanted students to have more resources at their fingertips. Our bibliographies strike a balance between classic work in the field and newer studies around any particular subject. If you are interested in reading more, the selected bibliography (along with footnotes through the book) can point to fruitful resources.

We hope that as you use this reader, you will develop a sense of the important difference that young people have made to the history of Canada. Our goal in putting this volume together was to "spread the word" about the history of children and youth not only in the Canadian context but around the world. Finally, we encourage you to think of your own childhood experiences as you read the chapters in this book. Where do you fit in to the history of children and youth in Canada? What experiences do you share with the young people you will meet in the pages to come? How are your generation and your circumstances different?

ACKNOWLEDGEMENTS

Without our contributors who have laboured in the history of children and youth, this volume would not have been possible. Their outstanding scholarship, assembled in this collection, gives life to a branch of history that is no longer in its infancy. That children and youth make a difference to Canada's past is clear and demonstrated in the powerful work highlighted here. For their patience and belief in our collective efforts, we are grateful. We are also delighted and amazed by the good humour and energy they put into building this sub-field of history. We would also like to offer our very sincere thanks to the editors and reviewers who have assisted in the production of the book, particularly Jodi Lewchuk and Tamara Capar, at Oxford University Press. Tara Tovell provided outstanding copyediting assistance and we are grateful for her expertise. We continue to value the enthusiastic support and hard work from Oxford University Press. They recognized in this collection what we did—an excellent opportunity to showcase the maturing field of the history of children and youth in Canada and to provide a rich teaching resource. We also acknowledge the various publishers who gave us permission to reprint articles here. And for their support of, and interest in, the work that we do, we are grateful for our colleagues in the Department of Educational Studies (Mona) and the History Department (Tamara) at the University of British Columbia.

As always, our families, John, Helen, and Nick (Tamara) and Eric, Sophie, and Will (Mona) encourage and sustain us. And they inspire us to do this work.

Mona Gleason
Tamara Myers

CONTRIBUTORS

Kristine Alexander holds the Canada Research Chair in Child and Youth Studies at the University of Lethbridge, where she is also an assistant professor of history and director of the Institute for Child and Youth Studies. Her scholarship focuses on young people, colonialism, and war in the early twentieth century. Her publications include studies of Canadian girls and the First World War, summer camps across the British Empire, the imperial and international history of the Girl Guide movement, and the epistemological and methodological challenges involved in doing archival research on childhood.

Bettina Bradbury has retired from the Departments of History and Gender, Sexuality and Women's Studies at York University in Toronto and now lives in New Zealand. Her current research into issues of inheritance in nineteenth-century British settler colonies builds on her study of the legal, social, and cultural aspects of marriage and widowhood in her most recent book, *Wife to Widow. Lives, Laws and Politics in Nineteenth-Century Montreal* (Vancouver: UBC Press, 2011).

Tarah Brookfield is an associate professor of history and youth and children's studies on the Brantford campus of Wilfrid Laurier University. She is the author of *Cold War Comforts: Canadian Women, Child Safety, and Global Insecurity* (Wilfrid Laurier University Press, 2012). She has also published book chapters and articles about Canadian women's war resistance and participation in wars, children's fear of nuclear war, and the history of orphanages and adoption. Her latest projects are a history of the Grindstone Island's Peace Institute and revisiting the history of women's suffrage in Ontario.

R. Blake Brown is an associate professor of history and Atlantic Canada studies at Saint Mary's University. He is the author of *Arming and Disarming: A History of Gun Control in Canada* (University of Toronto Press, 2012), and *A Trying Question: The Jury in Nineteenth-Century Canada* (University of Toronto Press, 2009). His current research examines the history of medical malpractice law in Canada.

John Bullen (1952–1989) was a pioneer in the history of children, labour, and social welfare. He graduated with a PhD from the University of Ottawa, where he taught undergraduate courses in Canadian History. He also taught at Erindale College and McGill University.

While a teacher at the Labour College of Canada, John worked with trade unionists who had little academic background. His published work explored the lives of labouring children in Canada over the nineteenth century and he was committed to producing historical work that furthered the interests of social justice.

Nic Clarke is the assistant historian, First World War, at the Canadian War Museum. He completed his doctorate in Canadian history at the University of Ottawa in 2009. His research focused on disability and health in Canada and the Canadian military during the Great War period. Nic's book, *Unwanted Warriors: The Rejected Volunteers of the Canadian Expeditionary Force*, was published in October 2015. *Unwanted Warriors* is the first study to provide a detailed description of the evolution of physical standards for service and the increasingly complex categories of fitness developed by Canadian military authorities as the war continued. In addition to his work on the First World War, Nic has also published articles on the treatment of people with disabilities in late-nineteenth- and early-twentieth-century Canada.

Tim Cook is a historian at the Canadian War Museum, an adjunct research professor at Carleton University, and a former director for Canada's History Society. He was the curator for the First World War permanent gallery at the CWM and has curated additional temporary, travelling, and digital exhibitions. He is the author of 8 books and over 50 academic articles. He is a member of the Order of Canada.

Sarah de Leeuw (UNBC and UBC), a human geographer and a creative writer, is an associate professor in the Northern Medical Program, part of UBC's distributed Faculty of Medicine. Her work, which often focuses on intimate geographies and creative or artistic practices, considers colonialism and disparities between Indigenous and non-Indigenous peoples, especially in British Columbia. Along with a new book of poetry (*Skeena*, Caitlin Press, 2015) de Leeuw recently co-edited *Determinants of Indigenous Peoples' Health in Canada: Beyond the Social* (Canadian Scholars Press, 2015). She is currently a Michael Smith Foundation for Health Research Scholar and a Research Associate with the National Collaborating Centre for Aboriginal Health.

Magda Fahrni is an associate professor in the Department of History at the Université du Québec à Montréal. She is the author of *Household Politics: Montreal Families* *and Postwar Reconstruction* (University of Toronto Press, 2005, awarded the Canadian Historical Association's Clio-Québec Prize in 2006); the co-author of the 3rd edition of *Canadian Women: A History* (Nelson, 2011); and the co-editor, with Esyllt Jones, of *Epidemic Encounters: Influenza, Society, and Culture in Canada, 1918–20* (UBC Press, 2012) and, with Robert Rutherdale, of *Creating Postwar Canada: Community, Diversity, and Dissent, 1945–75* (UBC Press, 2008). She is currently writing a history of risk and accidents in turn-of-the-twentieth-century Montreal and a history of families in Canada from New France to the present.

Sarah Glassford teaches in the Department of History at the University of New Brunswick. Her book *From Battlefields to Blood: The Canadian Red Cross Society, 1885–1970* is forthcoming from McGill-Queen's University Press in 2016. Her research on the senior Red Cross sparked an interest in its popular children's wing, the Junior Red Cross, which has since blossomed into an interest in "the difference kids make" in history more broadly. She is co-editor of the Canada's First World War series on ActiveHistory.ca, and is currently researching rural Canadian women's war work during the First World War as well as continuing to explore the evolution of the mid-twentieth-century Junior Red Cross.

Mona Gleason teaches in the Department of Educational Studies at the University of British Columbia. She is the author of *Small Matters: Canadian Children in Sickness and Health* (McGill-Queen's University Press, 2013) and *Normalizing the Ideal: Psychology, Schooling and the Family in Postwar Canada* (University of Toronto Press, 1999). Her co-edited collections include *Rethinking Canada: The Promise of Women's History*, 4th, 5th, and 6th editions; *Lost Kids: Vulnerable Children and Youth in Twentieth-Century Canada and the United States* (UBC Press, 2010); and *Children, Teachers, and Schools in the History of British Columbia* (Detselig, 2003). Articles based on her more recent work have appeared in *Childhood: A Global Journal* and *History of Education Quarterly*. With Penney Clark, she is co-editor of *Historical Studies in Education/Revue d'histoire de l'éducation*. Her latest research, funded by a Spencer Foundation grant, explores children's schooling in remote rural locations in interwar British Columbia.

Jessica Haynes has a PhD in Canadian history from Carleton University. Her doctoral thesis explored the impact of the birth-control pill on married women in English Canada, from 1960 to 1980. This topic intersects with her broader research interests in women's history,

social history, and medical history. An article based on her master's thesis, examining child-rearing advice to Canadian parents in the 1960s and 1970s, was published in *Histoire sociale/Social History* in 2011. She currently works for Global Affairs Canada.

Rhonda L. Hinther teaches Canadian and public history at Brandon University. She is the co-editor (with Jim Mochoruk) of *Re-imagining Ukrainian Canadians: History, Politics, and Identity* (University of Toronto Press, 2011), and the author of *Perogies and Politics: Radical Ukrainians in Canada, 1991–1991* (University of Toronto Press, 2016). She is also co-editor (with Karen Busby) of University of Manitoba Press's Human Rights and Social Justice series. Her current research focuses on familial and community responses to the internment of leftists in Canada during the Second World War.

Barbara Lorenzkowski is an associate professor in the Department of History at Concordia University. She is the author of *Sounds of Ethnicity: Listening to German North America* (University of Manitoba Press, 2010) and has published several book chapters and articles on the history of migration and trans-nationalism. Her current research explores the social spaces of childhood in Atlantic Canada during the Second World War. Based on around 90 oral history interviews, this project examines the small spaces of childhood, children's mobility in the city, and children's sensuous geographies in the wartime city.

Linda Mahood teaches in the history department at the University of Guelph. She is author of *The Magdalenes* (Routledge, 1990, 2012), *Policing Gender, Class, and Family*, (UCL, 1996), and *Feminism and Voluntary Action*, (Palgrave, 2010), and co-editor of *Social Control in Canada* (Oxford, 1999). She has published numerous articles on the social histories of gender, sexuality, and youth and child welfare. Her current research is on baby boom youth culture rituals, notably hitchhiking and youth hostelling.

Heidi MacDonald is an associate professor and past chair in the Department of History at the University of Lethbridge. She has two areas of research: 1930s Canadian youth transitioning to adulthood, and religious women (nuns) in Atlantic Canada since the 1960s. Her publications have appeared in *Acadiensis: Journal of Atlantic Canada*; *Histoire sociale/Social History*; and the *Canadian Journal of Sociology*, as well as in several edited collections.

Ian Mosby is currently a postdoctoral fellow at McMaster University's L.R. Wilson Institute for Canadian History.

His first book, *Food Will Win the War: The Politics, Culture and Science of Food on Canada's Home Front* (UBC Press, 2014) was awarded the Canadian Historical Association's 2015 Political History Book Prize. Mosby's recent research, uncovering a series of government-sponsored nutrition experiments conducted primarily on children attending Canada's notorious Indian residential schools, received widespread national and international media attention. This research has since been the subject of articles in publications ranging from *Nature* and the *Canadian Medical Association Journal* to the *Washington Post* and the *Literary Review of Canada*.

Roderick MacLeod is an independent researcher specializing in the history of the Anglo-Protestant population of Quebec, particularly education. An ongoing research project with historian Mary Anne Poutanen resulted in *A Meeting of the People: School Boards and Protestant Communities in Quebec, 1801–1998* (McGill-Queen's University Press, 2004) and several studies on the experience of Jews within Quebec's Protestant school system, including an online graphic novel (*Kids on Strike at Montreal's Aberdeen School, 1913*) in English, French, and Yiddish. He has also served as a historical consultant on public history projects aimed at engaging children and youth, including "Mapping the Mosaic" (Quebec Anglophone Heritage Network, 2012) and "Island of Stories" (Quebec Federation of Home and School Associations, 2013).

Tamara Myers is an associate professor in the history department at University of British Columbia. She is the author of *Caught: Montreal's Modern Girls and the Law, 1869–1945*, co-editor of *Rethinking Canada: The Promise of Women's History*, 6th and 7th editions, and is a member of the research collective The Montreal History Group. She is currently working on two research projects involving the history of children and youth: one on the Miles for Millions walkathons (about youth activism and global consciousness) and the other a cultural history of policing children in mid-twentieth-century North America. Her recent work has appeared in *Diplomatic History*, the *Journal of the History of Children and Youth*, and the *Journal of the Canadian Historical Association*.

Jane Nicholas teaches in the Department of Sexuality, Marriage, and Family Studies at St. Jerome's University in the University of Waterloo. She is the author of *The Modern Girl: Feminine Modernities, the Body, and Commodities in the 1920s*, and the co-editor of *Feminist Pedagogy in Higher Education: Critical Theory and Practice* (with Tracy Penny Light and Renee Bondy) and *Contesting Bodies and Nation in Canadian History* (with Patrizia Gentile). She is currently revising a book manuscript on the history of the freak show in Canada for publication.

E. Lisa Panayotidis is a professor in the Werklund School of Education at the University of Calgary. Her main research interest focuses on late–nineteenth- and early–twentieth-century visual culture and notions of spatiality and the body in higher education contexts. With Paul Stortz she is co-editor of *Women in Higher Education: 1850–1970: International Perspectives* (Routledge, 2015); *Cultures, Communities, and Conflict: Histories of Canadian Universities and War* (UTP, 2012); and *Historical Identities: The Professoriate in Canada* (UTP, 2006). Funded by an SSHRC Insight Grant, she investigates how Canadian university campuses between 1850 and 1950 have spatially shaped the identities, subjectivities, and representations of their various dwellers.

Mary Anne Poutanen teaches in the Programme d'Études sur le Québec and at the McGill Institute for the Study of Canada at McGill University. She is a member of the Montreal History Group and of the Centre de recherches interdisciplinaires en études montréalaises. Her co-authored graphic novel, *Kids on Strike at Montreal's Aberdeen School, 1913* appears in English on the website www.cjhn.ca/wpp-images/JPLA/EducationKits/KidsOnStrike.pdf and has been translated into French and Yiddish. Her present research project focuses on a student strike at the Baron Byng High School in 1934.

Paul Stortz is an associate professor in the department of history at the University of Calgary. He teaches philosophy of history, history of education, cultural theory, and history of multiculturalism, race, and gender in twentieth-century Canada. His research interests, currently funded by an SSHRC Insight Grant, are in the history of higher education, focusing on the professoriate and academic and intellectual cultures. With E. Lisa Panayotidis, he is co-editor of *Women in Higher Education: 1850–1970: International Perspectives* (Routledge, 2015); *Cultures, Communities, and Conflict: Histories of Canadian Universities and War* (UTP, 2012); and *Historical Identities: The Professoriate in Canada* (UTP, 2006). He is also editor-in-chief of *History of Intellectual Culture*, a peer-reviewed international open-access journal.

TIMELINE OF EVENTS IN CHILD AND YOUTH HISTORY

1620 > Missionaries from France began laying the groundwork for the residential school system.

1685 > Govenor Brisay de Denonville writes about his concern that boys in New France were being corrupted by too much hunting and trading.

1722 > Intendant's ordinance issues tax revenue for the care of *enfants du Roi* and penalizes concealing pregnancies and giving children to Amerindians.

1779 > Orphans Act, Upper Canada

1822 > Montreal General Hospital opens children's ward.

1827 > Guardianship Act, Upper Canada

1849 > Toronto Protestant Orphans' Home established.

1851 > Apprentices and Minors Act of 1851, Upper Canada

1866 > Halifax establishes an industrial school for boys.

1867 > Canadian Federal Government sponsors two residential schools established pre-Confederation, Ontario.

> Sacred Heart School at Fort Providence (NWT) established.

1871 > Compulsory education achieved at elementary level in Ontario.

> Twenty-three orphanages in operation in Canada.

1873 > Augustine Shingwauk, an Objibway leader, helps establish the Shingwuak Home boarding school.

1875 > Criminal Procedures Act amended to allow courts to sentence offenders as old as 16 to provincial reformatories instead of penitentiaries.

> Infants' Home founded in Toronto.

> Mount Allison becomes the first university in the British Empire to issue a degree to a woman.

1877 > Industrial Schools Act, ON

1878 > Andrew Mercer Ontariio Reformatory for Females established.

1879 > J.W. Langmuir's recommendations lead to more reform options for girls under 14 at the Andrew Mercer Reformatory in Ontario.

1882 > Dr Thomas J. Barnardo initiates sponsorships of thousands of children to emigrate to Canada.

1883 > Sir John A. Macdonald (prime minister and minister of Indian affairs) authorized the creation of three residential schools for Aboriginal children in modern day Alberta and Saskatchewan.

1884 > Ontario Factory Act restricts age and hours of work for children; exempts "family work."

> Ontario legislature passes an act to establish industrial schools for boys under the age of 14.

1885 > Act to Encourage Agricultural Education, Nova Scotia

1887 > Ontario school board formally integrates kindergarten into the public school system.

> Victoria Industrial School established (closes in 1934).

1889 > Toronto Police Commission enacted a by-law requiring street vendors younger than 16 to be licensed by the police.

1890 > Royal Commissiion on the Prison and Reformatory System of Ontario established: particularly concerned with "preventing and curing juvenile delinquency."

1891 > Of all Canadian children between 10 and 14, 13.8 per cent are gainfully employed.

> Children's Aid Society founded in Toronto.

> *Report of the Prison and Reformatory System*, Ontario recommends that curfews be implemented to curb juvenile delinquency.

> Total enrolment in publicly controlled elementary and secondary schools is 942,500.

1893 > Act for the Protection and Reformation of Neglected Children, Ontario.

1894 > First Ontario Conference on Child-Saving

1896 > Vancouver Ladies Hockey Club formed.

 > Ontario legislation allowing high school boards to promote military instruction for boys.

1900 > *Sex and Self* series published.

1901 > J.J. Kelso helps secure the establishment of 30 Children's Aid societies in Ontario.

 > Milk Depot established in Montreal; Goutte de lait clinics open across the province.

1904 > Ontario closes its Reformatory for Boys at Penetangishene.

 > G. Stanley Hall's *Adolescence: Its Psychology and Its relation to Physiology, Anthropolocy, Sociology, Sex, Crime, Religion, and Education* published.

1906 > Montreal municipal board of health supports the first systematic medical inspection of school pupils in Canada.

1907 > Vancouver Juvenile Protective Association established by Vancouver citizens.

 > Montreal's Sainte-Justine Hospital founded in an attempt to combat infant mortality.

1908 > Juvenile Delinquents Act

1909 > Strathcona Fund established by British high commissioner to Canada, Sir Donald Gordon Smith, Lord Strathcona.

 > Boy Scouts established in Canada.

 > Winnipeg opens the first juvenile court in Canada under the Juvenile Delinquents Act.

1910 > Boy Scouts' sister organization, Olave, established

1911 > All provinces able to receive funds from the Strathcona Trust and the federal government for physical education in schools.

 > Industrial Education Act, Ontario

1912 > Montreal holds a child welfare exhibition.

 > Montreal Juvenile Delinquents' Court opened.

1913 > Big Brothers Association established in Toronto.

 > Children's Protection Act; Ontario, restricting age a child could engage in any street trade or occupation.

 > *Winnipeg Free Press* publishes 64 articles condemning bilingual education.

1914 > Big Sisters Association established in Toronto.

 > Eight supervised playgrounds in Torono, compared to none in 1909.

 > First National committee on Boys' Work formed.

 > Junior Farmers' clubs established in Ontario.

1915 > First child health centre opened in Toronto by Dr Charles Hastings.

 > Dr Helen MacMurchy appointed Ontario's first inspector of the feeble-minded.

1916 > 30 June: "Better Schools Day" in Saskatchewan, part of a drive for overall education reform in the province.

1918 > Montreal Board of Health organizes a separate division of child hygiene for Montreal schools.

 > Dr C.K. Clarke helps to organize the Canadian National Committee for Mental Hygiene.

 > Child Welfare Association of British Columbia formed.

1919 > Adolescent School Attendance Act, Ontario

 > Act for the Promotion of Technical Education in Canada

1920 > British Columbia adopts one of the most comprehensive mothers' pensions programs in North America.

1921 > Ontario Parents Maintenance Act; requires that children help support their families.

> Of all Canadian children between the ages of 10 and 14, 3.2 per cent are gainfully employed.

> Children of Unmarried Parents Act

> Night Employment of Young Persons Act, BC

> From 1921 to 1923, the federal health department distributes 220,000 copies of Helen MacMurchy's *The Canadian Mother's Book*.

1922 > Canadian Society for the Study of Diseases of Children established.

> The Empire Settlement Act

> *Handbook of Child Welfare in Canada*, by Dr Helen MacMurchy, published.

1923 > Total enrolment in publicly controlled elementary and secondary schools reaches 1,939,700.

> Junior Red Cross clubs established in the early 1920s in Canada, enrolling 75,000 children by 1923.

1924 > *Declaration of the Rights of the Child* endorsed by the League of Nations.

> Marriage Act amended in Saskatchewan and Alberta to prohibit marriage under the age of 15 and require consent for those under 18.

1927 > Publication of the White List of appropriate films for non-adults by the Canadian Council on Child and Family Welfare.

> Ontario Minors' Protection Act

> Nova Scotia Training School for Mentally Retarded Children established.

1928 > Ontario Apprenticeship Act

> The Life and Health Sanitarium—Where the Sick Get Well established (later known as the Ideal Maternity Home and Sanitarium).

1929 > Juvenile Delinquents Act amended.

1931 > Canadian branches of Easter Seals launch public campaign about the pasteurization of milk to prevent the spread of tuberculosis.

1932 > *The End of the Road*, film produced by the Social Hygiene Council of Canada, "one of the most powerful and graphic educational pictures ever to be filmed."

1933 > Christie Pits riot, Toronto

1936 > Needy Mothers Assistance Fund, Montreal

1937 > Ontario Society for Crippled Children founded.

> Junior G-Men of Canada founded (Vancouver).

> Dominion–Provincial Youth Training Programme launched by King government.

> Easter Seals opened the first camp for children with physical disabilities.

1940 > Maternity Boarding House Act, Nova Scotia

> King government establishes the Canadian Youth Commission.

1942 > Canadian Youth Congress declared illegal under the Defence of Canada Regulations

> Montreal curfew bylaw passed.

1943 > Compulsory school law introduced in Quebec.

> Montreal police expose baby farms, illegal operations where custody of babies was surrendered for payment.

> National Physical Fitness Act

1944 > Mackenzie King's speech promises social security from birth to death.

> First Canadian Teen Town established in Penticton, BC

> The Committee on Public Welfare establishes a Special Committee on Juvenile Delinquency, Toronto.

> City Council in Toronto invokes the Children's Protection Act in an attempt to deal with concerns about youth activity at night.

> Toronto Board of Education includes venereal diseases education in Ontario curriculum for grades 10 and 12.

1945 > Ideal Maternity House is ordered to be closed (but William and Lila Young continue to fight for their business).

> First appearance of teen advice column "If You Take My Advice," by Mary Starr, in the *Toronto Star*.

1946 > Day Nurseries Act

> Youth employment centre prototype established in Toronto.

> RCMP begins working with local police forces in support of local Kiwanis boys clubs in Ontario.

1947 > Montreal police force establishes Police Juvenile Clubs.

1949 > Welfare Council Youth Services, Toronto, subcommittee on gangs alerts the public about the severity of the gang problem.

> Federal government agrees to provide funding to the British Columbia school board for the education of Aboriginal students.

> Bill 10 amended section 207 of the Criminal Code to broadly and vaguely include crime comics in the same category as obscene literature.

1950 > *A Date with Your Family*, popular educational film for adolescents

> Ontario Royal Commission on Education argues that masculine virtues such as duty, loyalty, courage, endurance, and discipline are key to building a strong post-war society.

> Publication of *Childhood and Society*, by Erik Erikson.

1951 > First National Conference on the Rehabilitation of the Physically Disabled

1952 > Senate Special Committee on Salacious and Indecent Literature

1953 > Northern Affairs and National Resources established: end of missionary control over Aboriginal education.

1955 > UNICEF boxes introduced on Halloween, carried by trick-or-treating children.

> Department of Northern Affairs and National Resources expands residential school system even as the federal government is working toward closing schools in southern Canada.

> Toronto women establish the Parents' Action League to combat so-called sex crime.

1957 > Ottawa convent school expels eight students for attending an Elvis Presley concert.

> Ontario opens Canada's first mental hospital for children.

> Financial reform of residential school funding: end of the "per-capita" system and implementation of a more "businesslike" plan.

> Thistletown Regional Centre, the first institution for children and youth suffering from mental illness, opened near Toronto.

1958 > Completion of A. Lenore Schwalbe's "Negro and partly-Negro wards of the Children's Aid Society of Metropolitan Toronto" (MSW Thesis, University of Toronto, 1958).

> Social Planning Council of Metropolitan Toronto conducts research into five of the city's six maternity homes for unwed mothers.

1959 > Declaration of the Rights of the Child adopted by the United Nations.

1961 > Bill C-131 passed; federal government agrees to "encourage, promote, and develop fitness and amateur sport in Canada."

1962 > Federal minister of justice established a Committee on Juvenile Delinquency

1965 > A Five-Year Education Plan for the Northwest Territories and Northern Quebec—1965–70

1966 > Canada Assistance Plan passed.

1970 > Royal Commission on the Status of Women established.

1971 > Corporal punishment abolished by Toronto School Board.

1973 > The International Labour Organization passes Convention 138 on Minimum Age for Admission to Employment. Canada has yet to sign.

1974 > First Nations women campaign against transracial adoption.

1976 > Coalition of Provincial Organizations of the Handicapped and the Autism Society of Canada formed.

1981 > Canadian Association for the Advancement of Women and Sport (CAAWS) established.

1984 > Young Offenders Act replaces the Juvenile Delinquents Act.

1986 > Canadian Supreme Court requires mentally handicapped girl's consent for sterilization.

1988 > Ideal Maternity Home and Sanitarium scandal uncovered in Nova Scotia.

1990 > Phil Fontaine, Grand Chief of the Assembly of Manitoba Chiefs, calls for a national inquiry into the residential school system.

1991 > First National Conference on Residential Schools

2003 > Youth Criminal Justice Act replaces the Young Offenders Act.

2004 > Proposed juvenile curfew in Montreal sparks protests.

2006 > Indian Residential Schools Settlement Agreement

Introduction

MONA GLEASON AND TAMARA MYERS

The least powerful in our society often leave little trace of their lives. This was especially true of children, and of childhood more generally, prior to the digital age. A child's birth and death might be recorded; an exceptional feat or tragedy might make headlines in a local newspaper; the paraphernalia of childhood activities (songs, toys, pledges, games, artwork) might be kept or remembered; and in modern Canada, their compulsory attendance at school might be duly recorded. Even with the popularization of photography, we are left with small fragments of a life and often more questions than answers. The image above, for example, captures a moment in these children's lives. Who are they? What are they doing and why? What meanings can we draw about childhood from this candid shot? How can we use this remnant of their childhood experience to tell their stories? What does it say about the larger society in which they lived? Can we write a history of life's most fleeting stage?

This photo is one of more than a thousand taken by Toronto photographer Joan Latch-ford in the late 1960s of a gruelling one-day, marathon-distance fundraiser known as the Miles for Millions.[1] Although Latchford did not provide details regarding the individual lives of the children in this image, she created an astonishing pictorial archive of children and youth that invites our analysis. We know from newspapers that this walkathon was enormously popular among elementary and high school students.[2] From Latchford's pictures, such as the one included here, we can see that kids at a fairly young age walked without parents or obvious supervision. And despite initial enthusiasms, the photographic record suggests that it was not an easy or entirely enjoyable effort. From the litter scattered on the ground we can imagine that a great number of youth had already come through this location and that a different sensibility from our own existed about trash! We might assume that the foregrounded children are siblings and that the sister, in holding her brother's hand tightly, was responsible for him. Behind them are throngs of teenagers. The image reveals therefore an age and racial diversity in the walkathon efforts, and perhaps in 1960s student activism in general. What we don't know is who these children are, how far they walked, how much money they raised, and what it meant to them.

Although children and childhood pose seemingly insurmountable challenges to history, historians are undaunted. For several decades, but especially recently, historians have laid the groundwork for a history of children and youth in Canada. We gather evidence about children from adults and read "against the grain," teasing out the fragments of children's experiences and presence in sources. This practice, employed by women's and post-colonial historians, involves reinterpreting documents created by the powerful (in our case, adults) for what they can tell us about the marginalized or powerless (children). And whenever possible, we think creatively about what evidence children leave behind and how to evaluate it. We also turn our attention to the question, What are some of the major ways that young people have contributed to historical change in Canada?

***

This thematically organized collection of histories on children and youth illuminates the importance of young people to the making of modern Canada. It is also possible, of course, to consider the contributions of young people to historical change in more traditional, temporal terms. In the late nineteenth century, British North America was radically reinvented from a series of colonies into a new Dominion. Accompanying this political innovation, industrialization, immigration, and urbanization transformed the nature of the country and the way that people lived. Following Confederation in 1867, politicians in Ottawa set about nation-building; this feat was in part a state-formation exercise, requiring new forms of democratic rule and institutions, but it was also an aggressive project of occupying the vast geography that lay between three oceans, one that demanded the recruitment of new populations and the dispossession of Indigenous peoples considered to be in the way of progress. By the turn of the century, leaders of the Dominion of Canada boasted a bright future for this young country, proclaiming the cities of Montreal and Toronto as its industrial heart, the Prairies as its breadbasket, and the transcontinental railway as its spine. These political, economic, social, and cultural transformations that made Canada modern simultaneously shaped childhood and were shaped by youth. The National Policy—focused on settling the West, industrialization, and population growth—didn't ignore children; they were central to its success. Children, as historians of childhood assert, are the "missing link" in this history: young people lie at the heart of the modern nation-state's development.[3]

The emergence of childhood as a discrete life-cycle stage predates Canada's emergence as an independent country, but nation-building had everything to do with children as malleable subjects. For example, in order to foster a new generation of citizens wed to the new nation, governments established schools where "Canadian" values would be learned and would over-ride other influences on the younger generations. When Canadian politicians and elites em-barked on the colonial project to rid the fertile west of Indigenous peoples, it targeted youth, desiring to acculturate Aboriginal peoples by removing children to residential schools. Cana-da's industrial engine was predicated on resource extraction and cheap labour: from the earliest industrial developments, children and youth gave their labour power to this economic revolu-tion. As concerned citizens, known as reformers, decried the poor state of children brutalized by industrial society, policy-makers expanded their reach by setting up new systems of welfare and governance to protect and police the nation's youth.

If childhood was central to the making of modern Canada in the late nineteenth and early twentieth centuries, adolescence would gain social and political prominence by the 1910s and 1920s. Increasingly compulsory schooling and protective labour legislation stretched childhood (as a dependent state) to around 12 years of age. Adolescents—whom experts at the turn of the century demarcated into a separate age category—often worked for wages but increasingly spent their teen years in the nation's high schools. They also contrib-uted to modern popular culture as both consumers and producers: in throngs they embraced new leisure pursuits—dancing, movie-going, sports, and clubs.[4] And as young people they, like their younger brothers and sisters, were perceived as representing the nation's future. Given the high stakes for both the nation and its young, modern states like Canada fixated on young people's moral lives and the rights they ought to embrace. Over the course of the twentieth century, adolescents became involved both intellectually and physically in adult spheres, especially at times of war and over issues like humanitarianism and peace. This came in the form of conformity and nationalism on the one hand and acts of resistance on the other. For Canadians, being modern meant paying attention to age.

Our decision to study and create a history of children and youth comes from an interest in and commitment to historical work, but it also speaks directly to the place of children in our own society. If current obsessions over youth are any indication, children and adolescents, es-pecially their well-being and endangerment, are central to contemporary life and politics. From widespread sexual and physical abuse, to the demobilization of children from soldiering in wars around the world, to dramatic and extreme parenting trends, it appears that the kids aren't, in fact, all right. Or at least that kids today make for an anxious adult world.[5] In 2014, two advo-cates for the rights and safety of children and young people won the Nobel Peace Prize. Kailash Satyarthi is credited with saving over 80,000 children from forced labour, and Malala Yousafzai, the youngest recipient in the history of the prize, remains a strong and vocal advocate for girls' education, having survived the brutal Taliban attempts on her life in her native Pakistan.[6] The recognition of their efforts is, of course, a significant indicator of the value placed on the young in our contemporary world. This recognition, nevertheless, also brings into sharp relief the depths of hardship and misery that continue to be the lot of many children around the world. In this book, we connect contemporary concerns, treatment, and experiences of childhood and adolescence with the past, illuminating both continuities and ruptures.

Turning to contemporary Canada, we might ask, What do we know about children to-day and what can that information tell us about childhood? Statistical information provides us with a useful place to start. In 2013, Statistics Canada reported that the total population of the country had reached 35,158,304 people. Young people between the ages of 0 and 19 years of age numbered 7,853,129, representing almost one quarter of the total population.[7] Female children made up just less than half of this total number.[8] The population of Canada is nevertheless aging rapidly. In 2011, 14.4 per cent of the population was 65 years of age or older. By the year 2021, Employment and Social Development Canada projects this percentage to rise to 18.5 per cent and, by 2031, to 23 per cent.[9] In 2001, those aged 0 to 19 in Canada numbered 7,778,865 out of a total population of 30,007,090, or 30 per cent, while in 1976, young people 0 to 19 numbered 8,341,000 out of a total population of 22,993,000, or 36 per cent.[10] In comparison to the post-war baby boom years, this downturn is even more significant. In 1956, for example, young people aged 0 to 19 numbered 6,388,000 out of a total population of 16,081,000, representing close to 40 per cent of the population of the country at that time.[11] Across the country, median age varies considerably. In 2013, Newfoundland and Labrador had the highest median age in Canada, at 44.2 years, and Nova Scotia was home to the highest proportion of seniors, at 17.7 per cent, and the lowest share of people under the age of 19 years (14.3 per cent). Nunavut had the youngest population in the country, with close to 31 per cent of its population under the age of 15 years.[12] Aboriginal children continue to be a growing proportion of all children in Canada. In 2006, for example, 20 per cent of all children in the country were Aboriginal.[13] Of the immigrant population who came to Canada in the last five years, 19.2 per cent were children aged 14 and younger (mostly from Asia, followed by Africa, the Caribbean, and Central and South America). Another 14.5 per cent of this newcomer population was between the ages of 15 and 24.[14]

Despite these significant numbers, the total overall population of young people in Canada has nevertheless declined over time. What has remained constant, or perhaps even increased, however, is concern on the part of adults over the status of the young. Even a cursory survey of the recent popular headlines and scholarly studies suggests that young people remain firmly on the radar.[15]

In 2011, the Organisation for Economic Co-operation and Development (OECD) released its "Better Life Initiative," comparing information for 36 countries, including Canada, across 11 dimensions that it deemed "essential to well being, from health and education, to local environment, personal security and overall satisfaction with life, as well as traditional measures such as income."[16] Across all dimensions, Canada scored extremely high, suggesting that it is a remarkably positive place in which to grow up. In data generated in 2013 by the Canadian Institute for Health Information comparing Canada and other OECD countries, Canada performed well on most measures of health behaviours in young people, particularly in terms of access to nutritious food and on perceived health status (i.e., self-reporting on personal feelings of healthfulness).[17] In the realm of education, the recent OECD Programme for International Student Assessment (PISA) comparisons of achievement in mathematics, reading, and science among 15-year-olds found that Canadian youth ranked consistently in the top 5 to 7 per cent in each subject area.[18]

In other respects, however, concern over young people in Canada is justified. Child poverty is a serious issue in Canada and one that continues to be largely ignored by those in positions of power.[19] It is an issue shaped not only by class but by race. Compared to non-Aboriginal children, a greater proportion of young Aboriginal children were living in low-income families in 2006. This is particularly true in urban centres across the country where "over half (57%) of First Nations children in census metropolitan areas (CMAs) were living in low-income families, as were 45% of Inuit children and 42% of Métis children. This is compared to 21% of non-Aboriginal children in CMAs."[20] The fact of Canada's racist present (and equally racist past) adds to these and other challenges faced by Aboriginal youth. In a 2008 roundtable report focused on issues most salient to enhancing the lives of young people in Aboriginal communities, top priorities for positive change that emerged were more culturally informed education, health initiatives that include not only individuals but whole communities, reforms to criminal justice practices, and a reformed partnership between government and Aboriginal communities.[21] Indeed concern for the health standards of children and youth has emerged as a global phenomenon. In 2012, the World Health Organization estimated 1.2 million deaths among adolescents that year, most of them from causes that could have been prevented or treated. Whereas maternal mortality used to be the main cause of death for girls aged 15 to 19 globally, for example, that cause has now been surpassed by suicide.[22]

Along other measures, the outlook is similarly bleak. Despite falling youth crime rates, in 2012 the Canadian federal legislation, Bill C-10, reversed a century of juvenile justice reform. Employing a retrograde strategy to put more young people in jail by expanding both the crimes for which youth could be incarcerated and the length of sentences, this "tough-on-crime" legislation came at a time when police-reported crimes were down to 1973 levels—and many countries were rethinking such an approach to young offenders.[23] This approach is even more cruelly ironic given that young people tend more often to be the victims of crimes, particularly at the hands of those closest to them. While the rate of family violence has decreased slightly in the last decade, it continues to take an inordinate toll on women, girls, and young people in general. In 2014, violence in family settings accounted for just over one quarter of all police-reported violent crime. Half of the just over 85,000 victims of family violence were a current or previous spouse of the accused and nearly one in five were victimized by a parent. Female victims of family violence (56 per cent) were more likely to be victimized by a spouse than male victims (31 per cent). Male victims however, were more likely to be assaulted by a parent (24 per cent) or an extended family member (18 per cent). Men were also more likely to be the perpetrator of violence when compared to female victims (15 per cent and 11 per cent, respectively).

In all categories, victims were overwhelmingly female. According to 2014 Canadian Centre for Justice statistics, females, regardless of age, were at a greater risk of family violence than males. The rate of family violence against females (327.6 per 100,000 population) was double that of males (157.7). The gap between male and female rates of family violence increased with age until age 30 to 34 years, at which point the difference was greatest, with rates of family violence against females (579.4) more than three times that of males (192.3). Spousal violence is most often cited in rates of police-reported family violence among female victims. These victims are most commonly assaulted by a spouse (56 per cent) rather than by other family members.[24]

In 2014, children and youth represented 17 per cent of all victims of police-reported violent crime. Family violence accounted for 31 per cent of these crimes against young people. Female children and youth are more likely to be victims of police-reported family violence.[25] As a recent UNICEF report claimed, violence against children and youth is an international phenomenon that, despite more recent recognition of its pervasive nature and impact, remains largely undocumented and unreported.[26]

The victimization and death of teenaged girls in particular *is*, however, a phenomenon that the media seems eager to report on, if only to sensationalize it for its audience. The cases of Amanda Todd, Serena Vermeersch, and Tina Fontaine in Canada are only the most recent manifestations of this violence against young women and the ensuing obsessive reportage. Todd was 15 years old when she was relentlessly bullied online and sexually exploited by an older man; she took her own life in October 2012 after posting a YouTube video documenting her torment and inability to find meaningful help.[27] Although media reports referred to 17-year-old Serena Vermeersch's murder in Surrey, British Columbia, in September 2014, as a "random attack," it was nothing of the sort. She was victimized by sex offender Raymond Caissie—labelled by the

Canadian Parole Board as at "high risk" to reoffend despite his release from prison in March 2013—because she was young and female.[28]

The body of Tina Fontaine, a 15-year-old member of the Sagkeeng First Nation, was found in the Red River in Winnipeg, Manitoba, on August 17, 2014.[29] Tina was in the care of Manitoba's Child and Family Services when she was reported missing a week before. Her death sparked renewed anger among First Nations and other Canadians who have long called for action in response to the over 1,200 murdered and missing Aboriginal girls and women reported since 1982. Despite widespread demands for a public inquiry on the part of the Assembly of First Nations, the Native Women's Association of Canada, all provincial premiers and territorial leaders, and thousands of Canadian citizens, the then Conservative government, led by Stephen Harper, refused to act. An editorial in *Maclean's* magazine, a national publication typically supportive of the right-wing policies of the Stephen Harper regime, likewise pushed the former prime minister to act, bluntly reminding the government that "as a recent RCMP report showed, [an Aboriginal girl in Canada] is five times more likely than her non-Aboriginal counterpart to meet a violent end at the hands of another."[30] Prime minister Justin Trudeau promised that the Liberal government would act decisively to implement improvements for First Nations communities, including setting up an inquiry into murdered and missing Aboriginal women. While many were hopeful that he would act promptly, it took almost a year for the inquiry to be established.[31]

Overt hostility and violence, careless and intentional disregard, alongside mounting attention to the young, shape not only our present but our past. Canadian historians of childhood and youth provide depth and breadth on issues that we grapple with today, historicizing demographic and institutional change, the transformation of ideal childhoods, and prescribed youthful norms, while searching for evidence of children's experience.

The History of Children and Youth in Canada— Where Have We Been and Where Are We Going?

In this collection of readings, we explore some of the major themes that currently characterize the field of the history of children and youth. These themes include children and work; children and political struggle; gender socialization; the role of danger and the law; war; health, disability, and the body; residential schooling reconsidered; global childhoods; and the making of youth culture. We believe that a thematic approach rather than a more traditional temporal approach enables readers to immediately appreciate the broad range of foci that characterizes this growing field. In addition, a thematic methodology underscores the areas in the field still wide open to historical exploration. The themes, as we suggest in this section, grew out of the field's original association with social history. As we learned more about those typically excluded from traditional historical accounts, such as women, the working class, and people of colour, questions arose about the role of young people. What difference did they make to these histories? Neil Sutherland's 1976 groundbreaking history of the progressive reform impulse to improve the state and status of the nation's children, *Children in English-Canadian Society: Framing the Twentieth Century Consensus*, was arguably the first major study to focus on young people.[32] More generally, interest in the history of children and youth in Canada grew out of the work of historians in related fields such as the history of the family, education, welfare, and delinquency studies.[33] This foundational work helped to establish young people's presence in these, and other, social history themes.[34] This scholarship represented what would come to be known as the first wave of historical work in the field, emphasizing the history of adult attitudes toward childhood. Much of it examined the role of the state and the classist, racist, and gendered assumptions behind child-centred initiatives and child rescue. In particular the treatment of babies and the implementation of government policy on infant health and welfare marked an early and major development of the field and continues to be sustained by those interested in the subject of adoption.[35] The Canadian colonial project, including residential schooling for Indigenous youth, complemented these reformist impulses and was central to the ambition of "rescuing" childhood from poverty and dissipation.[36]

Beginning in the 1980s, valuable edited collections helped to begin to crystallize the field as a unique focus within the broader field of social history. The earlier collections by Joy Parr, Patricia Rooke and R. Schnell, and Russell Smandych, Gordon Dodds, and Alvin Esau, traded on familiar themes of the family economy, schooling, child welfare, and delinquency. Nancy Janovicek and Joy Parr's 2003 collection emphasized adult–child relations and included primary sources generated by adults about children. In 2010, Mona Gleason, Tamara Myers, Leslie Paris, and Veronica Strong-Boag edited a collection of essays devoted to the historical vulnerability of children that more explicitly engaged with the central goal of the second wave of historical writing on young people: to explore their perspectives on, and contributions to, change over time.[37]

This second wave of historical work has been as fruitful as its predecessor. Early work by Joy Parr on child migrants, Jennifer Brown on children born of mixed-race unions in the fur trade era, John Bullen on child workers (included in this volume), Tim Stanley on student strikers, and Lucille Marr on church organizations for youth, encouraged historians to consider age as a significant and revealing category of analysis. In doing so, their scholarship revealed historical agency on the part of young people. Sutherland's second monograph, *Growing Up*, exemplifies another major methodological goal in the development of the field: to locate the experiences and voices of children.[38] Historians have revisited more traditional topic areas and time periods, delving into the experience of war and post-war periods, looking for, and finding, traces of young people.[39] They have also brought attention to young people's experiences in more controversial topic areas, demonstrating that sexuality, bodies, and embodied histories include the young.[40] They have read archival materials, like court records, "against the grain," interviewed adults about their childhoods, and used memoirs, visual culture, and material culture to deepen our understanding of children as both historical subjects and historical actors.[41] Scholars continue to tackle the many opportunities for further research in a number of areas, including more regional representation and more attention to children from non-dominant groups, such as Indigenous, working-class, immigrant and refugee, and gender non-conforming children, studying them apart from the professionals who intervened in their lives.[42]

Most recently, two areas in particular, adoption and fostering studies, and the history of children labelled with physical, emotional, and behavioural disabilities, exemplify these trends. A particularly important facet in the historiography concerned with adoption and fostering is its global scope and the prominent place of race, especially that of black children and the 1960s "scoop" of Indigenous children.[43] These histories confirm Canada's contributions to a global circulation of babies and children in the post–World War II era through the lenses of transnational adoption and the symbolic child.

Scholarship that focuses on children labelled with disabilities in the past has concentrated not only on bringing the traditionally marginalized into the historical record, but also on making substantial contributions to critical disability studies that challenge the medical model of disability and reopen questions of the tenacity of eugenics-inspired reform. This work has demonstrated how families and individual children both confronted and complied with broader social attitudes that were often aggressively marginalizing. Nic Clarke, for example, broke new ground with his essay (included in this volume) on the history of children with intellectual disabilities in British Columbia at the turn of the twentieth century. Clarke challenges the idea that all children have been conceptualized and treated as "precious." Given its constant importance in the history of children and youth generally, education and schooling have provided a significant focus for new scholarship that highlights the experiences of children labelled with disabilities. This work has made major contributions to unearthing the history not only of children often pushed outside the boundaries of "normal" but also of how and why adults contributed directly to the marginalization of these children.[44]

Children's and teen's pastimes have also drawn the attention of scholars. Sharon Wall's study of summer camps, for example, explores how adult interpretations of developmental psychology were expressed in camp programming. Wall is careful also to include the experiences of children themselves in her analysis. Young people's associational lives—evident in clubs like Girl Guides, Boy Scouts, and the Junior Red Cross—have likewise been the focus of historians. They also help us understand the meanings children derived from such leisure pursuits and citizenship training exercises.[45] The importance of youth culture and consumption has also given rise to new approaches and subject matter, exemplified by Linda Mahood's study of the rebellious countercultures of youthful hitchhikers in the 1970s (included in this volume).[46]

For all its growth and development, the history of children and youth has also had its share of methodological and interpretive conundrums. There remains the challenge of fragmentary evidence and what to do with the pieces that are found. How can historians use these remnants to tell children's stories? How do historians ensure that children, often seemingly powerless and silenced in history, are not merely "objects" of our studies but rather are treated as fully functioning human beings?[47] The successive waves of historical work recounted here, from a focus on adults' attitudes regarding, and their treatment of, young people, to a focus on young people's perspectives on their own lives perhaps edges us closer to resolving these conundrums. They also, however, reveal new ones. The now familiar desire on the part of historians to find and amplify "children's voices" as a measure of their historical agency is not without risk.[48] Historians, for example, need to carefully avoid over-sentimentalizing and generalizing the perspectives of young people. They must avoid trapping the history of young people in a compensatory, bi-naried, and undifferentiated mode, only meaningful as it differs from, or mimics, adult experiences and values, and insufficiently differentiated according to both familiar categories of analysis (such as race, class, gender, sexuality, and ablebodiedness) and new and evolving categories of analysis (such as size and age).[49] The essays assembled in this volume begin to address many of the difficult questions of interpretation and methodology we have posited here.

Contributions to This Volume—What Difference Do Kids Make to the History of Canada?

Contemporary headlines and statistics about young people illustrate the power of the categories "child" and "youth" to inspire adult action, for better or worse. As historians of bodies/medicine/education and policing/delinquency/regulation, respectively, and having been deeply influenced by feminist history, we use our work to explore the worlds that adults create, their production of the meaning of childhood and adolescence, and the responses of the young in the past. We have found that turning our analytic lens to children and youth helps to shed light on how age matters. In *The Difference Kids Make*, we have assembled a collection of research essays that help to define how the youngest, and often assumed to be most vulnerable and dependent, of our society have in turn contributed to the making of Canadian history. All the while, we keep an eye to how age is a relational category and so necessarily speaks to adult worlds.

As the social history of the 1970s and '80s reshaped our understanding of the Canadian past, giving rise to a rich historiography on labour, women, immigrants, and ethnic groups, some historians asked what difference age made.[50] John Bullen's and Bettina Bradbury's doctoral work in the 1980s made a simple but profound challenge to labour history that had heretofore been consumed by the industrial workers, the shop floor, and the strike: that most members of working-class families participated in the family economy, regardless of age.[51] In their contributions to this volume, Bullen and Bradbury show that children made a critical economic difference to families as they collected coal, cared for siblings, and sold what they could on street corners. The essays by Roderick MacLeod and Mary Anne Poutanen and Rhonda Hinther also emerge from a labour history tradition that used intersectionality (the simultaneous consideration of multiple identities like class, gender, and ethnicity) to examine working-class plight and protest. Rarely has the literature pointed to children's political activity, much less their strike action. In the cases discussed here, the young generation asserted itself, surprising adults and parents alike.

Like labour historians, women's historians revolutionized the study of Canada with gender analyses. Several decades of women's and gender history have been remarkably fruitful, as the proliferation of studies of girls and women attest.[52] Masculinity studies was slower to emerge in Canada, but as Blake Brown, Tim Cook, and Heidi MacDonald show in this volume, a focus on the socialization of boys and the coming of age of young men deepens our understanding of how boys' culture was imbued with militarism and how economic hard times profoundly affected traditional and accepted pathways to manhood.[53] Since gender is a relational phenomenon, these contributions to the history of boys and young men in Canada in turn have implications for girls and young women as well. Both Kristine Alexander and Tamara Myers explore such implications. By illuminating girls' contributions to Canadian history, whether in the context of the Girl Guides or the juvenile justice system, they highlight the methodological issues associated with finding the perspectives of those most often excluded from archival collections.

Early histories of childhood and youth focused on institutions, from orphanages to schools and universities, to incarceration facilities. Many institutions were seen as reformist or progressive innovations, intended to make society a better place for young people. More recent histories of university life, like that offered here by E. Lisa Panayotidis and Paul Stortz, ask new questions about these enduring institutional settings. How, for example, did students experience university life? Did they simply reproduce the cultural norms of the elite or was the university an incubator for the nascent emergence of a distinctive "youth culture" that would continue to be refined over the twentieth century? Race and class, these authors make clear, mattered in how historians answer such complex questions. In institutional settings like the residential schools, the growth of a strong youth identity and culture was not high on the agenda. Sarah de Leeuw's and Ian Mosby's essays in this volume point to the morally bankrupt and criminal residential schooling experiment that was meant to "uplift" Aboriginal children. Focusing on the perspective of children incarcerated in these institutions helps to correct the impression that residential schooling was about policy more than people, as the recently completed Truth and Reconciliation Commission has proved.

Historians have asserted that by the late nineteenth century an ideal childhood emerged that kept youngsters at a safe distance from the harsh adult world. This largely meant children were to be spared paid work and military service. For many youth, however, compulsory schooling and protective labour legislation did not reshape childhood in this way. Until recently it was assumed that children had little to do with wartime Canada, except as inconsequential bystanders. The essays included here by Tim Cook, Sarah Glassford, and Barbara Lorenzkowski point to the fact that not only did children play symbolic roles in generating a sense of a future to fight for, but also, in practical terms, their recruitment on the home front and for the battlefield of the twentieth century's world wars shows the fallacy of the idea that war did not directly involve children. As historians reveal how age mattered during wartime, they also show how war sets the gendered nature of the involvement of children and youth in high relief.

Historians of childhood and youth have long been preoccupied with the meaning and definition of childhood. In the twentieth century, the notion of "normal" childhood emerged at the hands of medical, social science, legal, and educational experts who turned to children's behaviour and bodies to proclaim both the normal and the abnormal. The prescriptive child, constructed in the discourses of adults, lay at the heart of much education and socialization of young people as well as regulation and discipline. This process of inclusion and exclusion influenced the experiences of children and their families, as Mona Gleason's article on children's medical treatment and education shows. The consequences of the exclusion of certain children from the privilege of being considered normal is starkly drawn in Nic Clarke's essay on "mentally deficient" children, Jessica Haynes's consideration of the babies born to mothers who had taken thalidomide, and Jane Nicholas's research into children presented as "freaks" on the side show.

Belonging and citizenship are major concepts driving social history, especially that of mobile populations. As historians have adopted Viviana Zelizer's notion that children became more precious in the modern period as their economic value declined, they have searched for material to help explain how certain children came to belong within their societies and in effect gained access to a kind of nascent citizenship. This involved tracing how some children were left behind, as Nicholas, de Leeuw, Mosby, Clarke, and Haynes show, and also how children were recruited into belonging and embracing a Canadian youthful identity. Tim Cook's piece on underage soldiers shows how desperately boys wanted to belong to the masculine world of representing and defending one's country. In the post–World War II period, as Myers, Glassford, and Tarah Brookfield demonstrate, voluntary endeavours like fundraising for the world's hungry, were paths to citizenship and belonging. The powerful metaphor that "children are the future" operated in this vein as children were seen as "seeds of destiny" and as embodying the hope for a more peaceful world. Linda Mahood's exploration of teenagers and hitchhiking in the early 1970s also trades on the broader theme of youthful citizenship and belonging. While many Canadian adults were perplexed and appalled by the large number of transient youth roaming across the country during this period, young people themselves understood it as an opportunity to learn about their country and themselves.

A feature of modern Canada, then, was that groups of adults took to heart the "best interest of the child," the definition of which was shaped by the times and the subject position of the adult. The essays in this volume therefore explore children and youth, childhood and adolescence, in the context of medical science innovation, institution building, political organizing, and even the development of cultural sites like carnivals, Girl Guides movements, and moving picture houses. Perhaps most profoundly, these essays complicate blanket claims to alleged "advances" in medical science and education on the part of adults. The history of thalidomide—an innovation in medical science intended to cure pregnant women's morning sickness—is a case in point. This is a history that went horribly wrong, as Jessica Haynes reveals, and that tells us as much about the presumptions, prejudices, and arrogance of adults as it does about healthy babies at mid-twentieth century. Similarly, Ian Mosby's work on the nutritional experiments on Aboriginal children in residential schools deepens our understanding of the extent of the unethical and criminal conduct of adults in a colonial setting. The essays included in this volume, lastly, help to encourage discussions about the methodological challenges that confront historical work on young people. Kristine Alexander, Jane Nicholas, and Magda Fahrni, for example, address the methodological challenges of centring children in historical interpretation—acknowledging gaps in source materials and also the spectre of exploiting vulnerable children by using their tragedy, as in the case of the Laurier Palace fire, or commercial images of their "freak show" bodies, to write history.

We encourage readers to engage with the history of children and youth assembled in this volume by considering our study questions and the primary documents provided by the essays' authors. How do they help deepen your understanding of Canadian history? What new interpretations and new understandings of young people do they inspire? We hope that you'll be motivated to discover new resources with which to pursue fresh avenues in the history of children and youth. And we invite you to join us in asking questions of the past as if age mattered.

Notes

1. Joan Latchford, photographer, private collection. Interview with Joan Latchford, Tamara Myers, 9 December 2010, Toronto.

2. See Tamara Myers, "Blistered and Bleeding, Tired and Determined: Visual Representations of Children and Youth in the Miles for Millions Walkathon" in this volume.

3. Steven Mintz, "Why the History of Childhood Matters," *Journal of the History of Childhood and Youth* 5, 1 (Winter 2012), 16.

4. Cynthia Comacchio, *The Dominion of Youth: Adolescence and the Making of Modern Canada, 1920–1950* (Waterloo: University of Waterloo Press, 2005).

5. Examples are plentiful. On iterations of sexual abuse of youngsters see the recent scandals in Rotherham, England, www.theguardian.com/uk/rotherham (Accessed 7 October 2014); on pressure to demobilize child soldiers, see http://fullcomment.nationalpost.com/2013/11/11/romeo-dallaire-and-shelly-whitman-remember-the-child-soldiers-forced-into-battle-and-killed-too (Accessed 7 October 2014); for examples of extreme parenting trends and critiques of "helicopter parenting," see, for example, the "Tiger Mom" phenomenon born from a book by Amy Chua, http://online.wsj.com/articles/SB10001424052748704111504576059713528698754 (Accessed 7 October 2014); www.slate.com/blogs/xx_factor /2014/07/15/debra_harrell_arrested_for_letting _her_9_year_old_daughter_go_to_the_park .html; on claims that the current generation of young people might be dubbed "Generation screwed," see www.cbc.ca/news/canada/generation -screwed-youth-struggle-for-jobs-home-ownership -1.2450281 (Accessed 7 October 2014).

6. http://nobelpeaceprize.org (Accessed 14 October 2014).

7. Statistics Canada, "Canada's population estimates: Age and Sex, 2013," *The Daily*, 25 November 2013, p. 5.

8. Total number of male children was 4,031,148 and total number of female children was 3,821,981. Ibid.

9. Employment and Social Development Canada, "Canadians in Context—Aging Population," www4.hrsdc.gc.ca/.3ndic.1t.4r@-eng.jsp?iid=33 (Accessed 1 October 2014).

10. For 2001 census data, see Statistics Canada, 2001 Census, Standard Census Data at www12 .statcan.gc.ca/english/census01/products/high light/SAC/Page.cfm?Lang=E&Geo=PR& Code=01&Table=1a&StartRec=1& Sort=2&B1= Age&B2=Counts (Accessed 24 September 2014); Historical Statistics of Canada, Section A: Population and Migration, www.statcan.gc.ca/pub/11-516-x/sectiona/4147436-eng.htm#1 (Accessed 23 September 2014).

11. Historical Statistics of Canada, Section A: Population and Migration, www.statcan.gc.ca/pub/11-516-x/sectiona/4147436-eng.htm#1 (Accessed 23 September 2014).

12. Statistics Canada, "Canada's population estimates: Age and Sex, 2013," *The Daily*, 25 November 2013, p. 5.

13. Statistics Canada, Social and Aboriginal Statistics Division, *Aboriginal Children's Survey, 2006: Family, Community and Childcare—Analytical Paper* (Ottawa: Statistics Canada, 2008), p. 6.

14. Statistic Canada, "Immigration and Ethnocultural Diversity in Canada—National Household Survey, 2011," Ministry of Industry, 2013, p. 15.

15. One measure of this interest is the rise in Critical Youth Studies (CYS) within the last decade. CYS draws together international scholars in history, sociology, geography, philosophy, anthropology, social work, psychology, women's studies, ethnic studies, sexuality studies, and others who share an academic interest in the study of children, youth, and their cultures. See, for example, Shirley R. Steinberg and Awad Ibrahim, *Critical Youth Studies Reader* (New York: Peter Lang, 2014); Derek Kassam, Lisa Murphy, and Elizabeth Taylor, eds., *Key Issues in Childhood and Youth Studies* (New York: Routledge Press, 2010); Amy L. Best, Ed., *Representing Youth: Methodological Issues in Critical Youth Studies* (New York: New York University Press, 2007); James E. Côté and Anton Allahar, eds. *Critical Youth Studies: A Canadian Focus* (Toronto: Pearson Education Canada, 2005). In the popular press, see Tralee Pearce, "Why the first 2000 days of a child's life are the most important," *Globe and Mail* (Thursday, 27 September 2014) www.theglobeandmail.com/life/parenting/why-the-first-2000-days-of-a-childs-life-are-the-most-important/article4572762 (Accessed 30 September 2014); Ivan Semeniuk, "How poverty influences a child's brain development," *Globe and Mail* (January 25, 2013) www.theglobeandmail.com/technology/science/brain/how-poverty-influences-a-childs-brain-development/article7882957/?page=all (Accessed 30 September 2014); Sarah Boesveld, "Child labour or just chores? Debate rages after Saskatchewan bans kids from working on family farm," *The National Post*, August 11, 2014 http://news.nationalpost.com/2014/08/11/debate-rages-after-saskatchewan-bans-kids-from-working-on-family-farm (Accessed 1 October 2014).

16. OECD Better Life Index www.oecdbetterlifeindex.org (Accessed 2 October 2014).

17. Canadian Institute for Health Information, "Benchmarking Canada's Health System: International Comparisons—Executive Summary" (21 November 2013) p. 6.

18. Pierre Brochu, Marie-Anne Doussing, Koffi Houme, and Maria Chuy, *Measuring Up: Canadian Results of the OECD PISA Study—The Performance of Canadian Youth in Mathematics, Reading and Science. 2012 First Results for Canadians Aged 15* (Council of Ministers of Education: Toronto, 2012). "The Canadian results in reading are consistent with those observed in mathematics. Results in 2012 confirmed Canada's consistently high level of achievement in this foundational area, with only five countries out of 65 surpassing Canada's average score. As was the case in mathematics, all provinces with the exception of Prince Edward Island performed at or above the OECD average. Students in British Columbia performed particularly well in reading, exceeding even the Canadian average. A computer-based assessment (reading of digital texts) was also administered to a subset of Canadian students for the first time in PISA 2012, and overall only four countries out of the 32 participating achieved a higher score than Canada on this component" (pp. 47–8).

19. On the United Nations report concerning the continuation of high rates of child poverty in Canada, see www.cbc.ca/news/canada/british-columbia/poverty-in-canada-has-child-s-face-un-report-says-1.1137445 (Accessed 8 October 2014); on British Columbia having the highest rates of child poverty in Canada, see www.cbc.ca/news/canada/british-columbia/b-c-has-highest-child-poverty-rate-in-canada-report-1.2440909#Report%20Card (Accessed 8 October 2014).

20. Statistics Canada, Social and Aboriginal Statistics Division, *Aboriginal Children's Survey, 2006*, p. 6.

21. Government of Canada, Policy Research Initiative, "Aboriginal Youth in Canada: Emerging Issues, Research Priorities, and Policy Implications," (Government of Canada: Ottawa, 2008) www.horizons.gc.ca/sites/default/files/Publication-alt-format/2009-0005-eng.pdf (Accessed 8 October 2014).

22. World Health Organization, "Executive Summary," *Health for the World's Adolescents: A Second Chance in the Second Decade* (Geneva: WHO Press, 2014), p. 2. http://apps.who.int/adolescent/second-decade/files/1612_MNCAH_HWA_Executive_Summary.pdf (Accessed 14 October 2014).

23. Anne Mehler Paperny, "Tory 'tough-on-crime' bill has youth advocates worried," *Globe and Mail online*, July 18, 2011; Gloria Galloway, "Crime falls to 1973 levels as Tories push for sentencing reform," *Globe and Mail online*, July 21, 2011. John Ibbitson, "Crime bill first on Tory agenda," *Globe*

and Mail online, September 18, 2011; Editorial, "The Conservatives' crime obsession is not magnificent," *Globe and Mail online*, September 20, 2011.

24. Statistics Canada, "Family Violence in Canada: A Statistical Profile, 2014," (Ottawa: Canadian Centre for Justice Statistics, 2016), pp. 21–2.

25. Statistics Canada, "Family Violence in Canada: A Statistical Profile, 2014," (Ottawa: Canadian Centre for Justice Statistics, 2016), pp. 25–6.

26. United Nations Children's Fund, *Hidden in Plain Sight: A Statistical Analysis of Violence Against Children*, UNICEF, New York, 2014.

27. Gillian Shaw, "Amanda Todd's mother speaks out about her daughter, bullying" *Vancouver Sun* (October 14, 2012). www.vancouversun.com/news/ Amanda+Todd+speaks+about+daughter+death/ 7384521/story.html (Accessed 1 October 2014).

28. Tara Carmen, "Parole board considered Raymond Caissie at high risk for violence," *Vancouver Sun* (September 24, 2014). www.vancouversun.com/ news/Parole+Board+considered+Raymond +Caissie+high+risk+violence/10232917/story. html (Accessed 1 October 2014).

29. That Tina's remains were left in a place where the perpetrator hoped she would be forgotten, or at least never found, is emblematic of the treatment of many Aboriginal girls and women victimized by violence in Canada. www.winnipegsun. com/2014/09/13/searching-for-answers-volun- teers-plan-to-dredge-red-river-sunday (Accessed 8 October 2014).

30. Editorial, "Why the PM should call an inquiry into missing Aboriginal women," *Maclean's* (August 26, 2014). www.macleans.ca/politics/ottawa/national -inquiry-into-missing-and-murdered-aboriginal -women (Accessed 1 October 2014).

31. www.cbc.ca/news/aboriginal/police-forces-need -culture-change-trudeau-1.3428530 (Accessed 9 June 2016).

32. Neil Sutherland, *Children in English-Canadian Society: Framing the Twentieth Century Consensus* (Toronto: University of Toronto Press, 1976). For an early bibliography of the literature, see Jean Barman, Linda Hale, and Neil Sutherland, comps. *History of Canadian Childhood and Youth: A Bibliography* (Westport, Conn.: Greenwood Press, 1992); for a recent bibliographical dis- cussion of the Canadian historiography, see Mona Gleason and Tamara Myers, "History of Childhood in Canada," in Heather Montgomery, eds., *Oxford Bibliographies in Childhood Studies* (New York: Oxford University Press, 2014). Oxford Bibliographies URL: www.oxfordbibliographies .com. Entry URL: http://bit.ly/1keaowa.

33. On work that charts the development of a state child welfare bureaucracy in English and French Canada, see Cynthia Comacchio, *"Nations Are Built of Babies": Saving Ontario Mothers and Children, 1900–1940* (Montreal and Kingston: McGill- Queen's University Press, 1990); Robert McIntosh, "Constructing the Child: New Approaches to the History of Childhood in Canada," *Acadiensis* 28 (Spring 1999): 126–40; Dominique Marshall, *The Social Origins of the Welfare State: Québec Families, Compulsory Education, and Family Allowances, 1940–1955*. Trans. Nicola Doone Danby (Waterloo: Wilfrid Laurier University Press, 2006). Originally published in French as *Aux origines sociales de l'État-providence* (Montréal: Presses de l'Université de Montréal, 1998); Renée Joyal, ed., *Entre surveil- lance et compassion: L'évolution de la protection de l'enfance au Québec* (Sainte Foy: Presses de l'Univer- sité du Québec, 2000); Denyse Baillargeon, *Babies for the Nation: The Medicalization of Motherhood in Quebec, 1910–1970*. Trans. W. Donald Wilson (Waterloo: Wilfrid Laurier University Press, 2009); on the family and education see Jean Barman, "Schooled for Inequality: The Education of British Columbia Aboriginal Children," in Jean Barman, Neil Sutherland, and J. Donald Wilson, eds., *Children, Teachers and Schools in the History of British Columbia* (Calgary: Detselig Enterprises, 1995); Claudette Knight, "Black Parents Speak: Education in Mid-Nineteenth-Century Canada West," *Ontario History* 89 (December 1997): 269–84; Mona Gleason, *Normalizing the Ideal: Psychology, Schooling, and the Family in Postwar Canada* (Toronto: University of Toronto Press, 1999); Jean Barman and Mona Gleason, eds., *Children, Teachers, and Schools in the History of British Columbia* (Calgary: Detselig Enterprises, 2003).

34. Early exemplars of this vast historiography as it pertains to children and youth include: Joy Parr, ed. *Childhood and Family in Canadian History* (Toronto: McClelland & Stewart, 1982); Bettina Bradbury, ed., *Canadian Family History: Selected Readings* (Toronto: Copp Clark, 1992); Bettina Bradbury, *Working Families: Age, Gender, and Daily Survival in Industrializing Montreal* (Toronto: McClelland & Stewart, 1993); Chad Gaffield, "Children, Schooling, and Family Reproduction in Nineteenth-Century Ontario," *Canadian Historical Review* 72, 2 (1991): 157–191; Harley D. Dickinson, "Scientific Parenthood: The Mental Hygiene Movement and the Reform of Canadian Families, 1925–1950," *Journal of Comparative Family Studies* 24 (Autumn 1993): 387–402; Robert M. Stamp, "Teaching Girls Their 'God Given Place in Life': The Introduction of

Home Economics in the Schools," *Atlantis* (Spring 1977): 18–34; Celia Haig-Brown, *Resistance and Renewal: Surviving the Indian Residential School* (Vancouver: Tilicum Library, 1988); Jean Barman, *Growing Up British in British Columbia: Boys in Private School* (Vancouver: University of British Columbia Press, 1984); Patricia E. Roy, "'Due to their keenness regarding education, they will get the utmost out of the whole plan': The Education of Japanese Children in the British Columbia Interior Housing Settlements during World War Two," *Historical Studies in Education/Revue d'histoire de l'éducation* 4 (1992): 211–31; Paul Bennett, "Turning 'Bad Boys' into 'Good Citizens': The Reforming Impulse in Toronto's Industrial Schools Movement, 1883 to the 1920s," *Ontario History* 78 (1986): 209–32; Manfred Prokop, "Canadianization of Immigrant Children: Role of the Rural Elementary School in Alberta, 1900–1930," *Alberta History* 37 (Spring 1989): 1–10; Timothy J. Stanley, "White Supremacy, Chinese Schooling, and School Segregation in Victoria: The Case of the Chinese Students' Strike, 1922–23," *Historical Studies in Education/Revue d'histoire de l'éducation* 2, 2 (Fall 1990): 287–305; Jean Barman and Neil Sutherland, "Out of the Shadows: Retrieving the History of Urban Education and Urban Childhood in Canada," in Ronald K. Goodenow and W.E. Marsden, eds., *The City and Education in Four Nations* (Cambridge: Cambridge University Press, 1992); D. Owen Carrigan, *Juvenile Delinquency in Canada: A History* (Toronto: Irwin, 1998).

35. See especially Cynthia Comacchio, *Nations are Built of Babies*; Denyse Baillargeon, *Un Québec en mal d'enfants: La médicalisation de la maternité au Québec, 1910–1970* (Montreal: Remue-Ménage, 2004); Karen Balcolm, *The Traffic in Babies: Cross-Border Adoption and Baby-Selling Between Canada and the United States, 1930–1972* (Toronto: University of Toronto Press, 2011); Karen Dubinsky, *Babies Without Borders: Adoption and Migration Across the Americas* (Toronto and New York: University of Toronto and New York University Press, 2010).

36. Rosalyn N. Ing, "The Effects of Residential Schools on Native Child-Rearing Practices," *Canadian Journal of Native Education* 18 (Supplement, 1991): 65–118; Jean Barman, "Schooled for Inequality: The Education of British Columbia Aboriginal Children," in Jean Barman, Neil Sutherland, and J. Donald Wilson, eds., *Children, Teachers and Schools in the History of British Columbia* (Calgary: Detselig Enterprises, 1995); J.R. Miller, *Shingwauk's Vision: A History of Native Residential Schools* (Toronto: University of Toronto Press, 1996).

37. Joy Parr, ed. *Childhood and Family in Canadian History* (Toronto: McClelland & Stewart, 1982); Patricia Rooke and R.L. Schnell, eds., *Studies in Childhood History: A Canadian Perspective* (Calgary: Detselig Enterprises, 1982); Russell Smandych, Gordon Dodd, and Alvin Esau, eds., *Dimensions of Childhood: Essays on the History of Children and Youth in Canada* (Winnipeg: Legal Research Institute of the University of Manitoba, 1991); Nancy Janovicek and Joy Parr, eds., *Histories of Canadian Children and Youth* (Don Mills, Ont.: Oxford University Press, 2003); Mona Gleason, Tamara Myers, Leslie Paris, and Veronica Strong-Boag, eds. *Lost Kids: Vulnerable Children and Youth in Twentieth-Century Canada and the United States* (Vancouver: University of British Columbia Press, 2010).

38. Joy Parr, *Labouring Children: British Immigrant Apprentices to Canada* (Toronto: University of Toronto Press, 1980); Jennifer S.H. Brown, "Children of the Early Fur Trades," in Joy Parr, ed., *Childhood and Family in Canadian History* (Toronto: McClelland & Stewart, 1982); Timothy J. Stanley, "White Supremacy, Chinese Schooling, and School Segregation in Victoria: The Case of the Chinese Students' Strike, 1922–23," *Historical Studies in Education/Revue d'histoire de l'éducation* 2,2 (Fall 1990): 287–305; Lucille M. Marr, "Church Teen Clubs, Feminized Organizations? Tuxis Boys, Trail Rangers, and Canadian Girls in Training, 1919–1939," *Historical Studies in Education/Revue d'histoire de l'éducation* 3,2 (Fall, 1991): 249–67; Neil Sutherland, *Growing Up: Childhood in English Canada from the Great War to the Age of Television* (Toronto: University of Toronto Press, 1997).

39. Lewis, Norah, "'Isn't this a terrible war?': The Attitudes of Children to Two World Wars," *Historical Studies in Education/Revue d'histoire de l'éducation* 7, 2 (Fall, 1995): 193–215; Mark Moss, *Manliness and Militarism: Educating Young Boys in Ontario for War* (Toronto: Oxford University Press, 2001); Tamara Myers and Mary Anne Poutanen, "Cadets, Curfews, and Compulsory Schooling: Mobilizing Anglophone Children in WWII Quebec," *Histoire sociale/Social History* 37 (Nov. 2005): 367–98; Susan Fisher, *Boys and Girls in No Man's Land: English-Canadian Children and the First World War* (Toronto: University of Toronto Press, 2010); Kristine Alexander, "An Honour and a Burden: Canadian Girls and the Great War," in Sarah Glassford and Amy Shaw, eds., *A Sisterhood of Suffering and Service: Women and Girls of Canada and Newfoundland during the First World War* (Vancouver: University of British Columbia Press, 2012); on the post-war and Cold

War period, see Mary Louise Adams, *The Trouble with Normal: Postwar Youth and the Making of Heterosexuality* (Toronto: University of Toronto Press, 1997); Dominique Marshall, "Canada and Children's Rights at the United Nations, 1945–1959," in Greg Donaghy, ed., *Canada and the Early Cold War, 1943–1957* (Ottawa: Department of Foreign Affairs and International Trade, 1998); Tarah Brookfield, *Cold War Comforts: Canadian Women, Child Safety, and Global Insecurity* (Waterloo: Wilfrid Laurier Press, 2012).

40. Steven Maynard, "'Horrible Temptations': Sex, Men, and Working-Class Male Youth in Urban Ontario, 1890–1935," *Canadian Historical Review* 78, 2 (June 1997): 191–235; Jean Barman, "Encounters with Sexuality: The Management of Inappropriate Body Behaviour in Late-Nineteenth-Century B.C. Schools," *Historical Studies in Education* 16 (Spring 2004): 85–114; Tamara Myers, "Embodying Delinquency: Boys' Bodies, Sexuality, and Juvenile Justice History in Early-Twentieth-Century Quebec," *Journal of the History of Sexuality* 14 (2005): 383–414.

41. In reading court records, "against the grain" historians reinterpret legal documents created by adults—such as juvenile court records—to detect any hint of agency and perspective of youth caught in that system. Gaston Desjardins, *L'amour en patience: La sexualité adolescente au Québec, 1940–1960* (Montréal: Presses de l'Université du Québec, 1995); Mona Gleason, "Disciplining the Student Body: Schooling and the Construction of Canadian Children's Bodies, 1930 to 1960," *History of Education Quarterly* 41, 2 (2001): 189–215; Mona Gleason, "Race, Class, and Health: School Medical Inspection and 'Healthy' Children in British Columbia, 1890 to 1930," *Canadian Bulletin of Medical History* 19 (2002): 95–112; Joan Sangster, *Girl Trouble: Female Delinquency in English Canada* (Toronto: Between the Lines, 2002); Sylvie Ménard, *Des Enfants sous surveillance. La Rééducation des jeunes délinquants au Québec (1840–1950)* (Montréal: VLB éditeur, 2003); Louise Bienvenue, *Quand la jeunesse entre en scène. L'Action catholique avant la Révolution tranquille* (Montréal: Boréal, 2003); Cynthia Comacchio, *The Dominion of Youth: Adolescence and the Making of Modern Canada, 1920–1950* (Waterloo: University of Waterloo Press, 2005); Tamara Myers, *Caught: Montreal's Modern Girls and the Law, 1869–1945* (Toronto: University of Toronto Press, 2006); Sharon Wall, *The Nurture of Nature: Childhood, Antimodernism and Ontario Summer Camps, 1920–1955* (Vancouver: University of British Columbia Press, 2009); Mona Gleason,

Small Matters: Canadian Children in Sickness and Health, 1900–1940 (Montreal & Kingston: McGill-Queen's University Press, 2013); on visual culture see Brian J. Low, *NFB Kids: Portrayals of Children by the National Film Board of Canada 1939–89* (Waterloo: Wilfrid Laurier University Press, 2002); Loren Lerner, ed., *Depicting Canada's Children* (Waterloo: Wilfrid Laurier Press, 2009); Tamara Myers, "Blistered and Bleeding, Tired and Determined: Visual Representations of Children and Youth in the Miles for Millions Walkathon," *Journal of the Canadian Historical Association* 22, 1 (2011): 245–75.

42. Robert McIntosh, *Boys in the Pits: Child Labour in Coal Mines* (Kingston and Montreal: McGill-Queen's University Press, 2000); Juliet Pollard, "A Most Remarkable Phenomenon: Growing Up Métis: Fur Traders' Children in the Pacific Northwest," in Nancy Janovicek and Joy Parr, eds., *Histories of Canadian Children and Youth* (Don Mills, Ont.: Oxford University Press, 2003); Anika Stafford and Mona Gleason, "Referred for Special Service: Children, Youth, and the Production of Heteronormativity at Alexandra Neighbourhood House in Postwar Vancouver," in Tracy Penny Light, Wendy Mitchinson, and Barbara Brookes, eds., *Bodily Subjects: Essays on Gender and Health, 1800–2000* (Kingston and Montreal: McGill-Queen's University Press, 2014): 227–44.

43. Veronica Strong-Boag, *Finding Families, Finding Ourselves: English Canada Encounters Adoption from the Nineteenth Century to the 1990s* (Don Mills, Ont.: Oxford University Press, 2006); Veronica Strong-Boag, *Fostering Nation? Canada Confronts Its History of Childhood Disadvantage* (Waterloo: Wilfrid Laurier University Press, 2010); Karen Dubinsky, *Babies Without Borders: Adoption and Migration across the Americas* (Toronto: University of Toronto Press, 2010); Karen A. Balcom, *The Traffic in Babies: Cross-Border Adoption and Baby-Selling between the United States and Canada, 1930–1972* (Toronto: University of Toronto Press, 2011).

44. Gerald Thomson, "'Through no fault of their own': Josephine Dauphinee and the 'Subnormal' Pupils of the Vancouver School System, 1911–1941," *Historical Studies in Education/Revue d'histoire de l'éducation* 18, 1 (Spring 2006): 51–73; Jason Ellis, "'Inequalities of children in original endowment': How Intelligence Testing Transformed Early Special Education in a North American City School System," *History of Education Quarterly* 53, 4 (November 2013): 401–29; Jason Ellis, "'All Methods—and Wedded to None: The Deaf Education Methods Debate and Progressive

Educational Reform in Toronto, Canada, 1922–1945," *Paedagogica Historica* 50, 3 (2014): 371–89; Karen Yoshida, Fady Shanouda, and Jason Ellis, "An Education and Negotiation of Differences: The 'Schooling' Experiences of English-speaking Canadian Children Growing Up with Polio during the 1940s and 1950s," *Disability & Society* 29 3 (March 2014): 345–58.

45. See for e.g., Alexander and Glassford in this volume.

46. Children and youth as consumers of culture is a growing focus in the field. See, for example, Katie Rollwagen, "Eaton's Goes to School: Youth Councils and the Commodification of Teenage Consumer," *Histoire Social/Social History* 47, 95 (2014): 683–702. Historians are also interested in the place of children and youth in broader histories of consumer culture. See Braden Hutchinson, "Gifts and Commodities: Second-Hand Toys, Marginal Consumers and the Marketization of Philanthropy in Interwar and Early Postwar Canada," *Journal of the History of Children and Youth* 7, 3 (2014): 462–84.

47. See the points in this regard raised by Willem Frijhoff, "Historian's Discovery of Childhood," *Paedagogica Historica* 48 (2012): 11–29. We are indebted to an anonymous reviewer for this citation.

48. On using empathetic inference as a method in the history of children and youth, see Mona Gleason, "The Power of Empathetic Engagement: History Education and the History of Children and Childhood," *The History Education Network/historie et education en reseau* http://thenhier.ca/en/content/power-empathetic-engagement-history-education-and-history-children-and-childhood-mona-gleason (Accessed 15 October 2014).

49. On avoiding the agency trap see Mona Gleason, "Observations on the Limits of 'Children's Voices.'" Society for the History of Children and Youth. Posted on July 2, 2013. http://shcyhome.org/2013/07/guest-post-mona-gleason-and-the-limits-of-childrens-voices (Accessed 15 October 2014); see also Mona Gleason, "Avoiding the Agency Trap: Caveats for Historians of Children, Youth, and Education," *History of Education* 45, 4 (2016): 446–59.

50. For an overview of these history fields see Bryan D. Palmer and Joan Sangster, *Labouring Canada: Class, Gender, and Race in Canadian Working-Class History* (Toronto: Oxford University Press, 2008); Mona Gleason, Tamara Myers, and Adele Perry, eds., *Rethinking Canada: The Promise of Women's History*, 6e (Toronto: Oxford University Press, 2010); Vic Satzewich and Nikolaos Liodakis, eds., *"Race" and Ethnicity in Canada: A Critical Introduction*, 3e (Toronto: Oxford University Press, 2013).

51. See Bullen's "Hidden Workers;" and Bettina Bradbury, *Working Families: Age, Gender, and Daily Survival in Industrializing Montreal* (Toronto: McClelland & Stewart, 1993).

52. See the work of Lynne Marks, Joan Sangster, Jennifer Brown, Mary Anne Poutanen, Denyse Baillargeon, Andrée Lévesque, Constance Backhouse, Tamara Myers, Veronica Strong-Boag, Cynthia Comacchio, Becki Ross, Franca Iacovetta, Marlene Epp, and Jane Nicholas.

53. Kathryn McPherson, Cecilia Morgan, and Nancy M. Forestall, eds., *Gendered Pasts: Historical Essays in Femininity and Masculinity in Canada* (Toronto: Oxford University Press, 1999); see also Mark Moss, *Manliness and Militarism: Educating Young Boys in Ontario for War* (Toronto: Oxford University Press, 2001); Christopher Greig, *Ontario Boys: Masculinity and the Idea of Boyhood in Postwar Ontario, 1945–1960* (Waterloo: Wilfrid Laurier University Press, 2014).

1 Working Children

Editors' Introduction

Canadians live in an era that supports an individual's right to a childhood free of labour. But this is a fairly recent development. Modern Canada's industrial development and its agricultural and resource sectors depended on a cheap labour source that inevitably involved children. Prior to the advent of provincial compulsory schooling acts (Ontario was first, in 1870), which legislated children's attendance at school, they worked in the factories, farms, mines, and homes of an industrializing nation.[1] Juvenile immigration programs that saw thousands of British young people come to Canada were labour migration schemes by another name; most migrants became farm hands or domestic workers.[2] During the First and Second World Wars, the patriotic notion that everyone must pull his or her weight for the Allies meant child labour was acceptable, even admirable, and the question of exploitation not spoken of.[3] It is indisputable that children contributed to the making of industrial Canada; importantly, in working-class households the wages and unpaid labour of young people were key to the family economy. Historians John Bullen and Bettina Bradbury, whose essays are included in this chapter, were among the first to take seriously the vital if often overlooked contributions children made to working-class family survival.

Since the nineteenth century, child labour has been a contentious issue, and in the twentieth century it has been central to the discourse concerning children's rights. The stories of newsboys and adolescent prostitutes, often the most public faces of child labour in the nineteenth century, underscore the physical exploitation and danger that youth employment poses to young people. Yet the historiography on working children cautions us to avoid falling into the trap of sentimentalizing history by only highlighting children's victimization. John Bullen's classic essay about child labour shows children's persistence and competence as economic contributors across the nineteenth century. Necessity and custom trumped protective labour laws and reform discourses about idealized childhood (featuring play, not work).[4] In his history of the boys who worked the pits in Cape Breton, Robert McIntosh does not shy away from demonstrating how being of "tender age" did not spare boys the brutality of the industry. Yet he imbues the boys who went into the coal pits with resourcefulness and dignity—two characteristics that are typically left out of sentimental approaches to labouring children.[5] Street children seeking to augment the family economy or line their own pockets became a favourite subject of journalists and child welfare reformers at the turn of the twentieth century, as the image of the "little girl with a bag of coal" suggests. From the collection of a prominent Ontario child advocate,

J.J. Kelso, this image speaks volumes about children's contributions to the family economy as often unwaged and clever, if not cunning.

Middle-class men and women who believed that labour endangered childhood and children's moral and physical health, and stymied their future used images of child workers and working-class children in general to garner sympathy. Those who took up the issue, known as reformers, embraced an ideal of childhood that would feature education not work. Their photographs and news stories presented the harshest aspects of industrialization's punishing effects on the working poor in order to change public opinion and encourage lawmakers to better protect the vulnerable. Most famous among these reformers was Lewis Hine, an American "muckraking" journalist whose photos depict working boys as prematurely aged and working girls as small and vulnerable.[6]

In recent histories of working families, attention remains on family composition, which necessarily affects child labour. Bradbury's essay shows how being raised in a single-parent household is not a new experience; according to the 1901 Census, in that year about 1 in 20 Canadian children grew up with a lone parent. Most of these parents were women, and because of the economic disadvantage women faced at the turn of the twentieth century, these children's lives would be structured by poverty. This, in turn, would shape the nature of childhood—whether it was spent at work or school.

Both of the essays in this chapter point to the importance of considering the active contributions of young people for what they can tell us about the history of the family, the economy, and childhood.

By the middle of the twentieth century, child labour had become an issue of international concern. In 1959, the United Nations adopted the Declaration of the Rights of the Child, which opened the door to but did not directly address the question of child labour. In 1973, the International Labour Organisation, a United Nations agency, adopted Convention 138 regarding the minimum age for admission to employment, a piece of legislation that has as its goal the "total abolition" of child labour. In 1999, Convention 182 on the Worst Forms of Child Labour specified the need to protect children from hazardous work and exploitation, specifically the trafficking in children for sex. Canada has yet to endorse Convention 138.

Notes

1. R.G. McIntosh, *Boys in the Pits: Child Labour in Coal Mining* (Montreal: McGill-Queens University Press, 2000); Sandra Rollings-Magnusson, *Heavy Burdens on Small Shoulders: The Labour of Pioneer Children on the Canadian Prairies* (Edmonton: University of Alberta Press, 2009); John Bullen, "Children of the Industrial Age: Children, Work, and Welfare," PhD dissertation, University of Ottawa, 1989; Bettina Bradbury, *Working Families: Age, Gender and Daily Survival in Industrializing Montreal* (Toronto: McClelland & Stewart, 1993).

2. Joy Parr, *Labouring Children: British Immigrant Apprentices to Canada, 1869–1924* (London: Croom Helm, 1980).

3. The issue of exploitation is a major theme in recent publications on child labour. See Nigel Goose and Katrina Honeyman, eds., *Childhood and Child Labour in Industrial England, 1750–1914* (Farnham, UK: Ashgate, 2013).

4. In *Working Families*, Bettina Bradbury showed similar results for Montreal, where an intricate system based on class, gender, and need shaped who worked and when. If child labourers were "hidden workers," they were hiding in plain sight. Bettina Bradbury, *Working Families: Age, Gender, and Daily Survival in Industrializing Montreal* (Toronto: McClelland & Stewart, 1993).

5. R.G. McIntosh, *Boys in the Pits: Child Labour in Coal Mining* (Montreal: McGill-Queen's University Press, 2000).

6. Hines's images are readily available on the web. See, for example: www.loc.gov/pictures/collection/nclc.

Hidden Workers: Child Labour and the Family Economy in Late-Nineteenth-Century Urban Ontario

JOHN BULLEN

The secret of a successful farm, wrote Canniff Haight in 1885, lay in "the economy, industry, and moderate wants of every member of the household."[1] Haight was simply repeating the conventional wisdom of the age in his recognition that all members of a farm family, including children, contributed to the successful functioning of the household economy. Haight and many of his contemporaries, however, would not have applied the same description to families in urban-industrial centres. The movement of the focus of production from farm to factory, many social analysts believed, decreased the interdependency of the family and offered individual members a greater number of occupational choices.[2] According to this interpretation, a typical urban family relied solely on the wages of a working father and the home management of a mother for its day-to-day survival. This notion of the difference between rural and urban families survived into the twentieth century and surfaced in a number of standard historical works. As late as 1972, for example, Blair Neatby wrote: "The urban family . . . bears little resemblance to a rural family. On a family farm children can make a direct economic contribution by doing chores and helping in many of the farm activities. . . . In the city only the wage-earner brings in money: children . . . become a financial burden who add nothing to the family income."[3] Like many myths of modern civilization, these perceptions of the urban family rested primarily on outward appearances and vague unfounded suppositions.

In the past fifteen years, social historians have uncovered patterns of urban survival which indicate that many working-class families, like their counterparts on the farm, depended on "the economy, industry, and moderate wants of every member of the household," including children, to meet the demands of city life. Several well-known primary and secondary sources describe in graphic detail the onerous trials of youngsters as wage-earners in the manufacturing and commercial establishments of large industrial centres such as Montreal, Toronto, and Hamilton.[4] But child labour was by no means limited to factories and shops. Children also performed important economic duties in their homes and on city streets as a regular part of their contribution to the family economy. This article concentrates on youngsters between the ages of seven and fourteen who worked outside of the industrial and commercial mainstream of late-nineteenth-century urban Ontario, usually for no wages, but who still contributed in important ways to the day-to-day survival of their families. The latter part of the paper includes a brief examination of the special circumstances of foster children.[5] The article will describe the various types of work children performed, evaluate the contribution youngsters made to the family or household economy, determine the extent to which economic responsibilities affected a child's opportunities for personal development and social mobility, and judge the reaction working children elicited from middle- and upper-class members of society. Such an examination illuminates the social and economic structure of urban-industrial Ontario in the late nineteenth century, and casts light into the shadowy corners of urban poverty, business practices, reform mentality, and class structure.

Urbanization, like its companion, industrialization, marches to its own rhythm; it does not unfold in carefully planned and even measures. In the latter decades of the nineteenth century, Canada's

Source: From *Labour/Le Travail*, 18 (Fall 1986): 163–187. Reprinted by permission of the publisher.

urban population increased at roughly three times the rate of the general population, a pattern that struck stalwarts of agricultural society with worry and despair.[6] *The Globe* acknowledged the trend in 1894, but conceded: "The complaint about the continual movement of population from country to city is a good deal like a protest against the law of gravitation."[7] Urbanization could take several forms. Many sons and daughters of Ontario farmers, victims of land exhaustion and exclusionary inheritance customs, recognized the diminishing promise of rural life and fled to the cities in search of work and spouses with whom to begin their own families. In other instances, immigrant families, mostly from the cities and countryside of Great Britain and continental Europe, settled in Canadian cities in the hope of escaping poverty and oppression. In the latter case, fathers and older sons often emigrated first and sent for remaining family members once employment and residence had been established.

All newcomers to the city discovered an environment and value system starkly different from rural society. While there is no question that life on the farm rarely resembled the bucolic paradise portrayed by romantic novelists, the city's emphasis on materialism, competition, standardization, and consumption constituted virtual culture shock for many recent arrivals. Skilled and unskilled workers alike adjusted their lives to the vagaries of the factory system, the business cycle, and the seasons, in an attempt to eke out a living above the poverty line. All workers lived in fear of unemployment, which struck especially hard in winter when outdoor work was scarce and the higher costs of food and fuel could wipe out a family's modest savings. Poor families huddled together in crowded and ramshackle rental units that lacked adequate water and sanitation facilities. For some demoralized labourers, the local tavern or pool hall provided the only escape from a working life of long hours, dangerous conditions, and abysmally low wages. In the face of these oppressive conditions, workers instinctively turned to the one institution that had served their ancestors so well for generations—their families. Although old rural traditions did not survive the trip to the city completely unscarred, workers still found their most reliable and effective support system under their own roofs. Within this scheme, children played a critical role.

In most working-class homes, children assumed domestic responsibilities before they reached the age of eight.[8] Their first duties usually took the form of assisting in the daily upkeep of the home. At any hour of the day, youngsters could be found sweeping steps, washing windows, and scrubbing floors. In neighbourhoods where dirt roads, animals, wood stoves, coal furnaces, and industrial pollution were common features, keeping a home even relatively clean and liveable could require several hands and many hours of labour. In the absence of fathers whose work kept them away from home ten to fifteen hours per day, six days a week, busy mothers frequently called upon children to make minor repairs to poorly constructed houses.

Other common children's chores contributed in a more direct sense to the day-to-day survival and economic status of the family. Youngsters routinely gathered coal and wood for fuel from rail and factory yards, and fetched water from community wells for cooking and washing. To supplement the family's food supply, children cultivated gardens, and raised and slaughtered animals. What home-produced food the family did not consume itself, children could sell to neighbours or at the market for a small profit. In an age when sickness could spell disaster for a family, youngsters provided care for ill family members and sometimes offered themselves as substitute workers. It was also common for older children to assume the duties of a deceased parent, girls frequently taking up mother's responsibilities and boys stepping into father's shoes. On occasion, parents lent their children's services to neighbours in return for nominal remuneration or future favours. Although youngsters who worked in and around their home did not normally encounter the dangers associated with industrial life, in at least one case a young Ottawa lad who was gathering wood chips outside of a lumber mill succumbed to his youthful curiosity and wandered into the plant only to meet his death on an unguarded mechanical saw.[9]

Children filled useful roles at home in at least one other crucial area—babysitting. Many working-class families found it necessary to depend on second and third wage-earners to keep themselves above the poverty line. In some cases, especially in families where children were too young for formal employment, economic need forced mothers to set aside their daytime domestic duties and take up employment outside the home. The introduction of machinery in sectors such as food processing and the textile industry created jobs for unskilled female labour, although it also depressed the general wage level and guaranteed that female earnings in particular would remain pitifully low. Such industries, along with retail stores, welcomed this cheap labour force with open arms. Wage-earning mothers, consequently, placed even greater housekeeping and other domestic responsibilities onto the shoulders of their children. Most importantly, mothers enlisted older children to babysit younger siblings in their absence. In cities where day nurseries were available, even the smallest cost proved prohibitive for many working-class families.[10] These duties took on particular importance in the households headed by the single parents, male and female.

In most cases, children's duties around the home were divided according to sex. Girls more often babysat and attended to housekeeping matters within the confines of the home while boys commonly performed tasks outside the home. This practice was consistent with both rural traditions and the sexual discrimination characteristic of urban life. A typical example can be found in the diary of Toronto truant officer W.C. Wilkinson. Paying a call on the Stone family in 1872, Wilkinson discovered thirteen-year-old Elizabeth cleaning house with her mother while her eleven-year-old brother Thomas was busy helping their father in the garden.[11] Sexual categorization, however, was not impenetrable. Families that lacked children of both sexes simply handed chores over to the most capable and available member. In these instances, domestic necessity conquered sexual stereotyping.

The frequency and regularity with which working-class families called on their younger members to assist in a wide variety of domestic duties highlights the continuing importance of children as active contributors to the family economy. This practice also reveals that working-class families could not rely on industrial earnings alone to provide all the goods and services demanded by urban life. The entrance of mothers into the wage-earning work force undoubtedly disrupted traditional family relations. But the family responded rationally by shifting responsibilities to other members. Single-parent families adjusted in the same manner. Children's chores usually corresponded with a sexual division of labour, except in cases where this was impractical or impossible. Unfortunately, not all observers recognized the significance of youngsters' work in and around the home. Truant officer Wilkinson, for example, complained in 1879 that "in many instances children were kept at home for the most *frivolous* reasons by their parents, such as to run messages, assist in domestic duties, cut wood, and many such reasons that I am compelled to accept, although reluctantly, as the law at present only requires the[ir] attendance four months in the year."[12] (emphasis added)

Working-class parents had more pressing concerns than truancy on their minds when they kept children at home to perform important economic duties. In some cases, children's domestic responsibilities included participation in home-centred industries that formed a branch of the notorious "sweat shop" system. The term *sweat shop* usually described a tiny workplace, sometimes attached to a residence, where a predominantly female and child labour force toiled long hours under contract or subcontract, producing saleable materials for large retail or wholesale outlets. A federal government inquiry in 1882 found sweat shops "sometimes being in the attic of a four-story building, at others in a low, damp basement where artificial light has to be used during the entire day."[13] The same investigation noted: "The rule, apparently which is observed by employers, is, not how many hands should occupy a certain room or building, but how many can be got into it."[14] The ready-made clothing industry, in particular, depended on sweated labour. In the simplest terms, this work extended and exploited the traditional role of women and girls as sewers for their own families. Workers discovered that they could earn a few extra dollars through this nefarious trade by fulfilling contracts in their own homes, or by bringing home after a regular shift unfinished material produced in a factory or workshop located elsewhere. In both cases, children accounted for a substantial portion of the work force.

The Globe found this to be a common practice among working-class families in Toronto as early as the 1860s:

> . . . frequently the industrious efforts of a whole family are employed to fill the orders of the employers. Often, in such instances, the child of eight or nine summers is made a source of material help in the construction of the coarser descriptions of men's garments that are now prepared for the ready-made clothing market. In the same way the female head of the house, a group of daughters, and, perhaps, the male members of the family, if no better occupation is available, turn in to assist the father in adding to their means of support.

The same article described one family that worked on clothing contracts sixteen to eighteen hours per day, six days a week.[15]

More than decade later, in 1882, a federal government inquiry studied the conditions of 324 married female workers. The investigation revealed that 272 women performed most of their work in their own homes. The women explained that in this way they could elicit the assistance of older children and watch over infants at the same time. Of the original 324 women, 255 worked in the clothing industry.[16] Three years later, federal inspector A.H. Blackeby reported that he encountered difficulty amassing information on the wool industry specifically because so much of the work was done in private homes.[17]

In 1896, a petition from the Trades and Labour Congress moved the federal government to appoint Alexander Whyte Wright to undertake a thorough investigation of the sweating system in Canada. Wright visited factories, workshops, and private homes in Halifax, Quebec, Montreal, Ottawa, Toronto, and Hamilton. He found appalling conditions and paltry wages to be the rule in factories and shops but discovered that workers toiled longer, earned less, and suffered more in their own homes: "When a comparison is made . . . between the condition of the people who work in contractors' shops and the conditions which attend the making of garments in private homes, the advantage is, in a marked degree, in favour of the former system.[18] Wright encountered scores of children working in excess of 60 hours per week in converted bedrooms, kitchens, and living rooms. Home labourers competed with contractors for available work, thus, in Wright's words, "bringing the wages down to the lowest point at which the employees can afford to work."[19] Furthermore, most employers paid by the piece, a practice that encouraged longer hours and a faster pace of work, and discouraged regular rest periods. Wright's report also revealed that home workers occasionally needed to carry damaged materials to the employers, "frequently losing half a day because of having to make an alteration which in actual work only requires a few minutes of time. To avoid this they are often willing to submit to a fine or reduction of wages far in excess of what the making of the alteration would be worth to them."[20] Even in unionized shops where hours of labour were restricted, Wright discovered workers anxious to bring material home to accumulate some precious overtime. "'The advantage of having the assistance of their families," he pointed out, "is a further inducement."[21]

Four years after Wright filed his report, a young Mackenzie King undertook a similar investigation on behalf of the postmaster-general. King found sweat shop conditions to be the norm in the carrying out of government clothing contracts: ". . . by far the greatest part of the Government clothing was made by women and girls in their homes or in the shops as the hired hands of subcontractors. . . . In some cases the different members of the family assisted in the sewing, and in a great many cases, one, two, three or more strangers, usually young women or girls, were brought from the neighbourhood and paid a small sum for their services by the week or piece."[22] Like Wright before him, King discovered that private homes, not factories or workshops, exhibited the harshest working conditions. Children routinely assisted in the sewing process and worked as carters carrying material between home and supply houses. King also reported that home workers were required to supply their own thread, a cost which he claimed composed "a substantial fraction of the gross earnings received."[23] Many shop workers brought unfinished material home at night and completed their work with the help of their families. King concluded: "It was pretty generally conceded that, except by thus working overtime, or by the profits made by the aid of hired help, there was very little to be earned by a week's work."[24]

Home sweat shop workers received no protection from government. Although the Ontario Factories Act of 1884 and the Shops Act of 1888 restricted the age and hours of child workers in industrial and commercial establishments, both pieces of legislation specifically exempted family work from any type of regulation. Thus, in 1900, Mackenzie King could write: "When clothing has been let out to individuals to be made up in their homes, with the assistance only of the members of the household, there was absolutely no restriction as to the conditions under which the work of manufacturer had to be carried on."[25] When the Ontario government's Committee on Child Labor reported seven years later, the situation looked much the same. Wrote the commissioners: "In poor neighbourhoods in cities the practice of employing children [in private homes] is very common. The sweat shop has been termed the nursery of child labour."[26] Unlike Wright and King, these government inspectors seemed not to realize that these conditions were not the creation of cruel parents who enjoyed subjecting their children to long hours of mind-numbing work. The iniquity lay in the callousness of a competitive economic system that mercilessly squeezed workers for the last drop of their labour power while building private fortunes for retail outlet owners, such as the renowned Canadian businessman Timothy Eaton. Business practice, not family practice, underlay this widespread suffering.

The example of the residential sweat shop demonstrates that the rural tradition of family work in the home survived in the city. But new circumstances forced this old custom to undergo a severe transformation. In one sense, the image of parents and children working together invites a comparison to the shared family responsibilities characteristic of rural society. But the urban sweat shop was a long way from the country quilting-bee. Clothing contracts violated the privacy of working-class homes and subjected adults and children to strenuous conditions over which they had little influence. Long hours of tedious labour brought a minimal return. Workers danced to the demands of a consumer market while competing contractors systematically drove wages down. Middlemen turned the sweat shop system into a chain of command that featured lower wages and harder working conditions with each successive downward link. Naturally, children occupied the bottom position in the work hierarchy. Yet it is apparent from the evidence collected by Wright and King that child workers proved to be the decisive factor in the economic feasibility of many contracts. This observation exposes the cruel paradox of child workers in a competitive labour market: the more the sweating system exploited the free or cheap labour of children, the less of a chance adults faced of ever receiving a fair wage for their own work.

In other areas, working-class families used their homes as bases for personal service industries. Young children carried laundry to and from their homes while older siblings assisted in washing and ironing. In cities where young single men and working fathers temporarily separated from their families composed a significant proportion of the population, the services of room and board were always in wide demand. Family-run boarding houses daily called on children to change sheets, clean rooms, serve meals, and wash dishes. Some homes took in extra customers, or "mealers," at the dinner hour, often resulting in several sittings per day. In other instances, children prepared and carried homemade lunches to workers at their place of employment. One Hamilton woman who as a child helped her aunt and uncle operate a boarding house reminisced about her youth with telling detail: "Others were a family. We were a business. . . . I couldn't take friends home. . . . I always seemed to be so busy working that I never had time to really make friends."[27] Although these home-centred industries rose above the conditions of residential sweat shops, child workers still made significant contributions, and sacrifices, on a regular basis.

Reaching beyond the perimeters of the home, many working-class children added to the family coffers through their participation in a variety of street trades. Nineteenth-century families immensely enjoyed socializing in public, and downtown streets always bristled with activity and excitement.[28] A police survey of 1887 uncovered approximately 700 youngsters, the vast majority of them boys, who regularly performed, polished shoes, or sold newspapers, pencils, shoelaces, fruit, or other small wares on the streets of Toronto.[29] W. McVitty, chief constable of Ottawa, reported in 1890 that the streets of the capital city supported approximately 175 newsboys but very few girls.[30] Some children, under instruction from their parents, simply begged for money from passers-by.[31] There is plentiful evidence as well of teenage prostitution.[32] Collectively, these youngsters composed a unique and vibrant street culture which occasionally exhibited elements of ritual and hierarchy. Of all the young street vendors, one group stood out—the newsboys.

Newsboys were serious businessmen, not simply charity cases trying to scrape together a few pennies like the other waifs and strays common to city streets. Some of these lads lived on their own in cheap boarding houses or at the Newsboys' Lodging and Industrial Home in Toronto, or its Catholic counterpart, the St. Nicholas Home. These privately run institutions attempted to provide independent newsboys with decent accommodation and moral and industrial training. At the Newsboys' Lodging and Industrial Home, 10¢ per day bought supper, bed, and breakfast, while $1.30 per week fetched full room and board. Many free-spirited boys, however, bristled at the home's regular curfew of 7:00 p.m., and extended curfew of 9:00 p.m. two nights a week, and sought its services only during the most desperate of the winter months. The majority of newsboys lived with their parents and pounded the streets daily as part of their contribution to the family economy. A small percentage of boys delivered door to door, but the greater number worked late into the evenings selling on the street. Some lads worked alone, while more experienced boys headed up teams of sellers. A common trick of a newsboy was to approach a customer with a single paper claiming that it was the last one he had to sell before heading home. If the unwary citizen fell for the con, the newsboy then returned to his hidden pile of papers and repeated the trick. Newsboys stationed themselves near the entrance of hotels, where they undersold the stands inside, and always stood out prominently, along with other young street traders, around the train station.[33] A passive visitor to Toronto, unable to resist the persistent overtures of the newsboys, bootblacks, and fruit vendors, would at least leave Union Station well informed, well-polished, and well fed.

In some instances, the earnings of a newsboy shielded a poor family from utter destitution. When W.C. Wilkinson inquired into the absence from school of fourteen-year-old William Laughlan, the lad's mother told him: ". . . the boy was the principal support to the house, the father having been ill for a long time. The boy carried out papers morning and evening."[34] This entry from Wilkinson's diary also indicates the importance of children as substitute wage-earners. In his notebooks, newspaper reporter J.J. Kelso speculated that some newsboys, who he estimated earned between 60¢ and $1.00 a day, fully supported their parents.[35] Despite their importance as wage-earners, the vast majority of newsboys, bootblacks, and other street vendors occupied dead-end jobs that promised no viable future employment. Although some business skills could be learned on the street, only a tiny percentage of enterprising newsboys managed to climb the professional ladder. Moreover, the "privation, exposure, and irregular life" that characterized the street traders' existence frequently led to petty crime and permanent vagrancy.[36] In the estimation of W.H. Howland, the reform mayor of Toronto, "it was ruinous to a boy to become a newsboy, in nine hundred and ninety-nine cases out of a thousand."[37] J.J. Kelso added: "The profession of selling newspapers is in my opinion pernicious right through."[38]

Newsboys and other young street vendors attracted the attention of a new group of middle-class social reformers and self-styled child-savers. These individuals objected to the presence of so many roughly hewn youngsters on public streets and feared that extensive exposure to the harsher elements of city life would turn vulnerable children into vile and irresponsible adults. This, in turn, would place greater burden on the public purse through the maintenance of jails and houses of refuge. In an attempt to ameliorate this situation, J.J. Kelso and other leading philanthropists petitioned the Toronto Police Commission in 1889 to adopt measures to regulate the street traders. Kelso and his cohorts succeeded, and the resultant law, enacted in 1890, required newsboys and other vendors under the age of sixteen to apply for a licence, and forbade boys under eight and girls of any age to participate in the street trade at all. To qualify for a badge, a boy had to maintain a clean criminal record, avoid associating with thieves, and attend school at least two hours per day. In addition to having their privileges revoked, violators could be fined or sentenced to the industrial school or common jail. Although over 500 boys applied for licences in the first year, the police failed to enforce the regulations rigorously and the law quickly fell into disuse.[39] Two years later, the Toronto Board of Education established special classes for newsboys, but met with little success. In both cases, reformers failed to recognize the enormous distance between controlled orderliness as prescribed by law and the burden of poverty. Irrespective of the intentions of social legislation, many working-class families depended on the contributions of children.[40] Furthermore, the arguments reformers put forward in favour of regulation revealed a deeper concern with public morality and family values than with the economic circumstances of newsboys and their families. This attitude is especially evident in the extra restrictions placed on girls, the future wives and mothers of the nation. Susan Houston's comment on child beggars is equally applicable to newsboys and other young street vendors: ". . . it was their habits rather than their condition that roused the ire of reformers."[41]

Ironically, middle-class reformers had no farther to look than their own neighbourhoods if they wanted to observe the conditions of child workers.

Although little information exists on the work experiences of the natural children of the middle class, there is a substantial body of material that describes the role foster children played in middle-class homes. The care of orphans and vagrant children had always posed a delicate problem for civil authorities. From the early years of Upper Canadian society, officials usually dispensed with parentless and needy youngsters by arranging apprenticeship agreements for them. By the mid-1800s, private charitable institutions such as the Protestant Orphans' Home provided shelter and training for helpless children until placements could be found for them or until they reached an age of independence. By the latter years of the nineteenth century, however, new perceptions of child welfare had emerged. Most reformers now agreed that only the natural setting of a family provided dependent children with a fair opportunity to develop proper social and moral values. Parentless youngsters and those whose natural family settings were found to be unwholesome or inadequate were now to be placed in foster homes where they would be treated as regular members of another family. In this way, reformers hoped to reduce the public cost of child welfare and at the same time prevent the creation of a future vagrant and criminal class. The primary institutional expression of this view was the Children's Aid Society (CAS), the first Canadian branch of which appeared in Toronto in 1891 as a result of the initiative of J.J. Kelso. This approach gained ground in 1893 when the Ontario government sanctioned the activities of the CAS with the passage of the Children's Protection Act and appointed Kelso as the superintendent of neglected and dependent children.[42]

Although the CAS preferred to place its charges in the countryside, in the belief that the wholesomeness and honest toil of farm life would develop moral and industrious habits, a small percentage of older children ended up in lower middle- and middle-class urban homes where they performed the normal roster of domestic duties. Despite the society's efforts to insure that each child placed out would receive elementary education and affectionate treatment, a youngster's ability to perform work around the home often proved to be the decisive factor in his or her placement. In a circular letter dated 15 September 1893, J.J. Kelso instructed CAS agents to be wary of homes that treated foster children as servants, a practice which he admitted was "altogether too common among those who apply for the care of dependent children."[43] A second letter, dated 22 April 1894, warned about parents with young children of their own who used their CAS wards as live-in nursemaids.[44] The demand for child workers also revealed itself through the report of a representative of the Girls' Home in Toronto who stated that her institution received twenty times the number of requests for girls between the ages of ten and thirteen as it did for girls five or six years old.[45]

The CAS must accept partial blame for the numerous instances in which its wards ended up as nothing better than underpaid domestic servants in comfortable urban homes. Although its members unquestionably exhibited genuine concern for the welfare of neglected youngsters, the CAS, like most child-saving agencies of the time, believed fervently that early exposure to work and discipline would guarantee the development of an upstanding and industrious citizenship. The society's literature unambiguously stated that "girls at twelve years of age, and boys at fourteen, should become self-supporting."[46] For children twelve years of age and over, the society used a special placement form that committed the child to domestic service in return for modest payment. The CAS's unbending adherence to the work ethic created a hazy atmosphere that clouded the distinction between healthy work habits and child exploitation. Even if the CAS had developed more stringent regulations pertaining to the type of work children could perform in the home, it would have been impossible to enforce them. Although the Children's Protection Act provided for the creation of local visiting committees with the authority to monitor foster homes, J.J. Kelso reported in 1894 that the province's 25 to 30 active committees represented well less than half of the needed number.[47]

Canadian households in search of cheap domestic labour could also look to anyone of a dozen or more charitable institutions that specialized in the placement of British children in Canadian homes. From the time that Maria S. Rye arrived at Niagara-on-the-Lake in 1869 with a party of young orphans, the demand for British children always outpaced the supply.[48] By 1879, approximately 4,000 British youngsters were living and working with Canadian families.[49] This number would exceed 70,000 by 1919.[50] Like the Children's Aid Society, the British agencies preferred to send children to the countryside, but they also faced an overwhelming demand from city households for older girls to perform domestic work. In most cases, prospective guardians took few measures to camouflage their desire for help around the house. Moreover, correspondence and newspaper advertisements referring to available youngsters frequently emphasized the children's abilities to perform specific domestic tasks.

The best known of the child immigrants are the home children who arrived in Canada under the auspices of philanthropist Dr Thomas John Barnardo.[51] A second group of children, which journeyed to Canada in the late 1880s and early 1890s under the watchful eye of social worker Charlotte A. Alexander, has also left useful records.[52] Alexander primarily handled girls between the ages of 10 and 14, many of whom found places with families in urban Ontario. Some of Alexander's girls joined in home-centred industries, such as 11-year-old Jane Busby who helped her mistress produce waistcoats.[53] The vast majority of girls, however, assumed the normal responsibilities of domestic servants or nursemaids. Although an extremely competent and hardworking girl could increase her wages from a starting salary of $2.00 a month to $9.00 after a few years' service, she still earned less than a regular domestic servant. In a letter to a friend, young Maggie Hall described a typical work day:

> I have to get my morning's work done by 12 o'clock every day to take the children for a walk then I have to get the table laid for lunch when I come in then after dinner I help to wash up then I have to give the little boy his lessons then for the rest of the afternoon I sew till it is time to get afternoon tea and shut up and light the gas then by that time it is time for our tea after which I clear away get the table ready for Miss Smith's

dinner then put the little boy to bed & after Miss Smith's dinner I help wash up which does not take very long then I do what I like for the rest of the evening till half past nine when we have Prayers then I take Miss Smiths hot water & hot bottle, the basket of silver & glass of milk to her bedroom shut up & go to bed which by the time I have done all it is just ten.[54]

The letter's lack of punctuation perhaps unintentionally corresponds with the rapid pace of Maggie Hall's work day.

The letters among the Charlotte Alexander papers disclose a life of hard and tedious work that offered little in the way of security and opportunity. Alexander negotiated each placement individually, thus failing to insure that her girls would all receive the same treatment. This practice also left many girls at the mercy of particularly demanding guardians. Although Alexander obtained signed indentures for most of her placements, she had no regular visitation system which would allow for verification of the contract. Many guardians complained of the children's rough manners and poor work habits. Others unilaterally altered the terms of the agreement if the girl did not meet their expectations. Extremely dissatisfied customers simply returned unwanted girls to Alexander, or shunted them off to other residences. When children complained of unfair treatment, Alexander encouraged them to be tolerant and reminded them of how fortunate they were to have a position at all. Many children clung to their placements out of fear that another position would present even greater hardships. All girls suffered from a basic insecurity that accompanied the performance of unfamiliar duties in a strange environment. As Joy Parr has stated: "To be young, a servant and a stranger was to be unusually vulnerable, powerless and alone."[55] One letter among the Alexander papers unintentionally projects a vivid image of how onerous life could be for a working child. Lamenting the recent death of a foster child, a friend wrote to Charlotte Alexander on 29 June 1888: "Poor dear little Ada Hees passed away from this cold world— what a happy change for the dear child."[56] In the

temporal sense, a more brutally frank assessment of the life of a working child would be hard to imagine.

In private homes and on public streets, children in late-nineteenth-century urban Ontario routinely performed a variety of important economic duties that directly contributed to the successful functioning of the family or household economy. Youngsters not only assisted their families in this way, but in many cases provided valuable services to a demanding urban clientele. In working-class neighbourhoods, the widespread practice of child labour exposed the poverty and insecurity that plagued many families which could not rely on industrial wages alone to meet the demands of urban life. At the same time, the use of youngsters as regular or auxiliary workers denoted a family strategy that was both rational and flexible in its response to new and challenging circumstances. In the short term, working-class families could depend on children to add the last necessary ingredient to their formula for survival. In the long term, youngsters paid the price. The most significant of these costs lay in the area of education.

By the latter half of the nineteenth century, most children in Ontario enjoyed free access to primary education. But this held little promise for youngsters whose economic responsibilities at home prevented regular attendance at school. School inspectors repeatedly identified the non-enrolment and irregular attendance of working-class children as the education system's primary problem. A Toronto School Board census of 1863 revealed that of 1,632 children between the ages of five and sixteen not registered to attend school, 263, or 16.1 per cent, regularly worked at home during the day. Only full-time employment appeared more frequently on the chart as an explanation for nonattendance. This category contained 453 youngsters, or 27.7 per cent of the total. Of the remaining 7,876 registered students, only middle- and upper-class children posted a record of regular attendance.[57] Ultimately, the irregular school attendance of workers' children exposed the class bias of urban-industrial society. In Hamilton in 1871, for example, Ian Davey has shown that working-class children attended school far less regularly than did the sons and daughters of entrepreneurs. Youngsters from female-headed households occupied the bottom position.[58] Children of the working class were thus denied the full opportunity of personal development and social mobility that regular school attendance offered other youngsters. Although school attendance among working-class children improved near the end of the nineteenth century, youngsters from the middle and upper classes still enjoyed their traditional advantage. Mandatory attendance laws, first passed by the Ontario legislature in 1871 and strengthened in 1881 and 1891, affected the situation little.[59] Even when parents exhibited awareness of attendance laws, which was infrequent, such regulations proved unenforceable and irrelevant to families dependent on children's work.

This view of public education, of course, rests on the premise that working-class children had something tangible to gain by attending school. This is an arguable point in historical circles. Harvey Graff claims that for many children "the achievement of education brought no occupational rewards at all."[60] Michael Katz, Michael Doucet, and Mark Stern offer an identical assessment: "School attendance played no role in occupational mobility."[61] These authors contend that "ascriptive" conditions, such as class, ethnicity, sex, and geographic stability, exerted greater influence on social mobility than did education. This argument, however, largely depends on data drawn from the middle decades of the nineteenth century, a period when neither the public school system nor the urban-industrial labour market had advanced much beyond their formative stages. Early school promoters unquestionably placed greater emphasis on social control than they did on the creation of occupational opportunities for working-class children.[62] By the latter decades of the century, however, less obsessive school boards injected more skill-oriented programs into the educational curriculum, such as bookkeeping and commercial arithmetic.[63] This development occurred at the same time that the urban-industrial labour market began to place a premium on these and other basic academic skills. The rapid growth of the white-collar work force sustains this argument. In 1898, Imperial Oil Canada employed only

11 white-collar workers. This number grew to 6,000 by 1919. In addition, public service employment in Canada increased from 17,000 in 1901 to 77,000 by 1911.[64] Although policies of social control and other "ascriptive" conditions remained dominant factors in late-nineteenth-century society, improvements in school curriculum, coupled with the opening of new sectors in the labour market, increased the value of education for working-class children.[65] Lastly, it can be argued that if education did not provide workers' children with opportunities for upward mobility, it at least offered them lateral mobility in the form of a greater number of occupational choices within their own class.

One further dimension to the school issue warrants brief examination—the question of technical and manual training. By the 1890s, most Ontario schools offered these programs to boys, while girls were invited to study domestic science.[66] School officials claimed that technical and manual training provided boys with practical skills and guaranteed them a secure place in the job market. Trade unionist Daniel O'Donoghue disagreed. Testifying before a royal commission in 1890, O'Donoghue declared that Ontario's labour unions were "unanimously opposed to manual training in the schools."[67] In O'Donoghue's estimation, these programs lacked the depth and detail necessary to turn out competent workers. A careful reading of O'Donoghue's testimony, however, reveals that his real concern was that these programs would flood an already crowded labour market, thus driving wages down and threatening the control of the workplace skilled workers had traditionally exercised through strict regulation of the apprenticeship system. Significantly, O'Donoghue did not suggest that the school board improve the quality of its programs. Rather, he recommended that young people be sent to work on farms. Between the lines, one can detect O'Donoghue's hope that this practice would remove these children from the labour market altogether. Moreover, not all unionists shared O'Donoghue's opinion. In 1901, the secretary of the Plumbers' and Gas Fitters' Union sent a letter to the Toronto School Board commending it on its programs of manual training.[68] This position was more consistent with the labour movement's traditional support of general primary education, as evidenced by numerous resolutions and petitions submitted to all levels of government.[69]

Discussions of the actual value of education aside, it appears that most parents believed that their children had something to gain by attending school. This is suggested by the strikingly high enrolment figures recorded by almost all urban school boards. Working-class children dutifully registered for school at the beginning of each semester, but found it impossible to maintain regular attendance in the face of economic pressures at home. In an attempt to combine economic responsibilities with educational opportunities, many working-class families sought, and received, special consideration from local school boards. Inspector James Hughes reported in 1874: "We have in Toronto a considerable number of Pupils who desire to be absent regularly for a part of each day, either as newsboys, or to perform some necessary work at home."[70] J.B. Boyle, Inspector of Public Schools in London, Ontario, reported that parents withdrew their children from school when the family economy demanded extra workers: "Sometimes they become errand boys in shops, or they sell papers, or they do what they can."[71] Lastly, children who attended school irregularly missed the full benefit of the new physical education and health programs most schools offered by the late 1880s.[72]

Children who worked at home or on the street instead of attending school received little compensation in the form of job training. The street trades and sweat shop industries in particular exposed youngsters to elements that were both socially and physically harmful while offering no promise of occupational advancement. Although contractors often relied on the ruse of apprenticeship to encourage home workers to exploit their own children, the only opportunities associated with such labour were missed opportunities. Home-centred enterprises also deprived working-class children of the solace, privacy, and security that most middle- and upper-class youngsters enjoyed as a matter of natural right.

Social legislation and various reform movements had little immediate impact on the conditions of working children. In their attempt to make society safe for middle-class values, and at the same time guard against future costs of public welfare, reformers concentrated more on the symptoms of social maladies than on their causes. Legislation could set standards for proper social conduct, but it did little to relieve poverty. Most reformers, of course, did not view the unequal distribution of wealth and power as the root cause of social problems. In most cases, they preferred to blame the poor for their own condition. W.C. Wilkinson and the Toronto Public School Board, for example, believed that "lack of proper control by parents" was the source of irregular school attendance among working-class children.[73] Yet Wilkinson himself had recorded numerous instances of school-aged children performing important economic duties at home. Wilkinson and his cohorts might have arrived nearer to the truth had they set their sights on business elites whose hold over economic power forced many working-class families to stretch their resources to the limit simply to survive. Even trade unions exercised little influence over the conditions of many working-class families. Indeed, evidence shows that union time restrictions in clothing workshops that paid by the piece forced employees to continue their work at home with the assistance of their families.

New charitable organizations such as the Children's Aid Society unquestionably rescued numerous youngsters from the clutches of poverty and neglect by placing them in the care of benevolent and compassionate foster parents. But records left by the CAS and other child welfare agencies sadly indicate that many foster children ended up as underpaid domestic servants in middle-class homes. In addition to shouldering the burdens common to all working children, these youngsters also bore the cross of class prejudice. While labouring children in working-class homes performed economic duties directly related to their family's survival, foster children provided personal service for the affluent. They were as much a symbol of a successful household as they were a component of it.

One group of historians has argued that "the family is an institution which industrialization shaped by removing the home from the site of the workplace."[74] Most others would agree in principle.

Once free from the production-oriented nature of farm life, the family could devote more time to social development and material consumption. Yet for many children from lower-class families, work and home remained one, and the greater social and economic opportunities that allegedly accompanied urban life never materialized. Urban poverty forced many working-class households to apply the rural tradition of shared family responsibilities to meet the challenge of city life. But the transposition was not an easy one. Urban-industrial life provided less insular protection than the farmstead and presented workers with a greater number of competing forces. Consequently, old customs were forced to adapt to new and demanding circumstances. Despite the different pattern of social and economic relations forged by urban life, country and city still shared one common feature: in many lower-class neighbourhoods at least, work in and around the home remained a family affair.

Notes

1. Canniff Haight, *Life in Canada Fifty Years Ago* (Toronto 1885). Cited in Michael S. Cross, ed., *The Workingman in the Nineteenth Century* (Toronto 1974), 34.

2. Late-nineteenth-century writers commonly saw their society in transition from a rural-agricultural setting to an urban-industrial one. This simple dichotomy facilitated discussion of new social developments and emphasized the threat to tradition posed by emergent urban-industrial life. Modern historians, taking into account the growth of capitalism and waged labour, have offered a more complex and sophisticated analysis of social change. Michael Katz, Michael Doucet, and Mark Stern, for example, construct a three-stage paradigm which claims that "North America shifted from a peculiar variety of mercantile-peasant economy to an economy dominated by commercial capitalism to one dominated by industrial capitalism." *The Social Organization of Industrial Capitalism* (Cambridge, MA 1982), 364. Despite these more complex undercurrents of social transition, most late-nineteenth-century workers identified with the rural–urban praxis. Historians develop comprehensive theories of social change over time; workers deal with the realities of life from day to day. This paper focuses on the second set of concerns.

3. Blair Neatby, *The Politics of Chaos: Canada in the Thirties* (Toronto 1972), 45. E.P. Thompson writes: "Each stage in industrial differentiation and specialisation struck also at the family economy, disturbing customary relations between man and wife, parents and children, and differentiating more sharply between 'work' and 'life'. . . . Meanwhile the family was roughly torn apart each morning by the factory bell . . ." *The Making of the English Working Class* (New York 1963), 416.

4. See for example *Report of the Commissioners Appointed to Enquire into the Working of Mills and Factories of the Dominion, and the Labour Employed Therein,* Sessional Papers. 9, XV, no. 42, 1882; *Report of the Royal Commission on the Relations of Capital and Labor in Canada* (Ottawa 1889), (hereafter *Royal Labor Commission); Annual Reports* of the Quebec Department of Labour; and *Annual Reports* of the Inspectors of Factories for the Province of Ontario. Among secondary sources, see Terry Copp, *The Anatomy of Poverty: The Condition of the Working Class in Montreal 1897–1929* (Toronto 1974); Bettina Bradbury, "The Family Economy and Work in an Industrializing City: Montreal in the 1870s," *Canadian Historical Association Historical Papers* (1979); Fernand Harvey, "Children of the Industrial Revolution in Quebec," in J. Dufresne et al., eds., *The Professions: Their Growth or Decline?* (Montreal 1979), reprinted in R. Douglas Francis and Donald B. Smith, eds., *Readings in Canadian History: Post-Confederation* (Toronto 1982); Gregory S. Kealey, *Hogtown: Working Class Toronto at the Turn of the Century* (Toronto 1974), also reprinted in Francis and Smith; Eugene Forsey, *Trade Unions in Canada 1812–1902* (Toronto 1982); Michael J. Piva, *The Condition of the Working Class in Toronto—1900–1921* (Ottawa 1979); and Bryan D. Palmer, *A Culture in Conflict: Skilled Workers and Industrial Capitalism in Hamilton, Ontario. 1860–1914* (Montreal 1979).

5. The youngsters chosen for examination here by no means exhaust all possibilities. Children also worked in institutions such as orphanages, asylums, industrial schools, and reformatories. See Patricia T. Rooke and R.L. Schnell, *Discarding the Asylum: From Child Rescue to the Welfare State in English-Canada (1800–1950)* (Lanham 1983); Harvey G. Simmons, *From Asylum to Welfare* (Downsview 1982); Susan E. Houston, "Victorian Origins of Juvenile Delinquency: A Canadian Experience," in Michael B. Katz and Paul H. Mattingly. eds., *Education and Social Change: Themes From Ontario's Past* (New York 1975); and Susan E. Houston, "The Impetus to Reform: Urban Crime, Poverty and Ignorance in Ontario 1850–1875," (Ph.D. thesis, University of Toronto, 1974). These children have not been included as subjects of this paper on the grounds that they did not belong to families or households in the conventional sense of those terms.

6. In 1851, Ontario's rural population stood at 818,541 and its urban population at 133,463. By 1901, at 1,246,969,

the rural population was still greater, but the urban population had increased dramatically to 935,978. Source: Canada, Bureau of the Census. *Report on Population*, 1, (1901). In Toronto alone the population increased from 30,775 in 1851 to 144,023 by 1891. Source: Gregory S. Kealey, *Toronto Workers Respond to Industrial Capitalism 1867–1892* (Toronto 1980), 99.

7. *The Globe*, 1 April 1894.

8. Most of the following examples are drawn from Toronto Board of Education Records, Archives and Museum (hereafter TBERAM). W.C. Wilkinson Diaries, six vols., 1872–74; TBERAM, Management Committee Minutes, 1899–1901; Hamilton Children's Aid Society, Scrapbook of Clippings, vol. I, 1894–1961, Hamilton Public Library, Special Collections; Susan E. Houston, "The Impetus to Reform;" and Alison Prentice and Susan Houston, eds., *Family, School and Society in Nineteenth Century Canada* (Toronto 1975).

9. Testimony of John Henderson, manager for J. McLaren & Company Lumber Merchants, Ottawa, *Royal Labor Commission*, Ontario evidence, 1139-9.

10. "Annals of the Poor (the Creche)." *The Globe*, 4 January 1987.

11. TBERAM, Wilkinson Diaries, vol. 2, entry for 7 October 1872.

12. Toronto Board of Education, *Annual Report of the Local Superintendent of the Public Schools* (Toronto 1874), 45.

13. *Report of the Commissioners Appointed to Enquire into the Working of Mills and Factories*, 4.

14. Ibid., 7. See also *The Globe*, 23 September 1871, and "Toronto and the Sweating System," *The Daily Mail and Empire*, 9 October 1897 (part two).

15. "Female Labour in Toronto: Its Nature—Its Extent—Its Reward," *The Globe*, 28 October 1868.

16. *Report of the Commissioners Appointed to Enquire into the Working of Mills and Factories*, 10–11.

17. "Report of A.H. Blackeby on the State of the Manufacturing Industries of Ontario and Quebec," XVIII, Sessional Papers, 10, Report 37, 1885, 31.

18. Alexander Whyte Wright, *Report Upon the Sweating System in Canada*, Sessional Papers, 2, XXIX, no. 61, 1896, 8.

19. Ibid., 9.

20. Ibid., 11.

21. Ibid., 8.

22. W.L. Mackenzie King, *Report to the Honourable the Postmaster General of the Methods adopted in Canada in the Carrying Out of Government Clothing Contracts* (Ottawa 1900), 10.

23. Ibid., 19.

24. Ibid.

25. Ibid., 28.

26. Ontario, *Report of Committee on Child Labour 1907* (Toronto 1907), 5.

27. Interview conducted by Jane Synge. Cited in Irving Abella

and David Millar. eds., *The Canadian Worker in the Twentieth Century* (Toronto 1978), 98. See also C.S. Clark, *Of Toronto the Good* (Montreal 1898), 62.

28. Conyngham Crawford Taylor, *Toronto "Called Back" From 1888 to 1847 and the Queen's Jubilee* (Toronto 1888), 189.

29. Public Archives of Canada (hereafter PAC). J.J. Kelso Papers, MG30 C97, vol. 4.

30. *Report of the Commissioners Appointed to Enquire into the Prison and Reformatory System of Ontario* (Toronto 1891), 372-3, (hereafter *Prison Reform Commission*).

31. See PAC, J.J. Kelso Papers, vol. 4; PAC, Children's Aid Society of Ottawa, MG28 184, Minutes, 1893–1906; and "Industrial Schools," *The Globe*, 4 November 1878.

32. See J.J. Kelso, *Second Report of Work Under the Children's Protection Act for the Year Ending December* 31, 1894 (Toronto 1895), 12; *Hamilton Spectator*, 23 January 1894; C.S. Clark, *Of Toronto the Good*, 136; and *Prison Reform Commission*, testimony of W.H. Howland, 689; David Archibald, staff-inspector, Toronto Police Force, 701–2; and J.J. Kelso, 724.

33. These descriptions of newsboys are drawn primarily from PAC, J.J. Kelso Papers; *Prison Reform Commission*, testimony of J.J. Kelso. 723-9, and George Alfred Barnett, superintendent of the Newsboys' Home, Toronto, 729-30; Ontario *Report of Committee on Child Labor;* "The Tag System Abortive," *The Toronto World*, 22 November 1890; "The Waifs of the Street," *The Globe*, 18 April 1891; "The Industrial School," *The Telegram*, 18 April 1878; "'Around Town," *Saturday Night*, 10 (21 November 1896); C.S. Clark, *Of Toronto the Good:* J.J. Kelso, *Protection of Children: Early History of the Humane and Children's Aid Movement in Ontario 1886–1893* (Toronto 1911); and Karl Baedeker, *The Dominion of Canada* (London 1900). I am indebted to David Swayze for bringing this last source to my attention.

34. TBERAM. Wilkinson Diaries, vol. 5, entry for 9 December 1873.

35. PAC, J.J. Kelso Papers, vol. 8.

36. Ontario, *Report of Committee on Child Labor, II*.

37. *Royal Labor Commission*, Ontario evidence, 161.

38. *Prison Reform Commission*, 723. Various police chiefs across Ontario upheld the views of Howland and Kelso. See *Prison Reform Commission*, testimony of W. McVitty, chief constable of Ottawa, 372-3, and Lieut.-Col. H.J. Grasett, chief of police, Toronto, 700. See also Ontario, *Report on Compulsory Education in Canada, Great Britain, Germany and the United States* (Toronto 1891), 89.

39. "The Waifs of the Street," *The Globe*, 18 April 1891.

40. Undoubtedly, some newsboys pursued their profession as a matter of personal choice, preferring the small income and independence of the street to the demands and discipline of the school system.

41. Susan E. Houston, "Victorian Origins of Juvenile Delinquency," 86.

42. For a thorough discussion of the new approaches to child welfare, see Patricia T. Rooke and R.L. Schnell, *Discarding the Asylum;* Andrew Jones and Leonard Rutman, *In The Children's Aid: J.J. Kelso and Child Welfare in Ontario* (Toronto 1981); Neil Sutherland, *Children in English-Canadian Society: Framing the Twentieth Century Consensus* (Toronto 1976); Richard Splane, *Social Welfare in Ontario: A Study of Public Welfare Administration* (Toronto 1965); Jane-Louise K. Dawe, "The Transition from Institutional to Foster Care for Children in Ontario 1891–1921." (M.S.W. thesis, University of Toronto, 1966); and Terrence Morrison, "The Child and Urban Social Reform in Late Nineteenth Century Ontario 1875–1900," (Ph.D. thesis, University of Toronto, 1971).

43. PAC, J.J. Kelso Papers, vol. 4. Kelso also mentioned this problem in his *First Report of Work Under the Children's Protection Act, 1893 For the Six Months Ending December 31 1893* (Toronto 1894), 26.

44. Ibid.

45. *Proceedings of the First Ontario Conference on Child-Saving* (Toronto 1895), 59.

46. J.J. Kelso, *First Report of Work Under the Children's Protection Act,* 27.

47. *Proceedings of the First Ontario Conference on Child-Saving,* 46.

48. See Wesley Turner, "80 Stout and Healthy Looking Girls," *Canada: An Historical Magazine,* 3, 2 (December 1975), and Turner, "Miss Rye's Children and the Ontario Press 1875," *Ontario History,* 68 (September 1976).

49. Ellen Agnes Bilbrough, *British Children in Canadian Homes* (Belleville 1879).

50. Neil Sutherland, *Children in English-Canadian Society,* 4.

51. A handful of informative monographs on the Barnardo children are now available. The best among them is Joy Parr, *Labouring Children: British Immigrant Apprentices to Canada 1869–1924* (Montreal 1980). For a more anecdotal approach, see Kenneth Bagnell, *The Little Immigrants: The Orphans Who Came to Canada* (Toronto 1980); Gail Corbett, *Barnardo Children in Canada* (Peterborough 1981); and Phyllis Harrison, *The Home Children: Their Personal Stories* (Winnipeg 1979).

52. PAC, Charlotte A. Alexander Papers, MG29 C58.

53. *Ibid.,* vol. 3, Indexed Register, 1885–93.

54. *Ibid.,* vol. 1, Maggie Hall to Miss Lowe, 13 February 1890.

55. Joy Parr, *Labouring Children,* 82.

56. PAC, Charlotte A. Alexander Papers. vol. 2, Alice Maude Johnson file, Mrs Coyne to Charlotte Alexander, 29 June 1888.

57. Toronto Board of Education, *Annual Report of the Local Superintendent* (Toronto 1863), 43. To avoid the impression that this period lacked normal youthful playfulness, it should be noted that Toronto truant officer W.C. Wilkinson regularly discovered youngsters engaged in the usual truant shenanigans of fishing, swimming, and attending the races. See TBERAM, Wilkinson Diaries.

58. Ian E. Davey. "Educational Reform and the Working Class: School Attendance in Hamilton, Ontario, 1851–1891," (Ph.D. thesis, University of Toronto, 1975), 187.

59. The Ontario School Act of 1871 required children seven to twelve years of age to attend school four months of the year under normal circumstances. In 1881, an amendment to the act required children seven to thirteen years of age to attend school eleven weeks in each of two school terms. In 1885, another amendment reduced compulsory attendance to 100 days per year. In 1891, attendance became compulsory for the full school year for all children between eight and fourteen years of age.

60. Harvey J. Graff, *The Literacy Myth: Literacy and Social Structure in the Nineteenth-Century City* (New York 1979), 75.

61. Katz, Doucet, and Stern, *The Social Organization of Early Industrial Capitalism,* 197.

62. For discussions of the motivations of early school officials, see Alison Prentice, *The School Promoters: Education and Social Class in Mid-Nineteenth Century Upper Canada* (Toronto 1977); Neil McDonald and Alf Chaiton, eds., *Egerton Ryerson and His Times* (Toronto 1978); and James H. Love, "Cultural Survival and Social Control: The Development of a Curriculum for Upper Canada's Common Schools in 1846," *Histoire Sociale/Social History,* 30 (November 1982).

63. See TBERAM, Management Committee Minutes, 1899–1901.

64. Gregory S. Kealey, "The Structure of Canadian Working-Class History," in W.J.C. Cherwinski and G.S. Kealey, eds., *Lectures in Canadian Labour and Working-Class History* (St. John's 1985), 28.

65. Combining "ascriptive" conditions and educational opportunities, J. Donald Wilson adds another dimension to the school question: "What happened to children in schools, how long they stayed in school, and how much they were influenced by schooling depended to a considerable extent on their ethnic and cultural background." "The Picture of Social Randomness: Making Sense of Ethnic History and Educational History", in David C. Jones et al., eds., *Approaches to Educational History* (Winnipeg 1981), 36.

66. Douglas A. Lawr and Robert D. Gidney, eds., *Educating Canadians: A Documentary History of Public Education* (Toronto 1973), 161, and Harvey Graff, *The Literacy Myth,* 210.

67. *Prison Reform Commission,* 739.

68. TBERAM, Management Committee Minutes, 14 February 1901.

69. For numerous examples see Eugene Forsey, *Trade Unions in Canada.* For a more detailed look at labour's view of technical and manual training, see T.R. Morrison, "Reform as Social Tracking: The Case of Industrial Education in Ontario 1870–1900," *The Journal of Educational Thought,* 8, 2 (August 1974), 106–7.

70. *Annual Report of the Normal, Model, Grammar and Common Schools in Ontario* (Toronto 1874), Appendix B, 84. Similar requests with positive replies can be found in TBERAM, Management Committee Minutes, 1899-1901.

71. *Royal Labor Commission,* Ontario evidence, 604-7.

72. See Neil Sutherland, *Children in English-Canadian Society:* Sutherland, "'To Create a Strong and Healthy Race:' School Children in the Public Health Movement 1880-1914." in Katz and Mattingly, *Education and Social Change;* and Robert M. Stamp, "Urbanization and Education in Ontario and Quebec, 1867-1914," *McGill Journal of Education,* 3 (Fall 1968), 132.

73. Archives of Ontario, responses to G.W. Ross's inquiry of July 1895 regarding revisions of the Truancy Act, RG 22, Acc. 9631, Printed Circular no. 47, W.C. Wilkinson, secretary-treasurer, Toronto Public School Board, to Hon. G.W. Ross, Minister of Education, 8 October 1895. I am indebted to Terrence Campbell, formerly of the Ontario Archives, for bringing this file to my attention.

74. Russell G. Hann, Gregory S. Kealey, Linda Kealey, and Peter Warrian, "Introduction," *Primary Sources in Canadian Working Class History 1860-1930* (Kitchener 1973), 18.

PRIMARY DOCUMENT

"Little Girl with Bag of Coal," c. 1900–1910

Source: Library and Archives Canada / PA-118224

Canadian Children Who Lived with One Parent in 1901

BETTINA BRADBURY

The men hired to enumerate Canadian households in 1901 recorded over 180,000 children under the age of 19—more than 100,000 of whom were under 15—living in a household with only one parent present.[1] Over two-thirds of these youngsters were living with their mother. These children with just one parent were in all parts of the country, in rural as well as urban areas and among all classes and cultural groups. Their ages, sex, history of schooling and work, and residential situations were diverse. So too were their parents' marital status. Bertha Whipley, aged 4, lived with her 34-year-old widowed mother Hattie, her two siblings, and her 72-year-old widowed grandmother, in Saint John, New Brunswick. Seventeen-year-old Elizabeth Brenton was listed as residing with her 66-year-old widowed father and five siblings in Cowichan, British Columbia. Her mother had likely been a local Cowichan woman, for all the children were listed, following the instructions for that census regarding people's racial origins, as "Cowichan English Breed."[2] Helen Mackitchen, who was 7, lived with her 8-year-old brother James and their 28-year-old mother, Mary. Mary was described as married, though no father was listed in their Hamilton dwelling. One-year-old Ace Hunter lived with his unmarried mother Mary Jane Hunter. She was a servant in the farm of a couple in their sixties in the Township of Edwardsburgh, Ontario. The enumerator in Warwick Township, Ontario, recorded that William Halsted, aged 14, was the adopted son of Alonzo Bitner, an unmarried, 40-year-old male farmer of German origin who shared his farm with two adult siblings. When Charles P. McRosite called at the one-room Nelson,

BC, home of the recently arrived Chinese immigrant whose name he transcribed as Juin Yen, he noted that this 40-year-old married man had one son living with him. Juin had arrived in Canada in 1898, Sing in 1899. There is no sign of Sing's mother. Immigration laws made it extremely difficult and expensive for men like Yen to bring their wives into Canada.[3]

Death, desertion or separation, birth out of wedlock, adoption, and racist immigration laws respectively left each of these Canadian children with just one parent. In the language preferred today by Statistics Canada, they were all the offspring of lone parents.[4] They constituted a significant minority of Canadian youngsters at the turn of the last century. Like Bertha, Helen, Ace, William, and Sing, roughly 6 per cent of children aged 5 to 9, and nearly 10 per cent of those aged 10 to 14, were living with only one parent when the census taker called (Table 1). Families headed by lone parents made up close to 12 per cent of all the families in Canada in which there were children in the home and the head was 55 or under (Table 4). The manuscript listings of families for the Canadian censuses, including those for 1901, allow historians to grasp some aspects of the lives of such children and their parents. They permit some answers to the question that family historian Cynthia Comacchio poses: "What about the children of single-parent, especially single-mother, families who worried so many experts due to the absence of a 'father figure?'"[5] It is possible to make rough estimates of how many children lived with a lone parent at the time the census was taken. And the estimates give us glimpses of these children's residential situations, of their schooling and wage-earning experiences, and of that part of family income that was earned through waged labour. Many more children than those visible at the time the census was taken

Source: From *Household Counts: Canadian Households and Families in 1901*, eds. Peter Baskerville and Eric Sager (Toronto: University of Toronto Press, 2006). © University of Toronto Press 2006. Abridged. Reprinted with permission of the publisher.

would have spent some time living in a single-parent family before the remarriage of a widowed parent or, briefly or permanently, when parents separated, disappeared, or, less frequently, divorced. Furthermore, the difficulties of raising children without a spouse meant that many youngsters who had only one parent were not living with a parent when the census was taken because they had been given up for adoption, placed in an institution, or sent away to relatives or to work.[6]

To spend part of one's childhood being raised in a single-parent family, then, is not a new feature of late-twentieth- and early-twenty-first-century childhood and youth, however much contemporary journalism and policy debates may cast it in that light. A significant proportion of Canadian children at the turn of the last century shared these experiences with children today. The 1901 census shows 8 per cent of youths aged 15 to 17 living only with a mother. Some 4 per cent were with their fathers. In the 1996 Canadian census 16 per cent of 15 to 17 year olds lived with their mothers only, while 4 per cent were with fathers.[7] Some characteristics of these children's lives were similar to those of the children of single parents today. Then and now the majority were raised by mothers rather than fathers, though the ratio of lone mothers to fathers has increased dramatically. And, as is true today, the children of lone mothers were especially likely to be raised in poverty. Many other aspects of their lives, however, were quite different.

This paper first looks briefly at historical research about single parenting and the children of single parents to sketch in some of the changing historical circumstances that influenced their visibility as well as the unravelling of their lives. It then examines the ways the process of census taking and database construction influence how we can explore the experiences of Bertha, Elizabeth, Helen, Ace, William, and Sing and other children raised by one parent. For the interactions between enumerators and the Canadians whose family situations they sought to transcribe influenced what we can now read from the pages these interactions produced.

Historians have paid surprisingly little attention to the history of such children, despite the important research on single-parent families being undertaken in sociology, social work, and other disciplines today and the ongoing popular and scholarly debates about the effects of divorce, in particular, on the young.[8] Most historical research in Canada has focused either on single mothers, rather than their children, or on the children of unwed mothers, and particularly on institutions created to shelter them during their pregnancies and to arrange adoptions.[9] In addition, four broad areas of historical writing provide important context that frames what we can see about lone parents and their children in the census of 1901. Studies of nineteenth-century charity, benevolent work, "child saving," and delinquency are critical to conceptualizing the reasons why many children would not have been living with their widowed or deserted mother or father when the census taker called and to understanding some of the institutional responses to one form of single parenthood—unwed mothers.[10] The research of scholars into the changing laws regarding marriage and motherhood, especially laws touching on women's rights in cases of desertion and cruelty, offers glimpses of the ways some widowed mothers struggled to care for and keep their children and of the changing framework of mothers' rights.[11] And the research of feminist family historians gives us some sense of the particular contours of the family economies of lone parents in the past,[12] while demographers have long explored illegitimacy and have more recently begun to investigate the impact of a parent's absence or death on household structures and on children's chances of survival.[13]

Widows and their children were invariably among those nineteenth- and early-twentieth-century poor who were considered "deserving" candidates for charity. Studies of benevolent institutions reveal that widows and deserted wives, their children, and orphans were among the main clients, both as inmates and as recipients of visits and users of soup kitchens.[14] This, of course, is not surprising given the difficulties many women faced raising children and finding employment that would pay sufficiently to support them and their family. Similarly, historians of early social-work agencies have been struck by the high numbers of single mothers in the agencies' case files and hence of the challenging lives many children in such families faced.[15] By the time the 1901 census was taken, child-saving reformers in most provinces had worked for several decades to create policies and institutions that would clear the streets of "dangerous children," remove some from parents deemed unworthy, and create separate educational and criminal institutions for delinquent or potentially delinquent youths. In Ontario, J.J. Kelso set the tone of much of the child-saving reform, first through his involvement in the creation of Children's Aid Societies, and, after 1893, as Superintendent of Neglected and Dependent Children. In that capacity he was empowered to implement the regulations of the Children's Protection Act, initiated that year by Oliver Mowat's Liberal government. This act provided for the punishment of people guilty of neglecting or exploiting children. It mandated that children who were considered "neglected" or who had no parents or guardians could be placed under the charge of Children's Aid Societies. Society workers were empowered to apprehend such children, supervise them, and take part in selecting foster homes for them. Similar ideas informed legislation in most other provinces. Outside Quebec, the dominant consensus about the best place for orphans and neglected children shifted away from a belief in institutional settings like orphanages to placement in families.[16]

John Bullen has demonstrated how the policies of these child savers deprived working-class families of their children's help in making ends meet by scrounging and selling on the streets.[17] The enforcement of truancy laws that prevented a child from earning could be especially difficult for single mothers, struggling as widows or deserted wives to secure sufficient family income. Furthermore, the focus on child removal and fostering meant that single parents faced the risk of losing their children if local Children's Aid Societies considered them neglected.

In the ways that Kelso and his bureaucrats discussed and publicized the dangers facing children, the children of widows and other single mothers slipped readily into the category of the problem child requiring rescue to a better home. In images, photos, and words the loss of a father, whether through desertion or death, was widely represented as a tragedy for the children that might lead only too readily to neglect, poverty, and incorrigible behaviour, even while widows were seldom targeted as vicious parents. "When the widow goes forth to drive the wolf from the door, neglect and vice seize upon the children," was the message of a sketch published in a turn-of-the-century report of the Department of Neglected and Dependent Children. Cleverly, in this representation of the problems of single motherhood, the widow retains elements of her place among the deserving poor. It is not her fault that her husband died, just as in another sketch in the report it is not the fault of the wife that her husband has deserted. Yet, at the same time, the effect on their children is clearly portrayed as a problem. If such children engaged in "such glaring evils as street-begging, peddling of small wares; youthful immorality and truancy," might they too not be rescued and find themselves among "upwards of a thousand children" whom Kelso boasted in 1899 had been transplanted "from a condition of misery and destitution into the homes of respectability and Christian culture."[18] In this child-saving, reform rhetoric of turn-of-the-century English Canada, to be without a father, or "motherless," was thus signified as one of the routes to neglect and crime that stigmatized single parents and their offspring. In Kelso's reports, children living only with their mother, or less frequently their father, were frequently featured in the vignettes describing the homes of problem children. Without actually blaming the mothers, vignettes such as these nonetheless linked mothers to child neglect.[19]

Such representations that linked single parenting, delinquency, and crime circulated widely, contributing to understandings of single mothers as problem parents that persist today. They hid the diversity of ways in which single mothers and fathers succeeded in raising children. The census of 1901 offers the possibility of getting a broader picture of the living situations of children in single-parent families. Yet the writing about new provisions for neglected and delinquent children should remind historians using the census that any offspring of single parents who were among the children "saved" would not be listed as living with their parent when the census taker called. This reshuffling of the child population into other people's homes through fostering means that only some children of single parents can be seen in the censuses.[20] Nor were foster homes the only places where the children of single parents might end up living. The very real challenges that many women and some men faced a century ago when they tried to raise children without a spouse did mean that some of their children were likely to engage in activities that were labelled as delinquent, as well as in criminal ones. Historians of delinquency and of industrial and reform schools have noted that disproportionate numbers of the youth arrested and institutionalized had widowed mothers.[21]

While research into juvenile delinquency and child saving suggests reasons why children might not have been living with a single parent, feminist research into provincial legislation touching on married women's rights suggests new ways in which some women could acquire some level of economic independence. Historians interested in legal history and state policy have sketched out the ways successive provincial politicians passed legislation over the second half of the nineteenth century that gave married women a claim on support from their husbands in some cases of separation, as well as the right to control their own earnings and property. Before the passage of Married Women's Property Acts, virtually all of a wife's property, including her earnings, belonged legally to her husband in the provinces outside Quebec, and in that jurisdiction such monies were administered by the husband, unless some separation of their property had been arranged through a marriage contract before marriage or a court order after. In the common-law provinces, successive acts gave wives the right to claim ownership of their own earnings and property, initially in cases of desertion, then by the 1880s in all marriages. Historians have begun to demonstrate how these acts increased the likelihood that married women would own property in their own names, and changed the ways husbands and wives decided about who should own what within families.[22] In the two decades before the taking of the 1901 census several provinces also passed legislation

that provided deserted wives who were able to locate their husbands with the possibility of taking them to court for a maintenance order. Such legislation contributed to public discussion about the problems such wives and their children faced. It also provided some relief for that minority of deserted wives who were successful in securing maintenance payments,[23] and raised the possibility that some married women would have the financial basis to imagine escaping marriages that were not working. No legislation modified the sex differential in earning capacity. Wages for women workers remained at half to two-thirds those of males, and only a small number of wives were likely to own the substantial property that would be required for them to be self supporting.

At the time the 1901 census was taken, then, major and contradictory changes were under way that would influence the lives of children with one female parent. Wives had a little more leverage in cases of desertion. They had gained control over monies they could earn or accumulate in other ways. But the state, through Children's Aid Societies and school truancy officers, was more interventionist in attempting to deal with children deemed neglected. It was well after this census, following the First World War, that feminists succeeded in convincing provincial governments that women raising children on their own deserved some kind of pension so they could keep their children at home, and thereby avoid fostering or giving them up to relatives, strangers, or institutions. In promoting Mother's Allowances or pensions for single mothers, feminists drew positively upon the long association of widows with the deserving poor, while building upon the child savers' insistence on families as the best place for children. In many provinces widows were the only lone mothers eligible for such allowances. Proponents continued to stress the dangers of delinquency in mother-headed families, blaming mothers while proposing support to keep them from working. In 1901, as in previous decades, widows, deserted wives, and unwed mothers who were supporting their own children had to rely on their own resources and initiatives, on support from kin and friends, or on charity.[24]

The significance of children's contributions to the family economies of lone parents has attracted the attention of feminist historians interested in widows and their children or in the fragility of male support. Such studies have shown the challenges women raising children alone faced because of women's meagre wage-earning possibilities. They have demonstrated how single mothers relied on the wage labour of their children and on domestic help from daughters as well as on the different roles sons and daughters played depending on whether the resident parent was their mother or father. Most such studies have been located within early industrial cities, and based on censuses or similar sources. Similar questions will be pursued in this article, though the focus here is more on the children than the parents and at the level of the whole country, including rural and urban areas.[25]

Apart from such works examining family economies, children who lived with only one parent have received surprisingly little attention from family historians. In early studies of families and households these children, like the widows, widowers, and other single parents raising them, frequently disappeared in paradigms and typologies that did not consider single-parenthood an important issue.[26] Single-parent families were frequently buried within the category of nuclear family, so that it has been too easy to slip from the argument that families have been predominantly nuclear in the history of north-western Europe to the understanding that nuclear families included two parents and their children.[27] Demographers, better armed with longitudinal techniques, especially family reconstitution, have succeeded in highlighting the impact of death and sometimes of remarriage on families. Yet they too have frequently chosen to focus on "completed" families—those where both parents live at least to the end of the wife's childbearing age. This decision also hides single-parent families, casting their patterns of fertility or family size outside the norm, and sometimes turning them into a methodological problem rather than a historical reality to be analyzed.[28] They become what Joy Parr has referred to as "the discordant bits, the parts of the past living space that our categories will not hold," which

she enjoins scholars of the history of childhood not to overlook.[29] Over the last decade several demographers have begun to give serious consideration to the presence of one or two parents as a predictor of children's survival rates. Recent literature reveals that not having a mother, especially for infants, made a significant difference to babies' survival rates.[30] If not having a mother could be a matter of life and death for newborns, what it meant for other children deserves serious attention.

The Children of Single Parents as Seen through the Lenses of the Census and Databases

The Canadian Families Project's 5 per cent sample of the 1901 census makes it possible to compare the lives of Bertha, Helen, Ace, William, and Sing and other children who were living with one parent when the 1901 census was taken with those in two-parent families. The category—child of one parent—is one that I have created. It includes those children 19 and under who were listed in the census as living with a person identified as their mother or father, but not with the other parent. These were the offspring of widows and widowers, of married men and women whose spouses lived elsewhere, and of a few divorcees. They included the biological and adopted children of single men and women. Behind the residential situations transcribed at the moment of census taking, and concretized in the schedules that we can consult today, lay multiple trajectories, tragedies, and traumas. Except for children whose parent had died, the reasons for the absence of a parent are often hidden. Invisible in the census, too, are the uncountable number of children for whom the death, departure, or disappearance of a parent had also meant separation from their remaining parent and placement with relatives or strangers or in institutions, although some appear as the adopted child of one parent. The census captures one moment in the life course of children. Most of what came before and all of what would follow can only be imagined.

While the marital status of men and women whose spouse died changed from married to widowed, and was noted as such in many legal and other records, there was no such designation for youth who had experienced the death of one or both parents. In the census, the only sign is the absence of one parent, or the official designation of their one parent as widowed. As a result this paper is not about children who had only one parent, but about those recorded as living with only one parent when the census was taken. I use several generic terms to refer to their parents—"lone parent," "single parent," "lone mother," etc.—consciously including in one category of more recent making the diverse forms of family breakup in the past, while specifying the parents' marital status when relevant.

Enumerators arrived at Canadian homes in 1900 to 1901 armed with their schedules, pens, and a set of instructions. They interpreted what they found both through the instructions they had been given and through understandings of family, household, gender, race, and class forged in their lifetime through their own experiences and contemporary debates. Perhaps, like the family historians who years later would take the forms they filled out and interpret them, they came to expect that most households would be composed largely of one family, most often two parents and their children. Certainly the instructions they received implied this. A family, they were told in section 42, "consists of parents and sons and daughters" in one "living and housekeeping community." Yet it seems unlikely that many of these men would have been very surprised at the numbers of homes they encountered where children were being raised by only one parent. Death rates were still high in 1901, though possibly lower than they had been several decades earlier. There were considerable regional variations.[31] Some of the enumerators were quite elderly men, if later debates about their need to hire carriages to go from house to house are to be believed.[32] Many men their age would have lost their parents before they reached adulthood. Some may also have been widowed themselves. More no doubt had relatives and friends who had experienced not only a parent's death before they reached adulthood, but also the death of a spouse. Nor were most Canadians unfamiliar with marriages that had gone awry. Many adults would have personally witnessed marriages

that did not work within their own kin group, or among their acquaintances. Husbands who drank, gambled, or simply disappeared leaving their wives to manage on their own became common currency during temperance campaigns as well as in debates about improving married women's rights to retain control of their own property during the 1880s and earlier.[33] Less likely perhaps was personal knowledge of women who had given birth out of wedlock, because strong social sanctions against such mothers led many to give up their babies.[34]

These men who were employed by the federal government as enumerators had an unprecedented opportunity to observe Canadian families within their homes and to ask sensitive questions about family relationships in order to do their job of recording the characteristics of the country's individuals, families, and households in the predetermined categories of their forms. What male enumerators recorded in the rigid columns of the census folios for their districts was based on their interpretations of the answers that the head of the household, or the person at home when they called, gave them. Respondents could be hazy about their age, or not remember their income. Some enumerators were sloppy in their recording or careless in their writing. Questions about marital status and parentage were unambiguous for most Canadians. Yet enumerators asking questions of single parents were sometimes on particularly sensitive terrain. Did Charles Irwin, the enumerator in poll 40 of Ward Four in Toronto, ask the 53-year-old widower Lainy whether the one year old he reported as his child was really his, or whether his 43-year-old single sister, or either his 19- or his 16-year-old daughter, was the biological mother? Or was co-operation on later questions so important, his respect for the family's privacy so great, or his desire to complete as many families in one day so urgent that he simply continued recording?[35] As far as we can tell, he did not ask about, but duly recorded little Arlene as William's daughter immediately after his two other daughters, Jane and Stella, and before his sister. Such decisions, forged in a brief interchange between enumerator and enumerated, have an effect on what historians using the records today can determine about single parenting.

William appears in the census as a widowed father, as he probably was. Yet it is also possible that one of the women in the household was Arlene's biological mother. Certainly, unless we are attentive to sexual divisions of labour in families, we neglect the likelihood that one or all three were actively involved in the day-to-day care and mothering of the little girl. And what happened when enumerators encountered children who were the result of incest? Then the circumstances of their conception would sometimes mean they were living with both parents.[36]

Some questions were better not asked, some answers better not given. Did enumerators verify whether women claiming to be widows were truly widowed or chose this designation as preferable to admitting to a departed husband, or to a birth out of wedlock? What did they ask married men and women whose spouses were absent to determine whether they should list their names among the family members present? Why did enumerator Armstrong list no one as head of the family when he arrived at the Hamilton home of James, Helen, and Mary Mackitchen, choosing instead to list her relationship to the head of family as "wife"? The three Mackitchens were recorded as the only residents of the small, three-room house on Chatham Street in Hamilton. Mr Armstrong does not seem to have suspected that Mr Mackitchen would return, for in cases where there was any "doubt," the instructions stated that the names of absent people should be recorded both on the family listing and on a separate special form, form A, and there is no indication he did this.[37]

At first glance, the instructions given to the enumerators seem to have been clear on this count. This was to be a *de jure* census, so any family members who were only temporarily absent should have been recorded with their families. Men temporarily working in lumber camps, or serving in the South African war, were to be recorded as if they were at home.[38] However, when marriages were in crisis, how long was a temporary absence? The difficulty of ascertaining permanent absences is recognized in the instructions to census takers. These acknowledge there is no fixed definition of "*de jure*." They provide ways for naming absent people who might return on the special form A, and frankly acknowledge the "room

for misunderstanding and error."[39] Decisions that enumerators made about absent spouses might well lead to an under-enumeration of marriage break-up. This was especially so in Quebec, for the instructions specified that "persons separated as to bed and board will be described as married." This form of legal separation was the only one recognized by the Catholic church in that province, where politicians and bureaucrats colluded to minimize the official count of broken marriages.[40] When enumerator Louis Girard found 28-year-old, married Maria Culliton and William Junior (1), Peter (4), and Maria (7), living in the home of the widow Catherine McIntyre in St Lawrence ward in Montreal, he recorded her as married, and a lodger and filled out form A to explain where her husband was.

Armed with their instructions, with the schedules for entering the information, and with information on the area they were to cover, these paid employees of the Canadian state attempted to slot the Canadian population into the categories that bureaucrats had decided were important.[41] Once inside any dwelling, one of the first decisions the enumerators had to make was about where the boundaries of families lay, for they were to identify each new family with its own number. Their instructions seemed clear enough. The family comprised parents and children "united in a living and housekeeping community." Households, in contrast, could "include all persons in a housekeeping community, whether related by ties of blood or not, but usually with one of their number occupying the position of head." Other members of the dwelling who did not live on their own, but rented rooms, or slept in the house, were to be included within the household.[42] How did these enumerators know which people were part of a shared housekeeping unit? How did they determine where these boundaries lay? Crucial to deciding this was the instruction that each member of a household be identified by their relationship to the family head. This had been asked for the first time in the previous census of 1891. Again, the instructions sound simple: "In column 6 the head of each family or household will be entered as such, and all others according to the relationship—as wife, son, daughter, servant, boarder, lodger, partner etc." Yet what happened when enumerators found a widow or a lone married woman and her children residing as lodgers in someone else's household? When were they considered as a separate family, and when simply recorded as lodgers? These decisions made so long ago in this private moment of recording may not seem very important now. But they made a difference to the total published count of families in Canada in 1901, and once they are transcribed into a database, they shape the ease with which we can identify lone parents and their children. The many lenses, filters, and interactions of the information gathering and recording process shape the ways we can see and understand very complex situations, captured at one moment of their evolution.

There is, of course, a further level of interpretation that also shapes what we can see of these families. Databases, like censuses, record information in predetermined categories and can be manipulated to make a variety of other ones. Errors can and do occur in data entry. Here, I have identified the children of single parents based on a constructed variable that indicates whether each person in the household had a mother or father present.[43] Similarly, single parents are identified through a variable that records whether or not each resident had a spouse in the household.[44] Overall, this method worked well to catch most single parents and their children. I have tried to correct as many errors as possible. Those that remain are unlikely to influence percentages at the national level, but risk doing so at the level of individual towns, small provinces, and in detailed analyses, where numbers are frequently too small for sophisticated analyses. For this reason, I have presented most data at the national level throughout the paper, except where dipping into local and more specific communities and cultural groups seemed critical. I have also kept the statistics simple and rounded out all the percentages. When I discuss statistical patterns I try to link them to the situations of individual children and especially to Bertha, Elizabeth, Helen, Ace, William, and Sing. Their stories remind us of the many different experiences of children of single parents a century ago. They reveal the ways the region they lived in, their racial and cultural backgrounds, age, class, and

gender, and the characteristics of the lives of their parent interacted to frame their lives as youngsters.[45]

With Whom Were Canadian Children Recorded as Living in 1901?

The vast majority of children in Canada in 1901 were recorded as living with two parents. This was the situation of 86 per cent of all children under 19. Yet, as reported above, over 180,000 were not. The proportion living with a lone parent increased with age. One-year-old Ace Hunter who lived with his unwed mother in 1901, was one of the roughly 4 percent of Canada's children under the age of 3 who lived with only one parent. Among children at James Mackitchen's age of 8 the percentage had doubled. The numbers increased steadily among older children as death, desertion, separation, and occasionally divorce created new categories of single parents and new living situations for their offspring. Elizabeth Brenton, at 17, and Sing Yen, at 18, were among over 13 per cent of Canadian youths their age listed as living with a lone parent (Table 1). At every age below 17, more Canadian children were living with one parent than there were in households with no parent present, a group that Gordon Darroch has recently studied.[46]

Patterns were pretty similar for boys and girls. For their parents, in contrast, gender differences were critical. In 1901, as today, many more youngsters were raised by their mothers than by fathers. Over six out of ten of these children lived with their mother. This figure is slightly lower than that found in the United States at the same time.[47] Some 6 per cent of Canadian youngsters at ages 10 to 14 were living only with their mother and about 4 per cent with their father. Among those aged 15 to 19, 8 per cent were with their mother, 4 per cent with their father (Table 1).

The information in the census, in combination with historical research in other fields, allows us to explain some of the reasons for the predominance of single mothers over fathers. A father's death was the main reason most children lived with only one parent. Among parents under the age of 55 who were raising children without a spouse, some 52

Table 1   Percentage of children in the 1901 sample living with single parents,
no parents, or two parents, in five-year age groupings

Age group	Mother only	Father only	Total with lone parent	Neither	Two
0–4	2	1	3	2	95
5–9	4	2	6	3	91
10–14	6	4	10	5	85
15–19	8	5	13	14	73
0–19	5	3	8	6	86
No. in sample	5,971	3,294	9,220	7,256	101,067

per cent were widows, 20 per cent were widowers, about 16 per cent were married women, and 7 per cent married men, while roughly 2 per cent were unmarried men or unmarried women. Well under 1 per cent were divorced.[48] (See Table 2.) Thus, in direct contrast to today, divorce was by far the least likely reason a child would find her- or himself living with only one parent. Eight- and 5-year-old John and Edith Cunliffe, who were recorded as living with their 31-year-old, divorced mother Katie Wilson, were among this small minority of children in Canada in 1901. Many more children, like 4-year-old Bertha Whipley or 17-year-old Elizabeth Brenton, had parents listed on the census as widowed. There were between two and three times as many widows as widowers raising children. Differences in age-specific death rates would explain some of this difference, as most wives were younger than husbands, making it likely that fathers would die first. More important, as I have argued in earlier work, were the difficulties that men whose spouses died faced attempting to raise children without a wife. It was extremely difficult for men to combine businesses or wage earning with raising children. And many did not have the domestic skills to run households and care for youngsters. For this, and other reasons, men were more likely to remarry following their spouse's death than were women. They were also more likely to give up their children to relatives or for adoption, or to place them in institutions.[49]

Thus, the offspring of male single parents are more likely to appear among those who had no parents in the household in which they were living when the enumerator called, or in institutions for orphaned or delinquent youth.

More surprising than the dominance of death as the reason children had only one parent is the large number of single parents who were married but not living with their spouses. Enumerators recorded that nearly one-quarter of the parents of these children were married, but as in the situation of James and Helen Mackitchen, or 18-year-old Sing Yen, they gave no indication of the second parent's whereabouts on the schedules.[50] The census offers no clues as to why their 28-year-old mother, Mary Mackitchen, was no longer living with her husband.[51] In contrast, when enumerator Louis Girard encountered 28-year-old Maria Culliton and her three children, William Junior, Peter, and Maria, aged 1, 4, and 7 respectively, living with the widow Catherine McIntyre on St Phillip Street in Montreal, he took care to fill out the special form that was meant to specify the whereabouts of those temporarily absent.[52] No entry explains why Sing Yen's mother was not living with him and his father in their one-room shack in Nelson. This was not information that interested a government whose policies had led to the situation where males outnumbered females by 22 to 1 in the BC Chinese community.[53] Both father and son had arrived in Canada after the

Table 2   Marital status of men and women 55 and under listed as offspring's only parent, Canada 1901 and United States 1900 compared

Sex and marital status	% of all Canada, 1901	No. in sample	% of sex	% in United States, 1900*	No. in sample
Widowed female	52.0	1,884	73.0	55.0	1,282
Married female	16.0	585	23.0	12.0	269
Unmarried female	2.0	72	3.0	3.0	77
Divorced female	0.5	17	0.5	1.3	32
Total females	71.0	2,558	–	72.0	1,660
Widowed male	20.0	741	69.0	24.0	551
Married male	7.0	240	23.0	4.0	91
Unmarried male	2.0	77	7.0	*	1
Divorced male	0.2	8	0.2	0.7	18
Total males	29.0	1,066	–	28.0	661
Total	–	3,624	–	–	2,321

*The U.S. figures are only for parents who were household heads. Coding and enumeration differences may also have made it less likely that unmarried males would be identified as parents, especially of adopted offspring.

Source: Linda Gordon and Sara McLanahan, "Single Parenthood in 1900," *Journal of Family History* 16, 2 (1991); CFP database, 5% 1901 sample. Reprinted by Permission of SAGE Publications, Inc.

imposition of a $50 head tax by the federal government in 1886. Perhaps they hoped to earn enough from their work as gardeners to bring Sing's mother out from China. Historians have made it clear that the head tax made it extremely difficult for men to bring their wives to Canada, unless they were among the diplomatic, merchant, and student groups exempted from the policy.[54] Sing Yen might well have never seen his mother again.

That nearly one-quarter of the single parents were married and raising their children without their spouse is a powerful reminder that long before Canada's divorce laws changed in the mid-twentieth century, men and women left marriages that were not working. Behind each such family there lies a history that might include the impact of racist immigration policies or the tragic stories of abuse, desertions, disappearances, bigamy, and informal and more formal separations that historians of the law have revealed through work in judicial archives.[55] A higher proportion of lone parents were married in 1901 than are evident in the fragmentary evidence provided in studies of earlier periods.[56] Perhaps decades of agitation by reformers and feminists seeking to publicize the plight of wives who were subject to abuse, combined with changes in married women's property rights and expectations of marriage, were making it more likely that some men and women would leave marriages that were not working. Possibly wives' relatively new rights to ownership of property and their wages were opening up new opportunities.

At the turn of the century, unwed mothers like Mary Jane, Ace Hunter's 20-year-old mother, faced strong pressure to give up their young. They were encouraged to do so by staff in the growing number of homes that provided temporary shelter for unwed mothers and their young along with adoption services. And they were pushed to do so in some provinces by punitive local relief and charity systems that denied them support. Historians have written much more about single mothers who used institutions than about such women as these, who "bore children unaided and unnoticed by public and private agencies." The unmarried mothers whom we can identify in the census were among the courageous minority who decided to keep their babies with them, were reported to the census taker as the child's parent when the enumeration occurred, and do not seem to have lived common law with a man. For, as Suzanne Morton has reminded historians recently, not all non-married mothers in the past "were single mothers."[57]

Bachelors fit less comfortably into contemporary understandings of single parenting in the past or the present than do unwed mothers. Yet, while 3 per cent of the lone mothers identified in the 1901 sample were unmarried women, some 7 per cent of the fathers appear to have been never married men who were the heads of their families and were raising children identified either as their son, their daughter, or adopted offspring. Some of these men may once have been married, yet reported that they were single either because that designation seemed to best suit the way they lived, or perhaps to deny their past relationship with wives who had left them. Others may have lived in common-law relationships with women who had died or moved on. A few look as if they were living in common-law relationships with women in the household who were described variously as "housekeeper" or "domestic," but were listed following the male head of household, a place normally reserved for wives. Enumerator George P. Thompson, in Nine Mile River, BC, either decided to be blunt, or was told to, for he listed the partner of 40-year-old gold miner Alexander Allan, 24-year-old Lucy McCarthy, explicitly as a "Kept Mrs." How long they had been together can only be guessed at from the children's ages. It is highly unlikely that the oldest boy, aged 12, was her son, given their ages. The four other youngsters, aged between a few months and 7, could well have been, in which case they were neither biologically nor socially the children of a lone parent.

Similar ambiguities surrounding the question of biological and social parenting abound for the children being raised in many of these bachelor-headed families. Over half these men were farmers and were listed as the heads of their families. Nearly half shared their farm house with their widowed mothers. A further fifth lived with siblings. In some cases it is unclear which household member was the child's biological parent. David Horn, for example, was a 53-year-old farmer in Reach Township, Ontario, and was identified as never married. Six-year-old Ray Horn was listed as his son. The household also included David's 31-year-old sister, Flora, his 22-year-old brother, and a widow, "Phemie," listed as 67 years old and as the mother of the family head. What we can tell about this family from the census is a good reminder of the limits to historians' ability to interpret what we find in the census. If Phemie was indeed David's mother, then either their ages are wrongly recorded, or he was born when she was only 14 years old. Nor is there any way to verify from this source that Ray was indeed the son of David, rather than of his sister, Flora, let alone to identify whom, if anyone, he considered his primary parent or parents. More important than missing genealogical information is the glimpse we get of these families where unmarried men and their widowed mothers, sisters, and other relatives raised children together on farms and elsewhere in Canadian cities and towns.

About 25 per cent of these children who lived with unmarried men were, like, William Halsted, listed as adopted, compared to only 2 percent of the offspring of all the male lone parents. The designation of many of these children as living with a never married, male, single parent results from the combined effect of the way enumerators reported the children's relationship to the family head and of how the Canadian Families database has been set up to link children to their parents. The designation of 14-year-old William Halsted reveals the situation of one such child in 1901 and the ways these two factors combine. He was listed as the adopted son of the family head. Alonzo Bitnet, aged 41, was recorded the head of the family and also as the proprietor of the farm. Yet, Alonzo lived with an older brother George, aged 42, and his sister Mary, aged 34. There is no indication that any of the siblings had ever married. William, then, is living with three adult siblings. He may have been adopted by Alonzo, or he may have been indentured to work on their farm. For, as Joy Parr has shown, indentures were much more common than adoptions for the orphans and semi-orphans sent from the streets of England by child-saving reformers to work on Canadian farms.[58] Certainly William's background as a child who arrived in Canada in 1890 from urban England suggests the profile of the youngsters sent by Dr Barnardo's and other child-saving groups. Should he be considered as the child of a single parent? No mother was listed in the dwelling, though Mary likely filled this role. I have considered these youngsters as the children of single parents, though they fit uneasily within the broad definition of a single-parent family. Their situations serve to remind us of the range of past family forms and of how people formed their own families in many ways that diverged from dominant ideologies.

Variations by Region, Residence, and Race

Youngsters living with one parent lived in small towns, big cities, rural townships and parishes and unorganized areas from coast to coast. Despite vast differences in the sex ratios of Canada's cities and provinces in 1901 and differential death rates, there are only minor differences between the proportions of children of lone parents in cities and rural areas, or different provinces.[59] In Canada's largest urban areas, where populations were over 20,000 people, about 8 per cent of all children under the age of 15 lived with one parent compared to 6 per cent of those in rural areas.[60] These rates are similar, but slightly lower than those reported in the United States census of 1900, where the equivalent figures were 9.3 and 8.3 per cent respectively (Table 3).[61] Among children around the age of William Halsted, who was 14, the rural–urban differences were slightly greater, with roughly 12 per cent of city children aged 10 to 14 living with one parent, compared to about 9 per cent of those in rural areas. Some urban areas had higher rates than others. In Ottawa, London, and Saint John over 15 per cent of 10 to 14 year olds were with

one parent, and there were disproportionately more with mothers than elsewhere. Local economic possibilities, demographic regimes, and variable support systems would influence these relatively minor variations. Joy Parr has shown that the textile and knit goods town of Paris, Ontario, attracted and retained lone mothers because of the earning opportunities. Indeed, of the 33 Paris households that fell into the 5 per cent population sample, some 9, or 27 per cent, were headed by lone mothers.[62] Apart from such labour-market-related differences, rates in Canada's larger cities and smaller towns were pretty similar. Nor should we be very surprised at the relatively small differences between cities, or between rural and urban areas. Death of a parent made over three-quarters of these youngsters into semi-orphans. Differential death rates no doubt explain some of these divergences. So would the migration of single parents into cities after a spouse's death, desertion, or departure to take advantage of a greater range of work and charitable opportunities or the anonymity of urban life. Yet family support was so critical for many men and women raising their children alone that it seems likely the majority remained where they were, taking advantage of any equity they had invested in their homes, farms, and neighbourhood relationships as they faced the challenges of raising their kids without a spouse.

The experiences of Canadian children appear to diverge most from those revealed in one American study in the higher proportion in Canada being raised by fathers, especially in rural areas (Table 3). This may be in part because I considered youngsters, like William Halsted, who were adopted by a bachelor as the offspring of a lone parent. It also reflects the significant number of widowers who were farmers. Fathers running farms were unlikely to leave rural areas when their wives died or left them. Their farms were the basis of their livelihood and of their children's future. And their children were also their most valuable support in the work of the farm and the farmhouse.

Provincial differences, like those between rural and urban areas, are small, intriguing, and difficult to explain (Table 4). We have seen that across the country as a whole just under 10 per cent of all 10- to 14-year-olds lived with just one parent (Table 5). Rates were lower in Quebec and British Columbia, at about 8.6

Table 3   Children 15 and under in Canadian cities and rural areas,
compared with the United States (%)

| | Canada, 1901 | | United States, 1900 | |
	Cities over 20,000	Rural	Urban	Rural
Two parents	88.6	90.4	85.5	86.5
One parent	8.0	5.8	9.3	8.3
mother	(75)	(58)	(71.6)	(70.9)
father	(25)	(42)	(28.1)	(28.3)
No parents	3.5	3.4	–	
Other relatives	–	–	2.4	3.5
Other	–	–	2.8	1.8
No. in sample	30,996	65,481	7,539	26,222
Total	95,997		33,761	

Table 4   Percentages of families headed by lone parents or a couple,
all families with children where head is under 55

	Single female	Single male	Male head with spouse	Total
BC	7.4	3.7	89.0	842
Territories	7.4	4.2	88.4	909
Unorg. Terr.	19.2	8.9	71.9	146
Manitoba	5.7	4.4	90.0	1,608
Ontario	9.5	3.1	87.4	13,254
Quebec	6.4	3.4	90.2	9,709
NB	7.3	3.7	89.0	1,888
NS	9.6	3.6	86.8	2,531
PEI	10.5	4.4	85.2	526
Canada	8.2	3.4	88.4	–
Total	2,568	1,069	27,776	31,413

per cent, and higher in the Unorganized Territories (13.1 per cent), Prince Edward Island (11.2 per cent) and Ontario (10.7 per cent). The Territories and PEI stand out for having higher proportions living only with their mothers or only with their fathers than other regions, while Ontario stands out for having relatively high proportions living with their mothers but one of the lowest rates of father-headed lone-parent families. These differences seem to point to the ways that variable economic opportunities, support systems, death rates, sex ratios, and family norms and practices could combine to make it more or less likely that children in different regions would live with one rather than two parents. The apparently higher rates of single parenting in the Unorganized Territories may well be partially the result of sloppy enumeration. Yet in this vast region, peopled predominantly by the First Nations and Métis, they probably also reflect different cultural practices of marriage and the mobility of the population, combined with the inability of enumerators to understand different family cultures or to fit them into the usual definitions.[63] Quebec's high rates of two-parent families suggest the power of Catholic discourse in deterring men and women from leaving their spouses and in convincing unwed

mothers to give up their babies, as well as in encouraging remarriage. Quebec's lone parents were more likely to be widowed and less likely to be married and separated than those in any other province. These differences may also reflect higher death rates as well as the choice of enumerators to list separated couples together even when they had been apart for over a year.[64]

Whether one counts the percentages of children (Table 5) or the proportion of families with children who were headed by a single parent, Prince Edward Island stands out for higher rates than any other part of the country except the Unorganized Territories (Table 4). This was also the province with the highest rates of non-marriage among women and among the highest for men. Michelle Stairs's research on spinsters and bachelors in Prince Edward Island reveals that it was not uncommon for unmarried men and women to adopt nieces and nephews, integrating them into their lives and making them heirs. Our sample also suggests that such practices distinguish PEI from other provinces, though the small numbers in most provinces enjoin caution. Over 11 per cent of the single parents in the PEI sample population were unmarried men and women. In no other province does the percentage

Table 5 Variations by provinces/territories, children 10–14 only (%)

	Live with mother only	Live with father only	No parents present	Two parents present	Number in sample
BC	5.6	3.0	6.3	85.1	572
NB	6.0	4.0	5.5	84.5	1,876
NS	6.6	3.5	5.6	84.3	2,480
PEI	6.7	4.6	6.7	82.1	586
Ontario	7.5	3.2	5.1	84.3	11,404
Quebec	5.1	3.5	3.9	87.5	9,341
Manitoba	5.5	3.9	6.9	83.7	1,421
Territories	5.7	4.0	6.8	83.5	768
Unorg. Terr.	8.2	5.1	4.1	82.7	98
Canada	6.3	3.5	5.4	84.8	–
Total	1,799	988	1,413	24,346	28,546

reach even 6 per cent, though the rates are closest in the other Maritime provinces of New Brunswick and Nova Scotia (Table 6). Low marriage rates, high out-migration, and strong traditions of adoption and support in some families for unwed mothers thus seem to have combined in the Maritime provinces, and especially Prince Edward Island, leading to high rates of single parenting.[65]

In as much as the reasons why children had only one parent can be read from their parent's marital status, there were differences across the country. In the West, separations and desertions were much more likely to leave youngsters living with one married parent than in the East. In part this was no doubt the result of the younger age structure of the western population and the mobility of its population. It may also have been facilitated by more generous provisions in legislation regarding married women's property rights and spousal maintenance.[66] As one moves eastward across the country, the percentage of parents who were widowed increases and the relative weight of separations falls. And, in the Maritime provinces, there are many more unmarried men and women raising children, some of whom were nephews and nieces, some adopted, and some possibly illegitimate offspring whose true parents are rarely revealed.

The relationship between race and family structures has been the subject of major debates among U.S. historians seeking to interpret the high rates of single parenthood among African American women.[67] In Canada, by contrast, historians have focused more on the influence of origins or ethnicity on family structures. This is partially because nineteenth-century census takers asked people about their origins, but not about their racial background. Those responsible for creating the 1901 census, however, were particularly interested in capturing a wider range of identities and differences.[68] In framing the questions for the census they drew upon the messy range of ideas about race and ethnicity that were being promoted in contemporary anthropology and other sciences as well as in popular culture. The forms had separate columns for colour, race, language, place of birth, and nationality. In including all these possible sources of identity and difference, the census reflected the diverse contemporary meanings of race, which might include the whole human race, broad groupings associated with colour, as well as particular nationalities. The

Table 6 Marital status of single parents under the age of 55 in each province, mothers and fathers combined (%)

	Widowed	Married	Single	Divorced	Number
BC	55.5	40.2	2.2	2.2	92
Territories	56.7	38.4	3.9	1.0	104
Unorg. Terr.	39.0	58.6	–	2.4	41
Manitoba	66.7	30.1	3.1	–	159
Ontario	72.2	23.3	3.6	0.6	1,668
Quebec	77.7	17.3	4.0	1.0	943
NB	73.8	20.4	5.8	–	206
NS	73.6	20.1	5.7	0.6	333
PEI	67.9	20.5	11.5	–	78
Canada	72.4	22.7	4.1	0.7	–
Number	1,884	741	585	240	3,624

options regarding colour seemed simple. Enumerators were told there were only four possible designations "w," "b," "r," or "y." These were presented unambiguously as linked to designations assumed to be widely understood—Caucasians were white, Africans or negroes black, American Indians red, and Mongolians (Japanese and Chinese) yellow. In the separate column for "race" enumerators were to indicate "racial or tribal origin," and informed that while Scotch, English, or Irish were "true" racial terms, "American" or "Canadian" were not.[69]

Borrowing from and adding to the racist and patriarchal understandings of their times, the instructions explained to enumerators who might encounter children of mixed marriages that "among whites racial or tribal origin is traced through the father" while, in contrast, colour in the case of any children "begotten of marriages between whites and any of the other races will be classed as red, black, or yellow, as the case may be." People born of unions between Canada's original peoples and Europeans were to be designated as "breeds." The instructions specified how to describe such mixtures—"i.b." for Irish breed, "Chippewa s.b." for someone with one Chippewa and one Scottish parent. Enumerators seem to have taken great care to identify the children of such First Nations–European liaisons. What questions did the enumerator ask John Brenton that led him to list Elizabeth and her siblings as "Cowichan English Breed?" Enumerators looked, asked, and recorded according to their perceptions and the answers they received. Recent writing by Adele Perry, Sylvia Van Kirk, and others has revealed the long history and the extent of such interracial marriages among British Columbia's elite and more common people alike. One has to wonder how comfortable enumerator David Thomas felt about recording Elizabeth and all her siblings as "r" or as "breeds."[70]

The fascination with the minutiae of racial difference is at some level ironic, for the most significant revelation of the state's attempt in 1901 to anchor Canadians' identities in racial categories constitutes an important reminder about the whiteness and homogeneity of Canada's population a century ago. Over 97 per cent of Canadian children up to 19 were described as white and as of northern European "racial" background. First Nations and Métis children, identified either as red or as members of a First Nation, "breeds," or Métis, made up only 3 per cent of the children, and blacks and Asians constituted less than 1 per cent. The small numbers in all minority groups, and the even smaller numbers of lone parents and their children among them, make it risky to generalize about apparent differences in children's experiences, yet some differences are so compelling that they warrant highlighting briefly in the hope that other researchers will take up the subject in greater depth and draw on a wider range of sources. Sing Yen's experience of not living with two parents was one that was shared by many Asian youths. Of the 136 Asians under 19 in the sampled population, only 39, or 29 per cent, were recorded as living with two parents. Most of these were under 15. Some 13 per cent lived with single parents, mostly fathers. What distinguished this small number of Asian youngsters most from other Canadian children was that 59 per cent apparently lived without any parents at all (Table 7). In the dwellings in which they were enumerated they were described as domestics, companions, apprentices, and above all as lodgers and boarders. Here were young men, many of whom, like Sing Yen, had arrived in Canada from China in the previous two or three years. Their mother languages were Chinese, occasionally Japanese. Only some spoke English. Some may have been with relatives or friends, but did not succeed in conveying this to enumerators. Most appear to be part of a world of bachelors, cut off from family and most British Columbians by racism, language, and culture.

The small numbers in the sample suggest that the proportions of children and youth in single-parent families was somewhat higher among both First Nations and African Canadian families than among whites, although the differences for blacks are not as great as have been found in many U.S. studies. Nearly 11 per cent of First Nations children and 13 per cent of African Canadians under 19, compared to 8 per cent of children classified as white, lived with only one parent. In every group more children lived with their mothers than their fathers, but this difference was much more pronounced in the white population than among other groups. Non-white children were more likely to live only with their fathers than

Table 7   Variations by assigned "colour" in 1901 census: children aged 0–19 (%)

	Live with mother only	Live with father only	No parents present	Two parents present	Number in 5% sample
"Black"	6.5	6.3	8.7	78.6	462
"Red"	5.6	5.0	10.8	78.7	2,193
"White"	5.1	2.8	6.0	86.1	114,463
"Yellow"	8.1	4.4	58.8	28.7	136
Missing information	–	–	–	–	334
Total, aged 0–19	5.1	2.8	6.2	85.9	117,588

were whites. Among Canadian children recorded as white only 2.8 per cent of those aged 19 and under lived just with their father, compared to 4.4 per cent among Asians, 5 per cent among First Nations and Métis, and 6.3 per cent among blacks (Table 7). The reasons they had only one parent were different too. Lone parents in the small BC Asian community were, like Sing's father, most frequently married. Among blacks there were equal proportions of widowed mothers and fathers, whereas in all other groups widows predominated. This suggests both the possibility of higher death rates among black women than for other groups, and the possibility that more widowed black men neither remarried nor gave up their children. In First Nations and Métis groups across the country, the majority of single parents were widows and widowers (52 per cent), yet there were significantly more married men and women heading these families than among the "white" majority population—41 per cent compared to 22 per cent. And there were also more divorced parents recorded by enumerators in First Nations families. Again, these figures may result from a combination of enumerators acknowledging Indigenous marriage and divorce customs as well as errors in recording and calculations (Table 8). [. . .]

Table 8   Marital status of single parents under the age of 55 by assigned "race" (%)

	Asian	Blacks	First Nations	White
Widow	16	26	37	53
Widower	–	26	15	21
Married woman	17	26	25	16
Married man	67	5	16	6
Unmarried woman	–	5	4	2
Unmarried man	–	10	1	2
Divorced woman	–	–	1	1
Divorced man	–	–	2	–
Total in sample	6	19	131	3,461

Work and Schooling Patterns among the Children of Lone Parents

Gordon Darroch has shown that there were differences between the schooling and work experiences of children who were not living with any parents and of those that were—categories he refers to as "away" and "at home."[71] When "at home" is broken down to compare children of single mothers and fathers with those with two parents, further differences appear. Table 9 compares all children across Canada, distinguishing by the sex of the single parent and including children with two parents or no parents present. Such aggregate figures hide a range of variations and of divergent local possibilities, yet there are some interesting patterns. James Mackitchen, aged 8, and his sister Helen, 7, were both recorded as having attended school for six months in the previous year. Bertha Whipley (4), her sister Isabel (5), and their brother Sanjord (9) were not. The enumerator, Frederick Jones, reported that Sanjord could neither read nor write. Nor does it seem likely that Hattie their mother could help them gain even rudimentary skills, for she could only read, not write. The major possibility for any instruction at home lay with their grandmother, the 72-year-old widow Jerushah Whipley, who was recorded by the enumerator as a "boarder" and could read and write.

Hattie was unusual in keeping her 9-year-old out of school. Indeed lone mothers and fathers alike sent a slightly higher percentage of 5- to 9-year-old sons and daughters to school than did mothers and fathers living together or those raising other people's children. Sixty-three percent of the sons and daughters of lone mothers were reported to have attended school in the previous year, compared to 59 per cent of those with two parents (Table 9). And those that attended school reported attending for slightly longer—8.7 months for the children of lone mothers, 8.6 for those of lone fathers, compared to 8.4 months on average among the children with two parents. Lone parents struggling to balance childrearing with their other duties may well have embraced the possibilities that they hoped early education would offer. They would also have welcomed

schools as places where they knew their young children were watched over during the day. However, as their children aged, single parents and their young made different choices. These appear linked to the different challenges confronting men and women raising children on their own.

The gender of a child's single parent and the child's own gender were important in determining how early they would leave school and whether they would take on employment outside the home. The patterns of schooling and work of the offspring of single parents in 1901 appear similar in their broad patterns to those I found in Montreal between 1861 and 1891. First, many single parents likely embraced early school attendance for their youngest children in part because it helped with childcare during school hours. Once children passed the age of ten or so, however, a higher percentage of those with two parents remained in school. When girls had no mother, their lives were reshaped by their fathers' need for domestic assistance in the home. Girls became surrogate mothers to younger children as well as surrogate wives bearing much of the load of housework. When boys and girls had no father, and their mother had few resources, they were more likely to be sent to work at an early age.

Girls aged 10 to 14 who lived only with their fathers were somewhat less likely than other children to be in school, but were also less likely to be employed. Only 69 per cent of girls these ages who were living with their father were reported at school, compared to 78 per cent of those with two parents and 75 per cent of those living with their mothers only (table 9). At these ages, as I have argued elsewhere, the combination of not attending school and not being employed can be read at least in part as meaning they were contributing their labour at home, whether in the household or on farms.[72]

Ten- to nineteen-year-old sons and daughters of single fathers were less likely than other children their age to report either attending school or engaging in waged labour. In the Cowichan valley on the 45-acre farm of the 66-year-old widower John Brenton, it is likely that it was Elizabeth and Louisa Brenton who had ensured that for at least 6 months of the year their 12- and 10-year-old siblings were fed and dressed and went to school. These 17- and 15-year-old girls were among the 77 per cent of 15- to 19-year-old daughters of lone fathers who were listed as neither at school nor employed. They probably also did much of the food preparation and cooking for their father and their two older working brothers as well as cleaning their three-room house, though of course the census records no occupations or assessment of the value of such contributions. In contrast, the census lists their brothers as earning around $350 each, one as a miner and the other as a farm labourer. Added to their father's reported earnings of $650, this mixed Cowichan-English family looks extremely well off compared to those of many lone mothers.

While income may not have been a problem for the Benton family, it clearly was in many families headed by women. The need for cash drew some of their youngsters into the workforce earlier than children with two parents or just a father. Eleven-year-old William Rhoda seems to have just begun earning when he was enumerated in the home of his widowed mother in Almonte, Ontario. He and his two sisters were all listed as factory operatives in this mill town, where women and youngsters alike could find work more readily than in many other industries.[73] He had worked for only 1 month over the twelve months prior to the census. There is no indication that he had attended school during that time. His sister Roseanne who was 12, was reported as having worked for just four months, while 14-year-old Lillie had worked for ten. Their reported earnings of $9, $40, and $80 brought the total visible resources of this family headed by their mother, a 47-year-old English-born widow, to $129.

Among children 10 and 14 who, like the three Rhoda youngsters, lived with only their mothers, some 9 per cent of the sons and 5 per cent of daughters listed an occupation. Among those with a father or both parents only 3 per cent and 2 per cent respectively were depicted as employed. Once the sons and daughters of lone mothers reached 13 for boys and 14 for girls, the likelihood that they would have some kind of occupation increased more rapidly

Table 9 Percentages at school and working: children in single- and two-parent families

	Not at school or work			At school			At work or at work and at school		
	Mother	**Father**	**Two parents**	**Mother**	**Father**	**Two parents**	**Mother**	**Father**	**Two parents**
Girls									
0–4	99	100	100	–	–	–	–	–	–
5–9	36	34	41	63	66	59	–	–	–
10–14	20	29	21	75	69	78	5	2	2
15–19	56	77	65	20	15	21	24	8	13
Boys									
0–4	100	99	99	–	1	–	–	–	–
5–9	37	38	41	63	62	59	–	–	–
10–14	20	27	20	71	71	77	9	3	3
15–19	38	48	52	14	16	19	48	36	30

than for other children. At age 14, about 16 per cent of the daughters of lone mothers were employed, as were 23 per cent of the sons, compared with 5 per cent of daughters and 10 per cent of sons living with both parents. Among those aged 15 to 19, 24 per cent of the girls and 48 per cent of the boys living only with their mothers reported a job. This compares with only 8 per cent of the daughters of lone fathers and 36 per cent of their sons (Table 9).

The earnings of these children ranged from minimal amounts like the $9 that William Rhoda reported earning to significant contributions like those of Elizabeth Brenton's older brothers. On the average the 10- to 14-year-old daughters of widows contributed some $94 annually to family earnings, while sons added $127 (Table 10.). They did not contribute any more on average than the youngsters of two-parent families, but their earnings made up a larger part of family revenues. Older children could contribute more. The earnings of 15- to 9-year-old girls living only with their mother averaged about $154, sons roughly $206. In this age group the average contributions of both girls and boys were higher than those of either the offspring of lone fathers or those with two parents.

Conclusion

To be raised by one parent is not a new experience historically for Canadian children. True, most children whose lives we catch glimpses of through the census of 1901 were living with two parents. Thousands, however, were not. The Canadian Families database reveals some of the empirical details of their lives and allows analysis of how they differed from those of children

with two living parents at home. In 1901, roughly one in every twenty children at the age of five lived with a lone parent. Among those who had reached the age of 12 it was closer to one in ten. These children lived in all parts of the country—in farms and in cities and among all racial and ethnic groups. They were the offspring of widows, widowers, married men and women living separate from their spouses, unwed mothers, and bachelor fathers, as well as a few divorcees. Death rather than divorce had broken up most of their families. Yet nearly a quarter were living with one parent who was listed as married. The other was living elsewhere. This proportion is higher than I have found in earlier studies based on mid- to late-nineteenth-century censuses. Although further studies would be required to determine whether this increase in marital separations was a trend, it does raise the intriguing possibility of a shift in the ways women and men might have contemplated leaving an abusive or drunken spouse. Relatively recent changes to legislation that allowed married women to retain their own property and wages in most provinces, in combination with new acts that attempted to force fathers who deserted to support their wives and children, would have increased the numbers of widows and wives with some property of their own and hence provided a basis for self-support, however meagre. The much greater prominence of married women than of divorcees as lone parents is an important reminder that family break-up in the past is not best measured by looking at formal divorce.

What we can see of the children of lone parents through the lenses and interactions involved in the making of the 1901 census suggests that their experiences and lives were diverse. They were shaped by their parents' gender, marital status, wealth,

Table 10 Average annual earnings contributed by children living with mother only, father only, or two parents ($)

	Girls' average earnings			Boys' average earnings		
	Mother	Father	Two parents	Mother	Father	Two parents
10–14	94	187	104	127	99	113
15–19	154	138	144	206	201	195

location, cultural traditions, and networks of family and friends, as well as by their own age, sex, and skills. The records left by the census enumerators allow us to capture only some aspects of their lives, at one particular moment. These children and youths share with their counterparts today the greater likelihood of being raised by a mother on her own than by a father, though the numbers being raised at the turn of the last century by married men as well as by bachelors are striking. Then, as now, those living with mothers seem more likely to be raised in poverty than other youngsters, though the particular interest of the census takers in wage-earning hides the wide range of other ways most of these women supported their families. In 1901 few jobs paid women even two-thirds of a man's wages. Mothers Pensions and Family Allowances did not yet exist. Most local relief systems, like private charity, made moral judgments that made it much easier for widows than for women who were separated or unmarried to secure support. Few daycares existed to help lone mothers or fathers combine money earning with childcare and domestic labour. Relatives, older siblings, and housekeepers performed this work.

Children living with one parent were more likely than those with two to leave school early either to earn wages or to assist with domestic labour. They were also more likely than youngsters with two parents to live in homes that included relatives other than their parent, other families, and boarders. That there was a greater likelihood of all these differences between their lives and those of children with two parents does not mean that all children of single parents were poor, left school early, or lived in homes with others. The majority lived only with their mother or their father and other siblings. Most attended school for roughly the same amount of time as others of their age and class. The census cannot reveal whether such children fell disproportionately among the truants and delinquents that so concerned the reformers of their time. The range of their experiences suggests that there were many ways to be raised by one parent. Nothing in the *published* census reports for 1901 reveals anything about these youngsters' lives. The Canadian Families database makes it possible for researchers to examine all the information as it was recorded, and to relate variables to each other in ways that were impossible in 1901. The stories of Bertha, Elizabeth, Helen, Ace, William, Sing, and the other children whose lives we have peeped into here through the census lens are far from complete. Research in other kinds of sources can complement what can be grasped through the census returns. These youngsters shared the experience of living in 1901 with only one parent. They were divided in their cultures, racial and ethnic backgrounds, religions, and age. Their parents were of different classes, sexes, and marital statuses and could call on diverse familial, economic, and social assets. All of these contributed to shaping their experiences. These glimpses of Bertha, Elizabeth, Helen, Ace, William, and Sing offer powerful reminders that there is a long history in Canada of children being raised by one rather than two parents.

Notes

1. The Canadian Families Project's 5 per cent sample includes 5,850 children under 15 living with only a mother or a father, and 9,305 under 19. Assuming the sample is representative, there would have been approximately 117,000 children under 15 living with a lone parent and 186,100 under 19. I use the term "single parent" to refer to any adult identified as a child's mother or father and recorded as living without a spouse. I use it interchangeably with the preferred Statistics Canada term "lone parent." Thus single parent, in this context, includes widows, widowers, and married men and women whose spouses were not listed in the same household as well as unmarried men and women identified as the parents of children. A child of a single parent is any child for whom only one parent is identified in the household. The 1901 census was a *de jure* census, so enumerators were supposed to list people's usual places of abode rather than the place they were the day the information on them was written down. In principle, then, if the spouse of a married man or woman was not recorded in a household, they did not normally live there. Unfortunately for historians, we cannot investigate the questioning and answering between enumerators and Canadians that might have verified such recording.

2. Canada, Department of Agriculture, Fourth Census of Canada, 1901, "Instructions to Officers" (hereafter, "Instructions to Officers,"), article 53 told enumerators to describe "persons of mixed white and red blood . . . by the addition of the initial letters "f.b." for French breed . . .

For example: "Cree f.b." denotes that the person is racially a mixture of Cree and French." See discussion in a later section of the paper.

3. I have used the names that were written down by the enumerators as transcribed into the Canadian Families Project database, as it is unlikely any of these children would be alive today. However, in order to provide a minimal shield of privacy, I decided not to reference their location in the census. All references to individuals are drawn from the CFP 5 per cent sample and database.

4. This term was apparently first used by Statistics Canada in the 1970s to avoid some of the negativity associated with "single parent." No such nomenclature is used in the 1971 census. In 1981 the published census defines "lone parent" as referring to "a mother or father with no spouse present, living in a dwelling with one or more never-married children." Statistics Canada, 3-2, Profile, Series B, Census Tracts, 95-959, p. xv. See also S.T. Wargon, *Canadian Households and Families: Recent Demographic Trends* (Ottawa, 1979).

5. Cynthia Comacchio, "'The History of Us': Social Science, History, and the Relations of Family in Canada," *Labour/ Le Travail* 46 (Fall 2000), 214.

6. Gordon Darroch, "Home and Away: Patterns of Residence, Schooling, and Work among Children and Never Married Young Adults, Canada, 1871 and 1901," *Journal of Family History* 26, 2 (2001); Bettina Bradbury, "The Fragmented Family: Family Strategies in the Face of Death, Illness, Poverty, Montreal, 1860–1885," in Joy Parr, ed., *Childhood and Family in Canadian History* (Toronto, 1982).

7. Statistics Canada, "Families in Private Households with and without Children at Home, 1991 and 1996," www .statcan.ca. Linda Gordon and Sara McLanahan make the same point for the United States in "Single Parenthood in 1900," *Journal of Family History* 16, 2 (1991). There, the rates in 1900 were similar to those of 1960, with some 14 per cent of children under 14 living apart from their two parents in 1900, compared to 12 per cent in 1960. The 1901 CFP sample shows roughly 10 per cent of children under 14 living either with one or no parent.

8. Important exceptions include Kathleen Kiernan, Hilary Land, and Jane Lewis, *Lone Motherhood in Twentieth-Century Britain: From Footnote to Front Page* (New York, 1998); and Rickie Solinger, *Wake Up Little Susie: Single Pregnancy and Race before* Roe v. Wade (New York, 1992).

9. Andrée Lévesque, "Deviant Anonymous: Single Mothers at the Hôpital de la Miséricorde in Montreal, 1929–1939," *Canadian Historical Association Historical Papers*, 1984, 168–84; Marie-Aimée Cliche, "Morale chrétienne et "double standard sexuel": Les filles-meres à l'hôpital de la Miséricorde a Québec, 1874–1972," *Histoire sociale/Social History* 24, 47 (May 1991); Marie-Aimée Cliche, "Unwed Mothers, Families, and Society during the French Regime," in Bettina Bradbury, ed., *Canadian*

Family History: Selected Readings (Toronto, 1992); Peter Gossage, "Foundlings and the Institution: The Case of the Grey Nuns of Montreal," *Canadian Historical Association Historical Papers*, 1986; Peter Ward, "Unwed Motherhood in Nineteenth Century English Canada," *Canadian Historical Association Historical Papers*, 1981; Suzanne Morton, "Women on Their Own: Single Mothers in Working-Class Halifax in the 1920s," *Acadiensis* 21, 2 (1992); Karen Balcom, "Scandal and Social Policy: The Ideal Maternity Home and the Evolution of Social Policy in Nova Scotia, 1940–51," *Acadiensis* 31 (Spring 2002); Karen Bridget Murray, "Governing 'Unwed Mothers' in Toronto at the Turn of the Twentieth Century," *Canadian Historical Review* 85, 2 (2004). Several recent popular works address the question of homes for unwed mothers: Bette Cahill's *Butterbox Babies; Baby Sales, Baby Deaths: The Scandalous Story of the Ideal Maternity Home* (Toronto, 1992) was made into a popular television series and play. See also Anne Petrie, *Gone to Aunts: Remembering Canada's Homes for Unwed Mothers* (Toronto, 1998). The focus on unwed mothers and maternity homes is apparent in the American literature as well. See Regina G. Kunzel, *Fallen Women, Problem Girls: Unmarried Mothers and the Professionalization of Social Work, 1890–1945* (New Haven, 1993); and Marian J. Morton, "'Go and Sin No More': Maternity Homes in Cleveland, 1869–1936," *Ohio History* 93 (Summer/ Autumn 1984), 117–46.

10. Neil Sutherland, *Children in English-Canadian Society: Framing the Twentieth Century Consensus* (Toronto, 1976); P.T. Rooke and M.R. Schnell, *Discarding the Asylum: From Child Rescue to the Welfare State in English Canada, 1800–1950* (Lanham, MD, 1983); Joy Parr, *Labouring Children: British Immigrant Apprentices to Canada, 1869–1924* (Toronto, 1994).

11. Judith Fingard, "The Prevention of Cruelty, Marriage Breakdown and the Rights of Wives in Nova Scotia, 1880–1900," *Acadiensis* 23 (1993); Annalee Golz, "'If a Man's Wife Does Not Obey Him, What Can He Do?' Marital Breakdown and Wife Abuse in the Late Nineteenth Century and Early Twentieth Century Ontario," in Louis Knafla and Susan W.S. Binnie, eds., *Law, Society, and the State: Essays in Modern Legal History* (Toronto, 1994); Annalee Golz, "Murder Most Foul: Spousal Homicides in Ontario, 1870–1915," in George Robb and Nancy Erber, eds., *Disorder in the Court: Trials and Sexual Conflict at the Turn of the Century* (New York, 1999); Lori Chambers, *Married Women and the Property Law in Victorian Ontario* (Toronto, 1997); Constance Backhouse, "Married Women's Property Law in Nineteenth Century Canada," *Law and History Review* 6 (Fall 1988), 211–57; Philip Girard and Rebecca Veinott, "Married Women's Property Law in Nova Scotia, 1850–1910," in Janet Guildford and Suzanne Morton, eds., *Women's Worlds in the 19th Century Maritimes* (Fredericton, 1994); Peter Baskerville, "Women and Investment in Late-Nineteenth-Century

Urban Canada: Victoria and Hamilton, 1880-1901," *Canadian History Review* 80, 2 (1999); Christopher A. Clarkson, "Property Law and Family Regulation in Pacific British North America," *Histoire sociale/Social History* 30, 60 (1997); Annalee Lepp, "Dismembering the Family: Marital Breakdown, Domestic Conflict and Family Violence in Ontario, 1830-1920," Ph.D. diss., Queen's University, 2001; Christopher A. Clarkson, "Remoralizing Families? Family Regulation and State Formation in British Columbia, 1862-1940," Ph.D. diss., University of Ottawa, 2001.

12. Bettina Bradbury, *Working Families: Age, Gender and Daily Survival in Industrializing Montreal* (Toronto, 1993); Lorna McLean, "Single Again: Widow's Work in the Urban Family Economy, Ottawa, 1871," *Ontario History* 83, 2 (1991), 127-50.

13. Réal Bates, "Les conceptions prenuptials dans la vallée du Saint-Laurent avant 1725," *Revue d'histoire de l'Amérique française* 40, 2 (1986); Gérard Bouchard, "L'evolution des conceptions prenuptials comme indicateur de change-ment culturel," *Annales de démographie historique*, 1993, 25-50; Frans van Poppel, "Children in One-Parent Families: Survival as an Indicator of the Role of the Parents," *Journal of Family History* 14, 2 (2000), 269-90; Jacques Légaré and Jean-François Naud, "The Dynamics of Household Structure in the Event of the Father's Death: Quebec City in the 18th Century," *History of the Family* 7 (2001).

14. Janice Harvey, "Dealing with 'the destitute and the wretched': The Protestant House of Industry and Refuge in Nineteenth-Century Montreal," *Journal of the Canadian Historical Association* 12 (2001); Janice Harvey, "The Protestant Orphan Asylum and the Montreal Ladies' Benevolent Society: A Case Study in Protestant Child Charity in Montreal, 1822-1900," Ph.D. diss., McGill University, 2002; Bradbury, "The Fragmented Family"; James Pitsula, "The Relief of Poverty in Toronto, 1880-1930," Ph.D. diss., York University, 1970; Huguette Lapointe-Roy, *Charité bien ordonnée: Le premier réseau de lute contre la pauvreté à Montréal au 19e siècle* (Montreal, 1987).

15. Joy Parr notes that half of the Barnardo emigrant chil-dren were the offspring of widows or widowers and some 29 per cent were illegitimate. Parr, *Labouring Children*; Linda Gordon, *Heroes of Their Own Lives: The Politics and History of Family Violence, Boston, 1880-1960* (New York, 1988); Gordon and McLanahan, "Single Parenthood in 1900," 98.

16. Sutherland, *Children in English-Canadian Society*; Andrew Jones and Leonard Rutman, *In the Children's Aid: J.J. Kelso and Child Welfare in Ontario* (Toronto, 1981), 56-65; John Bullen, "Hidden Workers: Child Labour and the Family Economy in Late Nineteenth Century Urban Ontario," *Labour/Le Travail* 18 (Fall 1986), 163-88; Cynthia Comacchio, *The Infinite Bonds of Family: Domesticity in*

Canada, 1850-1940 (Toronto, 1999), 55-7; Jane Ursel, *Private Lives, Public Policy: 100 Years of State Intervention in the Family* (Toronto, 1992), 116-20, 333. André Turnel touches on some differences between Quebec and English Canada in "Historiography of Children in Canada," in Nancy Janovicek and Joy Parr, eds., *Histories of Canadian Children and Youth* (Toronto, 2003).

17. John Bullen, "Hidden Workers."

18. Ontario, *Seventh Report of the Department of Neglected and Dependent Children of Ontario* (Toronto, 1900), 5-6.

19. In the Annual Report for 1900 Kelso included seven small vignettes of problem families. Such vignettes were one of his ways of capturing public attention. Of the seven main ones, four either mentioned widows, or talked of moth-ers without any indication that there were fathers on the scene. *Neglected and Dependent* (1900), 10, 11, 15, 16, 39, 41, 47.

20. Sutherland, *Children in English-Canadian Society*.

21. Mary Odem, *Delinquent Daughters: Protecting and Policing Adolescent Female Sexuality in the United States, 1885-1920* (Chapel Hill, 1995); Mary Odem, "Single Mothers, Delinquent Daughters, and the Juvenile Court in Early 20th Century Los Angeles," *Journal of Social History* 25, 1 (1991), 27-43; Tamara Myers, "The Voluntary Delinquent: Parents, Daughters, and the Montreal Juvenile Delinquents' Court in 1918," *Canadian Historical Review* 80, 2 (1999), 253; Carolyn Strange, *Toronto's Girl Problem: The Perils and Pleasures of the City, 1880-1930* (Toronto, 1995), 135-9.

22. Backhouse, "Married Women's Property Law"; Chambers, *Married Women and Property Law*; Clarkson, *Remoralizing Families?*; Baskerville, "Women and Investment'; Girard and Veinott, "Married Women's Property Law in Nova Scotia."

23. Ontario, "An Act Respecting the Maintenance of Wives Deserted by Their Husbands," 51 Victoria, 1888, and "An Act Respecting the Maintenance of Wives Deserted by Their Husbands," *Revised Statutes of Ontario*, 1897, vol. 1, chap. 167, 1647-9; Clarkson, *Remoralizing Families*; Chambers, *Married Women and Property Law*.

24. Margaret Jane Hillyard Little, "No Car, No Radio, No Liquor Permit," in *The Moral Regulation of Single Mothers in Ontario, 1920-1997* (Toronto, 1998); Veronica Strong-Boag, "'Wages for Housework': Mothers' Allowances and the Beginnings of Social Security in Canada," *Journal of Canadian Studies* 14, 1 (Spring 1979): 24-34; Megan J. Davies, "Services Rendered, Rearing Children for the State: Mothers' Pensions in British Columbia, 1911-1931," in Barbara K. Latham and Roberta J. Pazdro, eds., *Not Just Pin Money: Selected Essays on the History of Women's Working British Columbia* (Victoria, 1984), 249-63.

25. Olwen Hufton, "Women without Men: Widows and Spinsters in Britain and France in the Eighteenth Century," *Journal of Family History* 9 (Winter 1984), 355-76; Christine Stansell, *City of Women: Sex and Class in*

New York, 1798–1860 (New York, 1986); Marilyn Cohen, "Survival Strategies in Female-Headed Households: Linen Workers in Tullylish, County Down, 1901," *Journal of Family History* 17, 3 (1992), 303–18; Gordon and McLanahan, "Single Parenthood"; Bradbury, *Working Families*.

26. Among the earliest articles internationally were Hufton, "Women without Men" and Michael Anderson, "The Social Position of Spinsters in Mid-Victorian Britain," *Journal of Family History* 9 (Winter 1984). An excellent counter to this trend is Peter Gossage's current research into step-parenting. See "Remarriage and Family Conflict in 19th Century Quebec," in Lori Chambers and Edgar-André Montigny, eds., *Family Matters: Papers in Post-Confederation Canadian Family History* (Toronto, 1998) and Peter Gossage, "La Marâtre: Marie-Anne Houde and the Myth of the Wicked Stepmother in Quebec," *Canadian Historical Review* 76, 4 (1995), 563–97. I develop some of my ideas about the ways typologies favoured by family historians hid single parents in Bettina Bradbury, "Widowhood and Canadian Family History," in Margaret Conrad, ed., *Intimate Relations: Family and Community in Planter Nova Scotia, 1759–1800* (Fredericton, 1995), 19–41. Key debates that have diverted family historians away from focusing on such children include the desire to determine whether most families were nuclear or extended in the past, and questions surrounding the patterns of leaving home.

27. This has been one of the legacies of Peter Laslett's approach and that of the Cambridge Group for the History of Population and Social Structure. Their most influential work remains Peter Laslett with Richard Wall, eds., *Household and Family in Past Time: Comparative Studies in the Size and Structure of the Domestic Group over the Last Three Centuries in England, France, Serbia, Japan and Colonial North America, with Further Materials from Western Europe* (Cambridge, UK, 1972).

28. For example, Gérard Bouchard explains that he has excluded families broken by the premature death of a spouse from most analyses in his important longitudinal study *Quelques arpents d'Amérique: Population, économie, famille au Saguenay, 1838–1971* (Montreal, 1996), 169–70. Exceptions in Canadian history include Danielle Gauvreau and Mario Bourque, "Jusqu'à ce que la mort nous sépare: Le destin des femmes et des hommes mariés au Saguenay avant 1930," *Canadian Historical Review* 71, 4 (1990) and Danielle Gauvreau, *Une ville et sa population au temps de la Nouvelle France* (Sillery, QC, 1991).

29. Joy Parr, "Introduction," in Janovicek and Parr, eds., *Histories of Canadian Children and Youth*, 3.

30. Van Poppel, "Children in One-Parent Families."

31. Before 1921 there was no national system of record-keeping, so estimates for these years rely on work based on the excellent Quebec parish registers or on the census. The latter are not considered very reliable. Roderic Beaujot

and Kevin McQuillan pull together early research to suggest that the crude death rate in Quebec went up between the 1860s and 1870s, then dropped by almost half by the 1920s. This may not have been the case elsewhere in the country. They argue that there is evidence of dramatically different death rates in different cities and regions. *Growth and Dualism: The Demographic Development of Canadian Society* (Toronto, 1982), 27–8. See also Warren E. Kalbach and Wayne W. McVey, *The Demographic Bases of Canadian Society* (Toronto, 1979).

32. Canada, House of Commons, *Debates*, 12 October 1903, 13699.

33. Chambers, *Married Women*, 72; Clarkson, *Remoralizing Families*, 205–16.

34. Andrée Lévesque, *La norme et les deviants: Les femmes au Québec pendant l'entre-deux-guerres* (Montreal, 1989); Marie-Aimée Cliche, "Les filles-mères devant les tribunaux de Québec, 1850–1969," *Recherches sociographiques* 32, 1 (1991), 9–42; Cliche, "Morale chrétienne et 'double standard sexuel'"; Patricia Tomic-Trumper, "The Care of Unwed Mothers and Illegitimate Children in Toronto, 1867–1920: A Study in Social Administration" Ph.D. diss., University of Toronto, 1986; Leigh Vallieres, "Continuity in the Face of Change: Institutions for Unwed Mothers in Toronto, 1870s–1930's," major research paper, York University History Department, September 1993; Caroline Evans, "Salvationism vs. Social Gospel: Contrasting Responses to Unmarried Mothers, 1874–1900," major research paper, York University History Department, 1996.

35. Enumerators were paid "by the piece" at 5 cents a head, "5cts a death, 25cts a farm, and 30cts a factory." In addition, they were allocated $3.00 a day when they went to receive instructions from the commissioner of their county. As expenses came in for approval in the years following the taking of the census, politicians debated the expenditures in minute detail, especially as the cost of taking this census rose from early estimates of $500,000 to over $1,200,000. See especially House of Commons, *Debates*, 1903, 13723, 4824, and 4820.

36. On incest see Joan Sangster, *Regulating Girls and Women: Sexuality, Family and the Law in Ontario, 1920–1960* (Toronto, 2001), and in particular her chapter "Incest, the Sexual Abuse of Children, and the Power of Familialism," in Janovicek and Parr, eds., *Histories of Canadian Childhood and Youth*.

37. "Instructions to Officers," 1901, article 71.

38. Many politicians were sceptical about the de jure method, for, as Bruce Curtis makes clear, it served a political purpose in placing people who were away working, etc., in their home ridings. On lumber camps, see *Debates*, 1903, 4830. On de jure versus de facto census taking, see *Debates*, 1900, 8433; 1901, 3058–83. Bruce Curtis, *The Politics of Population: State Formation, Statistics, and the Census of Canada, 1840–1875* (Toronto, 2001).

39. "Instructions to Officers," 1901, articles 69–79.
40. Ibid, articles 44, 49; *Household Counts: Canadian Households and Families in 1901*. Eds. Eric W. Sager and Peter Baskerville (Toronto: University of Toronto Press, 2007), 441–76.
41. Shortly after Confederation, the 1870 census bill delegated power for determining all details about when to take the census, what questions to ask, etc. to the bureaucrats by designating them as administrative matters. As a result, as late as June and July 1900, not even a year before the census was to be taken, Members of Parliament were asking what the questions would be and when it would be taken, and were not given definite answers. Curtis, *The Politics of Population*, 261; Debates 1900, 6343, 7642, 7786, 8433. The only major discussion about content in the House of Commons was about how to report nationality, origins, and language.
42. "Instructions to Officers," 1901, article 12.
43. I categorized unmarried children aged 19 and under using the variables MOMLOC (location of mother in the household) and POPLOC (location of father) into those living with only their mother, only their father, neither parent, or both parents.
44. Two methods of identifying these parents rendered the same results. The simplest uses SPLOC (0 if no spouse present) in combination with marital status and NBRCHILD, a variable that is described as counting the number of children in the dwelling, but appear to only count those of resident parents. Identifying single parents by the constructed variable LIVETYPE, which identifies family structures from the point of view of each person in the household (If LIVETYPE = 7, 8, or 18, that person is a single parent), and is based on the same variables, produces the same result.
45. Reminders of the inextricability and contextuality of identities have dominated much recent work in feminist history in ways that do not seem to have influenced quantitative historians intent on separating the influence of variables through various forms of regression. Elsa Barkley Brown and Nancy Hewitt suggest the metaphors of jazz and chemistry respectfully as way of conceptualizing these interactions in Brown, "'What Has Happened Here': The Politics of Difference in Women's History and Feminist Politics," and Hewitt, "Compounding Difference," both in *Feminist Studies* 18, 2 (1992).
46. Darroch, "Home and Away."
47. Gordon and McLanahan, "Single Parenthood in 1900," 99–100.
48. Throughout the paper I move back and forth between discussing the characteristics of the children and the attributes of the single parents. The former makes the children the unit of analysis. Analysis of parents' characteristics is limited to all parents under 55 with a child present in order to contain the discussion as much as possible to parents with non-adult children, and to avoid giving a misleading impression of the characteristics of single parents by counting those with several children several times.
49. That many men failed to save babies whose mothers died during or soon after childbirth is clear from the high death rates among infants living with their fathers that are reported in the studies surveyed by Frans van Poppel in "Children in One-Parent Families." I argue in *Working Families* that those men who did keep their children after their wife died, or they separated, frequently had daughters or other female kin of an age to assist them. On children and institutions see my "The Fragmented Family."
50. Some data-entry errors inflate this percentage. For example, when a husband was miscoded as female, the program that identified whether a spouse was in the household recorded the spouse as absent. I have tried to correct most of these, but anyone using the database should be aware of this error in the SPLOC column.
51. It is possible that she had never married, but had reported she was married to the census taker rather than admit to being single. This seems less likely, as her relationship to the head of the household is described as "wife," even though she was the only adult in the house.
52. "Instructions to Officers," 1901, article 71.
53. In the sample population, there were 963 Asians counted in BC, the vast majority of whom were from China. Of them, 920 were male. Eighteen of the 43 females were under 19; 14 were in their twenties. The rest were all under 50. Only 3 per cent of the males were under 15; 22 per cent were aged 15 to 24, while some 66 per cent were clustered between the ages of 25 and 49.
54. Among the population in BC identified as Chinese and captured in our sample there were 301 married men of all ages, compared to only 12 married women. One of these women was living with a child but no spouse, as were four men, including Juin. Most of the men apparently lived without wives or children, though enumerators appear to have had trouble being sure about relationships.
55. Kathryn Harvey, "To Love, Honour and Obey: Wife-Battering in Working-Class Montreal, 1869–79," *Urban History Review* 19 (1990); Lorna McLean, "'Deserving' Wives and 'Drunken' Husbands: Wife Beating, Marital Conduct, and the Law in Ontario, 1850–1910," *Histoire sociale/Social History* 35, 69 (2002); Lori Chambers and John Weaver, "Alimony and Orders of Protection: Escaping Abuse in Hamilton-Wentworth, 1837–1900," *Ontario History* 95, 2 (2003), 113–35.
56. In my study of two Montreal wards between 1861 and 1891, the proportion of lone parents who were women with children but no spouse present increased from 3 per cent in 1861 to 7 per cent in 1891. *Working Families*, 244.
57. Suzanne Morton, "Nova Scotia and Its Unmarried Mothers, 1945–1975," in Nancy Christie and Michael Gauvreau, eds., *Mapping the Margins: The Family and Social Discipline in Canada, 1700–1975* (Montreal and Kingston, 2004), 328.

58. Parr, *Labouring Children*, 86.
59. In looking at single parenting in the United States through the census of 1900, Linda Gordon and Sara McLanahan had expected to find vast regional differences, particularly between rural and urban areas, in large part because their previous research had viewed such children through the files of charity and social workers. They found only minor differences. They could only identify children whose parent was recognized as a head of family, so children in what they call subfamilies are not counted. They found that 8.3 per cent of children under 15 in rural areas and 9.3 per cent in urban areas lived with a single parent. "Single Parenthood in 1900," 102.
60. In 1901 these were Victoria, Vancouver, Winnipeg, London, Hamilton, Toronto, Montreal, Quebec City, Saint John, and Halifax.
61. Not too much should be made of differences between the US and Canadian figures. These studies are based on different definitions of rural and urban as well as different sampling techniques. The sample in the CFP database is a "stratified random sample by dwelling." On the implications of this see Michael Ornstein, "Analysis of Household Samples: The 1901 Census of Canada," *Historical Methods: A Journal of Quantitative and Interdisciplinary History* 33, 4 (2000). The source for the American data is Gordon and McLanahan, "Single Parenthood in 1901."
62. Joy Parr, *The Gender of Breadwinners*. In her study of unwed mothers in two US states, Mary Louise Hough argues that the economic and demographic structures of communities shaped attitudes to children born outside of marriage and hence influenced whether mothers kept them. "'I'm a Poor Girl . . . in Family and I'd Like to Know if You Be Kind': The Community's Response to Unwed Mothers in Maine and Tennessee, 1876–1956," Ph.D. diss., University of Maine, 1997, 18, cited in Morton, "Nova Scotia and Its Unmarried Mothers," 334.
63. It is likely too that the de jure method of taking the census caused confusion when men were away hunting or seeking work, and that the practice of having more than one wife in some aboriginal communities could lead to miscalculations regarding spouses present or absent. It would be interesting to know how men serving in the South African War were recorded.
64. It is also possible that the proportions are partially an artefact of the decisions of those involved in planning and executing the census. Enumerators were instructed to list couples who had separated as to bed and as married. Annalee Lepp has shown how the clerks in Ottawa changed references to divorced people from Quebec, re-inscribing them as married. However, unless the absent spouse was listed at home with the children, such situations would still portray a single-parent-headed family in the database. Serge Gagnon portrays a fairly casual attitude to informal separations on the part of priests in the early nineteenth century, as well as the double standard of priests in the early nineteenth century, as well as the double standard surrounding separations of body and goods, the only kind of separation recognized by the Catholic church in his *Marriage et famille: Au temps de Papineau* (Sainte-Foy, 1993), 227–43. See also Lepp, "Dismembering the Family"; and Marie-Aimée Cliché, "Les procès en séparation de corps dans la région de Montréal, 1795–1879," *Revue historique de l'Amérique française* 49, 1 (1995), 64–108.
65. Suzanne Morton reports that the rates of births to unmarried mothers were higher in Nova Scotia in the 1920s and 1940s than elsewhere in the country, at 4 and 8 per cent respectively, and reminds readers of the ways children "could be incorporated into the family and raised as a new sister or brother to the mother or adopted by relatives," "Nova Scotia and Its Unmarried Mothers," 328, 335.
66. Clarkson, *Remoralizing Families*, 196–8.
67. Herbert Gutman, *The Black Family in Slavery and Freedom* (New York, 1976); Suzanne Lebsock, "Free Black Women and the Question of Matriarchy: Petersburg, Virginia, 1784–1820," *Feminist Studies* 8 (1982); Claire Robertson, "Africa into the Americas? Slavery and Women, the Family, and the Gender Division of Labour," in David Barry de Gaspar and Darlene Clark-Hine, eds., *More than Chattel: Black Women and Slavery in the Americas* (Bloomington and Indianapolis, 1996).
68. As explained above, most decisions were made within the Department of Agriculture. In July 1900, however, members of the House did discuss the question of how identity should be captured on the upcoming census. A.A.C. Larivière stressed the importance of being able to distinguish between French Canadian, Acadians, and what he called French half-breeds, wanting them all to be counted as French. There was also some discussion of the importance of being able to trace the history of the diverse "races" of Canada. *Debates*, 16 July 1900.
69. "Race" was a fluid term, constantly evoked in different ways, yet always marking difference based on hierarchies that place whites in a place of privilege. Consensus was rare about its meanings. The results of its deployment were inevitably harmful to those deemed inferior. When Theodore Roosevelt wrote his four-volume epic *The Winning of the West*, which was published between 1889 and 1896, not long before the 1901 census, he argued that the American race was difference from its English forbears. See Gail Bederman, *Manliness and Civilization* (Chicago, 1995), 179.
70. Sylvia Van Kirk, "Tracing the Fortunes of Five Founding Families of Victoria," *B.C. Studies* 115–16 (1997–8), 148–79; Adele Perry, *On the Edge of Empire: Gender, Race, and the Making of British Columbia, 1849–1871* (Toronto, 2001); Jay Nelson, "'A Strange Revolution in the Manners of the Country': Aboriginal-Settler Intermarriage in Nineteenth-Century British Columbia," in John McLaren, Robert Menzies, and Dorothy E. Chunn, eds., *Regulating*

Lives: *Historical Essays on the State, Society, the Individual and the Law* (Vancouver, 2003).

71. Gordon Darroch, "Families, Fostering and Flying the Coop: Lessons in Liberal Cultural Formation, 1871–1901," in Eric W. Sager and Peter Baskerville, eds., *Household Counts: Canadian Households and Families in 1901* (Toronto: University of Toronto Press, 2007), 197–246.

72. Bradbury, *Working Families.*

73. In her important work, *The Gender of Breadwinners*, Joy Parr delineates the ways the Penman employers went out of their way to seek skilled female workers for their knitting mill in Paris, Ontario, and the resulting high proportion of female-headed households in the town.

PRIMARY DOCUMENT

International Labour Organisation, Convention 138 on Minimum Age for Admission to Employment, 1973 (abridged from Articles 1–18)

Preamble

The General Conference of the International Labour Organisation,

Having been convened at Geneva by the Governing Body of the International Labour Office, and having met in its Fifty-eighth Session on 6 June 1973, and

Having decided upon the adoption of certain proposals with regard to minimum age for admission to employment [. . .]

Noting the terms of the Minimum Age (Industry) Convention, 1919, the Minimum Age (Sea) Convention, 1920, the Minimum Age (Agriculture) Convention, 1921, the Minimum Age (Trimmers and Stokers) Convention, 1921, the Minimum Age (Non-Industrial Employment) Convention, 1932, the Minimum Age (Sea) Convention (Revised), 1936, the Minimum Age (Industry) Convention (Revised), 1937, the Minimum Age (Non-Industrial Employment) Convention (Revised), 1937, the Minimum Age (Fishermen) Convention, 1959, and the Minimum Age (Underground Work) Convention, 1965, and

Considering that the time has come to establish a general instrument on the subject, which would gradually replace the existing ones applicable to limited economic sectors, with a view to achieving the total abolition of child labour, and

Having determined that these proposals shall take the form of an international Convention,

adopts this twenty-sixth day of June of the year one thousand nine hundred and seventy-three the following Convention, which may be cited as the Minimum Age Convention, 1973:

continued

Article 1

Each Member for which this Convention is in force undertakes to pursue a national policy designed to ensure the effective abolition of child labour and to raise progressively the minimum age for admission to employment or work to a level consistent with the fullest physical and mental development of young persons.

Article 2

1. Each Member which ratifies this Convention shall specify, in a declaration appended to its ratification, a minimum age for admission to employment or work within its territory and on means of transport registered in its territory; subject to Articles 4 to 8 of this Convention, no one under that age shall be admitted to employment or work in any occupation.

2. Each Member which has ratified this Convention may subsequently notify the Director-General of the International Labour Office, by further declarations, that it specifies a minimum age higher than that previously specified.

3. The minimum age specified in pursuance of paragraph 1 of this Article shall not be less than the age of completion of compulsory schooling and, in any case, shall not be less than 15 years.

4. Notwithstanding the provisions of paragraph 3 of this Article, a Member whose economy and educational facilities are insufficiently developed may, after consultation with the organizations of employers and workers concerned, where such exist, initially specify a minimum age of 14 years.

5. Each Member which has specified a minimum age of 14 years in pursuance of the provisions of the preceding paragraph shall include in its reports on the application of this Convention submitted under article 22 of the Constitution of the International Labour Organisation a statement—

   (a) that its reason for doing so subsists; or

   (b) that it renounces its right to avail itself of the provisions in question as from a stated date.

Article 3

1. The minimum age for admission to any type of employment or work which by its nature or the circumstances in which it is carried out is likely to jeopardise the health, safety or morals of young persons shall not be less than 18 years.

2. The types of employment or work to which paragraph 1 of this Article applies shall be determined by national laws or regulations or by the competent authority, after consultation with the organizations of employers and workers concerned, where such exist.

3. Notwithstanding the provisions of paragraph 1 of this Article, national laws or regulations or the competent authority may, after consultation with the organizations of employers and workers concerned, where such exist, authorise employment or work as from the age of 16 years on condition that the health, safety and morals of the young persons concerned are fully protected and that the young persons have received adequate specific instruction or vocational training in the relevant branch of activity.

Article 4

1. In so far as necessary, the competent authority, after consultation with the organizations of employers and workers concerned, where such exist, may exclude from the application of this Convention limited categories of employment or work in respect of which special and substantial problems of application arise. [. . .]

Article 5

1. A Member whose economy and administrative facilities are insufficiently developed may, after consultation with the organizations of employers and workers concerned, where such exist, initially limit the scope of application of this Convention. [. . .]

3. The provisions of the Convention shall be applicable as a minimum to the following: mining and quarrying; manufacturing; construction; electricity, gas and water; sanitary services; transport, storage and communication; and plantations and other agricultural undertakings mainly producing for commercial purposes, but excluding family and small-scale holdings producing for local consumption and not regularly employing hired workers. [. . .]

continued

Article 6

This Convention does not apply to work done by children and young persons in schools for general, vocational or technical education or in other training institutions, or to work done by persons at least 14 years of age in undertakings, where such work is carried out in accordance with conditions prescribed by the competent authority, after consultation with the organizations of employers and workers concerned, where such exist, and is an integral part of—

(a) a course of education or training for which a school or training institution is primarily responsible;

(b) a program of training mainly or entirely in an undertaking, which program has been approved by the competent authority; or

(c) a program of guidance or orientation designed to facilitate the choice of an occupation or of a line of training.

Article 7

1. National laws or regulations may permit the employment or work of persons 13 to 15 years of age on light work which is—

(a) not likely to be harmful to their health or development; and

(b) not such as to prejudice their attendance at school, their participation in vocational orientation or training programs approved by the competent authority or their capacity to benefit from the instruction received.

2. National laws or regulations may also permit the employment or work of persons who are at least 15 years of age but have not yet completed their compulsory schooling on work which meets the requirements set forth in sub-paragraphs (a) and (b) of paragraph 1 of this Article.

3. The competent authority shall determine the activities in which employment or work may be permitted under paragraphs 1 and 2 of this Article and shall prescribe the number of hours during which and the conditions in which such employment or work may be undertaken.

4. Notwithstanding the provisions of paragraphs 1 and 2 of this Article, a Member which has availed itself of the provisions of paragraph 4 of Article 2 may, for as long as it continues

to do so, substitute the ages 12 and 14 for the ages 13 and 15 in paragraph 1 and the age 14 for the age 15 in paragraph 2 of this Article.

Article 8

1. After consultation with the organizations of employers and workers concerned, where such exist, the competent authority may, by permits granted in individual cases, allow exceptions to the prohibition of employment or work provided for in Article 2 of this Convention, for such purposes as participation in artistic performances.

2. Permits so granted shall limit the number of hours during which and prescribe the conditions in which employment or work is allowed.

Article 9

1. All necessary measures, including the provision of appropriate penalties, shall be taken by the competent authority to ensure the effective enforcement of the provisions of this Convention. [. . .]

Study Questions

1. According to these essays, how did family configuration and class shape the experience of childhood in the past?
2. In looking at the image of the girl who was collecting coal, imagine who was interested in taking her photograph and for what purpose. Is the photograph sympathetic to her and her coal gathering or is it critical? Does the image help us to think about children and their usage of urban space?
3. Look at the excerpt from the International Labour Organisation document. How do restrictions on child labour help us to understand the value of children in any given society? When is child labour acceptable today?

Selected Bibliography

Articles

Coulter, Rebecca Priegert, "Between School and Marriage: A Case Study Approach to Young Women's Work in Early Twentieth-Century Canada," in Nancy Janovicek and Joy Parr, eds, *Histories of Canadian Children and Youth*. Don Mills, ON: Oxford University Press, 2003: 88–99.

Darroch, Gordon, "Home and Away: Patterns of Residence, Schooling, and Work among Children and Never Married Young Adults, Canada, 1871 and 1901," *Journal of Family History* 26, 2 (Spring 2001): 220–50.

Hurl, Lorna F., "Restricting Child Factory Labour in Late Nineteenth Century Ontario," *Labour/Le Travail* 21 (Spring 1988): 87–121.

Neff, Charlotte, "Pauper Apprenticeship in Early Nineteenth Century Ontario," *Journal of Family History* 21, 2 (April 1996): 144–71.

Pollack, Eunice G., "The Childhood We Have Lost: When Siblings Were Caregivers, 1900–1970," *Journal of Social History* 36, 1 (2002): 31–61.

Rooke, Patricia, and R.L. Snell, "Childhood and Charity in Nineteenth-Century British North America," *Social History/Historie sociale* 15, 29 (1982): 157–79.

Sutherland, Neil, "'We Always Had Things to Do': The Paid and Unpaid Work of Anglophone Children between the 1920s and the 1960s," *Labour/Le Travail* 25 (Spring 1980): 105–41.

Books

Bradbury, Bettina, *Working Families: Age, Gender, and Daily Survival in Industrializing Montreal*. Toronto: Oxford University Press, 1993.

McIntosh, Robert, *Boys in the Pits: Child Labour in Coal Mining*. Montreal: McGill-Queen's University Press, 2000.

Parr, Joy, *Labouring Children: British Immigrant Apprentices to Canada, 1869–1924*. Montreal and London: McGill-Queen's and Croom Helm, 1980.

Srigley, Katrina, *Breadwinning Daughters: Young Working Women in a Depression-Era City, 1929–1939*. Toronto: University of Toronto Press, 2010.

2 Political Children

Editors' Introduction

The study of labour history exploded in the 1970s and 1980s when historians interested in the human experience of industrializing societies and modernity itself focused on class as a category of analysis. Many labour historians were concerned not only with labour and relational class identities but also with the important determinants of working-class experience—most particularly, gender, ethnicity, and race. Thus, many working-class historians use analytical frameworks we could call "intersectional." This perspective insists that while class structured lives, other identities simultaneously influenced the nature of working-class life. Canadian historians have found this especially significant given the critical importance of immigration and immigrant labour in Canada and the broad range of understandings about politics and culture related to them.

Historians such as John Bullen and Bettina Bradbury (see the previous chapter) insisted that labour history needed to take age into consideration. In their essays in this chapter, Rod MacLeod and Mary Anne Poutanen, and Rhonda Hinther go beyond the importance of children to the family economy to another crucial aspect of working-class history—political activity. Both essays show how the world of politics and strikes was not inhabited solely by adults. From a young age, working-class children were socialized within, and in time absorbed, the political contexts in which they were raised. Young people could also be found expressing an activist labour politics independent of their families.

Two particular groups of children are the focus of this chapter: Jewish schoolchildren in MacLeod and Poutanen's essay and radical Ukrainian youth in Hinther's. While the latter had access to distinct Ukrainian community schools, Jewish children in Montreal were assimilated into the Protestant school system, where they experienced anti-Semitism and general hostility to their cultural and political perspectives. Both sets of schoolchildren learned from adults' labour activism, and in the case of the Aberdeen student walkout, Jewish children initiated their own resistance to discrimination. Despite the belittling headline in a local paper—"Wee kiddies on the picket line"—the fact that this act of resistance made newspapers suggests how profound it was. Hinther shows how adults in the interwar period went to considerable effort to impart the importance of ethnic identity and radical labour politics to their children, and how in turn, youth helped to shape the movement.

Children's and youth activism might easily be dismissed as superficial or as a function of immaturity. Recent literature on the subject, however, including the essays here, proves that tremendous insight can be gained by exploring intergenerational political commitment and youngsters' expressions of it.[1] These essays are examples of the richness gained by marrying working-class and children's history. The 1927 image of the Ukrainian folk music class reminds us of the close relationship among young people's identity formation, cultural identity, and family tradition. This image suggests that pride in working-class Ukrainian culture included the politics of labour.

Note

1. See for example, several articles in the Winter 2012 issue of *Journal of the History of Childhood and Youth*.

Little Fists for Social Justice: Anti-Semitism, Community, and Montreal's Aberdeen School Strike, 1913

RODERICK MACLEOD AND MARY ANNE POUTANEN

Introduction

During the last week of February 1913, Miss McKinley called her Jewish pupils "dirty" and declared that they should be banned from the school. Her outburst triggered a political storm at Montreal's Protestant Aberdeen School, where Jews constituted the vast majority of the population. News of Miss McKinley's anti-Semitic tirade spread quickly from her grade six classroom to other senior students who subsequently called a general strike. Hundreds of Jewish pupils congregated in the park across the street from the school and organized pickets. Some of the strikers marched to the Baron de Hirsch Institute and to the newspaper office of the *Keneder Adler* to demand that action be taken against the teacher unless she apologized. Prominent Jewish community leaders negotiated with the principal and with the Protestant school board. Under pressure, Miss McKinley

"expressed her regret for having made inappropriate comments which were misunderstood by the children."[1] While this did not constitute an apology, the students agreed to return to class the following Monday leaving it to their elders to resolve the crisis with the school commissioners.

It is tempting to see this event as an example of youthful exuberance, not to be taken seriously as a genuine strike. Certainly most contemporaries appear to have paid it little heed. The school board minutes are silent. Although it did receive press coverage, the treatment of the strike is often dismissive. However, silence can speak volumes about adult fears engendered by student militancy. Deconstruction of public discourse and a closer analysis of the behaviour of the actors involved reveal a much greater level of complexity in the reactions of adults, which ranged from pride to outrage, embarrassment, and anxiety. The strike had long-lasting consequences for the Jewish community, for Protestant school board policy, and for the character of Quebec's education system.

Source: From *Labour/Le Travail*, 70 (Fall 2012): 61–99. Reprinted by permission of the publisher.

The Aberdeen students' actions were remarkable. They showed maturity in their understanding of "the strike" as a strategic response to perceived injustice, in their degree of self-confidence, and in their resolve, even when faced with mounted police, who had been called in to control the situation, and with possible reprisals from teachers and parents. We argue that the Aberdeen student walkout reveals a close connection between the strikers, the labour activism of their parents, and the working-class Jewish community along the St-Laurent Street corridor (otherwise known as "the Main"). The collective action of the Aberdeen pupils speaks to the historical agency of children and what the actions of youth can tell us about their community and its nurturing environment. Indeed, the level of organization and the rhetoric used by students at the Aberdeen School is not often seen in those children's strikes treated by historians in Canada and the United States.[2] The strike at the Aberdeen School resulted from deep-seeded grievances and demonstrated a precocious understanding of the basic tenets of labour politics learned at home and in the neighbourhood.

Although the concept of children's agency has not informed much writing by Quebec historians, Tamara Myers's ground-breaking studies of juvenile justice have been influential in our understanding of how children respond to discrimination.[3] As Robert McIntosh reminds us, historical accounts of children usually have centred on actions undertaken by others, adults in particular, which have rendered children as victims of society.[4] Until recently, childhood has been understood as a process of socialization into the adult world. The new sociology of childhood recognizes children as social actors and capable of reflexivity; thus, it gives children their voices rather than silencing them. Proponents of this approach argue that children must be "seen as active in the construction and determination of their own social lives, and the lives of those around them," and that "children are not just the passive subjects of social structures and processes."[5] Today, scholars of children and youth emphasize a plurality of childhoods across societies as well as over time, and a methodology that recognizes the significance of social context in kids' lives.[6] Children, they argue, must be considered from their own shared perspectives and their experiences with others in their social networks. Instead of perceiving adults, especially parents and teachers, exercising power over children in a variety of circumstances and places, sociologist Madeleine Leonard has suggested that we ought to see adults and children as negotiating the expectations they had of each other within families. Nonetheless, the notion of agency, which is essentially individualistic, should not imply an absolute lack of influence from family, community, or institutions. We argue that the response of the Aberdeen strikers to Miss McKinley's anti-Semitic comments is evidence of autonomous action, albeit within the limitations imposed by parental and institutional authorities.

Since we know so little about the Aberdeen students themselves, we reconstituted aspects of their lives through their relations with kin, peers, school authorities, and community leaders. We consulted English, French, and Yiddish-language newspapers, school board documents, and McGill Normal School registers. These sources present challenges in identifying the children who attended the school and their families, making sense of the contradictory interpretations of the events, and figuring out what became of the strike leaders. To determine the fathers' occupations, and thus the social-class origins of the students, we reconstituted as many families as possible. To create a manageable cohort for analysis, we examined a list of students who registered for the 1912–13 school year and matched these names against the databases of *Montréal Avenir du Passé* or *MAP*, the 1911 census, Lovell's Directory, and parish records. Through a careful reading of these historical documents, we have come to understand aspects of the children's motivations. Unfortunately, there are no written accounts by the actors themselves and only one photograph of the strikers.

The Jewish Community in Early Twentieth-Century Montreal

When the Aberdeen students walked out of school in late February 1913, the Jewish community had grown substantially since the turn of the century owing to waves of immigration from Eastern-Europe.

In 1911, 30,000 Jews called Montreal home; 10 years later, the population had grown to over 45,000.[7] Most were poor, Yiddish-speaking, and Ashkenazi. They had escaped poverty, political repression, compulsory military service in the Russian army, discrimination, and pogroms.[8] These newcomers contrasted sharply with the small number of long-established, English-speaking, and largely well-to-do Jewish Montrealers who had set down roots in Quebec following the Conquest. While the "uptowners" lived principally in middle-class enclaves such as Westmount and Outremont, new arrivals or "downtowners" clustered along the corridor of St-Laurent Street where they recreated *shtetl* life.[9] The uptowners were ambivalent about the newcomers. Given that the two groups differed sharply in terms of social class, political orientation, and culture, many in the original community were concerned that these Jewish immigrants would sully their hard-earned reputation with regard to the mainstream community, especially respectable anglophones.[10] The overwhelming needs of impoverished immigrants strained the existing resources of Jewish charitable institutions as well as relations between the established members and newcomers.

Anti-Semitism was a constant feature of life for Jewish Montrealers. Prejudice ranged from snubs and taunts to acts of violence to accusations that Jews were inassimilable and represented a threat to the Christian character of Canadian society. That most newcomers were poor reinforced the popular association of outsiders with wretchedness, crime, and disease—an association shared by much of the established Jewish elite. Class divisions within the urban Jewish community also took on a political character as working-class Jews came to protest their economic condition, increasingly rejecting cultural tradition in favour of secular militancy. To the wider society, such militancy simply added to fears that the Jewish community as a whole was a potential danger.

The years leading up to the Aberdeen strike saw a sharp increase in anti-Semitic incidents and the acidity of anti-Jewish discourse in Quebec. This malicious tide crested in March 1910, when notary Jacques-Edouard Plamondon addressed a gathering of the *Association Catholique de la Jeunesse*

Canadienne-Française in Quebec City and denounced Jews and Judaism, evoking no less than the ancient blood libel as evidence of inherent murderousness on the part of Jews everywhere. This speech, and its subsequent publication as a pamphlet, provoked several instances of street fighting and vandalism between Jews and Catholics. These incidents in turn spurred the provincial Jewish leadership to sue Plamondon for libel, claiming that such language incited violence against Jews which potentially threatened lives and at the very least livelihoods.[11] The case ultimately would be lost on the grounds that the courts did not recognize group libel, but solely a specific attack on an identifiable individual. Plamondon's denigrations had not been of this nature. Even before the trial, however, which opened in May 1913, the case would have been an eagerly discussed topic throughout the Jewish community, by children as well as adults, both because of what was at stake and because the action of filing a suit on the grounds of defamation was itself unprecedented.

Despite such prejudices, immigrants set down roots and initiated strategies to manage on little income, while helping each other in the transition from the old world to the new. Stores, political and cultural institutions, synagogues, and neighbourhood parks served many functions, including places in which to exchange information and assist in the process of integration.[12] Immigrants purchased kosher food, clothing, shoes, along with Yiddish-language newspapers and books, at Jewish businesses which lined the Main. They utilized the services offered by existing community institutions such as Yiddish theatre, lending libraries, and mutual aid societies.

Life was not easy for young people but they found endless distractions in the neighbourhood that softened the harshness of poverty. Esther Goldstein Kershman writes fondly about her childhood, describing favourite activities and sites of play. Her own backyard attracted siblings, cousins, and friends who played in the space encompassing her parents and her uncle's triplexes. Children frequented green spaces where boys played baseball and girls organized picnics. At the Young Men's Hebrew Association, they attended nature study excursions, summer camp, swimming, and science lessons. Goldstein Kershman watched silent films at The Midway and vaudeville acts from the United States at the nearby Orpheum Theatre. The Main itself was a constant source of entertainment, a cornucopia of sounds, sights, and smells, where children (some of whom attended Aberdeen School) prowled in search of opportunities for urban amusement and for adventure:

> Nothing can ever taste as delicious as a sour apple you stole from one of the fruit stalls; so tart that it left you with a lingering velvety feeling in your mouth. Shops with shining fruits and vegetables, cheeses and delicacies from "back home" in Poland and Roumania or other sources—it was like the "shtetl" transplanted to Montreal. The crowds were busy, multi-lingual, buying, haggling, good-humoured people like in a trance. They filled the sidewalks, chatting, laughing, chewing on something, walking four-abreast, arm-in-arm, blocking the way for others.[13]

The children were also acutely aware that their parents were struggling in a new country to make ends meet. Many turned to the garment industry or *schmata* trade which had expanded northward from its earlier location around Notre Dame and St-Paul Streets; sweatshops spread along the Main as far as Mile End, allowing for a short trek to work.[14] That it was Jewish owners of garment factories who provided employment to newcomers, and Jewish socialist organizers who strove diligently to unionize the mainly Jewish needle trade workers, created further conflicts, tensions, and divisions within the community.

Growing hostility between employers and workers erupted in June 1912, when 4,000 tailors laid down the tools of their trade in firms of the Montreal Clothing Manufacturers' Association. The powerful Association refused to meet with the strikers and closed its shops. It then hired thugs (private detectives and off-duty city policemen who had been employed by factory owners) to physically attack picketing workers. The union organized

large rallies and parades in the heart of the *schmata* trade in protest. This strike was surely the substance of lively discussions around family kitchen tables, as well as on the streets, parks, and synagogues frequented by needle trade workers and their families. The acrimonious and bloody strike ended two months later in partial victory: manufacturers maintained their open shops; workers won a small reduction in hours of work and an increase in the rate of piece work. Even so, this labour dispute was critical to workers' growing class consciousness and solidarity, and it "marked the importance of Jews as major participants in the Montreal men's clothing industry, both as manufacturers and as workers."[15]

The tough economic situation was not to improve. After more than a decade of unprecedented growth, Canada plunged into an economic recession in the fall of 1912. Jewish residents of the St-Laurent Street corridor now had to contend with the uncertainty of employment and higher prices owing to inflation. Yet, despite the difficulties of everyday life associated with such economic uncertainty, immigrant Jewish families continued to send their children to elementary school, unlike the usual practice whereby working-class families temporarily withdrew their children from school during hard times. Jewish families placed great importance on educating their children, both to facilitate integration into the larger community and to encourage social mobility.

Aberdeen: A Protestant School

Montreal's Jewish families had been sending their children to Protestant schools since the 1870s. By 1913, certain schools had populations that were over 90 per cent Jewish. The growing number of Jewish students and the consequent demands for educational rights challenged, and potentially undermined, Protestant identity. Such claims touched a much cruder nerve within authorities than fears of social unrest: anti-Semitism was rarely expressed explicitly in the commissioners' discourse, but was never very far below the surface. Many school commissioners argued that Jews were, by definition, "outsiders" in both a legal and cultural sense.[16] Some Protestant parents refused to send their children to school, convinced that large numbers of Jews in the classroom diminished the curriculum's "Christian character."[17] Legal challenges led by lawyer Samuel W. Jacobs resulted in legislation passed in 1903 declaring Jews in effect had no educational rights. Although there were voices claiming that "persons professing the Jewish religion shall, for school purposes, be treated in the same manner as Protestants . . . and shall enjoy the same rights and privileges."[18] This legislation was regarded by the Jewish elite as the "magna carta" of Jewish education, marking the full acceptance of Jews within Quebec's public education system.[19] Even so, Protestant commissioners defiantly resisted any changes to its administrative structure, refusing to interpret the legislation as granting Jews any further rights beyond accommodation in schoolrooms.

Another source of aggravation was the treatment of Jewish children in Protestant classrooms. Although the school board had promised not to impose Christian teaching, the Protestant curriculum incorporated elements of Bible study into various subjects. Although the lack of defined religious instruction was traditionally seen as an attractive aspect of the Protestant school system to non-Christians, its more nebulous promotion of Christian values actually made it harder for Jews to find exemption from influence. During the 1900s Jewish families frequently complained that the board was not keeping its promise.[20]

It did not help relations within the classroom that virtually all teachers in the system were Protestant. Only a handful of Jews attended the McGill Normal School; by 1907 less than a dozen had received teaching certificates.[21] There is no evidence that any of them were hired by the school board. This lack of Jewish teachers was noted and decried in editorials and in letters to the editors of the *Keneder Adler* and the *Jewish Times*.[22] For Jewish children, having only Protestant teachers would not have been surprising given that every aspect of the school system—teaching personnel, administrators, and the curriculum—was Protestant. Schoolchildren routinely took at face value what teachers conveyed and Aberdeen students were presumably no different. And yet, it is not so difficult to imagine, given

the timing and substance of Miss McKinley's anti-Semitic remarks that her students might have looked around their classroom and noted that they were all Jews, and thus the target of her malice. Equally, it might have suddenly struck them that this Protestant teacher was the anomaly in the classroom and that her outburst was offensive. Quite possibly, from their perspective, the ground had shifted.

For their part, teachers in schools with large Jewish populations may have consistently felt a greater affinity with their Protestant employers, however fearful they might have been of the power they exercised over their lives, than with their young Jewish charges. For many teachers, facing a classroom of children from different ethnic, racial, or religious backgrounds would have been a daunting prospect. Furthermore, the teaching profession was as vulnerable as any other to prejudice and racism. Alton Goldbloom, future professor of medicine at McGill University, insisted that most of his Protestant teachers had no issue with their Jewish pupils, but recalled one who was "particularly venomous," constantly insulting him in public and wondering aloud what it was that made Jews "smell so bad."[23] Even well-meaning teachers would not have been immune from such prejudice. Most were young and distinctly ill-equipped to deal with urban diversity; certainly cultural sensitivity training was not a feature of the Normal School curriculum. Lack of experience, combined with a public discourse that was often overtly anti-Semitic, made the kind of incident that sparked outrage at Aberdeen School in 1913 all but inevitable.

The Strike

When Harry Singer, Frank Sherman, Joe Orenstein, Moses Skibelsky, and Moses Margolis heard Miss McKinley's remarks on that winter day in February 1913, they went to the principal to demand that the teacher apologize. Miss McKinley had allegedly said "that when she first came to the school it had been very clean, but since the Jewish children arrived the school had become dirty . . . and that Jewish children should be shut out of Aberdeen school."[24] Miss McKinley's tirade had touched a nerve. Aberdeen's Jewish students were often singled out and humiliated for being dirty. One child commented: "Should a Christian boy come to school in an unclean condition he was quietly sent home, but if a Hebrew lad turned up dirty he was sure to be told of it before the whole class and held up to ridicule." Accustomed as they were to such regular discrimination, the pupils were nevertheless struck by the blanket application of this accusation. Individually, students may have overlooked such countless petty putdowns, but by denigrating all Aberdeen's Jews, Miss McKinley had simply gone too far.

As the veteran head of several schools in working-class areas, including Aberdeen for fourteen years, Principal Henry Cockfield expected trouble from adolescent boys. Confronted by these five teenagers bringing an accusation against a teacher, Cockfield was inclined to take a jaundiced view of their sincerity and dismissed them as troublemakers. Frustrated, the boys met after school on Thursday, 27 February, and agreed to take action by calling a strike. In keeping with the logistics of labour protest that they had learned at home and in the community, the boys set out to mobilize the student body. By Friday morning the word had spread and growing numbers of students stood "about the school gates eagerly discussing the chance of success of their cause" and encouraging others to join their protest. Not knowing how long the strike would last, the five protest organizers suggested that classmates pick up their textbooks and scribblers; when they got to their class, however, they discovered that Miss McKinley had locked the door on them.[25] In response, the leaders sent a group of younger children throughout the school alerting anyone who might join their cause to what was taking place outside. The students then congregated in St-Louis Square across from the school. The strikers appointed the five boys who initiated the action as strike leaders, and resolved to uphold solidarity by not returning to class until authorized by the leaders to do so.[26] Some students were appointed to picket "as is the custom in all strikes."[27] They vowed as well to consider any strike-breaker a scab: "In those days, when the majority of the children were from working-class families, even the small children in the first grade felt contempt for scabs."[28]

At least 200 Aberdeen pupils joined the strike; some journalists have reported higher numbers, and Reuben Brainin of the *Keneder Adler* referred to "600 small soldiers."[29] That so many acted speaks to the close-knit community whence they came. The students knew each other very well. In 1913, the school had more than 1500 students with an average class size of 37. While such conditions may not have made for an ideal learning environment, they did permit students to network and conspire, and in this way build a sense of solidarity not unlike that of the factory floor. Moreover, these students all came from the same set of streets, often living next door to each other or even on separate floors of the same houses. The sense of solidarity was further expressed along the streets, green spaces, laneways, and even over backyard fences.

Who were these children? Of the 825 students who registered at Aberdeen for the 1912–1913 school year, we were able to link 121 students to the 1911 census and to city directories, thus allowing us to determine parents' occupations and therefore their social and economic status. These occupations indicate a preponderance of working-class families although some represent white collar jobs, management, and professionals. Notwithstanding the wide range of occupations, almost a third of the families had breadwinners who laboured as tailors. Likely all or most of these families would still be feeling the effects of the vicious tailor strike that had taken place only months before. No doubt this experience and others like it account for the readiness with which the Aberdeen students resorted to a call for militant action. It explains the ease with which they turned to the language of the strike: "uphold solidarity," "close ranks," "pickets," and "scabs." At the same time, the children were not simply mimicking their elders but rather were using these terms appropriately and effectively, revealing an understanding of the process of labour politics.

The strike leaders were all in grade six and aged 12 to 13. Their families originated in Eastern Europe, and two of the boys (Margolis and Singer) were born there prior to emigrating. Of the three born after the move, only Orenstein was born in Canada; Skibelsky's family was living in England at the time of his birth, while Sherman's was in the United States. Three of the strike leaders immigrated with their mothers as young children, the fathers having arrived earlier as was customary for those from Eastern European *shtetlekh*. Margolis and Skibelsky had fathers who were teachers, Orenstein's was a shopkeeper, and Singer's and Sherman's fathers were tailors. In the 1911 census, only one of the strike leaders' mothers was identified as a wage earner: Rebecca Margolis was an operator in a fur factory. Given that two of the fathers were teachers and two were tailors it is not surprising that these students would have been familiar with the politics of labour discourse. Joseph Orenstein's father self-identified as a shopkeeper in the 1911 census, but Lovell's Directory shows that in the years leading up to the strike he laboured in a variety of occupations that included grocer, pedlar, and presser. His work history would have given him a unique insight as small-business owner and wage labourer in the *schmata* trade. Joseph's oldest brother Henry had a similar labour experience; he worked for companies manufacturing clothing and shoes before managing the tony Cotter Boot Shop located on St James Street in the city's business district.

For journalist Reuben Brainin, Montreal's young strikers were inspired by "the literary evenings in Jewish institutions, of Jewish presentations which young people hear and absorb."[30] The Baron de Hirsch Institute on Bleury Street was at the heart of the community's cultural life and straddled geographically the divide between uptowners and downtowners. It was the principal social and educational centre and a venue for the kinds of events to which Brainin refers. The Institute offered day and night classes to young immigrants, housed a library of Yiddish as well as English books, and provided space for a variety of Jewish community organizations; it was part of the vibrant intellectual life, expressed in Yiddish, associated with labour unions, theatre, and bookstores along the Main. The *Keneder Adler*, Montreal's only Yiddish-language newspaper at the time, reflected this culture, at least to a certain extent. Although politically it was more liberal than socialist in outlook, and typically refrained from taking the lead in condemning factory

owners during key strikes, it was widely read by working families along the Main.[31] Identifying with these institutions reinforced a sense of the strike leaders' identity as Yiddish-speaking members of the working class. The local synagogues would also have provided social space to debate such political and social issues even while the strike leaders prepared for their bar mitzvahs. That these boys had either recently turned 13, or were about to, would have been a factor in taking a leadership role in the school as "men." This status, especially in 1913, would have earned them respect among the younger children in Aberdeen School, surely an important factor in rallying the rank-and-file.

As effective strike leaders, these young men inspired a sense of labour discipline on the picket line. By the afternoon of the strike, the crowds of children attracted reporters from most of the city's dailies as well as police: "Striking children lined the sidewalks and cheered lustily. A solitary foot policeman and one mounted officer paraded up and down the road trying to disperse the crowd, but as soon as the youthful strikers were moved from one part of the square, they gathered at another." Such tactics, typical of children trying to avoid trouble and escape adult authority, proved very useful in the context of the strike. Journalists reported that "the scholars behaved with almost perfect conduct; there was no booing or hissing, and not even one snowball was thrown."[32] Their apparent lack of fear was noteworthy, given that these children had witnessed the police brutality used against members of their families and neighbours during the recent tailors' strike and would have seen a police presence as intimidating.

Seeking solidarity with the larger Jewish community, some of the Aberdeen strikers marched to the offices of the *Keneder Adler*, where they found a sympathetic audience in its editor, Reuben Brainin. A Russian-born Hebrew essayist and scholar with a long career in Poland, Germany and the United States, Brainin had arrived from New York a year before to take up the position of editor-in-chief at the behest of the *Adler*'s owner and publisher, Hirsch Wolofsky. Brainin's editorials reflected not only the newspaper's support for the Jewish working class but also his own commitment to Jewish ethnic identity.[33] The Aberdeen strikers knew of him, expected a good reception, and were not disappointed. Although Brainin's sympathy for Jewish workers during the tailors' strike had been muted, given his opposition to creating divisions among the Jewish community, the Aberdeen school strike was clearly different.[34] It struck a chord with Brainin, who was already impressed by the cultural resilience of Jewish diaspora communities in North America, but had never seen this level of resistance to discrimination on the part of such youngsters. The students left convinced that their strike would receive positive coverage by Brainin in the community's newspaper. Any chance that the *Adler* might have presented the other side of the story was dashed when a reporter contacted the school later that day and Principal Cockfield refused to issue a statement.

Another group of Aberdeen students marched to the Baron de Hirsch Institute, located over a kilometre from the school, where they presented their case to representatives who agreed to call a meeting of the Baron de Hirsch's legislative committee to decide on a course of action. Knowing that the school authorities would never negotiate directly with children, the strikers were prepared to place their trust in this committee and to return to the strike. For all of their militancy, the strikers were also pragmatic, once again displaying wisdom beyond their years.

The legislative committee met at the Craig Street office of Samuel W. Jacobs, the prominent lawyer who would shortly prosecute the Plamondon case, and debated the children's actions. Jewish community leaders had mixed feelings about the strikers. On the one hand, because the strike was in reaction to anti-Semitism, they could hardly oppose its intentions; on the other hand, picketing children reminded them of the threat of labour militancy recently displayed in the bitter tailors' strike. In the end, the committee realized that they could not ignore the situation and so decided to appoint negotiators to intervene on the part of the students provided that they would return to school on Monday morning.[35]

Wishing to influence the outcome of this delicate situation, Herman Abramovitz, rabbi of the prestigious Sha'ar Hashomayim Synagogue located in Montreal's Square Mile, agreed to be one of the negotiators along with Jacobs. Abramovitz had a cautious response to the strike: "Whether there is any truth in what the boys say remains to be seen. [It would be] vastly unfair to make any move in this matter until I feel assured that the allegations made by the boys have some foundation of truth." Furthermore, Miss McKinley was a "young lady who has had close connection with the Hebrew community in the city for many years and was for some time a teacher in the Baron de Hirsch School. She has always been held in high esteem by those of the Hebrew race with whom she has come in contact."[36] Rabbi Abramovitz doubted that the teacher meant "the construction that the boys put upon the remark." Moreover, he placed the blame on the shoulders of the leaders, claiming that the strike could have been avoided if the students had taken their complaint to the proper authorities.[37] On the last point, the Rabbi was wrong; the leaders had in fact gone to the principal, and it was only after he had rebuked them that they resorted to calling a strike. The Rabbi's glowing description of the teacher is also inconsistent with Miss McKinley's behaviour in the Aberdeen classroom. Such a glaring contradiction suggests either that he was confusing her with someone else or that he was exaggerating her qualities out of a wish to downplay the validity of the boys' actions. These comments are reminiscent of the rhetoric associated with employers who typically characterize strikers' demands as unreasonable.

When these two prominent uptown residents arrived at the school by sleigh, the picketers cheered. To them, the presence of such high-powered figures indicated that the strike was being taken seriously. They likely expected that their cause would unite the community and did not see that their actions might have appeared as threatening to the Jewish establishment. While children generally do not welcome the prospect of adults meeting with a school principal, the Aberdeen strikers appear to have felt confident that Abramovitz and Jacobs would represent their position fairly on this matter. Before going into the school, the two men met with the strike committee in St-Louis Square. It may have been only a symbolic gesture, but to the young strikers it helped validate the legitimacy of their cause. Whatever Abramovitz and Jacobs's motivations, it is clear that they understood the need to recognize the chain of command in this dispute.

In the principal's office, Abramovitz and Jacobs were confronted by Cockfield's outrage over what he saw as the students' insolence. Called in to defend herself, Miss McKinley admitted that her comments had been inappropriate but maintained that they were misinterpreted by the students. The intransigence of principal and teacher appears to have convinced Abramovitz and Jacobs that the matter was more serious than they originally thought. Despite their ongoing concern for the social implications of children being on strike, they came to accept that on some level the students' action was justified given that the teacher's remarks at the very least bordered on anti-Semitism. Jacobs and Abramovitz presented Cockfield with two demands for the resolution of the strike: that Miss McKinley be transferred to another school and that the children be accepted back with no recriminations and without exception.[38] The irascible principal refused to make these concessions, claiming that it was a matter for the school commissioners. Learning that the school board would meet the following week, Abramovitz and Jacobs agreed to place the matter in the hands of the commissioners and left the school. The student strikers were apparently satisfied with this arrangement enough to agree to go back to school on Monday; once again, they cheered the community leaders as their sleigh disappeared down the street.[39]

Monday morning, however, when the children lined up in the school yard, Principal Cockfield called the strike leaders "out" and threatened to have them expelled. When journalists asked Cockfield what would happen to the leaders, he replied, "It is no business of the press what we do here in Aberdeen School."[40] Here again, Cockfield seems to have acted impulsively, displaying willfulness, and a lack of tact by snubbing Rabbi Abramovitz, Samuel Jacobs, and the press for no apparent reason other than to assert his rapidly diminishing authority over the situation. Likely, from the school board's perspective, both Cockfield and Miss McKinley had

become liabilities. The school commissioners found themselves faced with an embarrassing situation that threatened to present the Protestant school system in the worst possible light. However hostile some Protestant leaders were to the presence of large numbers of Jews within their schools, such overt anti-Semitism on a teacher's part or such incompetence and histrionics by a principal were unpardonable. That the school commissioners were prepared to concede to some of the strikers' demands in return for peace in the school yard, leads us to conclude that Cockfield was effectively silenced.

Jewish leaders at the Baron de Hirsch Institute felt "confident that the Commissioners will probe the alleged insult and give a sound judgement according to the facts of the case."[41] Curiously, however, the Aberdeen strike was not minuted at the March 6 board meeting. Whether the deliberations were held in camera or simply stricken from the record, the commissioners must have dealt with this delicate issue. Their silence suggests that they did not want the matter to be discussed further in the public domain. There was no more newspaper coverage of the Aberdeen School strike. Rabbi Abramovitz and Maître Jacobs did not press the issue; presumably they felt assured that the board would make concessions, such as not disciplining the strikers. After Cockfield's initial attempt to call the leaders out on the Monday morning, the matter appears to have been dropped. While we have no way of knowing this for certain, it is reasonable to assume that any punishment visited upon the students would have been publicized. Although the English-language newspapers might have agreed not to report on any recriminations against the students, one cannot imagine that Reuben Brainin of the *Keneder Adler* would fail to decry any mistreatment of the strikers.

This, however, was as far as the board would go for the time being. There is no indication that changes were made to the complement of teachers at the Aberdeen School. Miss McKinley does not figure in any of the transfers or retirements listed in the school board minutes in the weeks following the strike. Miss McKinley seems to have remained for the time being at Aberdeen School.[42] Although the students had set the teacher's removal as a condition for ending the strike, Rabbi Abramovitz and other Jewish leaders must have felt that the issue was not worth pursuing given the board's other concessions. Order was restored.

The strike provoked a variety of responses within the media, clearly demonstrating that the student conflict had alerted the adult world to the danger (or, in some cases, the advantages) of children who were willing to challenge authority. The *Montreal Gazette* was adamantly opposed to the students' strike call: "A big foot should be put down on any strike movement among scholars in public schools. Children are sent to school to be taught by teachers and not to dictate to them, as some of the learned youngsters think in these days of the idle strap and ruler. Let the juveniles wait till they grow up to be big men of 18 and 20 before they begin agitating and worrying old people of 30 and 40."[43] The language used in this article is deliberately demeaning, asserting the authority of responsible adults, and sanctioning the punishment of these children with strap, ruler, and the evocative "big foot." The *Montreal Herald* provided the most extensive coverage of any newspaper, featuring the strike on Saturday's front page, no less. It too used belittling language. One headline ran: "Wee Kiddies on Picket Duty at Aberdeen School Strike," accompanied by a photograph showing seven very young children standing in the snow.[44] Neither the image nor the headline conveys the seriousness of the strike with regard to the age of the leaders, the numbers involved, or the manner in which the strike was organized. This dismissive tone may well have masked anxieties about the potential radicalism of a new generation of workers brought up with strikes and militant labour rhetoric. The story was taken up in Toronto where *The Globe* provided background material on the confessional structure of education in Quebec, commenting that the Protestant board was not to be envied its task of having to accommodate pupils of widely varying origins.[45] The French-language newspapers were neutral in their coverage of the strike, providing very short descriptions of the incident without commentary. This position was typical when it came to issues between Protestants and Jews with respect to schooling. Editors did not want to insert a Catholic opinion into this conflict which had no relevance for the Francophone readership.

Although members of the Jewish elite were wary, many in the community supported the Aberdeen students. The *Canadian Jewish Times* depicted the strike as "novel in the annals of public instruction" and a "healthy symptom of Jewish nationalism." At the same time the editors drew a distinction between a teacher's off-hand remark and the views of the school board: "The teacher's oration we believe to be merely a slip of the unguided tongue [. . . and] are not prompted or sanctioned by her board."[46] The Yiddish press, less worried about upsetting the Protestant community or the English-speaking Jewish elite, was supportive of the strike. Nonetheless, Reuben Brainin played down the element of labour militancy and emphasized that the self-confident strikers were marching for Jewish dignity. Brainin was keen to see signs that the community was taking pride in a growing sense of identity. The Aberdeen students did not disappoint; the strike was "a major contribution to Jewish renaissance."[47] To Brainin, an understanding of this renaissance lay "hidden in the children's strike and more. The tender soul of the Jewish child would not dare revolt for so minor a matter if the threads of national rebirth were not weaving in their hearts."[48] There would have been no strike had these children not developed a sense of injustice and decided to stop making concessions to a system in which their identity was systemically suppressed: "Since schools were opened to Jews . . . every skulking teacher or professor had the right to stifle and insult the soul of a Jewish child . . . [while] his exilic parents always suppressed all that is Jewish in the child to the point of denial of his self." Brainin referred to this transformation as an assertion of honour: "The act of these children is an honour unto us. Many Christians will learn the new Jewish sense of honour."[49] Evidently, Brainin was projecting his own aspirations for the North American diaspora. Indeed, Aberdeen parents seem to have approved of their children's action, no doubt seeing in it a reflection of their own values; according to the *Globe*, they "encouraged the children to remain on the street."[50] The strike signalled to these working-class parents that their children had absorbed lessons in labour learned at home. To the elites, the strike signalled that the upcoming generation was prepared to challenge the authority of their elders in their quest for justice. To counter this challenge, Jewish elites were obliged to close ranks, assert their own authority, and downplay the significance of the children's actions.

Conclusion

Aberdeen's strikers made their own history. At a critical moment in the development of Montreal's Jewish community, when labour militancy, solidarity, and organization had reached unprecedented levels, when growing numbers of Jewish children began to present serious accommodation problems to the Protestant school system, and when the first concerted effort to mount a legal challenge to anti-Semitism had united Jews of all social classes, Aberdeen students marched. What might appear as a localized, momentary act of rebelliousness was in fact a course of action with landmark consequences for the world around it. Although adults appeared to demean or ignore its importance, they were conscious of the strike's serious potential challenge to authority, and worked to resolve the strike quickly. Both the Protestant school system and the Jewish community experienced significant changes in the months following the strike that were directly or indirectly related to the actions of the Aberdeen students. In looking back at the strike, they may well have been pleased with the social and legal changes that ensued.

The Aberdeen School strike marked a turning point in the history of the Montreal Protestant school system. Although the issue appears to have been whitewashed by the school authorities, they soon took clear steps to improve relations in the classroom. A crucial modification was the hiring of Jewish teachers. It was no coincidence that within weeks of the strike, the commissioners asked legal counsel to inquire whether it would contravene the provisions in the Education Act pertaining to the need for teachers to be vetted by Protestant clergymen. In June 1913, lawyers determined that the board had "the power to appoint Jewish teachers to its staff," and thus the commissioners agreed to

"consider applications for employment from Jewish women teachers who are otherwise duly qualified."[51] Members of the school board had managed to close their eyes to the issue despite frequent calls since 1903 by the public for change. They were also willing to tolerate anti-Semitic attitudes by teachers. But when the Aberdeen students responded publicly and militantly to Miss McKinley's outburst, the inappropriateness of having Protestant teachers instructing large classes of Jewish pupils could not be ignored. The following winter, Misses F. Novick, L. Chaskelson and Rebecca Smilovitz, all clearly identified as "Jewesses," were appointed to Montreal schools.[52] Within a decade of the strike, the board was employing over seventy Jewish teachers, hardly enough to go around all the schools on the Main, but a definite improvement over the situation at the beginning of the century. Despite continued pressure by the Jewish community, it would be a long time before the school board made further concessions such as recognizing the right of Jewish teachers to attend their high holidays without recrimination and moving high school dances from Friday to Saturday evenings.

The student strike also had an impact on the outlook of the Jewish community towards schooling. Since 1903, the elite had taken the position that attending Protestant schools was crucial to Jewish children's integration in North American society—or, more precisely, into the Anglo-Saxon world of the British Empire, which they respected for its values of "fair play."[53] Recent immigrants were more likely to value the preservation of Eastern European culture, including the Yiddish language, and to mistrust non-Jewish authority over their lives.[54] The more religious among such families had opted to send their children to the Talmud Torah School opened in 1896, and would help establish similar schools in the years following the Aberdeen strike; by 1917 there were five such schools, which joined to form the United Talmud Torahs of Montreal. More significant, in terms of its relation to the Aberdeen strike, was the growth in the support shown by non-observant Jews for independent schools. Members of the Poale Zion (Jewish socialist) movement, embracing ideas brought from Eastern Europe, had been critical for some time of the Jewish establishment's apparent willingness to continue negotiating with an unaccommodating Protestant school board. The opening in 1913 of the National Radical (later Peretz) Shul dedicated to the preservation of Jewish cultural heritage, and the creation the following year of the Jewish People's School, were clearly influenced by a rising sense of militancy that the Aberdeen School strike reflected.[55] For many years, these schools functioned only on Sundays and in the later afternoons on weekdays, as a supplement to regular classes in the Protestant system, but as of 1928 the Jewish People's School operated as a day school and the Peretz School would do so as of 1941. By the late 1920s, the supporters of these private schools would champion the formation of a separate Jewish school board, in fierce opposition to Maxwell Goldstein and others who continued to favour integration.[56] Even so, as the Protestant school board fought to reverse the 1903 legislation (successfully by 1928) and actively promoted separate schools, even a separate school system, the faith of the more liberal Jewish element in a comprehensive public school system was shaken.

The issue of Jewish representation on the Protestant school board also returned in the wake of the Aberdeen strike. Thanks to the efforts of the newly created Independent Citizens' League, clothing manufacturer Abraham Blumenthal had been elected to the Montreal city council in 1912, representing the St Louis Ward.[57] Two years later, at the end of a school commissioner's term of office, Blumenthal presented himself as a candidate for one of the three school board seats that the council appointed. He was not chosen, his candidature opposed by other members of the council. In 1916, when a second Jew, the popular world-champion skater Louis Rubinstein, was elected an alderman, Blumenthal attempted to have him appointed to the school board, again without success.[58]

The strikers themselves emerged as winners despite the odds; they were never publicly disciplined and they received an apology of sorts, even if they regarded it as insufficient. They did not succeed in having the objectionable teacher removed from the classroom, but they did set in motion a process that would result in much better Jewish representation among the public school teaching profession. They initiated the strike action without first securing permission from their parents, who nonetheless proved supportive. Likely, the strikers were aware of what they had achieved: by refusing to tolerate anti-Semitism, they drew the attention of their community to a systemic problem in the school system that had links to prejudice within the wider society. In so doing, they learned the value of taking action against injustice. The Aberdeen strike was also no doubt a transformative moment in their lives, the kind of incident that one often looks back on and recognizes as profoundly significant.

We have no way of knowing the long-term impact of being a student strike leader, but we have managed to glean something of their adult lives. In 1916, Moses Skibelsky emigrated with his family to the United States when his father accepted a position as principal of a Hebrew school in Chicago. Moses became a dentist and practised in Chicago for decades. Although he anglicized his name to Martin Bell, he married within his faith to Russian-born Esther and raised a daughter, Cyral.[59] Moses Margolis worked as a cloak operator and auto mechanic before enlisting (as Mack Margolese) in the Royal Canadian Dragoons in 1917 when he turned 18.[60] That for several years after the war Margolis was listed in Lovell's Directory only as "returned soldier" suggests that he had been injured or was unable to work. In 1921, Joseph Orenstein (he shortened his name to Oren) married Evelyn Yaphe, who was also a grade 6 student at Aberdeen School during the strike. The couple moved to Miami where Joseph operated a shoe store. According to his granddaughter, Joseph was the "least bigoted person" she had ever known. He employed an African-American worker as a "stock boy" with whom he sat and ate in the "Blacks-only" section of a segregated restaurant across the street from his store.[61]

These young men eventually anglicized their Jewish names—which may have been a nod to modernity, a means of pre-empting prejudice, or a practical business strategy rather than a rejection of their roots—but their actions in 1913 reflected a growing sense of Jewish identity. In this they were instrumental in rousing the community. Reuben Brainin spoke of the "national sensibility" that had "provoked their little fists."[62] To an extent, of course, Brainin read his own cultural interpretations into the children's actions whilst underplaying their political radicalism. In practice, the Aberdeen strike, like the tailors' strike the previous year, highlighted the deep class divisions within Montreal's Jewish community as well as, to a lesser extent, the differences between observant and non-observant Jews. It also highlighted the philosophical differences that would lead to long and bitter battles within the community over the values that constituted Jewish education, and over how and by whom such values should be imparted. Yet, in the end the Aberdeen strike proved an issue around which the entire community could rally, albeit cautiously in some cases. It may not have led directly to the creation of Jewish independent schools or the assertion of Jewish political rights, but it provoked critical deliberation. The student action served to remind Jews that they did not have to put up with the kind of discrimination, both veiled and explicit, that they swallowed every

day, proving to be one of the occasional cases where ethnic and religious solidarity prevailed. The conditions for mobilizing Yiddish-speaking members of the community were ripe, but it took the action of children to reinvigorate a growing movement to champion Jewish citizenship. The children were not only applying the values with which they were brought up but also affirming their importance as a means to effect change.

Going on strike confirmed the children's status in their own minds as members of the working class and connected them to their labour-activist parents. At the same time, resisting anti-Semitism bolstered their cultural identity, both in their neighbourhood and with the Jewish community at large. To an extent, they had grown up with this sense of identity, absorbing it at home, in the streets, and in the social life of the St-Laurent corridor, but it stood at odds with the broader notions of citizenship promoted in Protestant schools. The Aberdeen strike gave them the confidence to explore and express their own notions of citizenship predicated on Jewish identity, working-class solidarity, and a sense of social justice.

Notes

1. "Strike of Yiddish School children in Aberdeen School," *Keneder Adler*, 2 March 1913 (Translation: David Rome).
2. Timothy Stanley, "White Supremacy, Chinese Schooling, and School Segregation in Victoria: The Case of the Chinese Students' Strike, 1922–1923," *Historical Studies in Education* 2 (Fall 1990), 287–305 and Stanley, "Bringing Anti-racism into Historical Explanation: The Victoria Chinese Students' Strike of 1922–3 Revisited," *Journal of the Canadian Historical Association*, 13 (2002), 141–165. Donald R Raichle, "The Great Newark School Strike of 1912," *New Jersey History*, 106 (Spring-Summer 1988), 1–17. Shmuel Shamai, "The Jews and the Public Education System: The Students' Strike over the 'Flag Fight' in Toronto after the First World War," *Canadian Jewish Historical Society Journal*, 10 (Fall 1988), 46–53.
3. Consider *Caught: Montreal's Modern Girls and the Law, 1869–1945* (Toronto 2006) and numerous articles. Note also Valerie Minnett and Mary Anne Poutanen, "Swatting Flies for Health: Children and Tuberculosis in Early Twentieth-Century Montreal," *Urban History Review/ Revue d'histoire urbaine*, 36 (Fall 2007), 32–44. Outside Quebec, both Neil Sutherland and Mona Gleason seek out children's voices in interviews with adults about their childhood recollections and in textual sources such as diaries. See Sutherland, "Listening to the Winds

of Childhood," in his book, *Growing Up: Childhood in English Canada from the Great War to the Age of Television* (Toronto 1997), 3–23; Gleason, "Embodied Negotiations: Children's Bodies and Historical Change in Canada, 1930–1960," *Journal of Canadian Studies*, 34 (Spring 1999), 112–138. See also Elizabeth Gagen, "'Too Good to Be True': Representing Children's Agency in the Archives of Playground Reform," *Historical Geography*, 29 (2001), 53–64.
4. Robert G. McIntosh, *Boys in the Pits: Child Labour in Coal Mining* (Montreal 2000), 10.
5. Alan Prout and Allison James, "A New Paradigm for the Sociology of Childhood? Provenance, Promise and Problems," in Prout and James, eds., *Constructing and Reconstructing Childhood: Contemporary Issues in the Sociological Study of Childhood* (London 1997), 8. A growing body of literature since their path-breaking study includes Nick Lee, "Towards an Immature Sociology," *The Sociological Review*, 46 (August 1998), 458–482; Berry Mayall, "Toward a Sociology of Child Health" *Sociology of Health & Illness*, 20 (May 1998), 269–288; Gill Valentine, "Boundary Crossings: Transitions from Childhood to Adulthood," *Children's Geographies*, 1 (Number 1 2003), 37–52; Madeleine Leonard, "Children, Childhood and Social Capital: Exploring the Links," *Sociology*,

39 (October 2005), 605–622; Michel Vandenbroeck and Maria Bouverne-De Bie, "Children's Agency and Educational Norms: A tensed negotiation," *Childhood*, 13 (February 2006), 127–143; and H. Matthews, "A Window on the 'New' Sociology of Childhood," *Sociology Compass*, 1 (September 2007), 322–334.

6. Matthews, "A Window on the 'New' Sociology of Childhood", 325–326.

7. Gerald Tulchinsky, *Taking Root: The Origins of the Canadian Jewish Community* (Toronto 1992), 130, 158, 172.

8. Pierre Anctil, *Tur Malka: Flâneries sur les cimes de l'histoire juive montréalaise* (Sillery 1997), 59.

9. Anctil, *Tur Malka*, 55–74.

10. Sylvie Taschereau, "Echapper à Shylock: la Hebrew Free Loan Association of Montreal entre anti-sémitisme et intégration, 1911-1913," *Revue d'histoire de l'Amérique française*, 59 (printemps 2006), 460; Tamara Myers, "On Probation: The Rise and Fall of Jewish Women's Antidelinquency Work in Interwar Montreal," in Bettina Bradbury and Tamara Myers, eds., *Negotiating Identities in 19th- and 20th-Century Montreal* (Vancouver 2005), 176–177.

11. Tulchinsky, *Taking Root*, 250–53. Joe King, *From the Ghetto to the Main: The Story of the Jews of Montreal* (Montreal 2000), 98–99.

12. Sara Ferdman Tobin, *Traces of the Past: Montreal's Early Synagogues* (Montreal 2011), 45.

13. Canadian Jewish Congress Charities Committee, Esther Goldstein Kershman, "Echoes from Colonial Avenue," Unpublished manuscript, 2, 14, 17, 19, 24–25, 54.

14. Robert Lewis, *Manufacturing Montreal: The Making of An Industrial Landscape, 1850 to 1930* (Baltimore 2000), 177–182.

15. Tulchinsky, *Taking Root*, 212.

16. Tulchinsky, *Taking Root*, 139–140.

17. King, *From the Ghetto to the Main*, 135–136.

18. Quoted in King, *From the Ghetto to the Main*, 136.

19. David Rome, *On the Jewish School Question in Montreal* (Montreal 1986), 1.

20. Rome, *On the Jewish School Question in Montreal*, 39–40.

21. McGill University Archives, McGill Normal School Registers, RG.30, c.55, 2044B.

22. Rome, *The Drama of Our Early Education*, 130–131.

23. Quoted in Rome, *The Drama of Our Early Education*, 98.

24. Brainin, "Strike of Yiddish School Children in Aberdeen School," *Keneder Adler*, 2 March 1913.

25. Brainin, "Strike of Yiddish School Children in Aberdeen School," *Keneder Adler*, 2 March 1913.

26. Israel Medres, "The Children's Strike against Anti-Semitism," *Montreal of Yesterday*, 135.

27. Brainin, "Strike of Yiddish School Children in Aberdeen School," *Keneder Adler*, 2 March 1913.

28. Medres, "The Children's Strike against Anti-Semitism," 135.

29. Brainin, *Keneder Adler*, 4 March 1913.

30. Brainin, "Strike of Yiddish School Children in Aberdeen School," *Keneder Adler*, 2 March 1913.

31. Tulchinsky, *Taking Root*, 211, 224–5. In 1913, Yiddish-speaking Montrealers would also have read *Der Canader Yid* (*Canadian Israelite*), published in Winnipeg, and which has been described by Lewis Levendel as ranging from liberal to socialist. Lewis Levendel, *A Century of the Canadian Jewish Press: 1880s–1980s* (Nepean, Ontario 1989), 23.

32. "School Strikers Go Back to Desks," *Montreal Herald*, 1 March 1913.

33. Tulchinsky, *Taking Root*, 211; Rebecca Margolis, "The Yiddish Press in Montreal, 1900 to 1945," *Canadian Jewish Studies/ Études juives canadiennes*, 16–17 (2008–2009), 12.

34. Medres, "On the Eve of the Storm," *Montreal of Yesterday*, 144–145.

35. "School Strikers Go Back to Desks," *Montreal Herald*, 1 March 1913.

36. "School Children Call Strike but Only Six Respond," *Montreal Herald*, 28 February 1913.

37. "Scholars Strike at End," *Montreal Gazette*, 1 March 1913.

38. Brainin, "Strike of Yiddish School Children in Aberdeen School," *Keneder Adler*, 2 March 1913.

39. "School Strikers Go Back to Desks," *Montreal Herald*, 1 March 1913.

40. "Young Strikers Were Called Out from School Ranks," *Montreal Herald*, 3 March 1913.

41. "Young Strikers Were Called Out from School Ranks," *Montreal Herald*, 3 March 1913.

42. According to his son Stanley, Harry Diamond, one of the strikers, ran into the teacher at a movie theatre in the 1930s. Harry described the meeting as tense and her reaction frosty. (Interview conducted with Stanley Diamond, 31 May 2012.)

43. "Scholars Strike at End," *Montreal Gazette*, 1 March 1913.

44. "School Strikers Go Back to Desks," *Montreal Herald*, 1 March 1913.

45. "Jewish Scholars Have Been On Strike," *The Globe*, 3 March 1913.

46. "The Juvenile Strike," *Canadian Jewish Times*, 7 March 1913.

47. *Keneder Adler*, 9 March 1913.

48. *Keneder Adler*, 4 March 1913.

49. *Keneder Adler*, 4 March 1913.

50. "Jewish Scholars Have Been on Strike," *The Globe*, 3 March 1913.

51. English Montreal School Board Archives, Minutes of the Protestant Board of School Commissioners, 13 June 1913.

52. EMSB Archives, Minutes of the PBSC, 23 April 1914

53. Rome, *On the Jewish School Question in Montreal*, 1.

54. Rome, *On the Jewish School Question in Montreal*, 20.

55. Hershl Novak, *La première école Yiddish de Montréal, 1911–1914* (Québec 2009), 69. Novak refers to Simon Belkin, who

dated the city's first Yiddish school from 1911, but admits there is much uncertainty as to when the school actually opened. Accounts of the Jewish People's Schools give 1913 or 1914 as the dates when these schools began.

56. Rome, *On the Jewish School Question in Montreal*, 61.

57. Medres, *Montreal of Yesterday*, 118–120.

58. Rome, *On the Jewish School Question in Montreal*, 22.

59. National Archives and Records Administration, Washington, D.C., "Manifests of Passengers Arriving at St. Albans, Vermont, District through Canadian Pacific and Atlantic Ports, 1895–1954," M1464, in Library and Archives Canada, Records of the Immigration and Naturalization Service, Record Group 85; *1920 United States Federal Census*, Cook County, Illinois, Chicago Ward 12, T625-320, 1A, Enumeration District 675, Image

575; and *1930 United States Federal Census*, Cook County, Illinois, Chicago, 461, 18B, Enumeration District 1004, Image 38.0.

60. Library and Archives Canada, RG 150, Accession 1992–93/166, Box 5921—16, Soldiers of the First World War—Canadian Expeditionary Force, Mack Margolese.

61. Bibliothèque et Archives nationales du Québec à Montréal, Quebec, Vital and Church Records (Drouin collection), 1621–1967, Sha'ar Hashomayim, Folio 18, No. 32, Marriage of Joseph Orenstein and Evelyn Yaphe, 22 June 1921. We also draw on an email from Stanley Diamond describing a telephone conversation he had with Linda Slote Quick, 4 June 2012.

62. Brainin, *Keneder Adler*, 4 March 1913 (Translation: David Rome).

PRIMARY DOCUMENT

"Wee Kiddies on Picket Duty at Aberdeen School Strike"

WEE KIDDIES ON PICKET DUTY AT ABERDEEN SCHOOL STRIKE

Some of the children who were out doing picket duty at the Aberdeen School grounds yesterday, when two hundred Hebrew children went out on strike because of insults to their race, said to have been offered by a lady teacher.

Source: *Montreal Herald*, March 1913, from the Alex Dworkin Canadian Jewish Congress Archives

Raised in the Spirit of the Class Struggle: Children, Youth, and the Interwar Ukrainian Left in Canada

RHONDA L. HINTHER

Nadya Niechoda was born in Canada to a Ukrainian leftist family. Her parents were members of the Ukrainian Labour Farmer Temple Association (ULFTA) in Winnipeg during the 1920s and 1930s. They often took her to events at "the hall," where she witnessed speeches by leaders like Matthew Popovich and Matthew Shatulsky or performances of dancers, choirs, and mandolin orchestras. By the age of three, influenced by what she saw, Niechoda was ready to do her part for Ukrainian culture and the class struggle at home. "I used to sit on the bottom stair and play a make-believe mandolin on a broom, and sing The International," she explained.

Twice a week after school, she would also go to the Ukrainian Labour Temple for Ukrainian school. There, she learned to read and write in Ukrainian, and she and her fellow students honed their language skills by studying the poetic works of nineteenth-century Ukrainian literary greats Ivan Franko and Taras Shevchenko. The children also learned about local and world affairs and history, particularly that of Ukraine and the Soviet Union, and learned where they, as youngsters, fit in the class struggle. "Left or right—these terms were known to me from childhood," she recalled, "Left to me was good; right was the authorities sending my dad to work in a relief camp; left was the hall . . . right was a deportation order for our family." Members of the ULFTA came through for Niechoda and her family: "it was the people from this organization, supported by similar organizations, who launched a campaign so that the deportation order be rescinded." That same year, Niechoda's father bought her a real mandolin. Soon, thanks to

Saturday lessons at the hall, she remembered, "I was able to play The International…, though that did not stop me from playing Rock of Ages or Swanee River, and Ukrainian folk songs. How fortunate it was for me and the others that we were able to learn and study music at a time when it was so difficult for us to even survive."[1]

Niechoda's experiences represent those of many children during the interwar era who were born into or introduced to the ULFTA at an early age. They viewed and participated in Ukrainian-language concerts and plays, organized protests, read ULFTA newspapers, discussed political issues, and raised money to support a variety of causes. Though they would have been very young, the offspring of the first two waves of Ukrainian immigration to Canada (1891–1914, 1925–30) contributed in significant ways to the shape of the ULFTA community during the interwar years of the movement's history.

To expand our understanding of Canadian Leftist children's history, this article considers how class, ethnicity, age, and gender intersected in the lives of ULFTA youngsters. It combines a top-down and bottom-up approach to explore how youngsters, parents, ULFTA leaders, and Communist Party of Canada (CPC) officials all acted—together and apart, united and in opposition to one another—to build a vibrant radical Ukrainian young people's movement during Canada's interwar years. The structure of activities for youngsters reflected the priorities of parents and leaders. At the same time, however, children and youth (and their desires and interests—or, in some cases, lack of interest) were crucial in shaping their own work and influencing the movement's broader policies. As well, external factors—most notably the Canadian public school system and North American popular culture—also

Source: From Labour/Le Travail, 60 (Fall 2007): 43–76. Reprinted by permission of the publisher.

influenced patterns of youngsters' activities. So, too, did the CPC, a long-time ally yet oftentimes concurrent adversary, of the ULFTA.

The location of these youngsters at specific intersections of these power relationships meant that their experiences differed—at times significantly—from those of their parents, their public school classmates, other Ukrainian children (particularly those tied to one of the developing Ukrainian churches), and other leftist children. This article examines how discourses of gender, class, ethnicity, and age intertwined—unevenly and unequally—to shape the activities and experiences of these children and youth. The unevenness is key to our understanding; among the very young, gender, for example, typically mattered less in defining their experiences than did age, class, and ethnicity. As a child aged, however, they would become more aware of the gendered divisions that existed among adults (predicated on male dominance and female subordination). As youths, they would begin to be more formally trained and informally socialized (both explicitly and implicitly)—through their ongoing involvement with the movement—to take on (or challenge) similar roles as they entered young adult activities.

A rich literature exists on the value of an intersectional methodology. By considering class, ethnicity, and gender, Frances Swyripa has fruitfully interrogated the similarities and differences that emerged among nationalist and progressive Ukrainian women divided by politics.[2] Through her work on Jewish garment workers, Ruth Frager has illustrated how ethnicity, gender, and class converged, again, unevenly with external social, economic and political forces to shape and eventually undermine the attempts of Jewish garment workers to "bring about a fundamental socialist transformation."[3] Elsewhere, Katrina Srigley has aptly shown how gender could matter less than class, race, or ethnicity for women seeking employment in Depression-era Toronto. She underscores the strength of an intersectional methodology by reminding us "we need to make critical judgements about which identities emerge as more or less influential in shaping women's working lives in a given time and place, and at a particular phase of their life cycle."[4] The collected articles in *Sisters or*

Strangers: Immigrant, Ethnic, and Racialized Women in Canadian History, with their attention to categories such as race, ethnicity, class (and how and to what degree each was gendered) challenge and enrich our understanding of the complexities of women's experiences and immigration, nation-building, and citizenship.[5] [. . .]

This project also builds on existing work on the ULFTA and its relationship with the CPC. Viewing these studies from an intersectional perspective is especially useful, particularly where class and ethnicity are concerned. Historians and others have often labelled (and, at time, written off) the ULFTA as simply "pro-communist," often because they consider in their analysis only the activities of the organization's male leaders.[6] Many of the ULFTA's members and supporters certainly enthusiastically embraced the international and domestic proletarian struggle. Many—particularly the male leaders—were also Party members and leaders. However, this did not mean they lent wholesale, unquestioning, or unified support to the CPC and Comintern directives. In fact, for much of its history (especially during the interwar years), while attempting to work with the CPC, the ULFTA actively resisted and challenged the Party's repeated attempts to control or abolish activities, particularly those of a cultural nature, that the ULFTA members and supporters held especially dear. The type of "communism" these Ukrainian leftists embraced was inseparably cultural-political, combining priorities of Ukrainian cultural preservation and expression with a Marxist-Leninist political philosophy. This is not surprising. About Jewish socialists in Toronto, Ruth Frager has shown that "class consciousness and ethnic identity reinforced each other and intensified the commitment to radical social change." This is because, as she argues, "most had been radicalized not only in response to class oppression but also in response to the oppression they faced as Jews."[7] ULFTA members and supporters were not simply members of the working classes in Canada. They were Ukrainian members of the working classes and therefore experienced a dual oppression. Expression and defence of this Canadian-grown ethnic identity created a distinct brand of class-consciousness and socio-political resistance. Wherever possible, the ULFTA threw its wholehearted support behind Party initiatives. They would quickly withdraw or temper this support, however, whenever the Party began making demands that they cease or limit activities of a cultural nature, a frequent occurrence during the interwar years. Youngsters' activities are an important lens through which to understand the significant role of cultural-political activism and the movement's overall efforts to challenge and resist Party efforts to control and dictate the shape of the ULFTA. Ukrainian youngsters, in fact, were among the most loyal, often voting with their feet when the CPC came calling attempting to take over or redefine their activities.

Building the Interwar Ukrainian Left

Leftist Ukrainians created one of the most dynamic working-class movements in twentieth-century Canada. Radicalized by unfulfilled expectations of Canada, exploitation, and discrimination and often harbouring socialist and anti-clerical attitudes nurtured in the Old Country, many Ukrainian immigrants became labour activists, often through Ukrainian language-based socialist organizations. Their activism was manifest from the earliest years of Ukrainian immigration to Canada and would eventually centre in institutions known as Ukrainian Labour Temples, found across the country from Nova Scotia to British Columbia. Planning for the first Ukrainian Labour Temple—situated in Winnipeg's vibrant multi-ethnic working-class North End—began in 1918, and the hall opened in time to serve as an important organizing space during the Winnipeg General Strike of 1919. Soon after, under the auspices of the national Ukrainian Labour Temple Association (ULTA), which, by 1924 became the Ukrainian Labour Farmer Temple Association, Ukrainian workers erected or developed additional halls across the country.

Members and supporters accommodated themselves and mounted resistance to their experiences and circumstances as "ethnic" immigrants and workers. They developed an array of activities to address the experiences and realities of Ukrainian working-class life in Canada and to offer radical social, cultural, and political alternatives to the fledgling Ukrainian churches and developing right-wing Ukrainian nationalist organizations. Studies of leftist Jews, Finns, Hungarians, and others have noted the rich tapestry of social and cultural activities that were such a central part of defining these groups' left politics and "ethnic hall" socialism.[8] The Ukrainian leftists embraced similar patterns of activism, expressing their commitment to social justice in numerous ways. They employed traditional modes of activism including strike support, the publication of newspapers, and endorsing candidates for political office, particularly those from the CPC. At the same time—and perhaps most significantly—members and supporters of the Ukrainian Labour Temple also expressed their activism through a diverse array of other activities. To improve the lives of Ukrainian workers and address immediate issues of concern not attended to by the government the movement established institutions throughout the 1920s, such as the Workers Benevolent Association (WBA—a mutual benefit society that provided insurance and other financial services), and an assortment of newspapers, and literacy and language classes. During the Depression, the Ukrainian Labour Temple even acted as a makeshift soup kitchen and gathering space for displaced and unemployed workers. Cultural activities, such as Ukrainian embroidery, dance, theatre, cuisine, orchestras (especially mandolin orchestras), and choir, were also commonplace in the halls. Concerts and other gatherings featuring these activities routinely attracted sell-out crowds. Organizers used these events to illustrate complex political situations, encourage working-class solidarity, promote resistance, and further the struggle against economic and social injustice in Canada and abroad. Enormously successful, these activities served to establish the Ukrainian Labour Temple as one of the most popular and important interwar working-class institutions in Canada. The movement grew in the interwar era to encompass extensive numbers of members and supporters, female and male, children and adult. By the end of the interwar decades (before the federal government banned the ULFTA on 4 June 1940, severely circum-scribing its activities), it counted some 15,000 members working in 87 Ukrainian Labour Temples. Its two Ukrainian-language newspapers reached over 20,000 subscribers, and in its halls across the country, its Ukrainian-language dramas and concerts routinely played to full houses.[9] The interwar years were truly a golden age for Ukrainian cultural-political radicalism in Canada.

Like other contemporary radical groups, Ukrainian leftists developed a gendered discourse predicated on male domination and female subordination. Peasant village values brought from the "Old Country" influenced these models. Evident in a system of unequal power relations, these were further reinforced by Canadian manifestations of male gender privilege and female subordination, particularly within the CPC and other leftist organizations like unions, which were also deeply sexist and patriarchal.[10] From this grew a structured hierarchy that privileged men and their experiences, defining class and activism through a male lens of experience and opportunity. During the ULFTA's interwar years, men held virtually all leadership positions and were among its most visible supporters. Like other radical women, these Ukrainian women performed seemingly invisible but critical roles that ensured the movement's financial, organizational, cultural, and political survival. Despite these contributions, women endured frequent criticism for being "backward" or for failing to pursue male-defined methods of activism. At the same time, those who did wish to move beyond women's traditional sphere in the movement encountered hostility or contempt.[11] [. . .]

Despite ongoing power struggle, leaders of the ULFTA who were also Party members remained staunchly committed communists. Though they might disagree with the Party or its leaders and challenge policy, they still did what they could to integrate many of its initiatives into the programs of the ULFTA and its associated groups. Of course, they had to balance this carefully, taking into consideration what the ULFTA members and supporters would be willing to embrace or could easily implement without upset to the overall functioning

of cultural and organizational work. In 1931, for example, the Ukrainians accommodated through its cultural work. At that year's ULFTA convention, Matthew Shatulsky explained that choirs, orchestras, and drama groups must all take part in the turn and be "real shock-troop activists in the introduction of proletarian art to our stage. There is no 'art for art's sake.' To counteract this misleading bourgeois slogan we must raise the slogan: art in the service of the proletariat!"[12] To adhere to such a program was not difficult for many of the cultural forces of the ULFTA, given their existing tendency to fuse cultural expression with political content in plays and other performances. Easier to embrace was the mid-1930s Popular Front with its increased emphasis on social and cultural activities as a means through which to raise awareness and develop alliances in the name of fighting the rise of global fascism. The ULFTA was enthusiastic in supporting the Popular Front as the "community and neighbourhood activities"[13] it emphasized dovetailed easily with the work the progressive Ukrainian community had eagerly embraced throughout its history.

Scholars have offered a number of explanations for these Ukrainian leaders' behaviour. Some have argued that men like Popowich or Shatulsky, in opposing the party, were seeking to protect their own authority and power as leaders of the ULFTA and its related organizations. Others have shown how the ULFTA's failure to embrace the Party line—particularly in its calls for Ukrainians to take out formal membership in the Party—was related to fears of arrest and the very real possibility of deportation. Rejection of Party leaders' anglo-centricism and frustration with its ethnocentric attitudes has also been cited as a source of the Ukrainian left's resentment.[14] Somewhat underestimated, however, has been the pressure the Ukrainian left's leaders faced from the movement's base of members and supporters. When accepting or developing programs or policy, these leaders had to be mindful of the interests and concerns of its constituents for whom liquidation of the Ukrainian left, the dissolution of its cultural mandate, or integration of its members into the CPC were, to put it mildly, unappealing. Placing the experiences of children and youth front and centre allows us to consider this relationship from a more nuanced perspective. It helps to illuminate some of the additional pressures leaders faced when confronted with Party policy that challenged or threatened the ULFTA's cultural or social components. In this way, we gain a broader understanding of this community's political and cultural perspectives and the multifaceted ways in which members understood and carried out their activism.

Children of the Ukrainian Left

Children of ULFTA members and supporters most often had their first contact with the movement as babies or young children, brought by their parents to functions at or coordinated by a Ukrainian Labour Temple. Later, once they began attending public school, their parents would have enrolled them in after-school and weekend activities at a local ULFTA hall. Depending on age and the availability of programming in their particular locality, they would, perhaps between the ages of eleven and thirteen, graduate to participation in youth activities. The period of youth functioned as a much more transitional—and ambiguous—stage of movement life. When one ceased to be defined as a youth and began to be an adult within the context of the Ukrainian Labour Temple community had very little to do with age. Instead, the move from youth to adult activities had more to do with the whims, needs, and priorities of the male leadership of the movement and was contingent on the youngsters' life circumstances. Life milestones such as public school completion, injury or death of a parent, marriage, parenthood, the move into the workforce, and socio-economic context, also determined the transition point to adulthood.

Though there are clear differences characterising the categories of children and youth, it is nonetheless appropriate to discuss them in tandem since within both age categories, activities followed a similar pattern, existed for similar reasons, enjoyed similar status within the movement, and were together often distinct from the activities of adults. When discussed together, children and youth will be referred to as "youngsters" or "young people" for the purpose of this paper. Otherwise, when specific age categories of youngsters are discussed, "children" and "youth" will be used.

Ukrainian Worker Children's Schools

The Ukrainian left began to establish formal activities for youngsters with the opening of the Winnipeg Ukrainian Labour Temple in 1918. At the time, leaders and parents ascribed a great deal of importance to children's involvement. When the governments of the three Prairie provinces declared English as the sole language of instruction in public schools during the second decade of the twentieth century,[15] Ukrainian families there were forced to turn to outside institutions to provide Ukrainian educational and cultural experiences to supplement those taught in the home. Many parents also wanted their children involved in activities challenging the oppression Ukrainian and other, particularly immigrant, members of the working class faced upon their arrival to Canada. They also sought supervised, non-religious activities for their children after school and on weekends when parents had their own cultural-political activities to attend at the halls or when they needed to be at work. In response to these concerns, at the first convention of the Ukrainian Labour Temple Association, leaders established Ukrainian Worker Children's Schools (UWCS). Their purpose was "to teach the children of Ukrainian workers their native language, to give them the means in their native tongue to raise the consciousness of the workers, [and] to teach them to view the world through the eyes of the working class."[16] As the ULFTA expanded nationally over the course of the early 1920s, halls across Canada opened their own Ukrainian Worker Children's Schools. Throughout the 1920s and 1930s, schools constantly expanded, both in number and size and in terms of activities offered.[17] With interest in this work keen—on the part of both parents and the children themselves—the Ukrainian Worker Children's Schools enjoyed a striking degree of popularity. By the time the 1933 ULFTA convention took place, there were 45 schools functioning across Canada with some 2,000 students attending.[18] In 1937, the number of schools had grown to 54 with the number of students remaining steady at 1945.[19]

The Central School Board (CSB) of the ULFTA coordinated the schools at the national level and worked to ensure a standardized national curriculum. Thanks to this body, the schools tended to function in much the same manner regardless of locality (although remoteness of location could affect teacher availability and children's attendance rates). Typically, school organizers grouped children by grade or age in the Ukrainian schools, although this might also depend on a child's ability and knowledge of the language.[20] In most communities, the schools combined training in the Ukrainian language with musical and cultural training. "I attend the Ukrainian Workers Children's School where we learn our language, reading, writing, singing, and mandolin," explained Maria Tysmbaliuk of Kamsack, Saskatchewan in 1927, "Our teacher is Tovarish D. Prodaniuk.[21] He is now teaching us a play." She went on to explain, "we've mounted a few concerts, but the last one was cancelled because it was too cold and no one came." When organizer Tovarish Toma Kobzey came to inspect their school, she recalled, "He gave us a lot of questions on grammar and musical theory. He also advised us on proper behaviour and how to set a good example for others. He then asked us if we knew how to sing, so we did so."[22]

Throughout the interwar era, the CPC frequently criticised the UWCS for being too culturally centred, claiming that an emphasis on use of the Ukrainian language and culture distracted children from activities that the Party defined as of a more pressing political nature. Ongoing use of the Ukrainian language especially seemed to raise the ire of those working to Anglicize the Party. It is clear from their critiques, however, that the CPC understood or appreciated very little of the important ways in which the UWCS contributed to supporting the international proletarian struggle and how it integrated the Party line into its curriculum. Children attending the UWCS received, through cultural and language training, widespread exposure to Marxist-Leninism and analysis of the situation of the working class in Canada and abroad. This training,

which became especially intense with the onslaught of the Depression, was facilitated through a variety of means. Teachers made use of pro-working class, Ukrainian language newspapers, literature, songs, drama, and poems in their lessons. To make his classes more enjoyable, one teacher even had his students read popular "Children's literature to study individually," which he later interpreted for them "according to Lenin ideology."[23]

The CSB also encouraged teachers to supplement classroom lessons with hands-on experiences. For example, organizers instructed teachers in the 1930s to help students understand the plight of the unemployed and impoverished by planning field trips "to soup kitchens and forced labour camps." Many on the left used the latter term to describe the R.B. Bennett-established "relief camps" for single unemployed men, characterized by low wages and abysmal and isolated working conditions. The CSB also told teachers to encourage children to analyse their home lives in the context of the Depression in order to understand what their role must be in the class struggle.[24] To practise their Ukrainian and journalism skills, organizers, teachers, and newspaper editors encouraged children to write stories about working-class exploitation for their school's "wall gazette" and for the movement's newspapers.

Organizers did not structure children's activities and roles along gender lines as women and men's were. Leaders and parents expected girls and boys to participate equally and enthusiastically. Some activities, however, were geared more towards children of a specific gender, which served to socialize girls and boys into their future gender roles in the movement. When the Women's Branch members taught traditional Ukrainian handicrafts like embroidery to students, for example, it was generally only the girls who participated.

Sometimes separate orchestra groups existed as well, though not necessarily because organizers considered a particular musical activity more appropriate for girls or boys. Often, it was simply a case of numbers. In Winnipeg, Ollie Hillman recalled, when mandolin instruction began in the early 1920s, significantly more girls than boys were involved in the mandolin orchestra. Eventually, the

UWCS teacher Vladislav Patek recruited the hall's boys into a separate "big band." Nor were the boys more advantaged in this case when it came to performance opportunities and status. In fact, the Winnipeg Girls Mandolin Orchestra was one of the most influential youngster's cultural groups in the ULFTA nationally—they embarked on several tours of eastern and western Canada during the interwar years, raising funds, class-consciousness, and organizational awareness.[25]

Like adults, the UWCS students worked under a rigorous schedule, often attending classes and rehearsals nightly and even on weekends during the September to June cultural season. While these children certainly had friends from public school and their neighbourhoods, generally speaking, few found they had the time for much play or other activity outside the parameters of the labour temples. Nick Petrachenko attended the UWCS at the Welland Ukrainian Labour Temple during the 1920s, and it was there that he spent the most time with his friends. He would hurry home after public school for a quick snack before his five o'clock Ukrainian classes. At seven o'clock, the class would end but he would often remain at the hall for drama practice. On weekends, there would also be meetings, concerts, plays, or social activities. Like Petrachenko, Hillman and her friends spent all of their spare time at the Winnipeg hall. "Every evening was filled—there would be Ukrainian school, orchestra, meetings," she explained. She, like many other children, loved attending and taking part in hall activities. The activities were so important to her and the others that they used to walk through all sorts of weather: "it was like life and death, we had to attend dancing and the other events."[26] Also a student in the 1920s, Nick Dubas called the Winnipeg Ukrainian Labour Temple his second home, stating that in fact, "I was at the hall more than I was at home. Sometimes I did poorly in [public] school because I was so involved with the hall." For Dubas, the close quarters of labour temple life led to the development of his most significant childhood friendships. "I had friends at [public] school," he explained, "but they weren't like my pals from the Ukrainian Labour Temple." Patterns like this

continued throughout the interwar years for children like Myron Shatulsky, Olga Shatulsky, Mary Semanowich, and Clara Babiy, who had similar experiences with the UWCS schedule in the 1930s.[27]

The students put their education to good use in the movement by helping to raise funds and ethnic and class-consciousness with or like adult members of the Ukrainian Labour Temples. They frequently attended or took part in plays and concerts put on by the adult branches at the halls. In 1922, for example, in the last act of a play about the Bolshevik Revolution performed at the Ukrainian Labour Temple in Winnipeg, children from the UWCS marched amidst downed telephone, telegraph, and light poles "with Red Flags singing the 'International'" among "Priests and Noblemen [who were] cleaning the streets, clothed in rags."[28] Sometimes the children were the main draw. In 1926, the Toronto Children's Mandolin Orchestra embarked on a tour of nine communities in remote northern Ontario and gave what one reviewer called, "some very fine concerts."[29] Their program featured a variety of songs reflecting the ULFTA's emphasis on musical rigour, its ethno-political interests, as well as a general international influence. Alongside traditional Ukrainian folk songs like "Katerina," "Postava," and "Zaporozhets," could be found the overture to "The Barber of Seville," "O Sole Mio," and, of course, "The International."[30] Their repertoire also included the Ukrainian version of the popular "Razom tovaryshi v nohu" ("Together Comrades"):

> All of us hail from the people,
> Children of labour and toil,
> "Fraternal union and freedom"—
> Let this be our battle call.
> Long have they held us in bondage,
> Starvation long did us waste,
> Our patience has finally ended,
> Now we'll ourselves liberate.[31]

In the end, according to the ULFTA newspaper *Ukrainski robitnychi visti* (*Ukrainian Labour News*), the trip was "a great success from both a moral and financial point of view."[32] Tours like this and those of the Girls Mandolin Orchestra wherever they played inspired many ULFTA groups. Often, in their wake during the 1920s, lay newly minted children's orchestras in even the most remote communities where these youngsters had performed.

The Higher Educational Course

The popularity and expansion of the UWCS highlighted an important deficiency in the movement. From the earliest days, it was clear that a lack of trained organizers and teachers plagued the movement. For work with youngsters to flourish, the ULFTA needed to develop a cadre of activists possessing appropriate skills and experience. To confront this serious problem, the movement's national leadership in Winnipeg developed what came to be known as the Higher Educational Course (HEC) and recruited promising young people to take part. While the first course in 1923 had only had 13 students attending, subsequent courses tended to attract anywhere from 25 to 44 students.[33] Between 1923 and 1938, five HECs took place, graduating more than 100 students in total.[34] The course was so popular, organizers moved it to Parkdale, Manitoba on the outskirts of Winnipeg where the WBA owned a large facility that housed orphaned Ukrainian leftist children and older men, too aged or infirm to look after themselves.[35] Organizers were optimistic about the training program, which they viewed as key to the movement's growth and influence among Ukrainian immigrants and their offspring.

"In a word—the Higher Educational Course is our forge," ULFTA leader Toma Kobzey explained in 1923, "which sends out hammer-wielding smiths to smash the rampant ignorance of the workers."[36] That Kobzey chose to use such a masculinist image is no coincidence. It speaks forcefully to the male-dominated left, its celebration of hammer and fist imagery, and to the sexism prevalent among Ukrainian leftists (and other contemporary radical groups). Young men were the most desirable HEC students. The resulting student bodies, then, were a physical manifestation of these views. The students of the 1923–24 HEC were all male. The 1925–26 course saw three women participants. Through the 1930s, this pattern continued. Of the 28 students who completed the course in 1936, only

9 were women. Two years later, 9 women and 29 men took part.[37] Many women were selected only once they had proven themselves exceptional and, often, only then in the absence of a suitable male candidate. Mary Skrypnyk, then of Hamilton, Ontario, was one of the few young women who attended the HEC in 1938. She became a student only after the Hamilton Ukrainian Labour Temple's first choice, a boy, had to turn down the opportunity because his father had passed away, and he needed to remain in town to support his mother. At the time of her selection, many members were displeased. "I was told the course would be wasted on me because I was a girl," Skrypnyk—who ended up making her career with the Ukrainian left—recalled.[38] Skrypnyk, and her cohort of young women at the course, were among those who, by challenging gender roles and seizing opportunity, would establish themselves as important leaders in the movement during World War II and into the post-war period.

To attend a ULFTA HEC demanded temporal and often financial commitment from students. Once they were selected, some students paid for the course themselves, though more often individual branches, the national office of the ULFTA, and the WBA would cover the cost of transportation, teaching materials, and room and board.[39] For many participants, the time they spent at an interwar HEC was worthwhile; it was likely the only opportunity they had for further education and training in Canada. The promise of a position as an organizer, journalist, or teacher in a Ukrainian labour temple somewhere in Canada—though still poorly paid—opened up alternative job possibilities beyond those typically available to young Ukrainian women and men in domestic service, resource industries, or the agricultural sector. It also gave them the opportunity to meet and mingle with a new group of like-minded young people; several even met their future spouses through the course.

A young woman or man who attended an HEC received training in a variety of subjects designed to develop their abilities as well-rounded teachers and organizers. Courses of a political nature were a priority. John Boyd, who studied at the 1930 HEC led by Matthew Popovich, remembered a curriculum that "included . . . history and geography and . . . political economy and Marxism."[40] The intention of this line of teaching, as 1936 course participant Kosty Kostaniuk explained, was "designed to give them a broad understanding of what was happening around them."[41] Students also learned various practical ways to organize branches and activities. At the 1926 HEC, for instance, classes engaged in role-playing exercises. One student, cast in the role of organizer, would be responsible for organizing the remaining members of the class who played the parts of unorganized workers or farmers. In other situations, students would conduct mock meetings or lectures to teach them how to set up and run WBA and ULFTA branches and Ukrainian Worker Children's Schools. Students also learned techniques to help revive faltering branches.[42]

Balanced against the political and organizational aspects of the course was the other priority of the ULFTA, the maintenance of Ukrainian cultural life in Canada. In addition to political and organizational lessons, students were also educated about the Ukrainian language and Ukrainian culture. Courses in Ukrainian grammar, history, and literature were fixtures of the schools. Students also studied Ukrainian music, drama, and dance. Above all, they learned how to teach these subjects properly and how to coordinate cultural groups within the ULFTA.[43] When the course finished, participants would often demonstrate what they had learned to the ULFTA members and supporters in halls in the Winnipeg vicinity. After their exams in 1936, the students of the Higher Educational Course put on a revolutionary play called "Destruction of the Black Sea Squadron" at the Transcona Ukrainian Labour Temple, while the 1938 group performed "some fine singing, duets, trios, quartets and larger groups" at their farewell concert.[44]

Most HEC graduates would be immediately assigned to work in various branches across Canada. Others would be groomed for leadership positions in local branches or as touring organizers or journalists. Kostaniuk, for example, was assigned to the Fort William Branch. Some fortunate male students in the 1930s even had the chance, once they demonstrated their potential at the HEC, to study

in Ukraine. Mike Seychuk, for example, was sent with three other students to Kharkiv, Ukraine, to attend the Red Professorship after taking part in the 1929–30 HEC.[45]

The *Sektsia Molodi* and *Yunats'ka Sektsia*

The students selected for the HEC were nearly always drawn from the ranks of the ULFTA's Youth Section. Often linked to the activities of the UWCS, organizers designed the Youth Section to teach youngsters how to function as formal ULFTA branch members. The first incarnation of the Youth Section, *Spilka Ukrainskoi Robitnychoi Molodi*, or SURM (League of Ukrainian Working Youth) came into being in February of 1924 at the ULFTA Convention. Response was immediate, and over the course of the year, 12 branches formed across Canada with a total membership of 445.

Despite—or perhaps because of—its immediate success, however, pressure from the CPC acted as a direct challenge to the SURM's existence. The CPC feared that the growing strength of the Ukrainian-language SURM would undermine its own English-language Young Communist League. As such, by 1925 the CPC successfully demanded that leaders of the ULFTA abolish the SURM to pressure Ukrainian Youth to join the YCL. Ultimately, the effort was a failure as only a few of the former SURM's leaders ended up participating in the YCL. Resistant to the prospect of working not within the Ukrainian cultural-political milieu of the ULFTA but through the CPC, others, according to an RCMP source, "drifted away," choosing "to not belong to any of the organizations."[46] This acute rejection forced the CPC to recognize the desire for and value of a separate Ukrainian youth organization. At the 1926 ULFTA Convention, CPC National Secretary Jack Macdonald himself urged the ULFTA to reorganize a youth branch, albeit one, which he argued, should be led by Ukrainian youth who were also members of the YCL. The ULFTA happily obliged, and the *Sektsia Molodi* (Youth Section) was born.[47]

With a significant degree of autonomy from the CPC restored, the *Sektsia Molodi* enjoyed another wave of phenomenal growth. Over the course of the latter half of the 1920s, it, like the Ukrainian Workers' Children's Schools, expanded into numerous communities across Canada. By 1927, the ULFTA boasted 32 youth branches and 1,508 members in its youth division.[48] In 1931, the ULFTA even created a *Yunats'ka Sektsia* (Junior Section) modelled on the *Sektsia Molodi* for children aged seven to ten, too young for the *Sektsia Molodi* but eager for a branch of their own.[49]

Organizers deliberately structured both the *Sektsia Molodi* and *Yunats'ka Sektsia* like adult branches to teach children how to run an organization, hold meetings, and fundraise. Skypnyk, who was assigned to the *Yunats'ka Sektsia* during the late 1930s, "tried to make it a small organization for children, like a smaller model of the larger organization."[50] Like many adult branches, membership meetings for the young people's sections generally took place on Sundays. As one former member recalled, realizing there was a distinction between themselves and the religious—Ukrainian or otherwise—children, the *Yunats'ka Sektsia* children used to refer to it as their Sunday School.[51] Instead of the religious instruction that took place in church, however, in these groups youngsters would learn like adults, about Marxist-Leninism, the international proletarian struggle, and how to elect executives, hold meetings, pay dues, plan events, and raise money. In this way, these youngsters, who straddled two worlds—that of the Ukrainian left and that of the multi-class and multi-ethnic world outside the hall—drew on their radical culture to make sense of what they were doing vis-à-vis other children in their neighbourhoods and public schools.

Branch activities for youngsters mirrored in intensity those of women and men, reflecting a combination of organizational, political, and social activity. As one young member of the *Sektsia Molodi* branch in Sault Ste. Marie, Ontario explained in 1927, their branch had held in their three months of existence, "five administrative meetings, seven group readings, [and] two concerts independently." They had also coordinated "seven concerts with their Finnish comrades, one annual meeting with the election of the new executive, [while at

the same time] collecting money for a library."[52] The *Sektsia Molodi* and *Yunats'ka Sektsia*, like adult groups, were also encouraged to assist other ULFTA branches in fund-raising for the press, the organizational fund, and other labour-related projects. Many youngsters enjoyed the pace of organizational activity, but stuck around as well because of the important social elements inherent to these young people's branches. Mike Seychuk, a *Yunats'ka Sektsia* member in Winnipeg during the late 1920s and early 1930s, recalled his hectic schedule: "On weekends, we would spend time at the Ukrainian Labour Temple in a group meeting or on an outing; we would have socials in the evening with kids from the Transcona or East Kildonan Ukrainian Labour Temples." A favourite wintertime activity for Seychuk's group involved making a 12 kilometre "trek" east from their North End Winnipeg hall to meet their cohort at the Transcona hall.[53]

There were differences between youngsters' branches and adult branches, however. Most significantly, the young people's branch activities were not organized along gender lines. While organizers might, in some instances, develop activities with more appeal for girls or boys, overall youngsters were not forced to adhere to rigid definitions of femininity or masculinity, nor were they confined, like their parents, to branches and activities based on whether they were male or female. Both girls and boys were encouraged within their groups to play executive and committee roles, and girls often held key leadership positions such as president.[54]

Like the UWCS and the HEC, the *Yunats'ka Sektsia* and *Sektsia Molodi* seemed to enjoy a strong following and a great deal of popularity. Growth in the 1920s continued into the 1930s. By the time the 1933 ULFTA convention rolled around, the membership of the *Yunats'ka Sektsia* and *Sektsia Molodi* totalled 1,528 and 1,050 respectively. At the 1937 ULFTA Convention, the *Yunats'ka Sektsia* reported having more than 2,000 members,[55] while the *Sektsia Molodi* was shown to have grown to 1,800 members nationwide.[56]

Despite the sections' prolific expansion, their existence continued in some ways to be precarious. Struggles with the CPC cropped up sporadically throughout the 1930s, threatening to alienate Ukrainian youngsters from ULFTA branch work. Clearly, the role the CPC wanted the YCL to play in relation to the *Sektsia Molodi* continued to be contentious, and leaders of both the ULFTA and the CPC had to tread carefully. In a 1935 ULFTA-published Ukrainian language article entitled "What the Relationship Should Be Between the YCL and the Youth Section, ULFTA," Seychuk outlined these existing tensions and attempted to find common ground for the two organizations. He explained that a lack of understanding of the differing purposes of the YCL and the *Sektsia Molodi* led to "misunderstandings and antagonism between the two groups." Attempting to clear this up, Seychuk argued that the task of the *Sektsia Molodi* was "to nurture culture-educational activity amongst the Ukrainian youth preparing it for the class struggle," while the YCL, particularly through its Ukrainian members, was meant "to show leadership to all revolutionary (labour) mass organizations of youth, including the Youth Section of the ULFTA." While clearly supporting the idea of a close and hierarchical connection between the YCL and the *Sektsia Molodi*, Seychuk went on to warn both groups, but especially the YCL, to act carefully and respectfully, asserting much antagonism had been generated by the views of YCLers that the *Sektsia Molodi* was "an unnecessary organization."[57]

Clearly Comintern and Party policy around the early 1930s "turn" and the mid-to-late 1930s Popular Front period intensified the pressure the Party placed on youngster's groups like the *Sektsia Molodi*. While many in the ULFTA leadership sought to follow Party directives as closely as possibly, most realized that this would be impossible, given the continued contempt the Party held for the ULFTA's cultural mandate and interests and the importance ULFTA members and supporters placed on these ideals. Understanding the pressures they faced, many ULFTA leaders sought compromise between both sides. These efforts took on several forms when it came to the *Sektsia Molodi* and, in reality, few real shifts took place in the youth group despite the dramatic rhetoric the Party and ULFTA leaders were then employing. Throughout the 1930s, ULFTA

leaders continued to encourage youngsters to join not only the *Yunats'ka Sektsia* or *Sektsia Molodi* but also the Young Pioneers or the YCL. At the same time, in the same direction the women's and men's branches were being pushed by the Party, the ULFTA and CPC tried to encourage youngsters in the *Yunats'ka Sektsia* and *Sektsia Molodi* to collaborate with other young people's organizations in order to gain new contacts and recruits for the class struggle.[58] By the mid-1930s Popular Front period little had changed as members of the *Yunats'ka Sektsia* and *Sektsia Molodi* continued to be encouraged by both the Communist Party of Canada and the ULFTA leadership, in the name of a "United Front Against War and Fascism," to form alliances with other young people's organizations. In a gesture to the Party, to conform to this newest agenda, delegates to the Sixteenth National Convention of the ULFTA in 1937 voted to change name of the *Sektsia Molodi* to the *Federatsia Kanadsko-Ukrainskoi Molodi* (Canadian Ukrainian Youth Federation) in an effort to appeal to a wider constituency of Ukrainian youth.[59] Despite the name change, however, many of the day-to-day activities of young people remained the same—centred in the ULFTA—as they had in the 1920s and early 1930s. This sloganeering, therefore, seemed to represent more of an effort by Ukrainian leaders to placate the Party without making any fundamental—and potentially unpopular—shifts with regard to the work of the Ukrainian children and youth. Moreover, while evidence to indicate the success of this initiative is scant, given other Ukrainian groups' hostility to the Ukrainian left, it is unlikely that their children were drawn en masse to the CUYF.

Many young people did become more politically active and aware during the 1930s, likely from a combination of Party pressure, ULFTA training, and their own real life experiences growing up in working-class, immigrant neighbourhoods. Some, like *Sektsia Molodi* member Fred Zwarch, actively advocated the program set out by the Party. In 1936, Zwarch, supporting the Party's calls for a Popular Front, wrote to *Unite the Youth*, a bilingual (Ukrainian and English) magazine published in 1936 in honour of the tenth anniversary of the

Sektsia Molodi. He exhorted young people to use drama, sporting events, social activities, and educationals to build up "a genuine mass non-party youth organization" made up "of not only young Communists, but also of young Socialists, Cooperative Commonwealth [Federation] youth, students and all other progressive-minded youth . . . who are willing fighters against war and fascism and for the general welfare of the young generation."[60]

Most young people, unlike Zwarch, continued to centre their political expression and cultural activity with the ULFTA. Moreover, though politicization and activism throughout the 1930s took on a greater urgency in all facets of the ULFTA, the methods the movement used to carry out these activities remained largely unchanged, as did the popularity of activities for children and youth. Throughout the 1930s, in addition to conducting their activism through Ukrainian school, orchestras, and plays, children and youth increasingly supported strikes, joined protests against war and fascism, marched in May Day parades, and raised funds for various causes related both to the ULFTA and the Party.[61] The *Sektsia Molodi* in Broad Valley, Manitoba, for example, explained that they took part "in the struggle against the tax sales, relief grievances, [and] bailiff sales."[62] Concerns for conditions in Western Ukraine, peace, and protests against the rising clouds of imperialist war were also added to the list of issues with which the ULFTA was preoccupied during the Depression. With adults, children and youth shared these concerns and were central to protests and actions taken in support of these causes.

While the CPC/YCL connection hung over the movement bullying the *Sektsia Molodi*, so, too, were ULFTA leaders challenged in the field of work with youngsters in other ways. One of the reasons ULFTA organizers feared aggressively insisting that children and youth toe the Party line was because they were well aware that many youngsters were fully prepared to leave when the *Yunats'ka Sektsia* or *Sektsia Molodi* failed to adequately address their interests. While still ensuring that the ULFTA's political-cultural objectives were being met, organizers had to work hard to hold young people's attention

and keep them coming to meetings and functions. Nowhere was this more evident than where the "Educational" was concerned.

The "Educational" was one of the most important components of the *Yunats'ka Sektsia* and *Sektsia Molodi* mandate. *Yunats'ka Sektsia* and *Sektsia Molodi* "Educationals" were similar to those that took place in adult branches, usually consisting of a lecture by a ULFTA leader or a group reading of a ULFTA newspaper. Speakers would try to teach youngsters how to be good, class-conscious, Ukrainian young people. They would do so by discussing the history of the Soviet Union, Ukraine, and other issues relevant to working-class Ukrainian children and youth. Like some adults, some youngsters enjoyed and were profoundly influenced and politicized by these lessons. "The Youth Section has given me a correct outlook on the world so that now I can understand the reasons for the present hardships and sufferings of the working class and the working class youth in particular," explained *Sektsia Molodi* member Nick Hrynchyshyn in 1936. "But more than that," he asserted, "it has shown me the way out of these present miserable conditions and the way to a happy new world."[63]

Not all youngsters were as moved by the "Educationals" as Hrynchyshyn, however. Many youngsters found the "Educationals"—and even many branch activities—dull. They demonstrated their ennui in a number of ways: by offering suggestions to improve branch life or, if this proved too difficult, leaving the organization. Membership loss was clearly a constant problem, as a letter from *Sektsia Molodi* member M. Dembitski illustrates. In 1931, he wrote to an organizational newspaper on the topic of "Why are Some Members Leaving the Youth Section" in an effort to produce change. He argued that members stayed away because the meetings were simply not interesting. He suggested that, in order to keep members engaged, the *Sektsia Molodi* needed to spend less time holding meetings, paying dues, and emphasizing "slogans" in terms of educational work.[64]

Others argued that, given the competition the movement faced from popular culture when it came to retaining children's interest, the labour temples needed to make use of new technology and present the class struggle in more novel and engaging ways. This seemed a particularly important tactic during the Popular Front period, as the movement tried to attract a greater variety of Ukrainian children to its activities. In 1936, for example, Anna Gnit suggested following the lead of a church that used lantern shows to engage its child congregants. "Instead of showing scenes of Jesus," she proposed, "we can show them scenes from the life of the workers' and farmers' children in Canada and other countries, contrasting this with the life of the people in the USSR."[65] Nor did she feel it necessary that all such spectacles be imbued with class content, suggesting Mickey Mouse cartoons could also be shown. Similar ideas were implemented in many locales. Myron Shatulsky recalled going to the Winnipeg Ukrainian labour temple to see popular films. The movies, featuring Hollywood actors like Gene Autry or Jean Harlow, were shown on the hall's 35 mm projector Wednesday to Friday, and sometimes Saturdays if there was no ULFTA play scheduled.[66]

Physical Activity and Sports

The ULFTA leadership also turned to other means to keep children and youth engaged and active. The most important of these were sports. As sports historian Bruce Kidd has illustrated, Ukrainians did not bring to Canada "a strong sports tradition." Nonetheless, thanks to participation in sports at school or in their working-class neighbourhoods, and encouraged by the formation of the CPC/YCL-led Workers' Sports Association (WSA), many young Ukrainians eagerly embraced a variety of hall-led sports as their favoured form of leisure and activist activity. As a result, according to Kidd, Ukrainians eventually "made up the second most numerous ethnic group within the workers' sports movement."[67]

Ukrainian Labour Temples organizers viewed the presence of physical activity groups as crucial to recruiting and retaining a strong membership base of working-class-minded children and youth. Moreover, like the Ukrainian Worker Children's Schools, sports at the Ukrainian Labour Temples offered an important, labour-centred, radical alternative

to those provided by religious and quasi-religious groups like the Young Men's Christian Association (YMCA), Girl Guides, or Boy Scouts. "These are bourgeoisie clubs, the youths there are being cultivated in the bourgeoisie way," an organizer, speaking critically of the YMCA, explained in 1933, "They are absolutely kept in ignorance of the class struggle in the economic life of the people. Therefore we must support and build up our own Sports Club."[68] Sports were an important strategy local branches were especially encouraged to employ during the summer months, when the ULFTA cultural season and public school year ended. Organizers feared young people might drift away from the halls for good if they pursued activities (and made new non-ULFTA friends) outside the movement during their summer vacations.[69] Endeavouring to build the Comintern-mandated Popular Front during the 1930s, organizers held out great hope that sports might attract to the ULFTA young people from other Ukrainian, non-Ukrainian, and even non-leftist groups.[70] Most sports activities took place under the auspices of the *Sektsia Molodi*, and all halls eventually came to have some form of physical activity, though it varied according to locality and resources.

There is some indication that some sporting activities were organized along gender lines. Organizers especially believed that sports were an important way to attract and retain boys for the movement. At certain times, they believed that boys needed specific diversions because of extenuating social or economic circumstances. During the Depression in Welland, for example, Nick Petrachenko recalled, "all the young guys were unemployed at the time." Members of the Ukrainian labour temple suggested that a sports club be created for them so they would have something to do. Since there was no money to buy mats, the young men made some out of canvass and used them to perform "various exercises [and] gymnastics," and anyone in the area, "whether a member or not, could participate."[71] It is not clear whether the needs of unemployed girls were viewed in the same light. Even if they were playing the same sport, games or teams would sometimes be structured so as to separate the girls and boys. As Ollie Hillman recalled, this did not always necessarily reflect attitudes that certain sports were inappropriate for girls (either because they were deemed unfeminine or too rough) or that boys needed extra attention or resources. Rather, she explained, "the boys had their own sports because they were heavier."[72] In many instances, though, gender divisions were not guaranteed; girls and boys often could and did play together.

A variety of sports were popular with these Ukrainian children. In the summer, children commonly played baseball, hiked, or took organized nature walks. At ULFTA picnics, track and field events were also popular.[73] In the winter, youngsters often tobogganed or skated. In Winnipeg, Mike Seychuk and the *Sektsia Molodi* formed a skating club: "We got a boxcar from the CPR for a vacant lot, put a heater in there, and this was our club room. We got old boards from people and built a rink. The city flooded it for us and we had a skating rink for the whole winter."[74] Year round, by far the most popular and widely practised sporting activity was gymnastics (also called "acrobatics"). This is because they were relatively easy to organize, and many children—from the youngest to the oldest—could take part at a single time (as opposed to team sports where participant numbers were more limited), and the activity could easily accommodate girls and boys together.[75] Moreover, gymnastics could be politicized more easily and more overtly than other sports, which might only offer organizers the chance to teach youngsters the value of collective activity. Children often, for example, performed their routines at concerts and festivals, events that helped to raise money and generate new members for the ULFTA. At the same time, it was easy to incorporate—as many groups often did—Soviet or communist symbols into these acts.[76] These performances were often as well received and impressive as regular concerts or plays, apparently even to those who were not ULFTA boosters. "It was really marvellous and the place was packed, many went home without seeing it due to a lack of space," recounted an anonymous RCMP eyewitness informant of a February 1933 Winnipeg Sports Club gymnastics performance. "They had young children performing acrobatics wonderfully, boys and girls and grownup boys and girls, together," he enthused,

"The performances were astonishing and must have had careful preparation. Many membership forms were being filled out all over the audience."[77]

Svit molodi and Boyova molod

While all halls across Canada attempted to integrate some degree of activity for young people into their local programming, such activities did tend to vary in both consistency and size according to the nature of the Ukrainian community in its vicinity. Halls in urban centres like Winnipeg, Edmonton, or Toronto typically possessed a larger membership base than did more-isolated farming communities or smaller resource towns, from which to draw children and youth to activities. Generally, these communities were better able to support the cost of a teacher to coordinate classes and groups. Smaller halls, especially those in rural areas, tended to have a more difficult time organizing and maintaining young people's activities. Distance between farm families, inadequate financial resources (which became magnified for many halls during the Depression), and a lack of teachers qualified to carry out the ULFTA educational mandate meant functions for children and youth in many areas were, at best, sporadic, if they existed at all.[78] One of the ways the ULFTA attempted to alleviate this problem was through the publication of a variety of Ukrainian language newspapers to serve its various membership constituencies. Just as it did for adults, so, too, did the movement print a special newspaper for youngsters. *Svit molodi*, or *The Youth's World*, was created in 1927 to serve the needs of the *Sektsia Molodi*. Prior to the founding of *Svit molodi*, special pages in the women's paper, *Robitnytsia* (*Working Woman*), had been devoted to serving young people, particularly children. *Svit molodi* seemed to fill a void; by 1929, it boasted over 3700 subscribers across the country.

Like the adult papers, *Svit molodi* was, at heart, a teaching and recruitment tool geared to the politicization of youngsters. From it, young people learned about Marxist-Leninism, the fight for workers' rights (both locally and around the world), and the ULFTA's interpretation of current events. Its articles, poems, letters, and features supplemented and reinforced lessons children and youth learned at hall schools (and, leaders hoped, undid bourgeois lessons learned in public schools), in cultural activities, and in *Yunats'ka Sektsia* and *Sektsia Molodi*. Articles like "First of May—A Day to Fight," which appeared in the April 1932 issue, explored labour history, contemporary conditions for workers, and government oppression, encouraging youngsters to take part in the international proletarian struggle.[79] Because it was in Ukrainian, *Svit molodi* provided young people with literature to practise and hone their Ukrainian language skills, opportunities not afforded them in public school. This was especially critical for children and youth living in remote rural communities where access to Ukrainian school might be nearly impossible. *Svit molodi* was also interactive. Youngsters could both read features and write their own letters and articles for publication.

Svit molodi also worked as an essential tool for inter-branch communication and building the movement, much in the same way the adult papers functioned. To carry out their responsibilities in corresponding with the paper, youth branches were expected to elect a press correspondent, called a *Yunkor* or *Yunkorka*—as both boys and girls were encouraged to hold the position—to write to the paper detailing their activities. Organizers hoped that, by reading what other groups were doing, young people would be similarly inspired to be active in their localities. "I'm in the third grade of the Ukrainian Workers Children's School," wrote eleven-year-old *Yunkor* Wasyl Ravliuk of Coleman, Alberta, in 1927, "There aren't many of us, but we're doing a lot of work. We've already performed the play 'The Little Blacksmiths' and are preparing for a concert." Ravliuk went on to thank the Women's Branch for the post-play supper they prepared for the children which helped to raise funds for a branch library. He closed with commendations for the group's instructor: "Our teacher A. Zablotsky works very hard to turn us into intelligent children who don't hang out on the streets."[80]

Svit molodi represented a further and significant attempt at autonomy from the CPC on the part of the ULFTA. It was another effort to resist Party control and attempts at Anglicization of the Communist left. The Party, of course, expected all young people, including the Ukrainians, to read its English-language organ, *The Young Worker*. As we know, however, Ukrainian leaders and parents wanted their children to be fluent in Ukrainian language and culture as well as proletarian politics. Creating a paper to facilitate this seemed a natural step. It is not surprising that, like other areas of activity, the CPC tried to dictate the shape and content of *Svit molodi*. Again, like ULFTA leaders in other circumstances, the editors of *Svit molodi* attempted to find common ground with the Party without compromising the paper's Ukrainian cultural and political integrity. For example, the paper routinely carried advertisements for *The Young Worker*, and encouraged members of the *Sektsia Molodi* to subscribe to and read it and take part in its fundraising campaigns.[81] The paper also featured advertisements reminding youngsters to "Join the Ranks of the YCL!" and articles instructing them to "Step Up to the Ranks of the Young Communist League and Young Pioneers!"[82] As part of the early 1930s "turn," the name of *Svit molodi* was even changed to *Boyova molod*, or *Militant Youth* to better address the "revolutionary movement . . . sweeping the world."[83] During the 1930s the paper increasingly took on a more radical tone, partly because of Depression conditions and partly because many of those young leaders who wrote for the paper held membership in both the *Sektsia Molodi* and YCL.

Language: Ukrainian or English?

Despite its best efforts to train youngsters in the Ukrainian language, however, the ULFTA saw signs early on that it was losing the linguistic battle. The UWCS, cultural activities, and even *Svit Molodi* were no match for North American popular culture, the public school system, and the youngsters' multi-ethnic neighbourhoods where the common language of communication among Jewish, German, Russian, Polish, Ukrainian, and other working-class young people was English.[84] Even those youth whom leaders hoped would move to the forefront of the movement often had a great degree of difficulty functioning in Ukrainian. Young Bill Philipovich, for example, struggled to compose his autobiography and application for the 1936 Higher Educational Course because it had to be in Ukrainian.[85] For many young people born to Ukrainian immigrant parents, then, a language-based generation gap of sorts was created at home and at the hall.

In the interwar period, the language problem was less pronounced than it would become for the movement during the post-war era. Nonetheless, during the 1930s it was becoming noticeable that there was an issue with communication in the Ukrainian language as far as many children and youth were concerned. The ULFTA recognized this problem and attempted to moderate the effects of the process of assimilation in several ways. In doing so, it continued to reassert its autonomy from the Party. Though it could have simply directed young people to read the English language CPC papers or join the YCL, little to no positive Ukrainian content could be found there. The ULFTA thus refused to accept that as a solution, hoping to keep children and youth within a Ukrainian milieu. Sometimes leaders continued to demand that youngsters try to communicate and carry out their organizational work in the Ukrainian language regardless of their comfort level or ability. This was little more than an awkward and ultimately ineffective solution, however. "While this forced the young people to learn to express themselves in Ukrainian," former *Sektsia Molodi* member Misha Korol recalled, "it also held back many who found the language a big obstacle."[86]

In other instances, particularly as the 1930s wore on, the ULFTA encouraged compromise between the use of English and Ukrainian to ensure that children and youth would join and remain with Ukrainian Labour Temple activities. Leaders urged halls to create libraries that incorporated both English and Ukrainian materials. They also instructed youth organizers to conduct meetings and other activities in the language in which young members were most comfortable. The organizational newspaper *Ukrainski robitnychi visty* (*Ukrainian Labour News*) even incorporated a section for youth during the mid-1930s that made use of both English and Ukrainian in articles and correspondence.[87]

At the same time, to command and hold the attention of youngsters the ULFTA encouraged the proliferation of Ukrainian cultural activities for which language skills were unnecessary. One of the most important was Ukrainian folk dance. Nineteen twenty-six saw the first performances of Ukrainian folk dancing in the halls. That same year in Winnipeg, the ULFTA held Ukrainian folk dance courses. The following year, the ULFTA National Convention voted to include folk dancing as a new activity for Ukrainian school students.[88] Within a year, folk dance groups and classes sprang up among ULFTA groups across Canada, including Ottawa, South Porcupine, Edmonton, Fort Frances, to name but a few.[89] Folk dancing offered another means through which to politicize children and youth while at the same time imparting in them a strong sense of Ukrainianness. The folk dances, modelled on traditional regional Ukrainian dance styles, were not in and of themselves political. However, that children and youth danced them in a country overtly hostile to Ukrainians and that these performances were used to raise money to fund the ULFTA's (and sometimes the Party's) activities imbued them with a radical political purpose. Folk dancing developed as and remained one of the most consistently popular pursuits for youngsters. It lingers as one of the sole activities attracting children and youth to the Ukrainian Labour Temples today.

Conclusion

The interwar era was, in many ways, a period of cultural and organizational prosperity for the ULFTA, particularly where its activities for children and youth were concerned. A youngster growing up in the Ukrainian left during the 1920s and 1930s experienced a distinct type of radical childhood thanks to the particular ways in which definitions of class, ethnicity, age and, to a lesser extent, gender converged to shape their identities. Their sense of Ukrainianness distinguished them from other radical children, while the class consciousness their parents, leaders, and teachers tried to instil set them apart from other Ukrainian children (especially those from nationalist or religious families). At the same time, age differentiated them from their adult counterparts and, for girls in particular, offered some advantages over their mothers in terms of equal access with boys to organizational opportunities. Childhood—to a certain age—gave girls some freedom to pursue positions and activities in the movement unavailable to women. As a child reached adulthood, however, gender roles became more rigidly defined and enforced. Young men were expected to put their skills to work for the main ULFTA branch or its related organizations. Most young women—unless they had the opportunity to teach thanks to HEC attendance—would find their labours directed towards the women's branch.

Leaders and parents worked to impart in young people a strong sense of Ukrainianness and understanding of the proletarian situation. Reflected in these efforts was the adult hope and expectation that children would grow up with an intense and ongoing commitment to the Ukrainian left, the class struggle, and Ukrainian culture and history, becoming enlightened and active Ukrainian leftist adults. Young people, too, made important contributions to the shape of the movement, particularly where their own activities and experiences were concerned. Leaders had to work hard to accommodate youngsters' interests and needs—particularly their demands that activities be fun and, increasingly later, in English—while still maintaining integral movement values. As a result, organizers often reworked activities to keep them attractive to children and youth while trying to remain true to the cultural and political milieu of the radical Ukrainian community during the interwar years.

To maintain the movement's Ukrainian integrity, leaders also continually and successfully fended off CPC efforts to Anglicize and control the Ukrainian left's organizations and activities. Though the Party did influence the shape of youngsters' activities to some degree, rarely did this rework these activities in any sort of dramatic or fundamental fashion. In the end, the Party was fighting a battle it could not win. Communist officialdom neglected to appreciate that for a group fighting not only economic but also ethnic and social oppression, the Party line (as manifest or proscribed) could not fully satisfy the needs of the Ukrainian leftist, be they female or male, child or adult. This is because it failed to address their oppression as both Ukrainians and members of the working class. Heaping ethnocentric criticism on these Ukrainians—calling them backward, conservative, "right-wing deviationists"—for what were radical cultural-political pursuits only served to reinforce the need for a separate sphere of work.

Overall, the efforts of leaders and the encouragement young people received from parents to attend events at the hall paid off during the interwar era. From the time of their official inception with the advent of the ULTA at the end of the Great War to the early months of World War II, groups for leftist Ukrainian children and youth thrived across the country. Many who came of age in the 1920s and 1930s continued to support the movement in which they had grown up, opting to become members of adult branches at the halls or, most often in the case of young men, leaders at the national level of the movement.

Notes

1. Nadya Niechoda, "Autobiography," Canadian Society for Ukrainian Labour Research (CSULR) Symposium: "Forgotten Legacy": Contributions of Socialist Ukrainians to Canada (Winnipeg 1996), 4–7.

2. Frances Swyripa, Wedded to the Cause: Ukrainian-Canadian Women and Ethnic Identity, 1891–1991 (Toronto 1993).

3. Ruth Frager, Sweatshop Strife: Class, Ethnicity, and Gender in the Jewish Labour Movement of Toronto, 1900–1939 (Toronto 1992), 216.

4. Katrina Srigley, "'In Case You Hadn't Noticed!': Race, Ethnicity, And Women's Wage-Earning in a Depression-Era City," Labour/Le Travail, 55 (Spring 2005), 69–105.

5. Marlene Epp, et al., eds., Sisters Or Strangers?: Immigrant, Ethnic and Racialized Women in Canadian History (Toronto 2004).

6. The Communist question is evident in Jaroslav Petryshyn, Peasants in the Promised Land: Canada and the Ukrainians, 1891–1914 (Toronto 1985); John Kolasky, The Shattered Illusion: The History of Ukrainian Pro-Communist Organizations in Canada (Toronto 1979); Kolasky, Prophets and Proletarians: Documents on the History of the Rise and Decline of Ukrainian Communism in Canada (Edmonton 1990); Marco Carynnyk, "Swallowing Stalinism: Pro-Communist Ukrainian Canadians and Soviet Ukraine in the 1930s," in Lubomyr Luciuk, et

al., eds., *Canada's Ukrainians: Negotiating an Identity* (Toronto 1991), 187–205; Orest Martynowych, *The Ukrainians in Canada: The Formative Years, 1891–1924* (Edmonton 1991); Donald Avery, "Divided Loyalties: The Ukrainian Left and the Canadian State," in Luciuk, et al., eds., *Canada's Ukrainians*, 271–287; and Paul Yuzuk, "The Ukrainian Communist Delusion," in *The Ukrainians in Manitoba: A Social History* (Toronto 1953), 96–112.

7. Frager, *Sweatshop Strife*, 212.

8. For some examples, see Carmela Patrias, *Patriots and Proletarians: Politicizing Hungarian Immigrants in Interwar Canada* (Montreal 1994) and Patrias, "Relief Strike: Immigrant Workers and the Great Depression in Crowland, Ontario, 1930–35," Franca Iacovetta, et al., eds, *A Nation of Immigrants: Women, Workers, and Communities in Canadian History* (Toronto 1998), 322–358. See also Paul Michler, *Raising Reds: The Young Pioneers, Radical Summer Camps, and Communist Political Culture in the United States* (New York: Columbia University Press, 1999), and Ester Reiter, "Secular 'Yiddishkait': Left Politics, Culture, and Community," *Labour/Le Travail* Vol. 49 (Spring, 2002), pp. 121–46, and "Camp Naivelt and the Daughters of the Jewish Left," in Marlene Epp, Franca Iacovetta, and Frances Swirypa, eds., *Sisters or Strangers: Immigrant, Ethnic, and Racialized Women in Canadian History* (Toronto: University of Toronto Press, 2004).

9. For more information on the ULFTA's general history, see Peter Krawchuk, *Our History: The Ukrainian Labour-Farmer Movement in Canada, 1907–1991* (Toronto 1996) and my doctoral thesis, "'Sincerest Revolutionary Greetings': Progressive Ukrainians in Twentieth Century Canada," Ph.D. Thesis, McMaster University, 2005.

10. It is important that we not fall into the ethnocentric trap of viewing the Ukrainian left as a much more deeply patriarchal culture than was the Anglo-Celtic culture and hence the Anglo-Canadian left. Certain studies have emphasized the Ukrainian leftists' male chauvinism while not sufficiently subjecting the Anglo-Canadian left to the same degree of scrutiny. See for example, Joan Sangster, *Dreams of Equality: Women on the Canadian Left, 1920–1950* (Toronto 1989).

11. For a more detailed description of women's experiences with the ULFTA, see Joan Sangster "Robitnytsia, Ukrainian Communists, and the 'Porcupinism' Debate: Reassessing Ethnicity, Gender, and Class in Early Canadian Communism, 1922–1930," *Labour/Le Travail*, 56 (Fall 2005), 51–89, and my doctoral thesis, "Sincerest Revolutionary Greetings."

12. Kolasky, *The Shattered Illusion*, 278.

13. Sangster, *Dreams of Equality*, 126.

14. For more detailed discussion of the CPC-ULFTA connection, consult the standard sources cited above authored by Sangster, Avery, and Avakumovic. See also Ian Angus, *Canadian Bolsheviks: The Early Years of the Communist*

Party of Canada (Victoria 2004) and, especially, Jim Mochoruk's yet unpublished paper, "It's Not Easy Being Red: Ukrainian Canadians and the Communist Party of Canada in the 1920s."

15. Mary Ashworth, "Ukrainian Children," *Children of the Canadian Mosaic: A Brief History to 1950* (Toronto 1993), 77–80.

16. "Report on the State of Study and Education in the Ukrainian Worker-Children's Schools,"10th Convention ULFTA, February 4–6, 1929, translated by L. Stavroff; Peter Krawchuk, *Our History: The Ukrainian Labour-Farmer Movement in Canada, 1907–1991* (Toronto 1996), 245.

17. In 1927, for example, the ULFTA National Convention voted to include folk dancing as a new activity for Ukrainian schoolchildren. "Re AUUC—Montreal, P. Que.," 20 January 1956, Library and Archives Canada, Records of the Canadian Security Intelligence Service [hereafter LAC, CSIS], RG 146, Volume 3757: "AUUC—Case History Canada," Part 1.

18. Translation of Ukrainian Labour News, 18 March 1933, LAC, CSIS RG 146, Volume 3758: "AUUC, Women's Section, Canada," Part 1.

19. "Sixteenth Convention of ULFTA," 8 May 1937, LAC, CSIS RG 146, Volume 3792: "AUUC: Winnipeg, Manitoba," Part 8.

20. Ollie Hillman, interviewed by Rhonda L. Hinther [hereafter RLH], August 1999.

21. Special comment should be made about the terms "Tovarishka," "Tovarish," and "Tovarishky/Tovarishy" the female, male, and plural versions of the title "Comrade" which was often used in interwar documents to address and describe members and supporters. This study deliberately retains the Ukrainian transliteration of these terms so as not to lose the complexity of its meaning for the Ukrainian left community. Their use is significant not only for obvious political overtones, but also because the terms can be translated as "friend." This is especially important for understanding the ways in which the Ukrainian left defined what it meant to be Ukrainian in relation to the "Ukrainianness" espoused by other Ukrainian groups in Canada. The use of "Tovarishka" and "Tovarish," in addition to linking the Ukrainian left with the international proletarian struggle, acted as a rejection of what they perceived as the elitist, imperialist overtones of the terms "Panya" and "Pan" ("Lady" and "Lord") by which other more conservative Ukrainians in Canada tended to greet each other. Thus, these terms epitomize this particular Ukrainian community's attempts to create a more egalitarian set of social relations in the Canadian context.

22. *Svit molodi*, March 1927, translated by L. Stavroff.

23. "Report on the 1931 Convention, ULFTA," LAC, CSIS RG 146, Volume 3792: "AUUC—Winnipeg, Manitoba," Part 12; *Svit molodi*, March 1927, translated by L. Stavroff; *Programa Pratsi i Navchannya v URDShkola.*

[Teaching Guide for Ukrainian Worker-Children's Schools] (Winnipeg, 1932), Stavroff Private Collection (Toronto), translated by L. Stavroff; Krawchuk, Our History, 191.

24. Programa Pratsi i Navchannya v URDShkola, [Teaching Guide for Ukrainian Worker-Children's Schools].

25. Hillman interview; Peter Krawchuk, ed., Our Stage: The Amateur Performing Arts of the Ukrainian Settlers in Canada (Toronto 1984), 71–79.

26. Programa Pratsi i Navchannya v URDShkola [Teaching Guide for Ukrainian Worker-Children's Schools]; Nick Petrachenko, interviewed by RLH, December, 1999; Hillman interview.

27. Nick Dubas, interviewed by RLH, June 1998. For other examples: Pearl Milan, interviewed by RLH, August 1999 and Olga Shatulsky, interviewed by RLH, May 1998.

28. "Re Ukrainian Labor Temple Association, Winnipeg, Concert Given at the Ukrainian Labor Temple, 25 November 1922," LAC, CSIS RG 146, Volume 3792: "AUUC—Winnipeg, Manitoba," File 1.

29. Ukrainski robitnychi visti, 14 September 1926 as quoted in Krawchuk, ed., Our Stage, 77.

30. Ukrainski robitnychi visti, 21 September 1926 as quoted in Krawchuk, ed., Our Stage, 77.

31. Translated from Ukrainian by L. Stavroff.

32. Ukrainski robitnychi visti, 21 September 1926 as quoted in Krawchuk, ed., Our Stage, 77.

33. LAC, CSIS RG 146, Volume 3792: "AUUC—Winnipeg, Manitoba," File 10; Krawchuk, "The Education of Leading Cadres by the ULFTA, 1920s–1930s," The Tenth Anniversary Publication of Conference Proceedings . . . (Toronto 1996), 32–36.

34. Kolasky, Shattered Illusion, 10.

35. For more detailed discussion of the Parkdale Orphanage, see Hinther, "Sincerest Revolutionary Greetings."

36. T. Kobzey, "What We Are Studying at the Higher Educational Course" in Nashi Sproby [Our Endeavours] (Winnipeg 1926), a Publication of the Students of the Higher Educational Course of the ULFTA, translated by L. Stavroff.

37. "Re ULFTA—Winnipeg, Higher Educational Course," 20 January 1937 and "Re ULFTA, Winnipeg," 14 January 1938, LAC, CSIS RG 146, Volume 3792: "AUUC—Winnipeg, Manitoba," Parts 7 and 8.

38. Olga Shatulsky interview; Mary Skrypnyk, interviewed by RLH, December 1998.

39. "Re: Foreign Bolshevik-Communist Organizations," no date [c. 1938], LAC, CSIS RG 146, Volume 3792: "AUUC—Winnipeg, Manitoba," File 8; "Re Seventh Convention of ULFT Assn., held in Winnipeg on January 25–26–27, 1926," LAC, CSIS RG 146, Volume 3835: "ULFTA, Seventh National Convention, 1926," File 8.

40. John Boyd, A Noble Cause Betrayed . . . but Hope Lives On—Pages from a Political Life: Memoirs of a Former Canadian Communist (Edmonton 1999), 7.

41. Kosty Kostaniuk, interviewed by RLH, July 1999.

42. T. Kobzey, "What We Are Studying at the Higher Educational Course," in Nashi Sproby [Our Endeavours].

43. LAC, CSIS RG 146, Volume 3835: "ULFTA Seventh National Convention, 1926." Also Dubas, Kostaniuk, Skrypnyk interviews; Bill Philipovich, interviewed by RLH, May 1998.

44. "Ukrainian Labour Farmer Temple Association—Winnipeg, Higher Educational Course," 26 October 1938, LAC, CSIS RG 146, Volume 3787: "ULFTA—Winnipeg," File 8; LAC, CSIS RG 146, Volume 3792: "AUUC—Winnipeg, Manitoba," File 7.

45. Mike Seychuk, interviewed by RLH, June 1998; Peter Krawchuk, "The Education of Leading Cadres," 32–36.

46. LAC, CSIS RG 146, Volume 3835: "ULFTA, 7th National Convention, 1926."

47. "Youth, A Focal Point of Pride and Concern," Ukrainian Canadian, 15 April 1968.

48. Svit molodi, March 1927, translated by L. Stavroff.

49. Krawchuk, Our History, 389; Boyova molod, September 1932, translated by L. Stavroff.

50. Skrypnyk interview.

51. Joyce Pawlyk, interviewed by RLH, August 1999.

52. Svit molodi, March 1927, translated by L. Stavroff.

53. Seychuk interview. See also Pawlyk and Skrypnyk interviews.

54. Svit molodi, October 1927; Ukrainian Canadian, 15 May 1952.

55. Krawchuk, Our History, 394, 399.

56. "Report on 1937 Convention, ULFTA," LAC, CSIS RG 146, Volume 3792: "AUUC: Winnipeg, Manitoba," Part 8.

57. Mike Seychuk, "What the Relationship Should Be Between the YCL and the YS ULFTA," Nasha Pratsia [Our Work], 5 February 1935, Organizational Bulletin of the Central Committee of the Youth Section, ULFTA, Stavroff Private Collection (Toronto), translated by L. Stavroff.

58. "Extracts from the 'Reports and Resolutions of the Twelfth Convention of Ukrainian Labour Farmer Temple Association in Canada' held 15–20 July 1931, in the Ukrainian Labour Temple at Winnipeg," LAC, CSIS RG 146, Volume 3792: "AUUC: Winnipeg, Manitoba," Part 11.

59. "Report re: ULFTA Convention 1937," LAC, CSIS RG 146, Volume 3792: "AUUC: Winnipeg, Manitoba," Part 7.

60. Fred Zwarch, "Towards a United Front of Youth Against War and Fascism" in Unite the Youth, c. 1936, Stavroff Private Collection (Toronto).

61. See for example Niechoda, 4–7.

62. J.O., "Five Years," in Unite the Youth.

63. Nick Hrynchyshyn, "What the Youth Section ULFTA Has Given to Me and What It Can Give to You" in Unite the Youth.

64. Letter written by M. Dembitski, Svit molodi, February 1930, translation by L. Stavroff.

65. Anna Gnit, "For a Progressive Children's Movement" in Unite the Youth.

66. Myron Shatulsky, interviewed by RLH, June 1998.

67. Bruce Kidd, "'Workers' Sport, Workers' Culture," in The Struggle for Canadian Sport (Toronto 1996), 164.

68. Report "re Ukrainian Labour Farmer Temple Ass'n, Winnipeg–Sports Club Performance, Feb 2," February 3, 1933, LAC, CSIS RG 146, Volume 3792: "AUUC—Winnipeg, Manitoba," File 6.

69. *Svit molodi*, March 1927; May 1929, translated by L. Stavroff.

70. *Resolutions of the Provincial Conference of ULFTA Youth Section, September 1–2, 1934* (Toronto 1934), Stavroff Private Collection (Toronto), translated by L. Stavroff; "Report re Ukrainian Labour-Farmer Temple Ass'n Schools and Instructional Methods," 2 Oct 1934, LAC, CSIS RG 146, Volume 3792: "AUUC—Winnipeg, Manitoba," File 7.

71. Petrachenko interview.

72. Hillman interview.

73. Vera Woremiuk, interviewed by RLH, June 1998. Also Seychuk, Hillman, and Petrachenko interviews.

74. Seychuk interview.

75. John Boyd, email to author, 19 July 2007.

76. See *Album of the Workers Trading Cooperative Limited* (Toronto 1933).

77. Report "re Ukrainian Labour Farmer Temple Ass'n, Winnipeg–Sports Club Performance, Feb 2," February 3, 1933, LAC, CSIS RG 146, Volume 3792: "AUUC—Winnipeg, Manitoba," File 6.

78. LAC, CSIS RG 146, Volume 3835: "ULFTA, Seventh National Convention, 1926."

79. *Svit molodi*, April 1932, translation by L. Stavroff.

80. *Svit molodi*, March 1927, translation by L. Stavroff.

81. *Nasha Pratsia* [*Our Work*].

82. *Svit molodi*, June 1930, translated by L. Stavroff.

83. *Boyova molod*, June 1932, translated by Orysia Zaporazan.

84. Myron Shatulsky interview.

85. Philipovich interview.

86. Michael Korol, "AUUC Youth Discussion: 28 Years' Experience of Youth Movement," *Ukrainian Canadian*, 1 May 1953.

87. *Resolutions of the Provincial Conference of ULFTA Youth Section, September 1–2, 1934*; *Nasha Pratsia* [*Our Work*].

88. "Re AUUC—Montreal, P. Que.," 20 January 1956, LAC, CSIS RG 146, Volume 3757: "AUUC—Case History Canada," Part 1.

89. Krawchuk, ed., *Our Stage*, 86–88.

PRIMARY DOCUMENT

Winnipeg Folk Dancing School, 1927

Source: AUUC—WBA Archives, Winnipeg, Manitoba. With permission from the WBA Archives.

Study Questions

1. How were children and youth in the twentieth century able to express themselves politically?
2. Describe the children in the *Montreal Herald* newspaper photo and the image from the Winnipeg Folk Dancing School. How do the children and youth in the pictures compare and contrast?
3. The authors insist that we take children's agency into account when writing history. What are the benefits and limitations of this concept of agency?

Selected Bibliography

Articles

Hill, Janice, "Politicizing Canadian Childhood Using a Governmentality Framework," *Social History/Historie sociale* 33, 65 (2000): 169–82.

Hinther, Rhonda L., "'They Said the Course Would Be Wasted on Me Because I Was a Girl': Mothers, Daughters, and Shifting Forms of Female Activism in the Ukrainian Left in Twentieth-Century Canada," *Atlantis* 32, 1 (2007): 103–13.

Kennelly, Jacqueline, "Learning to Protest: Youth Activist Cultures in Contemporary Urban Canada," *Review of Education, Pedagogy, and Cultural Studies* 31, 4 (2009): 293–315.

Moses, Nigel Roy, "Establishing Precedents: Women's Student Activism and Social Change in the (Canadian) National Union of Students, 1972–1979," *Historical Studies in Education/ Revue d'histoire de l'éducation* 22, 2 (Fall 2010).

Myers, Tamara, and Joan Sangster, "Retorts, Runaways and Riots: Patterns of Resistance in Canadian Reform Schools for Girls," *Journal of Social History* 34, 4 (2001): 669–97.

Naylor, James, "Socialism for a New Generation: CCF Youth in the Popular Front Era," *The Canadian Historical Review* 94, 1 (March 2013): 55–79.

Prokop, Manfred, "Canadianization of Immigrant Children: Role of the Rural Elementary School in Alberta, 1900–1930," *Alberta History* 37 (Spring 1989): 1–10.

Shamai, Shmuel, "The Jews and the Public Education System: The Students' Strike over the "Flag Fight" in Toronto after the First World War," *Canadian Jewish Historical Society Journal*, 10 (Fall 1988): 46–53.

Stanley, Timothy, "White Supremacy, Chinese Schooling, and School Segregation in Victoria: The Case of the Chinese Students' Strike, 1922–1923," *Historical Studies in Education/ Revue d'histoire de l'éducation* 2 (Fall 1990): 287–305.

Books

Ashworth, Mary, *Children of the Canadian Mosaic: a Brief History to 1950*. Toronto: OISE Press, 1993.

Bagnell, Kenneth, *The Little Immigrants: The Orphans Who Came to Canada*. Toronto: Macmillan of Canada, 1980.

Kohli, Marjorie, *Golden Bridge: Young Immigrants to Canada, 1883–1939*. Toronto: Dundurn Group, 2003.

Parker, R.A., *Uprooted: the Shipment of Poor Children to Canada, 1867–1917*. Bristol, UK: Policy Press, 2008.

3 Socializing Boys: Masculinity and Violence

Editors' Introduction

Today, Canadians live in a culture saturated with violence. War, genocide, rape, mass killings, and their representations in our popular culture—movies, videogames, Twitter, YouTube channels—suggest a connection between gender—especially masculinity—and violence. The question of whether boys are "naturally" violent or taught to be so is a contemporary obsession of parents, educators, and policy-makers. In this chapter, we turn to the history of boys and weaponry to see what "historicizing" masculinity and violence can teach us. The two essays explore historical aspects of what we might call "the culture of violence" in Canada, particularly since the turn of twentieth century, in terms of its relationship to boys. Both pieces show how, a century ago, the path to manhood for boys involved guns and killing for one's country and empire. That is, boys were to embrace violence of a particular kind, in a specific context, in order to demonstrate that they were worthy citizens and men.

R. Blake Brown explores how ideas about proper boyhood at the turn of the century closely paralleled those of upstanding men, particularly as they pertained to Britain's aggressive pursuit of empire. The primary document accompanying Brown's essay, a 1904 advertisement for the Stevens Firearm Company, demonstrates how boyhood was a central focus in the promotion of guns. As the ad makes clear, the boy who practised shooting would soon become a "crack shot" and the envy of his friends. Adult gun culture, including hunting, rifle shooting, woodcraft, military drill, and eventually firearm ownership, was promoted to boys through popular organizations, schools, consumer culture, and with the state's eager co-operation. Imperialism, consumer capitalism, and the state's legal framework fostered popular acceptance of guns as part of growing up for boys. The promotion of gun culture as boyhood culture established a particular kind of boy as the ideal: a boy willing and able to go to war to defend Britain's (and therefore Canada's) interests, a boy who avoided the "feminizing" forces of modern city life, a boy not part of the immigrant classes who were often branded as inherently and criminally "violent and un-British." Given this context, the enlistment of around 20,000 underage boys into the Canadian militia during the Great War (1914–18), Tim Cook's subject here, seems inevitable and unsurprising.

Tim Cook's article on the involvement of underage boy soldiers in Canada's Expeditionary Force overseas shows that participation in the war effort—even by the "too young"—was supported by government, by broader societal norms, and by boys themselves. The two essays in this chapter therefore have interesting connections. Brown explores the deep-seated attachment to guns and gun culture that marked boyhood in the early decades of the twentieth century. Cook pulls this thread forward, mapping out how dominant masculine norms of the willing soldier citizen, proficiently trained in defending British values and hungry to avenge fallen comrades, played out in the lives of boys who went to the battlefields of France and Britain. The primary document that accompanies Cook's essay, sheet music for a very popular 1916 patriotic song written by Gordon V. Thompson, reminds us that girls were also implicated in social and cultural pressure to support war and soldiering, albeit it in different ways. Cook is careful to avoid casting the underage soldiers merely as victims of adult pressure, government betrayal, or cultural propaganda. Instead, he provides a detailed analysis of why underage boys were attracted to military service and how military and governmental agencies, as well as the boys' own families, responded to their service.

"Every Boy Ought to Learn to Shoot and to Obey Orders": Guns, Boys, and the Law in English Canada from the Late Nineteenth Century to the Great War

R. BLAKE BROWN

I am the famously funny toy;
Made with a special view to destroy.[1]

In 1899, Stephen Leacock poked fun at the lies parents told (and tell) children at Christmas. He described a young boy, Hoodoo McFiggin, bursting with excitement prior to opening each gift delivered from Santa Claus, and who, oddly, remained excessively cheerful as each present turned out to contain a practical item, such as a toothbrush or a Bible. Leacock's story included a wish list of what young McFiggin, and presumably other Canadian boys at the time, dreamed of acquiring. The boy "prayed every night for weeks that Santa Claus would bring him a pair of skates and a puppy-dog and an air-gun and a bicycle and a Noah's ark and a sleigh and a drum."[2] To modern eyes, this list may seem unremarkable. However, the

Source: From *Canadian Historical Review*, 93, 2 (June 2012): 196–226. Reprinted with permission from University of Toronto Press (www.utpjournals.com).

assumption that an "air gun" was a suitable gift for a boy was relatively new. In the late nineteenth century, Canadians encouraged young people to develop familiarity and skill with weapons.[3] The after-effects of inculcating a gun culture in young people remains with us, as anyone who has surveyed the armoury of toy guns at every Toys "R" Us well knows.

From the late nineteenth century to the Great War, firearms became a key part of boy and male youth culture in English Canada.[4] While firearms had long been useful tools for rural Canadians to hunt, kill pests, protect property, and sometimes commit crimes, in the late nineteenth century guns became more than practical implements—they became desired consumer items. Two factors contributed to the growing nexus between guns and young people before the Great War. The first was an interwoven set of cultural assumptions concerning manhood and imperialism. By the 1890s, imperialist sentiments had infused the growing interest in hunting, advocates of which celebrated the value of rifle shooting on the ground that it made boys into ideal British men. Worries about both the alleged feminization of urban youth and boys' lack of discipline also motivated proponents of military drill and rifle training. The perceived value of rifle shooting thus led governments to encourage training for school-age children in shooting. The second factor was economic. Businesses heavily marketed cheap, mass-produced arms in this period. Gun manufacturers and retailers employed several aggressive sales techniques, such as emphasizing that using firearms could inculcate manly virtues, and redefining some weapons as toys to make them into acceptable and desirable consumer items.

The use of weapons by boys and youth led to a number of apprehended social ills. Critics complained of accidental shootings. Some people also expressed environmental concerns, including the belief that young people armed with small rifles decimated animal populations. In addition, a few Canadians worried about the long-term effects of militarizing a generation of youth. Given the state's interest in encouraging gun use by boys and youth, however, legislative efforts to limit access to firearms were minimal. In 1892 and 1913, the Canadian government passed Criminal Code provisions that placed modest limitations on to whom certain weapons could be sold, but the widespread assumption that some kinds of arms were acceptable for most boys and youth helped ensure that these measures frequently went unenforced.

How guns became playthings for young people is largely unexplored in the Canadian and international historiography. Also, unlike in the United States, scholars have given little attention to the history of firearm regulation in Canada.[5] A full examination of firearms, gun control, and young people requires drawing from, and contributing to, a diverse set of historiographical literatures relating to hunting, environmentalism, militarism, consumer culture, imperialism, gender, state formation, legal change, social reform, and youth culture. The analysis is divided into four parts: a survey of the arms available to Canadian youth by the early twentieth century; a consideration of the cultural attitudes expressed regarding boys, youth, and guns; a

discussion of the perceived dangers of these weapons; and, finally, an examination of governments' responses to the apprehended dangers of arming a generation of young people.

Firearms for Boys

The appearance, functionality, and cost of arms available to boys and youth changed dramatically by the early twentieth century. Technological advances, for example, revolutionized pistols. The most important innovation was the creation of multi-shot "revolvers." Such arms declined markedly in price through the 1870s and 1880s, in part because of the excess manufacturing capability developed in the United States during the American Civil War. By the early 1880s, Toronto and Winnipeg retailers sold various kinds of revolvers, some for $1.50 or less.[6]

"Toy pistols" also became available in Canada. These pistols took several forms. Some were small calibre (.22 calibre) guns that fired blank cartridges. Others exploded a detonating wafer charged with a fulminating compound.[7] These extremely cheap "toys" were sold in the 1880s in the United States, often to celebrate the Fourth of July. Many Canadian retailers also offered such toy guns. For example, as early as 1869 one Halifax merchant advertised a "patent revolver for boys" as "quite a new and ingenious Toy, which can be fired five times in succession."[8] By the end of the nineteenth century, many other retailers carried toy pistols. The Consolidated Stationery Company of Winnipeg, for example, advertised toy pistols in 1900 and 1901 as a means of celebrating Victoria Day, while Simpson's included a cap gun in its Christmas 1906 catalogue.[9]

Air rifles also appeared in Canada. The air gun was long deemed an "assassin's weapon" because of its ability to fire almost silently. American companies, however, reshaped public opinion about such guns when they began to mass produce and market inexpensive air rifles. In 1888, the Plymouth Iron Windmill Company manufactured the first all-metal air gun. The company subsequently changed its name to the Daisy Manufacturing Company, began developing new models, including repeating air rifles, and slowly consolidated its market position. At first, businesses did not usually target children; instead, they often advertised air guns as suitable for adult entertainment. For example, in 1896 the Griffiths Corporation appealed to middle-class men and women, suggesting that air guns "furnish excellent amusement for lawn or parlour." The company's air guns sold for one dollar and up.[10] This low price was not unusual. A new Daisy air rifle could be purchased for just ninety-nine cents in Saint John in 1896, while in 1913 one Edmonton retailer offered several models ranging in price from $1.10 to $1.98.[11] Youth could graduate from air rifles to more powerful arms, especially .22 calibre rifles. A number of companies produced such rifles, the small size of which often created the sense that they could be safely handled by young people. Like air rifles, such guns were inexpensive. Eaton's, for example, offered .22 calibre rifles for as little as two dollars in 1899.[12]

A Fertile Field for Boys and Guns

An interconnected set of cultural attitudes concerning masculinity, modernity, imperialism, militarism, and hunting led many English Canadians to accept and even encourage the use of arms by young people. For example, imperialist sentiment was perceptible in Canadians' growing interest in hunting with firearms. As John MacKenzie notes, hunting was "a mark of the fitness of the dominant race, a route to health, strength, and wealth, an emblem of imperial rule, and an allegory of human affairs."[13] Imperialists saw hunting as having the added benefit of improving the martial skills of Canadians. Men learned to track prey, subsist in natural settings, and, most importantly, shoot at moving targets. Deer, moose, bears, or rabbits would, in wartime, be replaced by enemy soldiers. Sport, especially hunting, was thus "ideal training for the manly game of war."[14] This assumption encouraged efforts to give boys access to firearms.

A number of Canadians also believed too many urban boys led sedentary lives that provided little opportunity for differentiation between the sexes. The sense of uncertainty created by the social adjustments of the late nineteenth century seemed to require a return to "core" cultural values, which, for many, meant socializing young people in how to be manly men. The growth of hunting as a pastime reflected this concern. Middle-class, urban Canadian men took cues from British gentlemen in advocating sport hunting as a respectable, manly activity. British sport hunters (and their Canadian counterparts) were part of a movement for outdoor middle-class recreation at a time when reformers decried cities as unsanitary and rife with poverty. Urban residents thus sought out "pure" outdoor recreation. As the size of the middle class grew, so did the pool of potential recreational hunters responding to a desire to demonstrate their manliness in the face of the modern industrial, urban world.[15] This interest in hunting had important ramifications for the regulation of firearms, as most men encouraged young people to shoot as well.

Imperialist sentiment also resulted in renewed interest in the militia and military affairs throughout English Canada—a trend that led to efforts to make arms available to youth. By the 1890s, various journalists, politicians, and militia leaders argued that Canada could support Britain effectively in future wars only if Canadian men developed acumen in rifle shooting. As well, those worried over a possible attack by the United States believed that marksmanship using modern magazine-loading rifles was key to defending Canada. Canadians' limited experience with armed conflict strengthened the desire to create an armed citizenry. A key lesson taken from the Anglo-Boer War of 1899–1902, for example, was that future conflicts would be won by armies of amateur citizen-soldiers trained to be crack rifle shots. According to the magazine *Rod and Gun in Canada*, for example, the "great lesson of the South African war" was that "every Briton must know how to shoot."[16] This emphasis on shooting skill led to efforts to train boys and youth to practise with rifles. The idea of instructing boys in military drill was not an entirely new idea, but more calls to train young people in rifle shooting found expression as imperialist sentiments intensified in the 1890s.[17]

Military drill and rifle shooting, like hunting, were also responses to concerns that modern urban life threatened the masculinity of men and youth. Exercise and participation in martial activities could stem moral and physical decay and encourage good character. Military drill, for instance, was believed to combat youth delinquency. Many urban residents expressed concern that boys loitered in the streets, made lewd remarks, spit tobacco, and violated middle-class ideals of proper behaviour. Such commentators called for lessons in good posture, healthy living, and obedience to authority. Training in the mass use of particular kinds of violence would create order by inculcating morality, manliness, and an ability to resist the evil temptations of the city.[18]

These attitudes led to efforts to train boys in the art of war. Boys' brigades represented an early effort to uplift youth in poor areas by blending recreation with military training. In Montreal, Major Fred Lydons enlisted into a boys' brigade young people who pledged abstinence and accepted military obedience. The group purchased rifles and drilled. Two other organizations proved even more important. First, the scouting movement begun by Robert Baden-Powell came to include rifle training. Baden-Powell's Scouting for Boys appeared in Canada in 1908, and by 1910 Canada had approximately 5,000 Scouts, a figure which climbed to 13,565 by September 1914. As several historians have noted, scouting was an imperialist organization influenced by muscular Christianity, anti-modernist sentiments, and middle-class ideas of hunting. Generally catering to boys between the ages of 11 and 14, scouting sought to turn boys into good citizens and good soldiers by inculcating patriotism and imperialism.[19] Baden-Powell, in fact, suggested that scouting was good training for war. He encouraged boys to shoot, writing in Scouting for Boys that "every boy ought to learn to shoot and to obey orders, else he is no more good when war breaks out than an old woman."[20] Some scouts practised target shooting in Montreal before the Great War. Following the outbreak of war, Baden-Powell published Marksmanship for Boys, in which he outlined how boys could receive the Red Feather award if they proved they could drill and shoot. The Canadian scouting movement awarded hundreds of marksmanship badges during the war.[21]

Even more important than Scouts in inculcating the importance of shooting was the cadet movement, which grew quickly with the support of

Canadian governments. In 1898, Ontario promised to grant 50 dollars to any school board that had a cadet corps of at least 25 boys. Ottawa integrated the cadets into the militia system with the 1904 Militia Act, which allowed Ottawa to provide cadet corps with arms. Minister of Militia Frederick Borden entered negotiations with the provinces to incorporate military training in schools as part of a national system so that every boy would learn to use a rifle. Borden's efforts received a boost with the establishment of the Lord Strathcona Trust designed to encourage drilling, physical training, and shooting in public schools. The cadet movement picked up even more steam after Sam Hughes became minister of militia following the 1911 election. Hughes increased the federal budget for cadets from $93,000 in 1912 to $400,000 in 1913, and ordered several thousand .22 calibre Ross rifles for cadets. By 1914 the number of cadets had reached almost 45,000.[22]

Gun retailers and manufacturers buttressed state efforts encouraging young people to shoot. The industrial manufacture of firearms resulted in excess production capacity, and businesses responded by marketing their goods more aggressively. Firearms thus became another commodity in the emerging Canadian consumer market. According to Keith Walden, business "tried to persuade individuals that personal identity depended not on geography, family background, religious values, occupation, or similar things, but on choices made among consumer goods found in the market-place."[23] Eaton's was a leader in the shift toward consumerism, a product of what David Monod calls the "retailing revolution" of the late nineteenth century that witnessed the emergence of "a national market, large-scale production, and mass merchandising."[24] Eaton's used large department stores, aggressive newspaper advertising, and mail-order catalogues to take advantage of a growing demand for consumer goods. Guns promised profits to retailers such as Eaton's, which sought to sell firearms to hunters, target shooters, and children and youth.[25]

This is not to say that retailers and manufacturers attempted to sell all kinds of weapons to boys and youth. In particular, businesses did not market pistols to young people, sensing such weapons were too dangerous. Such guns, however, were widely sold to the general public, with the result that some fell into young hands. Many hardware and second-hand stores carried handguns, and Canadian retailers followed the example of American stores in developing a mail-order business in revolvers.[26]

While retailers deemed pistols too dangerous for young people, businesses aggressively marketed other types of arms to children and youth, especially air guns. Retailers often described or portrayed such guns as toys. Eaton's employed this approach for a time, including air guns in the toy section of its 1892–3 Fall-Winter catalogue, while a Victoria retailer sold a variety of "military toys" in 1897, including Daisy air rifles. Eaton's shifted air guns to the firearm section of its catalogue in 1902, although the primary market for the air guns remained boys, as evidenced, for instance, when Eaton's called the King Air Rifle "a splendid rifle for boys" in 1910.[27] Many other retailers continued to advertise air rifles as toys. Simpson's included air rifles in the toy section of its 1906 Christmas catalogue, while a Red Deer, Alberta, retailer in 1914 advertised an air rifle as a "good toy for boys 7 to 15 years old."[28] Other retailers did not overtly claim that air rifles were for boys, but advertised them beside toys, thus implicitly suggesting the suitability of air rifles for young people.

A number of businesses suggested that young people could safely handle air rifles by offering them as compensation for selling products. This practice, according to Gary Cross, stemmed from toy-makers' realization that "children had limited financial autonomy," but "unlimited desires."[29] In Ontario, for example, boys could receive a free air rifle for selling twelve boxes of Dr Groves's Famous Stomach, Kidney, and Liver Pills. Businesses advertised similar offers in almost all parts of Canada, including in small-town newspapers, thus ensuring the availability of air rifles to boys and youth in smaller communities and rural areas. For example, a Toronto company offered a Daisy air rifle to boys in Wetaskiwin, Alberta, who sold forty sets of greeting cards.[30]

Businesses also actively marketed .22 calibre rifles to boys and youth in the early twentieth century. While retailers did not call such arms toys,

they placed advertisements beside or among toys, or named and described the guns with the intention of appealing to young people. Eaton's, for example, called the Stevens .22 "Little Scout" rifle a "splendid little rifle for boys or youths."[31] The J. Stevens Arms & Tool Company of Massachusetts consistently targeted youth in its Canadian advertisements. In 1902, the company portrayed boys shooting and recommended some of its models for "younger shooters."[32] The Canadian Ross Rifle Company also began to produce and market a .22 calibre "cadet" rifle, describing it as a "splendid arm for training boys or men" that was "perfectly safe."[33]

Companies sought to make firearms attractive consumer items for young people by emphasizing the beauty of their guns. C. Flood & Sons of Saint John described its air rifle as "the handsomest air rifle in the world,"[34] while the Western Specialty Company of Winnipeg offered a "genuine Steel, Black Walnut Air Rifle, handsomely nickelled and polished" to anyone who sold twelve Japanese silk fans.[35] Retailers also employed the ultimate symbol of the new consumerist mentality, Christmas, to sell air guns and .22 calibre rifles. Toronto's Charles Stark & Co., for instance, suggested in 1904 that as a Christmas present nothing was "nicer for a boy than a small .22 calibre rifle,"[36] while in 1910 Eaton's listed air guns and small game rifles as desirable "Gifts for Lively Boys" at Christmas.[37] Gun manufacturers enticed parents to purchase weapons for their children using Christmas. The Stevens Arms Company showed Santa Claus carrying a rifle and told parents that Santa would be speeding over rooftops "loaded down with Stevens Firearms for the youths of the land."[38] In employing the holiday season to market guns, retailers and manufacturers thus sought to take advantage of the burgeoning Canadian consumer culture.

Retailers also emphasized that owning or using a gun could transform boys into men. Given the cultural context in which many Canadians both celebrated imperialism and saw hunting and rifle shooting as antidotes to the deleterious effects of modern urban life, retailers advertised guns to boys with images and language that suggested using arms signified manliness and/or love of empire. The Stevens

Arms Company emphasized the role of firearms in turning boys into men in blunt terms: "Make a man of your boy by giving him a 'Stevens'; he will surely appreciate it, and you will add to the education of your son."[39] Businesses promoted the role of guns in bringing together father and son, thus allowing for invaluable bonding and the transfer of wisdom regarding how to be a man. A common suggestion was that arming your son would instill in him manly qualities, such as independence, self-sufficiency, and an ability to protect personal property, all of which were desirable characteristics in a liberal nation.[40]

These marketing strategies, combined with the growth in hunting and rifle shooting by adults, resulted in a substantial increase in the number of weapons entering Canada. Gun imports were valued at $93,015 in 1897, then began a rapid ascent, to $180,072 in 1901, to $459,878 in 1904, and to $900,031 in 1913.[41] These figures include all kinds of firearms, not only the value of guns used by young people, but nevertheless suggest a substantial increase in the availability of weapons in Canada prior to the Great War.

The Dangers of Boys and Guns

> Willie had a new toy pistol,
> Loaded it, and felt no doubt;
> But the doctor, with a twist'll
> Probe most of the fragments out.[42]

By the early twentieth century, Canadian boys and youth had available to them a veritable arsenal of weapons. Mass produced and cheap, revolvers, toy pistols, air guns, and .22 calibre rifles found their way into the hands of young people from coast to coast. The accessibility of these weapons, however, led to various concerns, including fears of gun accidents, worries over environmental destruction, and apprehension about creating a generation of violent youth.

Accidents were the biggest concern. Although it is impossible to quantify the problem, it is apparent that weapons of all sorts caused injuries and deaths. For example, cheap revolvers sometimes found their way into the hands of children, often with disastrous results. In the nineteenth century,

there was no legislation dictating that revolvers be stored safely or be unloaded when not in use, nor was there any age restriction (prior to 1892) regarding who could be sold a pistol. Not surprisingly, children got their hands on guns, and, beginning in the late 1870s, newspapers contained numerous stories of tragic pistol accidents.[43] In reflecting on one accidental shooting, a coroner's jury in 1901 thus called attention "to the careless way in which the revolver and cartridges were left lying around where children could get access to them."[44] Charles Allan Stuart of the Supreme Court of Alberta also heavily criticized the availability of handguns. "It is beyond my understanding why a revolver is allowed to be sold," he mused.[45] The Globe expressed concern as well, suggesting that "the unguarded revolver has more victims to its discredit than smallpox or any other infectious diseases." It thus made an appeal: "Let moral and social reformers consider the revolver."[46] The reference to moral and social reformers was telling, indicating that some people believed that the regulation of pistols should become part of the broader effort to more closely regulate society.[47]

"Toy" pistols proved a concern as well, for such guns caused a substantial number of injuries and deaths in the United States and, to a lesser extent, in Canada. In 1880, the Chicago Daily Tribune damned the toy pistol as the "most prolific of all sources of accidents to children."[48] Reports from across the United States explain the Daily Tribune's assertion. For example, in 1882 toy pistols led to the death of 28 boys in several American cities. Fatalities occurred in a number of ways, but most stemmed from "lockjaw" (tetanus) acquired when boys stuffed gravel, slate pencils, or old nails down the barrel to create projectiles, then accidentally or intentionally shot themselves or others with these makeshift bullets. Even without such projectiles, some toy guns could burn or break the skin if fired at close range.[49] The injuries and deaths caused by toy pistols led several American jurisdictions to ban the sale of such guns.[50]

Canadians noted accidents with toy pistols in the United States, Britain, and Canada, and cautioned against the use of such guns.[51] After a youngster shot a toy pistol at another boy in British

Columbia in 1880, the justice of the Victoria police court warned that toy pistols could kill if fired at close range at a vital part.[52] *Pleasant Hours*, a Methodist journal, declared in 1884 that "the toy pistol has been conceded to be a more dangerous weapon in the hand of the thoughtless boy than the real pistol."[53] Nova Scotia physician and senator William Johnston Almon said he had seen "a good many accidents happen from toy pistols," and he had "known children's eyes to be put out and severe wounds to be inflicted." Almon later told his fellow senators that he wanted to prohibit the sale of toy pistols because he had treated two boys who had injured themselves with toy pistols loaded with stones.[54]

Twenty-two calibre rifles and air guns were also deemed dangerous. Air rifles resulted in a spate of accidents. One example can illustrate the problem. In 1907, two boys in Toronto went down Dufferin Street with an air rifle. They came across a six-year-old boy and told him to raise his hands. The air rifle went off, striking the child in the eye.[55] Such accidents led to warnings, such as when the *Manitoba Morning Free Press* suggested that air guns were "exceedingly dangerous weapons in the hands of careless boys."[56] There were also many accidents involving .22 calibre rifles. For example, in 1910 a 13-year-old Montreal boy stumbled, causing the discharge of the .22 calibre rifle he carried, and the bullet lodged in the hip of his 14-year-old companion.[57] Such accidents led the *Cayley Hustler* of Alberta to complain about the frequency of accidents and to suggest that many men and boys were unaware of the dangers of guns, and "should be forbidden to handle a rifle at all for generally some one else is the victim of their ignorance."[58]

While accidents were the major concern, some Canadians also expressed worries that toy pistols encouraged boys to become too attached to real guns. *The Globe*, for example, believed that toy pistols contributed to the tendency of young men to arm themselves. The manufacturers and vendors of toy pistols had to accept blame because these "suggestive playthings breed in children a desire to handle the genuine article, and are thus directly answerable for many lamentable happenings."[59] A writer in Edmonton made a similar complaint in 1906. A

young man described being surprised by a boy pretending to rob him with a toy pistol. The writer condemned the use of realistic toy arms: "Does it not seem altogether beyond belief that any man in his right senses, after all the warnings we have had in the shape of murders and accidents, should allow his son the possession of even a supposedly harmless air gun, knowing how one thing leads to another?" "Firearms," he concluded, "and small boys have, or should have, no thing in common."[60]

Another complaint was that boys from cities used small rifles in suburban areas to shoot indiscriminately at animals and property. A newspaper from rural Ontario, the *Temiskaming Speaker*, discussed this problem in 1909 when it described an accident in which a man had been shot by a .22 rifle, presumably fired by a youth, while waiting on a railway platform. "Better to cut out the 'twenty two' and the 'air gun' entirely than have these accidents continue," concluded the *Speaker*.[61] A particular worry was that armed boys might destroy animal populations. In the first decade of the twentieth century, many Canadians expressed concern with the destruction of wildlife, and they deemed thoughtless boys to be part of the problem.[62] In Victoria, for instance, the Society for the Prevention of Cruelty to Animals discouraged boys and youth from slaughtering birds.[63] Complaints from the suburban areas of Toronto led the *Toronto Star* to suggest in October 1911 that the "annual invasion of the suburban districts by the city lad with his 22-calibre rifle has begun." The boy "goes out into the country bordering on the city limits and shoots squirrels, chipmonks [sic], birds, and anything that comes before his eyes," lamented the *Star*.[64] Thus, while Canadians generally encouraged boys to shoot, many believed there were reasonable limits to this activity that required enforcement.

Guns, Boys, and the Law

Canadians worried about the use of firearms by boys and youth at a time of growing concern with child safety. Social reformers in the pre-war period believed that the autonomy of young people had to be constrained in a rapidly changing social, cultural, and economic context. The result was, according to Cynthia Comacchio, the "expanded regulation of adolescence" with the purpose of "training the ideal, responsible, conscientious adult citizen."[65] As noted earlier, the goal of creating ideal citizens led to efforts to train young people to use firearms. Several provincial governments also enacted child protection legislation, established family courts, created evening curfews, and extended the period of compulsory schooling. In addition, the federal government passed the Juvenile Delinquents Act of 1908, which created the category of "juvenile" crime and empowered the state to deal aggressively with those deemed delinquent.[66] The concern that some boys had access to arms but lacked sufficient training or mental maturity, and the belief that young people might use guns for nefarious ends, led to efforts to regulate the availability of some weapons to some youth. The choices legislators made in framing these laws illuminates how they determined when youth had sufficient capacity to be entrusted safely with weapons, and how legislation sought to delineate boundaries between the problematic categories of "safe" and "unsafe" weapons and between "toys" and "firearms."

Some arms seemed easy to categorize as dangerous weapons. Legislators perceived revolvers to be so dangerous that few people, of any age, were permitted to walk about with such guns. In 1877, Parliament banned the carrying of pistols unless a person had a reasonable cause to fear an assault or injury to himself, to his family, or to his property. Ottawa also attempted to prevent accidents by dictating a fine of between 20 and 50 dollars (or up to 30 days in jail) for anyone who pointed a pistol or air gun at another person, whether loaded or unloaded, without a lawful excuse.[67]

Pressure for limiting young people's access to pistols emerged in the Senate by the late 1880s, and in 1892 the first Canadian Criminal Code prohibited the sale or gift of pistols (and ammunition for such arms) to anyone under the age of 16. This was the first time that Ottawa placed an age restriction on who could purchase guns. The government's decision to impose an age restriction was a typical response to perceived social problems in this period, a time when legislators imposed or altered the minimum age at which youth were allowed to leave school to enter the workforce, or to engage in sexual relations. An age restriction on to whom guns could be sold fits within this approach; it created a demarcation line between youth and adulthood that sought to prevent the use of pistols by reckless young people. The 1892 Criminal Code also prohibited the sale or gift of air guns to anyone under the age of 16.[68] This reflected the traditional sense that air guns were sneaky, unmanly, and potentially dangerous arms. In 1892, air rifles were not yet widely accepted as toys. As air rifles became defined as toys, however, the law would be frequently disregarded, as many people saw little potential harm in young people owning an air gun.

The 1892 legislation contained important loopholes that reflected attitudes toward other weapons and the ability of adults to successfully supervise armed boys and youth. One important loophole was that Ottawa did not ban the possession of air guns or pistols by those under 16. Parliament therefore allowed parents or organizations to place such guns in the hands of young people. Nor did the law ban the sale of rifles to youth. The widespread support for efforts to train boys and youth in rifle shooting and the mesh of ideas concerning imperialism, hunting, and manliness meant that the state would not completely disarm young people. Parliament thus made no effort to regulate weapons deemed beneficial, and boys and youth continued to have free access to rifles until 1913.

Occasional voices spoke out in favour of new laws, or, at the very least, stricter enforcement of the 1892 legislation. The *Winnipeg Morning Free Press*, for instance, complained that retailers disregarded the Criminal Code provisions, while in 1898 a coroner's jury examining an accidental shooting deprecated the practice of letting boys shoot and recommended a law forbidding children under 16 from handling all kinds of firearms.[69] In making a case for new laws, some commentators asserted that weapons were not toys. *The Globe* suggested that some people regarded a small calibre rifle "as a toy," an impression the newspaper tried to correct: "Many fatalities have resulted from a failure to appreciate or consider the strength and efficiency of the various makes of 22-calibre rifles, and something should be done to dispel popular ignorance in this regard."[70]

Given the widespread encouragement of shooting by boys and youth, such calls often went unheeded, and debates over the wisdom of allowing young people to have access to rifles were largely one-sided. This can be seen in a parliamentary debate stemming from rural objections to the policy of encouraging boys to shoot. There were concerns that military drill was so attractive to youth that it was drawing farm boys into cities. As well, a few parliamentarians suggested that boys need not be inculcated with militarism at too early an age. Ontario MPP Thomas Simpson Sproule expressed all of these concerns in 1903, and he asserted that there was "a possibility of carrying this military spirit a little too far."[71]

Advocates of teaching boys to shoot dismissed such claims by arguing that rifle practice created manly character and by drawing upon the rhetoric of imperialism. Sam Hughes asserted that wherever "you have a strong military spirit, you have more manhood in the youth of the country."[72] Frederick Borden also defended the policy of teaching boys to shoot. He quoted from literature suggesting that the discipline and exercise of rifle training would improve boys' "health, strengthen their moral fibre and add to their professional, industrial or labour value when they are attained to manhood and entered on the serious business of their lives."[73] Advocates of teaching youth to shoot thus saw nothing wrong with boys arming themselves with rifles, hunting small animals, practising target shooting, and pretending to be soldiers for the Crown. While accidents were a real concern, the perceived solution was to give boys more training in the use of arms, not less. For example, in a column devoted to women's issues, the *Victoria Daily Colonist* advised mothers to have their children trained to use firearms. While guns were dangerous, "a well-trained youngster will soon learn to be proud of the fact that he is trusted with a real gun."[74] Given the dominance of these attitudes, Ottawa took little action to prevent boys and youth from acquiring most weapons.

With Ottawa taking little action, municipal authorities sometimes tried to prevent young people from using guns in highly populated areas. Many municipalities had long-standing bylaws banning the discharge of firearms within municipal limits, and some youth found themselves charged under such laws, often after an errant shot harmed a bystander. In 1906, for example, a boy in Saint John had to appear in police court for violating a local bylaw after he purchased a mail-order air rifle and then accidentally shot another boy in the lip.[75]

Gun accidents involving children led individuals to seek remedies in the civil courts, with mixed results. In 1910, the Divisional Court of the Ontario High Court of Justice held merchants liable after they sold an air gun to a 13-year-old boy, who then promptly struck the daughter of a neighbour in the eye while attempting to shoot a bird.[76] In another case, from 1911, a 12-year-old boy accidentally shot another 12-year-old in the eye when they were out shooting together in Smiths Falls, Ontario. The father of the injured boy sought compensation through a negligence claim against the shooter's father who, according to the claimant, loaned the gun to his son. The trial court found in favour of the plaintiff, but the Divisional Court of the Ontario High Court of Justice reversed the lower court decision on the ground that the injured boy was bright and knowledgeable about guns and had been contributorily negligent when he walked in front of the gun before it went off.[77]

Despite the general acceptance of boys using rifles, Ottawa passed new legislation in 1913 to affect their access to these arms. The motivation for this change was twofold. First, the continuing problem of firearm accidents motivated legislators. Many members of Parliament came to the conclusion that rifles, even small calibre rifles, were not toys. They were weapons, albeit ones that youth should learn to use under the guidance of fathers or in an organization such as cadets. Second, legislators had become increasingly concerned about the use of guns by recent immigrants, and thus the limits on the sale of all firearms to young people represented an attempt to prevent immigrant youth, and boys in particular, from acquiring guns.

A general desire to pass new gun control measures grew in the early 1910s. This had much to do with the fact that the 1910 to 1913 period saw especially heavy rates of immigration, peaking at over 400,000 in 1913.[78] Many Canadians believed that the new immigrants who came from southern and eastern Europe were inherently violent and "un-British." In Manitoba, for example, Justice James Prendergast of the Manitoba Court of King's Bench deemed foreigners too quick to use revolvers, and he implored a grand jury to make a presentment asking for tougher gun laws. New immigrants were "introducing a custom from which we have been free in the past," for they were "indulging in the foolish practice of carrying firearms."[79] The grand jury agreed with Justice Prendergast, recommending stronger laws to regulate sales and to stop recreational shooting along the Red River and Assiniboine River.

Several provinces passed legislation designed to disarm immigrants in the early 1910s. Ontario acted first, enacting the Offensive Weapons Act in 1911, which stipulated that persons who sold a pistol or air gun to someone lacking a certificate issued under s.118 of the Criminal Code (which under the Criminal Code was needed to carry a handgun) or a permit from the superintendent of the Ontario Provincial Police or from a chief constable of a city or town were liable to fines, or to imprisonment for up to six months. Sellers also had to keep detailed records of handguns and air guns sold. The desire to target immigrants carrying guns was evidenced by the act's requirement that police make a report to the minister of the interior when they found foreigners with illegal weapons "with the view towards deporting such person under the Immigration Act."[80] Other provinces soon passed similar legislation, including Manitoba and Saskatchewan in 1912, and British Columbia in 1913.[81] Requiring a permit to purchase an air rifle caused some consternation. Toronto Deputy Chief William Stark, however, lauded the measure because the "supply of guns and air rifles to boys will be stopped." In his view, there were "altogether too many air rifles in the hands of careless boys. They are very dangerous, and very mischievous. No living thing, bird or squirrel, or anything else, is safe within the city limits, or the suburbs."[82]

The federal government eventually passed Criminal Code amendments in 1913 that largely copied these provincial acts. Ottawa made it an offence for anyone to sell any kind of firearm to a minor under 16, or to sell or give a pistol or air rifle to anyone under 16. Once again, there were important loopholes. Ottawa did not ban the possession of weapons by boys under 16—just the sale and/or gift of weapons—and thus allowed for parents or organizations to provide rifles to young people to hunt or to target shoot as part of an organized group.[83]

Conclusion

The period of the late nineteenth and early twentieth centuries was a key time in the formation of a relationship between young people and firearms. Imperialist sentiments led to efforts to encourage boys and youth to use rifles. Anti-modernist concerns also helped promote the use of guns, as many Canadians believed firearms could instill masculinity in a generation whose urban environment risked making them effeminate. The mass production and skilled marketing of inexpensive firearms further cemented the connections between guns, and boys and youth. Businesses redefined some arms, in particular air rifles, as toys. Other guns, such as small-calibre rifles, were clearly marketed to youth, but Canadians debated whether they were guns or toys. Despite widespread support for encouraging the use of firearms by boys and youth, the perceived spike in accidents caused by pistols, toy guns, air guns, and small rifles, and worries over the use of arms by immigrants eventually led to modest action. Ironically, the very factors that led Canadians to train young people to use guns, such as industrialization and urbanization, made it necessary to regulate weapons through state mechanisms and organizations like the Scouts and the cadet movement.

In the interwar period, Canadians would continue to struggle with this issue. There were many more complaints about gun accidents, property damage, and the possibility that using firearms or playing with toy guns risked creating a generation of violent youth. The same period, however, saw Ottawa exert less effort in encouraging young people to shoot. This decreased government involvement reflected many of the lessons taken from the Great

War that undermined the rationales for strengthening the relationship between boys and guns. The war destroyed the belief that conflicts could be won by citizen soldiers trained as expert rifle shots. Instead, it demonstrated the importance of massed artillery, tanks, aircraft, and machine guns. The war also sapped imperialism of much of its allure. As a result, efforts slackened to create a new generation of citizen-soldiers.[84]

This is not to say that the connection between young people and guns was broken. The marketing of toy arms, air guns, and small calibre rifles to boys and youth continued, and, in some respects, increased in intensity. Hollywood films, critics charged, encouraged a celebration of gun-toting gangsters. By the 1930s, retailers marketed air rifles and toy guns with advertisements influenced by the "cowboy craze" that swept North America. Millions of toy pistols allowed American (and Canadian) boys to celebrate alleged cowboy values, such as rugged manly individualism. After the Second World War, guns remained a staple part of Canadian toy catalogues and were often portrayed in popular culture as implements of humour (on shows like *Bugs Bunny*) or tools of valour (think G.I. Joe).[85]

The history of weapons laws and young people in the late nineteenth and early twentieth centuries also hinted at the challenges that advocates of gun control have long had to deal with: gun regulation is very difficult to enforce. Historians of social and moral reform note that police often shied away from implementing statute law to the letter. Limitations on police resources and the attitudes of individual officers toward the particular offence often meant that criminal activity, even when detected, went unprosecuted.[86] The regulation of guns and boys thus highlights what Sharon Myers has recently described as the "fractured, conflicted, confused, and apocryphal character of state regulation and response."[87] This is discernible in the implementation of the 1892 and 1913 laws. Authorities often failed to enforce the 1892 Criminal Code provision, and 20 years after the passage of the 1913 legislation several members of Parliament expressed surprise that the Criminal Code included a law limiting the availability of guns to boys and youth. Of the parliamentarians who knew about the provision, many stated that the ban was widely disregarded.[88] Preventing the use of guns by young people would thus prove challenging, perhaps because of the strong link between masculinity and firearms created earlier in the century.

Notes

1. "The Toy Pistol," *True Witness and Catholic Chronicle*, 9 Aug. 1882, 1.
2. Stephen Leacock, "Hoodoo McFiggin's Christmas," *Canadian Magazine*, Jan. 1899, 285.
3. Historians have made conceptual distinctions between boy and youth. As Cynthia Comacchio, among others, has shown, the term youth (and juvenile) came to refer to the transitional life stage between boyhood and male adulthood. This article considers the connection between weapons and both boys and youth, focusing on young people 16 years of age and under. Cynthia R. Comacchio, *The Dominion of Youth: Adolescence and the Making of a Modern Canada, 1920-1950* (Waterloo, ON: Wilfrid Laurier University Press, 2006), 2-3.
4. Analyzing the changing attitude to firearms and young people in all of English Canada is of course a challenging exercise. The research plan employed for the present article entailed an examination of a range of sources, including provincial and federal legislation, parliamentary debates, reported judicial decisions, department store catalogues, hunting and police periodicals, archival records of the scouting movement, and an array of digitized Canadian and American newspapers and journals. Unfortunately, these materials capture public discourse by adults over the use of arms by young people, but shed less light on how boys and youth thought about firearms. Ann McGrath has studied a related topic from the perspective of young people: "Playing Colonial: Cowgirls, Cowboys, and Indians in Australia and North America," *Journal of Colonialism and Colonial History* 2, no. 1 (2001): 1-27.
5. Attitudes towards toy guns in Cold War America have been explored by Angela F. Keaton, "Backyard Desperadoes: American Attitudes Concerning Toy Guns in the Early Cold War Era," *Journal of American Culture* 33, no. 3 (2010): 183-96. For studies of Canadian firearm laws in this period, see Samuel A. Bottomley, "Parliament, Politics and Policy: Gun Control in Canada, 1867-2003" (Ph.D. diss., Carleton University, 2004); R. Blake Brown, "'Pistol Fever': Regulating Revolvers in Late-Nineteenth-Century Canada," *Journal of the Canadian Historical Association* 20, no. 1 (2009): 107-38; Gerald Pelletier, "Le Code criminel Canadien, 1892-1939: Le controle des armes a feu,"

Crime, Histoire & Sociétés 6, no. 2 (2002): 51–79; Philip C. Stenning, "Guns & the Law," *Beaver* 80, no. 6 (2000–1): 6–7.

6. David A. Hounshell, *From the American System to Mass Production, 1800–1932: The Development of Manufacturing Technology in the United States* (Baltimore: Johns Hopkins University Press, 1984), 46–50; Lee Kennett and James LaVerne Anderson, *The Gun in America: The Origins of a National Dilemma* (Westport, CT: Greenwood, 1975), 83–107; *Globe*, 26 Aug. 1882, 5; *Winnipeg Daily Sun*, 16 Apr. 1883, 6; [Winnipeg] *Morning Telegram*, 26 July 1900, 2.

7. Firearms are frequently designated by the internal diameter of their barrel. A ".22 calibre" thus has a barrel with an internal diameter of .22 inches.

8. "Toys for the Million," *Halifax Citizen*, 2 Nov. 1869, 3.

9. "Celebrate!," *Commercial*, 12 May 1900, 1128; "Fire Works and Flags Commercial," *Commercial*, 11 May 1901), 864; *Simpson's Christmas Catalogue*, 1906, 92, Library and Archives Canada (LAC), www.collectionscanada.gc.ca/mailorder/029006-119.01-e.php?page_ecopy=n-lc006877.92&brws_s=1&brws=3&&&&&&&&&&. Also see "Spencer's Arcade," *Victoria Daily Colonist*, 10 Dec. 1897, 4.

10. "Air Guns," *Globe*, 22 Sept. 1896, 8. On the sale of air guns as parlour games in the United States, see Gary Cross, *Kids' Stuff: Toys and the Changing World of American Childhood* (Cambridge, MA: Harvard University Press, 1997), 24, 66. On Daisy, see Michael Landry, "It's a Daisy!," *Michigan History* 90, no. 1 (2006): 28–38.

11. *Saint John Daily Sun*, 20 May 1896, 7; *Edmonton Capital*, 5 Sept. 1913, 9. For other examples of inexpensive air guns, see *Cycling*, 10 June 1891, 155; *Toronto Star*, 17 Dec. 1901, 8; *Red Deer News*, 16 Dec. 1914, 4.

12. T. Eaton Co., *Spring and Summer 1899 Catalogue*, F229-1-0-17, Archives of Ontario (AO). Also see [Winnipeg] *Morning Telegram*, 26 July 1900, 2; *Red Deer News*, 21 Aug. 1912, 9; T. Eaton Co., *Fall and Winter 1913–1914 Catalogue*, F229-1-0-47, AO; *Red Deer News*, 20 Aug. 1913, 7.

13. John M. MacKenzie, "Hunting and the Natural World in Juvenile Literature," in *Imperialism and Juvenile Literature*, ed. Jeffrey Richards (Manchester, UK: Manchester University Press, 1989), 170. Also see George Colpitts, *Game in the Garden: A Human History of Wildlife in Western Canada to 1940* (Vancouver: UBC Press, 2002), 63–102; Greg Gillespie, "The Empire's Eden: British Hunters, Travel Writing, and Imperialism in Nineteenth-Century Canada," in *The Culture of Hunting in Canada*, ed. Jean L. Manore and Dale G. Miner (Vancouver: UBC Press, 2007), 42–55; John M. MacKenzie, *The Empire of Nature: Hunting, Conservation, and British Imperialism* (Manchester, UK: Manchester University Press, 1988); John M. MacKenzie, "The Imperial Pioneer and Hunter and the British Masculine Stereotype in Late Victorian and Edwardian Times," in *Manliness and Morality: Middle-Class Masculinity in Britain and America, 1800–1940*, ed.

J.A. Mangan and James Walvin (Manchester: Manchester University Press, 1987), 176–98.

14. R.G. Moyles and Doug Owram, *Imperial Dreams and Colonial Realities: British Views of Canada, 1880–1914* (Toronto: University of Toronto Press, 1988), 62.

15. Cynthia Comacchio, "Lost in Modernity: 'Maladjustment' and the 'Modern Youth Problem,' English Canada, 1920–50," in *Lost Kids: Vulnerable Children and Youth in Twentieth-Century Canada and the United States*, ed. Mona Gleason, Tamara Myers, Leslie Paris, and Veronica Strong-Boag (Vancouver: UBC Press, 2010), 53–71; Greg Gillespie, *Hunting for Empire: Narratives of Sport in Rupert's Land, 1840–70* (Vancouver: UBC Press, 2007), 35–59; Tina Loo, "Of Moose and Men: Hunting for Masculinities in British Columbia, 1880–1939," *Western Historical Quarterly* 32, no. 3 (2001): 296–319; Sharon Wall, *The Nurture of Nature: Childhood, Antimodernism, and Ontario Summer Camps, 1920–55* (Vancouver: UBC Press, 2009).

16. "Learn to Shoot," *Rod and Gun in Canada* 1, no. 10 (Mar. 1900): 194. For discussions of the role of the Anglo-Boer War in stirring and shaping Canadian militarism, see Desmond Morton, *A Military History of Canada*, 5th ed. (Toronto: McClelland & Stewart, 2007), 116–17; Mike O'Brien, "Manhood and the Militia Myth: Masculinity, Class and Militarism in Ontario, 1902–1914," *Labour / Le Travail* 42 (1998): 115–41; James Wood, *Militia Myths: Ideas of the Canadian Citizen Soldier, 1896–1921* (Vancouver: UBC Press, 2010).

17. Mark Moss, *Manliness and Militarism: Educating Young Boys in Ontario for War* (Don Mills, ON: Oxford University Press, 2001); K.B. Wamsley, "Cultural Signification and National Ideologies: Rifle-Shooting in Late Nineteenth-Century Canada," *Social History* 20, no. 1 (1995): 63–72.

18. Susan E. Houston, "The 'Waifs and Strays' of a Late Victorian City: Juvenile Delinquents in Toronto," in *Childhood and Family in Canadian History*, ed. Joy Parr (Toronto: McClelland & Stewart, 1982), 129–42; Lynne Marks, *Revivals and Roller Rinks: Religion, Leisure, and Identity in Late-Nineteenth-Century Small-Town Ontario* (Toronto: University of Toronto Press, 1996), 81–6; Steven Maynard, "'Horrible Temptations': Sex, Men, and Working-class Male Youth in Urban Ontario, 1890–1935," *Canadian Historical Review* 78, no. 2 (1997): 191–235; Moss, *Manliness and Militarism*, 112.

19. R.S.S. Baden-Powell, "The Boy Scout Movement," *Empire Club Speeches*, vol. 8 (1910–11), http://speeches.empireclub.org/62214/data?n=1; Garry J. Burke, "Good for the Boy and the Nation: Military Drill and the Cadet Movement in Ontario Public Schools, 1865–1911" (Ph.D. diss., University of Toronto, 1996), 122–34; Patricia Dirks, "Canada's Boys: An Imperial or National Asset? Responses to Baden-Powell's Boy Scout Movement in Pre-War Canada," in *Canada and the British World: Culture, Migration, and Identity*, ed. Phillip Buckner and R. Douglas

Francis (Vancouver: UBC Press, 2006), 121; Desmond Morton, "The Cadet Movement in the Moment of Canadian Militarism," *Journal of Canadian Studies* 13, no. 2 (1978): 59. On the role of scouting in inculcating cultural values, see Jeffrey P. Hantover, "The Boy Scouts and the Validation of Masculinity," *Journal of Social Issues* 34, no. 1 (1978): 184–95; J.O. Springhall, "The Boy Scouts, Class and Militarism in Relation to British Youth Movements, 1908–1930," *International Review of Social History* 16 (1971), 135–6; Allen Warren, "Popular Manliness: Baden-Powell, Scouting, and the Development of Manly Character," in Mangan and Walvin, *Manliness and Morality*, 199–216.

20. Quoted in Moss, *Manliness and Militarism*, 118.

21. Minutes of Executive Committee Meeting of Dominion Council, Canadian Boy Scouts, 16 May 1914, MG28-I73, LAC; Canadian General Council of the Boy Scouts Association, *Report of the Third Annual Meeting held in Ottawa*, April 21, 1917, MG28-I73, LAC; *Annual Report of the Canadian General Council of the Boys Scouts Association*, March, 1919 (Ottawa: n.p., 1919), 8, MG28-I73, LAC.

22. Ronald G. Haycock, *Sam Hughes: The Public Career of a Controversial Canadian, 1885–1916* (Waterloo, on: Wilfrid Laurier University Press, 1986), 140–1; The Militia Act, SC 1904, c.23, s.67; Morton, "Cadet Movement," 56–68; Wood, *Militia Myths*, 150–61, 279.

23. Keith Walden, *Becoming Modern in Toronto: The Industrial Exhibition and the Shaping of a Late Victorian Culture* (Toronto: University of Toronto Press, 1997), 125.

24. David Monod, *Store Wars: Shopkeepers and the Culture of Mass Marketing, 1890–1939* (Toronto: University of Toronto Press, 1996), 16.

25. Eaton's was among several Canadian companies operating mail order catalogues that offered inexpensive air rifles. See Carsley Co. Limited, *Spring and Summer 1902 Catalogue*, 134, LAC, www.collections canada.gc.ca/mailorder/029006-119.01-e.php?& page_ecopy=nlc006870.134&&PHPSESSID= rn4gtck1nhf2jmad3nfimaibj1; *Simpson's Christmas Catalogue*, 1906, 98, LAC, www.collectionscanada .gc.ca/cmc/009002-119.01-e.php?&page_ecopy=nlc 006877&&PHPSESSID=t7l6ubh7ib4gb7rt5hg3ckavs2.

26. For example, T. Eaton Co., *Spring and Summer 1899 Catalogue*. Eaton's continued to carry revolvers in its catalogues until 1913. On the sale of pistols by second-hand stores, see *Manitoba Daily Free Press*, 22 Oct. 1878, 4; "Killed the Girl Who Teased Him," *Toronto Star*, 29 Apr. 1902, 7; *Globe*, 30 Apr. 1902, 14; "Second-Hand Dealers," *Globe*, 15 June 1904, 11; G.H. Robinson to Wilfrid Laurier, 17 Mar. 1909, 153648, vol. 566, MG26G, LAC.

27. T. Eaton Co., *Fall/Winter 1892–93 Catalogue*, F229-1-0-6, AO; "Spencer's Arcade," *Victoria Daily Colonist*, 10 Dec. 1897, 4; T. Eaton Co., Fall/Winter 1902–03 Catalogue, F229-1-0-24, AO; T. Eaton Co., Spring/Summer 1910 Catalogue, F229-1-0-40, AO.

28. *Red Deer News*, 16 Dec. 1914, 4; Simpson's, Christmas Catalogue, 1906, 93, LAC, www.collectionscanada. gc.ca/mailorder/029006-119.01-e.php?&page_ecopy= nlc006877.93&&&&&&PHPSESSID=5os2sigmj5qm quunkli2jjsiu0. Also see *Red Deer News*, 9 Dec. 1908, 1; Edmonton Capital, 12 Sept. 1913, 9; "Business Locals," *Red Deer News*, 10 Dec. 1913, 8.

29. Cross, *Kids' Stuff*, 50–1.

30. *Calgary Weekly Herald*, 22 Mar. 1900, 7; *Globe*, 21 Apr. 1900, 3; *Calgary Weekly Herald*, 11 May 1900, 8; *Globe*, 23 Mar. 1901, 4; *Toronto Star*, 22 Feb. 1902, 3; *Globe*, 1 Nov. 1902, 4; "Free Rifle," *Globe*, 31 Jan. 1903, 4; *Globe*, 24 Feb. 1905, 11; *Twillingate Sun*, 30 Oct. 1909, 3; *St John's Evening Telegram*, 19 Nov. 1909, 3; *Twillingate Sun*, 27 Nov. 1909, 3; *Waterford Star*, 9 Dec. 1909, 6; *Toronto Star*, 22 Jan. 1910, 7; "Free to Boys," *Wetaskiwin Times*, 28 Mar. 1912, 3; *Rod and Gun in Canada* 16, no. 9 (Feb. 1914): 1001.

31. T. Eaton Co., *Spring/Summer 1911 Catalogue*, F229-1-0-42, AO.

32. *Rod and Gun in Canada* 3, no. 12 (May 1902). Also see *Rod and Gun in Canada* 4, no. 11 (Apr. 1904).

33. *Globe*, 17 Oct. 1914, 16. Also see "The Ross Rifle," *Rod and Gun in Canada* 18, no. 1 (June 1916): 69; Roger Phillips, *The Ross Rifle Story* (Sydney, NS: J.A. Chadwick, 1984), 47.

34. *Saint John Daily Sun*, 23 May 1896, 7.

35. *Grain Growers' Guide*, 15 June 1910, 2.

36. *Toronto Star*, 17 Dec. 1904, 9.

37. *Grain Growers' Guide*, 23 Nov. 1910, 15.

38. *Rod and Gun in Canada* 5, no. 7 (Dec. 1903). For other examples of retailers advertising guns as Christmas gifts, see "Xmas," *Globe*, 21 Dec. 1896, 10; *Red Deer News*, 9 Dec. 1908, 1; *Victoria Daily Colonist*, 20 Dec. 1908, 9; *Edmonton Capital*, 14 Dec. 1911, 11; "Xmas Gifts," *Red Deer News*, 16 Dec. 1914, 5; "Christmas Suggestions," *Globe*, 2 Dec. 1916, 8; *Bassano Mail*, 18 Dec. 1919, 10.

39. *Rod and Gun in Canada* 5, no. 7 (Dec. 1903).

40. Cross, *Kids' Stuff*, 111–12; Steven Mintz, *Huck's Raft: A History of American Childhood* (Cambridge, MA: Belknap, 2004), 217. After 1900, publishers (and advertisers) became more interested in targeting particular markets determined by gender. Russell Johnston, *Selling Themselves: The Emergence of Canadian Advertising* (Toronto: University of Toronto Press, 2001), 192–6. On liberalism and the connection between liberalism and consumption, see Donica Belisle, "Toward a Canadian Consumer History," *Labour / Le Travail* 52 (2003): 191–4; Ian McKay, "The Liberal Order Framework: A Prospectus for a Reconnaissance of Canadian History," *Canadian Historical Review* 81, no. 4 (2000): 616–78.

41. Tables of the Trade and Navigation of the Dominion of Canada, in Canada, *Sessional Papers*, 1897, 1901, 1904, 1913.

42. "Echoes of the Fourth," *Toronto Star*, 11 July 1905, 6.

43. For a small sample of such accidents, see "Fatal Firearms Accident," *Globe*, 30 Apr. 1877, 4; *Globe*, 5 Apr. 1879,

8; "Notes from the Capital," *Globe*, 8 July 1879, 1; "A Revolver Accident," *Globe*, 22 Apr. 1885, 6; "Accidentally Shot," *Globe*, 2 Apr. 1887, 16; "The Fatal Revolver," *Globe*, 3 Aug. 1888, 1; "Shot by a Boy," *Manitoba Daily Free Press*, 30 Nov. 1892, 1; "Boy Shoots His Sister," *Toronto Star*, 27 May 1901, 1.

44. "Thomas Ryan Was Careless," *Toronto Star*, 28 May 1901, 3.

45. "Judge Scores the Sale of Revolvers," *Manitoba Morning Free Press*, 17 Oct. 1912, 16.

46. *Globe*, 28 May 1901, 6.

47. On social and moral reform in the period, see Craig Heron, *Booze: A Distilled History* (Toronto: Between the Lines, 2003); Carolyn Strange and Tina Loo, *Making Good: Law and Moral Regulation in Canada, 1867–1939* (Toronto: University of Toronto Press, 1997); Mariana Valverde, *The Age of Light, Soap, and Water: Moral Reform in English Canada, 1885–1925* (Toronto: McClelland & Stewart, 1991).

48. "Sixteen-Cent Pistols," *Chicago Daily Tribune*, 4 July 1880, 7.

49. "The Deadly Toy Pistol," *Chicago Daily Tribune*, 29 July 1880, 3; "The Deadly Toy Pistol," *New York Times*, 16 July 1881, 4; "The Deadly Work of the National Toy Pistol," *Chicago Daily Tribune*, 12 July 1882, 2; "The Toy Pistol Pursuing Its Deadly Course," *Chicago Daily Tribune*, 13 July 1882, 7; "Twenty-Eight Toy Pistol Deaths," *New York Times*, 21 July 1882, 2; "Toy-Pistol Tetanus," *Quarterly Epitome of American Practical Medicine and Surgery*, March 1882 (New York: W.A. Townsend, 1882), 512–13; "The Toy Pistol Again," *Medical Standard* 24, no. 7 (July 1901), 347–8; C.H. Claudy and Clarence Maris, "The Deadly Toy Pistol," *Technical World Magazine* 11, no. 1 (1909): 476–82.

50. "General Notes," *New York Times*, 26 July 1882, 4; "The Toy Pistol Prohibited," *New York Times*, 7 July 1883, 1; "Chicago Bars Toy Pistol," *New York Times*, 11 Nov. 1903, 1; "A Safe July 4," *Toronto Star*, 29 June 1912, 11.

51. For examples, see "Latest from London," *Globe*, 28 July 1877, 8; "American Mail," *Victoria Daily Colonist*, 8 Aug. 1880, 3; "American Mail," *Victoria Daily Colonist*, 26 July 1881, 3; *Canada Presbyterian*, 26 July 1882, 475; "The Toy Pistol," *Globe*, 24 Mar. 1884, 6; "The 'Toy Pistol' Again," *Globe*, 22 Oct. 1887, 1; "Local Briefs," *Globe*, 30 July 1892, 12; "Dangerous Toy Pistols," *Wetaskiwin Times*, 23 Aug. 1901, 2; "Lad Shot with Toy Gun," *Toronto Star*, 2 Sept. 1902, 7; "What It Costs to Celebrate Independence Day," *Advertiser and Central Alberta News*, 9 July 1908, 4; "Uncle Sam's Fourth," *Claresholm Review*, 10 July 1908, 1; "What It Costs to Celebrate Independence Day," *Wetaskiwin Times*, 16 July 1908, 6; *Victoria Daily Colonist*, 6 July 1909, 13; *Maritime Medical News* 21, no. 8 (Aug. 1909): 316.

52. "Municipal Police Court," *Victoria Daily Colonist*, 12 Oct. 1880, 3.

53. "Toy Cigars," *Pleasant Hours*, 23 Feb. 1884, 30. Also see

"Notes and Comments," *Toronto Globe*, 31 July 1882, 4; *Globe*, 6 July 1883, 4; "Warning to Little Boys," *Victoria Daily Colonist*, 24 Feb. 1888, 4; "Men and Things," *Victoria Daily Colonist*, 23 July 1903, 4; "In Woman's Realm," *Victoria Daily Colonist*, 19 Mar. 1908, 8.

54. Canada, *Senate Debates* (4 Apr. 1889), p. 429 (Hon. William Johnston Almon); Canada, *Senate Debates* (25 Feb. 1890), p. 140 (Hon. William Johnston Almon).

55. "Played Wild West," *Globe*, 26 Oct. 1907, 1. For a sample of accidents involving air rifles, see "Police Court," *Saint John Daily Sun*, 14 June 1906, 2; "Boy Shot in the Eye," *Montreal Gazette*, 20 Jan. 1910, 6.

56. "The Law on Air Guns," *Manitoba Morning Free Press*, 12 Nov. 1898, 12.

57. "City and District," *Montreal Gazette*, 12 May 1913. For a sample of other incidents, see "Shot in the Eye," *Globe*, 5 Nov. 1895, 10; "Shooting Accident at London," *Globe*, 14 Apr. 1900, 20; "Another Shooting Accident," *Globe*, 30 May 1901, 12; "Hamilton Boy Killed," *Globe*, 7 Sept. 1903, 1; "Boy Sportsman Killed," *Globe*, 20 July 1904, 9; "Hamilton Boy Shot," *Globe*, 20 Mar. 1905, 1; "Shot through the Brain," *Globe*, 11 July 1905, 1; "Another Gun Victim," *Montreal Gazette*, 17 Dec. 1908, 11; "Youth with Rifle Kills Companion," *Globe*, 27 Oct. 1913, 8.

58. "Accidentally Shot," *Victoria Daily Colonist*, 23 Sept. 1896, 5; "Shot through the Head," *Victoria Daily Colonist*, 29 Oct. 1897, 2; "Gun License," *Victoria Daily Colonist*, 11 Jan. 1901, 7; *Cayley Hustler*, 20 Sept. 1911, 5.

59. *Globe*, 23 May 1885, 9.

60. "Bad Boys at the Bijou," *Manitoba Morning Free Press*, 24 Mar. 1896, 6; *Globe*, 6 Aug. 1887, 4; "Influence the Imagination," *Educational Journal* 5, no. 16 (Jan. 1892): 604; "The Mirror," *Saturday News*, 13 Jan. 1906, 4.

61. "Boys Handling Fire Arms," *Temiskaming Speaker*, 29 Oct. 1909, 1. Also see "The Boy and the Gun," *Temiskaming Speaker*, 8 Nov. 1912, 1.

62. The history of wildlife protection has been studied by J. Alexander Burnett, *A Passion for Wildlife: The History of the Canadian Wildlife Service* (Vancouver: UBC Press, 2003); Colpitts, *Game in the Garden*; Janet Foster, *Working for Wildlife: The Beginning of Preservation in Canada* (Toronto: University of Toronto Press, 1978); Tina Loo, *States of Nature: Conserving Canada's Wildlife in the Twentieth Century* (Vancouver: UBC Press, 2006).

63. "Engaged in a Noble Work," *Victoria Daily Colonist*, 4 Nov. 1903, 6. Also see British Columbia, *Eighth Report of the Provincial Game Warden and Forest Warden, 1912* (Victoria: Government Printer, 1913), O6–O7.

64. "Small Boys with Rifles a Menace in the Country," *Toronto Star*, 26 Oct. 1911, 17; "The Killing of Birds," *Toronto Star*, 7 May 1904, 6; "The Boy and the Gun," *Toronto Star*, 6 Nov. 1911, 6; "Firearms in Suburbs," *Toronto Star*, 24 Oct. 1913, 1.

65. Comacchio, *Dominion of Youth*, 28.

66. Dorothy E. Chunn, "Boys Will Be Men, Girls Will Be Mothers: The Legal Regulation of Childhood in Toronto and Vancouver," in *Histories of Canadian Children and Youth*, ed. Nancy Janovicek and Joy Parr (Don Mills, ON: Oxford University Press, 2003), 188–206; Dorothy E. Chunn, *From Punishment to Doing Good: Family Courts and Socialized Justice in Ontario, 1880–1940* (Toronto: University of Toronto Press, 1992); Comacchio, *Dominion of Youth*, 29; Tamara Myers, *Caught: Montreal's Modern Girls and the Law, 1869–1945* (Toronto: University of Toronto Press, 2006); Tamara Myers, "Nocturnal Disorder and the Curfew Solution: A History of Juvenile Sundown Regulations in Canada," in Gleason et al., *Lost Kids*, 95–113.

67. An Act to Make Provision against the Improper Use of Firearms, S.C. 1877, c.30; Brown, "'Pistol Fever,'" 127–9.

68. Canada, *Senate Debates* (4 Apr. 1889), pp. 427–9; (9 Apr. 1889), pp. 449–50; The Criminal Code, S.C. 1892, c.29, s.106(1); Chunn, "Boys Will Be Men," 194. In 1890, British Columbia banned most boys under 14 from carrying a gun without the accompaniment of his father or guardian. An Act to Prevent Minors from Carrying Fire-arms, S.B.C. 1890, c.18. This was increased to those under 16 in 1913. Firearms Act Amendment Act, 1913, S.B.C. 1913, c.23.

69. "The Law on Air Guns," *Manitoba Morning Free Press*, 12 Nov. 1898, 12; *Toronto Star*, 27 Sept. 1898, 3. Also see "Children and Firearms," *Toronto Star*, 29 Apr. 1896, 2. Accidents with air guns led the Toronto Board of Police Commissioners to make renewed efforts to enforce the law forbidding boys under 16 from acquiring air guns. "The Boy and the Gun," 7.

70. "The Deadly Flobert," *Globe*, 25 Nov. 1913, 6. Concern with safety led Eaton's to note that Stevens .22 calibre "Little Scout" rifle was "Not a toy," but was a "safe dependable gun." T. Eaton Co., *Spring/Summer 1913 Catalogue*, Winnipeg ed., F229-2-0-17, AO.

71. Canada, *House of Commons Debates* (29 May 1903), p. 3773 (Thomas Simpson Sproule, MP). Also see "The Mail Bag," *Grain Growers' Guide*, 27 May 1914, 23.

72. Canada, *House of Commons Debates* (29 May 1903), p. 3777 (Sam Hughes, MP).

73. Canada, House of Commons Debates (10 July 1905), p. 9120 (Frederick Borden, MP). Also see "Let the Boys Shoot," *Victoria Daily Colonist*, 26 May 1890, 3.

74. "Let the Boys Shoot," 3; "Feminine Fancies and the Home Circle Chat," *Victoria Daily Colonist*, 8 Mar. 1908, 22; "Young Sportsmen," *Strathmore Standard*, 6 May 1914, 3; "Young Sportsmen," *Gleichen Call*, 14 May 1914, 7.

75. "Had Received No Authority," *Globe*, 17 Sept. 1887, 20; "Lad Had Air Gun, Mother Censured," *Toronto Star*, 24 Mar. 1906, 7; "Police Court," *Saint John Daily Sun*, 14 June 1906, 2; "Youth with Rifle Kills Companion," *Globe*, 27 Oct. 1913, 8.

76. Fowell v. Grafton, [1910] 22 Ontario Law Reports 550, upholding Fowell v. Grafton, [1910] 20 Ontario Law Reports 639; "Responsible for Gift," *Edmonton Capital*, 12 Apr. 1910, 8.

77. Moran v. Burroughs (1912), 10 Dominion Law Reports 181.

78. John Herd Thompson, *Ethnic Minorities during Two World Wars* (Ottawa: Canadian Historical Association 1991), 3.

79. "Grand Jury against Weapon Carrying," *Manitoba Morning Free Press*, 8 July 1911, 17; Canada, *House of Commons Debates* (27 Jan. 1911), pp. 2557–59 (Hon. E.N. Lewis, MP).

80. The Offensive Weapons Act, S.O. 1911, c.66, s.5.

81. The Offensive Weapons Act, S.M. 1912, c.57; The Offensive Weapons Act, S.S 1912, c.24; Offensive Weapons Act, S.B.C. 1913, c.83.

82. "Permit Is Now Necessary for Keeping an Air Rifle," *Toronto Star*, 21 Apr. 1911, 1.

83. The Criminal Code Amendment Act, 1913, S.C. 1913, c.13, s.5.

84. Comacchio, *Dominion of Youth*, 114. There were, however, efforts to encourage cadets in the Second World War. Tamara Myers and Mary Anne Poutanen, "Cadets, Curfews, and Compulsory Schooling: Mobilizing Anglophone Children in WWII Montreal," *Histoire sociale / Social History* 76 (2005): 367–98.

85. Keaton, "Backyard Desperadoes," 183–96.

86. Greg Marquis, "Vancouver Vice: The Police and the Negotiation of Morality, 1904–1935," in *British Columbia and the Yukon, vol. 6 of Essays in the History of Canadian Law*, ed. Hamar Foster and John McLaren (Toronto: University of Toronto Press and the Osgoode Society, 1995), 242–73.

87. Sharon Myers, "The Apocrypha of Minnie McGee: The Murderous Mother and Multivocal State in 20th-Century Prince Edward Island," *Acadiensis* 38, no. 2 (2009): 27.

88. Canada, *House of Commons Debates* (29 Mar. 1933), pp. 3526–31; Chief Constables' Association of Canada, *Forty-Third Annual Conference, Vancouver, B.C., September 22nd, 23rd, 24th and 25th, 1948* (n.p.: n.d.), 167–8.

Advertisement for Stevens Crack Shot Rifles, 1904

Source: Stevens Firearms Company

"He Was Determined to Go": Underage Soldiers in the Canadian Expeditionary Force

TIM COOK

Thousands of adolescents fought with the Canadian Expeditionary Force (CEF) during the Great War. Historians have overlooked their service because it has been difficult to distinguish them from their older comrades, since most of these young soldiers lied about their age in order to enlist. A sense of adventure, peer pressure, and fierce patriotism impelled young and old to serve. Most underage soldiers who enlisted were 16 or 17 (and later 18 when age requirements were raised to 19), but at least one cheeky lad enlisted at only 10 years old, and a 12-year-old made it to the trenches.[1]

As many as 20,000 underage soldiers served overseas.[2] Canadians under the age of 19 constituted an important segment of the population during the Great War, one of the most traumatic experiences in Canadian history, but their history remains largely unknown.[3] Studying the reaction of these soldiers to the war effort and their interaction with parents, society, and the military forces reveals that young Canadians were approvingly incorporated into and became a significant part of Canada's war effort.

Enlistment

The British and Canadian military had a long history of accepting into the ranks a small number of boy soldiers and sailors in apprenticeship roles, often as buglers, drummers, and young sailors. These boy soldiers and sailors, some as young as 10 or 12, were taken on strength with the regiment or ship, where they were part of the regimental family, eating, serving, and sleeping in the same barracks. Within the family officers tended to take a paternal attitude to these boys, and educational activities were offered or foisted on them to improve their lot in life.[4] Strict discipline and corresponding punishment for flouting regulations were also a part of their service in the rigid hierarchy of military service.[5] They were also in harm's way, with boy sailors fulfilling a variety of roles on a ship and drummer boys leading men into battle.

In Canada, the King's Regulations and Orders for the Canadian militia specified that boys of "good character" between the ages of 13 and 18 could be enlisted as bandsmen, drummers, or buglers.[6] However, since the Canadian permanent force was a mere 3,000 before the war, there were very few boy soldiers, although the various and scattered militia units across the country had no compunction about turning to juveniles to fill their always thin ranks. Still, the vast majority of the thousands of adolescents who would enlist in the Great War were not pre-war boy soldiers, but chose to serve for a variety of reasons.

To understand the role of serving adolescents in the Great War, one must acknowledge the constructed nature of childhood.[7] For much of the nineteenth century, little thought or worry was given to the emotional life of young people or the necessity of a childhood filled with play and exploration. Childhood was hard and dangerous in working-class families. All children, no matter their class or ethnicity, were sadly acquainted with death in and out of the workplace. Few families escaped the tragedy of losing children or siblings to disease or accident. Education remained a privilege for most, with youngsters often pulled from schools to support the family. Yet these pre-war working boys and adolescents were also toughened by their hardship, and it was not uncommon for them to mobilize in

Source: From *Histoire sociale/Social History*, 41, 81 (May 2008): 42–74. Abridged. Reprinted with permission.

the workplace, demanding greater rights.[8] Despite their age, they were tough customers who eagerly embraced all aspects of their emerging masculinity, smoking, drinking, and fighting in a rough-and-tumble environment.

At the time, there was no accepted classification for what age designated a child or adolescent, although the state—both at the federal and provincial levels—attempted to define young Canadians through the creation of various forms of legislation. Since 1871, legislation had required that students stay in school until the age of 12, but by the decade before the war this had been raised to 14 or 16, depending on province, as well as on city and rural jurisdictions.[9] However, many young people left school before the legislation allowed and were employed in full-time jobs. There was legislation to control youth from flooding the market, both for their health and to defend against a dilution of the work force, but this, too, was applied differently across the country, no doubt affected by provincial economies.[10] While labour laws varied, delinquent children and adolescents were defined and normalized in the 1908 Juvenile Delinquents Act, in the attempt to punish transgressive behaviour by youthful deviants. Under the act, delinquents were classified as between the ages of 7 and 16 (18 in some provinces), but children under 12 were treated more leniently under the law.[11] Thus, in the eyes of probation officers and the courts, adolescents fell somewhere between the ages of 12 and 18. While state actors attempted to define childhood, adolescence, and adulthood, the constructed nature of these classifications was also shaped by region, class, and ethnicity. Most young Canadians were involved in adult activities long before the age of 18. Any attempt to define youth invariably led legislators into contested terrain, although 21 was the required age of adult citizenship.[12]

Since the late nineteenth century, women's groups, educational reformers, and a constellation of reform-minded Canadians had aimed to improve the lot of children's and adolescents' health and spiritual wellbeing, no matter their age.[13] These groups engendered vast improvements in society and helped to shape the nature of childhood by demanding that the state and society recognize the difference between adolescence and adulthood. While many adolescents were rescued from the gutters, some would soon march straight into the trenches.

Canada went to war in August 1914, carried forward by a swell of patriotic excitement. For some boys in menial jobs or back-breaking work, the transition from a brutal, dangerous industrial profession to the military was viewed as a safe move, especially since few expected the war to extend past Christmas. Trading coal dust for healthy marching did not raise the objections of many in society. Soldiers, both young and old, spoke approvingly of having three solid, if monotonous, meals. The $1.10 a day for privates, plus the chance to serve a seemingly noble cause, were also incentives that drew lads from across the country.

Like all Canadians, adolescents had a myriad of reasons to enlist. "When the war broke out . . . The country went mad!" recalled Bert Remington, who immediately enlisted at age 18, but with a physical appearance, in his words, of "five foot nothing and 85 pounds."[14] Adolescents were just as susceptible to the hyper patriotism of the period, yet, unlike older men, most did not have good jobs or a family to temper the heady thoughts of serving King and country. Added to these factors was the inherent belief by most young people that they were nearly indestructible.[15] Others had pre-war militia training that made them more inclined to serve and fight, and before the war some 40,000 school boys had enrolled in the cadets, an institution accused by critics of militarizing childhood and adolescence.[16]

Even those youth who did not march in khaki or carry the .22 cadet Ross rifle had, for the most part, been raised at home and in school on stories of victorious campaigns that had won Britain her empire. While class mitigated some of the messages, insofar as boys and adolescents of working-class families would likely be engaged in paid work rather than education, much of the popular culture of literature, music, and toys for male children was infused with ideals of manliness. Military service in the imperial ranks caught the imagination of most boys at one time or another. Parades, marches, and flag-waving were all normal activities at school or in the community. When war came, many adolescents were eager to carve out their own heroic future.[17]

Despite the sense of naive adventure and pre-war masculine culture, one cannot discount genuine patriotism and a belief in the widely disseminated liberal ideals underpinning the British war effort. Later in the war, some youngsters ached to avenge the loss of an older sibling or a father. One letter of the era from John Wright to Prime Minister Sir Robert Borden provides insight into other motivations:

> I am only a boy of 16 years and want to give my life for my country. I have tried many times and failed. . . . My Dad has been to the Front and now he is back again, and you have taken my brother, and now I am the only one left to do something for my country. And, Sir, if you only knew how I am going crazy to do something to gain honor. I am strong and healthy, I have never had any sickness in my life. I was just reading the paper this morning and saw that you said "Canadians must hold the line." They cannot do it without men. Please will you give me a position in that line. I don't call myself a man but I might help to hold that line. So please give me a chance, the line is more valuable than my life.[18]

Wright was not accepted into the ranks, despite his heart-felt desire to serve his country.

Multiple layers of masculinity thus drove adolescents to enlist. Like young John Wright, who ached for honour, sacrifice, and an opportunity to prove his manhood, young boys instantly became men in their own eyes and those of others by signing their names to the legally binding attestation form. A 16-year-old student was treated the same as the 25-year-old baker or the 29-year-old clerk. In moving from short pants to military trousers and puttees, an adolescent moved from being a boy to a man.

This embracing of adulthood began with enlistment. Across the country, hopeful men of all ages made their way to the armouries. While militia orders stipulated that recruits were to be between the ages of 18 and 45, overage and underage Canadians provided fabricated birth dates for official documentation to serve.[19] There was a loop-hole, however, as adolescents under the age of 18 could enlist if they had a parent's signed letter of consent.

Many parents waived their right to veto their son's choice. Activist and author Nellie McClung was filled with fear and anger when she watched the "first troops going away. I wondered how their mothers let them go." But then her son, Jack, who was also there to see the soldiers off, turned to her with expectant eyes, asking, "Mother, when will I be eighteen?"[20] It was a blow and a realization that the war would affect everyone, but especially the mothers left behind, forced to wait, worry, and watch their eager sons enlist for war. Jack would eventually serve overseas, with McClung's blessing; he survived, although in his mother's eyes he lost his youth on the battlefields of the Western Front.

Jack was lucky; thousands did not return. Percy McClare, who enlisted in April 1915, six weeks after his seventeenth birthday, wrote a pleading letter to his mother asking that she sign the consent form. He had been impressed by a recruiting sergeant who informed McClare "that the men at the [front] are happy as can be. . . . Said they had a Jolly time. All I need is your concent [sic]."[21] His mother eventually agreed to his service, as did many parents, who were no doubt pressured by patriotic messages in speeches and posters. As one recruitment poster aimed at the "Women of Canada" demanded: "When the War is over and someone asks your husband or your son what he did in the great War, is he to hang his head because you would not let him go?"[22] Many parents did not need such shaming techniques, as they firmly believed in the war, but it is also clear that some parents allowed their underdeveloped and too-young sons to enlist because they assumed their boys could not possibly be accepted into the ranks of men.[23] Most were soon shocked to find their sons in uniform. [. . .]

While adolescents showed up at recruiting stations clutching letters of consent, often they were turned down because of their size or unsuitability for soldiering. The age requirement of at least 18 seems to have been used as a guide rather than a rule, however, and no one in the heady patriotic environment of 1914 and 1915 inquired too deeply about the influx of adolescents into the ranks. Perhaps the arbitrary assignment of an age—18 and later 19—seemed at odds with the situation of most adolescents who were out of school and working in the capacity of young adults. Whatever the case, thousands of youths disregarded the rule, which was almost impossible to enforce since few recruits had birth certificates, and no one was required to produce one as proof of age. One should also not discount the prevalence of Canadians who did not know their own birth date. Nonetheless, bluster and brass often allowed many youngsters to elude serious scrutiny during the already inconsistent enlistment process, although parents had the right to pull their underage sons from the forces until the summer of 1915, when this privilege was quietly dropped after a court ruled that the militia had made a pact with a soldier, no matter his age.[24]

Queuing before the recruiting sergeant could be a nerve-wracking exercise. Forty-nine-year-olds with newly dyed hair and 16-year-olds standing erect and sweating under a borrowed jacket and bowler hat watched anxiously as recruiting sergeants jotted down their names and birth dates. Depending on the circumstances of the unit, and especially if it needed more men to hit its quota to go overseas, recruiting sergeants often turned a blind eye to an obviously too-young lad or the deeply lined face of an older man. [. . .]

Not all had their wishes come true. Thomas Raddall, who would later become an eminent Nova Scotia novelist and historian, remembered wearing his first pair of trousers at age 15. Having shed his children's clothes, he walked confidently into a recruiting station. "Several boys from Chebucto School had [already] done so and gone overseas," he recounted in his memoirs. "One of our neighbour's sons had enlisted at sixteen and was killed in France at seventeen. But I was recognized by the recruiting sergeant who knew my father [who would be killed overseas], and he told me bluntly to go back to school."[25] However, even if a soldier was turned down, since there was no cross-referencing of rejected men, a determined youth could and did move from regiment to regiment in search of one that needed to fill its quota. Rejection for an obstinate youth only meant a trip down the street or re-enlisting on another day, with a different sergeant and under a new name, and it was not uncommon to find soldiers who tried to enlist two or three times before they were accepted. Of the several thousand soldiers rejected as unfits and misfits in 1914 at the Valcartier training camp, a recent study suggests that hundreds enlisted later in the war when the forces were more desperate for men.[26]

The act of enlistment was a two-step process, and being accepted by officers and sergeants did not guarantee service. Recruits still needed to pass a medical examination. The quality of the inspecting medical officers varied at the armouries and depots across the country. Throughout the war, several hundred thousand potential recruits were turned down by medical officers—and this number might have been as high as 40 per cent of all who attempted to enlist.[27] Anything from poor eyesight to flat feet to bad teeth could keep a man out of the service. Age was a factor, but it stopped fewer men than it should have. It was not an easy task to distinguish adolescents from men. [. . .] Even so, it was not easy to justify the enlistment of Private Russell Mick with the 224th Battalion on March 17, 1916. He was allowed through at the age of 16, weighing 80 pounds and suffering from "infantile paralysis," which left him largely incapable of movement.[28] After arriving in England and going almost directly to a hospital, he was eventually returned to Canada as an "undesirable." [. . .]

The medical screening process remained notoriously unreliable throughout the war. A cursory visual inspection of the naked body was a humiliating event: sunken chests were poked, genitals examined, flat feet kneaded, eyesight tested through distance charts.[29] Thomas Rowlett, an underage signaller, enlisted in Nova Scotia with two pals. Both naked friends were asked the same question by the medical officer: "Are you 19 years old?" Both replied in the affirmative. To the taller one the medical officer nodded; the other he rejected with a dismissive glance.[30] While medical officers were experienced in sizing up a man or boy with a glance and a bit of prodding, this haphazard approach led to regular complaints in England that the weak, too-youthful, and aged were being accepted into the ranks. [. . .]

Searching letters from desperate parents evoking their rights under the law continued to pluck underage soldiers from their units, however, until the summer of 1915. Roy Macfie, who served with his two brothers, wrote home shortly after arriving in England: "There are two of the Cook boys from Loring here, and their mother sent to the General and told him that they were underage, and were not to go to the front so I think they will be sent home, they won't like it."[31] Sapper J.E. Lowe was likely even younger than the Cook brothers, having enlisted at 15 (although, of course, lying on his attestation paper, which gives his age as 18) as a bugler in a pioneer battalion. After six weeks in England, the tough little Lowe, who stood five feet, three inches but had been a pre-war miner, was sent home.[32]

While an undisclosed number of young Canadians were pulled from the ranks, either because of parents' letters or by officers who now realized that the firing line was not the place for an adolescent, hundreds and then thousands of underage soldiers pleaded and cajoled their way into overseas service. Some openly threatened that, if sent home, they would only sign up again under an assumed name. Many officers relented and allowed the adolescents to continue serving, but others would have none of it, and those under age were put on ships and sent home.

Youth has never liked to be told how to act, and this was especially true for those returned to a country gripped with hyper-patriotism as exhibited through war posters, recruiting sergeants, politicians, and patriotic groups that assaulted every young man with the same message: do your bit. One student at the University of Saskatchewan wrote to his mother that he had been pressured to enlist because the other students "make you feel like two cents if you don't."[33] Eminent Canadians roared that "to live by shirking one's duty is infinitely worse . . . than to die."[34] Many men, both young and old, would have echoed Armine Norris's statement, "I enlisted

because I hadn't the nerve to stay at home."[35] Norris was no coward and would be awarded the Military Cross for bravery in battle before being killed during the last months of the war.

The returned patriotic youth did not last long under this pressure. Opportunities were available to fight the "Hun" from the classroom floor through the writing of vitriolic essays, by throwing their increasing weight behind raising funds through the various patriotic movements, and, towards the end of the war, by working as "Soldiers of the Soil" to help farmers bring in the crops, but they could not avoid the increasingly aggressive questions and disapproving stares that lumped them together with other perceived slackers. Many re-enlisted, often under assumed names and against their parents' wishes. Enlisting under a false name meant that a soldier was effectively cut off from his loved ones. There would be no letters home, no news of the family, no death benefits should the worst occur. Those at home might never know what had happened to their sons should they fall in battle.

Overseas

The Canadian Division arrived in France in February 1915 and was joined over the next year and a half by three more divisions to form the Canadian Corps, some 100,000 men strong. From the start, the Canadians soon encountered the harsh subterranean world of the Western Front. Million-man armies constructed vast trench systems in aerially eviscerated farmers' fields. The infantry had to endure rats, lice, and frozen feet in the winter and the same insect and rodent tormentors, as well as flies and thirst, in the summer. All year round there was the constant wastage of the trenches, where men were killed by shell and bullet, sickness and poison gas.

In the firing line, an underage soldier was expected to be a soldier just like his elder mates. Certainly there was no distinction for the other death-dealing weapons that indiscriminately took lives in fearful numbers. Among the ranks, however, underage soldiers sometimes were treated differently by older men who often took younger ones under their wing. Canon Scott recounted the actions of one officer, who told Scott about his encounter with a young lad in his company:

> [We] had to hold on, in a trench, hour after hour, under terrific bombardment. [The officer] was sitting in his dugout, expecting every moment to be blown up, when a young lad came in and asked if he might stay with him. The boy was only eighteen years of age, and his nerve was utterly gone. He came into the dugout, and, like a child clinging to his mother, clasped the officer with his arms. The latter could not be angry with the lad. There was nothing to do at that point but to hold on and wait, so, as he said to me, "I looked at the boy and thought of his mother, and just leaned down and gave him a kiss. Not long afterward a shell struck the dugout and the boy was killed, and when we returned I had to leave his body there."[36]

Occasionally, very young soldiers were seen almost as mascots. Sergeant F.W. Bagnall remembered being worried about one 14-year-old in the ranks and his propensity to fall asleep while on sentry, which could result in a death sentence under military law. Although the lad displayed great bravery in battle, even winning a Distinguished Conduct Medal for going to the aid of a wounded soldier while under fire, he, like many adolescents, had the physiological disadvantage of needing more sleep due to a still-developing body. Bagnall recounted that before "the kid" was pulled out of the line for being too young, "every one made a fuss over him."[37]

In the mud and misery of the front-line trenches, officers often ensured that underage soldiers were excluded from the most dangerous duties like trench-raiding, but there were few safe places at the front. Infantryman William Now remembered that his commanding officer had removed an underage soldier from the front-line trenches to carry water in the rear. [. . .] While some adolescents were put in "bomb-proof" jobs in the rear, more often underage soldiers were treated the same as their older companions.

The trenches were foreign and frightening to Private J.D. Thomson of the 102nd Battalion, who wrote home a month before Vimy Ridge about his experiences in the trenches:

> water dripping through in places, and the mud in the bottom two inches deep. . . . We got a few sand bags which were lying in the corner, spread them in the mud, laid our rubber sheet on top, used our packs for pillows, lay down, and put the two blankets, (which we carried), over us with our coats on top, before we went to sleep my chum said, "Will you ever forget this Christmas Eve?"

Thomson had enlisted at 16 and was fighting in the trenches by 17. In his unguarded letter, he wrote: "I am a mere boy, but I thought I was a man, and now I know I have to stick to it." He signed his letter, "Not a Hero."[38]

Thomson was not a hero in the conventional sense, but heroic nonetheless. The quiet courage of doing one's duty while sick with fear was a trait not unique to underage soldiers, but countless references bear witness to how adolescents stuck it out. The story of the Owen brothers bears repeating. Three brothers enlisted, all underage: James was in the trenches before he was 16; his twin brothers, Iorwerth and Cecil, enlisted prior to their seventeenth birthday. The three sturdy farm lads, all between five feet, six inches and five feet, seven inches, had enlisted on the same day, adding between two and three years to their ages. They fought together in the 15th Battalion, and their first major battle was on the Somme, a bloody attack against a fortified trench system on September 26, 1916. Private James Owen later wrote that, during the night before the assault, "fear had my stomach tied in a knot. I could not eat and I remembered thinking that I was much too young to die. I felt that if I was older, say 20, and had seen something of life, I would not mind as much. . . . I also doubted my ability to engage a full grown German with the bayonet, but felt a bullet would make us more equal."[39] He made a promise to himself to keep one round in the chamber at all times. One can only wonder how many boys, despite their training and bravado, worried about how they would fare in battle against grown men. James survived the battle, although he was wounded; one of his brothers was not so lucky and was later found among the slain. [. . .]

Young soldiers continued to serve and endure with the help of their mates. The comradeship of the trenches was a key component in constructing and supporting the will to keep fighting through the most dire of circumstances. Not to let down one's companions drove many soldiers to hold on past their limits. It was no different for young soldiers, and perhaps even more important, since there was a desire among most adolescents to live up to the ideals of the masculine soldier. A.E. Fallen, a 17-year-old infantrymen serving with the 52nd Battalion, remembered his first time in the line, standing in mud and slush and wondering to himself, "I hope to God I can stand this. . . . I would have hated like hell to have cracked up as a kid."[40] He found the strength to endure, serving through some of the toughest battles of the war.

Issues of masculinity remained important for the young soldiers. There were norms and regulations to follow in emulating the masculine ideals. Young soldiers did not like to stand out as anything other than a companion in the ranks. Some obviously overcompensated. Nineteen-year-old Private John Lynch recounted that he and other young soldiers "wanted to impress the world with their toughness. We cursed louder, drank harder and behaved in a very boisterous manner, putting on a front for the veterans of the outfit, many of whom were older than our fathers."[41] While service conferred adulthood on young men, sometimes they felt the need to prove it. But the army saw no distinction and paid young lads as much as older men. As well, the young soldiers received the same rights and privileges in the trenches. The daily issue of rum, in itself a tool for reinforcing discipline, hierarchy, and masculinity, was not denied to underage soldiers. Signaller William Ogilvie, who had enlisted at the age of 17 from Lakefield, Ontario, testified, "We juniors learned the ropes from our older and more experienced comrades and though we younger ones

were far from serious drinkers, we were now caught up by the challenge."[42] The act of drinking was often understood to be one of the distinguishing marks between men and boys. Army-issued rum was powerful, syrupy, over-strength spirit that burned, as one soldier remarked, as if "he'd swallowed a red-hot poker."[43] After the first few sputtering attempts, an infantryman learned to hold his rum, and these young soldiers soon measured up to the group's expectations.

While rum was not withheld, neither was enfranchisement. "We had scores of fellows who had not yet reached voting age. We knew at least two who celebrated their sixteenth birthdays in France," remarked Fred Noyes, a stretcher-bearer. "Many gave 'official' ages which wouldn't have stood the test if the authorities had cared to investigate. . . . A remarkable feature of the election was the voting of our teen-old youngsters."[44] As well, young soldiers were sometimes elevated in rank above their older peers. Although it appears uncommon, there were cases like Corporal J.G. Baker of the 15th Battalion, who, at the age of 17, would have been in charge of a dozen men, all likely older.[45] John Hensley enlisted at the age of 16 in Halifax, serving through two years of warfare before he was killed at Passchendaele at the age of 18. During that time, he had risen to the rank of captain, responsible at times for 200 men in his company.

Of course, not all young soldiers survived the emotional and mental rigours of the trenches. Lieutenant William Gray recounted watching one adolescent come unstrung during a heavy drum-fire bombardment: "He laughed rather hysterically and babbled incoherently. Suddenly he jumped up, climbed into the open, his sole thought to get away but there, a scant hundred yards, we saw him fall."[46] While anecdotal evidence suggests that young soldiers often had a better chance of withstanding the psychological pressures of war, many soldiers eventually broke under the prolonged stress. One report on British courts martial revealed the shocking statistic that 32 minors had been executed during the war, and that 10 of them had used shell shock as a defence for why they had deserted from the front.[47] None of the 25 Canadians executed was underage, but for all soldiers, from the young in the prime of their lives to the ancient 39ers (the nickname for older men who had lied about their age), enduring the strain of war depended on the man, the circumstances, and the ability to draw on those internal and external resources.[48]

With the constant lack of sleep, the never-ending agony of scratching at lice, and the threat of dismemberment by shell fire, many soldiers eventually began to pray for their release from the front lines. Unlike older soldiers, however, underage ones had an escape route, since by 1916 trench rumours had swirled through the ranks passing on valuable information that underage soldiers could reveal their age and be pulled from the line. Corporal Harry Hillyer wrote to his sister about her son, only a few months before Hillyer was shot in the head and killed in battle:

> How old is Eddie? You know if he is under 18 you can claim him out by writing to the OC of the Regiment. I think you would be wise in doing so if his age warrants it as the fighting is liable to increase in fierceness from now on, in fact, we have noticed the difference already. This has happened in 3 cases quite recently in our own regiment. One of the boys claimed out is one of our best scouts but he is to go just the same although he was very loathe [sic] to leave us. Of course, it is immaterial to me, but if he was my brother I would not let him go through what is in store for us here.[49]

Adolescents who had enlisted and embraced the army life, who had even lied to get into it, were torn in a silent battle between doing their duty and supporting their comrades, and the release that they would have received by revealing their real age.

Bert Warren, who had enlisted at 17 in Toronto, recounted the horrific fighting at Passchendaele at the end of 1917. After surviving his first tour in the slush-filled trenches inhabited by the dead and barely living, Warren and a fellow underage soldier emerged from the quagmire frozen, terrified, and bewildered. His companion, who was smaller than Warren, who himself weighed a mere "128 pounds soaking wet," remarked, "I just made two trips, my first and my last. I'm going to write my father to get me out." He scribbled a letter off to his parents that night, but the unit went back into the fighting: "he didn't come out, a direct hit, never found anything of him."[50] Private James Owen, while recovering from the wound he received on the Somme, took the opportunity to write to his mother that she present his birth certificate to the military authorities for his release. He was not sure whether he would get his "ticket or not," but it was worth trying. He did, returning to his mother, who was still dealing with the reality that one of her other sons would never come home. Hundreds of others followed Owen. Many justified revealing their age because they had done their duty and it was time for others to fill their place. Others neither needed nor cared about justification and only wanted out. Either way, by late 1916 there was an appreciation that the Canadian forces had a problem with thousands of underage soldiers serving in the ranks.

Removing Underage Soldiers from the Trenches

In July 1916 J.W. Carson, the Canadian Minister of Militia's representative in England, notified the British War Office that he often received letters from parents claiming that their sons "are under age and joined without their authority" and now wanted them removed from the firing line.[51] The War Office wrote a sharp letter back to Carson, noting the regulations under Army Council Instruction No. 1186, which stated, "if a soldier is under 17, he will be discharged; if over 17 but under 18, he will be posted to a reserve unit; if over 18, but under 19, posted to a reserve unit until 19 and sent overseas."[52] These rules seemed clearly delineated, except that the War Office consistently broke them and was caught deceiving British Members of Parliament when assuring them that no underage soldiers were in the trenches. Parents of British soldiers who applied to have their sons removed from the firing line were routinely ignored; in other recorded cases, commanding officers refused to allow young soldiers to leave a unit or turned a blind eye to requests after following the wishes of soldiers who refused to go. Since 1915 a heated and rancorous public debate had raged in the United Kingdom about underage soldiers. Crusading MPs in the House of Commons demanded answers from the War Office.[53] The issue would not be resolved until 1917, when the War Office clamped down on units that allowed underage soldiers to serve near the firing line.

In Canada, by contrast, there was barely a whisper about the underage soldiers in the first two years of the war. Not until 25 April 1916 was the question even raised in the House. The prime minister was asked if there were any underage soldiers in the CEF, to which he replied that he "always understood that the policy is not to enlist boys under 18 years of age." His confusion over the age of recruits, 18 or 19, can be excused, since different units were following the Canadian or British regulations, but he agreed to look into the case. He appears to have never reported formally back to the House. However, this was enough for the MPs, and only a few sporadic additional questions arose over the next two years.[54] A question was again directed to the government on 1 February 1917 about an underage soldier, Noel Gazelle, who had enlisted at 16 but lied saying he was 18. The responsible minister, A.E. Kemp, noted that, because he had lied in a "legally binding" document, he was, in effect, trapped in the CEF.[55] Again, the House seemed to accept the answer, and few MPs raised any objections to a government that refused to allow its underage soldiers to leave the service while noting that its policy was not to enlist minors. [. . .]

In mid-1916 the Allies were reeling on all fronts, their armies battered. More soldiers were needed to replace those chewed up in the maw of war, and so the forces began to lessen enlistment restrictions that had kept men out in the past.[56] Height requirements dropped and even hitherto discriminations against visible minorities were modified to encourage enlistment. While age was not reduced, adolescents continued to find ways through the screening process. With thousands of young Canadians already overseas and more joining during the desperate recruiting drives of early 1916, it is clear that the issue of youth was wilfully ignored in the name of supporting the war. Or was it simply not seen as an issue? With most adolescents out of school and working by age 16, parts of Canadian society seem not to have viewed these adolescents as boys, but as men. This might have been further supported in the patriotic atmosphere of Canada, where every man was needed for service; boys would do as well as those of legitimate age. For instance, it was not uncommon for newspapers to praise the valour of young soldiers serving overseas. *The Globe* noted that Driver H.E. Brouse, a 15-year-old from Kingston, whose brother was a successful local hockey player, had been seriously wounded with the 72nd Battery, Canadian Field Artillery. The paper noted rather triumphantly that he was "Kingston's youngest soldier at the front."[57] The public elevated these young warriors into heroes, and the adolescents gladly accepted the mantle.[58]

New battalions raised from mid-1915 onward consisted of a shocking number of underage soldiers. An analysis of several dozen battalions in November 1916 revealed significant problems with the quality of the recruits: 45 per cent of the infantrymen in the 32nd Battalion and 44 per cent in the 92nd were classified as unfit, overage, or underage; the 69th Battalion, the worst, reached 53 per cent.[59] Among these unfits were hundreds of underage Canadians, who made up the highest grouping of unfits at 38 per cent, followed by overage men at 24 per cent, with the remainder falling under an assortment of maladies, deformities, and medical problems from flat feet and defective vision to weak hearts and tuberculosis.[60] [. . .]

Studies like these indicated that, by the end of 1916, some 5,020 identified adolescents were already in England, having been placed in reserve and training units until they reached the required age of 19.[61] Officers in the training camps, which were beginning to overflow with these lads, were looking for guidance on what to do with them. While these adolescents had been allowed to enlist in Canada at the age of 18 and even younger, an attempt to discourage this practice and unify the Canadian and British standards resulted in an OMFC order of

December 1916 that stipulated that only 19-year-old troops would be accepted into the ranks (except for 18-year-old buglers). It proved to be too little, too late, since these had been the informal rules in place in England since the start of the war.[62]

After the OMFC acknowledged the problem, a new order went out to the various Canadian commands and training units in January 1917 that all boys under 16-and-a-half, who were not buglers or drummers, were to be returned to Canada. Hundreds of boys were sent home.[63] There was a brief, mean-spirited attempt to have them pay their own ocean fare, but senior officials intervened and refused to punish patriotic youth, no matter how short their service.[64] Those older than 16 were to be attached to the 5th Division. As well, some 1,500 underage soldiers were also employed in the Forestry Corps, both in England and in France, but on the continent they were to be identified and only used in bush work far behind the lines.[65] By mid-1917 the Overseas Minister, Sir A. E. Kemp, noted in the House of Commons that, of the 63,046 men who had been discharged from the CEF, only 1,977 had been underage.[66] The vast majority of these boys remained overseas or in Canada, kept in uniform because of their usefulness.

Parents intervening to pull their children out of the line continued to experience difficulty.[67] Identifying a boy under 19 and even presenting evidence of his age did not always result in his release. Many overseas units ignored the OMFC order, delaying until evidence (usually a birth certificate) was presented to them on the Western Front. However, the wait could be weeks or months, and identified underage boys were being killed as their departure orders were delayed.[68] Private William Woods recounted the story of two young soldiers pulled out of the firing line by his battalion commander to comply with the OMFC rules during the battle of Fresnoy in May 1917:

> Some lads who were under age had been held back at the horse lines during this attack but someone ordered two of these boys to carry water up to us apparently without thinking that there would be no communication trenches through the previous No Man's

Land. One of these boys came through with two cans of water and he was crying, his mate had been killed on the way in.[69]

Reacting to the stalling tactics of front-line units, Adjutant-General P.E. Thacker ordered in October 1917 that, upon receiving a communication by a guardian that a soldier was underage, a unit was to withdraw the soldier in question from the firing line.[70] Despite GHQ's insistence, some units continued to contravene the order.

Front-line units were loath to lose these well-trained soldiers. Other officers worried that, if a soldier could be pulled out of the line for claiming to be underage, there would be a loop-hole for thousands and a convenient holiday from the front lines for thousands more who might abuse the system. Private Douglas Campbell, who had enlisted at the tender age of 14 years and 3 months and gave his occupation as farmer's son, was held back in his unit several times, despite a series of warning letters from GHQ. In the end, he was released; perhaps at five feet, nine inches, he seemed a far cry from a boy, and his medical discharge papers noted, "he is sixteen years of age but looks older."[71] In contrast, Private F.H. McGregor of the 102nd Battalion had enlisted at 15 after his father had been killed during the Battle of Second Ypres. At 17, he was pulled from the line; while his battalion did not want to let him go, the commanding officer finally agreed to allow him to leave because of his service and that of his family's sacrifice.[72] With GHQ pressing the issue from late 1917 onwards, hundreds of additional underage soldiers began to stream from the front lines to the rear.

If soldiers were to be withdrawn from the firing line and even from the rear areas, where were they to go? Some remained in France, sometimes even in battalion headquarters always within range of shellfire. More often they went to work on the lines of communication, the rear logistical areas, either bringing up supplies, supporting the infrastructure, or working in bases. Yet experienced combat soldiers were too important to be transformed into glorified scullery maids or regimental clerks, and most were pulled back to England to continue their training until they reached the appropriate age of 19, when they were sent back to their units. The temporary loss of the boys from the front was an impediment to operational efficiency, but one that would be overcome with the natural aging process. Young soldiers pulled out of the line in 1915 and 1916 would be back within a year or two, in time for the costliest fighting of the war.

Throughout 1915 and 1916 the underage soldiers were spread among units throughout England, receiving the same training as older men. However, in early 1917 at Shorncliffe, one of the primary Canadian camps, an 18-year-old was put on fatigue duty in a wet canteen, serving beer to his companions. Temperance groups reacted violently when word leaked out. They were already furious that beer was served at all in camps, but even more so upon hearing that "boys who volunteered to fight are really made into bar-tenders."[73] The adjutant-general of the forces responded quickly, ordering that underage soldiers could no longer serve in wet canteens, but this embarrassing incident was also an impetus for galvanizing support for the creation of a separate battalion, a unit to train and care for the adolescents in isolation from older men. [. . .]

On July 28, 1917, a special boys' battalion was formed and was soon renamed the Young Soldiers Battalion (YSB).[74] The YSB was commanded by Colonel D.S. Mackay, a doctor in civilian life and former commanding officer of the South Saskatchewan Reserve Battalion. By the end of summer, orders were posted that all infantry units were to transfer their underage soldiers to the YSB. Although the strength of the YSB was only 1,000 soldiers at maximum, those who could not fit in its ranks could be attached to the Canadian Army Medical Corps (CAMC) or railway and forestry units, but only in units situated out of harm's way.[75] Adolescents in other arms of the military, like the artillery or engineers, either resided in the reserve units or, in the last year of the war, found their way into the YSB. At the CAMC, these youth were trained as orderlies; in the railway and forestry corps, they were engaged in hard labour. They also freed up older men to move to the front.[76]

Despite natural aging, the number of enlisted boys rarely diminished in England since minors continued to arrive from Canada. In a three-month period, from October to December 1917, some 568 identified minors got off the transport ships and were almost immediately sent back to Canada.[77] That number, incredibly, would only have included those under 17-and-a-half, which meant that several times that number, all under 19, had also arrived and were fed into the training camps in England. It seemed the recruiters in Canada were taking anyone who applied in the months before conscription was brought into full effect. However, parents tracked down many of these boys, demanding their return. Again, the authorities in England blamed their counterparts in Canada for not being diligent or stringent enough during the selection process, as many of the under-17 recruits were obviously too young for service. While the overseas ministry and its general staff resented the burden of the underage soldiers, units in the firing line continued to acknowledge their value as fighting men.

For those young infantrymen older than 17-and-a-half but younger than 19 who arrived from Canada, or those coming from the camps or fighting units, their home would likely be the Young Soldiers Battalion. The training in England with the YSB was a mixture of military discipline, physical fitness, and education.[78] Creating an environment where proper morals could be inculcated was important to Mackay, and he established "cheerful, well furnished reading and games rooms."[79] The boys had access to a dry canteen filled with candy and treats, but the alcohol-serving wet canteens were out of bounds. It is unclear what some of the combat veterans thought of this concern for their welfare, especially after enjoying the privilege of the daily rum ration, but perhaps it was a fair trade for getting out of the trenches.

Weak, reedy boys were quickly transformed into hardened young men. The military training included bombing, musketry, and anti-gas precautions. The intensity was a shock to more than a few adolescents coming straight from Canada. "One day we were taken out to be taught bayonet-fighting," recounted Keith Fallis of the YSB. "They had straw men there. After you had done a certain amount of training about how to hold your rifle, then you had to practice taking a run and a jab at this straw man. "In, out, and on guard," is what the sergeant would shout. We were instructed to aim for the throat and stomach. I think more than half of us just couldn't eat our supper that evening."[80] Officers and NCOs offered detailed lectures on how to survive on the Western Front: it was old-hat for some of the young combat veterans who had been pulled from the trenches, but an eye-opening experience for adolescents who had just arrived from Canada.

As in France, the young soldiers were subject to the full military law. While Mackay evidently cared for his boys, he was a strict disciplinarian who handed out punishments when warranted. But the colonel was no martinet. When two of his soldiers had their belts stolen and were then arrested for being improperly dressed, he refused to charge them, as they were "smart, bright boys" who did not deserve this harassment.[81] Mackay held his ground even though the camp headquarters was demanding punishment to enforce discipline. Private C.A. Stranger, a long-service veteran who had enlisted at 15, had been pulled back from his unit in France to the YSB in early 1918. Unhappy at being away from the firing line, he deserted to go back to the front. He was caught and returned to the YSB, where the OC only gave him a slap on the wrist, even though headquarters again demanded that "severe disciplinary action . . . be taken against him." Mackay refused, not wanting to "break the splendid spirit shown by this man."[82] In other cases, Mackay worried about punishing youngsters who were "very 'childish' and not fully developed mentally."[83] A few of these young soldiers were sent home on his orders rather than be transferred to the front, where he believed they would not survive.

This paternalism was not coddling, which would never have been endured by youths who had recently embraced manhood, but an attempt to guide the soldiers to maturity. It was noted in battalion records that there was never an epidemic of bad discipline in the YSB. Colonel Mackay was firm if understanding, and he soon quieted down, in the words of one soldiers' publication, the "young monkeys [who] were a source of worry to many a commanding officer when scattered through the training camps."[84] He started building morale and confidence by getting new, matching uniforms. Then he pushed hard and succeeded in convincing authorities that growing adolescents had different dietary requirements than older men and was able to arrange for an official supplement to their rations.[85]

Mackay and his officers often exhibited a genuine paternal instinct towards their young soldiers. This was not unique within the YSB, as good officers also cared for their men in the field.[86] In the YSB, however, officers were often called on to perform parental roles. One indignant mother demanded that the commanding officer give her son, Private Gilbert Taylor, a stern talking to since he was spending his pay with "terrible extravagance." Mackay did, later writing to assure her that her son blamed his monetary exuberance on visits to London, and a fetching girl he had met while there, but promised to continue sending $15 a month of his assigned pay to his mother.[87]

In other cases, the senior officers of the YSB intervened to ensure that their young charges did not marry during their periodic leaves to the big city. Since commanding officers had to authorize marriages, they often withheld this permission until their young soldiers had a chance to ponder the consequences. At other times, as was the case with Private George Clifford, the OC refused to authorize the marriage unless "circumstances demand it" through a pregnancy. They did not, and Clifford remained single, although he had contracted a serious case of venereal disease by the end of the war.[88] He was in a minority, however. While there were occasional cases of syphilis among the adolescents, the VD cases within the YSB only ran at 2 per cent, about seven times less than the average for older Canadian troops.[89] There did not appear to be any extra worry or fear that these lads were contracting diseases, and no extra precautions were taken, even though Mackay hinted at his worry about the boys' "morals." The young soldiers continued to be treated as men insofar as there were no restrictions on their seeing the opposite sex.[90]

In addition to protecting the young soldiers' bodies, the senior staff of the YSB were also eager to see their charges prosper intellectually. School studies were encouraged through the Khaki University programme, which educated more than 50,000 Canadians during the war. One report noted, "All kinds of men are being reached. . . . There are . . . quite a number of school boys trying to complete Jr. Matric[ulation] . . . and keen young fellows looking ahead to the days when they will have to resume civilian employment."[91] In fact, there was a designated battalion schoolmaster who helped 64 adolescents pass Grade 4, with 21 having been deemed illiterate before enlisting.[92] Hundreds of other young soldiers were taught at more advanced levels. Schooling was important, and Colonel Mackay noted that, through education, his boys would "be more useful citizens on their return to civil life."[93] Like other soldiers in the CEF, the adolescents also received spiritual guidance, with mandatory church parades on Sunday.

Despite this education and training, the young soldiers moved inexorably towards their nineteenth birthday and their inevitable transfer to the front. Throughout the period of the YSB's existence, some 568 soldiers travelled through its ranks, eventually to serve in Europe.[94] The parades transferring the adolescents to new units were trying for officers and men, and by 1918 they occurred daily. When soldiers reached 18 and nine months, they spent a final three months of intense training in a reserve unit before being sent to fighting units at the front. [. . .]

By the summer of 1918, there was also a constant stream of requests by Canadian parents for their sons to be returned to them. Private John E. Rice had enlisted at 16 in January 1918, adding 16 months to his age. His angry mother wrote to the YSB in July of that year that "they had no right to except [sic] him in the first place. . . . He is under age and we need him on the farm. He can help our country by doing his work on the farm at home." Rice's parents had been trying to track him down for months, but had no idea "how to get him out."[95] His mother's persistence may have gotten him out of the ranks more quickly than most adolescents, and he was labelled "unserviceable" after his mother passed along his birth certificate and notarized declaration attesting to his age. John Rice was sent home in late September and discharged formally on November 20, 1918.[96] [. . .]

Most of the letters came from rural families imploring the military to release their sons for essential war work on the farm, especially from elderly or sick parents who could not find farm hands. Others, like Charlotte Sinclair, offered a "mother's pleading" to let her son Joe come home for a visit. He had enlisted underage, and she was desperate to see him before he went to France. "I don't want to take him out of the army, all I am asking is if he can be let to go home for a while. I think my prayer should be granted as I have already lost two of my sons." Mackay was forced to turn down her impassioned request, but wrote revealingly, clearly trying to find a military reason for his discharge, that, if she could provide more details, he would take up her request again.[97] Joseph Sinclair was not demobilized until after the Armistice. [. . .]

In cases where underage soldiers were training in England, often a year or two away from being sent to the front, it was hard to justify why they could not be sent back to Canada. Most often parents expressed a hope that the young soldier be returned home, but similar pleas were also made by sisters, aunts, legal guardians, and even older brothers serving in the trenches, who did not want their younger siblings to experience what they were enduring.

By June 1918 there were 1,269 identified soldiers under 18: 755 were in the YSB, 136 in forestry units, 131 in the medical corps, 99 in reserve units, and another 148 in other units. There were also 1,392 aged 18: 203 in the YSB, 212 in the medical corps, 80 in forestry units, 809 in reserve units, and 88 elsewhere.[98] No one knew how many more adolescents were overseas, but the "problem" was taking care of itself as they aged into men, or remained forever adolescents as they were killed and struck off strength. The steady pressure from parents forced Overseas Minister Sir A.E. Kemp to issue an order in June 1918 that all adolescents under 17 be returned automatically to Canada, and those under 18 returned to Canada if parents requested. The minister especially wanted to grant releases to those young soldiers who had "served in France or are not presently employed in any particularly useful occupation."[99]

For the first time, the Canadian military authorities in France did not object. The Allies had weathered the storm of the German March 1918 Offensive that had been launched behind a fury of shells, poison gas, and new infiltration tactics, but it had been a near-run. The British had been pushed back across the front, and in their desperation had been forced to call up 18-year-olds who were not fully trained. [. . .] The Canadians did not have to raid their underage soldiers, and many were soon being sent home, although not those who were over 18.[100]

By October 1918, with the Germans being pushed back on all fronts in renewed heavy fighting, Colonel Mackay recommended that his unit be disbanded and that the young soldiers be sent back to Canada. Constant letters from mothers demanding to know why their sons were being sent overseas at 19, when conscription under the Military Service Act was only taking 20-year-olds, left him convinced that his young soldiers should not bear the brunt of having enlisted before conscription.[101] Mackay told his superiors that, while the Khaki University courses had been useful, his "boys" should be returned to Canada to "settle their minds down to some kind of civil employment." To appease some of the more diligent army administrators, he also proposed, "If the war continues long enough, then these men can be given the privilege of re-enlisting on attaining the age of 20 years."[102] Mackay's recommendation carried weight, and it went all the way up to the minister, who signed off on it at the end of October.[103]

In early November the 981 members of the YSB moved to Kinmel Park in North Wales to begin demobilization. Inevitable delays were brought on by a shortage of shipping and strikes, and the young soldiers waited in the dreadful shantytown that sprang up around Kinmel. The food was bad; the accommodations were worse. Drill was half-hearted and disrupted as soldiers were less willing to engage in mindless activity.[104] The Armistice of November 11 did nothing to ease tensions, and bad feelings erupted into a riot ten days later.

Members of the YSB had been invited to a dance. Cleaned up and eager to meet some women, a group of young soldiers arrived at the dance, but were barred from entry by British officer cadets. The Canadians, many of them combat veterans, reacted badly. They fortified and armed themselves with alcohol, fence posts, and bricks, and then stoned the building. Shattered window panes alerted the British soldiers and women inside to the angry mob. A company of British officer cadets was called out with bayonets fixed and faced down the Canadians. The soldiers of the YSB were not cowed and refused to back down. There were some skirmishes, with both sides suffering casualties—some sustained bayonet wounds, others brick lacerations to the head, and one poor British cadet was disarmed and non-fatally run through with his own bayonet. After some bruises and blood, the young Canadians were eventually persuaded by their officers to return to their barracks, but with 65 panes of broken glass and the remnants of some 400 dishes lining the floor, the Canadians had made their point.[105] The British high command heard it. Most of the young Canadians were fast-tracked through the demobilization process and sailed home within a week.[106]

Conclusion

The Commonwealth War Graves Commission, tasked with caring for the graves of over a million British and Commonwealth service personnel, has a total of 1,412 identified Great War Canadian adolescents under the age of 19 in its care. Of these, 1,027 were 18 years old, 296 were 17, 75 were 16, and 14 of the dead were aged 15.[107] Most were killed on the Western Front. Since only about 61 per cent of the total CWGC entries show the age of death, however, it would be logical to assume that about 2,270 underage soldiers died during the war. Of course, the number was likely higher, since soldiers who enlisted at 16 or 17 but were killed at 19 would not be classified as underage soldiers in this exercise. They warrant some acknowledgement, even if their number is unquantifiable. Since there were roughly 60,000 Canadian deaths for those in service, one in 26 was an underage soldier. Extrapolating again, of the 424,000 Canadians who served overseas, one in 26 would yield a number of almost 16,300 underage servicemen. [. . .] While these figures are necessarily soft, considering that underage soldiers often enlisted using a false age, it is clear that the country had relied heavily on its adolescents during the Great War.

These underage soldiers grew proficient at hiding themselves in their units to escape detection during the war. However, in the post-war years, the adolescents were left increasingly in the forefront of the ever-dwindling ranks of surviving veterans as their more elderly comrades succumbed to age. By the beginning of the twenty-first century, as the last veterans marched into history, it appeared that these now ancient heroes representing the great mass of veterans were all boys when they fought in the Great War. That, of course, is untrue: the average age of the Canadian Great War soldier was 26.3.[108] But the notion of wasted youth, of a lost generation, remains a powerful trope surrounding the Great War.[109] The war "murdered the nation's youth and turned youth into murderers," recounted one bitter veteran in his post-war memoirs.[110] The loss of more than 60,000 Canadians, and perhaps especially those who were underage soldiers, forever marked a generation.

Most veterans survived, however. Crashing back to Canada in wave after wave in 1919, they found jobs scarce in the post-war years as a country mired in debt was little able to fulfil its promise of creating a "land fit for heroes." Furthermore, an 18-year-old who had seen two years in the trenches, prematurely aged and perhaps embittered, did not easily return to being a stock boy or even to live under his parents' roof and rules. There were also the wounded, among whom there would have been some 6,500 underage adolescents.[111] Some would

never be the same. William Mansley had enlisted at 14 in the second year of the war. At 4 feet, 11 inches and 95 pounds, he could not deny his youth, but still he served in the trenches with the Royal Canadian Regiment, even if it was only for the last three months of the war and to escape a jail term for stealing a bike. While in the trenches he suffered no physical wounds, but remained psychologically scarred and unable to hold down a job after the war, even though other veterans often tried to intervene on his behalf. In 1930 he wrote to Sir Arthur Currie, his former corps commander, "[O]wing to my age and sacrificing all in life, all I have now is my discharge and medals."[112] [. . .]

[. . .] While the young trench soldiers played a part in the conflict, the role of children in a patriotically infused, total war environment was even more encompassing. We know very little about this children's war, but we can recognize the 20,000 underage soldiers who enlisted in the CEF during the Great War, as well as the more than 2,000 who were left behind, buried in war cemeteries for King and country. Perhaps saddest of all are those young Canadians who lie in graves bearing false names, whose parents never had a chance to say goodbye. It is perhaps fitting to end with one of those young soldiers left behind: Private W.E. Dailey was 16 years old when he was killed on the Somme. His tombstone in the Sunken Road cemetery contains the words: "Mother's darling."[113]

Notes

1. Desmond Morton, *When Your Number's Up: The Canadian Soldier in the First World War* (Toronto: Random House, 1993), p. 279.
2. See the conclusion for an analysis of available data.
3. No work specifically analyses Canadian children and the Great War, although segments of that experience can be gleaned from surrounding texts, especially those relating to social reform, welfare, and purity movements. For a recent important work that offers some insight into the role of children, see Desmond Morton, *Fight or Pay: Soldiers' Families in the Great War* (Vancouver: University of British Columbia Press, 2004); also see Barbara Wilson, *Ontario and the First World War, 1914–1918: A Collection of Documents* (Toronto: Champlain Society for the Government of Ontario, University of Toronto Press, 1977); William Raynsford and Jeannette Raynsford, *Silent Casualties: Veterans' Families in the Aftermath of the Great War* (Madoc, ON: Merribrae Press, 1986).
4. A.C.T. White, *The Story of Army Education, 1943–1963* (London: George G. Harrap, 1963), chap. 2–3.
5. A.W. Cockerill, *Sons of the Brave: The Story of the Boy Soldiers* (London: Leo Cooper, in association with Secker & Warburg, 1984), pp. 41–44.
6. King's Regulations and Orders (1910), para. 243, 246. The Militia Act of 1904, which had amended that of 1868 and drew upon the long traditions of the citizen-soldiers in the Canadas and before that in New France, provided for a levee en masse for all male inhabitants of Canada between the ages of 18 and 60. See J.L. Granatstein and J.M. Hitsman, *Broken Promises: A History of Conscription in Canada* (Toronto: Oxford University Press, 1977), pp. 64–65.

7. For an analysis of children in Canadian history, see Cynthia Comacchio, *The Dominion of Youth: Adolescence and the Making of Modern Canada, 1920 to 1950* (Waterloo: Wilfrid Laurier University Press, 2006), and *Nations Are Built of Babies: Saving Ontario's Mothers and Children* (Montreal and Kingston: McGill-Queen's University Press, 1993); Robert McIntosh, *Boys in the Pits: Child Labour in Coal Mines* (Montreal and Kingston: McGill-Queen's University Press, 2000); Neil Sutherland, *Children in English-Canadian Society: Framing the Twentieth Century Consensus* (Toronto: University of Toronto Press, 1976); Joy Parr, *Labouring Children: British Immigrant Apprentices to Canada, 1869-1924* (Toronto: University of Toronto Press, 1994).

8. For an example of boy miners, see McIntosh, *Boys in the Pits*, chap. 7-8.

9. Marta Danylewycz and Alison Prentice, "Teachers' Work: Changing Patterns and Perceptions in the Emerging School Systems of Nineteenth- and Twentieth-century Central Canada," *Labour/Le Travail*, vol. 17 (Spring 1986), p. 140; R.D. Gidney, *From Hope to Harris: The Reshaping of Ontario's Schools* (Toronto: University of Toronto Press, 1999), p. 13.

10. Robert McIntosh, "Boys in the Nova Scotian Coal Mines, 1873-1923," in Nancy Janovicek and Joy Parr, eds., *Histories of Canada's Children and Youth* (Toronto: Oxford University Press, 2003), p. 77.

11. Joan Sangster, *Girl Trouble: Female Delinquency in English Canada* (Toronto: Between the Lines, 2002), pp. 15-16.

12. See Robert McIntosh, "Constructing the Child: New Approaches to the History of Childhood in Canada," *Acadiensis*, vol. 28, no. 2 (Spring 1999), for an overview of the literature.

13. See Ramsay Cook, *The Regenerators: Social Criticism in Late Victorian English Canada* (Toronto: University of Toronto Press, 1985); Sharon Anne Cook, *Through Sunshine and Shadow: The Woman's Christian Temperance Union, Evangelism, and Reform in Ontario, 1874-1930* (Montreal and Kingston: McGill-Queen's University Press, 1995); Comacchio, *Nations Are Built of Babies*.

14. Daphne Read, ed., *The Great War and Canadian Society: An Oral History* (Toronto: New Hogtown Press, 1978), pp. 90-91.

15. David Silbey, *The British Working Class and Enthusiasm for War, 1914-1916* (London and New York: Frank Cass, 2005), p. 81.

16. On the cadet movement, see Desmond Morton, "The Cadet Movement in the Moment of Canadian Militarism, 1909-1914," *Journal of Canadian Studies*, vol. 13, no. 2 (Summer 1978), pp. 56-69.

17. For the influence of pre-war literature and military messaging, see Mark Moss, *Manliness and Militarism: Educating Young Boys in Ontario for War* (Toronto: Oxford University Press, 2001); Michael Paris, *The Great War and Juvenile Literature in Britain* (Westport, CT: Praeger, 2004).

18. Library and Archives Canada [hereafter LAC], MG 30 E100, Sir Arthur Currie papers, vol. 3, file A-H, John C. Wright to Sir Robert Borden, April 18, 1918.

19. See Directorate of History and Heritage, 74/672, Edwin Pye papers, folder 4, Militia Order No. 372, August 17, 1914.

20. Nellie McClung, *The Next of Kin: Those Who Wait and Wonder* (Toronto: Thomas Allen, 1917), pp. 33, 48.

21. Dale McClare, *The Letters of a Young Canadian Soldier during World War I* (Kentville, NS: Brook House Press, 2000), p. 1.

22. Toronto, Archives of Ontario, C232-2-0-4-263, "To the Women of Canada" [poster]. See also Jeff Keshen, *Propaganda and Censorship during Canada's Great War* (Edmonton: University of Alberta Press, 1996), p. 42.

23. Peter Simkins, *Kitchener's Army: The Raising of the New Armies, 1914-16* (Manchester: Manchester University Press, 1988), pp. 182-183.

24. Colonel A. F. Duguid, *Official History of the Canadian Forces in the Great War, 1914-1919*, General Series, Volume I (Ottawa: J. O. Patenaude, Printer to the King, 1938), pp. 430-431; LAC, RG 9, III, vol. 2893, 160-33, clipping, *Montreal Gazette*, October 18, 1916.

25. Thomas H. Raddall, *In My Time: A Memoir* (Toronto: McClelland & Stewart, 1976), pp. 42-43.

26. I would like to thank Nicholas Clarke for sharing with me some of his research for his ongoing dissertation on rejected volunteers from the CEF.

27. See Ian Hugh MacLean Miller, *Our Glory and Our Grief: Torontonians and the Great War* (Toronto: University of Toronto Press, 2002), pp. 76-80; for the British process, which was similar to that of the Canadians, see J.M. Winter, *The Great War and the British People* (London: Macmillan, 1985), pp. 48-64.

28. Herbert Bruce, *Politics and the Canadian Army Medical Corps* (Toronto: William Briggs, 1919), p. 45; LAC, RG 150, accession 1992-93/166, box 6153-40, Mick Russell.

29. Ilana R. Bet-El, *Conscripts: Lost Legions of the Great War* (Stroud, UK: Sutton Publishers, 1999), pp. 33-35.

30. Thomas P. Rowlett, "Memoirs of a Signaller, 1914-1918" (Canadian War Museum Library, unpublished memoir, n.d.), pp. 12-13.

31. John Macfie, Letters Home (Meaford, ON: Oliver Graphics, 1990), p. 12.

32. See LAC, RG 150, Accession 1992-93/166, box 5768-11, John Lowe; L.C. Giles, *Liphook, Bramshott, and the Canadians* (Preservation Society, 1986), postscript.

33. John Thompson, *Harvest of War: The Prairie West, 1914-1918* (Toronto: McClelland & Stewart, 1978), p. 42.

34. Quote by Robert Falconer, president of the University of Toronto, cited in Keshen, *Propaganda and Censorship*, p. 23.

35. Armine Norris, *Mainly for Mother* (Toronto: Ryerson Press, n.d. [1919]), p. 133.

36. Frederick G. Scott, *The Great War as I Saw It* (Ottawa: CEF Books, reprint 2000), pp. 94-95.

37. Ex-Quaker, "Not Mentioned in the Dispatches," North Shore Press, 1933, p. 57.

38. Norah L. Lewis, ed., *"I want to join your club:" Letters from Rural Children, 1900–1920* (Waterloo, ON: Wilfrid Laurier University Press, 1996), pp. 220–221. For the experience of the trench soldier, see Richard Holmes, *Tommy: The British Soldier on the Western Front, 1914–1918* (London: HarperCollins, 2004); Denis Winter, *Death's Men: Soldiers of the Great War* (London: Penguin Books, 1979).

39. Canadian War Museum, 2002063–002, Owen Brothers papers, 436743, "The Somme" by Private James Hector Owen.

40. LAC, RG 41, Records of the Canadian Broadcasting Corporation, research transcripts for radio program Flanders Fields, vol. 15, 52nd Battalion, A.E. Fallen, 3/1–2.

41. John W. Lynch, *Princess Patricia's Canadian Light Infantry, 1917–1919* (Hicksville, NY: Exposition Press, 1976), p. 59.

42. William Ogilvie, *Umty-Iddy-Umty: The Story of a Canadian Signaller in the First World War* (Erin, ON: Boston Mills Press, 1982), p. 40.

43. LAC, RG 41, vol. 8, 7th Battalion, J.I. Chambers, 1/7. For the importance of rum to soldiers, see Tim Cook, "'More as a medicine than a beverage': 'Demon Rum' and the Canadian Trench Soldier in the First World War," *Canadian Military History*, vol. 9, no. 1 (Winter 2000), pp. 7–22.

44. F.W. Noyes, *Stretcher Bearers at the Double* (Toronto: Hunter Rose Company, 1937), pp. 175, 183. For soldiers' voting, see Desmond Morton, "Polling the Soldier Vote: The Overseas Campaign in the Canadian General Election of 1917," *Journal of Canadian Studies*, vol. 10 (1975), pp. 39–59.

45. Desmond Morton and Glenn Wright, *Winning the Second Battle: Canadian Veterans and the Return to Civilian Life, 1915–1930* (Toronto: University of Toronto Press, 1987), p. 74.

46. William Gray, *A Sunny Subaltern: Billy's Letters from Flanders* (Toronto: McClelland, Goodchild & Stewart, 1916), p. 164.

47. Gerald Oram, *Military Executions during World War I* (London: Palgrave, 2003), p. 62.

48. On Canadian executions, see Andrew B. Godefroy, *For Freedom and Honour? The Story of the 25 Canadian Volunteers Executed in the First World War* (Nepean, ON: CEF Books, 1998); Teresa Iacobelli, "Arbitrary Justice? A Comparative Analysis of Canadian Death Sentences Passed and Death Sentences Commuted during the First World War" (M.A. thesis, Wilfrid Laurier University, 2004).

49. Norma Hillyer Shephard, ed., *Dear Harry: The Firsthand Account of a World War I Infantryman* (Burlington, ON: Brigham Press, 2003), p. 204.

50. LAC, RG 41, vol. 10, 20th Battalion, Bert Warren, 2/10–11.

51. LAC, RG 9 III, vol. 36, file 8–I–125, J. W. Carson to Secretary, War Office, Whitehall, July 13, 1916.

52. LAC, RG 9, III, vol. 36, file 8–I–125, Army Council Instruction No. 1186 of 1916, June 13, 1916.

53. Van Emden, *Boy Soldiers*, pp. 178–182.

54. Hansard, House of Commons Debates, April 25, 1916, p. 3049.

55. Hansard, House of Commons Debates, February 1, 1917, p. 338.

56. For enlistment, see C.A. Sharpe, "Enlistment in the Canadian Expeditionary Force, 1914–1918: A Regional Analysis," *Journal of Canadian Studies*, vol. 18, no. 4 (1983–1984); Robert Craig Borden and Donald Loveridge, "Unrequited Faith: Recruiting the CEF, 1914–1918," *Revue internationale d'histoire militaire*, vol. 51 (1982); Paul Maroney, "'The Great Adventure': The Context and Ideology of Recruiting in Ontario, 1914–17," *Canadian Historical Review*, vol. 77, no. 1 (1996), pp. 62–98.

57. "Kingston's 15-year-old Soldier is a Casualty," *Globe* [Toronto], November 21, 1917, p. 13.

58. Morton and Wright, *Winning the Second Battle*, p. 25.

59. LAC, RG 9, III–A–I, vol. 90, 10–12–15, Reid, Adjutant General to Perley, OMFC, November 9, 1916.

60. LAC, RG 9, III–A–I, vol. 90, 10–12–15, Adjutant General, Report, November 8, 1916; Thacker to Deputy Minister, February 9, 1917.

61. LAC, RG 9, III–A–I, vol. 90, 10–12–15, Reid, Adjutant General to Perley, OMFC, November 8, 1916.

62. See Directorate of History and Heritage, 74/672, Edwin Pye papers, folder 4, OMFC Routine Order 45, December 18, 1916.

63. LAC, RG 9, III, vol. 2893, 160–33, memorandum, November 9, 1916; vol. 2750, 55–33, HQ–39–1–13, January 19, 1917; vol. 436, file 413–1, from OMFC to Adjutant General, January 19, 1917.

64. LAC, RG 9, III, vol. 436, file 413–1, Canadian Discharge Depot at Buxton to OMFC, Argyll House, January 31, 1917.

65. LAC, RG 9, III, vol. 2750, 55–33, A.G.4b.Canadians, 5–1–7, January 2, 1917.

66. Hansard, House of Commons Debates, July 6, 1917, p. 3096.

67. Hansard, House of Commons Debates, July 31, 1917, p. 4001.

68. LAC, RG 9, III, vol. 2859, 7–33, A.G. To G.O.C., September 20, 1917.

69. Canadian War Museum, 58A 1.8.5, William Woods papers, "A Private's Own Story of the First World War," p. 11.

70. LAC, RG 9, III, vol. 1087, file 252–4, pt. 2, Adjutant General to A.A.G. GHQ, 3rd Section, October 4, 1917.

71. LAC, RG 9, III, vol. 2750, 55–33, Disposal of Minors, May 17, 1917; RG 150, 1992–93/166, box 1428–42, D.C.M.B. Campbell.

72. LAC, RG 9, III, vol. 2275, file 5–30, pt. 2, Field Cashier to AA and QMG, 4th Canadian Division, August 17, 1917.

73. LAC, RG 9, III, vol. 1478, 144–1, Adjutant-General to GOC, Shorncliffe, May 21, 1917. For the wet canteen as a lightening rod for conflict, see Tim Cook, "Wet Canteens and Worrying Mothers: Soldiers and Temperance Groups in the Great War," *Histoire sociale/Social History*, vol. 35, no. 70 (June 2003), pp. 311–330.

74. LAC, RG, III-A-1, vol. 90, 10-12-8, Order 2483, September 18, 1917.

75. LAC, RG 9, III, vol. 2994, 16–13, Transfer of Boys to CAMC, October 5, 1917.

76. LAC, RG 9, III, vol. 2859, 11–33, A.G.3 to CGS, June 10, 1918.

77. LAC, RG 9, III, vol. 2859, 11–33, Brigadier-General, Adjutant-General, Canadians to Secretary, Militia Council, December 29, 1917.

78. LAC, RG 9, III, vol. 4708, 90/21, Young Soldiers' Battalion historical record, December 8, 1918. For details on training, see the YSB's War Diary in RG 9, III, vol. 4952.

79. LAC, RG 9, III, vol. 4708, 90/21, Young Soldiers' Battalion historical record.

80. Read, *The Great War and Canadian Society*, p. 132.

81. RG 9, III, vol. 1768, file U–1–13, pt. 31, OC, YSB, to HQ, Bramshott, May 17, 1918.

82. RG 9, III, vol. 1765, file U–1–13, pt. 16, report, July 5, 1916; Ferguson to HQ, Cdn Troops, Bramshott, August 5, 1918.

83. RG 9, III, vol. 1530, file 4–7, OC 8th Res Cdn BN to HA, 2nd C.R. Bde, February 2, 1918.

84. RG 9, vol. 4751, "The Young Soldiers' Battalion," *The Bramshott Souvenir Magazine*, p. 122.

85. RG 9, III, vol. 1765, file U–1–13, pt. 14, YSB to HQ, Canadians, Kinmel Park, October 30, 1918.

86. See Gary Sheffield, *Leadership in the Trenches: Officer-Man Relations, Morale and Discipline in the British Army in the Era of the First World War* (London: Macmillan, 2000).

87. RG 9, III, vol. 1766, file U–1–13, pt. 19, Mrs. Sarah Taylor to OC, YSB, August 12, 1918.

88. RG 9, III, vol. 1767, file U–1–13, pt. 29(b), Captain, YSB to OC, 21st Reserve BN, June 28, 1918; RG 150, 1992–93/166, box 1799-25, George Clifford.

89. See the medical returns in RG 9, III, vol. 1763, file U–1–13, pt. 5. For venereal disease rates in the CEF, see Jay Cassel, *The Secret Plague: Venereal Disease in Canada, 1838–1939* (Toronto: University of Toronto Press, 1987), p. 123.

90. RG 9, III, vol. 2220, file 1–26, pt. II, Young Soldiers' Battalion, October 21, 1918.

91. LAC, MG 30 D115, Henry Marshall Tory Papers, vol. 7, file 13, Laddie Millen, YMCA, Shorncliffe, May 22, 1918.

92. RG 9, III, vol. 4708, 90/21, Historical Record, Young Soldiers' Battalion, December 8, 1918.

93. RG 9, vol. 4751, "The Young Soldiers' Battalion," The Bramshott Souvenir Magazine, p. 122.

94. Report of the Ministry, Overseas Military Forces of Canada 1918 (London, 1919), p. 24.

95. RG 9, III, vol. 1764, file U–1–13, pt. 7, W. Schoolery to YSB, n.d. [received July 6, 1918].

96. RG 150, 1992–93/166, box 8222-50, J.E. Rice personnel file, 3033011.

97. RG 9, III, vol. 1767, file U–1–13, pt. 30, Charlotte Sinclair to War Office, June 6, 1918; RG 150, 1992–93/166, box 8942-46, Joseph Sinclair, 722296.

98. RG 9, III, vol. 2859, 11–33, Adjutant-General, Canadians to CGS, June 3, 1918.

99. RG 9, III-A-I, vol. 90, 10–12–8, Minister, OMFC to Secretary, Argyll House, June 5, 1918.

100. For Currie's courage in breaking up the 5th Division, see Hugh M. Urquhart, *Arthur Currie: The Biography of a Great Canadian* (Toronto: J.M. Dent & Sons, 1950), pp. 205–206; Tim Cook, "The Butcher and the Madman: Sir Arthur Currie, Sir Sam Hughes and the War of Reputations," *Canadian Historical Review*, vol. 85, no. 4 (December 2004), pp. 693–719.

101. The Military Service Act, which resulted in conscription of Canadian males aged 20 to 45, categorized the manpower available, with those single men aged 20 to 24 being the first conscripted. See Granatstein and Hitsman, *Broken Promises*, chap. 3.

102. RG 9, III, vol. 2220, file 1–26, pt. II, Young Soldiers' Battalion, October 21, 1918.

103. RG 9, III-A-I, vol. 90, 10–12–8, Thacker to Minister, OMFC, October 30, 1918.

104. Desmond Morton, "'Kicking and Complaining': Demobilization Riots in the Canadian Expeditionary Force, 1918–19," *Canadian Historical Review*, vol. 61 (1980), pp. 334–360.

105. For the YSB riot, see LAC, RG 24, vol. 1841, file GAQ 10–34F, Disturbances in Canadian Camps and Areas, 1918–1919.

106. The YSB was officially disbanded on December 7, 1918.

107. I am indebted to Richard Holt for compiling and helping to interpret the information from the Commonwealth War Graves Commission.

108. Morton, *When Your Number's Up*, p. 278.

109. For a discussion of the lost generation and the war dead, see Jay Winter, *Sites of Memory, Sites of Mourning: The Great War in European Cultural History* (Cambridge: Cambridge University Press, 1995); Jonathan Vance, *Death So Noble: Memory, Meaning, and the First World War* (Vancouver: University of British Columbia Press, 1997).

110. Pierre Van Paassen, *Days of Our Years* (New York: Hillman Curl Inc., 1939), p. 81.

111. The ratio of death to wounded was about one in four during the Great War, and surprisingly consistent among most armies.

112. LAC, MG 30 E100, Sir Arthur Currie Papers, vol. 23, file 92, Mansley to Currie, January 23, 1930 and February 17, 1930; RG 150, 1992–93/166, 5904–14, W. T. Mansley.

113. Martin Gilbert, *The Battle of the Somme: The Heroism and Horror of War* (Toronto: McClelland & Stewart, 2006), p. 177.

Sheet Music Cover for Gordon V. Thompson's
"I Want to Kiss Daddy Goodnight"

Gordon V. Thompson, "I Want to Kiss Daddy Goodnight." CWM 20020077-007
George Metcalf Archival Collection, Canadian War Museum.

Study Questions

1. What can you learn about the meaning of masculinity for men and boys in this early period by looking at the primary sources that accompany Brown's and Cook's essays? What kinds of characteristics or qualities are promoted through these materials?
2. R. Blake Brown focuses on the role of gun culture in the production of "ideal boys" at the turn of the century. Can we learn anything about "ideal girls" from this history?
3. Tim Cook's essay suggests that soldiering and "defending the empire" were considered noble pursuits in the past. Young recruits, he argues, underestimated or failed to appreciate the danger associated with warfare. Visit the Child Soldier International website at www.child-soldiers.org/ and consider what is similar and dissimilar about how the issues associated with child soldiers are framed in contemporary times.

Selected Bibliography

Articles

Frank, Blye, "Queer Selves/Queer in Schools: Young Men and Sexualities," in Susan Prentice, ed., *Sex in Schools: Canadian Education & Sexual Regulation*. Montreal: Our Schools/Ourselves, 1994: 44–59.

Hantover, Jeffery P., "The Boy Scouts and the Validation of Masculinity," *Journal of Social Issues* 34, 1 (1978): 184–95.

Hogeveen, Bryan, "'You will hardly believe I turned out so well': Parole, Surveillance, Masculinity and the Victoria Industrial School, 1896–1935," *Social History/Historie sociale* 37, 74 (November 2004): 201–29.

Macleod, David, "A Live Vaccine: The YMCA and Male Adolescence in the United States and Canada, 1870-1920," *Social History/Historie sociale* 11 (May 1978): 5–25.

Warren, Allen, "Popular Manliness: Baden-Powell, Scouting, and the Development of Manly Character," in J.A. Mangan and James Walvin, eds, *Manliness and Morality: Middle Class Masculinity in Britain and America, 1800–1940*. Manchester: Manchester University Press, 1987: 199–219.

Books

Brown, R. Blake, *Arming and Disarming: A History of Gun Control in Canada*. Toronto: University of Toronto Press, 2013.

Cook, Tim, *The Necessary War, Volume One: Canadians Fighting the Second World War, 1939–1943*. Toronto: Allen Lane, 2014.

Dummit, Christopher, *The Manly Modern: Masculinity in Postwar Canada*. Vancouver: UBC Press, 2008.

Greig, Christopher J., *Ontario Boys: Masculinity and the Idea of Boyhood in Postwar Ontario, 1945–1960*. Waterloo: Wilfrid University Press, 2014.

Greig, Christopher J., and Wayne J. Martino, *Canadian Men and Masculinities: Historical and Contemporary Perspectives*. Toronto: Canadian Scholars' Press, 2012.

4 Gender and Childhood

Editors' Introduction

Gender history explores the making of femininity and masculinity in the past. In any given context or time period, what it meant to be female and male often differed from how we understand these categories today. One's gender, then, is shaped by context, culture, time period, and also ideas attached to chronological age. This means that social ideals associated with femininity and masculinity have varied across age cohorts and over time, and have been used for differing purposes and agendas. Despite some shared expectations, feminine ideals were applied differently to, for example, a 4-year-old girl and a 50-year-old woman in the same era. A 9-year-old working-class boy in the nineteenth century was arguably far closer to the masculine ideal of competent breadwinner than was a 9-year old middle-class boy in post–Second World War Ontario. These nuances are important and they remind us that age, like gender, is socially constructed and needs careful historical analysis.[1]

The two essays in this chapter, by Kristine Alexander and Heidi MacDonald, take up some of these complexities directly, highlighting how masculine and feminine ideals play out in different contexts and with different consequences. Alexander tackles a methodological question central to gender history and the representation of young people in historical work: can we truly find and adequately represent girls' voices? This question, as Alexander points out, reflects the powerlessness of girls relative to men, women, and boys, which renders them often entirely excluded from archival collections. Their membership and participation in the Girl Guides, she reminds us, doesn't tell us how young people felt about the experience. Alexander tackles this challenge head on. Using post-colonial scholar Gayatri Chakravorty Spivak's argument that the subaltern—in Spivak's case, Indian women under British imperialism—were spoken for and not heard,[2] Alexander wonders if girls were not also subalterns with muted voices. In response, she carefully documents where and under what circumstances she finds girls' voices, and suggests that historians follow what Mona Gleason has called "empathic inference" to imagine how girls would have understood their guiding experiences.[3] The primary document that accompanies Alexander's essay, the logbook of the Hay River Girl Guide Company, invites us to venture into questions of voice and perspective. What can we learn about the girls' lives from the observations collected in the logbook? What remains a mystery?

Whereas Alexander wrestles with the pervasive lack of archival textual evidence for the experience of girls, Heidi MacDonald does not encounter such a stumbling block in her discussion of young men. MacDonald is able to draw on the writing of young men themselves, focusing on how economic hardship in the Great Depression threatened to trap them in a perpetual state of immaturity. The claim to adult status of the three men discussed here was threatened by economic hardship, and MacDonald shows precisely how dominant ideas about acceptable manhood in Depression-era Canada were defined primarily by autonomy and breadwinning status. Ideas about manhood, it is also important to point out, stood in stark contrast to ideas about being young. When the economic collapse made both autonomy and breadwinning difficult to achieve for Alan, Ole, and John, their sense of self and their claim to adulthood were threatened and diminished. An example of the archival letters analyzed by MacDonald accompanies her essay and enables us to experience first-hand the desperation and difficulty that these young men had in establishing security for themselves and their families. In particular, the letter from Ole (full name Helge), written in the winter of 1932, makes clear that he felt much anxiety about not being able to provide proper care for his ailing wife, Emily. The compromised ability to be a breadwinner left men like Ole in a liminal state, no longer boys or youth, but also not yet fully adult. MacDonald teases out in finer detail the strands of "coming of age" that constituted acceptable manhood in the Great Depression era, demonstrating the personal cost that young men paid for their failure to live up to societal expectations.

Both of the essays in this chapter remind us that gendered attitudes and behaviours shaped not only how people lived in the past but whether and what clues were left behind to reflect them. As targets of adult efforts to reproduce hegemonic, or dominant, relations of power, young people are key to our historical understanding of gender. The social construction of gender, like that of growing up, is made and remade through time.

Notes

1. On age as a category of analysis, see Leslie Paris, "Through the Looking Glass: Age, Stages, and Historical Analysis," *Journal of the History of Children and Youth*, 1, 1 (2008): 106–13. The classic study of girls in Canada is Veronica Strong-Boag, *The New Day Recalled: Lives of Girls and Women in English Canada, 1919–1939* (Toronto: Copp Clark Pitmann, 1988). See also Kristine Alexander, "Can the Girl Guide Speak? The Perils and Pleasures of Looking for Children's Voices in Archival Research," in Chapter 4 of this volume; Christopher J. Greig, *Ontario Boys: Masculinity* *and the Idea of Boyhood in Postwar Ontario, 1945–1960* (Waterloo: Wilfrid Laurier Press, 2014).

2. Gayatri Chakravorty Spivak, "Can the Subaltern Speak?," *Can the Subaltern Speak?: Reflections on the History of an Idea*, rev. ed., ed. Rosalind C. Morris (New York: Columbia UP, 2007).

3. For a valuable critique of "voice" in children's history analyses, see Mona Gleason, "Observations on the Limits of 'Children's Voices.'" http://shcyhome.org/2013/07/guest-post-mona-gleason-and-the-limits-of-childrens-voices.

Can the Girl Guide Speak? The Perils and Pleasures of Looking for Children's Voices in Archival Research

KRISTINE ALEXANDER

The history of childhood is written by adults and is often written about adults as well—about their hopes, their fears, and the ways in which they have sought to affect the future by educating and regulating young people. In large part, this is because archives are reflections of existing power relationships: they privilege the written word over the visual, the oral, and the material, the masculine over the feminine, elite white perspectives from the metropole over non-white and working-class voices from the peripheries, and adult perspectives over youthful ones. The power to exclude, as Rodney G.S. Carter has written, "is a fundamental aspect of the archive" (216), and girls' voices have been excluded especially often. This is even true of the archival collections of the Girl Guide movement, the world's largest voluntary organization for girls.

Since its establishment in England in 1909, the Guide movement has sought to mould, protect, and encourage generations of girls and young women. While its twenty-first-century incarnation identifies itself as a global humanitarian organization, whose empowered girl members volunteer to end poverty and violence in their communities and around the world, in the early twentieth century the official global vision of Guiding was an imperial one: a contradictory mix of gender conservatism, empowered citizenship, global sisterhood, and the British "civilizing mission."[1] By the 1930s, over 1.5 million girls within and beyond the British Empire had joined the movement and were wearing its uniforms, earning badges, and learning about camping and social service. Like the young readers discussed in Kristine Moruzi's article, these early-twentieth-century girls were encouraged to see themselves as part of a diverse and harmonious imperial and international sisterhood. The official program of Guiding was a product of adult anxieties and aspirations, but it also reflected ongoing and often unacknowledged negotiations among adults, adolescents, and children, as well as among local, national, imperial, and global contexts.

The Guide movement offered similar experiences and ideals to girls with vastly different identities and life experiences: during the 1920s and 1930s, the global Guide "sisterhood" included Jewish girls in Winnipeg and Toronto, Aboriginal girls at Canadian residential and day schools, middle-, upper-, and working-class girls in England, and students at mission schools in India. Whereas existing scholarship on the history of this organization is based mainly on adult-produced sources held in British and American archives, I have sought to expand our understanding of its history both geographically (by producing a multi-sited study of the movement's practices and ideals in early-twentieth-century England, Canada, and India) and by asking how girls and young women in these three distant and different places responded to the often contradictory ideals and practices of Guiding.[2] Their voices, perhaps unsurprisingly, were among the hardest to find among the many documentary traces the movement has left behind.

I am a historian by training, and my doctoral work on the imperial and international history of Guiding was based largely on archival research. And yet, as this article demonstrates, relying solely on the archive can obscure as much as it can reveal. My scholarly practice is therefore also informed by the close reading practices of literary criticism, the insights of art history and cultural studies, and the

Source: From *Jeunesse: Young People, Texts, Cultures* (Summer 2012): 132–44.

emphasis on understanding silences and power imbalances that characterizes post-colonial scholarship. Inspired by the methods of social and cultural history, I ask questions about discourse and practice, and about the often complicated relationships between the two. My work also engages with girls' studies and the new children's history, in that I aim to put girls at the centre of my research rather than focus simply on the prescriptions and descriptions of adults.

By studying the history of Guides in England, India, and Canada, I have sought to discover how ideas about girlhood travelled across borders and how these ideals were complicated and shaped by factors like race, class, and religion. Crucially, I also ask how girls themselves understood and responded to the adult-led activities and pedagogy of Guiding and how they used aspects of the movement in their own cultural practices. In some respects, my work (which includes analyses of Guide catalogues, consumer goods, radio programs, and films) examines Guiding as an early example of the globalized youth marketing practices discussed by Natalie Coulter. Moreover, like Moruzi's work on late-nineteenth- and early-twentieth-century girls' magazines, my scholarship is also concerned with print culture, the transnational circulation of texts, and the construction of an idealized international girl figure.

This essay, based on my own research experiences, discusses the frustrations and rewards of looking for girls' voices in archives across Canada, England, and India. This discussion will also provide insights about broader methodological and epistemological issues related to historical research, post-colonial scholarship, and children's studies. The title of my paper is a play on Gayatri Chakravorty Spivak's "Can the Subaltern Speak?"—a question that she ultimately answers in the negative. Whereas the subjects of Spivak's analysis were adult women who had been marginalized by race, gender, and the colonial context of British India, a number of scholars have argued that children are also subalterns—a colonized group, frequently seen as primitive or not fully realized, who are more often spoken for and about than they are allowed to speak.[3]

This is especially true of girls. Despite their practical and symbolic place at the heart of numerous debates about nation, empire, and modernity (through debates about the age of consent in India and fears about the "flapper vote" in 1920s Britain, for example), girls and young women have "by most usual criteria . . . acted from positions of relative powerlessness, marginality, and invisibility. And they have often been 'acted on'" (Maynes 116; see also Bannerji; Bingham; Driscoll). Studying girls, as Mary Jo Maynes has shown, reveals "the inadequacy of prevailing notions of historical agency" especially clearly (116). It also reveals the inadequacy of existing methods of archival collection and categorization, as girls' actions and choices are generally far less visible in conventional textual sources than are those of boys, women, and men. Some girls' voices are present in archival scraps and fragments: in marginalia, diaries, and other texts that are often not seen as important enough to mention in collection descriptions, catalogues, and finding aids. Moreover, just as their experiences were fragmented along the lines of geography, class, race, and politics, so have these factors affected which sources and whose ideas have been seen as important and worth preserving.

Both perils and pleasures, then, await the scholar who attempts to combine girl-centred analysis with archival research. While marginalized, spoken for, and acted upon, girls from Canada, India, England, and beyond were also sophisticated consumers of the gender-based program of "character training" offered by Guiding, yet we know relatively little about them. This article will ask three questions about the attractions and limitations of looking for girls' voices in colonial archives. First, how have issues of gender, race, language, and geography affected the production and preservation of documentary evidence? Second, what impact has the accidental and purposeful destruction of archival sources had on what we can know about young people's responses to this particular youth organization? Finally, in such an uneven archival landscape, what strategies are available to historians who want to produce works of child-centred scholarship?

Like a number of other twentieth-century voluntary organizations, the Girl Guides have largely held on to their own records in collections that often consist of both carefully selected documents and uncatalogued pieces that were acquired more haphazardly. Many sources related to the history of Guiding in Britain and across its former empire are kept at the Girl Guiding UK Archives, located on one of the upper floors of the central London headquarters of the movement, an imposing building on Buckingham Palace Road that testifies to the ability of the movement to acquire valuable property and align itself with elites. It was my experiences in various local and national Girl Guide archives that led me to consider how the collections on which my work is based have been—and continue to be—constructed, manipulated, and policed. The British Guide archives are looked after by a single employee whose duties include managing the archival collections, regulating access to documents, and working with volunteers (former Guides and Guide leaders, now mostly in their seventies and eighties) who run smaller local Guide archives, sometimes out of their own homes. This reliance on voluntary labour, a necessity for non-profit organizations with limited funds, means that vast quantities of Guide records face an uncertain future as the elderly, unpaid archive workers of the movement literally die off.[4]

Like some of the other records workers mentioned in Antoinette Burton's edited collection *Archive Stories*, the employee who was in charge of the Girl Guiding UK Archives during most of my time there often acted as a gatekeeper, "controlling and mediating my entry . . . by stressing what [she] thought was 'important' to" the archive and its contents (Ghosh 29). Concerned with race, gender, and young people's responses to Guiding's ideals and practices, I was less interested in photographs of the adult founders of the movement or members of the British royal family than I was in scrapbooks and photograph albums created by so-called "unimportant" girls and women. These albums were some of the richest sources I encountered, and I was saddened to learn that many similar texts, donated by former Guides from Britain and around the world, had been disposed of simply because the girls and women featured in the photographs could not be identified.

The Girl Guiding UK Archives, like the British suffrage archives that have been studied by Laura E. Nym Mayhall, had clearly been put together and catalogued with the goal of privileging one narrative and one "trajectory of experience while devaluing and obliterating any others" (236). This official narrative of Guide history is a story of female emancipation, interracial cooperation, and cheerful heterosexuality. Yet I also found myself unable to ignore the exclusions and silences that characterized this collection, having witnessed first-hand the destruction of documents whose contents were seen as unimportant or as threatening to the reputation of the organization.

In England, where Guiding and Scouting had been taken up by young people from all social classes by the 1920s and 1930s, the voices of middle-class, urban, and suburban white Protestant girls are the ones that are the easiest to locate, especially in logbooks or diaries describing what took place at the weekly meetings of the various Guide groups. These sources provided information about individual responses and specific local contexts, which makes them a valuable counterweight to the mountains of prescriptive literature produced by Guide headquarters. They were also often a joy to read, as, for example, was a handwritten logbook kept between 1928 and 1930 by Eileen Knapman, a Girl Guide from Battersea in South London. In the ruled pages of a small notebook, Knapman described the weekly activities of her Guide group while also using her writing to mock several aspects of the movement and to create a sense of ironic distance from some of its more stringent requirements and ideals. In particular, her description of being tested for the mandatory Child Nurse badge (one of the many attempts of the movement to teach girls about scientific motherhood) may be read as proof that she—like many of her contemporaries—was more ambivalent than enthusiastic about maternal training. On 23 January 1928, she wrote:

> two [of us] trotted down to Tennyson Street, in the pouring rain, with drooping hat brims, and hearts in [our] boots, to enter for the "Child Nurse" Badge. There were

heated arguments on the way, as to whether one puts a baby into a bath head or feet first, and whether a boy of one year, five months should be allowed to use a carving knife or a garden fork to eat his dinner.

Several months later, she made a similar comment about the seriousness with which the adult leaders of her group approached First Aid training. A few members of her company, she wrote, were tested for

> [the] Ambulance Badge, including two Swallows. We spent the evening first aiding imaginary broken limbs, cuts, bruises, and grit in the eye; we surpassed ourselves in artificial respiration [and] we answered questions on every emergency possible (and impossible!), from an ice accident, to the baby swallowing the new Austin 7!

Not all English girls, of course, wrote such detailed and entertaining accounts of their Guide experiences, and certainly only a fraction of their logbooks and diaries have ended up in archival collections. Thankfully, I was also able to find bits of information about other English girls' responses to Guiding in the everyday record books that were kept by the adult leaders of each individual company (even fewer of these appear to have been thought of as worth preserving, however). The mostly working-class membership of the 1st Foots Cray Guide Company from Southeast London, for instance, included several shop assistants and a dressmaking apprentice, the latter of whom quit in 1927 at the age of 16 because of a "loss of interest."[5] This defection from Guiding, along with the numerous other examples I encountered of adolescent girls leaving the movement, supports Claire Langhamer's argument that young wage-earning women in interwar England saw the years between leaving school and marrying "as a time of freedom and independence" (50), a period without responsibilities when many teenage girls believed that they were entitled to spend their leisure time however they liked.

A similar age-based pattern of attrition also characterized Guiding in interwar Canada, a rapidly urbanizing, white settler society whose federal government was committed (through a variety of initiatives, including the Scouts and the Guides) to the assimilation of non-British immigrants and Aboriginal peoples. Once again, the logbooks kept in provincial Guide archives (in Canada, these are also run by aging volunteers) are generally by native-born, Anglo-Celtic girls from cities, such as Winifred Thompson, head of the Nightingale Patrol from the 21st Winnipeg Company, which met at St Albans Anglican Church. Thompson was a more serious and matter-of-fact diarist than Eileen Knapman: of a Guide meeting on 22 October 1928, for instance, she noted that some members of her company played volleyball while others practised their "ambulance" skills, marching, and singing for upcoming public displays, and she wrote that St Albans Guides had recently earned badges in flag signalling, bed making, fire making, and "health rules." Her logbook is also proof of the importance of local conditions in Guide practice; on 14 January 1929, she noted that her company began one January meeting by running laps around the church hall—not to keep fit but to keep warm.

Guiding in Canada also included non-British immigrants as well as Aboriginal children, yet these girls are discussed most often in official texts as abstract representations of the "Canadianizing" value of Guide work. While in Canada to receive an honorary doctorate from the University of Toronto, Scout and Guide founder Robert Baden-Powell spoke at the 1923 Imperial Education Conference, where he claimed that Guides and Scouts had been "found particularly useful in the schools for Red Indian children, just as [they] had also proved useful in a like manner on the West Coast of Africa and in Baghdad" ("Scouts and Guides," 232). Guiding was also often explained as a "useful" way to assimilate non-British immigrants: on 14 May 1928, for example, the Captain of a company from the Manitoba town of Morden was commended at the provincial level for "trying to turn fourteen little German girls into good Canadians" (Minute book). Unlike Eileen Knapman and Winifred Thompson, these "Red Indian children" and "little German girls" (among numerous other examples) exist in Guide texts as abstract concepts or social problems to be solved. My research in Canadian Guide archives failed to uncover any sources created by these young people, and I have not even been able to learn a single one of their names.

I have, however, found bits of evidence of how a few Aboriginal, mixed-race, and immigrant children responded to Guiding in the diary kept by Monica Storrs, a British missionary who started Guide and Scout groups in northern British Columbia in the late 1920s. Like many of her contemporaries, Storrs was fascinated by the "racial" and "national" composition of her Guides and Scouts (and it is worth noting that she often used those terms interchangeably), counting them off in her diary as including Danish, "Italian (Roman Catholic)," American, French-Canadian, "halfbreed," English, German-Italian, "three-quarters Indian," and "real Scotch" (61–62).[6] One evening in March 1930, Storrs wrote that her Guides "practiced bed-making. . . . We had a few serious differences of opinion [including]: How often you should strip [the bed]. The general opinion was, that to do it every day, (as sometimes in England), is morbid if not hysterical. Here we arrived at a compromise of *at least* twice a week!" (73). Storrs's emphasis on teaching "proper" bed-making skills, when considered alongside her attempts to categorize the ethnically heterogeneous group of children who joined Scouting and Guiding, may be read as an attempt to use domestic and cleaning rituals to promote supposedly "superior" British lifeways in a settler society inhabited by Indigenous, mixed-race, and non-British peoples. Her Guides' insistence that such time-consuming labour was "morbid if not hysterical," meanwhile, provides evidence that these metropolitan ideals were contested and sometimes, in fact, rejected.

The formal connection between Guiding and Scouting and the Canadian Department of Indian Affairs, which got stronger as the twentieth century progressed, was especially evident in the formation of mandatory companies and troops at many Aboriginal residential and industrial schools (see, for instance, McCallum; Miller 277–80). I have looked for these girls' responses to Guiding in sources produced by adults, primarily in reports on Guide activities by residential school principals (submitted

to the Department of Indian Affairs) and in Guide magazine articles that alternately stressed the exotic nature and exemplary accomplishments of Aboriginal Guide groups (all while extolling the benefits of so-called Indian play for implicitly white young people). Aboriginal Guides won prizes especially often for first-aid work and needlecraft, an indication that Native girls could and often did use Guiding as "a means to practice 'culturally related behaviours' and . . . to continue distinct Aboriginal traditions" (McCallum 156; see also Haig-Brown).

In an essay that discusses Guiding and Scouting at Australian Aboriginal schools, Fiona Paisley notes that, while these organizations supported racial hierarchies and naturalized colonialism, "indigenous accounts of being in Scout and Guide troops focus on the escape from uniformity they afforded. Where the impact of being institutionalized has been remembered by the 'stolen generations' as predominantly traumatic, Scouting and Guiding appears as fun" (255). A number of oral history interviews conducted with the survivors of Canadian residential schools similarly focus on the pleasures and pride that involvement in Guiding could bring. Marguerite Beaver, who was a student in the 1940s at the Mohawk Institute residential school in Brantford, Ontario, recalled the following:

> Another thing we really liked—they had the Brownies and the Girl Guides. . . . And Lady Baden Powell come down there and we all went to the Tutela Park and the ones from the Mohawk Institute—I'll never forget, oh we were so proud—we won everything—the inspections for the Brownies and the Girl Guides, out of all the troops in Brantford. They used to take the ones that stayed there in the summer, they used to take them camping. I went with them one time when they went to Chiefswood [the childhood home of Mohawk poet E. Pauline Johnson] and we had a fabulous time. (qtd. in Graham 386)[7]

Beaver's words, I think, may be read as proof that some Canadian Aboriginal girls, like many of their "Guide sisters" across the British empire and the world, enjoyed and took what they wanted from the movement without necessarily agreeing or engaging with some of its broader ideological goals.

Girls in late colonial India also used Guiding for their own ends, although Indian Guides from the 1920s and 1930s are more difficult to trace than their Canadian and British counterparts because of the political and organizational changes that affected South Asia and its voluntary organizations in the decades after independence. In Delhi, I was received warmly at the headquarters of the Bharat Scouts and Guides (a coeducational organization since 1951), but soon learned that they had very few documents dating from before the 1980s. I had better luck at the Margaret Cousins Memorial Library in Sarojini Naidu House, the headquarters of the All-India Women's Conference, a voluntary organization established in 1927 to promote female education and social reform. The leaders of this organization described Guiding as a way to modernize Indian girlhood through physical culture and character training, and their annual reports and conference programs include references to Guides as honour guards and volunteer workers at AIWC events and conferences. In interwar India, a British colony with an enormous and varied population, most Guide companies were attached to schools, such as the Brahmo Girls School in Calcutta (which was attended by middle-class Indian girls sponsored by a Hindu social reform group called the Brahmo Somaj) and the Lawrence Royal Military School (an institution for the mostly working-class children of British soldiers).[8] The public and private archives I visited in London and Delhi did not contain any texts created by the girls (Hindu, Muslim, Parsi, British, or Anglo-Indian) who had been Guides in late colonial India. While female literacy was far lower there than in Canada and England, the fact that most Guide companies were based in schools means that this lack of sources is not a result of the women and girls who belonged to the movement being unable to read or write. Instead, I suspect, written records of the activities of the individual groups were simply not preserved for a variety of practical and political reasons, including the changes wrought by Independence and Partition

and the amalgamation of the Indian Scouts and Guides into a single coeducational body in 1951—an organization that, I suspect, was not especially interested in locating and preserving documents produced mainly by white women during the early twentieth-century period that Indian Guide leader Lakshmi Mazumdar, writing in the 1960s, called "a bitter struggle" for "national liberation" (38).

I have found a few traces of how that "struggle" played out among some girls and young women in South Asia during the late 1920s and early 1930s. The 1930 annual report for the British Guide Association, for example, included references to "a certain amount of trouble over Guides [in Kashmir] resigning for political reasons," "trouble in one company [in Bihar and Orissa] on the question of loyalty," and the regional reports from Bengal and the Central Provinces noted that "political unrest" had led to the suspension or disbandment of several companies (*Girl Guides*, 141–44). These were not the first instances of South Asian Guides and Guide leaders acting in support of the popular movement to free India from its colonial ties to Britain. In 1928, for instance, senior students at Brahmo Girls' School in Calcutta refused to make the Guide promise of loyalty to the King-Emperor (Mazumdar 85). Perhaps unsurprisingly, this incident was not mentioned in the "India" section of the 1928–1930 biennial report of the World Association of Girl Guides and Girl Scouts, which focused instead on uniforms, training camps, and the publication of Guide handbooks in vernacular languages. But I think the fact that the actions of the Brahmo Girls' School students are discussed in the official history of South Asian Guiding (written in the 1960s and reprinted several times in the late twentieth century) reveals the importance of these acts of resistance.

Some Girl Guides, then, do speak (though in ways that are always mediated) from the archives kept by their organizations in various national contexts. The production and preservation of evidence about girls' responses to the prescriptions and practices of Guiding reflects a number of past and present power imbalances: between English and other languages, white and non-white racial categories, the printed word and non-print forms of knowledge, and the imperial and organizational centre and peripheries. Age and gender are important here, too, as ideas about what counts as evidence and what is worth preserving continue to reflect gendered power relationships between children, adolescents, and adults. Our understanding of how girls made their own meanings and cultural practices out of Guiding is also shaped by the many photographs, letters, and other sources that have not survived, whether because of decolonization, organizational priorities, or the desire to suppress past aspects of the organization that may be seen as embarrassing or unsavoury.

This essay has also highlighted a few of the strategies available to scholars who want to bring girls from the margins to the centre of historical analysis. These include looking for sources produced by girls (while still reading them critically) and reading archival finding aids and adult-produced sources against the grain. Girl-centred historical research is also made richer by what Mona Gleason has called empathic inference—the ability to imagine what events and experiences might have meant and been like from the perspective of a young person. Photographs are other especially valuable sources of information, as they depict a far broader range of girls than do the textual records of the Guide movement. Yet while presenting a broad and relatively unstudied body of evidence, photographs of Girl Guides from across the British Empire and the world are also reminders of just how many girls' subjectivities and ideas we will never be able to know. In addition to looking for voices, then, historians of girls and the institutions that socialized them should also remember, as Spivak suggests, to measure silences (48).

Notes

1. The World Association of Girl Guides and Girl Scouts (WAGGGS) has developed a "Global Action Theme" badge that focuses on the Millennium Development Goals (MDGs) of the UN. These goals, determined in 2000–2001, are to eradicate extreme poverty and hunger; to achieve universal primary education; to promote gender equality and empower women; to reduce child mortality; to improve maternal health; to combat HIV/AIDS, malaria, and other diseases; to ensure environmental sustainability; and to develop a global partnership for development. To mark the hundredth anniversary of the start of Guiding, WAGGGS is hosting a series of "Young Women's World Forums," held in 2010, 2011, and 2012, at which Guides from around the world meet to discuss the MDGs and how to achieve them. For more on the Girl Guides and British imperialism, see Alexander, "Imperial Internationalism"; Proctor.

2. See my dissertation, "The Girl Guide Movement, Imperialism and Internationalism in Interwar England, Canada and India," which I defended at York University in 2010.

3. See McGillis and Khorana; Nodelman; Wallace. A similar point is also made by Ann Laura Stoler, who writes that "racialized Others invariably have been compared and equated with children, a representation that conveniently provided a moral justification for imperial policies of tutelage, discipline and specific paternalistic and maternalistic strategies of custodial control" (150).

4. This problem has attracted some attention in the United Kingdom, most notably through the Database of Archives of Non-Governmental Organizations (DANGO), an Arts and Humanities Research Council-funded project based at the University of Birmingham. DANGO's main focus is on the "new social movements" of the 1950s, 1960s, and 1970s, however, so it is not especially concerned with Guide sources from the early twentieth century.

5. As opposed to Brownies, which were for younger girls, and Rangers, which were for girls over 16, Guides were between the ages of 10 and 16; many British girls during this period started full-time work at age 14.

6. While Storrs's unselfconscious list of racial and ethnic categories jars with twenty-first-century sensibilities, it is worth remembering, as Daniel Coleman does, that for early-twentieth-century Canadians the sorting of people into racial groups was carried out without the looming consciousness of atrocity. They thought of the processes of racialized categorization (for immigration, for social intervention, for national definition) as civil acts—very often as recognition, respect, orderly government, and even as potential welcome. That these acts were based upon the assumption of British superiority was not immediately attached in their minds to the images of genocide as it is in ours—this despite the fact that a greater devastation had been, and was being, carried out in the Americas under European colonialism than that perpetuated under Nazism. (41–42)

7. Graham's book also includes excerpts from reports written by the principal of the Mohawk Institute during the 1920s and 1930s that discuss the positive impact of Guiding on female students; most of the interviews cover a slightly later time period.

8. Sanjay Seth also highlights what a small percentage of

Indian girls attended these schools, writing that "the quinquennial survey of education for 1927–37 found that only 14 percent of girls who enrolled in school proceeded to even reach the fourth grade, completion of which was conventionally defined as the minimal requirement for attaining literacy, and on the eve of Independence there were only 232,000 girls in high schools, compared to almost two million boys" (157).

Works Cited

Alexander, Kristine. "The Girl Guide Movement and Imperial Internationalism in the 1920s and 1930s." *Journal of the History of Childhood and Youth* 2.1 (2009): 37–63. Print.

——. "The Girl Guide Movement, Imperialism and Internationalism in Interwar England, Canada and India." Diss. York U, 2010. Print.

Bannerji, Himani. "Age of Consent and Hegemonic Social Reform." *Gender and Imperialism*. Ed. Clare Midgley. Manchester: Manchester UP, 1998. 21–44. Print.

Bingham, Adrian. "Stop the Flapper Vote Folly: Lord Rothermere, the *Daily Mail*, and the Equalization of the Franchise 1927–28." *Twentieth Century British History* 13.1 (2002): 17–37. Print.

Burton, Antoinette, ed. *Archive Stories: Facts, Fictions, and the Writing of History*. Durham: Duke UP, 2005. Print.

Carter, Rodney G.S. "Of Things Said and Unsaid: Power, Archival Silences, and Power in Silence." *Archivaria* 62 (2006): 215–33. Print.

Coleman, Daniel. *White Civility: The Literary Project of English Canada*. 2006. Toronto: U of Toronto P, 2008. Print.

Driscoll, Catherine. "Girls Today: Girls, Girl Culture, and Girlhood Studies." *Girlhood Studies* 1.1 (2008): 13–32. Print.

Ghosh, Durba. "National Narratives and the Politics of Miscegenation: Britain and India." Burton 27–44.

The Girl Guides Association (Incorporated by Royal Charter) Sixteenth Annual Report and Balance Sheet of the Committee of the Council for the Year Ending December 31st, 1930. Girl Guiding UK Archives, London.

Gleason, Mona. "The Historical Child." U of Lethbridge. 5 May 2011. Keynote speech.

Graham, Elizabeth, ed. *The Mush Hole: Life at Two Indian Residential Schools*. Waterloo: Heffle, 1997. Print.

Haig-Brown, Celia. *Resistance and Renewal: Surviving the Indian Residential School*. Vancouver: Arsenal, 1998. Print.

Knapman, Eileen. 8th Battersea Company Swallow Patrol Diary, 1928–1930. Girl Guiding UK Archives, London.

Langhamer, Claire. *Women's Leisure in England, 1920–60*. Manchester: Manchester UP, 2000. Print.

Marcus, G. E. "Ethnography in/of the World System: The Emergence of Multi-sited Ethnography." *Annual Review of Anthropology* 24 (1995): 95–117. Print.

Mayhall, Laura E. Nym. "'Creating the Suffragette Spirit': British Feminism and the Historical Imagination." Burton 232–50.

Maynes, Mary Jo. "Age as a Category of Historical Analysis: History, Agency, and Narratives of Childhood." *Journal of the History of Childhood and Youth* 1.1 (2008): 114–24. Print.

Mazumdar, Lakshmi, ed. *A Dream Came True*. New Delhi: Bharat Scouts and Guides, 1997. Print.

McCallum, Mary Jane. "To Make Good Canadians: Girl Guiding in Indian Residential Schools." M.A. thesis, Trent U, 2002. Print.

McGillis, Roderick, and Meena Khorana. "Introductory Notes: Postcolonialism, Children, and Their Literature." *Postcolonialism, Children, and Their Literature*. Ed. Roderick McGillis and Meena Khorana. Spec. issue of *Ariel* 28.1 (1997): 7–20. Print.

Miller, J.R. *Shingwauk's Vision: A History of Native Residential Schools*. Toronto: U of Toronto P, 1997. Print.

Minute book, Manitoba Council of the Girl Guides of Canada, 1925–1928. Girl Guides—Manitoba Council, 1926–1983, P 3467. Provincial Archives of Manitoba, Winnipeg.

Nodelman, Perry. "The Other: Orientalism, Colonialism and Children's Literature." *Children's Literature Association Quarterly* 17.1 (1992): 29–35. Print.

Paisley, Fiona. "Childhood and Race: Growing Up in the Empire." *Gender and Empire*. Ed. Philippa Levine. Oxford: Oxford UP, 2004. 240–59. Print.

Proctor, Tammy. "Scouts, Guides, and the Fashioning of Empire, 1919–1939." *Fashioning the Body Politic: Gender, Dress, Citizenship*. Ed. Wendy Parkins. Oxford: Berg, 2002. 125–44. Print.

"Scouts and Guides: An Address by the Chief Scout at the Imperial Education Conference." *Girl Guides' Gazette* Oct. 1923: 232.

Seth, Sanjay. *Subject Lessons: The Western Education of Colonial India*. Chapel Hill: Duke UP, 2007. Print.

Spivak, Gayatri Chakravorty. "Can the Subaltern Speak?" Rev. ed. *Can the Subaltern Speak?: Reflections on the History of an Idea*. Ed. Rosalind C. Morris. New York: Columbia UP, 2010. 21–78. Print.

Stoler, Ann Laura. *Race and the Education of Desire: Foucault's History of Sexuality and the Colonial Order of Things*. Durham: Duke UP, 1995. Print.

Storrs, Monica. *God's Galloping Girl: The Peace River Diaries of Monica Storrs, 1929–1931*. Ed. W. L. Morton. Vancouver: UBC P, 1979. Print.

Thompson, Winifred. Nightingale Patrol Logbook, 1928–1929. Archives of the Manitoba Council of the Girl Guides of Canada, Winnipeg.

Wallace, Jo-Ann. "De-Scribing *The Water Babies*: 'The Child' in Post-Colonial Theory." *De Scribing Empire: Postcolonialism and Textuality*. Ed. Chris Tiffin and Alan Lawson. London: Routledge, 1994. 171–84. Print.

PRIMARY DOCUMENT

Logbook of the First Hay River Girl Guide Company, 1934–1936

4 June 1934

"The company followed their first trail and had quite an exciting time, once they got the idea. The mosquitoes were fierce, which rather spoilt the enjoyment of the evening.

Marks brought forward P142 B 116

This evening P.26 B16"

12 June 1934

"Being a wet cold evening, we had our first indoor meeting since April. We began with prayers and a short word on the First Promise. Nature work on the life story of a Rabbit, with which animal we are all familiar, was followed by a lively game of Wandering Ball & then the Company had its introduction to First Aid & learnt to tie up cut fingers & stop bleeding. The evening closed with taps."

26 June 1934

"Meeting had to be postponed last week on account of extra clearing [? Or cleaning?] & the coming of the boat. Again we had to have our meeting indoors on account of wet weather. After a short talk, we revised the last lesson on First Aid & learned the large & small arm slings. Team games followed & the evening ended with prayers & Taps."

10 January 1935

"After a lapse of almost six months due to unsatisfactory behaviour on the part of the Guides [!!], we restarted on probation & had an opening meeting. Instead of patrols we are having Red & Blue Teams for the present. After an introductory talk, we played a team game, which was won by the Reds, 4-1, & then other games & generally had a very merry time."

24 January 1935

"The girls decided they would like to do Child Welfare, so we had the life size baby doll & had a preliminary talk on Baby's needs & took notes. We played a Guessing Game, sponsored by Mary Vitrewka, and then Musical Spoons, which Mary won twice. Mary Alison [Alisa?] read the closing prayers."

continued

7 February 1935

"We discussed the clothing of the toddler & had our three year old Sallie's wardrobe to inspect. We afterwards played a game on this subject & then saw the picture & read about the Canadian exhibit at the International Guide Handicraft Exhibition. There was quite a good photo of our doll."

21 February 1935

"We began Baby's daily routine today and bathed the baby. The girls were very adept at handling the doll. When baby was dressed in clean clothes & put to rest, we played a few games."

4 March 1935

"After further practice at bathing the baby, with other girls, we played games for a while. Discontinued on account of confirmation classes.

Marks: Pansies 8 Bluebirds 9"

23 August 1935

"Roll call drill was held, followed by teeth inspection, which was very satisfactory. An exciting Woodcraft sign competition followed, then testing & learning the Guide Law & Promise. We had a session of folk dancing & besides doing "Ninepins," began to learn "Brighton Camp." The Legend of St. George was told & the meeting closed in Horseshoe Formation with the Flag Song, Guide Prayer & Taps.

Marks: Pansies 24 Bluebirds 22"

30 August 1935

"After the opening exercises, the recruits were tested on Law & Promise while the others made alphabetical lists of growing things. A good practice of the Enrolment Ceremony followed, then the girls voted for colour party for the Dedication of our flags. Mary V. & Rebecca are to be bearers, with Mary A., Emily & Alice V. as guards. The light was failing & the "Distribution" approaching, so we closed with a story, the Guide Prayer & Taps.

Marks: Pansies 51 Bluebirds 41"

6 September 1935

"We had a final practise [sic] for the Dedication Service, in church & with our colours & Mr. Singleton. On returning to school, we were very pleased to be able to welcome Miss Goddard, our new nurse, who has been a Guide for some years, to our Company. Seven new members were enrolled, four having already been Brownies. The rest of the evening was in social vein, folk dancing & games being played, & the meeting closed with prayer & taps."

8 September 1935

"On this day, at the afternoon service, our Colours were dedicated, this being the first service of this kind in the N.W.T. The Guides & Brownies marched to church & during the singing of the first hymn, "The Church's one foundation," the two colours were carried down the aisle by a colour party of five, & placed on the Communion Table by Mr. Singleton, the girls taking their places in the front seat. The Dedication ceremony took place after the Third Collect [?] & the singing of "Fight the Good Fight." After the Consecration, the Children's Song was sung & Mr. Singleton preached on the First Guide Law, the test [??] being, "Be thou faithful unto death & I will give thee a crown of life." The Presentation of the colours was made after the last hymn, "O happy band of pilgrims," & the national anthem followed the Benediction. Owing to the heavy rain, it was not possible to carry the colours unfurled to & fro church, & the proposed photographs also had to be postponed."

13 September 1935

"We had a quiet meeting this evening & after Roll Call drill, part of the Company wrote letters to the Sanatorium Guides, with whom we correspond, while others worked on the dolls' outfit which Miss Sowden is taking to England, as a specimen of our handiwork."

20 September 1935

"Roll Call & inspection were followed by a Leaf Identification test, in which the patrols did well. We next had a book balancing race & good carriage competition, then bandaging practices. "The Girl Guide Song" arrived on the last plane, so we began to learn it, then danced for awhile & closed with the Guide Prayer & Taps.

Marks Pansies 23 Bluebirds 28"

27 September 1935

"No meeting—staff all busy."

continued

4 October 1935

"The Company was in a noisy mood, but settled down very well to learning more by the new International Method. Folk Dancing followed, then some simple First Aid. The girls were very sleepy, so we sang & dismissed early."

11 October 1935

"A very good meeting. Alice Vitanelsi & Naomi Krenezzi were able to be with us again, after several weeks of absence owing to illness. After Roll Call Inspection for smartness, we revised the morse learned last week, with good results. A lively game & then a talk, demonstration & practice of stopping bleeding. We sang for a time, danced, then had the story of St. Andrew & closed with Taps.

Marks: Pansies 24 Bluebirds 25"

17 October 1935

"We have changed our evening to Thursday for the winter. After Inspection we had a period of morse & learned the straight dot & dash letters & were then able to do several short words. A game of nature descriptions followed, then Company Drill & forming fours. We sang & learned the actions of the first verse of "The Girl Guide Song" & the girls think it is fine & did well. Folk Dancing, a game of "Fruit Basket" then the Guide Prayer & Taps, ended the evening.

Marks: Pansies 19 Bluebirds 14"

24 October 1935

"After Roll Call & a satisfactory inspection of ties & position of badges, we had a First Aid session, learning what to do for Burns & Scalds & revising the work already learned. Company Drill was followed by a morse test, which showed good results. We practised our song, then the girls chose to play "Pop goes the Weasel," after which we closed with the Guide Prayer & Taps.

Marks: B 5 P 5"

14 November 1935

"Halloween Party & flu intervened on the two previous Thursdays. After Inspection we revised morse & took up the subject of fainting. Rebecca suggested a hung fish as the equivalent of smelling salts! So much time went by on these two subjects, that after a short game of Air, Land & Sea, our time was up.

Marks: P 10 B 4"

28 November 1935

"We were all very tired, so the meeting was shorter & quieter than usual. After roll call & Company drill, we had a short first aid discussion on nosebleeding & grit in the eye, then had an observation test. We sang for a while, read & talked of the Chiefs messages for the Guides of Canada, then they begged for a story, after which we closed."

5 December 1935

"Roll call & inspection was followed by Company Drill, & then we revised the Ambulance Test, against the coming of Miss Goddard. We played a team game with the sand bags, which the Brownies made, then had a quiet & interesting time with jig-saw puzzles, a story on keeping promises & closed."

30 January 1936

"Influenza prevented us restarting earlier in the year. We began our session by renewing our Promises & pledging our loyalty to King Edward VIII, then the Girl Guide Pennant was presented to the winning patrol, the Pansies. As the gramaphone [sic] has now been mended, we were able to play the Folk Dance record which the Bishop has sent us & started to learn Rufty Tufty. A test on Guide Laws was followed by a game of Horseshoes, which the Pansies won 8–21, after which we closed with the Guide Prayer.

Source: Anglican General Synod Archives (Toronto).

"Being in Your Twenties, in the Thirties": Liminality and Masculinity during the Great Depression

HEIDI MACDONALD

The Great Depression affected everyone who lived through it, but different cohorts were affected in different ways. Unemployment and underemployment were particularly devastating to young men in their twenties, who were in transition from youth to adulthood. Author Hugh MacLennan (1907–1990) described this experience very neatly. Completing a Ph.D. in 1935, he was unable to find waged work for five months, and then accepted a school teacher's job for $25 a week.[1] MacLennan used the masculine metaphor of an airplane—with its exhilarating combination of speed, technology, and daring—to describe his generation's experience. A young man, he said, is like an airplane ready to take flight, but, "The essence of being in your twenties in the thirties was that no matter how well tuned-up you were, you stayed on the ground, or just above it, for 10 years."[2]

The movement from childhood, through youth, to full adulthood can be quite complex. Historian of childhood Harvey Graff asserts, "Normative theories' notions of a relatively linear progression from total dependency to full autonomy seldom approximate the actual paths taken by persons growing up."[3] Nevertheless, scholars, including Graff, identify major transitions/events associated with autonomy and the entrance into adulthood, including: exiting school, entering the workforce, moving away from the family of origin, marriage, establishing a household, and having children.[4] Unemployment, underemployment, and a lack of hope for a rapid economic recovery could seriously hinder all of these transitions, and thus many young men growing up during the Great Depression got stuck in a liminal phase between youth and adulthood.

Anthropologist Victor Turner explained that liminality made people vulnerable: "The attributes of liminality or *liminal personae* ("threshold people") are necessarily ambiguous, since this condition and these persons slip through the network of classifications that normally locate states and positions in cultural space. Liminal entities are neither here nor there; they are betwixt and between the positions assigned and arrayed by law, custom, convention, and ceremonial."[5] The lives of unemployed and underemployed men in their twenties, whom Turner would classify as "threshold people," were thus not merely stalled in a benign liminality; they were sometimes deeply and permanently affected by the Great Depression. Whereas MacLennan described his experience thirty years retrospectively in a rather resigned tone, this paper uses 1930s diaries and correspondence of three contemporaries of MacLennan's to consider how unemployment and underemployment impeded their transitions to adulthood and threatened their sense of masculinity. In the early Depression years, Alan Creighton (1903–1999) was a single, struggling Halifax poet; Ole Nissen (1903–1979) was a Danish immigrant farmer; and John Murphy [pseudonym] (b. 1902) was a husband, father, and successful author. These three subjects were close in age to Hugh MacLennan, and they each kept a candid diary in which they made connections between the economic crisis and their struggles to achieve adult status.

Twentieth-century adult masculinities vary according to race, class, sexuality, occupation, level of education, urban or rural residency, stage in the life course, and engagement with technology. And, of course, forms of masculinity are influenced by local, national, and world events. What was constant was the societal pressure to pursue hegemonic

Source: Reprinted with permission from the author.

masculinity. As Mark Moss notes of Victorian Ontario, "Farmer or factory worker, rural dweller or city inhabitant, man or boy, no male could escape the pressure to be manly."[6] R.W. Connell argues that with the late-nineteenth century expansion of industrial production, manliness was significantly associated with the heterosexual breadwinner model: "forms of masculinity [were] organized around wage-earning capacity, mechanical skills, domestic patriarchy, and combative solidarity among wage earners."[7] Urbanization, however, led to a new concern that modern conveniences and urban amenities were softening men, particularly those in clerical and management positions. An anti-modern antidote stressed rugged, wilderness forms of masculinity, which were mythologized in Canada around Tom Thompson, artist and backwoodsman.[8] What these two ideals—breadwinner and backwoodsman—had in common was autonomy, a key component of hegemonic masculinity.[9] For the generation who came of age during the First World War, enlistment was a clear way to prove one's masculinity, particularly with, as Moss explains, "virtually every facet of society teaching boys that the warrior was the ultimate masculine ideal."[10] There is irony in how, after the First World War, during the high unemployment of the 1930s, adult hegemonic masculinity was once again strongly tied to breadwinning, which has been convincingly documented by Canadian historians Nancy Christie, Cynthia Comacchio, Lara Campbell, and Margaret Hobbes.[11] Christie, for example, summarizes, "The Depression amplified previous notions that the male breadwinner was the economic head of the family."[12]

The impact of unemployment went beyond financial distress and affected gender systems. According to R.W. Connell, "The constitution of masculinity through bodily performance means that gender is vulnerable when the performance cannot be sustained."[13] In the 1930s, gender was vulnerable because so many men's performance of waged work could not be sustained due to high unemployment.[14] Those in transition from youth to adulthood were deemed especially vulnerable because they needed the experience of waged work to keep them on the path to respectable adulthood; if they fell off the path into disillusionment and laziness, they might never be good citizens. Canadians' engagement with this rhetoric in the 1930s was clearly played out in such magazines as *Maclean's*, *Saturday Night*, and *Chatelaine*. These magazines offer hundreds of grim references to liminal male youth whose masculinity and self esteem were endangered by lack of employment opportunities. One poignant example from a 1934 *Saturday Night* article described a kempt man in his early twenties who was trying to sell his shoes, which he no longer needed since he had lost his job. The author reflected, "The bright, helpful young man, full of ambition and willing to work for his living. This is youth, and this is what the depression is crushing."[15] The portrayal of the 1930s economic crisis as particularly harmful to young men, and the increasingly strong link between masculinity and wage earning demonstrates Christopher Forth's observation of how a specific kind of masculinity—the breadwinner ideal—can become the focus of loss and grief in a crisis.[16] The three subjects of this article all expressed their own grief over how unemployment and underemployment led to liminality, which in turn interfered with their progression to adulthood and their ability to demonstrate their manliness.

For young men in their twenties in the 1930s, lack of work was emasculating because financial independence was the key to achieving all the other events associated with normative adulthood, especially marriage and setting up a household. The Depression-era unemployment rate of approximately 30 per cent meant that many men in their twenties could not afford to get married, a trend reflected in the decreased rate of marriage in the 1930s, the increased average age of marriage, and the rise in illegitimate births.[17]

Such statistics reinforced the anecdotal evidence that gender systems among youth had weakened and needed correction. If employment was associated with masculinity, then unemployment was associated with femininity; for gender systems to continue in their traditional way, men absolutely had to be employed.[18] As Lara Campbell argues, "Employment was linked both to men's sense of masculinity and gender identity, but also to their position of authority and sense of 'validation' in the family. Unemployment therefore brought more than material insecurity: for men, it struck at the very heart of their status in the family and the community."[19]

Examining life writing allows us to analyze how individuals experienced—or at least portrayed their experience—of a period of time. The diaries and correspondence of the three men under study appear frank and relatively unfiltered. None seem to have been written with the expectation they would ever be published, and all were donated to archives after their deaths.[20] The diarists are notable for the degree to which they internalized hegemonic masculinities and measured themselves against such ideals. Scholars agree that there is no such thing as an authentic voice; diarists can filter their comments, censor themselves, and even create narratives that have no basis in reality. And of course, it is impossible to record all of one's daily thoughts and activities. Nevertheless, these particular examples of life writing reveal how the masculinity of three young men depended on breadwinning despite the economic crisis. The diaries of Creighton, Nissen, and Murphy are, in Philippe Lejeune's terms, both analytical and personal: they "explain situations in such a way that they can be understood by oneself later, or by an outside reader [. . . and] foreground the impulses of the soul and creates a dialogue with them."[21]

The diaries contain a relatively complete recording of the writers' various struggles with their careers and families. Creighton's diaries are particularly personal, even describing at length some of his dreams. While Nissen's diary seems very frank, his correspondence with his brother in Denmark, is considerably more restrained and paints with broad stokes his experience of farming in Canada. Only on a couple of occasions, when Nissen asked his brother for financial help, did he really let his guard down. It is obvious that all of the diarists under study omit material that must have been important to them as men in their twenties. Most notably, none of them mention sex, which is of great interest to scholars of masculinity today.[22] The choices each of the three diarists made to include or exclude

material, is in keeping with Lejeune's observation about nineteenth century adolescent girls' diaries: "in which sometimes the writer declares she will 'confide everything to her little notebook,' appear to be extremely self-censored. All that pertains to the body, to sexuality, remains outside the scope of the diary."[23] Life writing leaves us with many questions, yet these three examples reveal a great deal about masculinity and states of liminality in the 1930s.

Alan Creighton

In the fall of 1929, when the Depression began, Alan Creighton was 26 years old, single, and living with his parents in Halifax. After completing grade 10 in 1920, he studied painting and violin, attended business school, and worked as a shipping news and crime reporter for the *Chronicle Herald*. In 1923–24, he worked briefly in Detroit, first on the night shift at Chevrolet and subsequently as a piano player at a silent movie house. In the early Depression years, Creighton desperately wanted to be on his own, but his very small income from writing magazine articles and poetry—probably $15 a month—prevented him from leaving his parents' house. Preoccupation with health problems, including indigestion, depression, and the fear of nervous collapse, seems to have limited his life in many ways, yet in addition to writing, Creighton speaks of skating, swimming, painting, reading and going to movies.[24] He also enjoyed spending time in the country where his family summered, and where he received inspiration for his poetry.

Creighton's main endeavour in the early 1930s was writing nature-based poetry for Canadian newspapers and magazines. In 1930, for example, he recorded acceptances from the *Montreal Star*, *Canadian Forum*, and the *New Outlook*, each of which paid between ten and thirteen dollars. He regularly expressed frustration that it was so difficult to write and publish, and once published, he was discouraged by his meager earnings. In January 1931, he noted his goal to make five dollars a week,[25] which was minimal considering he also received a dental bill for seventeen dollars (which he paid for) and purchased a twenty dollar winter coat (which his father paid for) the same winter.

In the early 1930s, Creighton was keenly aware that his youth was fading and he was not fulfilling the role expected of a man his age. He expressed shame at his inability to sufficiently contribute to his family, and he understood that his inadequacy as a provider put him at the lowest place in the family hierarchy, even though his sense of entitlement informed him he should, because of his age, gender, and ability, be at the top.[26] In spring 1930, Creighton wrote grimly: "I am only playing a part in all this. . . . A sad, pathetic, *unmanly* part. I am a liability—a needless, *burdensome,* thing to the world."[27] Masculinity and femininity are relative, so it must not have helped Creighton's self esteem when his younger sister got a job as a hospital dietitian in April 1930, and then got married a few months later, while his own life seemed stagnant.

Despite his belief that a man should be independent, Creighton refused to seek a job other than writing. Even in the summer of 1931, when Creighton's brother Norman contracted tuberculosis and had to resign his job, and their father almost resigned from his job because of accelerating arthritis, Creighton never seems to have considered going out to work himself. He believed that under the right conditions he might succeed as a writer, rationalizing: "that's why I'm here *dependent* on my parents on the family for a time because I know this condition is necessary for my ultimate *independence.*"[28] His use of opposite words—dependence and independence—suggests his awareness of not living up to normative adulthood or masculinity.

Despite his writing's lack of remuneration, Creighton defended his devotion to it as the 1930s continued. Moreover, he developed an increasing sense of entitlement, articulating in 1933: "I need cultivation just as a piece of land needs cultivation. . . . I must not turn away from the task I set myself. . . . But I have done no societal wrong. In fact, as a poet, I am a needed factor in the community. When I am known, there will be no question of this. People who deride me now do not understand."[29] Again his comments show his awareness of normative masculinity. His claim, "But I have done no societal wrong," suggests feelings of guilt and shame. Moreover, his argument that in the future he will prove

wrong, "People who deride me now," reveal both his sense of being stuck in a liminal state, and his belief that he will progress out of that state. Lara Campbell argues that entitlement was a sensibility expressed by some unemployed men throughout the Depression, and became the rhetorical basis for demanding relief.[30] Creighton's sense of entitlement is similarly connected to his masculinity and his right to an income and autonomy, but it is also mixed with a sense of entitlement as an artist. He believes his family should bear the burden of his material needs while he is in the liminal phase, not just on the cusp of adulthood, but also on the cusp of becoming a successful writer. While writing poetry and fiction was not traditionally masculine employment,[31] becoming successful would mean more recognition, money, and autonomy, all of which affirmed masculinity.

No diary can contain a complete recounting of daily life and thoughts. Creighton's diaries are typical in following a few threads: his struggle to become a successful writer, challenges getting along with his family, and health concerns.[32] On the other hand, there are a few topics that a reader would expect to encounter in a male diarist in his late twenties, which do not appear. For example, many twentieth century male youth perform their masculinity through an interest in cars and women, yet Creighton records neither in his diaries.[33] Did he accept that he could not date or drive a car because of his economic instability, or was he lacking interest in both? He mused upon how he might become happier, asking "what stimulates or delights me?" His first response is "A nice intelligent girl. Pretty girls merely excite and thereby distract me."[34] Yet, no evidence in the diaries suggests that Creighton acted on these heterosexual feelings until he moved to Toronto in his mid thirties and met Christine Eyles, a musician who became his lifelong companion.[35]

Until he moved from Halifax in 1937 at the age of 34, Creighton depended financially, and to some extent emotionally, on his parents. His primary relationships were with his family, and particularly his brother Norman, with whom he enjoyed fishing, swimming, and experiencing nature. As a writer, would he have been just as frustrated in another decade? It is hard to determine, but knowing how the economic crisis hit the publishing industry, it seems likely that the Depression lengthened the period in which Creighton was unable to support himself as a writer. Creighton moved from Halifax to Toronto in 1937, the year his parents retired and moved to Hantsport, Nova Scotia. He was thus forced to move out of his parents' house, but he was also finally achieving success as a writer: he published his first volume of poetry in 1936 and began editing an anthology of Canadian poetry with Hilda Ridley when he moved to Toronto in 1937. In 1941, he began work at *Canadian Forum* Magazine and was assistant editor when Northrop Frye was editor between 1948 and 1952.[36]

In the early 1930s, Creighton was betwixt and between. He had completed only one of the major transitions or markers associated with adulthood: leaving school. He entered the workforce but never found steady or sufficiently lucrative employment, he left his family of origin only briefly when he worked in Detroit for a few months, and (it appears) he never dated. Creighton describes himself as a burden on his family, yet simultaneously he is defiant at the thought that he should do more. This paradox of shame and entitlement—he is, on one hand, not living up to the manliness expected of him, and on the other hand, rebellious because his creativity deserves respect—damages his sense of identity and masculinity. Creighton's experience was not his alone. In "Unemployed," a poem published in 1935, he grieves for his entire generation, expressing the simultaneous shame and entitlement, loss and longing felt by innumerable young men in the 1930s. While the first stanza ends, "We came on eager feet," the second and final stanza ends, "The living dead of youth!"[37]

Ole Nissen

When the Depression began, Ole Nissen was 26 and had arrived in Canada seven years previously from Denmark. His emigration was spurred both by the Western Canadian emigration posters he saw while visiting his brother in England, and by his boredom working for Danish State Railways since 1919.[38] Since arriving in Canada in 1922, Nissen worked on farms in Alberta, and in a restaurant in Vancouver. He had

been leasing a section of land (640 acres) near Hussar, Alberta since 1928, with 280 acres under cultivation. He had a very basic, 14 x 16 foot house, eight horses, and an old car. In addition to farming, Nissen had made 41 dollars the previous year from playing his violin at community functions. He had been dating the same girl for two years, and hoped to get engaged when he had more money; he was confident that she could "stand up to the life of a farm wife." As a wheat farmer, however, Nissen felt the effects of the Depression early and sold his farm in March 1930, explaining to his brother, "never has the USA or Canadian farmer ever been in so desperate a financial situation."[39] Nissen later reflected on his decision to sell his farm and most of his belongings:

> As spring [1930] moved closer, I got more and more agitated. I had to meet a debt of $226 for the new car and had no money; I had to plow 180 acres and had no fodder for my horses; the price of wheat stayed down; we did not get our cheque from the Wheat Pool. All in all the outlook was very miserable. Then one day I made a quick decision. I wanted to sell my outfit and go to work again. It took me a long time to find a reliable buyer; 3 different families wanted it but I was afraid they would not be able to pay me. So finally I sold it to Old Ross for $750. He got everything except my radio, blankets and instruments. . . . So I went back to Hussar again and here I sold my car to the bank teller, Harold French, for $450.[40]

Not only did Nissen dispose of everything he owned except his blankets and instruments, he also ended his engagement to Emily Peterson, his girlfriend of two years. He could not court her in good faith if he did not intend to marry her, and he was in no position to take on the responsibilities of a husband and breadwinner. When he learned just a few months later that Emily was engaged to another man who was rumoured to earn $300 a month, Nissen was jealous and felt his masculinity diminished.[41]

After selling his farm, Nissen worked on another farm for a modest income and then was fortunate to get work on a road crew that paid $90 a month in 1931. He was also fortunate that Emily's engagement had broken off and, with his decent income, he and Emily married that year. Emily continued to live with her parents on their farm while Nissen travelled with the road crew, saving money for a home for him and Emily. Well aware of the effects of the economic crisis on the Prairie and grateful to be progressing with his life, Nissen wrote to his brother in Denmark that he was better off than 70 per cent of the Canadian farmers even if [he] was almost broke."[42]

By 1931, Nissen had fulfilled many of the markers associated with adulthood: leaving school, moving away from his family of origin, and marriage. His plans for acquiring a home and starting a family with his 25-year-old wife had to be put on hold, however, because the provincial money for road crews dried up the following year. Without a reliable income the newly married couple had to live with her parents, rather than independently as they planned. The subsequent years were increasingly difficult. Nissen had moved to Canada to become a farmer, but was definitely failing. His pride as an adult male, symbolized by a clear break from depending on his family of origin, kept him from declaring any hardship to relatives in Denmark. For example, in November 1932, he wrote to his brother and sister-in-law: "Now don't think that we are dressed in rags, that we go hungry, or live on government welfare. Far from it. It's only that it takes everything I earn to keep us in food, clothes, and other necessities."[43] His masculine pride was further eroded, however, when Nissen was unable to pay the hospital and doctor's bill when his wife was scheduled to deliver their first child a few months later in March, 1933. Finally he appealed for his brother's help: "I cannot see how we are going to make out this winter and if at all possible, I beg you to try to see if you could send us some money. We have our back against the wall and I do not know what we can do when Emily has to go to the hospital next March 1. It is on account of Emily that I am writing to you—she has got to have good care in the days to come. . . . I have lost all my self esteem and can only think of Emily's welfare."[44] For Nissen, being the family breadwinner was a minimum standard that he was obliged to keep. When he could not bring in the money himself, he still recognized his role as primary provisioner, and with great hesitation, for the first time since leaving Denmark nine years before, asked his family to help. As such he was still providing for his wife and child, but he was devastated by having to compromise his full autonomy.

While Nissen's family sent $50, exactly enough to cover the medical bills when baby Norman Koenig was born, they also suggested that Nissen return to Denmark where they could take care of him. Though he claimed to have lost all his self esteem, Nissen retained enough pride to insist: "I cannot face the shame of coming back home, broke."[45] Nissen, however, received his family's request as a second defeat. The thought that his family in Denmark considered him unable to support his new family, was even more devastating than having to ask them for money. In both scenarios his lack of money was tied to shame over not fulfilling the masculine role expected of a young man in his twenties. Nissen had achieved the major markers of adulthood, including starting a family, however, in his own judgment he had failed because he was still financially dependent both on his wife's family and his own family in Denmark. He was a *liminal personae*; his path to adulthood was incomplete. In fact, it took a long time for Nissen to achieve financial independence, partly due to large medical bills arising from the birth of his second child, Joan, in 1937. He was even forced to obtain four boxes of relief apples in 1937, which must have been extremely difficult for him.[46] His liminality between dependence and autonomy, and his seeming regression from adulthood back to youth, wounded his sense of masculinity, which was so tied to financial autonomy.

John Murphy

When the stock market crashed in October 1929, John Murphy (b. 1902) was 27 years old and living in Northern Ontario. Just one year older than Creighton and Nissen, Murphy was much farther along the pathway to adulthood. One might argue that he had completed the transition, but Depression circumstances caused him to regress. In 1929, Murphy had been married for a year and á half to Annette [pseudonym],[47] who was five years his senior. Together they had an eight-month-old daughter. They lived in a rented house but did not have a car. Murphy had more than a decade of experience as a newspaper reporter and fiction writer. "Then," in Murphy's words, "the Depression struck. Markets began folding up. This was the end of the pulp magazine era."[48]

Murphy found it increasingly difficult to make money from commercial writing during the Depression and became anxious and depressed from the strain of being the family's sole breadwinner. He and Annette enjoyed being consumers. They regularly bought new clothes and decorated their home. As a freelance writer, he eagerly awaited cheques arriving in the mail, but was more often disappointed than pleased. This economic instability increased exponentially during the Depression, as did his drinking.[49] Unlike Creighton, who made very little money writing, Murphy received two cheques in the $300 range and two in the $500 range in 1930 and 1931, with numerous smaller cheques in between.[50] In each case he applied the cheques to bills, and in December 1930 he also purchased a new radio. The $525 cheque received in June 1931 was especially welcome with his second child born a month later. Despite earning a relatively good income, Murphy complained regularly about financial stress, noting in September 1930, "It is discouraging to be broke with so much stuff out. Have only a few dollars left." In November 1930 he wrote: "Absolutely broke now. Not a nickel in the house."[51]

September 1931 marked the first time Murphy had to borrow money from a bank to cover basic expenses. He gave up his downtown office two weeks later. Although Murphy's total income in the early 1930s was substantial by most standards, he and his wife could not cope with the unreliability, and they resented having to curb their spending habits. Unlike most men who worked outside the home, Murphy's sense of masculinity and self worth was more dependent on being externally and financially rewarded. While his healthy income during the 1920s validated his self-esteem, his confidence spiralled downward as his income decreased. Consequently,

his diary entries were regularly filled with shame at not being consistently able to provide for his family.

From 1932 onward, Murphy's diary entries refer bleakly to his finances: "18 May 1932 . . . Down to the last three bucks and no money . . . from any source. The worse spot we have even been in. . . . 25 May 1932 I'm damn near sick with worry for there doesn't seem to be any way out. . . . 31 May 1932 Still no mail, no relief, and no hope."[52] While there were a few small cheques in the next few months, Murphy's year end summary of 1932 focused on his financial worries: "It has been on the whole a hard year and I am tired and confused and a little afraid of what may come. The day was cold with a bitter north wind. . . . We sat by the radio and read until midnight. The sounds of other people having a good time make me envious."[53]

A consistent diarist, Murphy records both positive and negative events. He weaves threads about his varied existence as a writer, husband, and father. He also provides updates on such masculine amusements as playing poker, bowling, and drinking, and reports enthusiastically on attending hockey games.[54] Murphy did not have traditional employment and usually wrote at home, which was not easy with two small children, although masculine prerogative allowed his wife to perform the primary childcare during his work hours.[55] He expresses both frustration and determination about his struggle to write at home, such as "October 30 . . . One hell of a day, with the kids howling and squacking from morning until night but I slapped out 4,000 words first draft of the second article" and "1 March 1932 . . . Thought I would get a great deal of work done today. What a hope! Had to take [baby] out for an airing. Annette had people for tea, cord of wood arrived, and the day was wrecked."[56] The combination of increased stress, and an unstructured work environment within the home allowed him more time with male friends, whom Murphy often blamed for his excessive drinking. His references to drinking consistently focus on his guilt and shame over disappointing his wife, a very real thing in 1931 when she threatened to leave him after he stayed out drinking until dawn. Just before their second anniversary, Murphy observed: "22 April 1930 (Tues)

Just one of those days. No work done. Met [friends] and down town . . . for some drinks. Went down to [nearby town with friend] came back and the gang were here. Annette was wild and gave me the devil. Rather unpleasant." Similarly, a couple of months later: "14 July 1930 (Monday) . . . I was in the bank where I ran into [two friends]. Was around with them all afternoon and most of the night in a hectic spree. Didn't get home until nearly dawn. . . ."[57]

Murphy's hard work and willingness to write for whatever commercial markets were available afforded sufficient money for his family during the Depression. In fact, he was relatively well off even when he and Annette added two children to their family in the early 1930s. Nevertheless, the economic crisis wounded Murphy's sense of pride in his work and he exhibited signs of depression. He also expressed anxiety about not being able to keep up the pace of writing required to keep money coming in, about the Depression killing the publishing industry, about having to get a more formal job, and about his increasing abuse of alcohol. Murphy's discontent was partly connected to his inability to pursue what he most desired, which was to write a successful novel and to have a writing space apart from his family. Though he seemed embarrassed by his own contributions to fiction, he continued to write it as it offered dependable income. He also saved money by giving up his downtown office and working at home. Above all, he was adaptable, transitioning into other media in the latter years of the Depression. Despite his relative financial stability during the 1930s, Murphy still judged himself harshly for not making as much money in the 1930s as in the previous decade. In the 1930s he did not measure up to his own expectations as an adult male, writer, and breadwinner and expressed his frustration and shame in his diaries.

Conclusion

Alan Creighton, Ole Nissen, and John Murphy all struggled with "being in your twenties in the thirties." Surely they would have agreed with MacLennan's description: "You stayed on the ground, or just above it, for ten years." The Depression affected them outwardly as they adjusted to their reduced incomes and inwardly as their sense of masculinity and self-worth plummeted. Creighton and Nissen became stuck in a liminal phase between youth and adulthood, and Murphy seemed to regress from adulthood to youth. They all internalized hegemonic masculinity's expectation that adult men must provide for their families, or, if single, provide for themselves, even when unemployment rates were very high.[58] Measuring themselves against that expectation, these three young men believed they were falling short of adulthood. Their sense of masculinity was impaired by their liminality.

Liminality had its own continuum and was only loosely connected to biological age. Each of these three young men, aged either 27 or 28 years of age when the Depression began, understood normative masculinity according to his proximity to adulthood, as well as his employment and marriage status. When the Great Depression began in the fall of 1929, Alan Creighton, neither employed nor romantically involved, was the most youthful. Ole Nissen, who owned a small farm and had plans to marry a woman certain to be a good farm wife, teetered significantly toward adulthood. John Murphy, a successful writer, married for two years with an infant daughter, had entered adulthood. These young men's internalized notions of masculinity and proximity to adulthood were reflected and affirmed in how they coped with the financial crisis. Each reacted to his worst financial crisis in a way appropriate to his specific place on the path to adulthood. Creighton, the most youthful, continued to depend on his parents as he always had. Ole Nissen asked his family for exceptional, one-time financial assistance ($50 to pay a medical bill). John Murphy, who was farther along the path to adulthood, went to the bank for a loan. They reacted to financial stress according to what was socially expected of them, depending on their level of autonomy and proximity to adulthood.

Achieving—or not achieving—adulthood is not just about completing steps on a pathway, but also about acquiring a more nuanced sense of adult masculinity, which is different from youth masculinity. Because Creighton and Nissen were actively trying to enter adulthood, and Murphy was trying to maintain his recently acquired adult status, their ideals of adult masculinity are vivid and telling. In the 1930s, certain performances, such as driving a car and being a member of a union, were identified with adult masculinity. In fact, the three young men under study were self employed and therefore did not belong to a union, and only Ole Nissen owned and drove a car.[59] The three diarists did participate in numerous other gender systems inside and outside of their families that contributed to their masculinity, however. In particular, they performed their masculinity in relation to women, consumption, and work.

To differing extents, these three young men defined their masculinity in relation to women around them.[60] Like many men, they were guided in their performances of masculinity, by *not* being like women. Among the most-identified characteristics of femininity was emotionality.[61] While all three men wrote in their diaries about their shame at not being better providers, overall they sought to maintain rationality. The two married men in this study demonstrate this very clearly in relation to their spouses. Murphy treated his wife, Annette, as the emotionalist specialist in their partnership. He even projected his emotions on her, and worked out his own emotions by misappropriating what she felt about his actions, particularly around his excessive drinking. These extracts from Murphy's 1930 diary are typical:

> "17 May [1930] [. . .] Didn't get home until dawn. It was a mean trick to play on Annette and I've got to straighten up."
>
> "Aug 5 [1930] Everybody recovering from a bad night. [. . .] Annette is rather disgusted but has forgiven me."
>
> "24 Sept [1930] Didn't get in until 4am and Annette was sore. She has a right to be."[62]

Ole Nissen also tried hard to maintain rationality. Although he suffered both financially and emotionally in the early days of the Depression after having to sell his farm and cancel his engagement, he kept a stiff upper lip when writing to his brother in Denmark. Only when he hit rock bottom did he acknowledge that his self esteem was lost. When he finally admitted his emotional strain to his brother, he wrote only of his worry for his wife's health, an attitude which affirmed his masculine role as her protector. Alan Creighton was the most emotional of the three male diarists, commenting in half his entries about his angst around his career, place in the family, and path to adulthood. As a single, underemployed poet, Creighton may have felt fewer inhibitions on his emotions compared to Nissen and Murphy. He did noticeably lack enthusiasm, however, when his younger sister got a job and then married in 1930, perhaps finding that her success amplified his failure.

These young men's consumption habits were part of their masculinity. They all used their diaries like household account ledgers, noting purchases as well as money received.[63] Between 1929 and 1931, Murphy, who had the most money of the three, recorded buying a radio, clothes for him and his spouse, several pieces of furniture, and household amenities. Nissen's financial notations focused on selling; he sold his radio, car, and farm in the first two years of the Depression. Creighton, in keeping with his health concerns, carefully recorded his dental and medical bills. What is most notable about these young men's consumption habits, however, is their distress at being unable to afford suitable accommodations. Creighton desperately wanted to move away from his family, Nissen did not like living with his wife's parents, and Murphy was very frustrated that he had to live and work in the same building. All three men lamented the loss of true manliness because they could not maintain a separate independent household. They explained their unhappiness as the lack of freedom to live as they hoped, and which, to some extent, they felt entitled as adult men. Several historians have described the housing crisis of the 1930s. According to Cynthia Comacchio, "Doubling-up and overcrowding in accommodation were strategies of despair for many families, as moves to ever cheaper, smaller, and unhealthier lodgings became an everyday parade."[64] Historians have long equated masculinity with employment. The life writing of these three men suggests an equally strong connection between setting up a new household and masculinity, adulthood, and autonomy, and adds a new layer of understanding to the 1930s housing crisis.

The diaries of these three young men confirm other scholars' argument about the inseparable ties between work and masculinity. Ole Nissen's work as a farmer and roadbuilder required strength, endurance, and toughness and was therefore very connected to the image of the physically strong masculine body.[65] John Murphy and Alan Creighton, on the other hand, were both writers whose work required their brains more than their bodies, yet they portrayed their work in physical terms. Murphy's violent description of his writing process contributes to his masculinity: "30 Oct [1931] . . . I slapped out 4000 words first draft of the second article. . . . 5 Dec [1932] . . . Worked like fury and finished up the story . . . and I shot it out . . . just in time to make the mail."[66] Creighton describes his writing process in hurtful terms: "April 24 [1930] 'Release'— an unfortunate sullen creature that was painful to produce and on which I put a good deal of forced labour, was published in the April *Busy East*."[67] Creighton is also notable for placing his work in the context of a greater good, for which he saw himself as something of a leader: "March 11 [1931] . . . As for my goal, it is simply that of writing stories that are good stories. The tendency of my writing is (at present) towards human emotions and the human struggle for happiness. This is not an original subject but it is a powerful one, worthy, I think, of study and application . . . 12 May 1933 . . . as a poet, I am a needed factor in the community."[68] Of these three young men, Nissen is the only one whose work (on a farm and road crew) required strength and taxed his body, yet Murphy and Creighton, whose work was mentally but not physically challenging, copied

the language of physical labour, using verbs such as slap, shot, and forced. Because, as Christopher Forth argues, "What counts as acceptable masculinity in one domain would not necessarily hold true in others,"[69] one might expect different masculinities in these two very different kinds of work, yet Murphy and Creighton construct their work as comparable to work requiring physical strength and endurance.

These three young men's masculinity was constructed not just in terms of the work they did, but also in terms of the work performed by women around them. For the two married men, their manliness was heightened by their wives' lack of waged work. Being the sole family breadwinner offered these husbands and fathers more authority and thus a closer approximation of the masculine ideal of the interwar era.[70] This may have been important to Murphy in particular, as he was engaged in work for which he did not need to leave the house, and may have needed to distinguish himself from his wife, who was also at home all day.

For many male youth, the inability to enter adulthood in a timely manner damaged their sense of heterosexual masculinity and self esteem. Creighton, Nissen, and Murphy expressed their disenchantment at not becoming the full adults they wished to be. Only in the late 1930s did they consider that they were again making progress toward independence: Creighton moved away from his family to Toronto; Nissen moved out of his in-laws' home and leased a farm of his own; and Murphy regained his self-assurance and adult status—at least in his own mind—when he succeeded in finding new work, which he did outside his home. For Alan Creighton, Ole Nissen, and John Murphy, unemployment and underemployment in the early 1930s lengthened their phase of liminality between youth and adulthood and diminished their sense of masculinity.

Notes

1. Hugh MacLennan, "What It Was Like to Be in Your Twenties in the Thirties," Victor Hoar, ed., *Essays and Memoirs from Canada and the United States* (Vancouver: Copp Clark, 1969), 151.

2. MacLennan, "What It Was Like to Be in Your Twenties," 147.

3. Harvey Graff, *Conflicting Paths: Growing Up in America*

(Cambridge and London: Harvard University Press, 1995), 7.

4. Michael Schiebach, "Transition to Manhood: Effects of the Great Depression on Male Youth," *Adolescence* 20 (Fall 1985): 727.

5. Much of Turner's work focused on the Ndebu. Victor Turner, "Liminality and Communitas," in Victor Turner,

ed., *The Ritual Process: Structure and Anti-Structure* (Chicago: University of Chicago, 1968), 95.

6. Mark Moss, *Manliness and Militarism: Educating Young Boys in Ontario for War* (Oxford: Oxford University Press, 2001), 21.

7. R.W. Connell, *Masculinities* (Los Angeles and Berkeley: University of California Press, 2005), 196.

8. Christopher E. Forth, *Masculinity in the Modern West: Gender, Civilization and the Body* (New York: Palgrave MacMillan, 2008), 141, 157–166, and Ross D. Cameron, "Tom Thomson, Antimodernism, and the Ideal of Manhood," *Journal of the Canadian Historical Association* 10 (1999): 186.

9. If one accepts the broadest definition of masculinity as being "not femininity," (Connell, p. 70) autonomy is a very masculine ideal that can be paired with the feminine ideal of dependency. Autonomy can also be paired with dependence to distinguish between adulthood and childhood, as Harvey Graff does.

10. Moss, *Manliness and Militarism*, 20.

11. Nancy Christie, *Engendering the State: Family, Work, and Welfare in Canada* (Toronto: University of Toronto Press, 2000); Cynthia Comacchio, "'A Postscript for Father': Defining a New Fatherhood in Interwar Canada," *Canadian Historical Review* 78:3 (September 1997): 386–408; Margaret Hobbs, "Rethinking Antifeminism in the 1930s: Gender Crisis or Workplace Justice? A Response to Alice Kessler-Harris," *Gender and History* 5, 1, (1993): 4–15; and Lara Campbell, *Respectable Citizens: Gender, Family, and Unemployment in Ontario's Great Depression* (Toronto: University of Toronto, 2010), 57–83.

12. Christie, *Engendering the State*, 247.

13. Connell, *Masculinities*, 54.

14. To a lesser extent, previously unemployed women entering the waged workforce to compensate a family for the loss of men's wages, also affected femininity. See for example, Comacchio, "Postscript," 391, and Katrina Srigley, *Breadwinning Daughters: Young Women's Work in a Depression-Era City, 1929–1931* (Toronto: University of Toronto Press, 2010), 2.

15. Frank W. Beer, "He Sold His Shoes," *Saturday Night* (August 14, 1934): 3.

16. Forth, *Masculinity*, 6.

17. *Historical Statistics of Canada*, "Table B75-81: Number of marriages and rate, average age at marriage for brides and bridegrooms, number of divorces and rate, net family formation, Canada, 1921 to 1974," and "Table B1-14: Live births, crude birth rate, age-specific fertility rates, gross reproduction rate and percentage of births in hospital, Canada, 1921 to 1974." Available online: www.statcan.gc.ca/pub/11-516-x/pdf/5500093-eng.pdf. Social agencies, such as the YMCA, became very concerned that the postponement of marriage would lead to increased incidence of premarital sex. Dire warnings of how unemployment could increase immorality added to the angst and shame

of many young couples in the 1930s and impacted normative notions of masculinity.

18. Comacchio, "Postscript," 394.

19. Campbell, *Respectable Citizens*, 59 fn11.

20. As a writer, Alan Creighton may have hoped his diaries would be of interest in subsequent years, but no biography has ever been written of him and his diaries were never published. Ole Nissen's daughter published her father's correspondence with his brother in Denmark: Joan Walter, ed., *A Paradise for the Poor: Hussar, Standard and Caroline Alberta, Letters of Ole Nissen, 1923–37* (Alberta Records Publication Board, 2001). For each subject, I used the original diaries held at Dalhousie University Archives (Creighton), the Glenbow Museum and Archives (Nissen), and an Ontario university archives (John Murphy) that I will not name because the family requested that I use a pseudonym and avoid identifying material. The family claims that they intended to restrict the diaries while the archives has documentation confirming there are no restrictions.

21. Philippe Lejeune, "Spiritual Journals in France from the Sixteenth to the Eighteenth Centuries," Jeremy D. Popkin and Julie Rak, eds., *On Diary* (Honolulu: University of Hawai'i Press, 2009), 71.

22. In fact, the first evidence in Murphy's diary that his wife was pregnant was when he recorded: "6 March 1929 Paid hospital bill . . . and preparing to bring the family back home at last tomorrow." "Diary, 1929," John Murphy Collection. (I am not including the archival information in order to honour the family's request to exclude identifying material.) Nissen was equally reserved when hinting to his brother that he and his wife were expecting their first child, saying: "We have been married two years now and it is said that it happens in the best of families, so I may have some news for you soon." Ole Nissen to Gudrun and Alfred, 19 November 1932, Nissen Family Fonds, M 8809, Glenbow Archives, www.glenbow.org/collections/search/findingAids/archhtm/nissen.cfm. R.W. Connell placed considerable emphasis on a man's first sexual experience in oral interviews with Australian, American, and British men, in his well-known book, *Masculinities*.

23. Philippe Lejeune, "The 'Journal de Jeune Fille' in Nineteenth-Century France," *On Diary*, 132.

24. "Loose Papers, 1926–1945," files 1. 20; "Biographical Excerpts," file 6.10; "Report Cards and other Education-Related material," file 19.1, MS-2-701, Creighton Family Fonds, Dalhousie University Archives.

25. "22 Jan 1931," Diary 1931-32, box 1, file 22, Creighton Family Fonds.

26. "May 1930," Diary 1929-30, Creighton Family Fonds.

27. "20 June 1930," Diary 1929-30, box 1, file 21, Creighton Family Fonds. The emphasis is mine.

28. "7 Jan 1931," Diary 1931-32, box 1, file 22, Creighton Family Fonds. Creighton referred to other people's

illnesses as complicating his writing career. My emphasis in the quotation.

29. "12 May 1933," "Diary Excerpts" (retyped), file 6.12 Creighton Family Fonds.

30. Campbell, *Respectable Citizens*, 71.

31. Early in his career, Thomas Carlyle (1795–1881) had similar angst about the lack of manliness connected to being a writer. See Norma Clarke, "Strenuous Idleness: Thomas Carlyle and the man of letters as hero," Michael Roper and John Tosh, eds., *Manful Assertions: Masculinities in Britain since 1800* (London: Routledge, 1991), 25–43.

32. Philippe Lejeune, "The Continuous and Discontinuous," *On Diary*, 178–79.

33. Connell, *Masculinities*, 179, 196.

34. "12 May 1933," "Diary Excerpts" (retyped), file 6.12, Creighton Family Fonds.

35. "Alan Creighton Finding Aid," MS-2-701, Dalhousie University Archives (Halifax): www.library.dal.ca/DUASC/FindingAids/MS_2_701.

36. Ibid. and Norman Creighton, *Talk about the Valley*, ed., Hilary Sircom (Halifax: Nimbus, 2001), 3.

37. "Alan Creighton, "Unemployed," *Canadian Forum* 15, no 172 (January, 1935): 137.

38. Walter, *Paradise*, xiv–xv.

39. Ole Nissen to Gudrun and Alfred, 14 March 1930, Nissen Family Fonds. http://asalive.archivesalberta.org:8080/?proc=page&sess=ASALIVE-1200-dEX_s&dbase=documents_alberta&item=GLEN-32&page=29. Pre 1930s information from scattered correspondence, 1923-1929.

40. "10 May 1930," Diaries 1915–1956, box 2, file 7, Nissen Family Fonds. Glenbow Museum.

41. "16 June 1930," Diaries 1915–1956, box 2, file 7, Nissen Family Fonds. Glenbow Museum.

42. Ole Nissen to Gudrun and Alfred, 14 March 1930, Nissen Family Fonds, Glenbow Archives, http://asalive.archivesalberta.org:8080/?proc=page&sess=ASALIVE-1200-dEX_s&dbase=documents_alberta&item=GLEN-32&page=29.

43. Ole Nissen to Gudrun and Alfred, 19 November 1932, Nissen Family Fonds.

44. Ole Nissen to Gudrun and Alfred, 9 December 1932,

45. Ole Nissen to Gudrun and Alfred, 19 May 1933, Nissen Family Fonds.

46. Walter, *Paradise*, 145.

47. Diary, 1929 (note at back), John Murphy Collection.

48. [Autobiographical notes] "Genealogical and Biographical," John Murphy Collection.

49. 27 March 1930; 22 April 1930; 7 Nov 1930; 8 Apr 1931; 22 April 1931; 15 July 1931; 4 Aug 1931; 10 Feb 1931, 1930 and 1931 Diaries, John Murphy Collection.

50. 4 January 1930; 10 April 1930, 1930 Diary, John Murphy Collection.

51. 1 November 1930, 1930 Diary, John Murphy Collection.

52. 18 May; 25 May; and 31 May 1931, 1931 Diary, John Murphy Collection.

53. 31 December 1932, 1932 Diary, John Murphy Collection.

54. Scholars have explained attending sporting events as engagement in "spectatorship masculinity." Forth, *Masculinity*, 158 fn 65.

55. Comacchio, "Postscript," 396.

56. 1932 Diary, John Murphy Collection.

57. 1930 Diary, John Murphy Collection.

58. Campbell, *Respectable Citizens*, 60.

59. Forth has a very interesting discussion of cars and masculinity: Forth, *Masculinity*, 176–182.

60. Connell, *Masculinities*, 44, 68, 70.

61. Connell, *Masculinities*, 164.

62. 1930 Diary, John Murphy Collection.

63. Philippe Lejeune, "Counting and Managing," 51–52, *On Diary*.

64. Cynthia R. Comacchio, *The Infinite Bonds of Family: Domesticity in Canada, 1850–1940* (Toronto: University of Toronto Press, 1999), 127.

65. Connell, *Masculinities*, 55.

66. 1930 Diary, Box 20; 1931 Diary, John Murphy Collection. Forth, *Masculinity*, 158

67. Diary 1929–30, Creighton Family Fonds.

68. Diaries, 1931–32 and 1933, Creighton Family Fonds.

69. Forth, *Masculinity*, 3.

70. Comacchio, "Postscript," 391.

Nissen Family Fonds. See also Comacchio, "Postscript," 394.

PRIMARY DOCUMENT

Ole Nissen's Diary, excerpt, "Helge (Ole) Nissen to Gudrun and Alfred," 9 December 1932 (Translated from Danish)

Caroline, Alta., December 9, 1932

Dear Alfred!

It is only a short while ago since I sent you my last letter, so I'm sure you will be surprised to receive this second letter. To tell the truth I've been wanting to write you for the last week, but I could not seem to express my needs to write you. However, to start with, I cannot see how we are going to make out this winter; and if possible, I beg you to try and see if you could send us some money. We have our back against the wall and I do not know what we can do when Emily has to go to the hospital next March 1st. it will cost us $50 cash before she can come home again. To get the doctor to come out here will cost us $35, and the doctor says that she should go to the hospital, as she has not completely recovered from her sickness of a couple of years ago.

When last I wrote you everything looked pretty good. We bought the old Ford car for half the cost of the return to our farm. But by the time we got here, we had experienced a lot of trouble and expense. We had to buy a new tire and tube; our expenses were twice what we could have travelled for. Still it is not all bad now I'll have a car to get Emily to the doctor if it becomes necessary. However, the worst that happened was the mess the man who was supposed to look after the farm had left for us!

He had left the oats and wheat standing in the field, now soaked with snow. The horses and cattle were not taken care of and had broken down a lot of fences. They got into the grain field and had tramped most of the grain down. When he finally got around to haul the crop in, he threw it up on the top of the flat-roofed barn. There it lay, all in great heaps for rain and snow to further deteriorate what was left. One half of the ducks and geese have disappeared; and all I could do was to give him a good piece of my mind. Now I'll have to buy feed for over half of the winter. I had a horse that went lame last summer. When the snow came, it could not find any feed. The man let it wander around in the bush until it finally died. I was not so well acquainted here in this country. I'd had quite a lot to do with this man; he is a 30-year-old bachelor and was nice and willing when we worked together. He has a farm, and is my neighbour. He moved his things over in our house and lived here while we were gone. I now have no seed wheat or oats, but that is not the worst.

It is account of Emily that I'm writing you—she has got [*underlined in original*] to have good care in the days to come. So I turn to you, Alfred, and ask you the following: See if you can spare me a few dollars; talk to the rest of the family and ask them, too. I know that times are hard for you folks too, but I beg of you to see what you can do. I have lost all my self-esteem, and can only think about Emily's welfare. If you can help us, keep track of the money, and I will repay you as soon as I can. If we can hang on to what we now have, we might have a hope for the future. I can see how that we should have stayed here at home [*at Caroline*], and looked after things, but money was hard to come by, and it looked bad, no matter what we did. I will write to Lex myself, but I don't' know the addresses of many of the others. I hope you will think this over, and do as you think best.

From your devoted brother, Helge

PS. Love to all.

Source: M-8809-7, Nissen Family Fonds, Glenbow Museum.
With permission from the Glenbow Museum.

Study Questions

1. Even without primary sources produced by young people, historians can read more traditional sources with the perspectives, feelings, and priorities of young people in mind. Historian Mona Gleason has referred to this approach as "empathic inference." If we read the Girl Guide Logbook from the 1930s that accompanies Kristine Alexander's piece through the lens of empathic inference, what can we say about the experience of young Girl Guides? What are the strengths and weaknesses of this approach?

2. The young men coming of age during the Depression featured in Heidi MacDonald's essay were concerned about their ability to provide for themselves and their families as "breadwinners." Is the concept of "bread-winning" an issue for young men in our contemporary times? How is this concept connected (or not) to ideals of femininity and masculinity today?

Selected Bibliography

Articles

Chunn, Dorothy E., "Boys Will Be Men, Girls Will Be Mothers: The Legal Regulation of Childhood in Toronto and Vancouver," in Nancy Janovicek and Joy Parr, eds, *Histories of Canadian Children and Youth*. Don Mills, ON: Oxford University Press, 2003: 188–206.

Burke, Sara Z., "'Being unlike Man': Challenges to Co-Education at the University of Toronto, 1884–1909," *Ontario History* 93, 1 (Spring 2001): 11–31.

Gidney, Catherine, "Dating and Gating: The Moral Regulation of Men and Women at Victoria and University Colleges, University of Toronto, 1920–60," *Journal of Canadian Studies/Revue d'études canadiennes* 41, 2 (Spring 2007): 138–60.

Gleason, Mona, "Growing Up to Be 'Normal': Psychology Constructs Proper Gender Roles in Post-World War II Canada, 1945–1960," in Edgar-Andre Montigny and Lori Chambers, eds, *Family Matters: Papers in Post-Confederation Canadian Family History*. Toronto: Canadian Scholars' Press, 1998: 39–56.

Lenskyj, Helen, "Training for 'True Womanhood': Physical Education for Girls in Ontario Schools, 1890–1920," *Historical Studies in Education/Revue d'histoire de l'éducation* 2, 2 (Autumn 1990): 1–14.

Marr, M. Lucille, "Church Teen Clubs, Feminized Organizations? Tuxis Boys, Trail Rangers, and Canadian Girls in Training, 1919–1939," *Historical Studies in Education/Revue d'histoire de l'éducation* 3, 2 (Fall 1991): 249–67.

Schiebach, Michael, "Transition to Manhood: Effects of the Great Depression on Male Youth," *Adolescence* 20 (Fall 1985): 727.

Sethna, Christabelle, "The Cold War and the Sexual Chill—Freezing Girls Out of Sex Education," *Canadian Women Studies* (Winter 1997): 57–61.

Stamp, Robert M., "Teaching Girls Their 'God Given Place in Life': The Introduction of Home Economics in the Schools," *Atlantis* (Spring 1977): 18–34.

Warner, Anne, "A Hatchet in 'Lily-White Hands': The Intricacies of Femininity at Private Girls' Camps in Early Twentieth-Century Ontario," *Journal of Sport History* 39, 3 (Fall 2012): 507–25.

Warren, Allen, "Popular Manliness: Baden-Powell, Scouting, and the Development of Manly Character," in J.A. Mangan and James Walvin, eds, *Manliness and Morality: Middle Class Masculinity in Britain and America, 1800–1940*. Manchester: Manchester University Press, 1987: 199–219.

Books

Strange, Carolyn, *Toronto's Girl Problem: The Perils and Pleasures of the City, 1880–1930*. Toronto: University of Toronto Press, 1995.

Veronica Strong-Boag, *The New Day Recalled: Lives of Girls and Women in English Canada, 1919–1939*. Toronto: Copp Clark, 1988.

5 Endangered and Dangerous Children and Youth

Editors' Introduction

Early-twentieth-century industrializing Canada provided ample opportunity for children and youth to exert independence from adult authority. Sometimes this growing autonomy was derived from the working-class imperative that children work for wages or generate income any way they could, as John Bullen's essay in this volume attests.[1] Historians have noted that alongside industrialization came adult hand-wringing over the dangers modern society presented to young people, prompting the establishment of institutions to care for and constrain those who appeared neglected or abused by circumstance. With urbanization and industrialization came the growth of "cheap amusements"—dance halls, moving-picture houses, and other commercial establishments that were targeted at a youthful market.[2] The world beyond the home was a complex one that both endangered children and, according to some, produced dangerous youth.

In this chapter, Magda Fahrni and Tamara Myers use legal sources to explore endangered and dangerous youthful lives in Canada's most important early-twentieth-century industrial city, Montreal. Fahrni examines the inquiries into the tragic deaths of children in the 1927 Laurier Palace Theatre fire, illuminating working-class children's daily lives and the attempts to limit their autonomy in early-twentieth-century Montreal. She shows the centrality of commercial leisure pursuits in children's lives, and how children were willing to defy parental and legal authority to attend the cinema. The essay is premised on the need for new questions to be asked of the official investigations that ensued in the aftermath of the fire. In particular, Fahrni focuses on what the historical sources related to this event can tell us about the changing value of children in Montreal society. Her investigation also prompts us to ask difficult questions about the ethics of using historical sources produced by tragic events to further historical scholarship. The primary source that accompanies Fahrni's essay, a January 1927 *Montreal Daily Star* editorial entitled "The Funeral," suggests that even at the time of the tragedy, people struggled to make sense of the death of so many children, regardless of the circumstances and the desire to assign blame.

Whereas Fahrni uses coroner's reports, Tamara Myers relies on the Montreal Juvenile Delinquents' Court to explore the history of youth in her essay. When the juvenile court opened in 1912 it quickly became a mechanism for "catching" adolescent girls who deviated from social rules around sexuality. In the early twentieth century, adolescent girls exercised their autonomy by exploring their sexuality; this behaviour was promptly treated as sexual delinquency, which meant that many were caught in the juvenile court–reform school trap. Myers turns to the records of the court to see what officials made of "boyish badness" and boys' bodies. She finds that the court treated adolescent boys' sexual behaviour differently than girls', but that it still regulated their bodies by investigating and punishing their precocious sexuality. In particular, the court was interested in cases of incest (where boys were seen as predatory) and same-sex sexual acts (where the boys were seen as victims of men). This trend would intensify by the Second World War, as the accompanying 1939 primary source news piece from the *Canadian Police Gazette*, "Juvenile Delinquency in Montreal," foreshadows. In this article, the Montreal police force and concerned citizens call for new mechanisms of control to both protect and police young people.

The two essays in this chapter suggest that the law was instrumental in defining early-twentieth-century youth culture and behaviour. The primary sources—news articles that report on the funeral for the Laurier Palace fire victims and warn about juvenile delinquency—demonstrate the centrality of children to early-twentieth-century society. Fahrni, Myers, and this chapter's primary sources also point to how, despite rules and regulations, children exhibited autonomy and created subcultures that at times operated beyond the reach of parents and the law.

Notes

1. Timothy Gilfoyle, "Street Rats and Guttersnipes: Child Pickpockets and Street Culture in New York City, 1850–1900," *Journal of Social History*, 37, 4 (Summer 2004), 853–82; Bettina Bradbury, *Working Families: Age, Gender, and Daily Survival in Industrializing Montreal* (Toronto: Oxford University Press, 1993); Neil Sutherland, *Growing Up: Childhood in English Canada from the Great War to the Age of Television* (Toronto: University of Toronto Press, 1997).

2. Cynthia Comacchio, *The Dominion of Youth: Adolescence and the Making of Modern Canada, 1920–1950* (Waterloo: University of Waterloo Press, 2005).

Glimpsing Working-Class Childhood through the Laurier Palace Fire of 1927: The Ordinary, the Tragic, and the Historian's Gaze[1]

MAGDA FAHRNI

On 9 January 1927, a fire tore through the Laurier Palace. This was a cinema located in a French-speaking, working-class neighbourhood on the east side of Montreal, the metropolis of early twentieth-century Quebec and Canada. At the time of the fire, roughly 250 children were watching a Sunday matinée (*Sparrows*, a melodrama starring Mary Pickford, and a comic film called *Get 'Em Young*); before the afternoon was out, 78 children had perished, asphyxiated by smoke inhalation or trampled to death as they attempted to escape from the theatre. Despite provincial legislation that prohibited persons under the age

Source: From *Journal of the History of Children and Youth*, 8, 3 (Fall 2015): 426–50. Johns Hopkins University Press Journals. Reprinted with permission.

of 16 from attending motion pictures unless accompanied by an adult, most of these children were there alone or with young siblings or friends. The multiple official investigations that ensued called into question the safety of movie-houses, the morality of screening films on Sundays, and the wisdom of allowing children to watch movies at all. Brief mentions of the fire in academic histories have focused on the subsequent legislation prohibiting Quebec children from commercial cinemas altogether.[2]

There are other stories, however, that could be told about the events that took place at the Laurier Palace in January 1927. I have chosen here to use judicial archives (both criminal and civil), coroners' reports, the abundant documentation generated by the different official investigations—including the testimony of parents, siblings, and neighbours of the victims—, and the extensive press coverage of the fire and its aftermath to ask questions about working-class childhood in early-twentieth-century Montreal. In the pages that follow, I examine a number of themes: children's autonomy versus parental surveillance and authority; the place of commercial leisure and petty consumption in the lives of working-class children; and contemporary understandings of such tragic accidents as the Laurier Palace fire. I conclude this article by reflecting upon the promise and perils of what David Lowenthal has termed—somewhat pejoratively, I think—the "voyeuristic empathy" promoted by historians.[3] What are the ethics of using sources produced by tragedy—the extraordinary—to study the ordinary? Does the empathy generated when one examines the lives of children in the past compensate for what could be seen as the unseemly, even ghoulish, voyeurism in which historians participate? Are historians of youth, what one scholar calls "latter-day child savers,"[4] more likely than others to adopt a perspective reliant upon (or vulnerable to) such empathy?

The Ordinary: Childhood and Cheap Amusements in an Industrial Neighbourhood

The sources produced by this catastrophe give us some insight into relations between parents and children in Hochelaga, a working-class, principally French-speaking, industrial neighbourhood in Montreal. Although some parents had given their children permission to go to the movies that Sunday afternoon, most maintained that their children had defied parental authority and gone without their consent or their knowledge. Many children appear to have lied about their intentions, claiming that they were going ice-skating, or to visit relatives, or to work. This testimony thus raises questions about parental authority, children's autonomy, and the texture of everyday life in an early-twentieth-century industrial neighbourhood. The depositions also reveal conflicts of opinion between husbands and wives, and notably what appear to have been different degrees of willingness to incorporate new commercialized leisure options into child-rearing practices. The importance of older siblings (brothers as well as sisters) as child-minders is strikingly apparent in these sources, as is the degree to which neighbours were often, in fact, members of extended family. Finally, the testimony gathered in the wake of the Laurier Palace tragedy highlights the importance of paid work for these children and teenagers. Delivering messages, selling newspapers, and sweeping cinemas not only gave working-class girls and (especially) boys a certain, legitimate freedom to move about their neighbourhood free from parental surveillance, it also provided them with the means to participate, in a limited fashion, in the new opportunities for mass consumption available in an industrial city. I situate this episode in the abundant Canadian and international literature on the family, notably that which interrogates the relative autonomy of children and adolescents, such as the valuable work done by Cynthia Comacchio and Tamara Myers.[5] My discussion of this tragedy also draws on, and contributes to, the North American historiography of the creation of a youth market for what Kathy Peiss has called "cheap amusements."[6] Indeed, as historians such as Peiss, Comacchio, and David Nasaw have demonstrated, leisure, but especially commercial leisure, was a key factor contributing to the creation of a youth culture in the first decades of the twentieth century.[7]

"Toutes les rues d'Hochelaga, moins quelques-unes, dans le deuil," a headline in La Patrie read the day after the fire.[8] Almost all of the victims of the fire came from Hochelaga.[9] This was a largely francophone, industrial suburb a considerable distance east of the city centre, annexed to Montreal in 1883.[10] Most of the victims lived within a few streets of the Laurier Palace cinema: only 8 of the 78 children killed lived outside the limits of the neighbourhood (see Figure 1). Many of these children had been born in the neighbourhood; the baptismal records of fire victims born in the Paroisse de la Nativité de la Sainte-Vierge d'Hochelaga indicate that many of their godparents were also residents of the parish, underscoring the closely knit ties of kin and community in the neighbourhood.[11] Local men worked as longshoremen, painters, carpenters, joiners, tinsmiths, watchmen, shoemakers, day labourers, repairmen, machinists, foremen, brakemen, boiler-makers, drivers, milkmen, firemen, and policemen; many were employed by railway companies such as Canadian Pacific and Canadian National.[12] The Laurier Palace, situated on rue Sainte-Catherine East and the only cinema in the neighbourhood, was a small theatre that showed vaudeville and musical comedies as well as films and news-reels.[13] Going to the cinema, particularly on a Sunday afternoon, was a neighbourhood affair. Children attended the movies with siblings, or with cousins, or with classmates, most of whom also lived nearby. Some children went to the Laurier Palace after Sunday mass at the parish church; Judge Louis Boyer, who presided the Royal Commission struck in the wake of the fire, noted that this was common practice among both French-speaking and English-speaking Quebeckers.[14] Several employees of the cinema also lived in its immediate vicinity, literally around the corner from the theatre,[15] while employees of other neighbourhood businesses also attended movies at the Laurier Palace.[16]

As the news of the fire spread through the neighbourhood by word of mouth, reported by children who managed to escape from the theatre or by passers-by and policemen, ambulances and fire trucks careened through the streets and desperate parents and curious onlookers gathered in front of the burning cinema. Neighbourhood firemen (there was a fire station across the street from the cinema) and policemen (a police station was to be found just

around the corner) worked together with priests from local churches to extricate children trapped in the cinema stairwell, to administer artificial respiration to the living and the last rites to the dying.[17] The sense that this was a neighbourhood story was reinforced two days later when a funeral mass was delivered at the Église de la Nativité d'Hochelaga, the parish church, in front of 38 small coffins. Although thousands of onlookers travelled by streetcar from across the city to attend the mass, this appears to have been a tragedy that the residents of Hochelaga saw as particularly their own—what Montreal Archbishop Gauthier called "cette épreuve qui frappe Hochelaga et Montréal."[18] Additional funeral services the next day at the Église de la Nativité d'Hochelaga and two other neighbourhood churches acknowledged, structured and perhaps alleviated somewhat the grief and mourning into which the neighbourhood had been plunged.[19] A teaching sister belonging to the order of the Soeurs des Saints Noms de Jésus et de Marie described the tragedy as "une catastrophe épouvantable [qui] s'abattait sur le quartier d'Hochelaga, lui ravissant de nombreuses victimes." She noted that numerous neighbourhood schools had lost pupils in the fire.[20] The precedent of the deaths of schoolteacher Sarah Maxwell and 16 young pupils at Hochelaga School, just two blocks away from the Laurier Palace on rue Préfontaine, 20 years earlier, was frequently evoked by newspapers as another tragedy—indeed, another fire—in which neighbourhood solidarity had been forged.[21]

The tragedy at the Laurier Palace suggests some of the workings of family in this early-twentieth-century industrial neighbourhood. Those who testified to having been present at the Laurier Palace on 9 January unanimously agreed that very few adults were in attendance at the Sunday matinée. With a small number of exceptions, such as Arthur Gendron, a father of eight children who was sitting in the balcony that afternoon, or Juliette Desrosiers, who lived and worked next door to the theatre on rue Sainte-Catherine and watched the movies alone from the balcony, the theatre was filled with children and teenagers, including what one 18-year-old witness called "des petits bonhommes de douze, treize ans."[22] Municipal authorities and newspaper

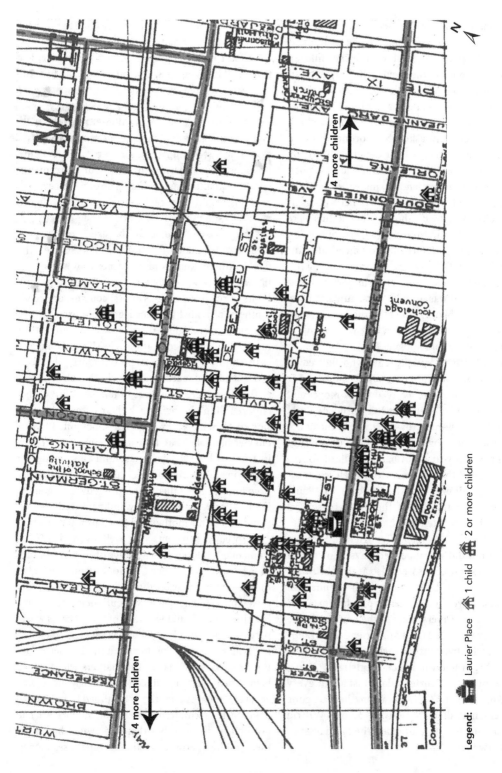

Figure 5.1 Homes of Children Who Died in the Laurier Palace Fire of 1927

Legend: 🏛 Laurier Place 🏚 1 child 🏘 2 or more children

Source: Based on a figure created by Isabelle Huppé. Background map courtesy Bibliothèque et Archives nationales du Québec. Icons ©iStock/Alex Belomlinsky

reporters made much of the fact that almost none of the victims had been accompanied by an adult, as the law required. The fact that most of the children had apparently gone to the movies that day without parental permission was another key element of the story. As heartbroken parents and others arrived at the city morgue to identify the body of their child, they were specifically asked by Coroner Edward McMahon whether their son or daughter had been accompanied by an adult and whether he or she had secured permission to attend the matinée.[23] In most cases (53 cases out of 78), it was the father who identified his child's body. Brothers of the victims were also asked to carry out this duty (9 times out of 78). Only four mothers performed the official identification of her child's body, one accompanied by her own sister, no doubt for emotional support. In other cases (10 in all), it was grandfathers, aunts, uncles, landlords, or neighbours who identified these small bodies—perhaps because such a task was too awful for their parents to contemplate?[24]

The children and adolescents who figured in this story appear to have exercised considerable autonomy—defined here as freedom of movement and the willingness to defy adult authority—, at least within the borders of their neighbourhood. Some of them had gone to the movie with siblings or cousins. Seven-year-old Albert Rémillard, for instance, attended the matinée with his eleven-year-old brother Philippe and their cousin "Ti-Paul" Bourguignon on the day of the fire.[25] In several instances, siblings attended the showing separately, alone or with their respective friends. Some of these children did not appear to have known that their brothers and sisters were also at the film. Other children attended the movie with friends and neighbours: 11-year-old Roger Arpin, for instance, who lived on rue Déséry, went to the Laurier Palace on 9 January with his 11-year-old friend Jean-Louis Falardeau, who lived just a block away on rue Préfontaine. Arpin told the Police Magistrates' Court that he went to the Laurier Palace just about every Sunday; on some of these occasions he had gone to the cinema alone.[26] Twelve-year-old Wilfrid Bigaouette, for his part, attended the Sunday matinée with two friends.[27]

Many children appear to have gone to the movie against their parents' explicit orders. Police officer Albert Boisseau and his wife, for instance, lost three children—aged 8, 11, and 13—in the fire. The children had obtained permission to go ice-skating and had instead gone to the cinema, despite the fact that they were explicitly prohibited from doing so and had in fact been punished by their father for attending a showing at the Laurier Palace a month previously.[28] Children who lied about their intended whereabouts clearly had a sense of which excuses or alibis would be acceptable to parents. Going to work, or going to look for work, was a perfectly satisfactory reason to be out in the streets alone. Thirteen-year-old Édouard St-Pierre, for instance, who died in the fire, had told his father that he was going with a friend to apply for work in a restaurant.[29] Visits to relatives, such as aunts, cousins, or grandmothers, provided another legitimate excuse to be at large in the neighbourhood.[30] Healthy wintertime pursuits such as ice-skating, sledding, or hockey gave children a reason to be outdoors;[31] brothers Wilfrid and Édouard Reid simply told their mother that they were going out to take a walk.[32] Other children didn't bother to ask their parents' permission or to make up excuses but snuck off: 10-year-old Germaine Pelchat, for example, went out to play in front of her family's house and then made her way alone to the cinema. Her nine-year-old brother Roméo, who was killed in the tragedy, had gone to the Laurier Palace separately and paid for his ticket using money his mother had given him for candy.[33]

To be sure, parents were well aware that unaccompanied children under the age of 16 were not supposed to frequent cinemas, and one wonders whether they hadn't been coached to tell the authorities that their children had gone without their permission. But then what should we make of the 30 cases where parents explicitly admitted to having given their minor children permission to attend the Laurier Palace unaccompanied?[34] Many of the fathers who testified before the Royal Commission presided by Judge Boyer several months after the fire claimed that they had opposed their children's cinema attendance, or had not known about it, but that their wives had given their children permission, and in some cases money, to attend the Sunday matinée.[35] Auguste Dumont, for instance, who lost two sons in the fire, thought that they had left the house to attend a hockey match. He claimed never to have given his children permission to attend the movies. His wife, however, testified that she had given the boys permission to attend the Laurier Palace on the Sunday in question, since it was the last day before the beginning of classes after the Christmas school holidays.[36] Seven-year-old Albert Rémillard, who appeared before the Coroner's Inquiry four days after the fire and before the Police Court Magistrates a week later, likewise testified that both permission to go to the Laurier Palace and money for admission had come from his mother. His father apparently thought that Albert and his brother Philippe had gone to their cousin's house.[37] Oscar Gravel, whose seven-year-old son Roland died in the cinema panic, testified before the Royal Commission "that he had always prohibited his children from attending movies, and admitted he did not see eye to eye with his wife on this matter."[38] Without endorsing the claim made by Quebec City police court judge Choquette to the effect that many women sent their children off to the cinema so that they could be free in the afternoon and play bridge,[39] it seems reasonable to assume that for many mothers carrying out their domestic labour in overcrowded flats, the movies offered some respite, a way of getting children out from underfoot, at least for a couple of hours. Some fathers attributed their ignorance of their children's whereabouts to their own regular absences from the house for work, for entire days and sometimes out-of-town for longer stretches of time. For example, the two teenage daughters of Pierre Coulombe, who lost his 11-year-old son Roger in the accident, continued to go to the movies against their father's wishes several months after the fire. *Le Devoir* reported that Coulombe explained his daughters' defiance by the fact that he worked in the United States six months a year; the newspaper noted that the girls' mother also worked outside the home.[40] But it is also possible that shifting blame to wives was a tactic designed to absolve fathers, the legal heads of households, from judicial responsibility.

Children's autonomy was not unlimited, but some children clearly did possess a certain freedom to move about the streets. They also possessed the ability to find the relatively small sums of money (10 cents per ticket, for children) needed to attend the movies. Some boys worked sweeping the Laurier Palace after the evening show, sometimes as late as midnight, in exchange for the price of admission.[41] Others delivered newspapers or ran errands for neighbours in return for cash.[42] Some adolescents, such as Laurette Francoeur, a 16-year-old girl who earned $20 per week and who was for all intents and purposes her widowed mother's sole support, had regular wages.[43] Other children were given the admission fee by their mother, their father, their grandparents, a sibling, or a boarder.[44] In at least two cases, parents hypothesized that their children had used their Christmas money to attend the movies on this early January afternoon.[45] Observers from outside the neighbourhood claimed that children sometimes stole, or begged, in order to secure the cost of admission.[46] Finally, the owners and managers of the Laurier Palace developed strategies for packing the theatre with children, regularly offering free admission to the first 50 children in line, distributing coupons in the neighbourhood allowing admission to the cinema for the reduced rate of seven cents, and holding rhubarb pie-eating contests, accompanied by reduced admission prices, on summer Saturday afternoons.[47]

Testimonies before the authorities give us some insight into the characteristics of an emerging youth culture. This was a heterosocial culture, as Kathy Peiss has argued about commercialized leisure in turn-of-the-twentieth-century New York City and Cynthia Comacchio about interwar English Canada.[48] Two-thirds of the fire victims were boys; one-third were girls.[49] This tragedy was thus an exception to the rule noted by American historian Arwen Mohun, to the effect that the "vast majority of accident victims in early twentieth-century America were men and boys."[50] Teenager Maurice Brown watched the film at the Laurier Palace with two 16-year-old girls, Annette Bisson and Alda Leduc, both of whom perished in the fire.[51] Children of all ages attended the movies: the victims of the fire were aged 5 to 18.[52] Testimonies also give us fragmentary evidence of behaviour that might have been considered delinquent in other settings or by other observers, but which appears to have been seen as normal by these children's peers. A teenage girl present at the matinée assumed, for instance, that the fire had been started by a small boy smoking.[53] Ten-year-old Germaine Pelchat, who lived around the corner from the theatre on rue Déséry, snuck into the theatre alone on 9 January without paying.[54] Another witness testified before the Police Court Magistrates that small boys habitually snuck into the Laurier Palace for free.[55]

Testimonies reveal a marked preference by these children for commercialized leisure, and particularly the cinema, despite competing options such as the activities for children organized by the parish priest on the Sunday afternoon in question.[56] Madeleine Guèvremont, aged 14, testified that she went to the movies whenever she could find the money, up to three or four times a week, even seeing the same movie several times. On the day of the fire, she had been at the Laurier Palace with her six-year-old cousin, Gaston Arpin, who died in the accident.[57] Commercial leisure created physical spaces in the city that were attractive to, and sometimes especially designed for, children and teenagers. These spaces, sites of "cheap amusements," also initiated children and youth into the culture of mass consumption: they were a category of persons to be protected, but also to be wooed.[58] Moreover, this emerging twentieth-century consumer culture was to some degree truly "mass": as Cynthia Comacchio notes about the 1920s, while the wages of working-class children across Canada remained crucial for the economic well-being of their families, these children nonetheless "appear to have retained some 'pocket money' to permit them a measure of involvement in the emergent popular culture that their middle-class peers were making their own."[59]

Adult commentators expressed mixed sentiments about commercial leisure in the wake of the fire. While husbands and wives, as we have seen, sometimes differed over whether the movies were an appropriate leisure activity for their children, many of them went to the movies themselves.[60] A few fathers were at the Laurier Palace that Sunday afternoon, and two of the boys present were accompanied by their grandfather.[61] Some commentators

proposed parks and playgrounds as a healthy alternative to dark, crowded movie-houses. Certain members of the Catholic and Protestant clergy and certain religious associations voiced their disapproval of children's movie attendance, especially on Sundays, but this condemnation was by no means unanimous.[62] Nor were lay authorities unanimous in their disapproval of children's movie-going habit, as we shall see. Union leaders argued that if children under the age of 16 were old enough to work, they ought to be able to attend the movies in their leisure hours.[63] Members of Quebec's legislative assembly debated not only the question of who should bear responsibility for the accident, but also what should be done. Not all members of the legislative assembly felt that theatres should be closed on Sundays, or that children should be prohibited from cinemas altogether.[64]

The fact that children exercised considerable freedom of movement within their neighbourhood should not be taken as a sign of parental negligence, or lack of affection, or of relations between parents and children that were strictly economic. Newspaper descriptions of parents identifying and claiming their children at the morgue, and of tragic funeral services in neighbourhood churches, testify to the profound grief of parents at the loss of their children, and of siblings at the loss of their brothers or sisters. Both fathers and mothers were described by reporters in the language of sentiment, as being wracked with sobs, inconsolable at the loss of their small children.[65] Parents of children killed in the fire gave their ages with great precision: 13 years and 4 days, for instance, or 11 years and 11 months.[66] Catherine Cournoyer is probably right to claim, as she does in her excellent M.A. thesis on childhood accidents, that parenting in working-class Montreal in the early twentieth century was characterized by a certain "laissez-faire." But as she notes, this laissez-faire coexisted with what appear to have been deep emotional attachments between parents and children.[67] The physical limits to laissez-faire were, I suggest, those of the neighbourhood: one could hypothesize that parents felt secure knowing that within the confines of Hochelaga, children would be supervised by neighbours (who were often relatives) and by local notables such as shopkeepers, police constables, and firemen. Both the fire itself and reactions to the tragedy suggest the resonance of neighbourhood in this industrial metropolis; both the pleasures and the perils of mass consumption were experienced in fundamentally local ways. The documentation produced by the Laurier Palace fire confirms the findings of recent studies of twentieth-century consumer culture—namely, that commercial leisure could both reinforce the very local identities of neighbourhood and help to engender a youth culture rather distinct from the world of adults.[68]

The Tragic: Risk and Understandings of the Accident

The Laurier Palace fire can also help us to explore the interpretive possibilities of the literature on risk and accidents. At the beginning of the twentieth century, Canadians and Quebeckers, like their counterparts in the United States and Western Europe, sought new kinds of explanations for accidents. Scholars such as Ulrich Beck, sociologist Anthony Giddens, and political philosopher François Ewald, working with the concept of "risk," have argued that the idea that accidents are preventable is relatively recent, a side effect or corollary of industrial modernity.[69] While accidents might once have been attributed to fate, the will of God, or simple bad luck, industrial modernity involved a concerted attempt to understand, control, and predict such occurrences. Once seen as inevitable, accidents were increasingly seen as avoidable. Under conditions of industrial modernity, both the state and members of civil society turned to science and technology in order to foresee and prevent seemingly random occurrences. Calculations and assessments of safety, and ideas of probability and preventative measures, were evident in factory inspections and safety legislation, in the actuarial sciences and the insurance industry, and in the emerging field of industrial hygiene. This belief in the possibility of controlling risk—what Jackson Lears calls "a modern culture of control"[70]—stemmed, according to Giddens, from "a grasp of the fact that most of the contingencies which

affect human activity are humanly created, rather than merely given by God or nature."[71] Accident prevention was thus one of a number of ways that contemporaries attempted to "tame uncertainty" or "discipline the future."[72] Statistics and what Jackson Lears calls "probabilistic thinking" rendered accidents predictable, as suggested in the paradoxical expression "an accident waiting to happen."

The reactions to this fire give us some sense of the attitudes of parents, children, and various other social actors toward accidents, or events defined as such. The official investigations carried out in the wake of the fire, along with the extensive newspaper coverage of the tragedy, reveal contemporary conceptions of acceptable levels of risk, of where risk was acceptable and for whom. Finally, these investigations and the newspaper coverage of the 1927 fire give us some insight into what sociologist Viviana Zelizer has called the "changing social value of children" at the turn of the last century.[73]

The Laurier Palace fire generated a lengthy process of inquiry and investigation. These various inquiries—municipal and provincial, criminal and civil, those that sought to understand what had happened and those that sought explicitly to lay blame—were closely followed and extensively covered in the press and provided readers with the opportunity to ponder the definition and meanings of an accident, the question of responsibility for an accident, and the possibilities of accident prevention. The inquiries called upon witnesses directly touched by the tragedy—parents, siblings, neighbours of the victims; employees of the theatre—but also upon "expert" witnesses such as architects, engineers, policemen, and firemen. These masculine technical experts relied upon, and recommended the implementation of, techniques of assessment, measure, and inspection. The extensive press coverage of these inquiries and testimonies was, for all intents and purposes, a form of risk education for the reading public. In its coverage of the fire, the press established discursive links with other kinds of urban dangers, particularly those involving children: the fire at the Hochelaga School 20 years earlier, for instance, or the everyday risk of traffic accidents.

The first of these inquiries was the Coroner's Inquest which, four days after the fire, heard over a dozen witnesses, including children, parents, cinema employees, and municipal employees, in order to determine, as Coroner Ed McMahon reminded the eight men who comprised the jury, "la cause de la mort pour voir s'il y a eu un crime de commis ou non." At the heart of this inquiry were reflections on what constituted an accident.[74] The fact that almost none of the victims had been accompanied by an adult, as the law required, and that most of the children had apparently gone to the movies that day without parental permission, was a key element of the inquest. We might see this as echoing what Viviana Zelizer has discovered for New York in the same period, that is, that the parents of children killed in automobile accidents were chided in the press for not supervising their children properly.[75] And yet parents were not McMahon's principal targets. After hearing the evidence, the Coroner's Jury concluded that the deaths of Édouard Saint-Pierre (the test case) and the 77 other children were neither natural nor accidental, but were due, rather, to third-party negligence. The municipal regulations regarding cinema safety and the provincial law regarding the mandatory accompaniment of children under the age of 16 had simply not been respected by the cinema owner and employees. The Coroner's Jury held Ameen Lawand, proprietor of the cinema, Michel Arie, manager of the cinema, and Camille Bazzy,[76] cinema employee, criminally responsible for the deaths of the 78 children and it referred the matter to the criminal courts.[77]

Termed "Syrians" in all of the primary sources, Lawand, Arie, and Bazzy were, more accurately, part of a Syrian-Lebanese community active in Montreal's world of small commerce. In the 1920s, the commercial heart of Montreal's Syrian-Lebanese community was located to the west of the Laurier Palace, along Notre-Dame East, between Gosford and Berri. The Lawand family owned several Montreal cinemas. At the time of the fire, the three accused men, British subjects all, had been in Canada for over 15 years. Nonetheless, they were surely viewed as "foreigners" (Arabic- and English-speaking), doing business in an overwhelmingly white,

French-speaking, and Catholic neighbourhood.[78] It is surprising that there is not more overt racism or xenophobia expressed in the press coverage of the fire; whether this is due to journalistic discretion or to the fact that the cinema owners were in all likelihood Christian—most early-twentieth-century Syrian-Lebanese immigrants to Montreal were—is hard to say. The preliminary inquiry into the manslaughter charge laid against Lawand, Arie, and Bazzi began 21 January and was presided over by Chief Justice Jérémie Décarie.[79] On 14 February, after several days' worth of hearings spread over several weeks, Décarie concluded that the three men would have to stand trial before the Court of King's Bench (Crown Side) at the next Assizes.[80] Their trial took place months later, in October. On 25 October, the Honorable Mr. Justice Wilson ruled that Lawand, Arie, and Bazzy were indeed guilty of involuntary homicide, that is, manslaughter. Lawand was sentenced to two years in the penitentiary and Arie and Bazzy to 12 months each at forced labour.[81]

Just over six months later, however, on 15 May 1928, the Court of King's Bench (Appeal Side) "quashed and set aside" the Guilty conviction, accepting the argument of the lawyers representing Arie, Bazzy, and Lawand that their clients' failure to respect municipal regulations and provincial laws could not be construed as the direct cause of the deaths of the 78 children.[82] In maintaining the appeal, the Honorable Mr. Justice Greenshields implicitly made space for the accidental: regardless of whether or not rules had been followed, the catastrophe of the Laurier Palace fire had simply "happened."

As the manslaughter charge against Lawand, Arie, and Bazzi wended its way through the court system, what appears to have been immense public pressure succeeded in convincing Liberal Premier Taschereau to strike a provincial Royal Commission on the Laurier Palace affair. Such a Commission was needed, an editorial in *La Patrie* argued, in order to resolve questions related to *moral* responsibility, beyond the jurisdiction of criminal courts.[83] Various municipal commissions had already been struck in the preceding weeks: within days of the fire, a municipal inquiry was undertaken by the Fire

Commissioner's Court, headed by Commissioner (and insurance expert) Emmett Quinn. This week-long inquiry concluded that the fire had not been intentionally set, that it was not due to individual criminal negligence, but that, rather, it was truly "accidental," and no doubt the result of a cigarette dropped into a hole in the balcony floor. Quinn called for more efficient and more vigilant inspections of movie-houses. Newspaper editorialists speculated that the cigarette had been dropped by a child wishing to hide the fact that he was smoking.[84] A commission of inquiry led by Montreal aldermen had also begun work shortly after the fire, but this municipal commission disbanded on 25 January 1927 when its members learned—with some relief, it appears—that a provincial Royal Commission was about to be appointed.[85]

From the outset, Premier Taschereau was determined that the provincial Commission investigate the question of movie-going at a province-wide scale, beyond the question of the Laurier Palace and beyond the city of Montreal. The commissioners, who began sitting on 26 April 1927, thus heard witnesses in Montreal, but also in Quebec City, St-Jérôme, and Valleyfield, the latter two chosen as representatives of small working-class towns.[86] Testimonials were provided by the same parents, children, neighbours, and municipal employees who had testified in the criminal trials, but also by safety experts, religious authorities, schoolteachers, and women's groups. Louis Guyon, Deputy Minister of Labour, was called upon to discuss the inspection of cinemas and show-halls; the screening of motion pictures in places that were not cinemas, such as church basements, convents, and private colleges; and the cooperation between provincial and municipal authorities. He argued in favour of keeping cinemas open on Sundays, and insisted upon the generally satisfactory nature of current legislation and regulations. The Laurier Palace disaster was, in his opinion, truly accidental.[87] Fire chief Raoul Gauthier, who came before the Royal Commission in order to discuss the inspection and the over-crowding of cinemas and theatres, also argued in favour of keeping cinemas open on Sundays, evoking the "riskiness" of alternative leisure pursuits.

Were cinemas to be closed on Sundays, he argued, children would play ball in the streets and thus risk being hit by cars—at a time when there were more and more cars on city streets. Montreal children, Gauthier claimed, turned the streets into "un vrai terrain de jeu."[88]

In all, the Commissioners, who sat until 30 June 1927, heard 427 witnesses and read hundreds of briefs and letters.[89] The Report of the Royal Commission, released on 30 August, struck a moderate tone. Boyer devoted most of his report to questions of inspections and safety, recommending, for example, the education of the public regarding appropriate behaviour in emergency situations, and an increase in the number of inspectors in buildings frequented by the public.[90] The final section of the Royal Commission's report, entitled "Moralité du cinema," seems strikingly out of place in this text that dealt largely with technical, rational concepts of safety, security, responsibility, causes, prevention, legislation and its enforcement. No doubt this was because at the eleventh hour, in early June, Boyer's mandate was suddenly broadened by Premier Taschereau to include questions concerning the morality of motion pictures.[91] Boyer had initially resisted pressures for the Commission to deal with the moral aspects of the cinema, preferring to restrict the inquiry to matters of safety and security. The Commission concluded that the Laurier Palace catastrophe was attributable to the panic caused by the fire, which had resulted from the negligence of an unknown person. It assigned no criminal or civil responsibility for the fire. Boyer explicitly opposed the wishes of those, like the Catholic Church hierarchy or the *Ligue du dimanche*, who favoured banning movie-going on Sundays, and allowed cinemas to remain open seven days a week. But he did recommend forbidding all children under the age of 16 from commercial cinemas, accompanied or not.[92] Its recommendation that cinemas be allowed to stay open on Sundays dismissed the suggestion that the cinema was "immoral," but its recommendation that children not be admitted to commercial cinemas, accompanied or not,[93] was an explicit argument that these cinemas were particularly "risky" for children. Moreover, Judge Boyer argued, parental authority was clearly insufficient in order to keep children away from the cinema; legislation was necessary.[94] The adoption of this legislation, a means of disciplining both parents and children, supports historian Mona Gleason's argument about the emergence of a "public child" in twentieth-century Canada.[95] One might also consider the political capital that Taschereau's Liberals stood to gain from this decision, a compromise (keeping cinemas open on Sunday, but closing them altogether to children) that avoided alienating Catholic voters or working-class voters, but that discounted the preferences of children, who were, obviously, non-voters.

Alongside the criminal trials and the official inquiries were claims pursued in the civil law courts. Claims for monetary compensation from the city were launched by the parents of 125 children killed or injured in the fire. These claims ranged from the $33 requested by R. Decelles to the $20,000 initially demanded by Auguste Dumont, and were justified on the basis of financial reasons such as "funeral expenses, hospital treatment, doctors' fees, clothing lost, and in the case of deaths, the monetary valuation on the life of the child as a future revenue bearer."[96] Arthur Paul, for instance, a longshoreman living in Hochelaga, sued the city for the death by smoke inhalation of his 12-year-old son, who had gone to the cinema without his father's permission. Paul alleged that the City was guilty of gross negligence for failing to ensure that the provincial law regarding the accompaniment of children under the age of 16 was respected. The $1,000 that he demanded from the city was to compensate a part of what he had spent on raising and educating his son, but was also intended to be an indemnity in recognition of his loss.[97] Auguste Dumont, of Tétreaultville, a neighbourhood a considerable distance east of Hochelaga, initially claimed more than any other parent of a Laurier Palace victim, seeking $20,000 for the loss of his two sons. Dumont, a painter, told the Royal Commission that he had thought that his two boys—Maurice, aged 16, and Jean-Marc,[98] aged 12—had gone out to play hockey, and that he had no idea how they had made their way to the Laurier Palace.[99] Both boys died of smoke inhalation. Their bodies were identified at the morgue by their brother-in-law, who claimed that Jean-Marc, at least, had

permission to attend the cinema. By the time Dumont's case reached the courts in July 1927, the total amount that he was requesting from the City of Montreal and from the cinema-owners, Najeeb and Ameen Lawand, had been reduced to $5,500 plus interest. Dumont argued that the cinema-owners had failed to respect municipal safety regulations and provincial laws regarding the admission of unaccompanied children to movie-houses, and that the City had knowingly allowed the cinema to continue operating regardless. Both were thus responsible for the deaths of the 78 children, including the two Dumont boys. In justifying the amount claimed, Auguste Dumont's lawyer cited the considerable expense invested in raising these boys and educating them—costs that had borne fruit, as at the time of their death, the boys were useful, intelligent, and in perfect health. The damages claimed were in order to compensate for the lost wages of the boys, but also to compensate for the funeral and other expenses associated with the mourning period. Almost two years later, in April 1929, the case was settled out of court.[100] Dumont vs. Lawand appears to have served as the test case for other parents who had launched civil suits.[101]

The claims for financial compensation reported in the city's daily newspapers show us parents both angry and active, as opposed to the tragic mourners depicted in journalists' descriptions of mass funerals, or the passive answerers of questions we find in the transcripts of the official inquiries. These claims speak to the economic value of these working-class children, as perceived by their parents. They also suggest, however, what Zelizer calls their "social value." In her analysis of civil lawsuits in turn-of-the-twentieth-century United States, Zelizer argues that compensation awarded by the courts to parents for the accidental death of their children was no longer just "the cash equivalent of the lost labor and services of a young child," but also reflected a new sentimental, emotional component to these children's worth.[102] Parents who filed claims in the wake of the Laurier Palace fire surely did so out of profound grief, frustration, and anger, out of a sense that someone had to bear responsibility for the tragic fate of their children. These lawsuits suggest conceptions of responsibility, negligence, and prevention considerably more developed than those Catherine Cournoyer finds in Montreal at the very beginning of the twentieth century.[103] However, Cournoyer notes that if a certain fatalism persisted regarding *household* accidents well into the twentieth century, parents were indignant when faced with the death of their children by automobile accidents.[104] It is this latter sentiment—this indignation—that we find in the reactions to the Laurier Palace fire. The claims that we see in 1927 represent, I would argue, the fact that parents saw the Laurier Palace fire as falling beyond the acceptable limits of risk. This fire was not part of the normal risks of childhood, in their eyes—even of an urban, working-class childhood that was often materially precarious. The father who explained to the Royal Commission that he never let his children go to the Laurier Palace but that he did let them attend movies at the Théâtre Napoléon, because the latter had a greater number of exits, suggests the constant calculation of safety and acceptable risks in which most parents were engaged.[105] (It also, evidently, suggests this father's desire to present himself as a "good" father.) Like the fire at the École Hochelaga, this one occurred somewhere that parents had seen as a relatively safe site for their children, free of danger.[106] The anger expressed over the fact that a cinema manager had apparently told children fleeing the fire to return to the balcony was due to the sentiment that the adults on the premises ought to have behaved as parents.[107] Moreover, even more than other accident victims, children were inherently innocent. Even though the official investigations revealed evidence suggesting that many of the children attending the cinema that Sunday had gone to the cinema without parental permission, or had lied to their parents about their whereabouts, or had snuck into the theatre without paying, there was clearly *no* desire to hold them responsible for their actions. Children, and their actions, were perceived as a collective responsibility. Moreover, in a socio-political context where, as numerous historians have pointed out, the lives and well-being of children were increasingly seen as key to the health of the nation (we might think here of child-saving campaigns, alongside

campaigns to reduce infant mortality), children's deaths were perceived, in Zelizer's words, as "a sign of collective failure."[108]

Press coverage of the fire appears to have fuelled what American historians Joel Tarr and Mark Tebeau have called "social anger" around safety issues.[109] This social anger was integral to the safety movement that had emerged, in Montreal as elsewhere, by the late 1920s: *la Semaine de prévention d'accidents* was organized in Montréal for the first time in May 1923, and the *Ligue de sécurité de la province de Québec/Quebec Safety League* was established that same year in response notably to the problem of traffic accidents.[110] This paralleled developments in the United States in the 1920s, where safety education movements, Safety Days, and Safety Weeks were established, also in response to children's deaths by automobiles and streetcars.[111] The LSPQ formed a committee of inquiry in the wake of the Laurier Palace tragedy and forwarded its recommendations regarding cinema safety (concerning entrances and exits, lighting, overcrowding, unaccompanied children, etc.) to the city's executive committee.[112] Arthur Gaboury, secretary of the LSPQ, also testified before the Royal Commission, declaring himself to be in favour of Sunday cinema-openings, despite the fact that he was a practising Catholic. Rather than closing cinemas on Sunday, he argued, cinema employees ought to undergo daily safety drills and the cinema-going public ought to be better educated as to safety procedures.[113]

The Laurier Palace, a small, neighbourhood cinema, was a place of work for a few people (the owner, the managers, the young female cashier, the ushers, the projectionist, presumably a piano player, the children who cleaned the cinema in exchange for free admission). For a much greater number of people, however, it was a place of leisure. American historian Arwen Mohun has argued that, "while many Americans saw accidents in streets and factories as the inevitable cost of progress, they were not willing to tolerate the same risks as consumers."[114] This, too, explains some of the outrage in the face of the Laurier Palace tragedy. Neighbourhood residents were probably all too aware of the risks of their workplaces (on the docks, in the factory, on the construction site), but as Mohun points out, risk-taking in the workplace was something that "could be compensated for by wages."[115] Neighbourhood residents were also undoubtedly aware of the risks of the city streets, increasingly crowded with automobiles. The cinema, however, may well have appeared to them to be an *inappropriate* site of danger, and the 1927 fire beyond *predictable* levels of risk. The fact that the Laurier Palace cinema was a small theatre in a working-class neighbourhood, far from the city centre, suggests, moreover, that it was less likely to be closely inspected by municipal authorities, and thus that in this particular situation, the working-class children of Hochelaga were at greater risk than those children frequenting cinemas downtown or in wealthier neighbourhoods.[116] The Report of the Royal Commission noted, for instance, that safety regulations were less likely to be respected in small theatres and in "les quartiers excentriques et ouvriers."[117]

Conclusion: On the "Voyeuristic Empathy" of Historians

Inasmuch as they can be understood through the sources studied here, contemporary views of the children who attended the movies in January 1927 are essentially sympathetic. Whether they were there with permission or not, accompanied by an adult or not, these children are not depicted as bad. There is no *Struwwelpeter* ("Shock headed Peter" or "Slovenly Peter") narrative here of poorly behaved children receiving their just deserts: these children are not nasty, merely young.[118] At worst, they are portrayed as mischievous, or misguided. But essentially, the children are depicted as innocent victims of the catastrophe, vulnerable to the larger forces that structure their existence.[119] To be sure, the sources examined here are all reading backwards: this horrific fire had turned all of the victims—those aged 17 like those aged 6—into children, and rendered all of them, including the defiant and disobedient ones, innocent.

The historian, too, sifting through the judicial archive and poring over contemporary press coverage, is led to grieve over these young children, these

small bodies. Like the adults who lived with these children, perhaps, the historian is led to lament their tragically early deaths, but also to admire their mischievousness—their insistence upon sneaking off to the cinema, sneaking in without paying, or sneaking a cigarette. As John Brewer has argued, empathy is in some ways the whole point of "history from below": seeing ordinary historical actors as the subjects of their own history, sentient beings, agents. Brewer suggests, furthermore, that the smaller the scale of the historian's study (the Italian *microstoria*; or *Alltagsgeschichte*, the German history of everyday life), the more likely the reader to empathize with these subjects of the past.[120] Adele Perry, inspired by anthropologist Ruth Behar, has recently reflected upon what she terms the "risks," but also the importance—more, the political necessity—of "historiography that breaks your heart."[121]

Yet the disastrous fire that took place at the Laurier Palace cinema also leads us to reflect upon the ethics of using sources generated by tragedy to study the everyday. Is this fascination with tragedy unseemly, even exploitative? Is it worse when the tragedy is merely a vehicle—an exceptional event productive of a paper trail—a means by which to understand the ordinary? Historian Jill Lepore, in her wonderfully titled essay "Historians Who Love Too Much," goes so far as to say that "If research is like stalking, a good and honest writer, however assiduous in pursuit of his prey, will still hesitate at the essential sordidness of the task at hand."[122] We might ask whether the methodological danger that David Lowenthal calls "voyeuristic empathy" is not particularly present in studies of the history of childhood—a trap that is less easily avoided when the historical subjects in which one is interested are almost inherently vulnerable. "The vivid intimacies [conveyed by historians] promote historical sympathy," Lowenthal writes, "but attenuate historical understanding, underscoring universal constants of human feeling while obscuring or ignoring the particular social and cultural trends that both link the past with, and differentiate it from, the present."[123]

Lowenthal is right, I think, to warn us of the risks of identifying with the emotions of actors in the past—the "universal constants of human feeling" of which he speaks. And he is no doubt right to argue that their feelings and sentiments were not the same as our own. But studying a catastrophe such as that of the Laurier Palace fire need not be exploitative. This event was a tragedy by any standards: those of 1927 like those of today. And a respectful analysis of this catastrophe helps us to understand the structures of power (age and social class in particular) that disadvantaged these 78 children.

The material that I've presented here allows us to see, in early twentieth-century Montreal, an emerging belief in the possibility of understanding, controlling, and predicting risk. Once seen as inevitable, accidents (seemingly random tragedies) were increasingly, in this period, seen as avoidable. This optimistic belief in the possibility of accident prevention—the possibility, not only of protecting oneself from the future, but also of *acting upon* the future—ought to be seen as part-and-parcel of the liberal vision of industrial capitalism. The concept of risk helps us to understand the ways in which accidents were, in the late nineteenth and early twentieth centuries, defined, measured, and

thus naturalized, normalized, routinized, and depoliticized.

And yet, as I've suggested here, this normalization and depoliticization coexisted with occasional outbursts of social anger, an anger fuelled particularly by the accidental deaths of children, by the sentiment—or the conviction—that such deaths should not be subject to cold calculations of risk. Such social anger was based on the premise that children were not individuals like any other individuals—that age made a difference. In the Montreal working-class neighbourhood at the heart of this analysis, children had not yet become "economically useless," to borrow Zelizer's expression. Some two decades before the principal legislation attempting to ensure the dependence of Quebec children—compulsory schooling, child labour laws, family allowances—, the paid and unpaid work of these children remained important to their family economies. But in the responses to the Laurier Palace fire, we do see an emerging conception of children as "emotionally priceless"[124] . . . or at the very least, an understanding of risk that took the specificities of childhood into account.

Notes

1. Very preliminary versions of some of this material were presented at the *Labouring Feminisms* conference held at the University of Toronto in 2005 and at the conference entitled *Modernité, citoyenneté, déviances et inégalités: Pour une analyse comparative des difficultés du passage à la modernité citoyenne* held in Córdoba (Spain) in 2006. My thanks to participants at both conferences, especially Suzanne Morton, for their useful comments on those papers. I would also like to thank Marc Ouimet and Yasmine Mazani for their research assistance; Thierry Nootens for initiating me into the fascinating world of judicial archives; and Isabelle Huppé for her most efficient map-making. Finally, I am grateful for the research funding provided by the Social Sciences and Humanities Research Council of Canada, for the intelligent comments on this article provided by my colleagues in the Montreal History Group, and for the constructive criticism provided by the journal's anonymous readers.

2. For example, Paul-André Linteau, *Histoire de Montréal depuis la Confédération*, 2e édition augmentée (Montréal: Boréal, 2000), 398; Cynthia Comacchio, *The Dominion of Youth: Adolescence and the Making of Modern Canada, 1920 to 1950* (Waterloo: Wilfrid Laurier UP, 2006), 168.

3. David Lowenthal, "The Timeless Past: Some Anglo-

American Historical Preconceptions," *The Journal of American History*, 75, 4 (1989), 1278.

4. Craig Heron, "Saving the Children," *Acadiensis*, 13, 1 (1983), 168.

5. Cynthia Comacchio, "Dancing to Perdition: Adolescence and Leisure in Interwar English Canada," *Journal of Canadian Studies*, 32, 3 (Fall 1997): 5–35; Comacchio, *The Dominion of Youth*; Tamara Myers, *Caught: Montreal's Modern Girls and the Law, 1869–1945* (Toronto: University of Toronto Press, 2006). The classic study of working-class families in Montreal is of course Bettina Bradbury's *Working Families: Age, Gender, and Daily Survival in Industrializing Montreal* (Toronto: McClelland & Stewart, 1993).

6. Kathy Peiss, *Cheap Amusements: Working Women and Leisure in Turn-of-the-Century New York* (Philadelphia: Temple UP, 1986).

7. Peiss, *Cheap Amusements*; Comacchio, *The Dominion of Youth*, esp. Chapter 6; David Nasaw, *Going Out: The Rise and Fall of Public Amusements* (Cambridge, Mass.: Harvard UP, 1999 [1993]). See also Nan Enstad, *Ladies of Labor, Girls of Adventure: Working Women, Popular Culture, and Labor Politics at the Turn of the Twentieth Century* (London; New York: Columbia UP, 1999).

8. "Toutes les rues d'Hochelaga, moins quelques-unes, dans le deuil," *La Patrie*, 10 janvier 1927. Translation: "Every street in Hochelaga, except for a few, in mourning."

9. "Les victimes du 'Laurier Palace' sont au nombre de 77," *Le Devoir*, 10 janvier 1927.

10. Linteau, *Histoire de Montréal depuis la Confédération*, 47.

11. Archives nationales du Québec à Montréal (ANQM), TP 9, S2, SS1, SSS2, Dossier no. 233, Le Roi vs Armeen Lawand, Camille Bazzi, Michel Arie. Sixteen extracts from the register of baptisms of the Paroisse de la Nativité de la Ste-Vierge d'Hochelaga were used as evidence at the preliminary inquiry into the manslaughter charges laid against Lawand, Arie and Bazzy.

12. See, for instance, the occupations of fathers and godfathers provided in the baptismal records, ANQM, TP9, S2, SS1, SSS2, Dossier no. 233, Le Roi vs Armeen Lawand, Camille Bazzi, Michel Arie.

13. See the daily advertisements in *La Presse*, e.g., 5 janvier 1927, p. 14.

14. Archives de la Ville de Montréal (AVM), VM 68, D3, Enquête au Bureau des Magistrats de Police, Témoignage d'Édouard Charles St. Pierre, 21 janvier 1927; *Rapport de la Commission royale chargée de faire enquête sur l'incendie du "Laurier Palace" et sur certaines autres matières d'intérêt général*, p. 13.

15. AVM, VM 68, D2, Enquête devant le Coroner. Déposition de Henri Lavigne, 13 janvier 1927; Déposition d'Ernest Carrière, 13 janvier 1927.

16. Juliette Desrosiers, for instance, who was at the Laurier Palace on January 9th, worked for Louis Marcil, the owner of Café Louis, located next door to the cinema. AVM, VM 68, D3, Enquête au Bureau des Magistrats de Police: Témoignages. Témoignage de Juliette Desrosiers, 25 janvier 1927, pp. 268-269; *Lovell's Montreal Directory 1926-1927*.

17. "Heroic Priests As Comforting Angels to Dying Children," *The Montreal Daily Star*, 10 January 1927.

18. "Le sermon de Sa Grandeur Monseigneur Gauthier," *La Patrie*, 11 janvier 1927. Translation: "This trial that has struck Hochelaga and Montreal."

19. "Sorrowful Scenes Again Witnessed As 21 Fire Victims Laid To Rest," *The Montreal Daily Star*, 12 January 1927.

20. Archives des Soeurs des Saints Noms de Jésus et de Marie, Chronique de l'école (1927), Incendie du Laurier Palace. Reproduced on-line in "Documents de l'école Hochelaga—Période 1920-1930," www.csdm.qc.ca/patrimoine/ecoles/H/banque_d/1920_30.htm, consulted 20 May 2005. Translation: "A dreadful catastrophe that has swept over the neighbourhood of Hochelaga, robbing it of many victims."

21. "Le sinistre du cinéma," *La Patrie*, 10 janvier 1927.

22. AVM, VM 68, D3, Enquête au Bureau des Magistrats de Police: Témoignages. Témoignage d'Arthur Gendron, 24 janvier 1927, p. 170; Témoignage de Juliette Desrosiers, 25 janvier 1927, pp. 268-269; Témoignage de Roméo Collin, 21 janvier 1927, pp. 99-100. Translation: "Little guys, 12, 13 years old."

23. AVM, VM 68, D2, Enquête devant le Coroner: Déposition d'Alex. Bazzy, 13 janvier 1927, pp. 69-70; Déposition de J.P. Boisclair, 13 janvier 1927, pp. 88-89.

24. ANQM, TP12, S2, SS26, SSS1, Enquêtes du Coroner, Dossiers, 1927. In two cases, the Coroners' Records do not indicate who identified the body.

25. AVM, VM 68, D3, Enquête au Bureau des Magistrats de Police, Témoignage d'Albert Rémillard, 20 janvier 1927, pp. 67-73. In his testimony before the Coroner's Inquiry a week earlier, however, Rémillard claimed that he had gone to the theatre alone that day. AVM, VM 68, D2, Enquête devant le Coroner sur l'incendie du Laurier Palace: Témoignages. Déposition d'Albert Rémillard, 13 janvier 1927, p. 113. Albert's father Édouard testified before the Coroner's Inquiry that the two brothers had gone to the theatre separately and that in fact each did not know that the other was there. AVM, VM 68, D2, Enquête devant le Coroner, Déposition d'Édouard Rémillard, 13 janvier 1927, p. 116.

26. AVM, VM 68, D2, Enquête devant le Coroner : Déposition de Roger Arpin, 13 janvier 1927, pp. 117-123; Déposition de J.L. Falardeau, 13 janvier 1927, pp. 124-127; AVM, VM 68, D3, Enquête au Bureau des Magistrats de Police, Témoignage de Roger Arpin, 20 janvier 1927, pp. 77-84.

27. AVM, VM 68, D3, Enquête au Bureau des Magistrats de Police, Témoignage de Wilfrid Bigaouette, 24 janvier 1927, pp. 204-211. See David Nasaw's discussion of children's high rates of movie attendance in the early twentieth century in the company of friends, in *Going Out*, esp. 169-170.

28. "L'enquête du 'Laurier Palace.' Le juge Boyer entend les témoignages des parents des victimes," *Le Devoir*, 30 mai 1927.

29. AVM, VM 68, D2, Enquête devant le Coroner, Déposition d'Édouard St-Pierre, 13 janvier 1927, pp. 5-7; AVM, VM 68, D3, Enquête au Bureau des Magistrats de Police, Témoignage d'Édouard Charles St. Pierre, 21 janvier 1927, pp. 6-10. On English-Canadian children's paid and unpaid work, see Neil Sutherland, *Growing Up: Childhood in English Canada from the Great War to the Age of Television* (Toronto: University of Toronto Press, 1997), esp. Ch. 6. Catherine Cournoyer also notes that paid work gave Montreal children the liberty to move about the city streets in "Les accidents impliquant des enfants et l'attitude envers l'enfance à Montréal (1900-1945)" (M.A. thesis, Université de Montréal, 1999), 83, 121.

30. Testimony of Cléophas Guérin, reported in "Si la police ne les voyait pas, elle faisait exprès," *Le Devoir*, 1er juin 1927.

31. Testimony of Edgar Gauthier, reported in "Camille Bazzy témoignera," *Le Devoir*, 31 mai 1927.

32. "Une série d'enfants à l'enquête," *La Patrie*, 31 mai 1927. See also the testimonies in "Enquête qui aurait des résultats," *La Patrie*, 30 mai 1927.

33. AVM, VM 68, D3, Enquête au Bureau des Magistrats de Police, Témoignage de Germaine Pelchat, 25 janvier 1927, pp. 264–266.

34. ANQM, TP12, S2, SS26, SSS1, Enquêtes du Coroner, Dossiers, 1927.

35. Testimony of Benoit Benoît, Alfred Arpin, Auguste Dumont, Albert Barry, Pierre Coulombe, reported in "Enquête qui aurait des résultats," La Patrie, 30 mai 1927; Testimony of Adélard Lavallée, reported in "Une série d'enfants à l'enquête," La Patrie, 31 mai 1927; Testimony of François Pesant, reported in "Camille Bazzy témoignera," Le Devoir, 31 mai 1927.

36. Testimony of Auguste Dumont, reported in "L'enquête du 'Laurier Palace.' Le juge Boyer entend les témoignages des parents des victimes," Le Devoir, 30 mai 1927; Testimony of Mme Auguste Dumont, reported in "Camille Bazzy témoignera," Le Devoir, 31 mai 1927; Testimony of Auguste Dumont, reported in "Enquête qui aurait des résultats," La Patrie, 30 mai 1927.

37. AVM, VM 68, D2, Enquête devant le Coroner, Déposition d'Albert Rémillard, 13 janvier 1927, p. 110; AVM, VM 68, D3, Enquête au Bureau des Magistrats de Police, Témoignage d'Albert Rémillard, 20 janvier 1927, p. 67–73; AVM, VM 68, D3, Enquête au Bureau des Magistrats de Police, Témoignage d'Edmond [sic] Rouillard, 20 janvier 1927, pp. 74–76.

38. Testimony of Oscar Gravel, reported in "Theatre Tragedy Survivors Give Evidence At Probe," The Montreal Star, 31 May 1927.

39. "On ordonne la fermeture d'un cinéma à Québec," La Patrie, 11 janvier 1927. Judge Louis Boyer, who presided the Royal Commission on the Laurier Palace, also claimed that some parents allowed their children to go to the movies whenever they wanted, out of a "désir de les parquer quelque part pendant qu'ils sont ailleurs ou de s'en débarrasser." Rapport de la Commission royale, p. 10.

40. "L'enquête du 'Laurier Palace.' Le juge Boyer entend les témoignages des parents des victimes," Le Devoir, 30 mai 1927.

41. Testimony of Frédéric Gagné, reported in "L'enquête du 'Laurier Palace.' Le juge Boyer entend les témoignages des parents des victimes," Le Devoir, 30 mai 1927, and in "Enquête qui aurait des résultats," La Patrie, 30 mai 1927; Testimony of Mme Paul Gervais, reported in "Le 'Laurier Palace' traitait bien certains officiers de police," Le Devoir, 1er juin 1927. Sixteen-year-old Ernest Carrière also watched movies for free in exchange for work around the theatre. AVM, VM 68, D2, Enquête devant le Coroner, Déposition d'Ernest Carrière, 13 janvier 1927.

42. Testimony of Rolland and Marcel Tellier, reported in "Camille Bazzy témoignera," Le Devoir, 31 mai 1927. And see Nasaw, Going Out, 169–170.

43. "Une autre action contre la ville et le Laurier-Palace," La Patrie, 8 juillet 1927.

44. Testimony in "Enquête qui aurait des résultats," La Patrie, 30 mai 1927.

45. Testimony of Willie Clément and of Mme Athanase Cournoyer, reported in "Enquête qui aurait des résultats," La Patrie, 30 mai 1927.

46. "Le cinema et la "journée catholique," Le Devoir, 30 mai 1927; "La nécessité des pompiers aux théâtres," La Patrie, 28 mai 1927; "L'admission des enfants au cinéma," La Patrie, 7 juin 1927. See also the testimony of Joseph Marquette, reported in "Si la police ne les voyait pas, elle faisait exprès," Le Devoir, 1er juin 1927. For one father's denial that his son stole in order to pay for the movies, see the testimony of M. Benoit Benoît reported in "Enquête qui aurait des résultats," La Patrie, 30 mai 1927.

47. "La preuve de l'admission des enfants est établie hors de tout doute," Le Devoir, 3 juin 1927.

48. Peiss, Cheap Amusements; Comacchio, "Dancing to Perdition."

49. 27 of the 78 victims (almost 35%) were girls. ANQM, TP12, S2, SS26, SSS1, Enquêtes du Coroner, Dossiers, 1926, nos 1351 à 1901; 1927, nos 1 à 290.

50. Arwen Mohun, "Designed for Thrills and Safety: Amusement Parks and the Commodification of Risk, 1880–1929," Journal of Design History, 14, 4 (2001), 292.

51. AVM, VM 68, D2, Enquête devant le Coroner, Déposition de Maurice Brown, 13 janvier 1927; AVM, VM 68, D3, Enquête au Bureau des Magistrats de Police, Témoignage de Maurice Brown, 21 janvier 1927, pp. 31–66.

52. "Près de 80 enfants meurent étouffés, asphyxiés ou brûlés au théâtre 'Laurier Palace,'" Le Devoir, 10 janvier 1927.

53. AVM, VM 68, D2, Enquête devant le Coroner, Déposition de Maurice Brown, 13 janvier 1927, pp. 90-108. On children smoking in the Laurier Palace, see also the testimony of Maurice Brown reported in "Une série d'enfants à l'enquête," La Patrie, 31 mai 1927, and the testimony of M. Labonté and of Conrad Ménard, reported in "Si la police ne les voyait pas, elle faisait exprès," Le Devoir, 1er juin 1927.

54. AVM, VM 68, D3, Enquête au Bureau des Magistrats de Police, Témoignage de Germaine Pelchat, 25 janvier 1927, pp. 263–264.

55. AVM, VM 68, D3, Enquête au Bureau des Magistrats de Police, Témoignage de Maurice Brown, 21 janvier 1927, p. 61.

56. "Soixante-dix-sept enfants s'écrasent à mort dans un cinema," La Patrie, 10 janvier 1927. On children choosing the cinema over church services, see also "L'enquête du 'Laurier Palace.' Le juge Boyer entend les témoignages des parents des victimes," Le Devoir, 30 mai 1927.

57. Testimony of Madeleine Guèvremont, reported in "La preuve de l'admission des enfants est établie hors de tout doute," Le Devoir, 3 juin 1927. See also the testimony of Alfred Arpin, reported in "Enquête qui aurait des résultats," La Patrie, 30 mai 1927.

58. Roy Rosenzweig, Eight Hours for What We Will: Workers and Leisure in an Industrial City, 1870–1920 (Cambridge: Cambridge UP, 1983), Ch. 8, "From Rum Shop to Rialto: Workers and Movies," esp. 194–198; Lisa Jacobson,

Raising Consumers: Children and the American Mass Market in the Early Twentieth Century (New York: Columbia UP, 2004); Cynthia R. Comacchio, *The Infinite Bonds of Family: Domesticity in Canada, 1850–1940* (Toronto: University of Toronto Press, 1999), 85–86.

59. Comacchio, *The Infinite Bonds of Family*, 87.

60. AVM, VM 68, D3, Enquête au Bureau des Magistrats de Police: Témoignage de Xavier Nadeau, 24 janvier 1927, p. 165; Témoignage d'Édouard Charles St. Pierre, 21 janvier 1927, pp. 6–10.

61. Testimony of Léopold Bouchard, reported in "Nouvelles dépositions de parents," *La Patrie*, 31 mai 1927.

62. *Rapport de la Commission royale*, pp. 13–18; Paul Laverdure, *Sunday in Canada: The Rise and Fall of the Lord's Day* (North Yorkton: Gravelbooks, 2004), 112–114.

63. "L'adolescent au cinéma," *Le Devoir*, 6 juin 1927.

64. Québec, *Débats de l'Assemblée legislative*: 13 janvier 1927, 18 janvier 1927, 20 janvier 1927, 9 février 1927, 2 mars 1927, 17 mars 1927.

65. "Soixante-dix-sept enfants s'écrasent à mort dans un cinéma," *La Patrie*, 10 janvier 1927; "Pathetic Scenes As Parents Visit Crowded Morgue," *The Montreal Daily Star*, 10 January 1927. As Jamie Bronstein remarks about press coverage of nineteenth-century workplace accidents, "The grief of surviving relatives was both omnipresent in the narrative and central to its interpretation." Jamie L. Bronstein, *Caught in the Machinery: Workplace Accidents and Injured Workers in Nineteenth-Century Britain* (Stanford: Stanford UP, 2008), 61.

66. AVM, VM 68, D3, Enquête au Bureau des Magistrats de Police: Témoignage d'Édouard Charles St. Pierre, 21 janvier 1927; Témoignage d'Edmond Rémillard, 20 janvier 1927.

67. Cournoyer, "Les accidents impliquant des enfants," ii, 100, 113–116, 121, 122, 153.

68. Rosenzweig, *Eight Hours for What We Will*, 172; Nasaw, *Going Out*, 168–171.

69. Ulrich Beck, *Risk Society: Towards a New Modernity* (London: Sage, 1992); Anthony Giddens, "Risk and Responsibility," *The Modern Law Review*, 62, 1 (1999); François Ewald, *L'Etat- providence* (Paris: Bernard Grasset, 1986). For a much more detailed discussion of the risk literature, see Magda Fahrni, "'La lutte contre l'accident.' Risque et accidents dans un contexte de modernité industrielle," 171–191, in *Pour une histoire du risque: Québec, France, Belgique*, ed. David Niget and Martin Petitclerc (Rennes, Presses universitaires de Rennes; Québec, Presses de l'Université du Québec, 2012).

70. Jackson Lears, *Something for Nothing: Luck in America* (New York: Viking Penguin, 2003), 19.

71. Anthony Giddens, *The Consequences of Modernity* (Stanford: Stanford UP, 1990), 32.

72. These two expressions are quoted in Patricia Jasen, "Breast Cancer and the Language of Risk, 1750–1950," *Social History of Medicine*, 15, 1 (2002), 19.

73. Viviana A. Zelizer, *Pricing the Priceless Child: The Changing Social Value of Children* (New York: Basic Books, 1985), 21; see also Neil Sutherland, *Children in English-Canadian Society: Framing the Twentieth Century Consensus* (Toronto: University of Toronto Press, 1976).

74. AVM, VM 68, Collection d'enquêtes sur l'incendie du Laurier Palace. VM 68, D2, Enquête devant le Coroner sur l'incendie du Laurier Palace: Témoignages (1927), Adresse de M. le Coroner aux jurés. Translation: ". . . the cause of the death to see if a crime was committed or not."

75. Zelizer, *Pricing the Priceless Child*, 37; Cournoyer, "Les accidents impliquant des enfants," 138–141, 155.

76. The names of all three are constantly misspelled in the sources : Camil, Camille, Bazzi, Bazzy, Arie, Arrie . . .

77. ANQM, TP9, S2, SS1, SSS2, Dossier no. 233, Le Roi vs Armeen Lawand, Camille Bazzi, Michel Arie; "Lawand, Bazzy et Arrie tenus criminellement responsables," *Le Devoir*, 14 janvier 1927.

78. "Lawand, Bazzi et Arie accusés de manslaughter puis relâchés," *La Patrie*, 14 janvier 1927; ANQM, TP9, S2, SS1, SSS2, Dossier no. 233, Le Roi vs Armeen Lawand, Camille Bazzi, Michel Arie. On Montreal's Syrian-Lebanese community, see the text produced for the Centre d'histoire de Montréal and entitled "Min Zamaan—Depuis longtemps. La communauté syrienne-libanaise à Montréal de 1882 à 1940," available at http://ville.montreal.qc.ca/portal/page?_pageid=2497,3090574&_dad=portal&_schema=PORTA L. David Nasaw discusses the harassment of "foreign" nickelodeon owners in the early-twentieth-century United States in *Going Out*, 177.

79. "Tous doivent contribuer à ce que cette enquête soit complète," *La Patrie*, 21 janvier 1927.

80. "Theatre Cases Go to King's Bench," *Montreal Daily Star*, 14 February 1927.

81. ANQM, TP9, S2, SS1, SSS2, Dossier no. 233, Le Roi vs Armeen Lawand, Camille Bazzi, Michel Arie.

82. ANQM, TP9, S2, SS1, SSS2, Dossier no. 233, Le Roi vs Armeen Lawand, Camille Bazzi, Michel Arie.

83. "Le Verdict," *La Patrie*, 14 janvier 1927.

84. "La deuxième enquête," *La Patrie*, 19 janvier 1927; "L'enquête sur l'incendie du "Laurier Palace," *Le Devoir*, 12 janvier 1927; "Le rapport de M. Quinn sur l'incendie," *Le Devoir*, 19 janvier 1927. On Emmett Quinn, see "Fire Commissioner Quinn," *The Gazette*, 10 February 1930.

85. "L'Enquête royale," *La Patrie*, 24 janvier 1927.

86. *Rapport de la Commission royale*, p. 2.

87. AVM, VM 68, D4, Commission royale d'enquête sur les causes de l'incendie du Cinéma Laurier Palace, Témoignage de Louis Guyon, p. 29.

88. AVM, VM 68, D4, Commission royale d'enquête sur les causes de l'incendie du Cinéma Laurier Palace, Témoignage de Raoul Gauthier, p. 17. Translation: ". . . a real playground."

89. "Nous nous demandons pourquoi notre population

devrait se ranger avec les autres provinces du pays, dernier refuge du puritanisme," *La Patrie*, 31 août 1927.

90. *Rapport de la Commission royale*, p. 24.

91. "Widen Scope of Theatre Inquiry," *Montreal Daily Star*, 6 June 1927. I have not dealt with early twentieth-century morality campaigns against the cinema here, as they have been amply treated by other historians of Quebec: see, e.g., Yves Lever, "L'Église et le cinéma: une relation orageuse," *Cap-aux-Diamants: la revue d'histoire du Québec*, 38 (1994): 24–29; Andrée Lévesque, *Making and Breaking the Rules: Women in Quebec, 1919–1939*, trans. Yvonne M. Klein (Toronto: McClelland & Stewart, 1994), 70–71; Myers, *Caught*, 67–68. My own interest is in the ways in which this fire was understood through the lens of risk. Translation: "Morality of the cinema."

92. *Rapport de la Commission royale*, p. 31; "Les gérants de théâtre sont satisfaits des conclusions tirées par l'Hon. Juge Boyer," *La Patrie*, 31 août 1927.

93. *Rapport de la Commission royale*, p. 31.

94. *Rapport de la Commission royale*, p. 10.

95. Mona Gleason, "From 'Disgraceful Carelessness' to 'Intelligent Precaution': Accidents and the Public Child in English Canada, 1900–1950," *Journal of Family History*, 30, 2 (2005): 230–241.

96. "Cent vingt-cinq réclamations pour les victimes du 'Laurier Palace,'" *Le Devoir*, 9 février 1927; "Panic Claims Total $500,000," *The Montreal Daily Star*, 9 February 1927.

97. "Il réclame mille dollars de la ville," *La Patrie*, 22 janvier 1927; ANQM, TP12, S2, SS26, SSS1, Enquêtes du Coroner, Dossiers, 1926, nos 1351 à 1901; 1927, nos 1 à 290.

98. The younger son is identified as Jean-Marc in documents produced by the Coroner, but as Marcel in the lawsuit. ANQM, TP11, S2, SS2, SSS1, 1927, Dossier 21 322, *A. Dumont vs N. Lawand et al.*

99. "L'enquête du 'Laurier Palace,'" *Le Devoir*, 30 mai 1927.

100. ANQM, TP11, S2, SS2, SSS1, 1927, Dossier 21 322, *A. Dumont vs N. Lawand et al.*

101. "Panic Claims Total $500,000," *The Montreal Daily Star*, 9 February 1927.

102. Zelizer, *Pricing the Priceless Child*, 139.

103. Cournoyer, "Les accidents impliquant des enfants," 2, 122–123.

104. Cournoyer, "Les accidents impliquant des enfants," 125.

105. Testimony of Joseph Tétu, reported in "Nouvelles dépositions de parents," *La Patrie*, 31 mai 1927, and in "Le cinéma meurtrier," *Le Devoir*, 31 mai 1927.

106. "Le sinistre du cinema," *La Patrie*, 10 janvier 1927. Louis Guyon, Quebec's Deputy Minister of Labour, alluded to the fire at the "école Maxwell" in his testimony to the Royal Commission presided by Judge Boyer. Like the Laurier Palace fire, the fire at Hochelaga School (renamed the Sarah Maxwell Memorial School when it was rebuilt

in 1908) sparked a campaign for the widespread inspection of theatres. AVM, VM 68, D4, Commission royale d'enquête sur les causes de l'incendie du Laurier Palace, Témoignage de Louis Guyon, 17 mai 1927, p. 3.

107. Cournoyer notes a similar anger towards adults responsible for the death of a child in a traffic accident. See "Les accidents impliquant des enfants," 133–134, 141.

108. Zelizer, *Pricing the Priceless Child*, 32.

109. Joel Tarr and Mark Tebeau, "Housewives as Home Safety Managers: The Changing Perception of the Home as a Place of Hazard and Risk, 1870–1940," in *Accidents in History: Injuries, Fatalities and Social Relations*, ed. Roger Cooter and Bill Luckin (Amsterdam: Rodopi, 1997), 222.

110. On the safety movement in Quebec, see Fahrni, "La lutte contre l'accident."

111. Zelizer, *Pricing the Priceless Child*, Ch. 1; Tarr and Tebeau, "Housewives as Home Safety Managers."

112. "Les réformes dans les cinémas," *Le Devoir*, 12 février 1927.

113. "En faveur du cinéma dominical," *Le Devoir*, 18 mai 1927.

114. Mohun, "Designed for Thrills and Safety."

115. Mohun, "Designed for Thrills and Safety," 303.

116. Zelizer notes the "greater vulnerability of lower-class children to accidental death" in *Pricing the Priceless Child*, 144; see also Cournoyer, "Les accidents impliquant des enfants," 77.

117. *Rapport de la Commission royale*, p. 24. Translation: "outlying and working-class neighbourhoods."

118. For an introduction to *Struwwelpeter* (Shockheaded Peter or Slovenly Peter), see the special issue of *The Lion and the Unicorn: A Critical Journal of Children's Literature* devoted to "Struwwelpeter and Classical Children's Literature," 20, 2 (1996). Many thanks to Margaret Steffler of Trent University for alerting me to the considerable body of work on *Struwwelpeter*.

119. Jamie Bronstein's analysis of the press coverage of nineteenth-century workplace accidents is instructive here. See *Caught in the Machinery*, 61.

120. John Brewer, "Microhistory and the Histories of Everyday Life," *Cultural and Social History*, 7, 1 (2010): 87–109.

121. Adele Perry, "Historiography that Breaks Your Heart: Van Kirk and the Writing of Feminist History," 81–97, in *Finding a Way to the Heart: Feminist Writings on Aboriginal and Women's History in Canada*, ed. Robin Jarvis Brownlie and Valerie J. Korinek (Winnipeg: University of Manitoba Press, 2012).

122. Jill Lepore, "Historians Who Love Too Much: Reflections on Microhistory and Biography," *The Journal of American History*, 88, 1 (2001), 139.

123. Lowenthal, "The Timeless Past," 1278.

124. The terms "economically useless" and "emotionally priceless" are to be found in Zelizer, *Pricing the Priceless Child*, 21.

PRIMARY DOCUMENT

"The Funeral," *Montreal Daily Star*, 11 January 1927

THE FUNERAL

It is doubtful if civilized man ever bared his head in the presence of a more pathetic funeral than that which wended its way through the street of Montreal today.

Children, every one of them—cut off at the very threshold of life—struck down with tragic swiftness in the midst of what for many of them was an accustomed weekly "treat." The cruelty of it—the crushing blow to their parents and loved ones—the profound sadness of today's impressive ceremony.

Not only all Montreal but all the North American continent and a greater part of Europe joined in the solemn obsequies. We cannot recall another case in which the keenly sympathetic attention of the world was so unitedly centred upon this city. Enquiries and expressions of condolence have poured steadily in from the four quarters of the earth.

Not all the victims were buried this morning. So colossal a catastrophe has compelled us to spend more than a day in burying our dead. It is like a battlefield—except that nothing save our own carelessness brought down the bolts of death.

No surer evidence of the deepness of our grief and the stunning nature of the shock could be given than the absence—as yet—of any great cry for punishment. This does not mean that the people of Montreal will not demand the fullest and most searching enquiry and the sternest administration of justice. The calamity is so great that we are conscious of a fear lest we be stampeded into injustice. There is no need to hurry—save in guarding against a similar horror elsewhere.

Our steps should be slow, sure—but relentless. If blame there be for this massacre of children, it will be a terrible blame—whether it fall upon those whose duty it is to enforce law, or upon those whose duty it is to make law.

MONTREAL MUST RENDER IT ABSOLUTELY IMPOSSIBLE FOR AT LEAST THIS KIND OF A TRAGEDY TO HAPPEN AGAIN.

Embodying Delinquency: Boys' Bodies, Sexuality, and Juvenile Justice History in Early-Twentieth-Century Quebec

TAMARA MYERS

Juvenile justice was born in the reform schools of the nineteenth century and matured in the juvenile courts of the early twentieth. From the outset, juvenile delinquency was a subjective concept, invoking gender, class, and racial understandings of behaviour and opening the door to the policing of a broad range of minor acts of adolescent recalcitrance. The gendered orientation of the juvenile justice system has perhaps been most striking because the acts that landed boys in juvenile institutions consistently differed from those implicating girls.

For girls, what connected their experience of juvenile justice through time and across cultural, religious, ethnic, and racial lines was the policing of their sexuality. The tight link between female deviance and sexuality is demonstrated in the juvenile court's obsession with and aim to contain girls' bodies. In short, girls embodied delinquency. The literature on gender and delinquency has amply proven that girls were constructed as *sex* delinquents, which overly determined their experience of juvenile justice.[1] Research into one of Canada's first juvenile courts, the Montreal Juvenile Delinquents' Court, provides ample evidence of girls' experience of sexuality—both coerced and consensual—and the juvenile court's comprehensive project to regulate it. Girls brought to juvenile court were sent for medical verification of the state of their hymens; in cases where medical reports condemned girls, they were required to submit to "sexual confessionals" and bare all to probation officers and the judge. So

many girls came forth with names of boys and stories of sexual experiences in dance halls, theatres, automobiles, and their neighbourhoods that one could well imagine that the libidinous adolescent male delinquent might also have been questioned about this behaviour. Yet, in juvenile justice history, the policing and protecting of boys' bodies and sexuality remain unexplored.

One is hard pressed to find mention of boys' sexuality—or the corporal dimension of their designation as delinquents—in the literature on boys and juvenile delinquency.[2] This absence is in part explained by the fact that official documents from juvenile justice institutions, like annual reports, are silent on the issue of boys' sexuality. Similarly, newspaper accounts largely ignored this aspect of boys' lives and delinquency. In fact, in early-twentieth-century Montreal the public image of the male delinquent was constructed purposely to elicit pity and compassion from the community and derive support for the new court, ostensibly a child "protection" agency. Thus images of delinquent boys tended to emphasize their prepubescent, sexless, and neglected state. Yet does historians' inattention to boys' sexuality in early juvenile justice confirm a silence in the archival record? Or have boys' bodies merely been overshadowed by the evidence and scholarly assumptions of a more problematic female adolescent body?

In this essay I turn to the Montreal juvenile court records, which provided me with countless stories of girls' sexuality, and ask, Where are the boys? I found a not insignificant body of evidence concerning boys' sexuality. The court's investigation of boys' sexuality was not routine, but from the outset in the 1910s the young male body became a factor in delinquency cases when associated with violence and what the court deemed "perversion," that is, homosexuality. This approach continued throughout the early twentieth century. By the 1940s, however, the court engaged in more widespread policing of boys' sexuality, focusing on boys' sexual agency and heterosexual (mis)adventures. In this way, the policing of boys' "immoral acts," as the court referred to them, began to parallel the policing of girls, though it diverged in two important ways: first, boys' immorality was investigated on a much smaller scale, and second, these investigations produced very different outcomes. Where girls were incarcerated, boys were sent home after promises to do better.

In early-twentieth-century Quebec juvenile justice authorities expected, tolerated, and normalized certain boyish badness when it confirmed the stereotypical behaviour of the incorrigible boy—recalcitrance at home, petty theft, public rowdiness, and even minor assault. Since the mid-nineteenth century delinquency among Montreal boys had animated discussions among politicians, municipal and penal reformers, and the press, leading to the establishment of provincial reform and industrial schools legislation in 1869. At that time, social commentators linked boys' "problem" of vagrancy and disorderliness to their abandonment by parents and families and their lack of education, justifying substantial sentences in reform institutions where they might obtain rudimentary learning and acquire industrial skills.[3] A long tradition of casting delinquent boys as more "in danger" than dangerous helped to shape the ethic of juvenile justice in Montreal that prevailed at the time of the inauguration of the city's first juvenile court in 1912. The juvenile court focused primarily on boyish behaviours that could be treated and on rehabilitating boys brought to court by their parents or the police. Once in court, probation officers probed the social and familial contexts of delinquency and in a limited way addressed the subject of boys' bodies. Although intent on analyzing boys' personal hygiene habits and moral condition, probation officers restricted their questions pertaining to sexual

behaviour to boys' masturbation practices. When faced with evidence of violent sexual behaviour or homosexuality, social, religious, and moral taboos led court officers to employ euphemisms to describe this behaviour.

Over the course of the first four decades of the juvenile court's work in Montreal the attitude of probation officers and other juvenile justice officials evolved, leading to more careful consideration of boys' bodies and sexuality. The situation had changed by the early 1940s because of several important factors relating to transformations in the experience of adolescence in Canada and Quebec. Like their American counterparts, Canadian adolescents during the interwar period had embraced a youth culture rooted in peer group identification and modern leisure pursuits. Alarmed parents and social commentators warned that the effect of this cultural shift was the loosening of sexual mores among the country's youth. The Canadian social work community, for example, declared adolescents' increasingly casual attitude toward sexuality to be one of the most pressing problems of the day.[4] The sources of these changes were many, but most commentators, from juvenile court judges to social workers to the clergy of the Catholic Church, identified French and American movies as the chief culprits and primary cause of adolescents' loss of their sense of modesty and decency. In Quebec the Catholic clergy and Christian women's groups worked to shore up weakening moral standards among working-class youth who had fallen victim to the pernicious foreign messages of films.[5]

During the Second World War focus on "bad" youth behaviour escalated as a delinquency panic, provoked by absentee parents, rising venereal disease rates, and concern for the future of the nation, led juvenile court officials, educators, and religious leaders to cast a more consistent gaze at adolescent behaviour and pushed the state and private agencies to police sexuality more vigorously. In an effort to "protect" the province's youth the Quebec government raised the age of juvenile delinquents from 16 to 18 in 1942, effectively expanding the category of juvenile. This older group brought with them to juvenile court more widespread sexual experience, forcing the court to examine more closely its role in policing the "immorality" of youth culture. The Montreal juvenile court's juvenile morality squad, consisting entirely of members of the city's police force, facilitated a shift toward closer examination of teenagers' social and sexual lives. As the court pursued sexually promiscuous boys in the 1940s, moreover, their behaviour was judged increasingly in terms of diagnoses of adolescent behaviour made by experts brought before the courts. By the era of the Second World War the Montreal juvenile court finally embraced the more widespread application of psychological testing and child development theories that acknowledged that post-pubescent adolescent boys entered a normal, though dangerous, period when rigid self-control was imperative and surveillance and regulation critical.

While juvenile justice history has been slow to problematize the male delinquent body, adjacent disciplines of masculinity studies, the history of sexuality, and education have opened the door to the possibility that boys' sexuality has a history, was part of their identity, and played a role at various moments in delinquency panics. From historical studies in education we learn of movements toward social hygiene instruction or sex education in the period after World War I. These movements promoted the belief that boys needed to be guided through puberty and past the threats of sexual depravity, disease, and racial degeneration, as outlined by Alexandra Lord.[6] Masculinity studies are also helpful in providing a context coincidental with the juvenile court era in which are found extensive campaigns to regulate masculinity and adolescent boys' bodies, including sexuality, as noted by Angus McLaren.[7] From the work of Steven Maynard we also know that the criminal justice system regulated gay male spaces and bodies.[8] Cynthia Comacchio's study of adolescence and leisure in the interwar period describes a moment in time when youth were problematized for seeking and shaping modern pleasure palaces and "dancing to perdition," in the words of one detractor. She suggests that anxieties over the youth problem in the 1920s linked crime and deviance to sexual license. Proper guidance for boys meant channelling boys' energies into various activities, from military training to healthy recreation and from sex education to the YMCA, and often into activities where men could provide models for boys.[9] Mary Louise Adams locates a sexualized youth problem in the post–World War II era and asserts that developing a proper heterosexual identity became critical in the adolescent years. She writes: "[Youth] identity and sexual identity came to be an inseparable pair."[10] Gaston Desjardins also identifies the post-war era as one loaded with prescriptive sexual messages to boys in Quebec.[11] Thus the period between the 1920s and the 1950s in Canada provides moments when boys, sexuality, and juvenile delinquency were linked within moral panics over youth behaviour.

In the literature on juvenile justice the policing of boys' sexuality is found within the confines of reform schools. The British boys' reformatories that Linda Mahood examined for her study of the policing of gender, class, and family suggest that the close watching of boys—the need to impart an ethic of self-control—meant that masturbation and homosexual activity were closely monitored and disciplined.[12] Similarly, Bryan Hogeveen, in a recent Ph.D. dissertation, has argued that in Ontario in the early twentieth century "working-class boys, in contrast to girls, were rarely arrested for violation of sexual mores," yet they were brutalized for demonstrating a lack of sexual control while incarcerated.[13]

Records from the Montreal Juvenile Delinquents' Court from the first half of the twentieth century—chiefly cases of immoral conduct—document the typical boy delinquent and the discursive rendering of male delinquency as well as the court's focus on sexuality. It seems clear that by the 1940s boys' bodies and sexuality were undeniably integrated into the juvenile justice system's approach to boyish badness. Court records not only permit a view as to how a regulatory body constructed and contained sexuality but also suggest contours of sexuality: where and when delinquent boys engaged in hetero- and homosexual activity, when pleasure was sought, and when boys used their bodies to assert their power through an emerging sexualized vernacular and through action.

Juvenile Justice and the Construction of Boyish Badness

The juvenile justice system in Canada, as elsewhere, was designed originally as a response to working-class male delinquency, especially the "waifs and strays" of urban life.[14] In fact, in the nineteenth century youthful male street culture became synonymous with juvenile delinquency.[15] A combination of the major features of industrial modernity—from urban poverty to cinemas to a decline in the power of the Catholic Church—resulted in the growing presence of boys in public space. The modern city drew boys onto the streets as vendors, newsboys, delivery boys, vagrants, and thieves. This growing public presence of minors elicited action on several fronts broadly directed at the amelioration and regulation of children's lives.[16] This ethic of child saving was rooted in a belief that urban, industrial society had rendered children at once more vulnerable and vicious, requiring grand solutions on the part of charitable organizations and the state. For example, gangs of idle, working-class boys in the streets of Montreal—Quebec's largest city—served as an impetus to establish schools under the Education Act of 1846. Another part of this reaction was the creation of the juvenile justice system. Its first gesture was the removal of youth from local jails to reform institutions. In 1869 the province of Quebec instituted legislation authorizing the establishment of reform schools for children under the age of 16. In the next decade two reform schools for delinquent youth, one for boys, the other for girls, opened in Montreal, and both were run by Catholic religious orders.

A second phase of juvenile justice began in the early twentieth century with a federal act concerning juvenile delinquents. The Canadian Juvenile Delinquents Act of 1908 introduced the new juvenile court, at once a replacement for the criminal court and a tribunal for neglected children. Under the act delinquents formed part of a new category of youth arraigned by the juvenile court system for behavioural difficulties, often at the behest of their parents.[17] This act and the municipally based juvenile courts that followed facilitated state regulation of the working class, not only children under the age of 16 in conflict with the law but also adults who were judged derelict in their parental duties. Central tenets of the new court included a rejection of the notion that children commit crimes and the substitution of enlightened "treatment" for punishment. Like their American counterparts, these Canadian courts signified a shift toward a more child centered system that promoted the superiority of a middle-class moral position.

In the 1910s the Montreal Juvenile Delinquents' Court charged thousands of boys with a variety of delinquent acts. Unlike other jurisdictions, this court was not overly concerned with truancy; compulsory schooling legislation was notoriously late in Quebec, coming only in 1943. The court was, however, interested that boys keep their jobs, obey their parents, and keep off the streets, especially at night. The juvenile court overwhelmingly targeted working-class boys, not only French Canadians and Irish Catholics but also English Protestants and a growing number of immigrant boys from southern and eastern Europe, including Jewish youth. Boys of the Roman Catholic faith were consistently in the majority, ranging from approximately 70 to 80 per cent of all cases.[18] During the last years of the 1910s more than a thousand formal cases were processed annually by the Montreal court, with boys comprising over 80 per cent of these cases. By the late 1930s boys' cases had grown to over two thousand per annum; this growth continued through the years of the Second World War.[19] Boys were typically brought to court for theft, disturbing the peace, incorrigibility, and vagrancy.[20] [. . .]

In the era in which the court opened juvenile justice was widely lauded for its preventive and protective potential. Child welfare reformers argued that the decriminalization of boys' crimes guaranteed the preservation of innocent childhood. In the press juvenile court officials promoted themselves as a charitable force and as genuinely concerned about delinquent boys. Montreal child savers spoke of the "peculiarity of the boyish temperament" and the necessity of "get[ting] at the hidden spring of this nature."[21] Through a lack of understanding, boyish badness meant that "some of the finest boys are in reformatories, because they possessed too much animal spirits." By reducing boys' crimes to "pranks and escapades" the personnel of the juvenile court and probation system asserted their ability to correct families and put boys back on the right track toward a "proper" childhood.

As a means of educating the public and promoting the new juvenile court, the local press was periodically invited to witness and report on its daily proceedings. With exuberance the Montreal newspapers wrote about François-Xavier Choquet (the "Children's Judge") and his staff of maternal probation officers. Throughout the 1910s newspapers presented in their stories the apparently fixed category of an uncomplicated boy delinquent: a preteenager, poor (as demonstrated by his shabby dress), and with no visible signs of "foreignness"—these were *canadien* (French-speaking and Catholic) or Canadian (English-speaking, Protestant or Catholic) boys. Through caricatures and melodramatic reporting reporters constructed the bad boy: "angelic faced" and prepubescent, he was "half ashamed, half defiant" and "burst into tears in front of the judge."[22] The press emphasized boys' innocence and youth and blamed their delinquent activities on negligent parents and the lure of the streets. Boys neglected by parents were led astray by the "bad company" they found on the street.[23] Even boys who were arrested for wielding firearms were presented as merely playing Wild West heroes, mimicking what they had seen at the movies.[24]

This gendered and sympathetic approach to delinquents was also generated by those who had a vested interest in portraying their work in the court as being in the best interest of the child and the community. While aiming to inspire confidence about this "child saving station," judges and probation officers also clearly identified delinquency's main cause to be working-class parents and their inability or unwillingness to train and supervise their own children.[25] [. . .] Judge François-Xavier Choquet, who headed the Montreal juvenile court during its first decade, asserted that delinquency began in the overcrowded, immigrant sections of the city where "ignorant" parents did not comprehend the "language and laws of the new land."[26] In justifying and promoting his approach to delinquency in the new court Choquet promised to impart wisdom

and moral guidance to children of the undisciplined and "foreign" working class. His assertions were impressionistic at best, for the majority of boys who came into his court were in fact born in Quebec.

In investigating cases probation officers went beyond an examination of the offence at hand, often listing the boys' habits and making general commentary on their lives. This contextualization of the offence, or perhaps trivializing of it, formed a cornerstone of twentieth-century juvenile justice and allowed the court to propose a moral judgment not only on boys' criminal behaviour but also on their circumstances. Certain adolescent boys' social proclivities were always noted: smoking, swearing, attending the cinema, and hanging about or running in the streets. In the 1910s Judge Choquet claimed that 95 per cent of boys who came before him smoked cigarettes, "becoming moral and mental wrecks from their use."[27] The Woman's Christian Temperance Union, active in the city's Protestant schools, likened tobacco smoking among boys to alcohol abuse in adults. Judge Choquet also joined a chorus of voices in Quebec that criticized the moving pictures industry. Choquet argued that the "cheap drama" of cinema should be minimized and that the industry's romanticization of crimes such as theft led children to temptation. [. . .]

[. . .] The juvenile court, like its predecessor, the reform school, was intended as a remedy for "street corner" life that fed upon neglected youth who attended neither school nor work and who committed petty offences and were destined for a life of crime. [. . . Court clerk Owen] Dawson declared that "the free and easy life of the streets does not tend to uplift the boy and many of them drift into idle ways," and he concluded that "idle youngsters" embraced "evil ways."[28] Both Dawson and Choquet complained that idleness indicated a dissipated life, compromising boys' potential as future citizens.[29]

This boy problem contained an element of urgency as it forecast dire news of unproductive, criminal adulthood. As children and youth were increasingly seen as state assets and future citizens, it was imperative that the juvenile justice system turn these delinquents around. Even though juvenile justice reinforced a category of delinquency based on chronological age, as citizens-in-waiting boys in Quebec needed to learn respect for familial and community authority, private property, and standards of moral decency. The main religious and cultural communities (French Catholic, English Protestant, and Jewish) saw the loss of their members to delinquency as particularly dire. [. . .] The personnel of the juvenile court, mostly Catholic, also decried the dangers of boys becoming lost to the parish and the father-headed family, noting that as boys moved beyond the parish they also refused to attend Sunday mass and obey their parents. These court personnel worried about the ramifications of such behaviour for the survival of the French Canadian "race."[30]

Sex and the Juvenile Court

While it is clear from the juvenile court records that working-class boys' tendency to hang about the streets all hours of the day and night inspired the court to discipline them, probation officers cast it in moral terms but never asked about the sexual aspect of this behaviour, nor did they typically sexualize it. This silence is important when placed in the context of the early-twentieth-century obsession with sexual knowledge and regulation. As historians of sexuality have noted, concern about children's sexuality had been a feature of Victorian society's preoccupation with national degeneration, a preoccupation centred on working-class children and expressed in gendered terms and about specific sexual activities. Girls elicited dramatic attention because precocious sexuality was perceived to lie at the heart of escalating juvenile prostitution rates. Boys, on the other hand, commanded attention because their lack of sexual self-control—as evidenced by the habit of masturbation—might lead them down the road to homosexuality; this threat was countered in a number of ways, including advice manuals, warnings, and even circumcision.[31] By the early twentieth century, with the discovery of and investigations into adolescence, masturbation among boys had become "normalized," and problematic sex was linked more closely to homosexual activity itself, which continued to be criminalized and pathologized. Thus, as the juvenile

courts opened, girls' precocious sexuality remained a general problem, but boys' sexual "deviance" was only narrowly construed. In short, delinquent sexualities were gendered and unevenly considered by the juvenile justice system. [. . .]

Whereas delinquent boys were singled out for their potential for citizenship, which meant at various times being respectable workers, good Catholic family members, and obedient subjects, girls were more problematic.[32] Protection and policing of girls and their participation as members of community and nation followed especially from their potential as mothers. In interwar Quebec French Canadian girls were identified as a weak link in the plan for *la survivance de la race* (the survival of the [French Canadian] race). The *jeunes filles modernes* (young modern girls) embodied delinquency as they turned to the marketplace, made their presence felt in public spaces downtown, foxtrotted on the weekends, ate not their mother's cooking but food made in "ethnic restaurants," and adopted a modern attitude that was expressed through their sexuality. As adolescent girls eschewed the model of passive femininity represented by their mothers, French Canadian nationalists forged a campaign to get them to embrace their subordinate class and gender position within the patriarchal family and "nation." Beginning in the 1910s and continuing through the 1940s, the court ordered "medical" examinations for girls as part of the background investigation into cases involving female juvenile delinquents. Male doctors examined each girl for the presence of a hymen and questioned her about the extent of her sexual experience.[33] A verdict of "virgin" would undoubtedly lead to an easier time with the judge, but most of the girls were in fact branded *déflorée* (deflowered or debauched). Under such circumstances the girls were obliged to defend their character in court against the "scientific" proof of their sexual delinquency—as evidenced by an incomplete or absent hymen. The probation officer then pressed these girls to disclose the names, places, and dates pertaining to the sexual indiscretions. This focus on the relationship between sexuality and delinquency was entirely gendered, as delinquent boys were almost always spared the same sexual interrogation and invasive physical examination. In fact, in 1924, for example, the court ordered 284 medical exams for 278 girls and only 6 boys, demonstrating that the "sexual confessional" was constructed virtually for girls alone.[34] At the same time, the case file for each girl might well have contained boys' names and their sexual activities upon which the court officials could have acted had they been interested in policing juvenile sexuality for both boys and girls.

What can we make of this first glance at the juvenile court's refusal to police the heterosexual sexual experience of boys? One way to comprehend the court's orientation is to see it as a continuation of nineteenth-century child-saving ideas and policies and as a function of gendered citizenship. As Susan Houston has argued for Toronto's delinquency problem in the nineteenth century, the street culture in which boys participated alarmed Victorian society because they "subsisted on the fringes of capitalist enterprise" and resisted developing the required work ethic.[35] [. . .] Nineteenth-century solutions to controlling sexuality elsewhere meant girls were incarcerated to prevent them from becoming prostitutes and boys were subjected to socialization techniques aimed at expending excess energy and producing bodies of self-control, meaning mostly sports but also scouting, military training, and instruction in social hygiene.[36] Similarly, Judge Choquet and probation officer Rose Henderson in Montreal advocated that sex hygiene be added to the school curriculum as a remedy to the delinquency problem, a proposal that did not receive a warm reception from the city's largest education administration, the Catholic School Board.[37] The ongoing preoccupation with appropriate and gendered roles for working-class youth—boys as future workers and citizens and girls as wives and mothers—meant that the juvenile justice system remained fixated on what stood in the way of achieving these norms. For boys that fixation meant that sexuality was only important to correct if it fell outside heterosexuality; for girls, the emphasis on protecting their reproductive future meant that even their precocious heterosexuality was dealt with severely. [. . .] Boys' bodies and sexuality, then, are much more in evidence in girls' sex delinquency cases than in the majority of boys' cases.

Boy's Bodies, Sexuality, and the Montreal Juvenile Court

How did the juvenile court, its judges, and its probation officers view boys' bodies and their sexuality? At first, their bodies were not probed, their sexual histories not taken. Only in very circumscribed ways did boys' sexual activities come to light. Masturbation was acknowledged as age appropriate, and the Montreal juvenile court probation officers assumed masturbatory habits among adolescent boys and commented little about it.[38] Much more distressing to the personnel of the juvenile court and thus recorded in greater detail in the historical record was homosexual or incestuous sexual behaviour. In short, the court constructed a dichotomy into which they fit boys: victim and predator. "Victims" were boys caught in homosexual acts (which nonetheless likely ranged from consensual to coerced); these boys were characteristically portrayed as young, innocent, and resistant to such sex. "Predators" were boys accused of incest.

Certain cases in the Montreal Juvenile Delinquents' Court suggest that boys as well as girls needed protection from worldly, lecherous men who lay in wait for them. [. . .]

When boys were caught in or confessed to homosexual sex the court worked to construct them as victims of adult men, often downplaying the sexuality of boys. Boys played a critical role in this process, offering "pardon tales" to excuse behaviour the court officers and police found repugnant and marshaling evidence that the larger structures shaping their lives were to blame for their delinquent acts.[39] Boys provided probation officers with fragments of their family lives, often including stories of broken homes and neglectful parents or guardians, that served as a warning to all of the consequences of an inadequate and unstable home life. Such is the case of Théodore F., a 15-year-old French Canadian boy who was arrested in the summer of 1918 in Viger Square, a popular gathering place in downtown Montreal.[40] The charge was vagrancy, since he had not been able to give a proper account of why he was in the square late at night. His was a story of poverty and neglect: his widowed mother had remarried a man who did not care for Théodore, thus

prompting a series of attempts to board the adolescent away from his home. First he was sent to a
man who worked at the tramway, then he was sent
to a boarding house run by a Madame Côté. With
no one properly looking after him he easily fell into
the "wrong" crowd. One July night at Viger Square
he met a man with whom he shared some beer and
whom he followed home that night. According to
the boy, this male "friend" attempted to commit an
indecent act upon him, but he refused and found his
way back to the square. By the time he arrived it was
very late, and the common police sweep of loiterers
resulted in his arrest and juvenile court appearance.
Théodore's experiences of maternal neglect and his
declaration that he had successfully spurned homosexual advances show his reliance on a model of
victimhood and innocence that fit neatly within the
preconceptions of the court officers.

The case of Thomas D. has similar elements,
although he confessed to doing "revolting things
not even animals did."[41] In the months before his
case was heard family "instability" had followed the
death of his mother, and Thomas had been sent to
live with an aunt. The 13-year-old French Canadian
boy ran away and was not found for three weeks. As
he told the story to the probation officer, he met and
stayed with a soldier who had recently arrived from
the front. This married soldier claimed his wife
was in England. Living hand to mouth, the soldier
and the boy stole what they could to survive. When
Thomas was arrested for theft the story of their involvement came out in the private office of the juvenile court's probation officer. Unlike girls' cases,
where the probation officer and medical examiner
were careful to describe sexual encounters in detail,
in this case the probation officer described them
in legal terms: simply put, the soldier was guilty of
"gross indecency." In this case Thomas, often referred to as *le jeune* (the young), was easily described
as a victim of the soldier, the "brute" and "lecher,"
who was held responsible for the arrangement. The
protective aspect of juvenile justice is clear in this
case. Any agency that Thomas wielded appears to
have evaporated in this juvenile justice process, and
he received a relatively short sentence of one month
in reform school, followed by probation.

In the case of the "lecherous" soldier and
Thomas D., Thomas was not recorded as having
complained about the soldier's actions; still, the
probation officer's repulsion was not even thinly disguised, and it is likely that Thomas received clearly the message that the role he was to play was as a
young victim. The 1910s coincides with increasing
state regulation of homosexuality in Canada. Police
used an 1890 law concerning "gross indecency" as a
weapon against homosexual behaviour, as they did
against the soldier. An ill-defined law, it was used to
police gay men for a broad range of behaviour that
even so much as hinted at physical intimacy.[42] Under the Criminal Code of Canada men charged with
homosexual offences were sent to medical doctors
for physical examination (for evidence of penetra-
tion), and by the 1910s courts began to also send
those charged to psychiatrists.[43] In addition, morality squads targeted well-known gay hangouts, where
consenting men were arrested for sexual behaviour
under the gross indecency laws.[44] In the context of
the escalation of surveillance and criminalization of
gay men the juvenile court constructed adolescent
boys as victims of adult male "perverts" and defined
itself as a court of protection. [. . .]

In the early years of the court adolescent boys
were considered libidinous, predatory, and therefore
responsible for sexual crimes only in very limited
situations, such as in cases of incest. When juvenile
court officials asked girls pointed questions about
their loss of virginity, a number of them revealed
that the persons "responsible" were their brothers.[45] From the girls' cases it does not appear that
the court used this information to police the sexual
behaviour of their brothers. It could be that the incident in question happened years earlier or that the
girl was simply not believed or that she was considered in some way equally responsible. Occasionally, the probation officer would note such activity if
the parents were aware and offered the information.
[. . .] Wilfrid C. was brought to court by his father in
May 1916 for refusing to attend school regularly and
staying out late at night. Like many other 15-year-
old boys who came before a judge, he testified that
his family had been "broken" by the death of his
mother a year earlier. His two older brothers lived

outside the home, leaving Wilfrid and his younger sister at home with their father. A letter from the boy's school testified to the fact that the widower had to work, leaving the children without proper supervision. The school authorities suggested placing the boy at an industrial school. Instead, Wilfrid agreed to work in a factory rather than attend school. Two months later Wilfrid and his father were back in court. It is not clear how the father knew that Wilfrid was raping his sister, but in July an investigation took place. Monsieur C. lodged a complaint stating that on the first day of July 1916 his son "did cohabit and have sexual intercourse with his sister . . . age 7 years." Wilfrid admitted to probation officer Marie Mignault that the incidents of incest numbered around twenty-five. A doctor was called to examine the seven year old. Recent injury and ample evidence of coitus, including a ruptured hymen, led the doctor to conclude that she had been the victim of sexual assault. Wilfrid's father wanted him severely punished. The boy's uncle (the brother of the dead mother) came to his defence, suggesting that this boy had been well behaved until he suffered the loss of his mother. After that time his father failed to care for him, leaving both children to fend for themselves from six o'clock in the morning until six o'clock in the evening. Led astray by bad friends, his uncle claimed, Wilfrid lost his way. The uncle, who was now caring for the seven-year-old sister, claimed that she had not suffered greatly: she still seemed virtuous and never spoke out of place. His recommendation to the judge was to send Wilfrid to an institution where he could learn a trade. Ultimately, the judge agreed, and Wilfrid was given three years in a reform school run by a Catholic male order.

World War II and the Heightened Sexual Policing of Boys: Boyfriends, Flashers, and Prostitutes

During the Second World War the attention of juvenile justice to boys' bodies and sexuality grew in intensity, and the court's protective stance gave way to more of a policing role. There is both continuity

and change in this period: older adolescent boys who allegedly abused younger children were marked as predators; sexual exhibitionism and sexual coercion were more prominent in the court; and finally, the juvenile court began to target boys' heterosexual behaviour, which heretofore had been restricted to female delinquency cases. The juvenile court's willingness to examine the sexual histories and experiences of boys was facilitated by changes within the juvenile justice system. [. . .] For example, a corps of police officers known as the Juvenile Morality Squad began working with the juvenile court. These officers collected young couples from parks, dance halls, and other public spaces, paralleling the work of the first female police officers who had operated on Montreal streets during the era of World War I as a sort of sexual delinquency squad.[46] [. . .]

Also of tremendous consequence, in 1942 the Quebec government expanded the age category of juvenile delinquent from those under the age of 16 years to those under 18. One of the results of the growing presence at the juvenile court of boys 16 years of age and older was the greater attention paid to their sexual behaviour. Complaints against these boys described "immoral acts" committed with girls under the age of 18. The attention paid to the girls' ages suggests that the court charged juvenile delinquents with immoral conduct as a substitution for age-of-consent laws. The latter could be found in the Canadian Criminal Code but were cumbersome to use in prosecutions; juvenile offences like immoral conduct were less so. Thus a pattern emerged where 16- and 17-year-old boys who were caught having sex with female minors were judged by the court to have behaved in a "scandalous, immoral [manner]."[47] The reshaping of the juvenile delinquency laws to include this older cohort of boys resulted in the presence in the juvenile justice system of a cohort of youth who likely considered themselves young adults, not juveniles, and more independent of their families, especially in social matters. Few offered pardon tales to excuse their "immorality"; impugning the reputation of any implicated girls was a more common defence.

Another critical coincidental change that focused the court's gaze on boys' sexuality was the psychological turn and the medicalization of delinquency, embraced much earlier by courts elsewhere but resisted in Montreal until the late 1930s.[48] By the 1940s most delinquents were seen by a court-appointed physician and a dentist; an increasing number were sent to a psychiatrist, especially those involved in sexual immorality. The court thereafter accepted adolescent psychology and the idea of proper sexual and social development and sought mental health expertise when hearing allegations of sexual aberration. [. . .] A strong link between delinquent activities, especially those considered "perverted" or "depraved," and psychological factors influenced the court's attitudes toward boys and permeated the vernacular of anti-delinquency moral reformers and probation officers.[49]

The actions of juvenile court workers reflected attitudes and concerns of the larger Quebec society. Like other North American cities, Montreal witnessed a mounting delinquency panic during the war that placed youth sexuality at the fore of home-front social problems. [. . .] In 1944 the director of the Municipal Service Bureau sounded the alarm over "moral degeneracy among teenage youth," which had its origins, he claimed, in the "sex talk that goes on among and between boys and girls at school," the pernicious messages in movies, and the beer and petting parties in the city's nightclubs.[50] A juvenile court lawyer told the author of La délinquance juvénile et la guerre (Juvenile delinquency and war) that youth had abandoned school to pursue pleasure and satisfy their passions.[51] These activities were noted as a particular problem among 16- to 20-year-old boys, who had suddenly higher wages and more freedom than before the war but less discretion.

As part of its response to the delinquency crisis Montreal hosted a national conference in 1944. The bilingual and multidenominational event, "Delinquency Prevention Week," began with the session "VD and Delinquents." Youth culture's loose morality struck a nerve when it found expression as venereal disease. During World War II Quebec was home to Canada's "most serious VD problem."[52] VD rates among male armed forces recruits were found to be alarmingly high in Montreal, and,

while anti-VD campaigns targeted women and girls, youth sent to juvenile court were increasingly suspected of carrying the disease. Tests for venereal diseases, such as the Neisser and versions of the Wasserman, were consistently used on "indecent" youth. The juvenile court took VD infection among delinquents very seriously: 14-year-old Alcide G., for example, was committed to the Bordeaux Jail for syphilis treatment rather than the boys' reformatory because of his highly contagious state.[53] Boys were also incarcerated if they refused to follow VD treatment.[54] The campaigns to eradicate the VD problem inspired more discussion about social and sexual hygiene and about the importance of parents and educators in prevention. [. . .]

By the late 1930s the Montreal Juvenile Delinquents' Court also began to explore more systematically the masturbation habits of delinquent boys. The information typically arose during the medical or psychological examinations of boys. Increasingly, however, probation officers commented on this aspect of boys' behaviour. Of particular concern were those boys who allegedly preyed upon younger boys, leading them into mutual masturbation sessions. These boys were viewed suspiciously by probation officers as Pied Pipers of immorality. At the root of the concern was a new and medicalized image of the predatory boy: a gang leader who could enlist boys into criminal activity and further immorality and whose behaviour was evidence of perversion or latent homosexuality. [. . .] The juvenile court took measures to separate the "gang leaders" from younger boys and to extricate them from the depraved living and moral conditions that were thought to have produced such behaviour.[55] [. . .]

In a case of indecent assault one implicated 17-year-old youth, Robert, "freely discussed" masturbating and stated to the probation officer that it and women "were all [his] gang ever talks about."[56] The probation officer considered the gang influence detrimental and largely though not solely responsible in this case. This group of young men whose hangout was a fish-and-chips stand became the source of all sexual knowledge and values for Robert due, it was claimed, to the vacuum left by his well-meaning but misguided mother. The gang created a culture that, according to the court, became impermeable to the better influences of home and family. In commenting on the family situation the probation officer remarked that this mother, "like so many parents, [. . .] thinks [Robert's] problem is largely solved when habits of modesty are established." While the parent proudly claimed that there was no sex talk in her respectable working-class home, the probation officer reported this as a failure and part of Robert's problem.

During the war constables of the Juvenile Morality Squad labelled certain cases of mutual masturbation "immoral conduct with a homosexual." These cases appear similar to others involving mutual masturbation except that the boys charged with homosexuality were older. In two separate cases of homosexuality in September 1944 the 16- and 17-year-old boys were described as having behaved immorally for months and were both incarcerated for several years.[57] The severe response was likely influenced by contemporary psychiatric perspectives on "perversion" and its complicated treatment. Sometimes the court sent boys accused of mutual masturbation to psychiatrists, looking for evidence of mental deficiency to explain the behaviour. In the case of a 13-year-old boy who was brought to court for mutual manual and oral masturbation with other boys the court psychiatrist found him to be "mentally inferior" and his sexual perversion—as evidenced by masturbation and homosexual tendencies—to be rooted in mental retardation.[58] In the cases mentioned above involving older boys, however, mental capacity was not noted as an issue or an explanation, and perhaps that was seen as justifying separating them from society ostensibly to put a halt to their homosexual behaviour. [. . .]

In the case of heterosexual sex the clinical language of the juvenile court record often cast the boy as a sexual predator, yet a closer examination reveals more complex adolescent interaction, intergenerational tension, and concern over public health and morality. By the early 1940s couples were picked up by the court's Juvenile Morality Squad or brought to court by parents, resulting in accusations launched at boys for allegedly encouraging girls to leave home and have sex with them. These relationships seem to range in nature, and those implicated were sometimes lovers and at other times mere acquaintances. In 1944 Jean-Paul L. was brought to court on a complaint of Madame A. Lecompte, a female probation officer, for immoral conduct with girls under the age of 18. His seduction of minor girls allegedly began in the city's shady restaurants and culminated in anonymous rooms rented for illicit purposes. Likely the probation officer's information came from girls' sex delinquency cases. Jean-Paul was sent for VD tests, and, finding that he was not infected, the court sent him home under the condition that he no longer seek out these questionable venues, pay a reasonable pension to his father, and behave honourably at work.[59] In another example, Bernard P. and his girlfriend, Gisèle, both under the age of 18, were brought to court to answer for immorality during the course of their four-month relationship.[60]

Often a parent intervened and brought the young people to court. Fifteen-year-old Lloyd, for example, encouraged Claire, aged 16, to "desert her home without permission and live with him in the streets, in the park, and in a rooming house in Montreal" in June 1943. This case revolves around an intergenerational struggle between Lloyd and his parents over his dating of Claire. The court was presented with a letter written by Lloyd to his mother, demanding that she give him written permission to marry Claire. She wrote back to him, telling him he was too young and that other girls would come his way. In court he admitted to the offence and was given a suspended sentence under condition that he "obey and listen to his parents, look for work and give his salary to his parents, stay away from Claire." To curb his maturing sexual desire and lust for marriage his curfew was set at 10 o'clock in the evening, and restaurants and pool rooms were forbidden to him.[61]

Familiar to "bad girl" histories is the role of parents in seeking out the court's aid, acting on the suspicion that their daughters might be sexually active. Parents of sexually delinquent girls also used the juvenile court to keep boyfriends away from their daughters. Seventeen-year-old Normand L. had both good and bad luck during World War II. He landed a job at a flour mill, earning almost as much as his father. During the summer of 1944, with cash in hand, he and his girlfriend frequented restaurants and cinemas in their small town outside Montreal. When their dating turned from "every night" to overnight, the 14-year-old girlfriend's father intervened. To discipline his daughter he sent her away to a convent in August. In October she returned home for a family visit and took the opportunity to get reacquainted with Normand. They travelled to downtown Montreal, where they rented a hotel room for a week. Her father then brought the sordid story to the juvenile court, asking that it proceed against Normand. In his interview with the probation officer Normand denied nothing and offered that he had taken precautions against getting his girlfriend pregnant. Ultimately, the solution was to separate the two; she returned to the convent, and he was sent back home, where he was instructed by the court to act honourably, give his salary to his parents, and return home by nine o'clock each evening.[62]

Parents also called on the court to make boys and young men accountable for their role in the pregnancy of unwed women. François P.'s mother told the court that he had made a girl under the age of 18 pregnant. This 18-year-old youth admitted to having sex with the girl but denied it had resulted in pregnancy. Painting her as promiscuous was not difficult, as the court read her pregnant body as evidence enough. His culpability could not be proved, yet the court did not let him go without assurance that he would not repeat his offence and would control his sexual urges. The judge demanded that he promise to keep away from the pregnant girl and live with an uncle who was understood as a better disciplinarian than his mother.[63]

In spite of the court's willingness to investigate boys' heterosexual sexual adventures by the 1940s, the treatment of the delinquents remained notably different for boys and girls. Roger, age 17, was caught one August morning with his 16-year-old girlfriend acting in an immoral fashion in Lafontaine Park. Jacqueline was sent for a gynecological assessment, where she denied to the doctor any sexual intercourse or even sexual touching, although the doctor's report claimed her hymen was "incomplete."

Both sets of parents were brought to court for judgment. The treatment of the two underscores the continued gendered differentiation in the court's treatment. Both were made wards of the court until the age of twenty-one and given a suspended sentence with certain conditions; this was commonplace and allowed parents to send their children, even in young adulthood, back to court if they broke these conditions. Jacqueline had to promise to stay away from public parks with dishonourable intentions and to behave honestly with all boys. Roger, on the other hand, was simply fined five dollars (upon default of which he would be sent to the detention house for 15 days).[64] [. . .]

Older adolescents allegedly disobeyed their own or others' parents, and so there is evidence that some parents bringing their children to the juvenile courts were looking for ways to bolster their waning authority and help to wrest boys from a youth culture from which they increasingly felt alienated and that they were powerless to contest. Roland, aged 17, was brought to court on the complaint of a young woman's mother. The probation officer found that he was a very bright, dedicated practitioner of the Catholic faith, but he aggravated his own mother by going out too much and coming in at 1:30 in the morning, if at all. This smoking, dancing, and detective novel–reading adolescent was also egotistical, but not deceitful, lazy, or easily led. His doctor's report revealed that he had gonorrhea, and he was thus placed for just under one month at the prison hospital, then released as a ward of the court under a promise to behave honestly with all girls.[65]

Some cases involving boys' immorality suggest that the investigations of the probation officer regarding boys occasionally began to mimic those of girls. Thirteen-year-old Marcel was brought to court in 1940 on a complaint of the mother of one of his friends, a twelve-year-old girl named Marie. The complaint against him charged that he was guilty of sexual immorality with a girl over the last six months. Implicated in this case were not only Marie and Marcel but also two other boys. The probation officer filed the usual forms, recording that Marcel was easily led, sociable, but not lazy or selfish and that he was not involved with drugs, cigarettes, or alcohol. What is surprising about the case is that the probation officer took a sexual history: Marcel admitted to collective masturbation sessions (having been introduced by an older boy in the past) as well as sexual intercourse with Marie, who "encouraged" him. She claimed to have been debauched by Marcel. His contrition and success in blaming the situation on Marie spared him from reform school, and he was sent home with a suspended sentence and made a ward of the court until the age of 21. Marie, on the other hand, was damned by her mother's admission that she frequented restaurants and was too often incorrigible and uncontrollable. This revelation, coupled with a bad reputation among neighbors, motivated the court to sentence her to four years in reform school.[66] This case points to obvious differences in the disposition of cases.

Another cluster of cases from the 1940s involves sexual threats or public exposure of the body. These cases involved sexually explicit language, exhibitionist behaviour, and boys considered a danger to other adolescents or themselves. The Montreal court, which had been very slow to utilize psychological or psychiatric tests or personnel, began to defer such cases to mental health experts. Although their actions were increasingly pathologized, no single discourse predominated as an explanation for boys' seemingly odd behaviour, and moral indignation and the rhetoric of sin and temptation found a place with medical explanations or attributions of environmental or hereditary weakness. Mental testing of delinquents remained irregular, though it became increasingly important over the course of the decade. [. . .]

Exhibitionism among boys was also taken very seriously by the juvenile justice system. Most were sent to psychiatrists to see if mental deficiency explained their actions. Sixteen-year-old Benny, who exposed himself on Jeanne Mance Street in the middle of the afternoon, was sent to the Mental Hygiene Institute (of Montreal), where he was found to be an imbecile, with a mental age of six and an IQ of 47.[67] Fifteen-year-old Frank was also brought to court for repeatedly exposing himself to girls in public. The court doctor found cavities (!) but concluded that his mental state appeared normal. The court then sent him to a psychiatrist, who proclaimed his immoral acts to be "stupid" and not the result of an insane mind. While a little behind mentally, it was concluded, he certainly knew that what he was doing was wrong. The psychiatrist recommended a sojourn to a reform school to straighten out this behaviour.[68] The court disagreed and sent him home as a ward of the court. In another case a 17-year-old who in the course of his job delivering the mail exposed his "private parts" to minors was found to be mentally unstable. His dominant problem, according to the psychiatrist, was masturbation, a symptom of his erotic obsession. This obsessional characteristic was understood as a sign of a developing neurotic personality disorder in this young man. Although his activities were thoroughly pathologized, the court and the psychiatrist believed he could be sent home on probation and with encouragement and guidance, be freed of his neurosis.[69]

In the 1940s the juvenile courts continued to hear cases involving boys and older men. By the 1940s, however, the boys were no longer seen simply as victims, and the court was willing to charge them with prostitution-related offences. Fifteen-year-old Gerard told of going with various men who paid him for sex (described as masturbation and oral and attempted anal sex). These men fed him, bought him drinks, and gave him small sums of money; one claimed to be worried that he wasn't dressed adequately. Like other boys he admitted to a habit of masturbation. The case ultimately turned on Gerard's home environment. The family, so poor as to be unable to provide Gerard with a proper education (his lack of clothing, it was maintained, prevented him from attending either school or mass), became the culprit. He was made a ward of the court until the age of majority and given a strict curfew of six o'clock in the evening, and his parents were ordered to dress him for school.[70] In another case from November 1944 unemployed 16-year-old Louis T. was arrested for soliciting men for purposes of prostitution. During the probation officer's interrogation Louis admitted that he was soliciting when the detectives caught him and tried to rationalize it by claiming he simply wanted some cash to spend the night at Danceland. It was Louis' second arrest for this charge and would likely have resulted in incarceration had he not successfully fled the jurisdiction.[71] [. . .]

Conclusions

Boys' bodies and sexuality played a role in the practice of juvenile justice history, and judges, probation officers, and parents recognized this corporal dimension of male delinquency, although that recognition developed slowly. It is true that in the early decades the sexual activities of boys did not fit with the predominant image of the delinquent child who was deserving of care and rehabilitation. Street-wise and working-class boys were worrisome for their lack of education, their history of neglect, and their susceptibility to temptation. In keeping with the construction of the court as a *conseil de famille,* or child-saving station, boys were seen as salvageable. Their activities were not sexualized by the early juvenile court in the way girls' delinquency was. The court initially chose to investigate only limited aspects of male adolescent sexuality: it heard stories of homosexual relations and constructed the boys as victims of adult predators in a climate increasingly hostile to homosexuality. Boys' experience of homosexuality, whether coerced or consensual, was taken as reversible and treatable, not unlike petty theft. Montreal's juvenile court did not pathologize or criminalize boys' sexuality, except when it was linked to violence or incest.

By the 1940s an older cohort of adolescent boys were brought to juvenile court for "immoral conduct" of a sort that heretofore was not generally policed. It is clear that the Montreal juvenile court used the juvenile offence of "immoral conduct" as a way to police premarital sexuality. By the Second World War, in the context of a delinquency panic, court officials had adopted a language that expressed concern for boys in the throes of an adolescent "crisis," where they were easily sexually excited by films and by what they witnessed on the streets.[72] Brought in by the Juvenile Morality Squad or by parents, boys were asked to explain their lewd behaviour, and they admitted to private and public sexuality. By that time the court regularly asked about a boy's masturbation habits. Masturbation indicated that discipline at home was lacking, yet the problem could

be fixed with proper school or church attendance. In cases where masturbation involved group activity probation officers aimed at breaking up the gang and eliminating further immorality and potential criminality.

Also by the 1940s sexual offences committed by juvenile delinquents were commonly ignored or trivialized, especially once a doctor had examined their perpetrators. Boys caught using an aggressive and sexualized vernacular or flashing their bodies in public were investigated by psychiatrists. Medical doctors also examined the boys' bodies, looking for evidence of sexual behaviour and venereal disease. The court and parents also recognized boys' role in the spread of venereal disease and the rise in the numbers of unmarried pregnancies. Thus boys' bodies and sexuality were medicalized and pathologized; yet the court did not follow one particular discourse on boys' sexuality but engaged competing discourses that pointed to mental or moral failings on the part of the boy or, indeed, his parents.

Notwithstanding the placing of boys' bodies and sexual activity on trial, juvenile justice continued to be gendered, especially when it came to disposition of cases. During the Second World War working-class adolescent boys, especially those over 15 years of age, easily found well-paying jobs, enjoyed independence from parents by serving in the armed forces or working in war-related industries. Their troublesome behaviour concerned the personnel of the juvenile court, but they, like teachers, social workers, and politicians, expected that adolescent boys would fill in for absent fathers for the duration of the war and assume a critical role in society after the war.[73] Thus, unlike girls, boys were interrogated and then sent home with an understanding that they would not repeat their offences, and parents promised to discipline them better. Also unlike girls, older boys were often fined for acting upon "normal" but inappropriate and immoral sexual urges. These fines functioned in two ways: first, to teach them that their actions had consequences, and second, that they would literally have to pay for their actions. In the end the court acknowledged juvenile males as sexual agents, as wage earners, and, paradoxically, as citizens old enough to contribute to society.

Notes

1. Anne Meis-Knupfer, *Reform and Resistance: Gender, Delinquency, and America's First Juvenile Court* (New York: Oxford University Press, 2001); Mary E. Odem, *Delinquent Daughters: Protecting and Policing Adolescent Female Sexuality in the United States, 1885–1920* (Chapel Hill: University of North Carolina Press, 1995); Meda Chesney-Lind, *Girls, Delinquency and Juvenile Justice* (Belmont, Calif.: Brooks/Cole, 1992); Linda Mahood, *Policing Gender, Class and Family: Britain, 1850–1940* (London: University College London Press, 1995); Ruth Alexander, *The "Girl Problem": Female Sexual Delinquency in New York, 1900–1930* (Ithaca: Cornell University Press, 1995).

2. There are, nonetheless, studies that examine in comparative fashion the gendered nature of delinquency. See Dorothy E. Chunn, "Boys Will Be Men, Girls Will Be Mothers: The Legal Regulation of Childhood in Toronto and Vancouver," *Sociological Studies in Child Development* 3 (1990): 94.

3. Jean-Marie Fecteau, Sylvie Ménard, Jean Trépanier, and Véronique Strimelle, "Une politique de l'enfance délinquante et en danger: La mise en place des écoles de réforme et d'industrie au Québec (1840–1873)," *Crime, Histoire & Sociétés/Crime, History & Societies* 1, no. 2 (1998): 75–110.

4. Cynthia Comacchio, "Dancing to Perdition: Adolescence and Leisure in Interwar English Canada," *Journal of Canadian Studies* 32, no. 3 (1997): 5–35, 25.

5. In 1919 Montreal's archbishop issued a pastoral letter on the issue, encouraging a women's organization, the Fédération nationale St-Jean-Baptiste, to invigorate the Ligue des bonnes moeurs (League for Good Morals). American "talkies," like dance clubs, were targeted by the Catholic Church in its campaign to preserve the morals of young people. See Andrée Lévesque, *Making and Breaking the Rules* (Toronto: McClelland & Stewart, 1994), 56–60.

6. Alexandra M. Lord, "Models of Masculinity: Sex Education, the United States Public Health Service, and the YMCA, 1919–1924," *Journal of the History of Medicine and Allied Sciences* 58, no. 2 (2003): 123–52.

7. See, for example, Angus McLaren, *The Trials of Masculinity: Policing Sexual Boundaries, 1870–1930* (Chicago: University of Chicago Press, 1997).

8. Steven Maynard, "'Horrible Temptations': Sex, Men, and Working-Class Male Youth in Urban Ontario, 1890–1935," *Canadian Historical Review* 78, no. 2 (June 1997): 191–235.

9. Comacchio, "Dancing to Perdition"; Cynthia Comacchio, "'The Rising Generation': Laying Claim to the Health of Adolescents in English Canada, 1920–70," *Canadian Bulletin of Medical History* 19, no. 1 (2002): 139–78.

10. Mary Louise Adams, *The Trouble with Normal: Postwar Youth and the Making of Heterosexuality* (Toronto: University of Toronto Press, 1997).

11. Gaston Desjardins, *L'amour en patience: La sexualité adolescente au Québec, 1940–1960* (Montreal: Presses de l'Université du Québec, 1995).

12. Mahood, *Policing Gender, Class and Family*, 112.

13. Bryan Richard Hogeveen, "'Can't You Be a Man?' Rebuilding Wayward Masculinities and Regulating Juvenile Deviance in Ontario, 1860–1930," Ph.D. diss., University of Toronto, 2003, 2 and chap. 5.

14. See, for example, Jean Trépanier and Lucie Quevillon, "Garçons et filles: Définition des problèmes posés par les mineurs traduits à la cour des jeunes délinquants de Montréal (1912–1950)," in *Femmes et justice pénale, XIXe–XXe siècles*, ed. Christine Bard et al. (Rennes: Presses Universitaires de Rennes, 2002), 341.

15. Susan E. Houston, "The 'Waifs and Strays' of a Late Victorian City: Juvenile Delinquents in Toronto," in *Childhood and Family in Canadian History*, ed. Joy Parr (Toronto: McClelland & Stewart, 1982), 131.

16. Peter C. Baldwin, "Nocturnal Habits and Dark Wisdom: The American Response to Children in the Streets at Night, 1880–1930," *Journal of Social History* 35, no. 3 (2002): 593–611. For literature on Canada see P.T. Rooke and R.L. Schnell, *Discarding the Asylum: From Child Rescue to the Welfare State in English Canada, 1800–1950* (Lanham, MD: University Press of America, 1983); Neil Sutherland, *Children in English-Canadian Society: Framing the Twentieth Century Consensus* (Toronto: University of Toronto Press, 1976); Renée Joyal, ed., *Entre surveillance et compassion: L'évolution de la protection de l'enfance au Québec* (Sainte Foy: Presses de l'Université du Québec, 2000).

17. Under this act a youthful lawbreaker, defined as between seven and sixteen years of age, was relieved of the "criminal" or "offender" designation and instead labelled delinquent. A juvenile delinquent was described as "any child who violates any provision of The Criminal Code, . . . or of any Dominion or provincial statute, or of any by-law or ordinance of any municipality." Canada, An Act Respecting Juvenile Delinquents, 7–8 Edward VII, chap. 40.

18. Annual reports of the Montreal Juvenile Delinquents' Court do not exist for all years of the period under study. For boys' cases in 1919: 1,116 (81 per cent) Roman Catholic; 164 (12 per cent) Protestant; 93 (7 per cent) Jewish; 8 (< 1 per cent) Orthodox. For boys' cases in 1922: 895 (70 per cent) Roman Catholic; 213 (17 per cent) Protestant; 147 (12 per cent) Jewish; 10 (< 1 per cent) Orthodox. For boys' cases in 1926: 1,316 (78 per cent) Roman Catholic; 200 (12 per cent) Protestant; 130 (8 per cent) Jewish; 33 (2 per cent) Orthodox; 2 (< 1 per cent) other. Archives nationales du Québec, Québec (hereafter ANQ-Q), Office of the Attorney General, Correspondence, E 17, files for 1919, 1922, and 1926.

19. Aggregate numbers can be found in the Québec an-nuaire statistique/Statistical Yearbook (1946); see also National Archives of Canada, Canadian Council on Social Development Fonds, MG I10, vol. 85, File: Juvenile Courts . . . 1938–41, "Questionnaire, Province of Quebec."

20. For a breakdown of offences committed by boys see Trépanier et Quevillon, "Garçons et filles," 343. As an example of boys' offences, a study of 100 boys' cases (10 per cent) before the Montreal juvenile court in 1918 revealed the following breakdown: 40 involved theft, 14 incorrigibility, 12 vagrancy, 5 breaking and entering, 4 assault, 4 desertion, 4 damage to property, 4 being neglected, 3 weapons, 3 selling papers without a licence or after hours, 1 forgery, 1 firecracker violation (according to municipal bylaw), 1 trespassing, 1 indecent act, 1 traffic violation (according to municipal bylaw), 1 riding a bicycle without lights, 1 smoking cigarettes in a public place. Archives nationales du Québec, Montréal, Fonds de la Court des jeunes délinquants de Montreal (hereafter ANQ-M, Fonds CJDM), files for 1918.

21. Montreal Daily Herald, 9 April 1909, J. J. Kelso of Ontario speaking about the need for a new juvenile court.

22. Montreal Herald, 8 June 1912.

23. Montreal Gazette, 4 October 1918.

24. François-Xavier Choquet, "The Juvenile Court," Canadian Municipal Journal 10, no. 6 (June 1914): 233.

25. See ANQ-Q, Office of the Attorney General, Correspondence, E 17, Annual Reports of the Montreal Juvenile Delinquents' Court (hereafter MJDC) for 1915, 1916, and 1924; Choquet, "The Juvenile Court," 232.

26. Choquet, "The Juvenile Court," 232.

27. Ibid.

28. Jean Trépanier, "Protéger pour prévenir la délinquance: L'émergence de la loi sur les jeunes délinquants de 1908 et sa mise en application à Montréal," in Joyal, Entre surveillance et compassion.

29. ANQ-Q, Office of the Attorney General, Correspondence E 17, Annual Report of the MJDC for 1916, 4; Choquet, "The Juvenile Court," 232.

30. See Sylvie Ménard, Des enfants sous surveillance: la rééducation des jeunes delinquents au Québec (1840–1950) (Montreal: VLB, 2003). On the reaction of the Jewish community see Tamara Myers, "On Probation: The Rise and Fall of Jewish Female Anti-delinquency Work in Interwar Montreal," in Negotiating Identities in Nineteenth- and Twentieth-Century Montreal, ed. Bettina Bradbury and Tamara Myers (Vancouver: University of British Columbia Press, 2005).

31. See Michel Foucault, The History of Sexuality, vol. 1, An Introduction, trans. Robert Hurley (New York: Random House, 1980); Robert Darby, "The Masturbation Taboo and the Rise of Routine Male Circumcision," Journal of Social History 36, no. 3 (2003): 737–57.

32. Joan Sangster, "Creating Social and Moral Citizens: Defining and Treating Delinquent Boys and Girls in English Canada, 1920–65," in Contesting Canadian Citizenship: Historical Readings, ed. Robert Adamoski, Dorothy E. Chunn, and Robert Menzies (Peterborough, Ontario: Broadview Press, 2002), 337.

33. This location was changed to the Detention House in subsequent years.

34. ANQ-M, Office of the Attorney General, Correspondence E 17, Annual Report of the MJDC for 1924.

35. Houston, "The 'Waifs and Strays,'" 131.

36. Ibid., 136. Mahood notes that Frank Mort suggests that this is the moment when "militarized conceptions of male sexuality" emerged.

37. Choquet, "The Juvenile Court," 233; Henderson, "Child Labour," 17.

38. Bastien Pelletier, "Les agents de probation à la cour des jeunes délinquants de Montréal, 1912–1949," master's thesis, Université du Québec à Montréal, 2000, 88.

39. Joan Sangster, "'Pardon Tales' from Magistrate's Court: Women, Crime, and the Court in Peterborough County, 1920–50," Canadian Historical Review 74, no. 2 (June 1993): 161–97.

40. ANQ-M, Fonds CJDM, 29 July 1918, Case #5166, Théodore F., 15 years old, arrested for vagrancy.

41. ANQ-M, Fonds CJDM, 27 March 1918, Case #4759, Thomas D., 13 years old, arrested for desertion. All translations from French are my own.

42. Carolyn Strange and Tina Loo, Making Good: Law and Moral Regulation in Canada, 1867–1939 (Toronto: University of Toronto Press, 1997), 85–86.

43. Steven Maynard, "The Emergence of the Homosexual as a Case History in Early Twentieth-Century Ontario," in On the Case: Explorations in Social History, ed. Franca Iacovetta and Wendy Mitchinson (Toronto: University of Toronto Press, 1998), 67.

44. Steven Maynard, "Through a Hole in the Lavatory Wall: Homosexual Subcultures, Police Surveillance, and the Dialectics of Discovery, Toronto, 1890–1930," Journal of the History of Sexuality 5, no. 2 (1994): 207–41.

45. See Tamara Myers, "'Qui t'a débauchée?': Female Adolescent Sexuality and the Juvenile Delinquents' Court in Early Twentieth-Century Montreal," in Family Matters: Papers in Post-Confederation Canadian Family History, ed. Lori Chambers and Ed Montigny (Toronto: Canadian Scholars Press, 1998), 377–94.

46. Tamara Myers, "Women Policing Women: A Patrol Woman in Montreal in the 1910s," Journal of the Canadian Historical Society n.s. 4 (1993): 229–45.

47. ANQ-M, Fonds CJDM, 10 November 1943, Case #5319.

48. The Montreal Juvenile Delinquents' Court's smaller, non-Catholic, English-speaking committee, which served Protestant and Jewish children, had accepted in the 1920s the involvement of the Montreal Mental Hygiene Institute. These psychiatrists were called upon by the Anglophone probation officers, and they also conducted research into delinquent populations through the court.

49. See, for example, R. P. Valère Massicotte, *La délinquance juvénile et la guerre* (Montreal: Oeuvre des Tracts, 1944), 6. In assessing rising juvenile delinquency rates he asks if the boy is mentally behind or "abnormal" and "unable to repress his perverted instincts."

50. Wright, "Juvenile Delinquency," 1.

51. Massicotte, *La délinquance juvénile*, 10.

52. Keshen, *Saints, Sinners, and Soldiers*, 136.

53. ANQ-M, Fonds CJDM, 20 February 1943, Case #3371.

54. ANQ-M, Fonds CJDM, 31 March 1943, Case #3696. Rosaire's case came back to the court in 1946 because of his refusal to take his medication for VD.

55. See David Niget, "Jeunesses populaires sous le regard de la justice: Naissance du tribunal pour enfants à Angers et Montréal (1912–1940)," Ph.D. diss., Université d'Angers, 2005, 420–21.

56. ANQ-M, Fonds CJDM, 6 November 1944, Case #7557.

57. ANQ-M, Fonds CJDM, 20 September 1944, Case #7309, Armand C., 16 years old; 18 September 1944, Case #7276, Roger D., 17 years old.

58. ANQ-M, Fonds CJDM, 7 November 1942, Case #2572, Jean G., 13 years old.

59. ANQ-M, Fonds CJDM, 31 March 1944, Case #6266.

60. ANQ-M, Fonds CJDM, 24 March 1944, Case #6214.

61. ANQ-M, Fonds CJDM, 28 June 1943, Case #4424.

62. ANQ-M, Fonds CJDM, 13 October 1944, Case #7435.

63. ANQ-M, Fonds CJDM, 4 July 1944, Case #6845.

64. ANQ-M, Fonds CJDM, 23 August 1943, Case #4761.

65. ANQ-M, Fonds CJDM, 9 August 1943, Case #4686.

66. ANQ-M, Fonds CJDM, 19 July 1940, Case #1333 and Case #1312.

67. ANQ-M, Fonds CJDM, 26 February 1943, Case #3420.

68. ANQ-M, Fonds CJDM, 1 March 1940, Case #375.

69. ANQ-M, Fonds CJDM, 9 February 1944, Case #5877; see also 20 June 1944, Case #6773.

70. ANQ-M, Fonds CJDM, 5 December 1940, Case #2378.

71. ANQ-M, Fonds CJDM, 3 November 1944, Case #7549.

72. ANQ-M, Fonds CJDM, 4 March 1943, Case #3476.

73. Tamara Myers and Mary Anne Poutanen, "Cadets, Curfews, and Compulsory School: Regulating Youth in WWII Quebec," *Histoire sociale/Social History* 38, no. 76 (2005), 367–98.

PRIMARY DOCUMENT

"Juvenile Delinquency in Montreal," *The Canadian Police Gazette*, June 1939

A problem of increasing seriousness in the City of Montreal is that presented by the alarming increase in juvenile delinquency. During the past few years the number of cases that have come before the courts has increases very heavily. In 1928, 700 boys and 70 girls were arrested in Montreal. Last year the figures were 1,343 boys and 126 girls. Discussing the matter recently, Mr Dufresne, Chief of the Police Department, said: "The situation here is very bad—far worse than the public imagines. Any public action to improve it can meet only with the approval of police." A few days ago Dr S. LaFortune, Governor of the Montreal jail, discussing the same matter, said: "I had had 30 years' experience as a practicing physician and 14 years as Chairman of the School Board behind me when I took over the jail, and frankly I found conditions in the juvenile delinquency field far worse than I expected."

With the object of attacking this problem in the most comprehensive manner possible, the general council of the Federation of the Leagues of the Sacred Heart of Montreal, representing 45,000 members, for the most part fathers of families, has addressed a petition to

continued

the Mayor, the Executive Committee, and the City Council, asking them to direct the Chair of Police of Montreal to appoint a juvenile morality squad. The Council points out that it has received information in the report of the Federation's committee on morality of a veritable campaign of corruption of youth, both boys and girls, and unhappily even among children; that the records of the Juvenile Court, of the reformatories and the homes for unmarried mothers, show an alarming increase in vice amongst young people; that a large number of parents neglect their duty of safeguarding the moral well-being of their children and allow them to roam the streets till all hours of the night; that an increasing number of corrupters of youth are at present carrying on their nefarious work; that the officers of the police force are well aware of the situation and deplore the fact that, in the present circumstances, they are unable, for want of numbers and jurisdiction, to deal with it in any efficient manner; that on the morality squad there are at present only two constables to deal with crimes involving juveniles, and that, from the experience of recent years, they declare it is absolutely impossible for them to handle the present epidemic of juvenile corruption.

The Council submits that the only practical solution in this unhappy situation is the establishment of a special juvenile morality squad, whose work will deal exclusively with cases involving juveniles, this squad to be composed of 15, 20, or 30 constables (according to the number deemed necessary by the executive committee and the police officials), married men of unquestioned moral integrity, of mature age, having jurisdiction over all sections of the city and especially in places where this work of corruption can be carried on, viz: parks, St Helen's Island, picnic grounds, beaches, public baths, theatres, pool rooms, dance halls, grills, restaurants, clubs, both private and public, and even private hospitals and private dwellings which have given cause for suspicion; that the constables be responsible to the Chief of Police alone; and that, if necessary, the municipal law be amended accordingly.

There is in these representations substantial cause for apprehension. The attitude of the police in the matter is sufficient warranty that the charges made are not exaggerated. Manifestly . . . our police force is not equipped to handle this problem. But it would be a very easy matter for the civic authorities to comply with the recommendations of the Council. In a matter so vitally affecting the development of the youth of this city, delay is not only dangerous, but reprehensible.

Source: "Juvenile Delinquency in Montreal," *The Canadian Police Gazette*, 14, 3 (June 1939), 10–11.

Study Questions

1. Referring to the two essays in this chapter, describe the "ordinary" habits of children and youth in early-twentieth-century Montreal.
2. Fahrni raises the ethical question of using tragic events to write history. What kinds of insights do we gain from using court records that reveal desperate moments?
3. How was delinquency gendered and why? Is the situation different today?

Selected Bibliography

Articles

Fahrni, Magda, "La Lutte Contre L'Accident: Risque et accidents dans un context de modernité industrielle," in *Pour une histoire du risque. Québec, France, Belgique*, eds., Magda Fahrni, David Niget, Martin Petitclerc. Rennes: Presses universitaires de Rennes; Québec, Presses de l'Université du Québec, 2012: 181–202.

Gleason, Mona, "From Disgraceful Carelessness to Intelligent Precaution: Accidents and the Public Child in English Canada, 1900–1950," *Journal of Family History* 30, 2 (April 2005): 230–41.

Romesburg, Don, "Wouldn't a Boy Do? Placing Early-Twentieth-Century Male Youth Sex Work in the Histories of Sexuality," *Journal of the History of Sexuality*, 18, 3 (September 2009): 367–92.

Books

Ménard, Sylvie, *Des Enfants sous surveillance. La Rééducation des jeunes délinquants au Québec (1840–1950)* (Montreal: VLB éditeur, 2003).

Myers, Tamara, *Caught: Montreal's Modern Girls and the Law, 1869–1945* (Toronto: University of Toronto Press, 2006).

Sangster, Joan, *Girl Trouble: Female Delinquency in English Canada* (Toronto: Between the Lines, 2002).

Zelizer, Viviana A., *Pricing the Priceless Child: The Changing Social Value of Children* (New York: Basic Books, 1985).

6 Children and War

Editors' Introduction

The involvement of young people in war, whether as armed combatants (see Tim Cook's essay in this volume), spies, lookouts, messengers, members of voluntary organizations, or subjects of propaganda, has been a feature of many, if not all, armed conflicts around the world. Considered in a rather superficial way, war would appear to be an entirely adult experience. However, this is far from the case, as both contemporary and historical experience make clear. In the present day, for example, non-governmental organizations such as Child Soldiers International (CSI), based in the United Kingdom, work to end the recruitment of youngsters into armies, demobilize those currently fighting, and secure their successful reintegration into their local communities.[1]

In their respective historical examinations of children's wartime experiences at home, Barbara Lorenzkowski and Sarah Glassford paint a detailed picture of the central role that the Second World War played in the lives of Canadian and Newfoundland children. Setting her essay in the context of St John's, Newfoundland, Lorenzkowski draws on 25 life-course interviews to move beyond superficial understandings of how children experienced the culture of war on the home front. The citizens of St John's, an active British seaport in the North Atlantic, acutely felt the daily presence of warships, sailors, and soldiers, both Canadian and American, not to mention the very real threat of German submarines. Lorenzkowski's essay powerfully details the geography of children's lives during the period, emphasizing that public and domestic space, significantly classed and gendered, was more than a mere backdrop to children's experiences. Through their life-course interviews, participants literally "map out" how spaces and places had a formative impact on their consciousness as they grew up under the threat of war. The primary source accompanying Lorenzkowski's essay, a 2007 oral history interview with William Abraham, who grew up in St John's, demonstrates not only the variety and importance of young people's contributions during the war, but also the vividness and gravity of these memories because they were lived in families and communities. This interview underscores the role that place can play in shaping children's experiences.

Sarah Glassford's essay, focused on young people's more formal contributions to the war effort through the Junior Red Cross (JRC), complements Lorenzkowski's focus on the everyday and informal lives of young Canadians in wartime. Accompanying Glassford's essay is an excerpt from a 1940 edition of the *Junior Red Cross News*, testifying to the array of activities JRC members engaged in and their commitment to these activities. Glassford echoes the question asked in 1919 on the eve of the First World War: in times of war, what is the role of children? Answering it was particularly tricky for organizations such as the Junior Red Cross, which had, in the wake of the brutality of the First World War, embraced the ethic of internationalism and peace. Glassford argues that the interwar emphasis of the Junior Red Cross on peace and international understanding clashed with older traditions and immediate demands, as the Second World War began, of fostering patriotism and war work. Children were acknowledged as central to the war effort even as they were positioned as harbingers of a more peaceful future.

Paired together under the thematic umbrella of children and war, this chapter's two essays demonstrate how varying primary sources—in this case, life-course interviews and more formal textual and institutional files—reveal complex responses to shared events. Lorenzkowski and Glassford emphasize that the war shaped children's lives while they were exploring their neighbourhoods on bikes or playing with friends as surely as it did through their more formal experiences in school and as members of organizations. Both authors insist that children actively engaged in the wartime society. Children were not only metaphors of a hopeful future but contributors to their communities in material ways.

Note

1. www.child-soldiers.org.

The Children's War

BARBARA LORENZKOWSKI

In examining the social history of the Second World War, historians have begun to rediscover age as a category of historical analysis.[1] The story which they tell, in remarkably similar terms, revolves around the mobilization of Canadian school-aged children and youth for the war effort as well as the moral panic that ensued as some children became latch-key "orphans," their soldier fathers fighting abroad, their mothers working long hours in war industries. "Juvenile delinquency" and "youth run wild" emerged as catchwords of a public discourse that juxtaposed the "good" children and the "bad."[2] While these studies have much to teach us about public perceptions of childhood, they reveal little about children's wartime experiences.

Children's own voices remain muted, taking public stage only in the carefully crafted cadences of high school yearbooks or the children's pages of national newspapers.[3]

Yet, if we listen to the "winds of childhood"—as they rustle in childhood memoirs, echo in letters, and ring through oral history interviews—the history of the children's war unfolds along very different narrative lines.[4] As the Canadian writer Janet Lunn notes in her memoir, "Those war years are a very long time ago now and my wartime memories are jumbled in my mind like photographs in a box." Her memories of "newspaper pictures of battles and heroes" mingle with "stories of terrible deprivations in Britain." Memories that taste of adventure—"the ration books, songs, movies, radio programs, the sailors who came to us for home-cooked meals, and the air raid drills"—are "all mixed up" with

Source: From *Occupied St. John's: A Social History of a City at War*. Ed. Steven High (Montreal: McGill-Queens University Press, 2010)

the haunted thoughts of "our neighbour who died on 'The Death March from Bataan,' my cousin Paul, and the boy who came home without his legs."[5] Wartime memories, in other words, do not come packaged in a tidy, linear narrative, and nor do these memories necessarily linger in the social space that historians have probed most extensively, namely the schools. More typically, the story of the children's war, as it is remembered from the vantage point of adulthood, reveals itself in a series of vivid images and vignettes.[. . .][6]

This chapter draws upon 25 life-course interviews conducted by a team of research assistants in St John's in the late summer and fall of 2007.[. . .][7] The chorus of voices that emanates from these interviews is moving not only for its individual "melodies" which were modulated by the story-teller's age, gender, class and religion, but also for its collective evocation of growing up in a city at war. Elsewhere across the continent, as the historian Neil Sutherland has suggested, the war "merely formed the background to the day-to-day immediacy of [children's] lives." But in St John's—as in the seaports of "Montreal, Halifax, Sydney, . . . and, later, Prince Rupert and Vancouver"—the lines between home front and battlefront blurred as children watched warships lining up in the harbour or received word of ships torpedoed in the Battle of the Atlantic, with sailors on board who had joined their family for Sunday dinner just weeks earlier.[8] When George Ledrew stated that "we were part of the war zone in the western hemisphere," he spoke for many of our interview partners for whom memories of the war loomed large—so large indeed that the immediacy of the war in children's lives is tangible even across a temporal divide of more than six decades.

In order to disentangle the many strands of childhood that were so tightly interwoven with larger threads of religion, class, and gender, this chapter charts the maps of childhood in ever-widening concentric circles.[9] After probing children's geographies in the 1930s and 1940s, it turns to the social spaces inhabited jointly by boys and girls as they witnessed the coming of the war and the subsequent transformation of "small-town" St John's into a city that seemed to be in perpetual motion,

with warships crowding the harbour, platoons of servicemen parading on the streets, and servicemen "invading" family homes as boarders and frequent dinner guests. The study then maps the gendered worlds of childhood; for gender sharply demarcated the ways in which children experienced the war and interacted with servicemen stationed in town. Although girls and boys alike marvelled at the novel dinner guests who read teacups after dinner, helped youngsters with their French homework and took children out to the movies or sliding on the hills, only boys regularly interacted with sailors, soldiers and airmen beyond the realm of the family home. [. . .]

The final part of this study examines the city's invasion by motor vehicles that re-shaped local maps of childhood yet again as soaring traffic accidents prompted a public debate on which public spaces were appropriate for children and which were not. In foreshadowing later-century debates on the reformulation of public space into an adult space, within which children's movements would be tightly regulated, the stories of children's lives in wartime St John's tell both of the remarkable freedom in the city which children (and, particularly, boys) enjoyed and of subsequent attempts to curtail this freedom in the name of public safety. The new "geography of danger" emphasized the threat posed by speeding vehicles and sought to regulate and limit children's access to public space for the sake of their own protection.[10]

Children's Geographies

"The town," remembers Ann Abraham, "was so small before the war."[11] Small, too, was the harbour that would soon be crowded with corvettes and destroyers, making the "few outport schooners that still came in" looking "out of place now, small and unimportant," as Helen Porter recalls in her childhood memoirs.[12] Barely 2 kilometres long and 700 metres wide, the "snug, almost land-locked St John's harbour" was the heart of a city of 40,000 people whose principal stores clustered along Water Street.[13] From here, the cobblestone streets climbed the steep hills that surrounded the bay, each lined with "endless rows" of houses as Mona Wilson, Canada's Red Cross Assistant Commissioner, wrote to her sister Jane in September 1940.[14] To Wilson, who had just arrived in St John's to tend to the needs of Canadian servicemen, the rhythms of town seemed reminiscent of an earlier time. The clatter of horseshoes echoed in the roads as horse-drawn carriages delivered groceries and coals around town.[15] In the winter months, the horses strained to pull the carts, laden with coal, up over the hills. When the horses slipped on the icy streets, the drivers "would be beating and driving up the horses, and it was terrible," Ann Abraham recalls.[16] In the summer, the iceman made his rounds once a week and when he came, Eileen Collins remembers, "the kids would crowd around to ask for a chip of ice. That was your treat."[17] Cars were a rare sight on the streets, ruled by groups of youngsters from the neighbourhood who played until darkness fell.[18]

Many of our women interviewees recall rhythms of childhood that revolved around home, school, and church. Their younger selves did not question the strictures of religion that formed a "natural" part of their week. "You woke up on six in the morning," Ann Abraham remembers, "and your Sunday clothes were at the bottom of your bed, and you put them on, and you went to church."[19] Religion circumscribed their lives, curtailing both physical movement and vocal expression. "Being a Protestant, you were not allowed to skate or slide on Sundays," Patricia Winsor remembers, whereas Eileen Collins, who was educated by nuns, recalls the annual retreats of her youth. For an entire week, she and her sisters "couldn't speak, either at school or at home. And we listened to lectures, and read holy books, and went to the first mass of the day at 6.30 in the mornings. There were four girls in our family. Mum must have thought she was in heaven!"[20]

But since class, not religion, determined residency patterns in much of the city, children did play with youngsters of different denominations on their neighbourhood streets. "Even though half the street was Roman Catholic, and half was Anglican," recalls Tom Goodyear, "they were fairly close-knit." Once, as a boy, he walked into the neighbour's home next door to find the entire family kneeling on the kitchen floor. "And I didn't know what to do . . .

and I closed the door, and I went home, and I told my mother." He learned that his neighbours were saying the rosary. Later, his mother gently admonished him: "My son, it wouldn't have done you any harm if you had knelt down beside them. So, that's the type of woman that she was."[21] Jim Prim's best friend "went to a different school because he was not the same religion," while David Edwards took a Roman-Catholic girl to the school dance, despite his mother's persistent admonitions: "Dave, don't you think you could find a nice Spencer girl to take to the dance?"[22]

The oral history interviews at the core of this study provide tantalizing evidence that the stark denominational boundaries in 1940s St John's could be subtly subverted; for children did not necessarily abide by the rules of the adult world. [. . .] In creating communities of childhood, the children of St John's forged friendships across denominational boundaries.

Chasms of wealth separated the Water Street merchants and the city's educated elites from "the average Newfoundland worker, for whom life was a perpetual struggle against geography, the weather and mounting debts," as the historian David MacKenzie has written.[23] Children were well versed in reading markers of social class, be it an affluent neighbourhood address or the clothes worn by passer-byes that projected either respectability or poverty. The most inescapable sign of social status was their father's line of work. Working-class children whose parents had scrambled to send their firstborns to one of the city's private colleges dreaded the first day of each school year when they had to reveal their father's occupation. Forty years later, Helen Porter still remembers "the way everybody giggled, or nearly everybody, when someone like Vera or Freddie Smity replied, in a very low voice, a cook or a longshoreman." Her well-to-do classmates who came from families of wholesalers, manufacturer's agents, doctors, or general merchants also chuckled when Porter identified her father as "Chief Rater at the Freight Office." Each year, Helen's mother would emphasize her husband's formal title: "*Chief Rater*, don't forget. I'm not going to have them laughing at you." Each year, with the careless cruelty of children, Helen's classmates laughed anyway, although the girl never told her mother.[24]

In middle- and upper-class homes, children were barred from the front parlour when their parents entertained visitors. They quietly served tea or sat on the stairs, watching their parents hosting "Navy people" or the officers of the Quebec Rifles. Only the very young were admitted into this adult world, as was five-year-old Frankie O'Neil in her great-uncle's mansion who sat in her school uniform "on some officer's knees with my white bloomers just showing . . . passing out peanuts" to the guests.[25] More modest homes did not allow for such a clear delineation of adult and children's spaces. Here, domestic life revolved around the kitchen, often the only heated room in the house where the family's radio set brought news from the war.

Class determined the outer limits of children's worlds. Youngsters from affluent backgrounds enjoyed trips to the countryside in the family car, travelled to Britain on family holidays, and pictured their older selves pursuing higher education or professional training outside the country, thereby following in the footsteps of family members and friends who had studied at Bishop's University (Quebec) or trained as nurses at St Vincent's Hospital in New York.

Regardless of their social class, girls "knew" that their working years represented merely an interlude between school and marriage. [. . .] Without exception, the women and men who lived through the war years as children and youth describe mothers who worked as full-time homemakers. [. . .] To run a household with several youngsters was a time-consuming operation that invested mothers with great parental authority. In a recurrent theme, our interviewees describe their mothers as "efficient and organized," as the family's financial manager and "dominant decision-maker." As Jim Prim puts it succinctly, "Mother was devoted to us, and she called the shots."[26] With mothers being bound to the home by either custom or necessity, the traditional family remained intact throughout the war years. As a result, the moral panic over "eight-hour orphans" whose mother had found work in lucrative war industries never entered the public discourse in

Newfoundland. In six years of wartime coverage, the St John's *Evening Telegram* did not once evoke fears of an "epidemic" of juvenile delinquency—due to motherless and fatherless homes—that was a common refrain in Canadian and American newspapers [. . .][27]

With memories of the Great Depression still vivid in their minds, working-class children and youth in St John's measured their family's well-being in neither money nor consumer goods, but in food and occupational stability. "We never had any money, but we always had food," Helen Fogwill Porter remembers whose father was one of "a half dozen men—the most" from her south side neighbourhood who worked in an office. Each morning, he would dress up to work and put on his tie. Even when his salary was cut by 15 dollars during the depression, he invited beggars into the home "for a cup of tea" while his wife and mother-in-law offered them buns of homemade bread. Although money was tight, young Helen Porter felt secure in the knowledge that "My father had a steady job. If you had a steady job, you were respected and envied."[28] The barter economy that dominated Newfoundland's outports persisted in working-class neighbourhoods in St John's. "I often heard my mother saying that there were times before the war when father brought home fifty cents a week," Gilbert Oakley recalls whose father worked as a sail-maker on Water Street. And yet, "we always had plenty to eat." In the fall, when the schooners returned from Labrador, "people would bring salted salmon, salt cod fish, peach-berries. And they paid when they got their money."[29] In Jim Prim's family, whose breadwinner had gone to sea with an English merchant company, the pangs of hunger were held at bay by the vegetables grown and animals raised on his grandmother's farm in the west end. "We never had too much, but we always had enough to eat," Jim Prim says in a tribute to his "pioneer" grandmother who "taught me the fundamentals of farming and rearing animals and hard work. [. . .] Much like their contemporaries in British Columbia, whose childhood the historian Neil Sutherland has probed so perceptively, our interviewees—most of them born in 1920s and 1930s—"focused on the immediate aspects of their lives" and "took their circumstances, no matter how harsh, as a given in life."[30] They took pride in their families' self-sufficiency and described the casual back and forth in close-knit neighbourhoods.

It was in the home that the lives of adults and children intersected in patterns that were unique to each family. Given the young age of our interviewees during the war years, it is not surprising that both women and men situated their younger selves firmly within family networks. Women described how they turned to their mothers for advice and affection, while men fondly evoked father-son outings in which close bonds were forged. "Father," reminiscences Paul O'Neill, "was the kindest man I ever came across." Only once did he chastise his two young boys, whipping them with his slipper after their wild jumping destroyed the bed's spring box. "But this was the only time he ever raised his hands, and afterwards, he was full of remorse," Paul O'Neill smiles. "Mother, on the other hand, she did not spare the rod." By contrast, other male interviewees characterized their fathers as distant, aloof, and taciturn, while paying tribute to their warm and joyous warm mothers.[31]

Bonds of love and affection cut across gender lines. Helen Porter's father regularly took his daughter, a ferocious reader, to the local lending library "over" on the city's north side and celebrated her thirteenth birthday by inviting her along to Toronto where he was attending a railway convention. Patricia Winsor remembers her father, a police officer, as "a gentle giant" who treated the family to humorous stories about disorderly servicemen.[32] Indeed, whether children gravitated towards the collective "we" of their family or their peer group seemed to be a question more of class than of gender. In large working-class families that could afford neither house-maids nor nurse-maids to alleviate the burdens of home care, men and women stated matter-of-factly that "With a big family, the attention has to be spread around. You made your own way generally." Or, as Eileen Collins, put it, as a middle child in a family of five children "You are really ignored because mom and dad have been busy with the first two and take you for granted, but it is benign neglect, which is nice." Importantly, such

"benign neglect" did not preclude regular and affectionate interaction between parents and children.[33]

Age determined how far children were allowed to venture from the family home. When Eileen Collins and her siblings "stayed out after dark when we were small, mother would have—now, this sounds barbaric—but she would meet us at the door with a cord of the electric iron in her hand, and it was folded up, and as we each came in after dark we got a whack on the leg as we ran past her and up the stairs." As children grew older, the territory which they could explore on their own expanded, yet its outer limits remained defined by parental edicts so clearly understood that they rarely needed spelling out. James Walsh, for one, who freely roamed the farmlands which surrounded his family home, knew that he was not expected to "spend much time in the east end of the city at my age."[34] When a member of our interview team light-heartedly inquired whether his respondent ever "got into trouble," thereby hoping to elicit memories of mischievous childhood adventures, the answer illuminated the strictures of an earlier era that placed a high stake in personal reputation. As Jim Prim firmly stated, transgressions carried social repercussions. "When I was growing up, I never had any trouble and my friends never had any trouble. When somebody got into trouble with the police, they were marked. Very rarely did you hear of anybody getting in trouble with the police."[35]

Consumed by the rhythms of their own world, children paid little attention to the growing international tensions in Europe in the mid-1930s. Their fathers, in turn, were reluctant to share stories of their own battlefield experiences during the First World War. [. . .] David Edwards muses that "I don't remember my father talking much about the war," although his father's friends could sometimes be enticed to share carefully-edited stories, "They never told you stories about death or injuries or fellows being dismembered. Stories that they told were happy memories, little parties."[36] As the horrors of the battlefields did not lend themselves to "tales of heroism and danger," many World War I veterans lapsed into silence or sought out the company of fellow veterans.[37] Despite their father's reticence, the children who walked the city's streets encountered reminders of war's horrific toll. To this day, James Walsh can picture World War I veterans in St John's "with legs missing and arms missing" and their wooden legs painted green. [. . .] Little wonder that the young boy feared for his father when war was declared: "I thought I am going to lose my dad."[38] In fact, his father was spared from serving active duty. Age, poor health, or their status as married men with dependents prevented the fathers of our interviewees from enlisting, an experience shared by nearly half of the male volunteers in Newfoundland who were declared medically unfit during the years of the Second World War.[39] As their fathers supported the war effort by volunteering for public duty as air-raid wardens, children witnessed their brothers, uncles, cousins, and neighbourhood boys marching off to war, their absence a painful reminder of the all-encompassing nature of the conflict.[40]

A City at War

It is the voices they remember. When Britain declared war on Germany on 3 September 1939, Neville Chamberlain's radio address to the British nation was carried into homes across Newfoundland where eight-year-old David Baird listened "to the voice coming out of the radio," its solemnity lending a personal air to the abstraction that was war. "When the war was declared, it was a speech by Winston Churchill that I recall," remembers James Walsh who was only six at the time. "I didn't exactly recall what he had said but it was his voice that we heard. [. . .]"[41] The immediacy of the spoken word that emanated from radio sets captivated youngsters who also recall the grave countenance of adults. Fourteen-year-old Eileen Collins was staying at a teacher's summer house for a dance rehearsal as one evening she and her classmates "were all shooed out of the house and told not to come in until after the news was over. Her husband was listening intently to the news bulletin. This was when Poland was being invaded. That was my recognition that something was wrong with the world." [. . .] Whether it was the novelty of the medium or the fact that news travelled quickly on airwaves, the radio loomed large in childhood

memories. Eight-year-old Paul O'Neill never had a chance to perform the play he was staging with friends on 3 September 1939 as "Dad came down and said: 'There will be no audience there tonight. There is war in Europe. Newfoundlanders will be involved.' And we went down and listened to the radio."[42]

To listen to the radio was a communal act, with families gathering in kitchens and dining rooms and neighbours dropping by to listen to the news.[43] [. . .] "Once the news came on, there was no talking," Gilbert Oakley says, "You were not allowed to say a word."[44] In a similar vein, Patricia Winsor describes how "everything went quiet" once the radio was turned on. "The children were given a book to sit down and read so you didn't ask questions," as radio announcers analyzed troop movements and discussed the fickle fortunes of war.[45]

The radio also enlivened the sombre mood. Children listened to *Superman*, *The Inner Sanctum*, and, together with their parents, tuned into *The House of Peter McGregor*. "It was marvellous," Stuart Fraser says of the shows that brought American popular culture into the St John's households. "Every Sunday, these shows would be on and every Sunday in our house, we sat at the fire on a winter evening, and mother did her knitting, and dad did some wood-carving, and I played or read, and we listened to these shows."[46]

The American radio station Voice of the United States (VOUS) on Fort Pepperrell carried popular tunes into Newfoundland homes, offering an alternative to the Sunday hymns that had previously aired on the Voice of Newfoundland (VONF). "Music would cheer you up," says George Ledrew who, like other St John's youngsters, regularly tuned into VOUS. Children quickly memorized the patriotic tunes broadcast on the radio, singing songs of victory—"Keep the homefires burning" and the war's unofficial anthem "There will always be an England." [. . .]

Probably the most painful social change wrought by the war was the departure of the city's young men. Some grade 11 students marched straight from their high school graduation to the recruitment office, at the tender age of 17.[47] Before they left, "those slick-haired, eager-faced boys" had their photographs taken which later graced the pages of the St John's *Evening Telegram*. In her scrapbooks, which Helen Blundon lovingly assembled during the war, the faces of her brother, her cousin, her future husband and his two brothers and "boys from practically all over Newfoundland" gaze at the observer, their youthfulness as yet unmarred by the ravishes of the war. "Even those who came back," Helen Porter contemplates, "never wore quite the same expression on their faces again."[48] Pride and heart-break mingled as brothers, cousins, uncles, and boys from "our street" enlisted in the armed forces. "I was twelve years old, and I had four brothers, and it was such a traumatic time," remembers Vicki Cheeseman who, at 11 years of age, was the youngest of eight siblings. Two of her brothers went overseas, one of whom went "missing for quite a while in Africa," while an older sister worked as a nurse in London, England, as the city was reeling under sustained German bombing attacks. [. . .]

The war retained its glamour only if it remained at a safe emotional distance. When some of the older girls at Bishop Feild School joined the navy and air force, "we were so proud of them," remembers Ann Abraham. "When they left, we had a special prayer for their safe return." While young Ann marvelled at the transformation of her former schoolmates who proudly donned their uniforms, Helen Porter fell apart when her cousin Harold joined the Royal Navy, clinging "to him like a baby" when the time came to bid good-bye. "Harold and two of his brothers and just about every eligible man on the South Side . . . joined up," she remembers, "most of them in the Royal Navy, a few in the Merchant Marine. Growing up near the sea as they had done, ships were second nature to them; it seemed more natural to fight on the water than on a grubby battle field."[49]

[. . .] The Royal Canadian Navy quietly made its entrance into town in 1941 to make final preparations for the "Newfoundland Escort Force" that would soon shepherd large convoys of ships across the North Atlantic.[50] It was the far more dramatic arrival of the American troopship, the Edmund B. Alexander on 29 January 1941 that captured the public imagination.[51] Mothers, fathers, and uncles took youngsters down to the south side to admire the "big spectacle" which was only enhanced when the sailors gave a band concert on the wharf and then marched through town, handing out chocolate bars. To the children, memories of muscular American servicemen with white, strong teeth soon became associated with the taste of coke and chocolate bars, "the likes of which we had never seen in our lives."[52] On 7 April 1941 the troopship finally opened its gates to local residents who eagerly explored the troop ship, a captured German luxury liner.[53] For the next four years, the harbour would remain "a magnet for us kids," Paul O'Neill recalls. "We all felt we were in the front lines because of the ships and the convoys."[54]

[. . .] Whereas men's memories of the harbour are laced with a sense of adventure, women recall the harbour as a site of social occasions. So closely are memories of the war intertwined with the harbour that Eileen Collins took members of our interview team on an extended harbour tour, painting vivid pictures of wooden wharves—"rickety in many cases"—where, today, only concrete structures stand.[55] After mass on Sundays, Collins remembers, "mom and dad would take all for a walk" around the finger wharfs. "Dad had lived the first few years of his life on the South Coast, so he loved the water and the ships. And he always had a little chat with one of the skippers."[56] For Helen Porter, who grew up on the south side of St John's, the harbour was a place both poetic and prosaic. Her "memories of a clock-calm harbour, cloudless skies and thick clusters of blueberries on the Hill" mingle with "the smells of fish and oil and fat that drifted upward on certain winds" and the day her cousin "Dot and I watched some boys throwing stones at a plain, thick-lipped girl from the Battery because she, according to them, 'did it' with sailors."[57]

Most men on the south side worked for merchant companies, made barrels in small cooperages, or lined up at the wharves each morning "unloading coal or salt boats at Morey's or Wyatt's." Their children made the harbour their playground, transforming it into "a skating rink, a swimming pool, a place to catch tomcods, a place to skip stones." In the war years, southside boys too young to enlist made a fortune selling coke bottles to American servicemen, while southside girls skipped on the smooth surface of the wharves, regularly inviting "one of the free French fellows to come over and run into the ropes and skip a bit."

Parents placed few strictures on their children's play at the harbour, which they regarded as an extension of the neighbourhood. There were limits, of course, to parental indulgence. When Helen Porter and her cousin Dot took a ride on "a weatherbeaten old waterboat . . . our families feared we must be neophyte scarlet women to trust ourselves to a bunch of merchant seamen way outside the narrows where nobody would be able to hear you yell for help."[58] Wartime censorship prevented the local papers from evoking the sights and sounds of the harbour that figure so prominently in childhood memories of the war.

When the first American servicemen stepped off their troopship, the Edmund B. Alexander, in January 1941, the city's children marvelled at the newcomers' strange attire. "They had these huge, hooded jackets," chuckles Eileen Collins and "socks that were half an inch thick. We didn't know what to make of them." But, she continued, "as soon as they discovered that our climate, even in winter-time, was much milder than many had expected back home," they left their parkas in the closet and did not even put on over-shoes in the slushy St John's winters.[59]

Children and adults alike judged servicemen according to the clothes they wore, contrasting American style with the baggy, shabby uniforms worn by Canadian soldiers. As women and men remember in unison, the Americans were "dressed to kill," looked "very sharp," and impressed with their "lovely caps" and "jazzy uniforms."[60] "These guys were polite, beautifully dressed, well dressed," recalls Margaret Kearney, while young Helen Porter noted, with the sharp eyes of a 12-year-old, the closely cropped hair of the American soldiers and their strong, white teeth.[61] By contrast, Canadian uniforms attracted unflattering commentary as children—well versed in reading clothes as a marker of social status—described "baggy khaki pants brought in tight around the ankles, badly fitting tunics . . . and huge clumsy boots."[62] Such categorizing

was a popular pastime in wartime St John's where Canada's Red Cross Assistant Commissioner, Mona Wilson, charged with outfitting survivors of German submarine attacks, "always tried to find out in advance the nationality of the men who were coming in. If they were Norwegians, the largest sizes in clothes were laid out for the burly Scandinavian, if they were Chinese, the very smallest, and the brightest coloured shirts for the negroes."[63] [. . .]

At Christmastime, the local press encouraged the "[m]others of lads who are now abroad . . . to fill in the empty chair at the dinner table on Christmas Day" with "some other mother's boys," coaching its appeal for wartime solidarity in the language of universal motherhood, replete with the slogan "Let us invite a Service man."[64] Each year, on Christmas day, as Patricia Wilson remembers, "my father and I and my brother would walk down to Caribou Hut," a popular hostel for servicemen, to "take these gentlemen" home for Christmas dinner. In the privacy of their homes, children caught intimate glimpses of the sailors and soldiers stationed in town. "One Christmas," Patricia Winsor remembers, "a sailor had a really great, big, bushy red beard and my brother was paralyzed. He wouldn't go near him. He wouldn't sit at the table." Another year, a guest agreed to read tea cups after dinner, predicting the young girl's future with "almost frightening" accuracy. In meeting servicemen up close, children were impressed with gestures and appearances, recalling the politeness of a British officer who, even "in the stormiest days . . . always took off his hat before he came in through the door," or the hairy chest of the Canadian soldier who boarded with Patricia Winsor's family and stitched together a rain coat for his own little boy back home.[65]

Visiting servicemen acted as surrogate brothers for the young, cutting a Christmas tree in the woods, pulling it home on a slide, and stuffing the children's Christmas stockings with forbidden treats. When young Ann Abraham found chewing gum in her stockings on Christmas morning, it confirmed her belief in Santa Claus since her mother would never have slipped gum into the stockings. "My mother did hate chewing gum. . . . It was like a cow, chewing gum. It was a terrible thing." "It never entered my mind," adds Ann Abraham, that the "six burly sailors" who had walked into the house on Christmas Eve "had brought a whole lot of stuff for our stockings." The servicemen whom children encountered in their homes were not the "unruly men," described in reams of newsprint, but young fellows who "missed family and children," took joy in taking the children out sliding on a brisk winter afternoon and assisted Vicki Cheeseman with her French-language homework. That June, the young girl brought home a 98 in French.[66]

Children's frequent, if casual, encounters with servicemen put a personal face on the battles of war. Ann Abraham and David Edwards both remark on the haunting absence of young sailors who "had been at the house and they never came back. And you know that their ship had been sunk, whereas others would come back again."[67] As Mona Wilson, Canada's Red Cross Assistant Commissioner in St John's, scrambled to provide for the needs of survivors from German submarine attacks, whose number had reached close to 6,000 by 1943, children, too, learned about stories of death and survival.[68] For Margaret Kearney, the Battle of the Atlantic wore the face of Ted, a young sailor from Quebec, whom her mother had met at the servicemen hostel, the Knights of Columbus. Whenever his Corvette lay anchor in the harbour, Ted visited the Kearney's home. "The last time Ted came in," Margaret Kearney remembers, "he must have come through the front door—it must have been evening—and he sat right down in the den and did not speak to anybody. He just sat there. And mother stayed in the den with him (there was a fire in the den) and somebody made him a cup of tea, and he still did not speak. We learned later that there had been a terrible battle out in the Atlantic and that the Corvette had picked up as many survivors as it could. But it couldn't take any more and they had to leave servicemen in the water." [. . .]

Gliding through the dark waters of the Atlantic and attacking both civilian and military vessels, German submarines became synonymous with death and destruction. In keeping with the tenet of secrecy, sailors on shore leave in St John's had to cover up the names of their ships, proudly displayed on little rosettes they used to carry; for "you weren't supposed to know what ship was in port," as Ann Abraham remembers. Far more difficult to conceal was the destruction wrought by the Battle of the Atlantic as it freely floated on the waters of the harbour. When 10-year-old James Walsh visited the harbour in the early 1940s, he saw "ships in various states of destruction. I can remember one ship—the bow had been torpedoed—and I can remember a fisherman going right through with his boat." Gilbert Oakley, as well, was struck by the sight of the damaged boats in the harbour that had narrowly escaped a German submarine attack: "There was one that had a lot of paper on it, and there was a torpedo that went right through it. And the fishermen used to call them bomb-boats and they would bring sailors to the boats, tied in the middle of the harbour" for a fee of 20 cents so that they could inspect the damaged boats.

What the historian William Tuttle Jr has called a "flashbulb memory, the freeze-framing of an exceptionally emotional event down to the most incidental detail," captures some of the iconic moments that burned themselves into the memory of St John's youngsters, irrespective of their gender, class, or religion.[69] In 1942, disaster struck twice. On 14 October 1942, the ferry Caribou was torpedoed on its regular run between North Sydney, Nova Scotia, and Port aux Basques, Newfoundland, and sank in the Cabot Strait. Among the 130 victims were family friends, neighbours, and acquaintances, including the "really good friend" of Helen Porter's cousin Harold, the brother of one of Ann Abraham's classmates and a family friend of David Edward. The son of a widow, living across the street of James Walsh and his family, survived with only a broken arm, one among about 100 survivors who were pulled to safety from the frigid waters of the Atlantic. "He was in the Royal Navy and he was coming home when the Caribou was torpedoed," James Walsh remembers.[70] Stories quickly spread of men, women, and children "clinging to life rafts, pieces of wreckage, and the one lifeboat that managed to stay afloat. Some were crying, others were dying. Still others were shouting the names of loved ones, hoping to hear the reply 'I'm here!'

Some did."[71] Only six months after the sinking of the *Caribou*, 13-year-old Helen Porter accompanied her father to a railway convention in Toronto, a celebratory occasion that turned into "the most frightening experience of my life." To guarantee the ferry's safety, a destroyer and a Corvette sailed alongside while a plane flew overhead. In a raging storm, the journey took 13 hours. Porter begged her father to fly home after the convention, an impossible proposition given the family's tight finances.[72]

On 13 December 1942, one hundred people perished in a devastating fire that destroyed a local servicemen haunt, the Knights of Columbus hostel. Across town on this winter evening, children and adults were listening to *The Barn Dance*, a popular show that was broadcast every Saturday live from the servicemen hostel. "We were listening to it that night," Helen Porter recalls, "everybody listened to it, and suddenly you heard screams." "All of a sudden there was screams," remembers James Walsh, "and then we lost radio contact." As 11-year-old Paul O'Neill pulled away the heavy blackout curtains to glance out of the window of his home, children across town stepped outside onto the streets or "ran to the back of the house" to look at the sky. In strikingly similar terms, eye-witnesses describe "that red glow . . . in the sky" and recount apocalyptic scenes: "flames, smoke going up," "flames coming out of the sky," and flames so fiery that they "scorched all the houses on the other side of the road." [. . .] St John's youngsters would be able to recount, over six decades later, the sight, sound, and smell of the Knights of Columbus fire. More than even the arrival of the *Edmund B. Fitzgerald* or the sinking of the *Caribou*, the fire acted as a "flashbulb memory" that encapsulated the emotional intensity of the war years.

Gendered Spaces

[. . .] The campaign to mobilize children and youth for the war effort reached youngsters of either sex. Schoolchildren listened to principals who provided daily reports on the latest battles;[73] they prepared their very own "little diary of the war" by copying newspaper headlines into scrapbooks;[74] and they traced the movement of allied troops. "They used to have war maps," James Walsh recalls, "and every evening we used to sit around the living room with the war map on the floor and listening to the radio and hear the reports of the advance and sticking the flags in the area. We had this war map with flags plastered all over to indicate the advances made by the allies."[75] In predictably gendered ways, schools called upon girls to knit socks, make fruitcakes and, after the war brides arrived in mid-1945, assist the young mothers with children in tow. "I remember these poor creatures getting off the boat," Ann Abraham says, "and that was before the days of disposable diapers, and most of them had one or two babies with them. The smell of urine, it was terrible."[76] Meanwhile boys were called upon to join the cadets or collect aluminum and scrap metal for the war effort.[77]

Yet such organized mobilization was not what fired boys' imagination. In keeping with the tenets of boy culture, boys were drawn to public spaces where they could play and explore beyond the watchful eyes of adults. While teachers and principals dissected the fortunes of war, boys pictured—in colourful fashion—the fate of the German foe should he happen to fall into their hands. "On the way home from school, during wartime, we argued the war," Paul O'Neill remembers. "'What would you do with Hitler?' 'I put him into a hand-slicer and slice him slowly to pieces.'" With four other boys from the neighbourhood, Paul O'Neill sold candies and drinks and brought the proceeds to a local radio station that awarded each donation with a brief appearance on air: "'And now the Cochrane Street gang, what do you boys got?' 'We've got $5.23.' 'Wonderful, wonderful, that's for the boys overseas. We are buying smokes for the boys overseas.'" The time in the spotlight was short—"just long enough to say who you were and where you were from and how much money you made,"—but satisfying nonetheless. "We felt we were doing a great job for the war effort. We had one sale every couple of weeks," Paul O'Neill recounts.[78]

Nothing excited boys more than the enforcement of blackout orders and the staging of air-raid drills. "Every night," Stuart Fraser recalls, "I had to put up shades on the window—beaver-board—so that no light would show." Girls, as well, were "going around [the house] every night, putting up shutters and making sure drapes were closed," but only boys appear to have accompanied their fathers on their nightly rounds as wardens.[79] David Edwards describes "going out with [my father] in the neighbourhood, checking on the windows of our neighbours to see whether there was no light shining through. . . . And I remember the next day, my father saying: 'Now I have to go to Mrs. Brown and I have to go to Mrs. Whoever, tell her that last night, her lights were shining.'" Gilbert Oakley, in turn, who was only 12 years old at war's end, needed no formal appointment as warden: "When we were children and we saw lights coming out of somebody's window, we knock at the door and tell them. We are on the door telling them, there is light shining out."[80] The utter darkness into which the city plunged each night was punctuated only by air-raid drills that simulated a German bombing attack.

The drama of civil defence drew boys out onto public, darkened streets and the wide, open spaces of the countryside. By contrast, women's stories of blackout and air-raid drills unfold in the domestic setting of family homes and home-like schools where "the whole school would go down to the basement and have a concert" during an air-raid practice.[81] The boundary between "private" and "public," which a generation of historians has called into question, held more than rhetorical significance for children and youth in wartime St John's. In the sheltered space of the schools—themselves an extension of the world of domesticity—girls assumed warden duties of a kind by ringing the bells that signalled their classmates to head for the basement.[82] Yet they still moved and acted within a space built for children, but regulated by adults. The freedoms to wander, to explore, and to experiment that boys so confidently claimed as their own, were denied to girls, or, in the very least, severely circumscribed.

This is not to say that girls preferred to play indoors; for both girls and boys roamed the city's open spaces. On the eve of the Second World War, the rural outskirts of the city had not yet been swallowed by suburban developments and local children found nature just a stone-throw away. Eileen Collins encountered goats grazing on the hills of the south side when her father took the family for Sunday walks, while Ann Abraham remembers "running through thistle fields" with her friends and hiking and cooking meals on fire-sites with her fellow Girl Guides: "It was so easy. You were near enough to the country that you could do these activities."[83] When Vicki Cheeseman spent the summers on her grandparents' farm in Topsail, she "could ride the horse down the street to get a drink" after she had performed her household chores. At home in Bishop's Falls, she muses, "There was no such thing as indoors. Summer or winter, you played outdoors." Cars were few, everybody walked, and children roamed the streets and explored the rural outskirts far away from the watchful eyes of adults, but usually accompanied by groups of friends or, at the very least, a sibling. Then, as now, there was safety in numbers.

In her moving childhood memoirs *Below the Bridge: Memories of the South Side of St John's*, Helen Porter makes an eloquent case for a world of play that was inhabited jointly by girls and boys. "Here, then, is another way in which the South Side did not conform to the North American standard," she writes, describing how "most of the games we played were totally integrated. . . . One's status as a player depended more on skill and prowess than on sex."[84] Mostly, however, our interviewees describe worlds of childhood in which the other sex played a marginal role at best. "Girls!" laughs James Walsh, "They were a nuisance, early on. Especially, a buddy of mine who had a sister and she persisted in following us around. I recall he used to throw stones at her, trying to drive her away." "We never had much to do with girls," concurs Norman Crane. "They never went fishing with us. They used to screw up their faces when we'd put a worm on a hook. We were always out in the woods or up the South Side Hills and we were active outdoors."[85]

[. . .] The arrival of thousands of sailors and soldiers in wartime St John's provided boys with a stage on which to enact the rough-and-tumble world of boy culture. Stories of unruly servicemen reached the ears of Patricia Winsor in the tranquility of her home where her father, a policeman, regaled his family to tales of drunken sailors and soldiers who, once sobered up, began fighting with one another in overcrowded cells "because one was a navy and one a soldier" and "they were loyal to their uniforms." In the social world of boyhood, these figures of lore—and the material traces they left behind—assumed a tangible presence that spoke of danger, physical prowess, and naughty allure. Young Gilbert Oakley walked over to the site of an airplane crash and sifted through the broken pieces: "There were parts of the airplane everywhere, and I picked up a part of an aluminum pipe that had broken off." The boy painted his wartime souvenir yellow and held onto it "for years" afterwards. Meanwhile, in the city's northern outskirts, James Walsh marvelled at the soldiers, practicing manoeuvres in the countryside nearby his home. "You see them going through the farmland, and going with their rifles, and there was live ammunition all over the place. It's a wonder we weren't killed." Happily ignoring the danger, James Walsh and his friends picked up live ammunition, placed it into tree-holes, and "discharged the bullets" with a nail, placed atop a lengthy stick. Both boys began smoking during the war, a "manly" vice facilitated by the platoons of soldiers who littered the streets with cigarette butts. "You could pick them up on the streets," James Walsh recalls. "They were so cheap. They tossed them all over the place." Gilbert Oakley recalls asking an American soldier coming down the hill "for a cigarette and he gave us a cigarette each. . . . We used to go down to Water Street to pick up cigarette butts and my logic was: if anybody's got TB, they'd be out in the hospital, the sanatorium. And I had two boxes—one with matches, the other one for the big cigarette butts." As recent research has suggested, smoking remained a manly habit well into the 1940s, its puffs of white smoke and distinctive odour demarcating men's and women's spaces and, by extension, the social worlds of boys and girls.[86]

In wartime St John's, boys and men shared social spaces from which girls, by nature of their sex, were excluded. David Baird can recall the day he walked into "the boys' washroom with the showers" at his school, Bishop Feild's, "and there was a guy standing there, shaving, stripped to the waist, and he had the Lord's Prayer tattooed on his back. That was one of my first impressions. He must have been a sailor and

how he got into Bishop's Feild, I don't know. He must have walked right in." [. . .] Yet, above all, it was the washrooms that beckoned the youngsters. "They had toilets there," recounts Paul O'Neill, "and we'd love to go in there and read what was written on the walls. As kids, we thought it was marvellous because all these poems were written on the walls by naughty Americans." Thomas Doyal, in turn, "being of an inquisitive age," loved to lurk around the outside perimeters of "Camp Alexander" to befriend American servicemen stationed in town. "Soldiers being soldiers," he says, "we would be passed chocolate bars the likes of which we had never seen in our lives—O'Henry, Hershey Bars, and coke in bottles. And, of course, we'd be in seventh heaven and we go back day after day." One young soldier grew so fond of the boy that he kept in touch by correspondence, his three letters to Thomas Doyal—dated 30 July 1945, 1 October 1946, and 5 January 1947—lovingly preserved to this day.[87]

In a self-described "garrison town" in which Canadian and American servicemen peopled the streets, as did Allied sailors of every conceivable nationality, the men in uniform were never construed as dangerous in private or public conversations over childhood. On the contrary, if we are to believe the indignant writings in the *Evening Telegram*, it was the servicemen who required protection from "children carrying out a persistent campaign of cadging for coppers, cigarettes or various other things. Strangers, in particular the sailors and soldiers, are almost exclusively the objects of these attentions."[88] In his characteristic bluntness, "Spike," the public voice of American servicemen, wrote in the city's *Evening Telegram* that "there are, definitely too, too many ragamuffins, rascals and pests in general, in the form of small boys, who spoil the time with their everlasting begging."[89]

[. . .] Unlike boys' carefree interactions with servicemen, young women internalized rules of propriety that governed their behaviour at movie theatres, dancing halls, and servicemen hostels. "My older sister, Mary, worked as a volunteer hostess at the U.S.O.," Frank Kennedy writes in his memoirs, "and every night after work a different serviceman walked her home in the blackout. They never got inside the house, though, my mother saw to that."[90] To guard female virtue, parents and employers enforced curfews, meant to shield young women from the moral dangers of the night.[91] Despite these restrictions, women recall a freedom of movement that was palpable. "We had a freedom in the city," marvels Margaret Kearney. "We could walk anywhere in town. We could walk on Water Street in the evening at Christmas time and I never remember any aberrations. As young girls—grade 8 or 9—we would go to each other's houses and we would walk home, and we would leave their house at 11 o'clock in the evening and walk home and feel safe and not be frightened."[92] Eileen Collins, in turn, recalls the evening she "walked home in the dark with a flashlight," accompanied by two girlfriends. "So we were walking home, the three of us from a later movie. We dropped off Alice and when we got to Rawyln's Cross, all the troops were coming out from the airport, the party-goers. They were noisy. And we were scared and we started to run. When we stopped, there was this little sailor . . . and he said: 'Girls, if it made you feel any better, I would walk with you.' And he did. And Peg lived on Circular Road—her father was a judge—and there was a dark corner at the end of Circular Road, and we walked down and walked up, and we stood on the street talking for a few moments, and I thanked him. . . . He walked me home for protection, a little Canadian sailor. He was just so nice."[93]

Much like their younger brothers and cousins, young women knew the city's geography intimately. But where the city's public spaces spelled "excitement" for boys, young women who traversed the streets and walked after nightfall were keenly aware of the threats that might lurk in "dark corners" and apprehensively observed the drunken exuberance of partying servicemen. Even in adolescence, women's freedom of movement differed in kind from the free-wheeling exploits of the city's boys. Whereas boys enjoyed the freedom to roam, women cherished freedom from sexual assault.[94]

The "Traffic Problem"

Prior to the war, children in the country's capital were far more likely to spot horse-drawn carriages or the streetcar trolley making its downtown loop than automobiles.[95] At a time when the automobile revolution had transformed North American towns, cities, and the countryside, most Newfoundlanders continued to travel by either sea or the railway.[96] Cars were owned by taxi drivers or the wealthy, both of whom felt a communal obligation to ferry around their neighbours, a courtesy which local car-owners later extended to servicemen stationed in St John's.[97] The streets, rough as they were, seemed safe to the city's children who did not yet have to compete for public space with trucks or military vehicles.

The arrival of American and Canadian servicemen heralded a transformation of public space that youngsters watched with amazement. As Patricia Winsor marvelled, the Americans "had all these big tractors, pushing all this earth around. We had never seen anything like it in St John's." Jim Prim, too, recalled the "big, heavy trucks" that transformed previously quiet streets into busy thoroughfares, with motorized "Americans and Canadians going back and forth all the time."[98] Suddenly, St John's, too, did have a "traffic problem," as the St John's *Evening Telegram* wrote in August 1941, as neither drivers nor pedestrians seemed inclined to pay much heed to each other.

In a series of opinion pieces, "Spike"—the American serviceman writing in the columns of the *Evening Telegram*—dropped his usually light-hearted tone to urge the "drivers of motor vehicles, especially of military transportation, that in a few days, driving will be even more hazardous—due to the fact that school will be out. Children, even more than usual, playing in the streets. And children at play are apt to dash thoughtlessly out in the front of your machine—from nowhere in particular."[99] In the months to come, Spike repeatedly admonished the city's drivers to slow down and exert caution, an appeal that fell on deaf ears. By the end of [1941] . . . the "traffic situation in town" remained as perilous as ever. [. . .]

[. . .] It was pedestrians who paid dearly as drivers sped over cobblestone streets and the number of fatal traffic accidents soared. In June 1941, eleven-year-old Maud Bragg "was killed instantly on Saturday afternoon on Quidi Vidi road, east of the General Hospital, when she was hit by a bluish-green motor car which sped westward at a fast clip . . . the motor car hit the child and hurled her at a distance of 20 or 30 feet in front of her mother. The car proceeded without stopping."[100] A year later, an over-turning truck tumbled off the street near Waterford Bridge, smashing down on two brothers, aged seven and thirteen, who had been drinking from a well near the roadside. The younger boy died instantly; the older later succumbed to his injuries in St Clare's hospital.[101] In December 1942, seven-year-old Edna Stevens was hit by a car "going at a terrific speed" while walking with her aunt, Stella Kirby, on the sidewalk. The little girl, the *Evening Telegram* reported, was found dead underneath the car.[102] The fact that each accident was chronicled, as were the many near-misses, suggests how quickly and dramatically the rules of the streets had changed as St John's was being dragged, in the brief span of six years, from the age of horse and carriage into the automobile era.

In response to these new hazards, local opinion-makers sought to regulate and limit children's access to public space for the sake of their own protection. The new "geography of danger," to quote the human geographer Gill Valentine, emphasized the threat posed by speeding vehicles, the need for social and legal sanctions to reign in reckless drivers and the importance of banning children from the city's streets.[103] In the summer of 1941, a "Traffic Safety Campaign" instructed drivers in proper traffic etiquette and lobbied for stop signs at dangerous intersections in the vicinity of the Newfoundland Hotel.[104] [. . .] Meanwhile, the St John's *Evening Telegram* published children's ditties that encouraged safe road practices, such as the entry submitted by Freddy Pike on 3 Pleasant Street: "Stop! Look! And Listen! Before you cross the street! Use your ears and then your eye, And, then use your feet!" Yet such tame measures proved insufficient as vehicles crowded formerly quiet streets and drivers stubbornly refused to slow down. In exasperation, "Spike" recounted "several narrow escapes of school children, going to and from school, where drivers of motor vehicles simply ignored the kiddies and drove merrily on their way."[105] Yet newspaper reports also reveal the reluctance of pedestrians and children to yield the public space of the streets to motorized vehicles.[106] [. . .]

By 1942, public discussion shifted to the creation of new, sheltered spaces in which the young could play safely. Newspaper editorials now encouraged youngsters to restrict their play to the spatial confines of parks and playgrounds. "So imminent are the risks run by children sliding over streets and roads used by motor vehicles," wrote the *Evening Telegram* in January 1942, "that the practice should be prohibited." In condemning one of the most popular winter pastimes of the city's children, the paper pointed out that "Not an incline in the city is any longer safe for sliding. Winter traffic has become general and the number of vehicles in use has very considerably increased as the result of the various defence activities. For a child to shoot down over a hill intersected by thoroughfares along which conveyances of various kinds are constantly moving is nothing short of courting disaster." [. . .] In foreshadowing the public rhetoric of later decades, streets were declared dangerous and the city's children invited to play in "proper" children's spaces that were carefully supervised by adults. Warmly, the *Evening Telegram* endorsed the efforts of the *Children's Playground Association* which, for over 20 years, had sought to "provide the children with recreation in safety." As the writer reasoned: ". . . the streets are too dirty to be used as playgrounds. A hand or knee grazed by a fall on such a surface might mean blood poisoning or lockjaw, complaints with which no chances should be taken. Those dangers are far less likely in the grass-covered parks."[107] Yet, we may add, the "grass-covered parks" provided none of the excitement offered by city's unregulated public spaces. As the oral history interviews at the core of this study vividly attest, St John's children were not easily dissuaded from using the city itself as a playground, preferring the allure of "tent city" at Camp Alexander, the bustle of the Harbour, and their public interactions with servicemen to formal "recreation facilities" which the *Children's Playground Association* so valiantly promoted.[108]

Conclusion

In listening to childhood memories of the war, this chapter has examined what human geographers call "the child's 'ecology'—that is, the physical environment and 'social space' in which children grow up."[109] In the seaport city of St John's, children came of age in a self-described "war zone" where the Battle of the Atlantic left visible scars—both in the haunting absence of sailors whose ships had been torpedoed by German submarines and the damaged boats that floated in the harbour, having narrowly survived an encounter with the enemy. Laced with emotion, the immediacy of childhood memories of the war is striking indeed. For Helen Porter, the feeling of pure joy is forever tied to the moment when her cousin Harold "put down his duffle bag" in the lower hall, "looked up and grinned," having been missing for weeks after his ship, the H.M.S. *Firedrake*, was torpedoed by German submarines. "I won't attempt to describe what happened next," Porter has written. "Sometimes, when I'm trying to define happiness, joy, bliss, relief, I remember that night. But there are no words."[110] Over six decades later, our interviewees still recall the tastes, smells, sounds, and sights of wartime St John's, with the senses acting as agents of memory.

The recollections of our interviewees evoke the gendered worlds of childhood, allowing us to reconstruct how girls and boys moved through the city's public spaces. The "culture of boyhood" that saw boys freely roaming on streets and fields sharply contrasted with the spaces that girls identified as their own, namely the home and the school. It was in the family home that the worlds of childhood and the "ordinary adult world" connected—fleetingly so

for children who flourished in the culture of their peers, intimately so for others who were embedded in the rhythms of family life.[111]

Most tragically did these two worlds collide when speeding automobiles—driven by the urgency of wartime—clashed with children walking on sidewalks, drinking from roadside wells or riding their sleds on the city's steep street in wintertime. In contemplating the social costs of the "traffic problem," local opinion-makers recommended restricting children's play to parks and playgrounds. In merging with adult-regulated spaces, children's spaces were to be stripped of their free-wheeling, experimental, and daring characteristics—safer yes, but also infinitely more boring. Not incidentally, this vision of public order remained elusive during the war years. And yet, these early attempts to shield children from the dangers inherent in public spaces resonate with contemporary debates on children's uses of public space. As Gill Valentine has put it succinctly, children in much of the Western World have been "losing their freedom to be in public space both during the day as well as at night" since the 1970s, with "traffic squeezing children out of public space."[112] Here, then, is an unlikely cost of the "friendly invasion." In accelerating the automobile revolution in wartime St John's, the trucks, tractors, and military vehicles that invaded the city between 1939 and 1945 irrevocably altered children's geographies, making it ever more costly to roam the city's streets and, over time, gradually curtailing children's "freedom in the city."[113]

Notes

1. See, in particular, William M. Tuttle's *"Daddy's Gone to War": The Second World War in the Lives of America's Children* (New York: Oxford University Press, 1993), x.

2. Tamara Myers and Mary Anne Poutanen, "Cadets, Curfews, and Compulsory Schooling: Mobilizing Anglophone Children in WW II Montreal," *Histoire sociale/Social History* 38, no. 76 (2005), 367–98; Jeffrey A. Keshen, *Saints, Sinners, and Soldiers: Canada's Second World War* (Vancouver: University of British Columbia Press, 2004), 194–227; Christabelle Sethna, "Wait Till Your Father Gets Home: Absent Fathers, Working Mothers and Delinquent Daughters in Ontario during World War II," in Lori Chambers and Edgar-Andre Montigny eds., *Family Matters: Papers in Post-Confederation Canadian Family History* (Toronto: Canadian Scholars' Press, 1998), 19–37; M. Johnston, "The Children's War: The Mobilization of Ontario Youth During the Second World War," in Roger Hall, William Westfall and Laurel Sefton MacDowell eds., *Patterns of the Past: Interpreting Ontario's History* (Toronto: Dundurn Press, 1988), 356–380.

3. Christine Hamelin, "A Sense of Purpose: Ottawa Student and the Second World War," *Canadian Military History* 6, no. 1 (Spring 1997), 34–41 and Norah Lewis, "'Isn't this a terrible war?': The Attitudes of Children to Two World

Wars," *Historical Studies in Education/Revue d'histoire de l'éducation* 7, no. 2 (1995), 193–215.

4. I have borrowed the metaphor of the "winds of childhood" from Neil Sutherland who, in turn, encountered it in Gabrielle Roy's *The Fragile Lights of Earth*. See Neil Sutherland, *Growing Up: Childhood in English Canada from the Great War to the Age of Television* (Toronto: University of Toronto Press, 1997), 3–23. Although Sutherland does not devote a separate chapter to children's wartime experiences, his account is rich with childhood memories of the war.

5. Janet Lunn, "This isn't really a story. It's a collection of memories about a few years in my life," in Priscilla Galloway ed., *Too Young to Fight: Memories from Our Youth During World War II* (Toronto: Stoddart, 1999), 46.

6. As Neil Sutherland has suggested, "a series of unconnected but vivid vignettes suggests a childhood as yet not reflected upon or put in a final perspective and comes closer to the events of childhood, with all of their sensual and emotional freight." See Sutherland, *Growing Up*, 7.

7. These 25 interviews have been chosen from the project's total of 50 life-course interviews for their vivid memories of growing up—or coming of age—in wartime St John's.

8. Ibid., 203. Memorable wartime memoirs of children growing up in these seaports include Helen Porter, *Below the Bridge: Memories of the South Side of St John's* (St John's: Breakwater Books, 1979), Alan Wilson, "A Young Maritimer in the 1930s and '40s: A Memoir," in Hilary Thompson ed., *Children's Voices in Atlantic Literature and Culture: Essays on Childhood* (Guelph: Canadian Children's Press, 1995) and Budge Wilson, "To live in Halifax, Nova Scotia, is to be aware of the shadow of war—even in peacetime," in *Too Young to Fight*, 172–187. See also the oral history recollections in Emilie L. Montgomery, "'The war was a very vivid part of my life': British Columbia School Children and the Second World War" (M.A. thesis, University of British Columbia, 1991).

9. For recent explorations of the history of childhood in a Canadian context see, for example, Joy Parr, "Introduction," in Nancy Janovicek and Joy Parr eds., *Histories of Canadian Childhood and Youth* (Don Mills: Oxford University Press, 2003), 1–7 and Robert McIntosh, "Constructing the Child: New Approaches to the History of Childhood in Canada," *Acadiensis* 28, no. 2 (Spring 1999), 126–140.

10. Gill Valentine, "Children Should Be Seen and Not Heard: The Production and Transgression of Adults' Public Space," *Urban Geography* 17, no. 3 (1996), 210.

11. Interview with Ann Abraham, 11 August 2007.

12. Porter, *Below the Bridge*, 67–68.

13. Ibid., 5 and Paul Collins, "'First Line of Defence': The Establishment and Development of St John's, Newfoundland as the Royal Canadian Navy's Escort Base in the Second World War," *The Northern Mariner/ LeMarin du nord* 16, no. 3 (July 2006), 24.

14. Quoted in Douglas Baldwin and Gillian Poulter, "Document: Mona Wilson and the Canadian Red Cross in Newfoundland, 1940–1945, *Newfoundland and Labrador Studies* 20, no. 2 (2005), 284.

15. Interview with Stuart Fraser, 20 August 2007.

16. Interview with Ann Abraham, 11 August 2007.

17. Interview with Eileen Collins, 27 August 2007.

18. See, for example, the interviews with Norman Crane, 7 September 2007, Patricia Winsor, 29 August 2007, Eileen Collins, 27 August 2007, and Paul O'Neill, 13 September 2007.

19. Interviews with Margaret Kearney, 1 October 2007, Ann Abraham, 11 August 2007, Eileen Collins, 27 August 2007 and Patricia Winsor, 29 August 2007. See also the religious divisions described by British war brides who arrived in Newfoundland in the mid-1940s as described in G.J. Casey and Maura C. Hanrahan, "Roses and Thistles: Second World War Brides in Newfoundland," *Newfoundland Studies* 10, no. 2 (1994), 240-49.

20. Interviews with Patricia Winsor, 29 August 2007, and Eileen Collins, 27 August 2007.

21. Interview with Tom Goodyear, 27 August 2007.

22. Interviews with Jim Prim, 27 September 2007, and David Edwards, 28 August 2007.

23. David MacKenzie, "A North Atlantic Outpost: The American Military in Newfoundland, 1941–1945," *War & Society* 22, no. 2 (October 2004), 53.

24. Porter, *Below the Bridge*, 27–28.

25. Interviews with Margaret Kearney, 1 October 2007, David Baird, 12 September 2007, and Frankie O'Neil, 28 August 2007.

26. Interview with Jim Prim, 27 September 2007.

27. For a point of comparison see Keshen, Chapter 8: "The Children's War: "Youth Run Wild," in his *Saints, Sinners, Soldiers* and Tuttle, Chapter 5: "Working Mothers and Latchkey Children," in his *"Daddy's Gone to War."*

28. Interview with Helen Fogwill Porter, 28 August 2007.

29. Interview with Gilbert Oakley, 22 September 2007.

30. Sutherland, *Growing Up*, 24 and 47.

31. "My father rarely talked. . . . He never talked to me once. . . . He never talked much about anything."

32. Porter, *Below the Bridge*, 5. Interviews with Helen Porter, 28 August 2007, and Patricia Winsor, 29 August 2007.

33. Interview with James Walsh, 21 September 2007, and Eileen Collins, 27 August 2007.

34. Interviews with Eileen Collins, 27 August 2007, and James Walsh, 21 September 2007.

35. Interview with Jim Prim, 27 September 2007.

36. Interviews with Norman Crane, 7 September 2007, and David Edwards, 28 August 2007.

37. Wilson, "To live in Halifax, Nova Scotia, is to be aware of the shadow of war—even in peacetime," 173–74. For the chasms of communication that separated men on the battlefields from friends and relatives on the home front see Jeffrey Keshen, *Propaganda and Censorship during*

Canada's Great War (Edmonton: University of Alberta Press, 1996).

38. Interview with James Walsh, 21 September 2007.

39. In order to protect would-be volunteers from the taunts and ostracism that "slackers" faced, the government "began distributing rejection badges to those Newfoundlanders who had volunteered for active service." See Peter Neary, *Newfoundland in the North Atlantic World, 1929–1949* (Montreal: McGill-Queen's University Press, 1988),117. For the public censure meted out to "slackers" see the interview with Paul Neill, 13 September 2007 and Porter, *Below the Bridge*, 65–66.

40. Porter, *Below the Bridge*, 68.

41. Interviews with David Baird, 12 September 2007, and James Walsh, 21 September 2007.

42. Interviews with Eileen Collins, 27 August 2007, Helen Porter, 28 August 2007, Margaret Kearney, 1 October 2007, and Paul O'Neill, 13 September 2007.

43. As James Walsh recalls, "Occasionally, there would be other people in the house because not everybody at the time had a radio. We were one of the few people in our area who had a radio." Interview with James Walsh, 21 September 2007.

44. Interview with Gilbert Oakley, 22 September 2007. In a similar vein, Stuart Fraser recalled that "as a kid, you had to be quiet at 12 o'clock every day because the news was on." Interview with Stuart Fraser, 20 August 2007.

45. Interview with Patricia Winsor, 29 August 2007.

46. Interviews Paul O'Neill, 13 September 2007, and Stuart Fraser, 20 August 2007.

47. Interviews with Margaret Kearney, 1 October 2007, and Ann Abraham, 11 August 2007.

48. Interview with Helen Blundon, 28 August 2007, and Porter, *Below the Bridge*, 65.

49. Interviews with Patricia Winsor, 29 August 2007, Ann Abraham, 11 August 2007, and Helen Porter, 28 August 2007. See also Porter, *Below the Bridge*, 65.

50. Bernard Ransom, "Canada's 'Newfyjohn' Tenancy: The Royal Canadian Navy in St John's, 1941–1945," *Acadiensis* 23, no. 2 (Spring 1994), 45–71.

51. St John's *Evening Telegram*, "U.S. Troopship Now in Newfoundland Waters," 25 January 1941 and "St John's Extends Warm Welcome to American Troops," 29 January 1941.

52. Interviews with Margaret Kearney, 1 October 2007, and Thomas Doyal, 21 August 2007.

53. St John's *Evening Telegram*, "Plans Completed for Visit of the Public to American Troopship," 5 April 1941.

54. Interviews with Helen Porter, 28 August 2007, George Ledrew, 29 August 2007, and Paul O'Neill, 13 September 2007.

55. The piers fell victim to the national harbour reconstruction of the early 1960s that destroyed Helen Porter's south side neighbourhood; Porter, *Below the Bridge*, 124–25.

56. Interview with Eileen Collins, 27 August 2007.

57. Porter, *Below the Bridge*, 19.

58. Ibid., 4, 65, 1–2 and interview with Helen Porter, 28 August 2007.

59. Interview with Eileen Collins, 27 August 2007, and Gilbert Oakley, 22 September 2007.

60. Interviews with R.J. Gallaghar, 29 September 2007, Helen Porter, 28 August 2007, Eileen Collins, 27 August 2007, and Stuart Fraser, 20 August 2007.

61. Interview with Margaret Kearney, 1 October 2007; Porter, *Below the Bridge*, 71.

62. Porter, *Below the Bridge*, 71 and interview with R.J. Gallagher, 29 September 2007.

63. Quoted in Baldwin and Poulter, "Mona Wilson and the Canadian Red Cross in Newfoundland, 1940–1945," 203.

64. St John's *Evening Telegram*, 20 December 1941.

65. Interview with Patricia Winsor, 29 August 2007. It is no coincidence that the Christmas guests were mostly Canadian as American servicemen enjoyed many amenities, including excellent food, on the military base Fort Pepperrell.

66. Interviews with Ann Abraham, 11 August 2007, and Vicki Cheeseman, 30 August 2007.

67. Interview with Ann Abraham, 11 August 2007. See also David Edwards, 28 August 2007.

68. See, for example, Baldwin and Poulter, "Mona Wilson and the Canadian Red Cross in Newfoundland, 1940–1945," 287 and St John's *Evening Telegram*, 31 May 1941.

69. Tuttle, Jr, "Daddy's Gone to War," 3.

70. St John's *Evening Telegram*, 15 October 1942. See also the interviews with Helen Porter, 28 August 2007, Ann Abraham, 11 August 2007, David Edwards, 28 August 2007, and James Walsh, 21 September 2007.

71. As recalled in Frank J. Kennedy, *A Corner Boy Remembers: Growing Up in St John's* (St John's: Breakwater Books, 2006), 170.

72. Neary, *Newfoundland in the North Atlantic World*, 163 and the interviews with Helen Porter, 28 August 2007, and Ann Abraham, 11 August 2007.

73. Interview with George Ledrew, 29 August 2007.

74. Interview with Ann Abraham, 11 August 2007.

75. Interview with James Walsh, 21 September 2007.

76. Interview with Ann Abraham, 11 August 2007.

77. Interviews with James Walsh, 21 September 2007, and Gilbert Oakley, 22 September 2007. In addition, two of our male interviewees joined the Church Lads Brigade. See interviews with David Edwards, 28 August 2007, and Gilbert Oakley, 22 September 2007.

78. Interview with Paul O'Neill, 13 September 2007.

79. Interviews with Stuart Fraser, 20 August 2007, and Patricia Winsor, 29 August 2007.

80. Interviews with David Edwards, 28 August 2007, and Gilbert Oakley, 22 September 2007.

81. Interview with Helen Porter, 28 August 2007.

82. Interview with Patricia Wilson, 29 August 2007.

83. Interviews with Ann Abraham, 11 August 2007, and Eileen Collins, 27 August 2007.

84. Porter, *Below the Bridge*, 77.

85. Interviews with James Walsh, 21 September 2007, and Norman Crane, 7 September 2007.

86. Interviews with Gilbert Oakley, 22 September 2007, and James Walsh, 21 September 2007. See Davis and Lorenzkowski, "A Platform for Gender Tensions," 435.

87. Interviews with David Baird, 12 September 2007, Paul O'Neill, 13 September 2007, and Thomas Doyal, 21 August 2007.

88. St John's *Evening Telegram*, 16 July 1941.

89. St John's *Evening Telegram*, "NBC Flashes," 11 July 1941.

90. Kennedy, *A Corner Boy Remembers*, 161.

91. See, for example, Eileen Collins, 27 August 2007, Ann Abrahams, 11 August 2007, and Paul O'Neill, 13 September 2007.

92. Interview with Margaret Kearney, 1 October 2007.

93. Interview with Eileen Collins, 27 August 2007.

94. For making this connection, I am indebted to Brown, "Golden Girls," 249.

95. See, for example, the interview with Patricia Winsor, 29 August 2007.

96. This transformation is charmingly captured in Reynold M. Wik, *Henry Ford and Grass-roots America* (Ann Arbor: University of Michigan Press, 1973).

97. Interviews with Ann Abraham, 11 August 2007, David Edwards, 28 August 2007, and Don McClure, 23 September 2007; "NBC Flashes," St John's *Evening Telegram*, 26 July 1941 and 2 August 1941.

98. Interviews with Patricia Winsor, 29 August 2007, and Jim Prim, 27 September 2007.

99. St John's *Evening Telegram*, "NBC Flashes," 31 May 1941.

100. Ibid., "Eleven-Year-Old Child Victim of Fatal Accident," 2 June 1941.

101. Ibid., "One Child Instantly Killed, Brother Critically Injured," 7 July 1941; interview with Gilbert Oakley, 22 September 2007.

102. Ibid., "Three Persons Killed and Four Others Injured When Struck Down by Motor Car," 2 November 1942.

103. Valentine, "Children Should Be Seen and Not Heard," 210.

104. St John's *Evening Telegraph*, "NBC Flashes," 11 October 1941. These tentative beginnings were later formalized in "traffic control plans" for elementary schoolchildren who were shepherded across busy thoroughfares by senior college girls acting as traffic guards. See ibid., "Traffic Control for Children," 23 March 1944.

105. Ibid., 11 October 1941.

106. As "Spike" wrote in his column "NBC Flashes," "Pedestrians too, we think, should be a little more careful. Jaywalking always has been dangerous—always will be! And walking in the streets at any time—even though the sidewalks are wet—is bad business. Now that the snow is gone—is there any good reasons why the sidewalks shouldn't be used. Seems to us that the streets are crowded enough—without cars and trucks having to dodge people on foot too!" See ibid., 31 May 1941.

107. Ibid., "Children's Playground Association," 28 May 1942.

108. "Children's Playground Association," St John's *Evening Telegram*, 28 May 1942.

109. William M. Tuttle, Jr., *"Daddy's Gone to War": The Second World War in the Lives of America's Children* (New York: Oxford University Press, 1993), 94.

110. Porter, *Below the Bridge*, 67.

111. Nasaw, *Children of the City*, 24.

112. Gill Valentine, "Angels and Devils: Moral Landscapes of Childhood," *Environment and Planning D: Society and Space*, 14 (1996), 585–86.

113. Interview with Margaret Kearney, 1 October 2007.

PRIMARY DOCUMENT

Interview with William Pepperell Abraham, excerpt, c. 2007

In 1937, seven-year-old William Pepperell Abraham moved with his family from London, England to St John's, Newfoundland. The second youngest of four siblings, William grew up in "very much a clerical family." For six years, the family lived on Church Hill in a comfortable row house, nearby the cathedral where William's father worked as assistant to the Bishop. In 1943, after his father had been "enthroned as Bishop of Newfoundland," the family moved to the much grander quarters of the official bishop's residence on King's Bridge

Road. William Abraham recalls spending most of his boyhood in the St John's downtown area, roaming Gower Street, Bond Street, Water Street and Duckworth Street. In the summer holidays, the family relocated to their summer home in Brooklyn, Bonavista Bay. —The following are excerpts from an interview conducted with William Pepperel Abraham in the summer of 2007 by research assistant Kenny Hammond as part of the Occupied St John's project.

How did you get behind the war effort?

I wasn't old enough to be an air raid warden like my brother, but in school, there were various things. All through the province, the teachers all had war savings stamps in their desks to sell you—these were little blue stamps at ten cents' value—and you went up and wanted to buy some. And then you put these in, and when you got twenty-five, it meant the book was completed, and you could take it into the Newfoundland Savings Bank on Duckworth Street. [. . .] They would give you a receipt for it and pay you a certain amount of interest. [. . .] We got, I think it was typically at that time, fifteen cents [. . .] and our father made clear that ten cents of that should go towards buying a stamp every week. And spend the five cents as you wish, more or less! [Chuckles] [. . .] That was considered your contribution.

And then there were drives in the city from time to time. [. . .] Going around the city, collecting metal that would be useful for the war effort, things like old kettles or aluminum pots or something. They'd be collected by truck and then shipped. We heard, maybe just an urban legend, but we heard that the ship that was carrying this across the Atlantic, sadly, was one of the ones torpedoed. [. . .]

We collected magazines, *Life* magazines, *Look* magazines, *Reader's Digest*, all of the reading material, and it would be taken to the cathedral parish hall on Queen's Road, and on Saturday nights the group would get together and roll up and tie up bundles of say, you know, one *Life*, one this, one that, fairly heavy magazines, pretty heavy indeed. And at the cathedral, there was a long-standing group of men called the Cathedral Men's Bible Class, which met on Friday, on Sunday afternoons, but they had a boat, a succession of boats, actually, like small motorboats on the harbour. And when spring came they'd put them in the water again, and they'd been doing this for years, before the war even, taking around reading material and religious tracts to schooners that were tied up at the various wharfs.

But in the war, it became the main focus. [The] men from the cathedral, they weren't necessarily sailors with captain's certificates or anything, but handy and generous with their time and they would go down Sunday mornings and deliver out in the harbour and around the wharfs, these bundles, often throwing up a bundle onto a deck. And sometimes the shortage of reading material was so desperate, apparently, on these long convoys, sometimes people would practically be reduced to reading the label on a soup can. So these magazines were much treasured and almost pounced on as they landed on the deck. There must've been tons and tons of magazines that were distributed that way. [. . .]

continued

Did your family ever take in servicemen for dinners or suppers?

There was this bureau in St John's that you could ring up [. . .] especially at Christmas. And so, we wanted some British navy, Mother and Father coming from England, and our leaning was to ask for British sailors rather than Canadian. And the first year, because of Father's position as bishop, I guess, somebody went down through the list and thought, "Oh, well, he's quite an important man. We'd better send him three or four lieutenant commanders or captains or something." So the first group we had was probably three or four officers, and they were nice enough and we probably had roast turkey. [. . .] But afterwards these officers were kind of look-ing at their watches soon after lunch, "Well, I think we need to be moving on. We have another reception somewhere at three."

[. . .] So after that Father specified we want ratings, we want ordinary seamen. So every year after that during the war we had three or four navy ratings and they not only appreciated it, but sometimes were great fun. [. . .]

And we must've mentioned at some point that we had no real great shortages, but ob-viously some items were hard to get, like this hot mustard from England, Colman's dry hot mustard; it was hard to get it now. The next day, one of these men turned up with a two-pound tin of it from the ship's stores to sort of make sure that we had plenty of dry mustard for the rest of the war. We liked their friendliness, and they appreciated it. And we sometimes kept in touch when they'd be in port again. [. . .]

And I can remember sometimes there was one particular man who came and, you know, rather than feed him, his first [. . .] need was for sleep, and so Mother put him in a bedroom and we'd sort of or she or somebody would creep in from time to time, as he was sound asleep, and I think he slept for twenty-four hours before he had any need to get up and have a meal, you know? Just totally exhausted. [. . .]

Anything you think we are forgetting to talk about?

My mother and father had gone over to England; they both had aging parents that they hadn't seen since 1937, so they had what I now realize a rather scary journey, but they left in October '44 and went to Halifax, took a ship there and went in convoy across.

This was October '44; there were certainly U-boats still around. They got to England and they visited with their parents and other friends, and they stayed away from us, it must've been six or seven months.

We were boarded up, my brother and I, with a Mrs. Knoll on Cook Street and she had two sons over, with the 166th Regiment, so we kind of had the experience of realizing what it was like living in a home with two boys overseas.

It was good for them that they went because Father's father died in January '45, so he was able to be there to help bury him. And then just after my mother and father got back in May, her father died; we had a cable and I think it was on May the 8th, V-E Day. So I don't remember much in terms of St John's celebrations.

But by V-J Day, the end of the war in Japan and the Pacific, we were in Brooklyn, as usual that summer. And it was organized very quickly. It was decided that the children and the people of Brooklyn would walk into Lethbridge, which was [4.5] miles away, and there they would meet the children of people of Lethbridge who would've walked out to this bridge and we joined forces and go back [. . .], just a day thing. [. . .] There was a dance, and parades, and people festooned their bikes and the flags, so, that was the out port celebration of V-J Day.

Source: Transcription of interview with William Pepperell Abraham, excerpt, c 2007. From the Occupied St. John's Project. (Steven High, principal investigator); reproduction permission granted by interviewee.

Practical Patriotism: How the Canadian Junior Red Cross and Its Child Members Met the Challenge of the Second World War

SARAH GLASSFORD

During the 1938–39 school year, Canadian children from across the country, members of a school-based health and citizenship education program known as the Junior Red Cross, pooled their small individual donations to contribute to the creation and maintenance of an International Peace Garden straddling the Canada–United States border between North Dakota and Manitoba. The image of children co-operatively gardening across the world's longest undefended border held symbolic power for interwar adult Red Cross leaders and Peace Garden promoters and expressed their hope that children's international friendships could make lasting global

peace a reality. Only one year later, however, Junior Red Cross members were knitting for soldiers, donating their pocket money to the Junior Red Cross War Fund, and welcoming refugee children from Britain.

Children have long been used as visual metaphors and icons in major wars, political movements, and revolutions, as Karen Dubinsky has pointed out. Their perceived innocence and vulnerability have made them potent signifiers of need in a variety of media, from humanitarian aid campaign advertisements to political party propaganda.[1] Canada's entry into the Second World War in September 1939 therefore marked a crossroads in the two-decade history of the Junior Red Cross in Canada: there was symbolic power in any role the organization might take. But what *was* the proper response of

Source: *From the Journal of the History of Childhood and Youth*, 7, 2 (Spring 2014): 219–42. Reprinted with permission.

an internationalist, peace-promoting children's organization when the country's adults took up arms in a popularly understood "good" war? How should the Junior Red Cross respond, and would its child members embrace that response? In order to survive and thrive in a wartime context, adult leaders made some changes. Through strategies of avoidance, adaptation, and redirection, the Canadian Junior Red Cross shifted its focus from internationalism to voluntary service—aided by young Canadians' own productivity and desire to participate—and thereby managed to negotiate successfully the challenge posed by the Second World War to its peacetime internationalist agenda.

The international Red Cross movement began its humanitarian work in Europe during the 1860s, providing aid to sick and wounded soldiers of late nineteenth-century European wars. The distinctive Junior Red Cross (JRC) of the interwar years (1919–1939) originated in children's branches of the senior Red Cross which were organized in Canada, Australia, and the United States during the First World War. The successful mobilization of children in wartime led to the development of a separate "junior" Red Cross program in 1919; it quickly became a central element of the international Red Cross movement's new peacetime public health work around the world (although each national JRC remained autonomous). The new JRC diverged from its wartime roots to focus upon three key areas which adult organizers felt would make younger generations happy, productive, and peaceful citizens of their local, national, and global communities: health, voluntary service, and international friendliness (sometimes replaced by "citizenship").[2] During the 1920s and 1930s, the JRC was actively promoted in Canada by its parent organization, the Canadian Red Cross Society (CRCS), which had emerged from the First World War as Canada's leading wartime humanitarian aid agency and transformed itself in 1919 into an influential nation-wide peacetime public health body. The Canadian JRC program was not a stand-alone club, but was designed to be integrated by teachers into the school curriculum. Individual classroom teachers joined the movement slowly but steadily, until by the end of the 1938–39 school year

some 425,000 Canadian children between the ages of 5 and 18 (approximately 13 per cent of school-age children in Canada) were dues-paying members of over 14,000 JRC branches.[3]

Throughout the interwar years Junior branches met one or more Friday afternoons each month. They raised funds to support local health initiatives, observed the 12 rules of the health game, performed health-related plays, and tackled local service projects. Many classrooms and individual children also received the JRC's widely subscribed national children's magazine, *The Canadian Red Cross Junior* (hereafter *CRC Junior*), which reinforced the messages of health, voluntary service, and good citizenship through stories, dramas, articles, crafts, and games.[4]

After the devastation of the First World War, many internationally minded adults placed great faith in the power of children's international cultural understanding ("international friendliness") to assure peace and global harmony. JRC activities and educational materials reflected this belief, and offered a democracy-friendly alternative to communist or fascist youth organizations.[5] International correspondence between Juniors, and particularly the exchange of handmade portfolios showcasing a branch's home community and country, were key elements of this attempt to cultivate international friendliness among children. Canadian Juniors were frequent participants in these exchanges. The *CRC Junior* attempted to foster an internationalist outlook through articles profiling other countries, international JRC activities, and international figures who had made the world a better place through science, technology, philosophy, or the arts. The International Peace Garden project was another result of the prevailing internationalist outlook.

The outbreak of the Second World War in 1939 constituted a crossroads for the Canadian Junior Red Cross, because it set the program's interwar internationalism on a collision course with the wider Canadian Red Cross Society's history of serving as an outlet for Canadians' wartime patriotic impulses. *Internationally*, the Red Cross movement was neutral and impartial. However, by 1914 *national* Red Cross societies had been unofficially adopted as extensions of local patriotic feeling. In Canada, the First World War had established a tradition of Red Cross work as a means of contributing to the national war effort. When war broke out again in 1939, ordinary Canadians took it as given that supporting the CRCS, Canada's preeminent war charity, was a way to help Canadian troops. Moreover, the Second World War made itself felt to children: through the mass media, public spectacles, toys and books, adult conversations, and overseas correspondence, the war and its causes confronted and politicized children to varying degrees.[6] Although interwar Juniors likely associated the JRC only with its peacetime work, after September 1939 the pervasive presence of the wartime CRCS would quickly link the Red Cross and war work in their minds. These facts, combined with the Canadian JRC's origins in children's voluntary work during the First World War, made it almost inevitable that the JRC of 1939 would involve children in *some* form of war work. The questions that faced the CRCS, then, were not so much whether Juniors would engage in war work at all, but rather what kind of war work they would do, and how it would fit with the overall goals of the JRC.

No documents have survived to provide detailed insight into how much or how little debate went into this question. But comments such as that of Quebec JRC Supervisor Ruth Shaw—who pushed for continued international correspondence since "knowledge and sympathetic understanding of conditions and difficulties throughout the world are essential in the interest of world peace"—suggest that some leaders recognized the challenge presented by wartime.[7] The clearest indication of serious concerns among JRC leaders over how to navigate the altered national and international context is evident in the only known document to publicly and explicitly address the war and the JRC's place in it: an editorial in the October 1939 *CRC Junior* by its founding editor and long-time National JRC Director Jean E. Browne. Ontarian Jean Elizabeth Browne trained as both a teacher and a nurse before beginning her 28 years with the JRC in 1922. A humble, "quiet-spoken woman" noted by her colleagues for her "leadership, vision and modest tenacity," Browne was lauded

upon her retirement in 1950 as having "kept an unshakeable faith in young people" and their abilities throughout her career. Rather than "citizens of tomorrow," Browne believed "young people are citizens of today, with their own capabilities and capacities for contributing to our society."[8]

Browne's 1939 editorial reflected this personal philosophy: it offered an authoritative statement about the war, its causes, and how Junior Red Cross members should respond to it. It also set the tone for how all provincial divisions of the JRC handled the war years. She refrained from mentioning the names of the now-enemy countries and did not elaborate upon the events or ideologies involved. Her vague urging that children should contribute to "the sacrifices now being made [. . .] to this cause of liberty" suggests a personal belief in the necessity of the war, but she did not elaborate further. The Second World War challenged the prevailing western ideal of a "happy childhood" by threatening the safety and protection integral to it, and instead temporarily positioned children as vital workers for nations in crisis. However, since JRC leaders' belief that children were the keys to a peaceful future hinged upon children's perceived innocence and apolitical nature, Browne's silence on the politics of the war in 1939 (and thereafter) may reflect a desire to avoid politicizing them.[9]

Nonetheless, Browne outlined three specific ways children could help. First, they should keep themselves healthy, in order to be of use to their country now and in the future. Second, they should earn and save money to donate to Red Cross funds. These instructions show the influence of the interwar JRC emphasis on health and service, as well as the tradition of CRCS wartime assistance to sick, wounded, and captured servicemen. The personal health goal also hints that older youth might soon find themselves among the sick and wounded personnel being helped. But the most telling element of Browne's editorial appeared in her third suggestion. Despite her belief in the cause of "liberty" Canada was fighting for, Browne was loath to abandon the JRC's cultural internationalist role. "Do not give up your programme of International Friendliness," she wrote, for "the world needs friendliness and love as never before. Do not hate our enemies. Hatred is vicious and never accomplishes anything but harm." She closed by urging her young readers not to treat enemy alien children unkindly. "Let us put forth every effort to help our soldiers, and let us not show hatred in any form," she concluded.[10] Although Browne's editorial offered a model for handling the competing demands of internationalism and wartime patriotism, to some extent the managing of this dilemma was out of the hands of the Red Cross itself: classroom teachers were in ultimate control of what transpired in their Junior branches. Some had already established a tradition of mediating the provincial curriculum when it did not fit community needs or beliefs. Furthermore, school and organized extracurriculars comprised only one part of a wider array of information and experience available to children.[11] JRC teacher-directors therefore talked about the war and the Red Cross's part in it in whatever way they chose, while, drawing on their broader experiences, children came to their own conclusions. But despite national and provincial JRC leaders' inability to control the grassroots, they appear to have employed three informal (perhaps unconscious?) strategies for negotiating the shift to a wartime footing in those areas of the JRC they *could* control.

First, the realm of nationalism was avoided as much as possible. This did not come naturally, because ordinary Canadians—including those involved with the CRCS—saw wartime Red Cross work as patriotic labour for the nation and empire at war. However, the entire concept of wartime humanitarian aid through an international network of Red Cross societies hinged upon the concept of impartiality: the Red Cross as an organization did not take sides. The CRCS therefore tried to use Canadians' identification of the Red Cross with patriotic work to garner support but had to be careful not to compromise its official impartial status too flagrantly. This meant not discussing in official materials the opposing sides, ideologies at stake, or actual fighting. The CRCS simply took the existence of war as a given, and worked for humanitarian ends within that context. Likewise, the JRC avoided discussing the causes, aims, and potential outcomes of the war. Both the senior CRCS and the JRC promoted

an ethos of humanitarian service and personal sacrifice which appeared to transcend nationalism, but quietly relied upon Canadians' patriotic impulses to help motivate that service and sacrifice.

The *CRC Junior* magazine exemplifies this approach: during the Second World War it never provided any "war news" about the actual fighting and instead reported children's efforts to help Allied servicemen and civilian children, without ever mentioning the suffering (or existence) of children, soldiers, or prisoners of war from Axis countries. The suffering of bombed-out British children often appeared, but such discussions dwelt on separation from family members and the loss of one's home, clothes, and toys, rather than on physical harm. Although some of the plays and stories in the magazine had wartime settings or dealt with home front issues relevant to children, they largely used the war as a backdrop for conventional JRC topics like good health. War-related content included suggestions for JRC war work, reports of branch activities, and acknowledgements of Juniors' donations. Churchill, Roosevelt, Stalin, and Canadian Prime Minister W.L. Mackenzie King each received biographical treatment; articles about British architecture contained the odd remark about "ancient monuments of civilization" being "razed to the ground by ruthless bombs."[12] Yet the majority of each issue remained dedicated to health, nature, and serving others. This contrasts with not only the extreme example of wartime Japanese children's magazines (which cultivated a culture of sacrificial death) but also with Britain's *Journal of the Junior Red Cross* (*JJRC*) which, although similar in much of its content to the *CRC Junior*, regularly included articles detailing British military exploits and editorials relating to national and international news. Sociologists Berry Mayall and Virginia Morrow note that the *JJRC* explicitly encouraged British children to engage in Red Cross work as part of the larger national battle for freedom and argue that "this suggests that the [British JRC] organisation did not want to shield children from this war."[13]

The Canadian JRC's shielding efforts are apparent in *CRC Junior* cover art. Only 17 of the magazine's 60 wartime covers presented images that invoked the war, and only 5 of those 17 depicted military personnel—a shockingly low number given the ubiquity of uniformed men and women in public life at the time. Even these five were portrayed in a gentle, sanitized fashion. The other war-related images consisted of nurses and Red Cross volunteers, Red Cross flags, Princess Elizabeth Windsor, Winston Churchill, British children receiving JRC-supplied items, and a single "V" for a victory which was then nowhere in sight. The remaining forty-three covers offered traditional *CRC Junior* fare: romanticized animals, flowers, landscapes, and seasonal images. A perceived need to boost morale may have been responsible for the war-related covers, since fourteen of the seventeen appeared in 1941–1942—arguably the darkest years of the war for Canada and the Allies. Within the magazine's pages war-related content peaked from 1941 to 1943, then declined through 1944 and 1945. The victorious conclusion of the war passed without comment in the *CRC Junior*.

The second strategy evident in the wartime Junior Red Cross involved adapting its internationalism. Rather than repudiate this element (so vital to adult hopes for the future), JRC leaders put it on hold or transformed elements of the interwar program into more viable wartime forms. International correspondence and portfolio exchanges are a perfect example. Overseas correspondence was never officially suspended during the war, since JRC leaders believed it could counteract "the hatred and misunderstandings" inevitable in wartime, but it was altered. The JRC had existed in both Germany and Japan during the interwar years, but it was not possible to correspond with either after the declarations of war. Occupied countries were similarly off-limits, and communications with many others became impractical.[14] Some provincial divisions (such as Ontario) quietly removed the "international friendliness" subheading from their annual reports and did not talk about it for several years; others (such as Manitoba and Alberta) redirected their correspondence to other Canadian provinces or to the United States—retaining the concept of friendship across borders, while acknowledging the altered wartime context.

Jean Browne's decision to use the bulk of Juniors' donations for child-oriented relief work overseas demonstrates another transformed version of international friendliness. Rather than adding JRC donations to the CRCS pool of money being used for everything from medical supplies to comforts for combatant troops, Browne often used Junior-raised funds to provide food and clothing relief through neutral Red Cross channels to children in occupied Western European countries and to British children suffering the effects of the Blitz.[15] Again within the constraints of what would be publicly acceptable (no aid to Axis children), this child-helping-child model was a means of preserving some aspect of the international friendliness program in wartime. Despite the more limited range of countries eligible for international friendliness between 1939 and 1945, the basic message of caring for others did not fall upon deaf ears. A first grade branch in Ontario, whose six-year-old members needed help from their mothers to create the knitted quilt they sent overseas to British children, included a short letter with their donation in which they explained that they had saved their pennies to buy clothes for those who were bombed and that they said a little prayer for children overseas each day: "Dear God, so many now are sad / That we, who still are glad, / Now pray—God cheer them on their way." Since their prayer was the first verse of a poem which appeared earlier in the *CRC Junior*, their recital of it suggests adult intervention.[16] Nonetheless, these six-year-olds' act of saving pennies represents a significant show of empathy and care for distant children they would never meet.

The *CRC Junior* also modified its approach to promoting international friendliness during the war years. With such a diminished volume of international correspondence to report upon, it instead attempted to convey the impact of Canadian Juniors' efforts for children in Britain, the experiences of British war guest children living in Canada, and the work of Juniors in other Allied countries like Australia or the United States. In 1944 the magazine featured profiles of Chinese and Russian public figures—exotic individuals who happened to be wartime Allies at a crucial point in the war. The

"Our Friends in Foreign Lands" series profiled the customs and ways of life of people in eleven different European countries, all Allies, officially neutral, or occupied by Germany. The ensuing "Our Friends to the South" series profiled three Latin American countries similarly unobjectionable to Canadian readers.[17] Again, these series represented a compromised form of internationalism for the Canadian JRC, since they attempted to broaden children's knowledge of other lands and peoples but steered clear of enemy countries (which were never mentioned by name). Since editor Jean Browne must have known that North American comics, radio programs, and other child-focused media were heavy on pro-Allied propaganda, it is tempting to imagine she steered her own magazine's wartime approach to internationalism according to that familiar maxim: "If you can't say anything nice, don't say anything at all."[18] She, at least, would not further politicize children.

The third and most effective strategy used by Canadian Junior Red Cross leaders involved redirection. By foregrounding children's roles as active workers engaged in wartime voluntary service they skirted much of the tension between JRC peacetime internationalism and the CRCS national wartime mandate. Little organizational change was required to accomplish this shift; "I Serve" had been the Junior motto since the early 1920s, and for two decades Juniors had been raising money for community projects. By emphasizing the continuity of a service ideal which stretched back to the First World War, JRC leaders neatly sidestepped the loss of international friendliness as a primary focus of the program, as well as the fact that the *objects* of children's voluntary service were quite different in wartime. Both the Red Cross and provincial departments of education embraced this mobilization of child labour in wartime as a lesson in the value of hard work and self-sacrifice for a greater cause. Jean Browne described Red Cross work by Canadian youth as a form of "practical patriotism," and asserted that the wartime value of the JRC lay in inculcating this virtue in children. When in 1940 the Juniors of Toronto's Allenby School donated to the CRCS Soldiers' Fund the money they usually spent on Empire Day firecrackers, Browne

approvingly published the fact in the *CRC Junior* under the title "Real Patriotism."[19]

Children's desire to be part of the war effort engulfing the lives of the adults around them was exactly the kind of voluntary spirit the Red Cross wished to develop in them. In this respect, the JRC was aligned with a wider national shift in curricular emphasis during the Second World War. Rosa Bruno-Jofre notes, for instance, that the war introduced "the elements of unity, patriotism, and service" into a Manitoba citizenship curriculum which previously emphasized obedience, Christian faith, and democratic values. The war intensified an already existing concern with health and citizenship education, and the JRC was among the wartime school activities noted by contemporaries "for their contribution to development of wholesome community attitudes and improved citizenship."[20] For a country that believed itself to be fighting a war for the very survival of democracy, raising healthy children well-versed in the rights and responsibilities of a democratic society was a priority.

In line with the prevailing theories of parenting and education in early twentieth-century North America, Canadian JRC leaders and supporters also believed that structured, supervised activities were crucial to moulding children into disciplined, productive, moral adults. Organizers and teachers viewed the JRC as a desirably structured, wholesome, and patriotic outlet for children's energies in a time of war. In late 1939 Saskatchewan Minister of Education J.W. Estey called the JRC "the most appropriate channel through which the children of our schools may work," and asserted that Juniors had a special role to play, "since the conditions of war inevitably [would] create greater need for funds for work among the children of Canada, refugee children and the children of other countries involved in the struggle."[21] Who better to work for the benefit of suffering children, Estey implied, than other children? There was something powerful in the child-helping-child model beyond the tangible benefits of the aid itself. The symmetry and moral rightness of it was appealing; perhaps it also eased adult consciences to think that children's generosity could redeem a world thrown into disorder by their elders.

It was not only the child-helping-child symmetry which appealed to adults like Estey. The JRC also channelled youthful energy away from socially unacceptable pastimes. Tamara Myers's and Mary Anne Poutanen's research on the mobilization of anglophone school children in wartime Montreal makes clear the close relationship which existed between the perceived problem of growing juvenile delinquency and authorities' efforts to direct children's energies into patriotic work for the war effort. The moral panic over absent parents and a tomorrow-we-may-die attitude among the young likely influenced some schools' decision to adopt the JRC program. Its three pillars of health, service, and good citizenship offered a reassuringly civic-minded, constructive, and adult-supervised alternative to the spectre of unsupervised, destructive, immoral youth. The JRC was also a good fit for schools seeking organized programs to help compensate for the impact of underqualified teachers and crowded classrooms, both of which were results of the wartime migration of qualified teachers to war industry and the armed forces.[22]

Karen Dubinsky has noted that posters relating to war, political movements, and revolutions often feature children as politicized subjects in need of protection or saving. In contrast, images of Canadian JRC members published in a special December 1940 issue of the *Canadian Geographical Journal* (*CGJ*) devoted to the work of the CRCS depicted children as active agents. The magazine's photographs showed youth of various ages practicing first aid and home nursing techniques for use in wartime emergencies, engaging in woodworking or needlework to make items for sale or donation, performing plays to raise funds, knitting in groups, and proudly posing beside displays showcasing their handiwork.[23] The occasional Union Jack or red cross in the background visually linked these efforts to their Canadian, British imperial, and Red Cross contexts, but these images unmistakeably proclaimed that young Canadians were active workers for the Red Cross. This approach contrasted sharply with interwar publicity images of Juniors, when they were commonly depicted more passively: in costume after a health play, being weighed and measured, listening to others speak. The *CGJ* clearly made a particular statement about children and their relationship to humanitarian war work. Other wartime publications depicting the JRC followed a similar trend, highlighting the fact that, as Myers and Poutanen contend, in social terms children's value grew during the war: they were recognized as not only future soldiers, workers, and parents, but also as an important source of increasingly scarce labour in the meantime.[24]

What children did through their JRC service, although frequently small on an individual level, added up to a significant contribution overall, and child labour provided an important component of the CRCS's wartime humanitarian aid effort. By the end of the war, the CRCS estimated that Canadian Juniors had raised over $3,000,000 of the $80,647,874 in voluntary cash contributions received by the CRCS for various war-related service during the conflict. This amount was over and above the value of Juniors' in-kind donations of goods and labour. Juniors kept up their prewar health and local community service work at the same time, too, although in an altered context: instead of being described as a building block of a great future Canada (as was the case during the interwar years), children's health was now "one of our first lines of home defence," in the words of Canada's Governor General Lord Tweedsmuir.[25]

Juniors' monetary contributions are even more impressive in light of the methods used to obtain them. Although undoubtedly some children broke this rule, Juniors were "forbidden" to ask their parents for money or to canvass for donations. They were to raise the money through their own labour and/or through self-denial (for example, not spending pocket money on themselves).[26] To this end they mounted school concerts and plays; sold their own handmade toys, candy, or wooden items; published and sold school magazines; ran cloakrooms at local events; market gardened; and donated the gate receipts from school sporting events. This policy kept Juniors from competing with adult Red Cross canvassers in their communities, but more importantly held pedagogical value. Effort and sacrifice were critical components of the voluntary spirit and ethic of service the JRC attempted to instill in children. The caption "Young Canada in Training" which accompanied the *CGJ* photo spread of Juniors suggests that contemporaries outside the CRCS (in this case, the magazine's editorial staff) also saw young Canadians' JRC work as a tangible lesson in good citizenship. Educationally speaking, the JRC fit well with a shift in curricular emphasis which had swept Canada in the late 1930s. "Projects" and "learning by doing" were newly in vogue, and Red Cross work offered excellent hands-on training in wartime citizenship and voluntary service.[27]

The three strategies of avoidance, adaptation, and redirection helped both the junior and senior wings of the Canadian Red Cross to negotiate the challenges of being both a neutral humanitarian organization and a patriotic one. However, it seems likely that the subtle differences between the *Canadian Red Cross* war effort (focused on humanitarian aid) and the Canadian war effort (focused on winning) were lost on all but the oldest and most sophisticated of Canadian Juniors. After all, the distinction was rather fuzzy for many adults. Some children may have reasoned that the most humanitarian thing to do was to win the war and therefore end it; for others, perhaps war work was war work regardless of the framework in which it took place. We have no record of how individual teacher-directors explained JRC war work to their students or what students thought as they went about their tasks. Children's broader day-to-day experiences also shaped their understandings of JRC work, quite possibly more than did the explanations of their teachers. Happily, glimpses of children's understandings surface in the pages of the *CRC Junior*. Although publication implies tacit adult approval, such submissions remain the work of children themselves and offer valuable clues.

The blurring of national and Junior Red Cross goals is evident in a composition by seventh grade student Mildred Stein of Toronto, whose essay "How Children Can Serve the Empire" appeared in the March 1940 issue of the *CRC Junior*. Mildred (who was probably about thirteen years old) argued that "We, the children, should and can unite to perform the duties which are required of us" in wartime;

these duties included staying healthy, getting an education, and practising thrift and economy. "While these may be only minor items," she earnestly concluded, "they help us to do our part in winning this war." On a similarly patriotic note, the students of the "Be a Help" JRC branch in Stratford, Ontario, reported that they sang a prayer each day seeking God's protection for Canada's servicemen. Hygiene and love of country mingled in an anecdote reportedly based on a true story about two Juniors washing their school's dirty Union Jack flag. The story, sent in by the Merrymakers branch of Vancouver, British Columbia, portrayed one student telling another: "You know the Junior Red Cross stands for cleanliness and patriotism." Maria Metcalfe, a Junior from Glace Bay, Nova Scotia, included both "the valiant men of Britain" fighting for "the International right" and "the Red Cross Workers" who were "standing by to do their share" in her poem on the theme of victory, in 1942.[28] Young Canadians understood the JRC in their own ways, and freely integrated elements into their JRC experience which fell outside of the official parameters.

Perhaps because of this flexibility, the wartime Canadian Junior Red Cross grew dramatically. Enrolment nearly doubled from 425,000 members in 14,000 branches in 1939, to 772,037 members in 26,031 branches by the end of the 1940–41 school year. The 1941 membership represented roughly 7 per cent of the total Canadian population (11,507,000) and 25 per cent of all Canadians aged 5 to 19.[29] This dramatic increase—one quarter of all eligible Canadian children and youth doing war work through a single humanitarian agency—indicates that many children and teachers responded to the opportunity offered by the JRC. But the JRC was far from universally adopted. The Milton (Ontario) High School Board, for example, resented JRC work collecting clothing and supplies "as an improper intrusion on instruction time," and rejected a proposal for a Red Cross fundraising dance because it felt there were already enough school dances.[30] Despite some resistance of this kind national JRC membership grew and remained high. By the 1944–45 school year it sat at approximately 842,000 members in 29,000 branches from coast to coast. If JRC leaders feared a loss of members if the organization did not take on war work (which seems reasonable given the many other groups enlisting youth for war work), JRC membership growth after 1939 suggests that the shift in emphasis suppressed this potential threat.[31]

In their Montreal study, Myers and Poutanen highlight both the normalization of "devotion to the war effort" and "the coercive nature of this mobilization." Powerful, pervasive forces urged young people to actively engage in the war effort, whether they liked it or not. Accordingly, there was a strong element of coercion involved in children's JRC participation: it was run by their classroom teachers, at least partly during school hours; most children probably accepted it as just another required school activity. It seems likely that teachers initiated the enrolment of most JRC branches, particularly among younger children. However, this does not mean that children could not also be willing—even enthusiastic—participants. In Mary Peate's memoir of her teenage years in Second World War–era Montreal, she relates the initial lack of enthusiasm she and her friend Cath felt when Cath's mother suggested they scour the basement for salvage items. That reluctance turned to willingness when Cath's mother reminded them that salvage drive proceeds would be used to entertain the troops. Many young Canadians probably exhibited similarly mixed responses to the prospect of JRC work. William Tuttle's study of American children in the Second World War shows that when framed by patriotic wartime rhetoric, even small tasks could make children feel they were making a difference, thereby boosting their sense of pride and self-worth and increasing their enthusiasm.[32]

The JRC National Director administered the JRC War Fund, so we cannot attribute any agency to Canadian children in terms of the chosen recipients of their hard-earned money. However, at the branch level the JRC was run in at least semi-democratic fashion, following parliamentary procedure. Teacher-directors were intended to serve as guides, while Juniors elected officers and took responsibility for their service projects and health activities. The youngest Juniors (five years old) would have needed a great deal of direction, but older children gained greater influence over their activities. In rural one-room schools older children likely took the leadership roles while younger children helped as they were able. We can therefore, within certain limits, speak of children's agency within the JRC. As James Marten argues about children of the American Civil War era, it seems reasonable to assume that many children "insisted on getting involved" because they saw themselves "not merely as appendages to their parents' experiences but as actors in their own right in the great national drama." JRC war work gave children an officially sanctioned, publicly recognized space in which to act and provided an opportunity for adults to recognize their agency.[33]

Although hardly conclusive evidence, the persistently high JRC enrolment throughout the war suggests that the program was liked by students. Unlike an unpopular math lesson, the JRC was not officially part of any provincial curriculum, so teachers were free to opt out at any time. No doubt they would do so if the program went over like a lead balloon. High school–age JRC members are a useful case in point. Organizers had struggled unsuccessfully throughout the 1930s to gain a significant foothold in high schools. Wartime provided the breakthrough, bringing tens of thousands of high school–age youth into the JRC fold: from 19,197 adolescent members in 1939–40, to 61,406 in 1942–43. It is hard not to read this growth—in combination with reports of high school Juniors showing "great initiative and leadership"—as, at least in part, a surge of enthusiasm for JRC war work among those old enough to understand what was going on, but still too young for many forms of wartime service.[34]

In her study of two Ottawa, Ontario, high schools during the war, Christine Hamelin finds that these students took on "serious responsibilities and acquired a remarkable sense of purpose." The presence of their older peers in the armed forces, as well as the distinct possibility of their own military service (both boys and girls) in the near future, led the teens to pour their energies into War Savings Stamp drives, cadet training, and Red Cross work. A letter published in the January 1941 CRC Junior from the secretaries of seven JRC branches in the Hon. J.C. Patterson Collegiate Institute in Windsor, Ontario, suggests that for these high school students their JRC involvement was teacher initiated but enthusiastically embraced. "Miss Wagg, our supervisor," the letter stated, "has explained your work to us and also our duties and we are all anxious to start work. '*We are proud and willing to do all we can to serve our country.*'" Jean Browne claimed that this letter was "typical of hundreds of letters received at Junior Red Cross headquarters."[35]

Quebec JRC Supervisor Ruth Shaw attributed children's hard work for the JRC in her province to "a keen desire to do all in their power to help the fighting forces, air raid victims and refugees in England," and Prince Edward Island Director Verna Darrach observed that the island's Juniors had proven "most enthusiastic in their war effort." This may have been merely wishful thinking on the adults' part, but Darrach's word choices offer a clue to the situation on the ground. In 1942 she subtly indicated children's preference for war work over their ordinary JRC health activities by choosing the word "outstanding" to describe children's contributions to JRC war services. The ordinary peacetime activities she described as merely "well-maintained."[36] Children's initial enthusiasm for war work (before war weariness inevitably set in) and sense of playing an important role were no doubt boosted by the supportive response their efforts received from the adults around them. Voluntary work also served as "emotional labour" for Juniors, providing a welcome occupation in the face of worry, fear, or grief. A 1941 column in the yearbook of Glebe Collegiate in Ottawa asserted that Glebe students "all feel some sort of glow knowing that some concrete evidence of our willingness to . . . help has been shown." Tangible tasks helped those too young to fight deal with the tensions and frustrations of wartime, the student author explained, unknowingly echoing American psychiatrist J. Louise Despert, who noted at the time that "participation in the war effort" served as "a powerful mechanism to allay anxiety."[37]

These children of wartime proved capable and diligent workers, and, whether coerced or voluntarily given, their labour for the Red Cross produced significant results. Juniors' donations were put to use by adults in a range of tangible humanitarian aid projects of which children could be proud. In 1941, JRC leaders used $15,500 from the JRC War Fund to purchase five mobile kitchens for use with British fire fighters and civilians suffering from the nightly bombing raids of the Battle of Britain; another $5,000 purchased 2,500 blankets for bombed-out British civilians. At the end of the year the balance of the fund was earmarked as a contribution to a new CRCS project: more than a dozen nurseries for orphaned British children under the age of five who had sustained bombing injuries. The financing of these nurseries and provision of clothing for their occupants became the main form of "war service" for the JRC in 1942.[38] JRC funds also provided musical instruments, writing supplies, and dental equipment to servicemen in enemy POW camps. After 1943 Junior funds were sent through neutral International Red Cross channels to help relieve starving children in Greece, Belgium, Yugoslavia, Poland, France, India, Norway, China, Russia, and the Netherlands. While the absence of enemy countries on this list is not entirely surprising, it is notable that the $140,000 worth of relief sent overseas by the JRC in the first few months *after* the end of the war was directed to the children of Holland, France, Norway, and Poland. Given the dire situations in Germany, Italy, and Japan, the absence of former enemy countries among the post-war recipients is disappointing from the standpoint of truly neutral humanitarianism. Clearly the concept of the "neutral child" upon which JRC international friendliness had rested in the interwar years had its limits.[39] Presumably adult leaders believed that some compromises to maintain public support were still necessary so soon after the war.

Sick and wounded servicemen recuperating in military hospitals—the traditional recipients of Red Cross aid—received Junior assistance as well in the form of small gifts made by children to provide a bit of Christmas cheer. Quebec Juniors made 38,615 sewn or knitted articles (clothing and medical supplies) to be sent overseas in 1942 alone. By the end of the war Juniors had made hundreds of thousands of wooden arm splints for the Surgical Supplies Division of the Department of National Defence, and children's salvage drives had helped earn thousands of dollars for war-related Red Cross services.[40]

The Nova Scotia JRC report for 1942 records the kinds of humble, local, everyday efforts in which many Canadian children likely engaged. "Gave gifts to a Corvette, Gave [sic] party for soldiers stationed on duty," reported one local branch; "Made arm bands for A.R.P. workers," "barrells [sic] of apples were sold at recess periods," and "sawed wood for a Red Cross Auxiliary," reported others. Boys and girls of all ages learned to knit for the troops, and they made or bought complete outfits for bombed-out British children. Some Juniors welcomed British children evacuated to Canada as war guests. Although children co-operated in a wide variety of projects, their labour sometimes followed traditional gender divisions, such as one Nova Scotia branch which reported that "Some boys delivered milk, worked on a farm wherever necessary, girls looked after children while mothers attended Red Cross meetings."[41]

Other common activities included writing letters to servicemen overseas, buying and selling War Savings Stamps and Certificates, visiting or entertaining servicemen in convalescent hospitals in Canada, and creating quilts and afghan blankets for children overseas. Sisters Lucienna and Marilyn Wismer, raised on a farm near Amherstburg, Ontario, still remember knitting simple red quilt squares at school for the JRC during the war. Anticipating the UNICEF campaigns of the post-war period, some Manitoba Juniors collected pennies for the War Fund instead of treats, as they went door-to-door on Halloween. The emphasis on service was more than simply a coping mechanism in the face of the wartime challenge to internationalism: the JRC directly engaged children as active workers for the humanitarian cause, and their efforts were held up as an exemplar for their elders. Juniors' impressive output "should act as a stimulant for we adults to increase our efforts in this great work," wrote British Columbia Division President G.C. Derby in 1941.[42]

The national patriotic fervour of wartime and the senior Red Cross tradition of acting as an outlet for citizens' patriotic impulses easily swamped the more internationalist, peace-promoting tendencies of the interwar Canadian JRC, as young Canadians were mobilized into the mainstream of patriotically perceived senior Red Cross work. But although the Second World War saw the JRC turn much of its attention to war, many adult leaders clung doggedly to their belief in its peaceful, internationalist potential. International correspondence continued throughout the conflict—albeit with fewer countries—and adult organizers eagerly anticipated the post-war re-establishment of relationships between Canadian Juniors and their counterparts elsewhere.[43]

The dream of children creating a more peaceful future lived on in some adults' minds, despite the disruption of the war. In 1944 Nova Scotia JRC Director Elizabeth Browne argued that the enduring value of the JRC lay in its role of providing "training for Good World Citizenship" through giving young people responsibility, and helping to inculcate "emotions of altruism." The result, she argued, was to "help young people to be 'better kids in a better world.'" Similarly, Margaret Palmer, British Columbia's provincial JRC Director, believed that Canadian children's wartime service, and their demonstrated willingness to help less fortunate children at home and overseas, was a promising sign that Canada's "citizens of tomorrow" would be "the kind of men and women who [would] be able to maintain lasting peace in the years to come."[44]

Adult JRC leaders did their best to facilitate this goal. After the cessation of hostilities, the JRC War Fund was renamed the JRC Service Fund, its purpose now to provide whatever was most needed by children in countries ravaged by the war. In addition to these gifts of cash or purchased medicine and foodstuffs, Canadian Juniors continued to make and send articles of clothing and bedding overseas in the immediate post-war period. The international correspondence program quickly resumed on its old footing, to the satisfaction of provincial directors.[45] International friendliness among children thus appeared to bloom once more, amid the still smouldering ruins left by the war.

The unbounded optimism of interwar Canadian Junior Red Cross leaders, however, had been tempered by the experience of the Second World War, so swift upon the heels of the First. In the post-war period organizers plainly still believed that international friendliness among children had a vital role to play in shaping the world of tomorrow, but they no longer considered it a cure-all. The 30 million Juniors of 1946, living in 53 countries around the world, seemed eager to correspond with one another, observed New Brunswick JRC Committee members, and their interactions could "create a spirit of friendship and goodwill amongst young people" which was "much to be desired." But, they warned, it could "by no means be considered a solution to war and unrest." Adult efforts to physically rebuild Europe and the Far East and to psychologically rehabilitate the children caught up in these war zones would be paramount. The Second World War did not kill the belief in children's centrality to future world peace and prosperity: the post-war work of UNICEF and adoption of a new international declaration of children's rights in 1959 made this clear.[46] The war had, however, subdued the unbridled utopianism of the most ardent supporters of JRC international friendliness. Friendship was only a first step.

This glimpse into the history of the Canadian Junior Red Cross is a very specific case study of one particular organization and its struggle to adapt to changing contexts and remain true to both peacetime and wartime traditions. But when considered in the context of the myriad other youth organizations actively engaged in wartime work at the same time, it also raises a larger question: when war and violence are a reality, what is a child's proper role?[47]

The Canadian JRC chose to keep silent on some issues, adapt its internationalism, downplay nationalism, and heavily emphasize voluntary service—the so-called practical patriotism of humanitarian aid to the armed forces, civilian refugees, and particularly to other children suffering the effects of war. Within this adult-approved space, Canadian children and youth made real sacrifices of time and money which were translated (with adult help) into important humanitarian aid.

Millions of children were evacuated, displaced, interned, bombed, starved, and conscripted during the war, but most Canadian children never faced such trauma.[48] Safe in Fortress North America, they instead offered voluntary service. This contrast may have helped rationalize children's war work: it was relatively innocuous and in many cases explicitly humanitarian, as opposed to the direct violence, fear, and destruction faced by children elsewhere. Regardless of whether we agree or disagree with the JRC's solution to its wartime challenges we need look no further than the youthful revolutionaries who participated in the recent "Arab Spring" to recognize that young people exert agency in times of crisis and are implicated in very tangible ways in war, revolution, and conflict. Paradoxically, such involvement holds the potential to both strengthen and destroy them. In today's uncertain, globalized world juggling on-the-ground realities with the ideals of peace and internationalism remains as fraught with moral complexity as it was in 1939.

Notes

1. Karen Dubinsky, "Children, Ideology, and Iconography: How Babies Rule the World," *Journal of the History of Childhood and Youth* [hereafter *JHCY*] (Winter 2012): 10–11; Karen Dubinsky, *Babies Without Borders: Adoption and Migration across the Americas* (Toronto: University of Toronto Press, 2012), chapter 1.

2. Sarah Carlene Glassford, "Marching as to War: The Canadian Red Cross Society, 1885–1939," (Ph.D. diss., York University, 2007), 133–36; *Fourteenth International Red Cross Conference, Twelfth Meeting of the Board of Governors of the League, Brussels, October 1930—Reports of the League Secretariat* (Paris: League of Red Cross Societies, 1930), 83–84. In Canada, the JRC promoted health, service, and *citizenship*—which included

contributing to the international community. Using "citizenship" instead of "international friendliness" meant that after 1939 the Canadian JRC could shift its focus but use consistent language.

3. Canadian Red Cross National Archive, Box 1, File 1.1, "The Canadian Red Cross Society 1914—and After," 8; Dominion Bureau of Statistics, "Table 5: Population by Age Groups and Sex, Census of 1941, with Estimates (as at June 1), 1942–49," *Canadian Year Book 1951* (Ottawa: King's Printer, 1951), 125. See also Nancy M. Sheehan, "Junior Red Cross in the Schools: An International Movement, a Voluntary Agency, and Curriculum Change," *Curriculum Inquiry* 17, no. 3 (1987): 247–66.

4. The magazine appeared monthly from September to June.

By 1938 monthly circulation reached 33,743 copies, but because siblings and classrooms shared copies, readership was larger. Circulation notice, *CRC Junior*, March 1938, 2.

5. Akira Iriye, *Cultural Internationalism and World Order* (Baltimore: Johns Hopkins University Press, 1997), 3; Kristine Alexander, "The Girl Guide Movement and Imperial Internationalism in the 1920s and 1930s," *JHCY* (Winter 2009): 37–63; Julia F. Irwin, "Teaching Americanism with a World Perspective: The Junior Red Cross in the US Schools from 1917 to the 1920s," *History of Education Quarterly* (August 2013): 255–79; Diana Selig, "World Friendship: Children, Parents, and Peace Education in America between the Wars," in *Children and War: A Historical Anthology*, ed. James Marten (New York: New York University Press, 2002) [hereafter Marten, ed., *Children and War*], 135–46; Rhonda L. Hinther, "Raised in the Spirit of the Class Struggle: Children, Youth, and the Interwar Ukrainian Left in Canada," *Labour/Le travail* (Fall 2007): 43–76.

6. John F. Hutchinson, *Champions of Charity: War and the Rise of the Red Cross* (Boulder, CO: Westview Press, 1996), 256; Glassford, "Marching as to War," chapters 3–7; James Marten, *The Children's Civil War* (Chapel Hill: University of North Carolina Press, 1998), 3.

7. Ruth B. Shaw, Appendix VII, "Junior Red Cross Report," *Annual Report 1942* (Montreal: Quebec Division CRCS, 1943), 51–52; Ruth B. Shaw, Appendix VI, "Junior Red Cross Report," *Annual Report 1944* (Montreal: Quebec Division CRCS, 1945), 54. Girl Guide leaders faced similar challenges. See Kristine Alexander, "The Girl Guides, Imperialism and Internationalism in Interwar England, Canada, and India," (Ph.D. diss., York University, 2010), conclusion.

8. "Cross-Section: Personalities in the News," *Despatch*, March 1950, 12.

9. Jean E. Browne, "Dear Juniors," *CRC Junior*, October 1939, 3; on children's innocence/promise see Dubinsky, *Babies Without Borders*, 15–16, 131. Such depoliticization also informed the 1920s American JRC health program discussed in John F. Hutchinson, "The Junior Red Cross Goes to Healthland," *American Journal of Public Health* 87 (1997): 1816–23.

10. Jean Browne, "Dear Juniors," 3.

11. Rosa Bruno-Jofre, "Citizenship and Schooling in Manitoba, 1918–1945," *Manitoba History* 36 (1998): 31; Barbara Lorenzkowski, "The Children's War," in *Occupied St John's: A Social History of a City at War, 1939–1945*, ed. Steven High (Montreal & Kingston: McGill-Queen's University Press, 2010), 113–50.

12. Nina Holland, "Lost Treasures," *CRC Junior*, March 1941, 21.

13. Owen Griffiths, "Japanese Children and the Culture of Death, January–August 1945," in Marten, ed., *Children and War*, 160–71; Berry Mayall and Virginia Morrow, *You Can Help Your Country: English Children's Work During*

the *Second World War* (London: Institute of Education, University of London, 2011), 209–10. The unstudied Second World War–era American JRC makes North American comparisons impossible.

14. W.O. Banfield, "Annual Report of the Junior Red Cross in British Columbia for the School Year 1938–1939," *Annual Report 1939* (Vancouver: BC Division CRCS, 1940), 1–2. The Japanese JRC was founded in 1922: www.jrc.or.jp/english/about/history.html. The German JRC, founded in 1925, was dissolved by the Nazis in 1937: www.drk.de/ueber-uns/geschichte/ zeitleiste.html. Quebec JRC annual reports show that the province's wartime international correspondence was reduced to roughly eleven percent of pre-war levels.

15. Alberta Division CRCS, "Report of Executive Officers," *29th Annual Report 1943* (Calgary: Alberta Division CRCS, 1944), B-8. The Allied blockade of Germany made humanitarian relief for European civilians nearly impossible, but the International Committee of the Red Cross and League of Red Cross Societies, both based in neutral Switzerland, used national Red Cross society donations to provide some relief in occupied Europe, particularly to children. Caroline Moorehead, *Dunant's Dream: War, Switzerland and the History of the Red Cross* (New York: Carroll & Graf, 1998), 387–92.

16. V.K. Greer, "Junior Red Cross," *Annual Statement 1941* (Toronto: Ontario Division CRCS, 1942), 31; Mariel Jenkins, "A Prayer," *CRC Junior*, November 1939, 3.

17. Profiles included Josef Stalin, Sun Yat-Sen, and Chiang Kai-Shek. "Our Friends in Foreign Lands" ran 1942–1943; "Our Friends to the South" appeared in spring 1944.

18. William J. Tuttle, Jr., *"Daddy's Gone to War": The Second World War in the Lives of America's Children* (New York: Oxford University Press, 1993), 148–61; Robert Wm Kirk, *Earning Their Stripes: The Mobilization of American Children in the Second World War* (New York: Peter Lang, 1994), 33–54; Juliet Gardiner, *The Children's War: The Second World War through the Eyes of the Children of Britain* (London: Portrait, with the Imperial War Museum, 2005), 144–45.

19. Canadian, American, and British youth were all directed toward community service in wartime, although the French Catholic school boards of Quebec did not encourage war-related school activity because of their own ambivalence and a wider French-Canadian hostility toward the war. Tamara Myers and Mary Anne Poutanen, "Cadets, Curfews, and Compulsory Schooling: Mobilizing Anglophone Children in WWII Montreal," *Histoire sociale/Social History* (November 2005): 367–98; Mayall and Morrow, *You Can Help Your Country*, chapter 8; Tuttle, Jr., *"Daddy's Gone to War,"* chapter 7; Nicole Sedgwick, "'More than Ever Now Our Minds Require Defences': Ontario's Primary Schools during the Second World War" (MA thesis, Carleton University, 2010). Quotation: Jean E. Browne, "The Junior Red Cross," *Canadian Geographical*

Journal (December 1940): 325–27; "Real Patriotism," *CRC Junior,* September 1940, 21.

20. Bruno-Jofre, 28–29; R.S. Patterson, "Society and Education during the Wars and Their Interlude: 1914–1945," in *Canadian Education: A History,* eds. J. Donald Wilson, Robert M. Stamp, and Louis-Phillipe Audet (Scarborough, Ontario: Prentice-Hall, 1970), 378.

21. Cynthia Comacchio, *The Dominion of Youth: Adolescence and the Making of Modern Canada, 1920 to 1950* (Waterloo, Ontario: Wilfrid Laurier University Press, 2006), chapter 7; Jennifer Robin Terry, "'They 'Used to Tear Around the Campus Like Savages': Children's and Youth's Activities in the Santo Tomas Internment Camp, 1942–1945," *JHCY* (Winter 2012): 98; J.W. Estey quoted in Saskatchewan Division CRCS, *Annual Report 1939* (Regina: Saskatchewan Division CRCS, 1940), 14.

22. Myers and Poutanen, "Cadets, Curfews, and Compulsory Schooling," 367–98; Jeffrey A. Keshen, *Saints, Sinners, and Soldiers: Canada's Second World War* (Vancouver: UBC Press, 2004), 204–26.

23. Photos accompanying Jean E. Browne, "The Junior Red Cross," 322–27.

24. Myers and Poutanen, "Cadets, Curfews, and Compulsory Schooling," 371.

25. Ruth B. Shaw, Appendix VI, "Junior Red Cross Report," *Annual Report 1945* (Montreal: Quebec Division CRCS, 1946), 50; CRCS, "Statistical Highlights of Services—Canada and Overseas," *Annual Report for the Year 1945* (Toronto: CRCS, 1946), 171. This $3,000,000 is equivalent to $39,717,391.30 in 2012 Canadian dollars: Bank of Canada Inflation Calculator, www.bankofcanada.ca/rates/related/inflation-calculator. Quotation: Saskatchewan Division CRCS, *Annual Report 1940* (Regina: Saskatchewan Division CRCS, 1941), 15.

26. Jean E. Browne, "The Junior Red Cross," 325–27.

27. C.K. Rogers, "Report of the Junior Red Cross Committee Year Ending December 31st, 1941," *Committee Reports Year 1940* (Winnipeg: Manitoba Division CRCS, 1942), n.p.; Patterson, "Society and Education," 378.

28. All examples from *CRC Junior*: Mildred Stein, "How Children Can Serve the Empire," March 1940, 11, 22; "Hymn for Our Soldiers," January 1941, 22; "They Also Serve—A True Story," February 1941, 6; Maria Metcalfe, "Victory Song," March 1942, 16.

29. CRCS, "Report of the Junior Red Cross for the School Year 1940–41," *Annual Report for the Year 1941* (Toronto: CRCS, 1942), 52; Statistics Canada, "Population and Growth Components (1851–2001 Censuses), www.statcan.gc.ca/tables-tableaux/sum-som/; Dominion Bureau of Statistics, 125.

30. Charles M. Johnston, "The Children's War: The Mobilization of Ontario Youth During the Second World War," in *Patterns of the Past: Interpreting Ontario's History*, eds. Roger Hall, William Westfall, and Laurel Sefton MacDowell (Toronto: Dundurn Press, 1988), 367, 378

note 42.

31. CRCS, "Statistical Highlights of Various Red Cross Services in Canada and Britain," *Annual Report for the Year 1944* (Toronto: CRCS, 1945), 158; CRCS, "The Year 1945—Canadian Branches and Membership," *Annual Report for the Year 1945* (Toronto: CRCS, 1946), 170; Anne Millar and Jeff Keshen, "Rallying Young Canada to the Cause: Anglophone Schoolchildren in Montreal and Toronto during the Two World Wars," *History of Intellectual Culture* 9, no. 1 (2010/11): 10–12, www.ucalgary.ca/hic.

32. Myers and Poutanen, "Cadets, Curfews, and Compulsory Schooling," 369–70; Mary Peate, *Girl in a Sloppy Joe Sweater: Life on the Canadian Home Front during World War II* (Montreal: Optimum Publishing, 1988), 94; Tuttle, Jr., *"Daddy's Gone to War,"* 112.

33. Marten, *Children's War,* 5; Mayall and Morrow explore this theme in the English context.

34. Shaw, *Annual Report 1944,* 53; NB Division CRCS, "Canadian Junior Red Cross Society Report 1942," *Annual Report of Division (Including Branches) for the Year Ending December 31, 1941* (Saint John, New Brunswick: NB Division CRCS, 1942), 1.

35. Christine Hamelin, "A Sense of Purpose: Ottawa Students and the Second World War," *Canadian Military History* 6, no. 1 (1997): 35, 38; "Proud to Serve Our Country," *CRC Junior,* January 1941, 22. Original italics.

36. Ruth B. Shaw, Appendix V, "The Junior Red Cross Quebec Provincial Division—Report of the Supervisor for the Year 1940," *Annual Report 1940* (Montreal: Quebec Division CRCS, 1941), 71; Verna G. Darrach, "Junior Red Cross Report," *Annual Reports—1940* (Charlottetown, Prince Edward Island: PEI Division CRCS, 1941), 3; Verna G. Darrach, "Junior Red Cross Annual Report for 1942," *Annual Reports for the Year 1942* (Charlottetown, Prince Edward Island: PEI Division CRCS, 1943), n.p.

37. Bruce Scates, "The Unknown Sock Knitter: Voluntary Work, Emotional Labour, Bereavement and the Great War," *Labour History* (Australia) 81 (2001): 29–49; *Lux Glebana* 1941, p. 17, quoted in Hamelin, "A Sense of Purpose," 36; J. Louise Despert, quoted in Tuttle, Jr., *"Daddy's Gone to War,"* 124.

38. Saskatchewan Division CRCS, *Annual Report 1941* (Regina: Saskatchewan Division CRCS, 1942), 14; Saskatchewan Division CRCS, *Annual Report 1942* (Regina: Saskatchewan Division CRCS, 1943), 16.

39. BC Division CRCS, "Report of the Provincial Junior Red Cross Committee—1945," *Annual Report 1945* (Vancouver: BC Division CRCS, 1946), 46; on the "neutral child" see Dominique Marshall, "Children's Rights and Children's Action in International and Domestic Welfare: The Work of Herbert Hoover Between 1914 and 1950," *JHCY* (Fall 2008): 351–88.

40. Saskatchewan Division CRCS, *Annual Report 1943* (Regina: Saskatchewan Division CRCS, 1944), 16; Shaw, *Annual Report 1942,* 53; Verna G. Darrach, "Junior Red

Cross Annual Report for 1943," *Annual Reports for the Year 1943* (Charlottetown, Prince Edward Island: PEI Division CRCS, 1944), n.p.

41. Elizabeth O.R. Browne, "Report of the Junior Red Cross—Nova Scotia Division for the School Year 1941–1942," *28th Annual Report* (Halifax, Nova Scotia: NS Division CRCS, 1943), 2; Elizabeth O.R. Browne, "Report of the Junior Red Cross for the School Year 1942–1943," *29th Annual Report* (Halifax, Nova Scotia: NS Division CRCS, 1944), 3.

42. Conversations with my maternal grandmother Lucienna Wismer Jones Pattison and my great aunt Marilyn Wismer Kettlewell in January 2009 supported the findings in Mary Elizabeth Nowlan, "Junior Red Cross Volunteer Knitting in Winnipeg School Division No. 1 During and Immediately After World War II (1939–1946)," (MSc thesis, University of Manitoba, 1996); C.K. Rogers, "Report of the Junior Red Cross Committee Year Ending December 31st, 1942," *Committee Reports Year 1941* (Winnipeg: Manitoba Division CRCS, 1942), n.p.; G.C. Derby, "President's Annual Report," *Annual Report 1941* (Vancouver: BC Division CRCS, 1942), 4.

43. C.K. Rogers, "Report of the Manitoba Junior Red Cross for the School Year 1943–44," *Committee Reports Year 1944* (Winnipeg: Manitoba Division CRCS, 1945), 1.

44. E.O.R. Browne, "School Year 1942–1943," 5; Elizabeth O.R. Browne, "Report of the Director of Junior Red Cross—For the School Year 1944–1945," *Annual Report for the Year 1945* (Halifax, Nova Scotia: NS Division

CRCS, 1946), 22; Margaret Palmer, quoted in "Report of the Provincial Junior Red Cross Committee—1944," *Annual Report 1944* (Vancouver: BC Division CRCS, 1945), n.p.

45. Mrs. Hendry McLellan and Marion B. Bates, "Junior Red Cross Annual Report," *Annual Report for the Year 1945* (Saint John, New Brunswick: NB Division CRCS, 1946), 2.

46. W.H. MacKenzie and Marion B. Bates, "Junior Red Cross Annual Report," *Annual Report for the Year 1946* (Saint John, New Brunswick: NB Division CRCS, 1947), 2; Tara Zahra, *The Lost Children: Reconstructing Europe's Families After World War II* (Cambridge, MA: Harvard University Press, 2011), 1–23; Marshall, "Children's Rights," 351–88; Dominique Marshall, "Humanitarian Sympathy for Children in Times of War and the History of Children's Rights, 1919–1959," in Marten, ed., *Children and War*, 184–99.

47. Janie Hampton, *How the Girl Guides Won the War* (London: Harper Press, 2012); Lisa L. Ossian, "'Too Young for a Uniform': Children's War Work on the Iowa Farm Front, 1941–1945," in Marten, ed., *Children and War*, 254–65; Keshen, "Rallying Young Canada," 202–4; Gardiner, *The Children's War*, 133–45; Kirk, *Earning Their Stripes*, chapters 3–4.

48. Children's wartime experiences are recounted in Emmy Werner, *Through the Eyes of Innocents: Children Witness World War II* (Boulder, CO: Westview Press, 2000). The exceptions in Canada were Japanese-Canadian children, who were interned with their parents.

PRIMARY DOCUMENT

"Junior Red Cross News," *Canadian Red Cross Junior*, 1940

Balanced Giving

We are interested to know that many Junior Red Cross Branches in Canada are carefully considering the needs to be met and are then balancing their donations accordingly. Typical examples of this follow:

The members of the *L'Ordre de Bon Temps Branch of Grade 8, Williamson Road School, Toronto,* undertook to put on a candlelight carol service in their school just before Christmas. It was an evening performance and the public were invited. An admission fee was charged. The

continued

Juniors wore surplices and had most impressive stage settings, consisting of Christmas trees and mammoth white candles set on standards. In addition to impressing the public with what Juniors could really accomplish, they cleared the sum of $40.00 which they apportioned as follows,— $10.00 to the Crippled Children's Fund, $10.00 to the Red Cross Relief Fund, $20.00 to the Soldiers' Fund of the Red Cross.

The same Juniors undertook a unique type of Christmas service. They invited as their guests a girl and boy of their own age from a district in another part of the city where Christmas treats are rare. They prepared a Christmas tree with beautiful and suitable presents for the guests. It is hard to say who enjoyed this event more, the guests or the hosts.

The secretary of the *Little Long Lac Branch* describes the activities of the Branch in a letter sent to Headquarters: "We have had two silver teas and were quite successful in making $11.50. In answer to a plea to the Senior Red Cross in Port Arthur, 12 pounds of 4-ply heather Scotch fingering were sent to us. So far we have been knitting scarves and sleeveless sweaters for the soldiers. At a hockey game sponsored by the Red Cross here, six of our members took up a silver collection and succeeded in making $37.50. Of this we are contributing $25.00 to the Senior Red Cross in Geraldton, as they sponsored the game and gave us the proceeds. We are also giving $5.00 of it to the Crippled Children's Fund. At Christmas our Service Committee gave a doll and some fruit to a small girl dying of tuberculosis of the bone. She is past doctors' help and comes of a poor family.

"This is a fair outline of our work and we are now thinking of making a portfolio to send to India."

The Beaver Club of East Ward School, Pembroke, reports as follows:

"We, the members of the Beaver Club of East Ward School, take this opportunity of sending you a postal note for the amount of five dollars ($5.00) to be used as follows: $1.00 to pay our membership fee, $2.00 for the Crippled Children's Fund, $2.00 to the Soldiers' Fund. Some of this money was donated by our members and the rest obtained by selling 'non-run kits.'

"We are anxious to help the good work of the Junior Red Cross and are saving all the money we can for that purpose."

Be a Help Branch

The "Be a Help" Branch of St Joseph's School, Stratford, Ontario, has more than vindicated its choice of name. The following letter from the Reverend Sister Ethelrida tells an interesting story of excellent social service carried on in their own community:

"The pins and other material for the Junior Red Cross, St Joseph's School, Room III, 'Be a Help' Branch were received with much pleasure by the pupils.

"We are enclosing the dollar fee, and wish that it could be more.

"Perhaps you would like to hear of our activities since our last letter.

"We provide reading material for the soldiers who are in the hospital. One hundred and seventy magazines were sent, also the daily and weekly papers. A bundle was sent each week.

"Each child brought a toy for the Christmas Welfare baskets. There were sent to the Scout shops to be distributed. Shoes and rubbers were provided for a child who was unable to attend until proper footwear was provided.

"Three overcoats and underwear were given to one family who were in need of them. Two suits, mackintoshes and bloomers were provided for another family, and an overcoat and shoes to an old man who needed them badly.

"Five baskets of fruit were sent to the soldiers in hospital and two to members of our Junior Red Cross, who were also in the hospital.

"At Christmas we made up nine individual boxes, each box contained fruit, candy, candy cane and an individual present in each box. These were done up in the usual Christmassy papers with tags attached. Seven were sent to the hospital for seven soldiers who did not receive a personal box from home, one was sent to an invalid who lives near by, and the ninth to one of our Junior members who was in the hospital owing to an appendicitis operation.

"There are only 38 in the class and 40 per cent of their parents are on part time work, so the pennies are scarce but they are anxious to help and do the best they can.

"When the Health Rules were given to the members before they signed, one little boy, who is very pale and has been in the hospital for some time said, 'Sister, I can't sign that.' I said, 'Why?' 'Well,' said he, 'we have to promise to eat vegetables and I just hate them.' We compromised. I said, 'Well, just start taking a spoonful at a time, and after a while you will be asking for more.' He has been eating the vegetables since November, and I think his cheeks are showing the result."

Source: "Junior Red Cross News," *Canadian Red Cross Junior* 21, 4 (1940): 2.

Study Questions

1. Barbara Lorenzkowski's essay inspires questions about the central role of memory in histories of young people. How is Lorenzkowski's reliance on childhood memories particularly important for gleaning information about the home front during wartime? What is revealed using this method that might otherwise remain hidden from history?

2. Read over the *Canadian Red Cross Junior* news page from 1940 that accompanies Glassford's essay. What does the variety of activities that members of the Junior Red Cross engaged in during the Second World War tell us about the agency and initiative of young people as historical actors?

3. In the affluent countries of the Global North, contemporary childhood is rarely associated with war. What assumptions about children and childhood make this association difficult or uncomfortable? How do the essays in this chapter challenge our feelings of discomfort in this regard?

Selected Bibliography

Articles

Alexander, Kristine, "An Honour and a Burden: Canadian Girls and the Great War," in Sarah Glassford and Amy Shaw, eds, *A Sisterhood of Suffering and Service Women and Girls of Canada and Newfoundland during the First World War*. Vancouver: University of British Columbia Press, 2012.

Burke, Garry J., "Good for the Boy and the Nation: Military Drill and the Cadet Movement in Ontario Public Schools, 1865–1911." Ph.D. diss., University of Toronto, 1996.

Dirks, Patricia, "Canada's Boys: An Imperial or National Asset? Responses to Baden-Powell's Boy Scout Movement in Pre-War Canada," in Phillip Buckner and R. Douglas Francis, eds, *Canada and the British World: Culture, Migration, and Identity*. Vancouver: UBC Press, 2006: 111–28.

Johnston, Charles M., "The Children's War: The Mobilization of Ontario Youth during the Second World War," in Roger Hall, William Westfall, and Laurel Sefton MacDowell, eds, *Patterns of the Past: Interpreting Ontario's History*. Toronto: Dundurn Press, 1988: 356–80.

Kiefer, Nancy, and Ruth Roach Pierson, "The War Effort and Women Students at the University of Toronto, 1939–45," in Paul Axelrod and John G. Reid, eds, *Youth, University, Canadian Society: Essays in the Social History of Higher Education*. McGill-Queen's University Press, 1989: 161–81.

Lewis, Norah, "'Isn't this a terrible war?': The Attitudes of Children to Two World Wars," *Historical Studies in Education/Revue d'histoire de l'éducation* 7, 2 (Fall 1995): 193–215.

Mainville, Curt, "The Middlemore Boys: Immigration, Settlement, and Great War Volunteerism in New Brunswick," *Acadiensis* 42, 2 (2013).

Montgomery, Emilie L., "'The war was a very vivid part of my life': The Second World War and the Lives of British Columbia Children," in Jean Barman, Neil Sutherland, and J. Donald Wilson, eds, *Children, Teachers and Schools in the History of British Columbia*. Calgary: Detselig, 1995: 161–74.

Morton, Desmond, "The Cadet Movement in the Moment of Canadian Militarism, 1909–1914," *Journal of Canadian Studies* 13, 2 (Summer 1978): 56–69.

Springhall, J.O., "The Boy Scouts, Class and Militarism in Relation to British Youth Movements, 1908–1930," *International Review of Social History* 16 (1971): 125–58.

Books

Cockerill, A.W., *Sons of the Brave: The Story of the Boy Soldiers*. London: Leo Cooper, in association with Secker & Warburg, 1984.

Fisher, Susan, *Boys and Girls in No Man's Land: English-Canadian Children and the First World War*. Toronto: University of Toronto Press, 2010.

Moss, Mark, *Manliness and Militarism: Educating Young Boys in Ontario for War*. Don Mills, ON: Oxford University Press, 2001.

McClare, Dale, *The Letters of a Young Canadian Soldier during World War I*. Kentville, NS: Brook House Press, 2000.

7 Regulation and Children's Embodiment

Editors' Introduction

The regulation of children's bodies has long been a major feature of Canadian history. Particularly over the nineteenth and twentieth centuries, the growth of the nation state involved the construction of systems of social welfare as well as schooling, urbanization, and shifting domestic arrangements that would focus attention on the management of values regarding acceptable childhoods and children's physical bodies. The regulation of young bodies was central to this broad transformation as children felt the impact of the rise of new specialties in medicine, law, and psychology that focused on defining, protecting, policing, and treating the ailments of childhood and adolescence.[1]

This chapter's essays, by Mona Gleason and Jessica Haynes, consider the embodied regulation of children and their families and how they responded to it. Gleason focuses on children's medical treatment and health education over the early decades of the twentieth century, while Haynes explores the fate of mothers and babies at the heart of the 1960s thalidomide drug scandal. Both essays focus on the regulation of children's bodies, whether in the doctor's office or the classroom, by parental negotiation or legal and political constraint.

The socialization of children into bearers of community values and beliefs has been a constant, and contested, preoccupation of adults, both lay and professional. Class, race, gender, and ability played important roles in determining whether children and their families experienced social inclusion or exclusion. In her contribution, Gleason considers how turn-of-the-twentieth-century medical professionals and health educators understood healthy, "normal" children's bodies and how this in turn shaped children's experiences. Excerpts from 1906 and 1911 health textbooks used in Canadian schools accompany Gleason's essay and give us a glimpse into how embodied care and pedagogy was also infused with powerful messages about, among other things, gender and race. Combining historical evidence from professional medical journals, training manuals, and curriculum documents with the oral histories of 11 adults who grew up in various regions of Canada, Gleason identifies a critical tension between how adult professionals understood the needs and capacities of young people and how youth and their families responded.[2]

Against the backdrop of the thalidomide drug crisis of the 1960s, Jessica Haynes, anticipating Nic Clarke's essay in the next chapter, challenges us to consider what history reveals about children's stereotypical construction as precious. The reaction to babies born with the physical effects of thalidomide exposure, Haynes argues, takes its place within the much longer history of eugenics in Canada. In their discussions of "thalidomide babies" in the popular press, journalists, parents, medical and psychological professionals, and the general public drew on arguments about embodied normalcy as a prerequisite for a healthy and happy existence. The primary document that complements Haynes's article, a front-page photo from the *Toronto Daily Star* of 26 July 1962, gives us a window into how the media positioned families and children dealing with the effects of the drug. The essential message propagated about such families was that they were forced to deal with tragedy and shame because their child was abnormal, not because society was ruthlessly discriminatory.

Like other essays in this collection, this chapter's contributions challenge readers to consider the possibilities and limits of children's agency. The interaction between youth and adults, particularly adults in positions of social authority, requires careful consideration by historians.[3] Clearly, as these essays demonstrate, children were never merely victims of adult actions or neglect. Nor, however, could they escape the considerable strictures placed on them by virtue of their young age and small size.

Notes

1. See for example, Allan Moscovitch and Jim Albert, eds., *The Benevolent State: The Growth of Welfare in Canada* (Toronto: Garamond Press, 1987); Carol Baines, Patricia Evans, and Sheila Neysmith, *Women's Caring: Feminist Perspectives on Social Welfare* (Toronto: McClelland & Stewart, 1991); Cheryl Warsh and Veronica Strong-Boag, eds. *Children's Health Issues in Historical Perspective* (Waterloo, ON.: Wilfrid Laurier University Press, 2005); Cynthia Comacchio, *The Dominion of Youth: Adolescence and the Making of Modern Canada* (Waterloo: Wilfrid Laurier Press, 2006); Veronica Strong-Boag, *Finding Families, Finding Ourselves: English Canada Encounters Adoption from the Nineteenth Century to the 1990s* (Don Mills, ON: Oxford University Press, 2006); Veronica

Strong-Boag, *Fostering Nation?: Canada Confronts Its History of Childhood Disadvantage* (Waterloo: Wilfrid Laurier, 2010); Karen A. Balcolm, *The Traffic in Babies: Cross-Border Adoption and Baby Selling Between the United States and Canada, 1930 to 1972* (Toronto: University of Toronto Press, 2011); Tarah Brookfield, *Cold War Comforts: Canadian Women, Child Safety, and Global Insecurity* (Waterloo: Wilfrid Laurier Press, 2012).

2. See also Mona Gleason, *Small Matters: Canadian Children in Sickness and Health, 1900–1940* (Montreal and Kingston: McGill-Queen's University Press, 2013).

3. Mona Gleason, "Avoiding the Agency Trap: Caveats for Historians of Children, Youth, and Education," *History of Education* 45, 4 (2016): 446–59.

"Lost Voices, Lost Bodies"? Doctors and the Embodiment of Children and Youth in English Canada from 1900 to the 1940s

MONA GLEASON

In 1915, a story entitled "The Little Brother" appeared in *The Canadian Nurse*, the premier journal of nursing practice in English Canada until well into the 1980s. Dramatizations of nursing care were a regular feature of the journal. The story of "The Little Brother," penned by Vancouver writer Rene Norcross, revolved around the hospitalization of Mah Too, a 14-year-old Chinese boy who had arrived in Vancouver a month before. Very early in the short tale, the author makes it clear that the presence of Chinese patients in Vancouver hospitals at the beginning of the twentieth century was not unusual. "Indeed," the narrator suggests, "there was some inclination to regard them as unavoidable nuisances to be dealt with as kindly and patiently as possible."[1] But Mah Too was young and vulnerable and singled out for his "astonishing prettiness." Eventually, Mah Too's condition deteriorated and the young boy requested that he be allowed to return to Vancouver's Chinatown with his brother, Mah Soon. The doctor's response to this request foreshadowed the boy's fate: "Confound it, that means cutting in half what little time he has left. . . . He'll be put into a six by eight hovel with an atmosphere you could cut with a knife and fork and a jabber like a sawmill going on day and night."[2] The hospital surgeon listening nearby offered a sage response: "Perhaps that's what he misses." Mah Too's request was granted and within a week of returning home, he was dead. The story ends here.

The treatment of Mah Too in "The Little Brother" mirrors many of the complexities and contradictions that accompanied medical encounters between adult experts and young people in English Canada over the course of the twentieth century. Although the explicit message delivered in the story revolved around the tragedy of Mah Too, the implicit subtext suggested a lesson steeped in the racial politics of the day: it reminded readers of the superiority of white Western conceptions of health and well-being. Mah Too's death had little to do with the youngster's bleak health prognosis and much to do with his inability to adapt to the expectations of culture. Racial inferiority, as surely as pneumonia or tuberculosis, contributed to his demise. From the perspective of the white medical establishment, Mah Too's shortcomings set in motion a tragic journey into darkness, dirt, and death.

If we try to imagine Mah Too's motivations for leaving the hospital with his brother, for these are never made explicit in the story itself, very different kinds of interpretations emerge. Family and home, for example, often occupied a central place for young people of all backgrounds faced with professionalized institutional care. The prospect of facing a ser-

ious illness in an unfamiliar setting in which his presence was merely tolerated undoubtedly terrified Mah Too and perhaps made his illness seem unbearable. However circumscribed and modest, the boy's decision to leave the hospital and return to his home in Chinatown marked a kind of "knee high agency" or at least a yearning for cultural safety in the midst of the hegemonic demands, advice, and beliefs, however well intentioned, of white adult experts.[3]

Mindful of the interpretive power represented by the perspectives of young people as historical actors in their own right, this chapter brings into conversation two sources from roughly the first half of the twentieth century: the published writings of doctors, nurses, and educators on the medical treatment of children's bodies, and the oral histories of adults who grew up in English Canada over roughly the same period. I explore how adult experts understood the bodies of children and how adults remember their bodies in childhood, particularly the medical care of their bodies at the hands of adult professionals. I argue that the embodied management of children, particularly marginalized children, and their varied responses to this management, forged, sustained, and challenged hierarchies and social divisions based on class, race, and gender. This management and responses to it on the part of youngsters and their families deepens our understanding of the role of age in the production and contestation of unequal relations of power in the modern nation state.

Adult memories are gleaned from a set of 11 oral history interviews conducted between 2001 and 2004 in which aspects of learning to be healthy, going to a doctor or traditional healer, or familial folk medicine were queried.[4] Historians are well aware of the problems and limitations associated with oral histories. They counsel caution in using memories that can be unreliable and fallible, and that tend to reconstruct rather than recollect a life. Paul Thompson, in particular, warns us about the need to recognize the inevitable concerns of the present embedded in stories about the past.[5] In the absence of a rich reserve of sources that try to reflect, however imperfectly, the perspective of young people on their experiences, oral histories remain a valuable source. Despite the dangers inherent in the politics of representation, they nonetheless have the potential to give voice to the traditionally voiceless—to children generally, to girls, to First Nations peoples, and to working-class girls and boys. Historians must use them carefully, with healthy skepticism and in conjunction with other kinds of data. All historical sources, after all, have their own unique flaws.

As quintessential "lost children," youngsters outside the boundaries of white, middle-class acceptability also remain largely on the margins of English-Canadian historiography. Much of the foundational scholarship on the history of English-Canadian children's health and welfare over the early decades of the twentieth century has focused on the broad contours of statistical improvements in infant mortality rates and rates of contagious disease infection over the first four decades of the twentieth century in Canada.[6] Subsequent studies detailed the work of medical professionals, legal and urban reformers, and state-sanctioned social welfare departments and networks in their quest to use modern scientific understandings of health and welfare to shape policy, education, and parenting behaviour.[7] As the state became increasingly dependent on the health of its citizens, improvements in sanitation and public health took aim at families and children judged inadequate. From the point of view of a growing cadre of health and social welfare professionals, bringing families up to socially acceptable standards of domestic life, health, education, and employment ensured a strong national citizenry. As Cynthia Comacchio has argued, however, even though experts believed that "nations were built of babies," the needs and preferences of families, or even their best interests, did not always result from health and welfare interventions.[8]

A number of scholars have laid bare the erroneous notion that all children and youth benefited equally from improvements in medical science and life expectancy in the twentieth century. Mary Ellen Kelm, Tina Moffat, and Ann Herring, for example, have shown how the effects of colonization, settlement, and racism resulted in high rates of infant death in First Nations communities over a period otherwise characterized by the triumph of medical science.[9] In the case of adopted children, Veronica Strong-Boag's

recent work in the English-Canadian context reminds us that social premiums placed on "perfect, healthy children" stigmatized those outside this ideal as much as it was a goal for all Canadian youngsters regardless of life circumstances.[10] Attuned to the difference that class, religion, gender, and other markers of social identity made, Tamara Myers has documented how increasing medical authority in the juvenile courts in twentieth-century Montreal often made "modern girls" into "delinquent bodies."[11]

As embodied subjects rather than merely objects in this long history of health and welfare intervention, the perspectives of children and youth remain conspicuously absent from sustained historical analysis in the English-Canadian context.[12] In a recent international collection of essays dedicated to historical perspectives on children's health, the editors lament that "young voices and opinions remain for the most part missing . . . we very much wished for their inclusion and we deeply regret their ultimate omission."[13] The responses of racialized, working-class, and disabled children suffer particularly from under-representation in historical analysis. Their perspectives on their experiences with health professionals, with illness and recovery, and with their bodies add a complicating layer to historical portraits of the period that offer an uncomplicated narrative of the triumph of medical science over high rates of infant and child mortality. This essay attempts to find the lost voices and bodies of young people, particularly those youngsters from minority and working-class backgrounds who typically appear in historical narratives as objects of medicalization. By repositioning young people as subjects in this narrative, they emerge as social actors in the production, reproduction, and, in some places, interruption of dominant social relations.

Doctors, Nurses, and the Problem of Small Bodies

Early in the twentieth century, social reformers, in large part white and middle class, worked to reconstitute childhood as a time deserving of special protection. As Veronica Strong-Boag, Neil Sutherland,

Robert McIntosh, and others have summarized, ideal childhoods, and consequently ideal children, came to be characterized by vulnerability, dependence, protection, segregation, and delayed responsibility.[14] This "needs" orientation could have unintended consequences; it could be malevolent as well as benevolent and was often characterized by an ambivalence about *which* children deserved attention and *what* form that attention should take. The emerging urban and capitalist social order that unfolded over the course of the twentieth century in English Canada developed in a context of eugenics, potent ideas about white racial supremacy, solidifying class hierarchies, gendered and able-bodied biases, and the dominance of Protestant Christianity as the only true religion. This context had enormous consequences for the increasingly professionalized and public management of children's health and welfare. For their part, youngsters were vitally important to the production and maintenance of hierarchical social relations.

Historians in English Canada, following very much along the lines of explanation offered in other national contexts, suggest that specialized interest in the health and welfare of youngsters was nurtured through the convergence of public health reform and concern about high rates of infant mortality in the early years of the twentieth century.[15] As Neil Sutherland has shown, at the turn of the century, approximately one out of every five to seven babies born died in the first year or two of life. This was a state of affairs largely accepted as tragic but not yet a matter of public concern. "What actually prevailed," Sutherland explains, "was a vague but generally unstated sense of inevitability and resignation."[16] In 1916, prominent Toronto physician Dr Alan Brown would note "how frequently one hears the assertion that delicate infants should not live . . . in fact, some go so far as to state that it interferes with the law of natural selection which is the survival of the fittest."[17]

By the end of the First World War, however, this resignation faced challenge for a complex range of reasons: increased understanding of the need for public health reform, concerted medical effort on the part of dedicated medical professionals to confront and eradicate infant and maternal mortality, and lingering eugenic fears of race suicide. The death toll exacted by the First World War, along with the arrival of large numbers of new immigrants, fostered home grown anxieties about the health of the white population. Eugenics, the "cultural policing of the country's 'genetic stock,'" lent its support to numerous welfare initiatives to ensure that middle-class standards of health were either adhered to or, at the very least, represented the ultimate goal for families in English Canada.[18] Thus, infant and maternal welfare movements, dominated by white, Protestant, middle-class reformers and professionals, struggled to reduce the abysmal infant mortality rate in the early decades of the twentieth century.[19]

Doctors were central to this growing attention to the health of the nation's babies. With increasing momentum behind pediatrics as a recognized medical specialization over the turn of the nineteenth century, professional medical writing in the form of textbooks and journal articles focused specifically on the needs of young patients. Conditions of the body "peculiar to, chiefly found during, infancy and childhood," as one textbook writer characterized them, were increasingly understood as warranting separate attention.[20]

Textbooks on pediatrics used in Canadian medical schools, such as Kenneth Fenwick's 1889 *Manual of Obstetrics, Gynaecology, and Paediatrics*, clearly show that notions of normalcy and health were not characteristics readily associated with small bodies. Given the high infant mortality rate with which doctors had to contend, anxiety surrounding the preservation of life in the early years was understandable. Notwithstanding this concern, the intensity of assumptions about children's embodied volatility in the writings of medical professionals is striking: children's feeding is highly problematic, they suffer from "nervous complaints" that come on without warning, they are unreliable sources of information about their own health and are not to be trusted by doctors, and they need to be closely monitored for any number of conditions.[21] Fenwick, for example, conveyed the impression that children—based on assumptions about their small, young bodies—were principally medical problems: "In childhood the tissues are softer, more vascular, and more succulent; the glandular, lymphatic and capillary systems are extremely active; the skin and mucous membranes are softer; more delicate and more sensitive; the brain is large, vascular, and almost fluid in consistency; there is excessive nervous excitability due to want of controlling power; and reflex sensibility is excessively acute."[22] Fenwick was certainly not alone in this presentation of young bodies, particularly infant bodies, as pathological. "One should point out," remarked Dr George Smith, "and emphasize the frailty of the material one is working with. Anatomically the infant lends itself to infection. The organs are small and almost fragile. The distance from the nose to the lung is very short. The physiological and mechanical resistance to oncoming infection is slight."[23] In *Diseases of Childhood* (1926), Hector Charles Cameron warned, "at the moment of birth there is risk both of trauma and infection."[24] Young children, Cameron states, are born vulnerable to a triad of complications that vex the doctor and parent alike throughout childhood: this triad consists of "dietetic disturbances, infections, and severe emotional unrest."[25] "The metabolism of all children, just because they are children," advised Cameron in the *Canadian Medical Association Journal* of 1931, "is less stable than that of later life."[26] Alan Brown, physician-in-chief at Toronto's Hospital for Sick Children, and Frederick Tisdall, his colleague there, advised doctors in *Common Procedures in the Practice of Paediatrics* that "the physical examination of infants and children presents many problems quite distinct from those encountered in the examination of adults."[27] Young patients, they advised, needed thorough inspection from head to toe. Judging the child's cry—its intensity and tenor—was a valuable tool for the diagnosing doctor. Further, "Much information can be obtained by observing the child while the mother is being questioned. If the patient is crying vigorously or taking an interest in its surroundings you know at once that it is not acutely ill. In regard to the character of the cry, with a little practice it is possible to determine whether it is due to the patient being hungry or in pain or whether it is merely the result of fright or temper."[28]

Doctors, it would seem, were right to be very cautious around young, small bodies. Not only were children vulnerable to any number of physical threats, they did not give up their secrets easily. As Fenwick reminded his readers, the diagnosis of medical problems was hard enough in adults, never mind the additional complications that infants and children presented for practitioners: "The task is one which requires patience, good nature, and tact for the helpless silence of the infant, the incorrect answers of the older child, the fright, agitation, or anger produced by your examination, or even mere presence, render it difficult to detect the real aberration of function."[29]

Challenges to the provision of good health posed by small bodies were mitigated by middle-class affluence, according to the advice of doctors. In professional conceptions of good health, minimal standards of housing and cleanliness were solidly middle class. Consider the advice of Dr A. Grant Fleming, offered in 1929, and typical of the era and beyond: "Individual health depends essentially upon the individual's practice of what we call 'personal hygiene.' Even in our age of organization, we expect that we must consider our bath, our bed-time, and our open bed room window as personal responsibilities. Modern inventions have given us conveniences that greatly assist and make reasonably easy the practice of personal hygiene."[30] Running water, separate bedrooms with windows, new household gadgets, choices about sleep—for all the veneer of scientific objectivity, good health and personal hygiene were thoroughly steeped in middle-class habitus.

That the working class, and in particular the racialized working class, did not participate in such middle-class habitus made them particularly "unhealthy." Professional practitioners tended to conceptualize these "other bodies" as in need not simply of good advice but of significant health salvation and reformation. The story of Mah Too is a stark testimony to the racialization of health status and its recuperation by middle-class white health professionals in early-twentieth-century Canada. Another example is offered in a feature story entitled "In the Children's Ward," written by B.E.A. Philmot for *The Canadian Nurse's* April 1909 edition. In her account of the various children and families encountered on the ward, intertwined issues of ethnicity and class come to the forefront. Readers learn of the fate of Dennis, a three-year-old boy of working-class Irish descent, early in her observations. According to the nurse, "We undressed him by main force and put him in the tub. He evidently, to judge by his struggles, thought we were going to drown him. Probably he had never seen so much water collected in one place before. Also he dreaded to part with that outer covering of dirt; it had been his own for so long it was well-nigh impossible to take it from him."[31] Although Dennis eventually "learns" to be a proper patient, he cannot simply wash away his ethnic and class identity. Drawing on entrenched stereotypes of Irish-Canadians, the author notes that the boy will likely become "a prize-fighter one day for he had just the figure for it!"[32]

Racialized assumptions about the inferiority of Aboriginal peoples on the part of some professional medical practitioners over the course of the century had a direct impact on the care and treatment they received, or did not receive. That Aboriginal children made seemingly ideal specimens for health exhibition and experimentation, particularly during the second half of the twentieth century, was belied by fact that they often suffered for want of medical attention. "There was no doctor at the Indian villages of Klemtu and Kitamaat, and these places were not receiving much in the way of medical attention," reported Florence Moffatt, a nurse at the R.W. Large Memorial Hospital on Campbell Island, in British Columbia, in the 1940s. When Moffatt visited these neglected villages, she struggled, often unsuccessfully, to help keep her patients alive: "I treated more than 40 people with penicillin and mild sedatives. One young girl had a severe ear infection following a mastoid operation. I had taken her to the hospital, but the infection had been too severe and too long-standing, and she died shortly afterward."[33]

When medical attention was forthcoming, it could run the risk of reifying racist stereotypes of Aboriginal people at best, and seriously compromising their health status at worst. In the late 1940s, for example, an "Indian Baby Show," initiated by the Indian Affairs health nurse responsible for overseeing the Coast Salish peoples of British Columbia, sought to respond to the "commonly held white belief that Indian parents neglect their children and

that Indian children in particular suffer from poor nutrition, inadequate clothing, and poor hygiene." The resulting baby show displayed several classes of baby contestants, "set up and judged by a doctor and nurse as to which child was the healthiest."[34] Writing about her nursing experiences in the Arctic during the 1930s and 1940s, Margery Hind reported on a study of the "effects of white man's food upon Eskimo children" undertaken by the Toronto-based white nurse stationed there. Each morning, the children "received a bowl of porridge, half a pint of rich milk, a pilot biscuit, a vitamin pill and a spoonful of cod liver oil. . . . these children are weighed regularly, and a special note is made of their ailments."[35] In a large study of the nutritional status of the First Nations of James Bay published in the prestigious *Canadian Medical Association Journal* in 1948, the authors suggested that "many characteristics, such as shiftlessness, indolence, improvidence, and inertia, so long regarded as inherent or hereditary traits in the Indian race, may at the root be really the manifestation of malnutrition. This is of concern not only to the Indian but to the white population, as any attempt to eradicate tuberculosis in Canada must include the institution of preventative measures for everyone. In addition, from the economic standpoint a group of people in poor health tends to be a liability rather than an asset to the nation."[36]

Such evidence of the "scientific" study of Aboriginal children's health appeared to unfold in tandem with their virtual neglect by professional medical practitioners in other contexts, such as the residential schools.[37] While "science" aided in the discovery of new explanations for Aboriginal peoples' seemingly "natural" characteristics, it did nothing to challenge the racist assumptions that undergirded such thinking.

Small Bodies in Schools

While doctors approached small bodies as problems to be solved, educators in the same period approached the body and health as pedagogical imperatives. More so than professional medical practitioners, educators in schools were uniquely placed to impart specific lessons about good health to children. Compulsory schooling, as historians have documented, represented an unprecedented opportunity to educate children about "proper" standards of morality, industry, cleanliness, and bodily care.[38] State-supported public schooling became a powerful site for the inculcation of citizenship and something of a health laboratory for the treatment and prevention of illness in children. The provision of public schooling for children spread across the country just before the period under study, starting with Ontario by the mid-nineteenth century, Manitoba and New Brunswick in 1871, British Columbia in 1872, Newfoundland and Nova Scotia in 1874, the North-West Territories in 1901, and Alberta and Saskatchewan in 1905. In Quebec, legislation in 1868 created the Ministry of Public Instruction, which was abolished in 1875. Coexisting with this was the Council of Public Instruction, created in 1856 and divided into two separate denominational committees (Catholic and Protestant), which included both clergy and laypeople.[39]

At the turn of the nineteenth century, the notion of science contained in discussions of germ theory, eugenics, and sanitation in health texts authorized in English-Canadian curricula reflected a dominant social order steeped in Christian moral values and an acceptance of personal responsibility for poor health. Ideas about the primacy of heredity intimated that particular children—those associated with undesirable social characteristics—had to be more vigilant in their personal health habits than those considered more fortunate. Whether through ignorance, wickedness, or wilful disobedience, then, poor health was presented as at least partly a matter of choice. As Dr A.P. Knight, professor of physiology at Queen's University in Kingston, Ontario, and author of *The Ontario Public School Hygiene* (1910) wrote, "If you have followed the teachings of this book thus far, it must be clear to you now that our lives from birth until old age are shaped largely by two great influences: (1) by what we inherit from our parents, grandparents, or other ancestral relatives, and (2) by our environment, that is, by our surroundings."[40]

Health curriculum was offered as an antidote to ignorance and to unhealthy practices and was presented as a moral and religious duty. Adherence to traditional gender roles was a key avenue to the observance of healthful morality. In *The Essentials of Health: A Text-book on Anatomy, Physiology, and Hygiene* (1909), for example, children learned that

> what every boy and girl should aim to do is put his body under the control of his mind in matters relating to his own health. That is to say, he should so apply his understanding of the uses of the various organs of the human body and the effects of this or that treatment upon them, so that he is able for the most part to avoid those things which will be harmful to his health and cultivate those things which will help to upbuild his physical and mental manhood. . . . Control of our own bodies, then, based upon a proper understanding of them, is the first step toward the attaining of true manhood or womanhood.[41]

Girls and boys were encouraged to understand abstinence from alcohol, tobacco, and self-abuse as part and parcel of their healthful journey to appropriately gendered adulthood.[42] Girls would be expected to parlay healthful habits into motherhood and marriage, while boys would prepare for public roles of leadership and governance.[43]

In *How to Be Healthy*, a 1911 textbook co-written by Manitoban doctor J. Halpenny and approved for use in elementary and middle schools in British Columbia, Alberta, Saskatchewan, Manitoba, Quebec, Nova Scotia, and Prince Edward Island, good health and vigour were unmistakably moral virtues reserved for those who chose to live "a sensible, normal life." By extension, those who struggled with poor health were cast with the pall of immorality, bad choices, and weak wills. Students were instructed, "when real difficulties come to us, let us meet them manfully, and win or lose, but never hold onto them or brood over them. This is the cause of much ill health. Our right to be happy must not be interfered with by anything. . . . Once we begin to brood, our power to do difficult things and our course to face the trouble begins to fail. Thus we weaken ourselves." Failure to meet "real difficulties," particularly on the part of working-class whites, was interpreted as a matter of alterable ignorance.[44] In a paper presented at the Canadian Nurses Association meeting in Toronto in 1918, Dr W.W. Chipman noted, for example, that unfortunate babies have to "fight from the very start. . . . Their mothers fought before them—fought in poverty, in ignorance and neglect—to give them birth; and so in poverty, ignorance and neglect the child's life begins."[45]

Scholars have argued that school textbooks, including those used in furthering lessons in health, reflect a great deal about whose knowledge counted as meaningful in the past.[46] Like their medical school counterparts, public school textbooks promoted the ideological priorities of those powerful enough to drive the social agenda.[47] To intervene in the care and treatment of children's bodies—either in the doctor's office or in the classroom—was to inculcate, however imperfectly, moral values judged acceptable.

Bodies and Memory

From the perspective of professionals with the power and inclination to intervene in family life, the modernizing twentieth century rendered children vulnerable to death, disease, and malnutrition, and thus they needed saving, healing, and training. Even though domestic efforts to treat illness and cultivate healthfulness were routinely discouraged by professional medical practitioners, family members and neighbours typically responded first to the health needs of youngsters. In many cases, mothers were often the only source of medical treatment many children had, particularly in isolated or rural parts of the country. Although they occasionally found themselves at odds, both family members, particularly mothers, and professional medical practitioners understood the health needs of children as under their direct purview.

Interviews with adults who grew up in English Canada during the twentieth century deepen, complement, and complicate seemingly straightforward and uncontested constructions of white, middle-class hegemony. Conditions of poverty, for example, could easily compromise straightforward assumptions about healthy living. Such was the experience of a 93-year-old white male interviewee, born in Montreal in 1913 and raised among 12 siblings. He recalled conditions of poverty in a busy urban centre that made acceptable standards of hygiene and freedom from contagion a luxury rather than the norm. "Let's say that you go to the grocery," he remembered when asked about family routines surrounding hygiene, "you buy some rice, you buy some beans, you have to go through everything to remove the—not rats—the mice, all the manure of the mice, you had to clean all that, you have to remove it before you cook it. . . . Because in the grocery they would have everything in bowls, you know, and so you had all of those visitors."[48] Even the provision of middle-class assistance was often far from the ideal touted by professionals and reformers. A white interviewee recalled receiving city welfare in the form of food aid when her family moved to Toronto in the depths of the Depression. "They sent you a box of food," she recalled, "with what they considered staples, and that had to do you for the week. . . . you did get milk and you did get bread. And the box of food contained probably flour, and sugar, tea, probably some carrots or cabbage. And then once a week they would give you a package of meat, maybe a roast . . . so we were never hungry but we certainly weren't . . . I suppose in retrospect it wasn't too bad a diet except for the lack of fresh fruit and fresh vegetables."[49]

While medical professionals and textbook authors warned about the dangers of folk or home remedies, patent medicines, and general "quackery," many interviewees remembered their use in their homes. At school, health curriculum disparaged homespun medicine. In *Health Essentials for Canadian Schools*, for example, authors J. Mace Andress and Elizabeth Breeze warned students that "promises, like many others made by patent-medicine manufacturers[,] are deceptive, and the drugs they sell may be dangerous to health. It is always best to rely on the advice of a reliable physician."[50] Despite professionals' distaste for domestic doctoring, it was a memorable part of growing up for many children. If Jean Tierney, born in 1906 in Gladstone, Manitoba, had a stomach ache, her mother would tell her to put some salt in her hand and "lick it a little bit at a time . . . and that really worked."[51] Born in 1910 in Nova Scotia, another informant remembered wearing a camphor bag around her neck during the Spanish influenza outbreak of 1918. "After that [outbreak of 1918]," she concluded, "every winter almost we wore that little bag of camphor around our necks and we were healthy, we never had colds or anything."[52] In 1915, Dorothea Ingram, born in Vancouver, contracted diphtheria. She was five years old, and she remembered the health officials putting a big red card on the door of her house with the word "Diphtheria" printed on it. In a conversation over the backyard fence, the family's neighbour persuaded Dorothea's mother to allow her to try a home remedy on the child. Clearly breaking the quarantine order, the neighbour paid Dorothea a visit. "She came over and she had a big white feather—a chicken feather like, and a bottle of brandy. And she came over and painted all my tonsils and the inside of my mouth with it. And my mother said it just brought new life to me."[53]

Although the feather and brandy might have made Dorothea's experience unique, that her illness was treated at home by her mother and a neighbour was certainly not. For many adults who grew up in Canada during the twentieth century, mothers and other family members are vividly remembered as providing primary care for their sick and injured bodies during their childhoods. Visits to doctors, and occasionally to hospitals, are also remembered, but they stand out as unusual events, undertaken only when efforts at home proved inadequate or an injury was serious enough to warrant such drastic measures.[54]

Into the 1920s and well beyond, families continued to concoct their own folk remedies to check the spread of diseases. An informant born in the mid-1920s in Toronto remembered vividly her father's painting the outside of her and her siblings' necks with iodine to prevent sore throats. "Now that was a strange one," she recalled, "and, of course, you hated that because you went back to school with this great big brown throat from the iodine."[55] She also remembered that if any of the children had whooping cough, her father would seek out a newly paved road. "Somebody told my father that if we breathed in the tar it would stop the cough, so I remember him trekking us all out there and we had to stand there and breathe in this tar . . . and I don't know if it helped

or not!"[56] A male interviewee, born just after the Second World War, grew up in Peterborough, Ontario, with his father and grandparents. His grandparents, according to him, "had some strange ideas about home medicine. . . . [My grandmother] would take a teaspoon of raw ginger powder mixed with sugar and we'd have to eat that before we walked to school . . . we'd be spitting half the way!"[57] Another interviewee, born in the late 1940s on the Sugar Cane Reserve in Williams Lake, British Columbia, understood the preparation of medicine as informed by Secwepemc traditions. He recalled that his mother would often prepare remedies when someone got sick: "I think most of the remedies, my mom made them. And some of them were from different plants that she would gather. . . . Or, she would buy certain things and make things there was a hot kinda tonic that she made—I think it had ginger and honey and some other stuff in it."[58] These familial health strategies complicated the admonishments of doctors and official school health curriculum that privileged "science" over "superstition." Despite, or perhaps because of, the centrality of folk health remedies in many adults' childhood, textbooks took great pains to challenge such practices: "Great and unnecessary waste of life, health and vigour has resulted, and still results, from a neglect of scientific principles in regard to common things."[59]

For some children, the space between what health professionals held up as acceptable standards of healthful living and the actual conditions of life produced deeply unequal social relations. The child's experienced body and the adult's idealized body could be far apart indeed. A Métis woman who grew up in Saskatchewan in the 1930s recalled: "The teacher tried to teach us about daily hygiene like brushing your teeth after breakfast and I don't think any of the kids in my school owned a toothbrush—I know I didn't until I was twelve years old. . . . The teacher's idea of a good lunch was a sandwich, a couple of cookies or a cake, and an orange or an apple which most of us only saw once a year at Christmas time."[60]

First Nations children, in particular, could experience the imposition of white middle-class notions of cleanliness in especially malevolent ways.

Growing up on a reserve in Deseronto, Ontario, in the 1930s, a female First Nations interviewee placed the body at the centre of colonial relations. It was on the body that this relationship was made sensible to her and her Aboriginal classmates. She recalled,

> I went to this school and there was this [Aboriginal] boy in the school who was very, very dirty. And you know, I thought [this] the most humiliating thing when I got older—the teacher couldn't stand it so she got a tub of water and we would all take turns washing him—his back and his hair. . . . Isn't that awful? Oh, he didn't have his clothes off. He had his underwear on, but, kind of ridiculous . . . And, ah, I used to think as I got older that that was a really awful thing to do to him—so embarrassing.[61]

The white teacher enforced standards of cleanliness and, in the process, reinforced prejudices about the First Nations peoples as naturally disinclined to keep clean. Our interviewee made no distinction between learning about oppressive colonial relations and learning about the importance of "keeping clean." In her memory, the two were inextricably linked.

Within some families, the experience of illness could mark a time of mediated pleasure for youngsters. Depending on a wide array of factors, adult assumptions about children's vulnerability and incompetence could have positive effects. For one informant, it meant a welcome reprise in an otherwise hard existence. Introduced earlier, our 93-year-old male interviewee from Montreal remembered his time in a quarantine hospital with scarlet fever as a break in an endless cycle of work and poverty. When asked to tell us what he remembered feeling about the experiences, he said, somewhat sheepishly, "You know, it was the best time of your life! You could have good meals . . . the nuns were looking after that. . . . I was there for about forty days. . . . Yeah, when I was 14 years old it was easy to make friends, you know."[62]

Being sick occasionally challenged standard hierarchical relationships between adults and children and introduced quite different dimensions into them. Growing up in Winnipeg in the 1920s, Anna

Friesen remembered, "Softly Mother's hand felt my fevered cheeks, then rested lightly on my forehead. Then she pulled up my blanket and tucked it gently around me. After pausing motionless beside me awhile, she tiptoed away. I felt as if an angel had visited me, and my illness seemed inconsequential."[63] A female interviewee growing up in Vancouver some 30 years later had a similar tale to tell: "I do recall the times of illness as actually special times when I received my mother's sole attention. . . . as the last of five kids, I savoured the feeling of closeness it brought. . . . she (my mother) was always kind and patient when I was ill, and I will never forget the feeling of her small cool hand on my fevered brow!"[64] Ruth Cook, a Tsimthian woman born in 1931 near Prince Rupert, attended residential school and remembered that the experience of illness depended very much on context. At home, she recalled, "You never had to worry if you got sick . . . you always had an uncle or an aunt, or the grandparents were there to lend a helping hand."[65] Such memories suggest that, from the point of view of some children in particular circumstances, times of illness were not simply times of unmitigated grief. They could be far more complex, reflecting the centrality of family culture and of sentimentality in influencing children's experiences with health and illness.

Conclusion

From the point of view of those with considerable social power and responsibility, such as doctors, nurses, and teachers, children's bodies over the first half of the twentieth century were conceptualized as vulnerable and susceptible to serious medical problems. To intervene in the care and treatment of children's bodies—either in the doctor's office or in the classroom—was to inculcate not only good health but also acceptable moral values. Through the body, medical practitioners and educators attempted to legitimize and reproduce traditional hierarchies of power. When the discourse of professionals is positioned alongside the memories of adults, the fissures between them are imbued with additional meanings. On and through children's bodies, social acceptability, civilizing and colonizing techniques, interests of the state, and so-called "good health" were written, operationalized, and vied for space. The lived memories of adults who grew up in different communities in English Canada suggest that the family's primacy in the embodied care of children was often downplayed or disparaged even as it was employed for social reproduction.

The central thrust of this essay is to go beyond our understanding of children merely as objects of health and welfare interventions—of adult interventions—and to query how children's own embodied subjectivity—their voices and their bodies—gives us a deeper understanding of their role in the social production and reproduction of inequality over the first half of the twentieth century. The remembered body, made and remade in adult memories of growing up, "talks back" to objectifying processes, on the part of both twentieth-century health and welfare experts and historians who overlook or ignore these

voices. They show how adults inculcated social inequity through seemingly uncomplicated and positive processes—like health and welfare—and how young people responded to them.

The process of designating particular bodies as healthier, stronger, and more acceptable than others enshrined inequality deep in the flesh, and it began with the very young. Throughout the entrenchment of conventional medicine and the rise of the health professional over the course of the twentieth century, techniques to promote healthy normative bodies, constructed through adult assumptions, can be readily discerned. Through critical engagements with adult memories of childhood, however, we are privy to a more finely tuned accounting of how these unequal relations of power were woven—sometimes seamlessly but also often with great tension—into the process of growing up.

Acknowledgment

I wish to acknowledge the critical comments of members of the Lost Children workshop and the anonymous manuscript reviewers who helped vastly improve this essay, and the research assistance provided by Natalie Chambers and Lori MacFadyen.

Notes

1. Rene Norcross, "The Little Brother," *Canadian Nurse* 2 (1915): 43–38.

2. It was likely not lost on readers that the young brothers' names together suggested that Mah Too died "Too Soon." Norcross, "The Little Brother," 437.

3. In the workshop version of this chapter, Molly Ladd-Taylor encouraged me to explore more fully Mah Too's "rejection of the hospital cure" and to focus on what this signified about Mah Too's agency. I am grateful for her suggestion.

4. In total, 62 oral history interviews were conducted by me and two graduate students, Lori MacFadyen and Natalie Chambers, between 2001 and 2004; 11 of these interviews are used in this chapter. Interviewees were selected primarily through word of mouth and some limited advertising in retirement homes in Vancouver; Penticton, British Columbia; and Montreal. We relied primarily on a snowball effect in which those interviewed told friends and family who in turn contacted us. The interview was intentionally open-ended and asked participants for their childhood recollections of anything to do with health, health care, learning to be healthy, illness, and medical treatment. We asked only that participants be raised in Canada and born before 1960. Interviews were conducted in places suggested by interviewees. Most took place in

interviewees' homes or local coffee shops. The vast majority were conducted in person, with a handful conducted by telephone. References below to these interviews are cited as "Child Health Interview."

5. See, for example, Neil Sutherland, "When You Listen to the Winds of Childhood, How Much Can You Believe?" *Curriculum Inquiry* 22, 3 (1992): 235–326, and Paul Thompson, "Believe It or Not: Rethinking the Historical Interpretation of Memory," in Jaclyn Jeffrey and Glenace Edwall, eds., *Memory and History: Essays on Recalling and Interpreting Experience* (Lanham, MD: University of Toronto Press, 1976; Waterloo, ON: Wilfrid Laurier University Press, 2000). All subsequent citations are to the 1976 edition.

6. Neil Sutherland, *Children in English-Canadian Society: Framing the Twentieth Century Consensus* (Toronto: University of Toronto Press, 1976; Waterloo, ON: Wilfrid Laurier University Press, 2000). All subsequent citations are to the 1976 edition.

7. The most pertinent examples are Angus McLaren and Arlene Tigar McLaren, *The Bedroom and the State: The Changing Practices and Politics of Contraception and Abortion in Canada, 1880–1980* (Toronto: McClelland & Stewart, 1986); Agnus McLaren, *Our Own Master Race:*

Eugenics in Canada 1885-1945 (Toronto: McClelland & Stewart, 1990); Jane Ursel, *Private Lives, Public Policy: 100 Years of State Intervention in the Family* (Toronto: Women's Press, 1992); Katherine Arnup, *Education for Motherhood: Advice for Mothers in Twentieth-Century English Canada* (Toronto: University of Toronto Press, 1994); Carolyn Strange and Tina Loo, *Making Good: Law and Moral Regulation in Canada, 1867-1939* (Toronto: University of Toronto Press, 1997); and John McLaren, Robert Menzies, and Dorothy E. Chunn, *Regulating Lives: Historical Essays on the State, Society, the Individual and the Law* (Vancouver: UBC Press, 2002).

8. Cynthia Comacchio, *Nations Are Built of Babies: Saving Ontario's Mothers and Children, 1900-1940* (Montreal and Kingston: McGill-Queen's University Press, 1993).

9. Mary Ellen Kelm, *Colonizing Bodies: Aboriginal Health and Healing in British Columbia* (Vancouver: UBC Press, 1998); Tina Moffat and Ann Herring, "The Historical Root of High Rates of Infant Deaths in Aboriginal Communities in Canada in the Early Twentieth Century: The Case of Fisher River Manitoba," *Social Science and Medicine* 48 (1999): 1821-32.

10. Veronica Strong-Boag, *Finding Families, Finding Ourselves: English Canada Encounters Adoption from the Nineteenth Century to the 1990s* (Toronto: Oxford University Press, 2006).

11. Tamara Myers, *Caught: Montreal's Modern Girls and the Law, 1869-1945* (Toronto: University of Toronto Press, 2006).

12. Roger Cooter, "In the Name of the Child Beyond," in Marijke Gijswijt-Hofstra and Hilary Marland, eds., *Cultures of Child Health in Britain and the Netherlands in the Twentieth Century* (Amsterdam and New York: Rodopi, 2003), 287-96. As Cooter suggests, what continues to elude historian is "a history of children's own experience of illness and medicine" (290-91).

13. See Cheryl Krasnick Warsh and Veronica Strong-Boag, eds., *Children's Health Issues in Historical Perspective* (Waterloo, ON: Wilfrid Laurier University Press, 2005), 3.

14. See Patricia Rooke and R.L. Schnell, *Discarding the Asylum: From Child Rescue to the Welfare State in English Canada, 1800-1950* (Lanham, MD: University Press of America, 1983); Sutherland, *Children in English-Canadian Society*; Robert McIntosh, *Boys in the Pits: Child Labour in Coal Mines* (Montreal and Kingston: McGill-Queen's University Press, 2000); and Veronica Strong-Boag, "Getting to Now: Children in Distress in Canada's Past," in Brian Wharf, ed., *Community Work Approaches to Child Welfare* (Peterborough, ON: Broadview, 2002), 29-46.

15. Buford L. Nichols, Angel Ballabriga, and Norman Kretchmer, eds., *History of Pediatrics, 1850-1950* (New York: Raven Press, 1991); see particularly Buford L. Nichols Jr., "The European Roots of American Pediatrics," 49-54: Howard A. Pearson, "Pediatrics in the United States," 55-64; Silvestre Frenk and Ignacio Avila-Cisneros,

"Mexican Pediatrics," 65-76. On the connections made between public health and paediatrics see, for example, Chapter 13, "No Baby, No Nation: A History of Pediatrics," in Jacalyn Duffin, *History of Medicine: A Scandalously Short Introduction* (Toronto: Oxford University Press, 2006); and Russell Viner, "Abraham Jacobi and the Origins of Scientific Pediatrics in America," in Alexandra Minna Stern and Howard Markel, eds., *Formative Years: Children's Health in the United States, 1880-2000* (Ann Arbor: University of Michigan Press, 2002).

16. Sutherland, *Children in English-Canadian Society*, 57.

17. As quoted in Nora Moore, "Child Welfare Work," *Canadian Nurse* 12, 11 (1916): 634-35.

18. Sharon L. Snyder and David T. Mitchell, *Cultural Locations of Disability* (Chicago and London: University of Chicago Press, 2006), ix.

19. Sutherland, *Children in English-Canadian Society*; Comacchio, *Nations Are Built of Babies*.

20. Henry Ashby and G.A. Wright, *Diseases of Children, Medical and Surgical* (New York: Longmans Green, 1897), Preface. This volume was available through "A.P. Watts and Company, Medical Publishers and Bookseller to College St, Toronto."

21. Joseph Race, "Milk Supply in Relation to Tuberculosis in Ontario," *Public Health Journal* 6 (1915): 378-83; Nora Moore, "Child Welfare Work," *Canadian Nurse* 12 (1916): 364-65; Reginald H. Wiggins, "The Management of Posture in Children," *Canadian Medical Association Journal* 27 (1932): 47-51; D.E.S. Wishart, "The Problem of the Deaf Child," *Canadian Medical Association Journal* 44 (1941): 462-66.

22. Kenneth N. Fenwick, *Manual of Obstetrics, Gynaecology, and Paediatrics* (Kingston, ON: J. Henderson, 1889), 192.

23. George E. Smith, "The Prevention of Infection in Infancy," *Public Health Journal* 17, 8 (1926): 405-6.

24. Hector Charles Cameron, *Diseases of Childhood: A Short Introduction* (London: Oxford University Press, 1926), 6-7. This text was utilized by teaching staff at the University of British Columbia's Faculty of Medicine.

25. Cameron, *Diseases of Childhood*, 6-7.

26. Hector Charles Cameron, "Sleep and Its Disorders in Childhood," *Canadian Medical Association Journal* 24, 2 (1913): 239-44.

27. Alan Brown and Frederick F. Tisdall, *Common Procedures in the Practice of Paediatrics*, 4th ed. (Toronto: McClelland & Stewart, 1949), 7. The first edition of the work appeared in 1929. The fourth edition was revised with the arrival of sulpha drugs and to reflect "a better understanding of the fundamental principles of mineral metabolism" (Preface to 4th edition, n.p.).

28. Brown and Tisdall, *Common Procedures*, 7.

29. Fenwick, *Manual of Obstetrics, Gynaecology, and Pediatrics*, 193.

30. A. Grant Fleming, "The Value of Periodic Health Examinations," *Canadian Nurse* 25, 6 (1929): 284.

31. B.E.A. Philmot, "In the Children's Ward," *Canadian Nurse* 5 (1910): 176–77.

32. Ibid., 176.

33. Florence C. Moffatt "Forgotten Villages of the BC Coast: Hospital Life at Bella Bella," *Raincoast Chronicles* 11 (1987): 52.

34. John Dewhurst, "Coast Salish Summer Festivals: Rituals for Upgrading Social Identity," *Anthropologica* 28 (1976): 258.

35. Margery Hind, *School House in the Arctic* (London: Geoffrey Bles, 1958), 95.

36. R.P. Vivian, Charles McMillan, P.E. Moore, E. Chant Robertson, W.H. Sebrell, F.F. Tisdall, and W.G. McIntosh, "The Nutrition and Health of the James Bay Indian," *Canadian Medical Association Journal* 59, 6 (1948): 505.

37. See Kelm, *Colonizing Bodies*.

38. See Sutherland, *Children in English-Canadian Society*, 40–42.

39. On the history of schooling legislation in Canada, see J.D. Wilson, Robert M. Stamp, and Louis-Phillippe Audet, *Canadian Education: A History* (Scarborough, ON: Prentice-Hall, 1970), and E. Henry Johnson, *A Brief History of Canadian Education* (Toronto: McGraw-Hill, 1968).

40. A.P. Knight, *The Ontario Public School Hygiene* (Toronto: Copp Clark, 1910), 229.

41. Charles H. Stowell, *The Essentials of Health: A Text-book on Anatomy, Physiology, and Hygiene* (Toronto: The Educational Book Company, 1909), 253. This text was "prescribed for use in the Public and High Schools of British Columba" (Preface, n.p.).

42. On the significant of the temperance movement in Canada see Jan Noel, *Canada Dry: Temperance Crusades before Confederation* (Toronto: University of Toronto Press, 1995), and Sharon Anne Cook, *Through Sunshine and Shadow: The Women's Christian Temperance Union, Evangelicalism, and Reform* (Montreal and Kingston: McGill–Queen's University Press, 1995).

43. Wendy Mitchinson, *The Nature of Their Bodies: Women and Their Doctors in Victorian Canada* (Toronto: University of Toronto Press, 1991); Veronica Strong-Boag, *The New Day Recalled: Lives of Girls and Women in English Canada, 1919–1939* (Toronto: Copp Clark Pitman, 1988).

44. J. Halpenny and Lillian Ireland, *How to Be Healthy* (Toronto and Winnipeg: W.J. Gage, 1911), 54.

45. W.W. Chipman, "The Infant Soldier," *Canadian Nurse* 14, 12 (1918): 1453–63. Chipman's wife was active in another aspect of reform work: she rallied for women police officers in Montreal and reformatories for girls in the period. I am grateful to Tamara Myers for pointing out this connection.

46. Michael W. Apple and Linda Christian-Smith, "The Politics of the Textbook," in Michael W. Apple and Linda Christian-Smith, eds., *The Politics of the Textbook* (New York: Routledge, 1991), 1–21.

47. Bernd Baldus and Meenaz Kassam, "'Make Me Truthful, Good and Mild': Values in Nineteenth-Century Ontario Schoolbooks," *Canadian Journal of Sociology* 12 (1996): 327–58.

48. Child Health Interview, Participant #024, 3 February 2004, transcript, 10. (See note 4 above.)

49. Child Health Interview, Participant #006, 15 April 2004, transcript, 3.

50. J. Mace Andress and Elizabeth Breeze, *Health Essentials for Canadian Schools* (Boston, Montreal, and London: Ginn, 1938), 159. See also the discussion of the dangers of homespun health practices in J.W.S. McCullough, "Chatelaine's Baby Clinic: The Common Diseases," *Chatelaine* June 1934, 54, and Ross A. Campbell, "The Spastic Child," *Canadian Nurse* 42 (1946): 471.

51. Jean Tierney is a pseudonym. Child Health Interview, Participant #014, 9 March 2004, transcript, 12.

52. Child Health Interview, Participant #010, 28 July 2004, transcript, 2.

53. Dorothea Ingram is a pseudonym. Child Health Interview, Participant #024, 3 February 2004, transcript, 7.

54. Socialized health insurance was first introduced in the province of Saskatchewan in 1962 and had spread to the rest of the country by the mid-1960s.

55. Child Health Interview, Participant #006, 15 April 2006, transcript, 6.

56. Ibid.

57. Child Health Interview, Participant #007, 27 April 2004, transcript, 2.

58. Child Health Interview, Participant #002, 26 February 2004, transcript, 6.

59. This message of the superiority of medical science in treating matters of health and illness is conveyed in a number of texts. See, for example, Ontario Provincial Board of Health, *Manual of Hygiene for Schools and Colleges*; J.H. Halpenny and Lillian Ireland, *How to Be Healthy*, 174; and J. Mace Andress and W.A. Evans, *Healthy Citizenship* (Toronto: Ginn, 1935), 63.

60. Child Health Interview, Participant #004, 3 June 2004, transcript, 8.

61. Child Health Interview, Participant #001, 16 January 2001, transcript, 5.

62. Child Health Interview, Participant #012, 2 October 2001, transcript, 4.

63. Anna Friesen, *The Mulberry Tree* (Winnipeg: Queenston, 1985), 14.

64. Child Health Interview, Participant #005, 14 February 2004, transcript, 2.

65. Ruth Cook, "An Interview with Ruth Cook," in Dorothy Haegert, ed., *Children of the First People* (Vancouver: Tillacum Library, 1983), 24.

PRIMARY DOCUMENT

Excerpts from Health and Hygiene Textbooks Used in Canadian Public Schools in the Early Twentieth Century, 1906, 1911

Caring For the Hair: Girls with long, thick hair are sometimes careless about washing their heads; they do not know how much other people are judging them by the looks and the odour of their hair. Washed hair is light and fluffy, sweet and clean, while unwashed hair is solid and heavy, neither sweet nor clean. (p. 113)

Our Lungs: Some people used to think that a small waist made a woman look delicate and beautiful, but in these days we are sure that it makes her look ignorant and out of shape. We think so because we know what she has done to the inside of her body. She has squeezed up hundreds and thousands of air tubes and air sacs until they are like a useless sponge. When that happens, neither the lungs nor the blood can possibly get as much air as they need. (p. 140)

Source: Frances Gulick Jewett, *Good Health. The Gulick Series* (New York: Ginn & Company, 1906).

Our savage ancestors were lithe and alert. They had to be. Every cell in their bodies was active. Every minute of their lives they struggled for existence. Food was hard to get, and everywhere wild animals or wild men lay in wait for them. Thus their days were filled with physical labour. Thus nights, of necessity, were spent in sleep. How could they be anything else but healthy? . . . So seldom do we have to go back to nature for our needs that we are getting to expect almost everything ready made. Some even resent having to cook, and often breakfast foods are advertised as pre-digested. What will become of us? (p. 43)

Why are the people so stiff and clumsy? Because they eat food such as their savage ancestors ate—meats and other flesh-producing foods—yet they are not called upon to perform the same intense physical exercises. They eat fats, oils, and sugars in great abundance, and yet they house themselves in comfortable apartments and clothe themselves warmly. Their ancestors slept under the open sky, and in winter were clothed in rough skins. The men of this generation sit all day at their work. They ride home in crowded cars at night. Don't you see where our life is leading us? (p. 44).

Source: J. Halpenny, M.A., M.D. and Lillian B. Ireland, *How to be Healthy* (Toronto and Winnipeg: W.J. Gage, 1911).

Creating "Normal" Families: Thalidomide Babies and the Eugenics Agenda in Post-war Canada

JESSICA HAYNES

Popular images of 1950s and early 1960s North America stress stable nuclear families contentedly ensconced in new suburbs. Indeed, during the Cold War, "the ideal family was at once seen as a source of affectional relationships, the basis of a consumer economy, a defence against communism, and a salient metaphor for various forms of social organization."[1] With the Second World War behind them, Canadians began to start families, confident, more than ever before, that medical science could ensure them healthy and well-adjusted children. Though historians have detailed to some extent the illusory quality of this dream, few have examined the explosive impact of thalidomide.[2] Thalidomide was developed in West Germany in 1957 and went on sale in Canada in 1961. Hailed as a completely safe and non-addictive tranquilizer, the drug actually produced serious malformations in the unborn children of women who took it while pregnant. Throughout 1962, Canadians debated in the press the fate of these children, many of whom were born without arms or legs.

While scholars have stressed the increased emphasis placed on the psychological health of the family in this period,[3] reactions to the thalidomide babies, as they would come to be called, indicated that physical health remained deeply important to Canadians. In fact, the wholeness of the body was often seen as a prerequisite for psychological happiness and proper personality formation.[4] Babies affected by thalidomide ignited debates around abortion, mercy killing, and institutionalization, starkly revealing an unwillingness on the part of some to incorporate these physically different children into the ideal post-war family. Further, even efforts to help the children centred primarily on

providing them with prosthetic limbs which gave only the appearance of normalcy while, at times, diminishing mobility.

The readiness of some Canadians to destroy, dispose of, or otherwise erase physically imperfect children suggests that eugenic thinking continued to circulate after the Second World War. Eugenics, a term coined in 1883 by Francis Galton, borrowed heavily from Darwinian principles and, as defined by Galton, was "the study of the agencies under social control that may improve or impair the racial qualities of future generations, either physically or mentally."[5] Eugenicists concerned themselves with both encouraging the reproduction of the "fit"— usually understood as healthy, white, and middle class in North America—and decreasing the reproduction of the "unfit."[6] While eugenicists in Canada and elsewhere became very preoccupied in the interwar period with identifying and eliminating mental deficiency, which they labelled "feeblemindedness," they also discouraged the physically disabled from reproducing.[7] In eugenics, physical health remained a key factor for optimal reproduction.[8] Nazi Germany implemented eugenic policies to justify the sterilization and execution of those deemed "defective."[9] Though this is less well-known today, Alberta and British Columbia, motivated by the same concerns, implemented legislation in 1928 and 1933 to allow compulsory sterilization.[10]

Though the Alberta law remained in force till 1972, many Canadian scholars maintain that Nazism irreparably discredited eugenics.[11] However, historians in recent years have challenged this claim by exploring a continuing role for eugenics into the 1950s, 1960s, and 1970s. For example, Angus McLaren alludes to the growth of a "new eugenics" in the post-war period. He cites developing

Source: Reprinted with permission of the author.

reproductive technologies that allow for the detection of birth defects and their elimination through therapeutic abortions.[12] In many ways, this procedure was also advocated for thalidomide babies in 1962, even though confirmation of defect before birth was not as possible at the time. Additionally, in the 1950s and 1960s, many North American geneticists saw their discipline as an extension of eugenics. Thus, in their quest to eliminate bad genes, they "continued to speak in the language of eugenics, condemning past abuses but also taking for granted that reproduction was an act of social consequences and was legitimately a matter of social concern."[13] In the post-war US context, eugenicists, such as Paul Popenoe, began to focus much more on fostering eugenic families based on strict gender roles. Popenoe, a well-known marriage counsellor in the 1950s and 1960s, believed that "the male–female dichotomy was essential to the interconnected health and survival of the family, the nation, and western civilization."[14] Wendy Kline affirms in her book on US eugenics that Popenoe wished especially to encourage the growth of the white middle class. He and other eugenicists were primarily responsible for the pronatalism of the baby boom years.[15] Thus, eugenics survived the Second World War and continued to influence ideas about reproduction, family, and child-rearing.

Canadian historians have not discussed the impact of thalidomide in any depth. In his comprehensive overview of contraception, Angus McLaren briefly mentions that thalidomide increased self-awareness about the side effects of all drugs as well as fuelling arguments for abortion reform.[16] This essay will explore the latter claim in more depth. Barbara Clow has examined how the North American medical interpretation of pregnancy as an illness contributed to the impact of thalidomide.[17] She argues that pregnant women were perceived as prone to emotional disturbances and, therefore, were more likely to be prescribed tranquilizers.[18] Joel Lexchin, a medical doctor, mentions thalidomide briefly in his book on the Canadian pharmaceutical industry, *The Real Pushers*. He asserts that the thalidomide tragedy demonstrates starkly the unwillingness of the Canadian government to interfere against the pharmaceutical industry.[19]

There has been more analysis of thalidomide in the international context. *Suffer the Children: The Story of Thalidomide*, written by a team at the *Sunday Times* in London, remains an influential book. It details the problematic development of thalidomide by the West German company Grünenthal. The authors, many of whom covered the tragedy as it unfolded, seem to hold this company responsible for not only failing to properly test the drug but also attempting to repress initial reports of side effects. *Suffer the Children* goes on to introduce the victims of thalidomide and to discuss their legal battles to gain compensation from drug companies.[20] The book also briefly mentions the Canadian story.[21] Historian Rock Brynner and professor of anatomy and embryology Trent Stephens concur in many ways with the team from the *Sunday Times*. Their book, *Dark Remedy: The Impact of Thalidomide and Its Revival as a Vital Measure*, likewise condemns Grünenthal for its failure to systematically test the drug and its suppression of reports regarding birth defects.[22] As should be clear from this overview, these studies focus largely on the development and approval of thalidomide. The following essay explores the wider debates surrounding the future of thalidomide children in Canada. In order to trace reactions, I focus mainly on 1962, the year in which most Canadian thalidomide babies were born. To analyze this discourse, I draw on letters and articles from *Chatelaine*, the *Toronto Star*, *The Globe and Mail*, the *Ottawa Citizen*, and *The Vancouver Sun*. These newspapers provide a good national overview of reaction to these children.

History of Thalidomide and Disability in Canada

As mentioned above, thalidomide first appeared in West Germany in 1957. Though the negligence of Grünenthal and other involved drug companies has been the subject of much debate, there were certain testing options available at the time and in use that could have prevented the tragedy. Most strikingly, in light of the growing awareness that some substances could cross the placenta barrier, Grünenthal carried out no tests to determine the impact of thalidomide on pregnant women or animals.[23] Other companies showed much more diligence in this regard. For example, in the 1950s, Wallace Laboratories, a US firm, carried out extensive tests on meprobamate, a tranquilizer that would be marketed as Miltown. As well as performing long-term assessments of toxicity, Wallace Laboratories gave meprobamate to pregnant rats through gestation, birth, and nursing. The resulting litters were counted and studied. Though thalidomide does not cause visible deformities in rats, it does decrease litter size, an indication of teratogenic effects that were understood at the time.[24]

Despite a lack of systematic clinical tests, thalidomide was marketed as a safe sedative and sleeping pill.[25] Worldwide, it was sold under at least 37 different names and recommended for the treatment of a wide variety of problems, including colds, coughs, flu, asthma, headaches, anxiety, and sleeplessness.[26] Though not especially designed for pregnant women, many in this condition did end up taking it. Almost from the beginning of its distribution, Grünenthal began to receive reports of side effects, including constipation, memory loss, and, more seriously, numbness and paralysis.[27] According to the team at the Sunday Times, the company did its best to repress these reports and denied that thalidomide could cause such problems.[28] The drug was quickly marketed internationally and became available in Canada in April 1961. Here, two companies, the Cincinnati firm Richardson-Merrell and the Montreal company Frank W. Horner Limited, sold it under the names Kevadon and Talimol respectively.[29]

Meanwhile, doctors in Germany began to notice an alarming increase in birth defects. Initially unsure of the cause, they soon became suspicious of thalidomide.[30] Though Grünenthal resisted pressure once again, the drug was recalled in November 1961 in West Germany and Britain.[31] A month later, drug company representatives informed the Canadian government of possible evidence linking thalidomide to birth defects. However, officials continued to allow its sale until March 1962, at which point they asked the companies involved to withdraw the drug from the market.[32] Federal health minister J. Waldo Monteith justified this decision by saying reports on thalidomide's possible teratogenic effects had to be confirmed before action could be taken.[33] Dr C.A. Morrell, director of the Canadian Food and Drug Directorate, later claimed that the drug company representatives had minimized the significance of the recall in Britain and West Germany by blaming "bad publicity."[34] This statement alludes to the limited nature of drug regulation in Canada at the time. In the aftermath of thalidomide, it was widely reported that the Food and Drug Directorate lacked the staff and facilities to carry out their own studies on new drugs. Consequently, the government often relied on the research conducted by drug companies. Additionally, once a new drug was approved, the Food and Drug Directorate lacked the power to recall drugs at the time. They could only request that companies do so.[35] During the 11-month period of legal sales in Canada, over 4 million thalidomide tablets were sold.[36] An additional number of pills were also given out as samples.

To this day, scientists remain uncertain about precisely how thalidomide acts upon the developing fetus.[37] Nevertheless, in the summer of 1962, it became terribly apparent that it did. In all, there were 8,000 affected children born worldwide, in 46 countries. Deformities varied, but many victims had shortened arms or legs. Eye and ear problems also occurred, along with more serious internal malformations. At least 115 Canadian babies were affected by thalidomide; of these, 8 were stillborn and 33 died in their early months, leaving 74 survivors.[38] Many of these children were born in 1962. In light of the fierce debate provoked by the thalidomide babies and their enduring presence in collective memory, one might have expected the number to actually be much higher in Canada. Certainly those who lived through the events expressed some surprise that Canadian thalidomide babies numbered in the hundreds and not thousands. Indeed, writing in August 1962, Harold Weir of The Vancouver Sun argued that the panic over thalidomide was out of proportion to the danger it posed to mothers and their unborn children.[39] Regardless of the exact number, the alarm over these babies clearly tapped into wider concerns about science, drugs, and, of particular interest to this essay, the integrity of the body. Specifically, reactions to the physical differences of these children confirm that eugenic ideals persisted into the 1960s.

Despite this strong public response, children affected by thalidomide were by no means the first, or last, born in Canada who would have to negotiate a physical disability. According to the Canadian Sickness Survey of 1950–1, approximately 92,000 children under the age of 18, about 2 percent of all Canadian children, had a permanent physical disability of some kind. By the time the thalidomide children were born, services, though fragmented and variable, did exist for the treatment and rehabilitation of the physically disabled. For example, in 1922 the Canadian Junior Red Cross had set up a special fund to cover the costs of transportation, medical treatment, and orthopedic appliances for handicapped children.[40] Also, in 1949, Dr Gustave Gingras launched his Rehabilitation Institute in Montreal, which would become a key centre for children who had disabilities caused by polio and, later, by thalidomide.[41]

Particularly after the Second World War, and inspired in part by efforts to help veterans with disabilities, both provincial and federal governments became more involved in the provision of these services, traditionally the purview of voluntary organizations such as the Red Cross.[42] Some provincial governments began to offer more direct aid to polio victims in particular and, more generally, to subsidize existing voluntary programs. In sum, "[Charitable] Societies in some provinces [. . . remained] the major agencies for arranging and supplying services to orthopedically handicapped children, while in other provinces their role [. . . was] essentially to supplement the basic services made available by government agencies and voluntary hospitals."[43]

After the Second World War, the federal government also expanded its role in managing disability, though it did so primarily by funnelling more money to the provinces. In 1948, the government introduced the Crippled Children's Grant, which made money available to the provinces to improve and develop services for children with disabilities. Initially, the grant was for $500,000 each year. However, in 1960, it was merged with the Medical Rehabilitation Grant, first created in 1953, which brought the available total to $2,616,751.[44] Reflecting a desire to better organize rehabilitation services in Canada, the federal government also held a National Conference on the Rehabilitation of the Physically Handicapped in 1951. As a result of this meeting, and in the hopes of facilitating co-operation, the government appointed a National Co-Ordinator of Rehabilitation to work within the Department of Labour and to help the provinces with their programs.[45] In addition to these initiatives, in 1954, Parliament passed the Disabled Persons Act, which implemented means-tested monthly allowances for those aged 18 to 69 with permanently disabilities. The cost of the program was to be evenly divided between the provinces and the federal government. All provinces had signed the Act by 1956.[46] Finally, in 1961, the Vocational Rehabilitation of Disabled Persons Act offered equal cost-sharing to the provinces to cover services designed to train persons with disabilities so they could enter or re-enter the job market.[47]

Thus, the children born with deformities caused by thalidomide had options for aid. Federal officials seemed reluctant at first to offer any special compensation outside these established channels.[48] However, very quickly, perhaps reacting to public and political pressure, the federal government announced it would work with the provinces on an equal basis to cover the cost of surgeries, prosthetic devices, and rehabilitation for those children affected by thalidomide. Federal health minister Monteith was quick to clarify that the program would not have a means test.[49] In doing so, the government was recognizing that the public did not see existing programs as sufficient to meet the needs of families affected by thalidomide.

Abortion and Mercy Killing

As historians in both the Canadian and US contexts have noted, thalidomide stimulated debate over abortion.[50] In the early 1960s, abortion in Canada was illegal and permitted only when the life of the mother was threatened by the pregnancy.[51] Under these guidelines, between 1954 and 1965, only 226 therapeutic abortions were carried out in Canadian hospitals, while an estimated 50,000 to 100,000 illegal abortions were performed. Throughout the 1960s, an increasing number of doctors, some citing safety concerns, called for decriminalization.[52] Others in North America, stressing the benefits of compulsory sterilization, demanded legal abortions for eugenic reasons. According to historian Johanna Schoen, "advocates of eugenic abortion argued that the legalization of abortion would provide another avenue for preventing the birth of children who were likely to perpetuate social problems and become public charges." The possibility of eliminating birth defects, such as those caused by thalidomide, was often presented in these debates over abortion. While such legislation was never passed in North America, Nazi Germany and Communist China did impose abortions on women for eugenic reasons.[53] Though they would not have welcomed the comparison and certainly did not use the word "eugenics," some Canadians were clearly drawing on a similar rationale when they argued that abortions for mothers who took thalidomide would serve the interests of the nation.

In addition—a fact that has not been noted as much by historians—these children also stimulated a contentious discussion in the Canadian press over mercy killing, which was, and still is, prohibited under the Criminal Code.[54] This was actually not the first time that the issue of euthanasia for "defective" newborns had come up in the North American context. Though not referred to in the 1960s and apparently forgotten about even in the United States, a American doctor, Harry J. Haiselden, stirred up controversy in the 1910s by publicly admitting he had allowed "defective" infants in need of treatment to die. In championing this idea, inspired by eugenics, he even wrote and starred in a short film dramatizing one of those cases. Despite the popularity of eugenics, many Americans opposed this form of mercy killing. They insisted that "possession of a soul gave each human being equal inherent value [... and ...] defectives had social utility too."[55] Intriguingly, given that no one in the 1960s appeared to remember Haiselden's crusade, these same arguments

would re-surface in the Canadian debate over the thalidomide babies.[56] The similarity of rhetoric perhaps re-enforces the argument that eugenic thinking regarding "defective" newborns persisted in North America throughout the twentieth century.[57]

More memorably, the Third Reich, as mentioned above, implemented radical eugenic measures, including killing those considered physically or mentally unfit.[58] Though Canadians expressed revulsion over Nazi tactics, some felt that the thalidomide babies represented a case where the state should condone and even carry out mercy killing. Others supported only abortion in this situation and made no mention of euthanasia. Nevertheless, arguments in favour of both actions often centred on the perceived inability of the children to have fit, meaningful, useful, or happy lives without conventional bodies. In this way, Canadians were tapping into an existing eugenic discourse. Debate in Canada was stimulated not only by the rising incidence of Canadian thalidomide cases but also by the Sherri Finkbine drama in the United States. Mrs. Finkbine, mother of four and better known for her role on the popular children's television show *Romper Room*, appealed for a legal abortion in July 1962. In Arizona, as in Canada, abortions were only rarely permitted in cases where the mother's life was considered to be at risk.[59] Finkbine felt that she should be granted access to an abortion as she had taken thalidomide, purchased in Europe by her husband, and feared that her child would be deformed as a result. In her words, "The care and attention that this child would require—the added, heavy drain it would place on our limited income—couldn't help but deprive [our four children] of some measure of the care and love of both of us, to say nothing of their actual physical needs, the money for which would have to go for the constant care and attention our handicapped child would require."[60] Ultimately, the Arizona court denied the couple's request for an abortion and they went to Sweden to procure one.[61]

Though the subject of mercy killing was raised in conjunction with thalidomide babies from the time of their first appearance, another international case was of note here. In November 1962, Belgian mother Suzanne Vandeput, along with members of her family and her doctor, were charged with killing Suzanne's eight-day-old daughter, born without arms because of thalidomide. The group confessed to the crime, but all felt that, given the baby's deformities, they had had no choice. Mrs Vandeput, with the support of her mother and sister, had obtained a prescription for barbiturates from her doctor and laced the baby's milk with them. Her husband had done nothing to stop his wife or save his daughter. Mrs Vandeput was charged with voluntary homicide. If found guilty, she might face the death penalty, while the others were considered accessories to the crime. On the stand, Mrs Vandeput said, "If only my baby had also been mentally abnormal, it would have been different. . . . She would not have realized what her fate was, but she had a normal brain. She would have realized. She would have known. I would have had remorse all my life. There was nothing else I could have done."[62] Throughout the trial, public sympathy in Belgium seemed to lie with the defendants, particularly Mrs Vandeput. Perhaps reflecting this mood, all of the accused were acquitted.[63] Because of the worldwide nature of the thalidomide tragedy, and the existing debate in Canada over mercy killing, the Belgian trial garnered a great deal of Canadian media attention.

Some Canadians seemed to feel that deformed thalidomide children, many of whom lacked arms and legs, had no chance at anything approaching a normal life and would, in fact, only be a burden to those around them. Reducing or eliminating strains on the state through management of the population was an avowed goal of eugenicists.[64] Perhaps most intriguingly, many felt, as Mrs Vandeput would express months later at her trial, that the normal mental capacities of the thalidomide babies would only add to their misery in life. One might have thought that, given the emphasis placed on psychological and mental health in the post-war period, intact mental functions would have been seen as a blessing for all children but most particularly the physically impaired. Eugenicists in particular, and throughout the twentieth century, were preoccupied with mental faculties. However, it would be misleading to suggest that this focus meant that physical health became unimportant. On the contrary, many

Canadians, including doctors and even the parents of thalidomide babies, agreed with Mrs Vandeput and stressed the conventional physical body as a basic prerequisite for a happy life.[65] In July 1962, Dr Brock Chisholm, psychiatrist and former head of the World Health Organization, made headlines in several newspapers when he suggested that Canada should set up a Royal Commission to examine mercy killing and, more specifically, to determine if thalidomide babies should live or die.[66] In a CBC panel discussion on thalidomide, Dr Chisholm clarified his views that such children would lead unhappy lives.[67] In the *Toronto Star,* he declared that a Royal Commission was needed to decide "whether these limbless babies being born today are capable of living a satisfactory life without being a burden on society. If yes, then the child has every reason to live. If nothing but misery lies ahead for the child, then he has no reason to live."[68]

A self-identified handicapped person agreed with Dr Chisholm that physical deformities, such as those of the thalidomide babies, precluded a worthwhile life. As I will discuss below, most handicapped people who wrote in to newspapers, while admitting some physical impairment, defended their own lives as useful and happy. A notable exception was printed in the *Toronto Star* in August 1962. The letter, signed "Anonymous," was from someone with an abnormally short stature who claimed, based on this physical birth defect, to be able to speak for the thalidomide babies. According to the writer, "I am on the side of Dr Brock Chisholm. To allow the badly deformed to live beyond the period of birth is the worst of two evils. Their future will be full of snubbings, frustration, heartache and agony. Many of their own relations will shun them, even if their mental faculties are normal: they will be a burden to society. They will never know happiness if they are intelligent. I speak from experience."[69] Despite this rather grim picture, many Canadians, including those with physical disabilities, rejected eugenic calls for the elimination of those born like them and did not support abortions or mercy killings. I will return to their views later in this essay.

Others also expressed the opinion that thalidomide babies, though potentially of normal intelligence, could never be useful to society due to their physical differences. For example, *The Peterborough Examiner* argued that "[a] human being without limbs is a pathetic creature completely unable to care for itself in any way. To be condemned to a life of complete inactivity and perpetual dependence on others will be constantly painful and distressing to those without limbs and a dreadful trial to their parents."[70] Letter writer David G.R. Wilkinson called for legalized abortions in these cases and added that, as Mrs Susanne Vandeput would say later at her trial and like the anonymous writer cited above, the fact that thalidomide babies were not mentally impaired only made their situation more horrible. He said, "Society will purposefully and knowingly inflict a lifetime of bitter agony upon the limbless persons who will be allowed to mature, unable to help themselves. . . . The mental awareness of these limbless persons will constitute an even greater horror. They will know their agony."[71] A man named Ralph H. Braux in a letter to the *Toronto Star* in August 1962 also called for legalized abortion and euthanasia. As others had done, he highlighted the cost to society in raising such children.[72] A mother, writing to *The Vancouver Sun*, likewise supported abortions and asked "what value to anyone is the deformed child—a dreadful thing to itself; impossible in a family; needless, useless expense in an institution; and wasted effort for those paid to care for it."[73] These writers, in discussing the value of the children, were drawing on eugenic arguments that the unfit made intolerable demands upon the state. Finally, articulating eugenic principles explicitly, Harold P. Koehler wrote in a letter to the *Toronto Star* that thalidomide highlighted how modern medicine had undermined nature's control over the population. He explained that, until recently, "the struggle for survival has ruthlessly murdered the unfit." He seemed to be suggesting that governments had a responsibility to eliminate unfit life by allowing abortions and euthanasia.[74] This discourse demonstrates that physical health, even in a period preoccupied by psychology, remained fundamental to social acceptance. Additionally, the rejection of the thalidomide babies, based on their perceived lack of fitness and their anticipated dependence on

the state, reveals the enduring influence of eugenics in post-war society.

Many writing in the summer of 1962 seemed to feel that thalidomide babies represented a special, unwanted burden for their parents. Thus, they argued for abortion and mercy killings in the interest of protecting parents. It is important to note that these arguments were expressed before the killing of the thalidomide baby in Belgium. The *Toronto Star* received many such letters: K. Rutherford agreed with David Wilkinson, quoted above, and said that laws should relieve "mothers of the necessity of bringing limbless children into the world. To let such births take place is the worst cruelty that lack of imagination can inflict on helpless creatures."[75] D.G.P., calling for changes to the abortion law, argued that caring for deformed babies would negatively affect the health of the mothers.[76] Mrs May Burchard concurred, asserting that "[a]llowing such babies to live can have a disastrous effect on the mental health of the parents and the other children in the home, to say nothing of the bleak future of the afflicted children themselves. Yet we refuse to condone legalized abortion."[77] That the children might have normal or even extraordinary mental capacities was not seen by those on this side of the argument as sufficient reason for parents to raise them. Once again, this suggests a difficulty in imagining such children as members of the post-war Canadian family. They simply did not fit the idealized and eugenic parameters.

Parents of thalidomide babies were not silent in these debates. In fact, they had their own views about whether or not their children's physical differences should mean loss of life. Sometimes, perhaps surprisingly, they seemed sympathetic to eugenic arguments. At least one, Mrs Carl Beeston, mother of a thalidomide daughter, said in July 1962 that abortion should be permitted if the pregnant woman suspected she had taken thalidomide. She was quoted in *The Globe and Mail* as stating, "I don't see why a child should be brought into the world like that. They cannot lead a normal life, get married or have a career."[78] In the *Toronto Star*, Mrs Beeston also seemed to support the mercy killing of thalidomide babies. She stated that children like hers "shouldn't be allowed to draw their first breath." According to the *Star*, she felt mercy killing "is for the child's sake. A child shouldn't be expected to live a life of misery."[79] Thus, even thalidomide parents who loved their children questioned their worth to the point of endorsing abortion and mercy killing. In this way, they also subscribed to eugenic definitions of the "unfit."

The November 1962 trial of Mrs Vandeput again focused the attention of Canadians onto the question of mercy killing in thalidomide cases. Though, as we will see below, many Canadians were against Mrs Vandeput's actions, some felt they were justified and even commendable. A 16 November letter to *The Globe and Mail* by Gordon Arthurs reflected on the verdict in this case and proclaimed, "Humanity took a giant step forward when the courageous jury of Liege pronounced its verdict. A decision based on love and reason, not fear and superstition. No murder was committed by this mother, but rather an act of great compassion."[80] Writing to the *Ottawa Citizen*, Mostyn Paull reiterated that it was more compassionate to practise euthanasia in these cases.[81] And in a letter to *The Globe and Mail*, contributing to the discourse about useful lives advanced by Dr Brock Chisholm and others, F.L.M. urged people to "Put yourself in the place of the child. Whereas the odd crippled child may make a good life for himself, how many if they are normally intelligent must wish they had never been born. Surely true compassion would spare them their misery."[82]

As this discussion should make clear, there was a segment in the Canadian population who did not believe that thalidomide babies could ever lead useful, happy lives. They would mainly be "burdens" to their parents and society at large. Further, eliminating such children would actually represent progress for all humanity. This discourse, inspired by older eugenic ideas, underlines the emphasis placed on conceptions of the healthy, whole physical body as a prerequisite for happiness and success.[83] It also shows the unwillingness of some Canadians to integrate the physically different into the idealized nuclear family. There was, however, another current of opinion. An almost equal number of Canadians rejected the idea that a conventional body, including the usual appearance of limbs, was required for a

person to contribute to society. In making their case for thalidomide babies, they drew on a wide variety of arguments, including Christian morality, past precedents, and recent experiences in the Second World War. Though citing such seemingly diverse sources, the Canadians in this group were united in the belief that it was presumptuous and impossible for society to judge what body parts were required for a useful life.

Many who opposed abortion and mercy killing for the thalidomide babies simply refuted claims that these children could not possibly grow up to be happy and contributing members of society. Thus, they complicated eugenic distinctions between the "fit" and the "unfit." Though the debate over these issues was carried out throughout the summer and fall of 1962, many clearly felt compelled to write in the wake of the Belgian case. In constructing their arguments, they often referred to individuals who had overcome physical disabilities. One letter writer suggested that if mercy killing and abortion were allowed, remarkable individuals, such as Helen Keller, could be destroyed.[84] Using Canadian examples, Philip L. Copper discussed two young people in Edmonton with physical disabilities. He said 13-year-old Leonard Sealy was born without arms but could swim, dance, and play soccer. Even more strikingly, Trudy Mitchell was born with deformed limbs and one eye, but she "leads a happy and useful life, holding a job by day and doing voluntary community work at night."[85] In the wake of the trial of Suzanne Vandeput, during which her lawyer claimed there was no place on earth for the deformed baby, Rabbi W. Gunther Plaut of Holy Blossom Temple likewise commented, "I know of splendid artists who, having been born without hands, have learned to paint with their mouths and even with their feet, and who I venture to say would not look favourably upon a suggestion that . . . there was no possible place for them on this earth."[86] Robert F. DuMont, writing to *The Vancouver Sun* after the trial, added that many in West Germany alone were missing limbs but that they led "happy and useful lives with the aid of modern technology and artificial limbs."[87] It is interesting to note how often the words "happy" and "useful" are linked in this discourse.

As noted earlier, handicapped individuals and their families did not remain silent while others debated their utility. Whereas one writer to the *Toronto Star*, quoted above, argued for aborting and euthanizing those born like him, others reflected more positively on their lives. In doing so, they rejected the argument, inspired by eugenics, that the lives of the thalidomide babies would not be worth living. For example, in her letter to the *Toronto Star*, J. McKay wrote that both she and her sister were born with serious handicaps. However, "In spite of this, we have grown up as worthwhile and useful human beings, with good husbands and families." McKay urged the parents of thalidomide babies to be grateful that their children were born with normal intelligence. This stands in marked contrast to the opinions of Suzanne Vandeput in Belgium and other Canadians, who seemed to feel that normal mental capabilities would only make the children more miserable by making them aware of their shortcomings. McKay also noted that a lot could be done to help thalidomide babies.[88]

One mother of a handicapped child also wrote to the *Star* to argue against mercy killings. Nora Ludlow expressed sadness over the operations her 16-year-old daughter had had to endure but certainly did not feel she should not have been born. She said "Deformed and crippled children do not miss what they never had. They seek a chance at life and to be accepted as they are without pity. . . . When my husband and I look at our daughter, we see a pretty teenager full of fun, love, kindness. . . . We wouldn't have missed having her as she is for anything."[89] An editorial in *The Globe and Mail* also discussed the attitude of thalidomide parents. It said that many had chosen to accept and help their children. Further, the editor argued that the role of thalidomide children might be to draw attention to all children with handicaps. Indeed, "If the thalidomide babies impel Canadians to improve the lot of all deformed and retarded children, they will have lived more usefully than many. They will have helped to develop the whole man, who consists not only of the usual assortment of limbs and organs, but of a conscience."[90] The use of the expression "whole man" seems to be alluding to the opinions of some Canadians, cited above, that thalidomide babies lacked bodily integrity and, thus, could not be part of the nation. This editorial articulated a counter-argument expressed by others as well: that these children, though facing many challenges, could grow up to contribute to society. Indeed, this latter group, which included some physically handicapped individuals, questioned the strict equation made between conventional physical appearance and social worth. They also expressed dismay with the proposal, first promulgated by eugenicists, that the state should take upon itself the task of determining human worth.

Many of those opposed to abortion and mercy killing for thalidomide babies also alluded to Judeo-Christian values. Sometimes these sentiments were articulated alongside arguments about utility. Though seemingly different, both lines of reasoning rejected the right of society to judge those born physically unique. In his 2005 book *For Canada's Sake: Public Religion, Centennial Celebrations, and the Re-Making of Canada*, Gary Miedema argues that many Canadians still felt the country was defined by Christian values into the 1960s.[91] Certainly, many who wrote in to Canadian newspapers opposing abortion and mercy killing for thalidomide babies justified their stance as Christian. While still defending the potential of thalidomide babies to lead happy and useful lives, they also argued that practices such as abortion and euthanasia were counter to Judeo-Christian values and against God's will.[92] Some asserted explicitly that it should be left to God to determine who was worthy of life. In this way, they claimed that the Christian body, with or without all its typical limbs, was sacrosanct. Many also expressed an awareness of Nazi policies toward the disabled and infirm. Those who supported the rights of the thalidomide babies rejected the eugenic arguments described above and argued that Nazism, and by extension eugenics, represented the antithesis of Christian morality.

Canadians had strong reactions to the proposal of Dr Brock Chisholm that Canada set up a Royal Commission on mercy killing that would also be empowered to determine the fate of the thalidomide children. An editorial in the *Toronto Star* called this proposal revolting and opposed to Christian values.

The editor argued that Judeo-Christian morality maintained the right of all children to life and that, because of this principle, ignored most recently by the Nazis, "humanity owes the survival of many of its brightest figures, a surprising number of whom were born sickly or deformed."[93] Possibly also in response to Dr Chisholm's suggestion, letter writer Mrs B. Sullivan observed, "It is amazing to me that a number of people who live in our so-called Christian society which places so much emphasis on the rights of the human being, no matter how old, born, or unborn, are so overcome with pity for the children deformed by thalidomide that they want to kill them."[94] An August survey of Vancouver clerics found that many were actually divided on the subject of abortion in suspected thalidomide cases. While some felt access should be allowed, a Catholic priest, Reverend J.P. Carney, affirmed that "[a] child is a human being endowed with an immortal soul from the moment of its conception. No one but almighty God has the right to interfere with that child's chance for life."[95] Finally, a letter in the Ottawa Citizen, questioned more explicitly humanity's right to determine life or death for those born with physical deformities. Peter Morris asked, "Who is to say there is not a divine reason behind many things, including those who are born into this world without the so-called normal physical and mental endowments?"[96]

Perhaps not surprisingly, questions of Judeo-Christian morality continued to shape reactions in the wake of the thalidomide mercy killing in Belgium. Increasingly, supporters of abortion and euthanasia were likened to Nazis. According to Mrs Allan McPhail, less than 20 years after the Second World War, "we find our very own so-called Christians no less contemptible than the murderers of the camps at Dachau and Belsen." She argued that, while the Nazis murdered the aged and deformed, "Today the Finkbines of U.S.A. and the Belgian couples of Liege have publicly admitted to a no less shocking crime."[97] Robert F. DuMont, quoted above, added that the Belgian parents should not have destroyed the baby because it was not physically perfect. He commented that Hitler wished to create a perfect race but that, in this case, God's law should have trumped the will of the parents and the doctor.[98] Finally, Gary Doyl Gottlieb, writing to the Toronto Star in the aftermath of the Belgian trial, affirmed that Judaism likewise upheld the sanctity of life and God's unique right to determine who should live.[99]

Clearly, Nazi policies were often presented as the antithesis of a Christian morality that, according to some Canadians, protected the right of all children, no matter their physical condition, to live. They argued further that only God could decide the merits of a life. The Canadians in this group were plainly repulsed by those who called for the elimination of thalidomide-deformed children through abortion and euthanasia. They alluded to Nazis policies not only to discredit their opponents but also to express what they perceived, rightly, as a shared rationale in both Nazi programs and Canadian proposals to dispose of thalidomide babies. As a counterpoint, they stressed the spiritual component of life. They emphasized that the soul, endowed by God, was more important to the individual than the body. Therefore, they agreed with other Canadians that a complete set of limbs was not a requirement for a valuable life.

Abortion and euthanasia remain contentious issues in Canadian society. That these practices were linked to the fate of the thalidomide babies suggests a refusal by some to integrate the physically unconventional into the nation. They argued, drawing on older eugenic discourses, that quite simply these children would never lead useful lives—for them a requirement for happiness—without their limbs. Those who disagreed recounted success stories of the disabled and argued that Christian morality, the opposite of which was espoused by the Nazis, protected the sanctity of life, independent of a whole body. In the next section, I will explore the debate surrounding the institutionalization of thalidomide children. Though some Canadians did not condone abortion or mercy killing, they did think that these children would function better in institutional settings. The decision to remove these children from the home may, like calls for abortion and mercy killing, indicate a deep ambivalence, fostered in part by eugenicists, about having such visibly different children in post-war families.

Institutionalization

At the start of the twentieth century, institutions were seen as appropriate places for disabled children. However, increasingly in the post-war period, experts believed that even children with serious physical ailments, such as spina bifida, would be better off in some kind of family setting.[100] In espousing this attitude, they were part of a wider deinstitutionalization movement that "represented a well-intentioned effort to remove the mentally disabled, physically handicapped, mentally retarded, prisoners and other dependent groups from asylums and similar places of incarceration, in order to place them in community settings."[101] This movement, which began in the 1960s, articulated a growing consensus among health professionals that institutional care could be detrimental.[102] However, with the thalidomide babies, their parents, and the media seemed to still consider institutionalization a legitimate choice. Though presented as in the best interest of the children, one wonders if institutionalization represented a rejection of them. Especially initially, parents of thalidomide babies repudiated the idea of raising these children alongside their "normal" siblings. Newspapers debated the pros and cons of institutional versus home care. Even after most Canadian parents decided to keep their thalidomide babies at home, institutionalization was presented as a viable and legitimate option. Though not as extreme perhaps as abortion or euthanasia, placing physically different children in institutions would likewise erase them from the population.

One of the very first newspaper articles about a thalidomide baby detailed the rather sad story of a couple in Kitchener, Ontario, who asked the court to make their deformed baby a permanent ward of the Waterloo County Children's Aid Society. The baby was born without arms, and his father blamed pills taken during the pregnancy. In this case, the judge declared the baby a ward of the CAS because he agreed that caring for it would be too much of a burden on the mother.[103] According to the *Ottawa Citizen,* "The mother, described as under a severe strain, has never seen more than the child's head."[104] At the hearing, "A doctor who examined the child after birth suggested a foster home or institutional care because the child would be difficult to feed and would present severe emotional difficulties for the mother if she were to care for it."[105] Though the parents' decision to seek institutional care seems to have been exceptional, many did feel it should remain an option for parents of thalidomide babies. For example, in a *Globe and Mail* editorial printed the next day, the editor said society had a responsibility to these children and their parents, which meant, among other things, that the Children's Aid Society had to be open to receiving thalidomide babies.[106]

Other Canadians certainly felt that institutional care would be best for all members of a family touched by thalidomide. In August 1962, *The Globe and Mail* solicited opinions from Toronto health welfare workers on this issue. They found that views were fairly evenly split. I will discuss those who opposed institutional care below. Those in favour argued that "only special institutions could offer the personnel and facilities to equip properly the children for later life." One of the chief proponents of this kind of care was visiting British professor Leslie Hilliard, who had experience with mentally disabled children and added that thalidomide children would need intensive and early training in the use of artificial limbs. Miss Majorie Jenkins, Superintendent of Bloorview Hospital, a residential treatment centre for physically disabled children, emphasized the drawbacks of home life for the thalidomide child. She asserted, "If the child were with his own sisters and brothers at home, they would probably always be running off and leaving him alone."[107] Journalist Leonard Bertin reported Professor Hilliard's views on this subject. He stated, "To leave them with families untrained to look after their special needs can only cause anguish to parents, [Professor Hilliard] says. For the children so monstrously misformed, any attempt to bring them up as normal children will mean loss of their one chance to become, later, contributing members of their community. Deprived of limbs through which they learn during their first two years of life, their brains will inevitably deteriorate unless the deficiency is made up in some other way."[108] Thus, some Canadians asserted that only institutional care could mould deformed children into useful citizens. Such care also had the less clearly stated benefit of removing them from view, an appealing idea for a public influenced by eugenics and, therefore, deeply concerned with promoting the image of a healthy, productive nation.

As mentioned above and according to newspaper coverage, many parents did initially consider placing their physically deformed thalidomide babies in institutional care of some kind. A Sarnia couple, later identified as Mr and Mrs Case, discussed their struggle over the future of their son, born in May 1962 without arms or legs. Mrs Case apparently wept when she first saw her baby, and when interviewed two months later, the couple expressed the desire to place him in an institution. According to Mr Case, "It's not that we don't want our son—it's going to be hard to give him up now—but in a few years it would be much too hard for us to take care of him. It would be cruel to him and to any other children we might have to keep him at home."[109] Mrs Beeston, a mother of a thalidomide baby, also wanted to give her daughter up at first.[110] And Mr Bamber, a Victoria father, who will be quoted at length below, said his first inclination was to send his newborn son to an institution.[111] Thus it seems that, though almost all the couples would change their minds, institutionalization was considered a viable option and was, in fact, pondered openly by the parents of Canadian thalidomide babies in the days, weeks, and months after birth. They, along with other Canadians, argued that it would be impossible to raise these babies alongside other, healthy children they already had or hoped to have in the future. In this discussion, the privileging of healthy children and the removal of thalidomide babies from "fit" families reflected again the continuing appeal of eugenic priorities.

However, other Canadians asserted from the beginning that institutionalization was inappropriate for thalidomide babies. They seemed to feel that some home life would be far more beneficial for the physically disabled. In the *Globe and Mail* survey of Toronto health welfare workers cited above, a large number of respondents favoured home care. They argued that "placing mentally alert children—even though they were deformed—in institutions could

add mental injury to their physical injuries." Ward Markle, director of the Catholic Children's Aid Society, explained that institutionalization would be "the worst thing in the world for [thalidomide babies]. It's all right for mentally retarded children because they do not know the difference between their surroundings and the world outside. But the physically handicapped child requires home care and affection." Another welfare worker, Benjamin Schlesinger, concurred that institutional care could emotionally harm the child.[112] A November 1962 article in *Chatelaine* by Catherine Sinclair affirmed that most Canadian doctors preferred home care.[113] Thus, once again, the argument is being made that thalidomide babies, though physically damaged, had the same mental capacities as other children and, therefore, deserved the same love and care. Additionally, they had the right to be fully incorporated into their families and should not be shunted aside or made invisible. This perspective rejected the eugenic distinctions between "unfit" and "fit" that many Canadians seemed implicitly to apply to thalidomide babies and their siblings.

Some thalidomide parents immediately declared their intention to keep their babies, and almost all ultimately would state their desire to do so. In making this decision, they conformed more to the broader trend away from institutionalization and asserted that, contrary to eugenic prescriptions, physically disabled children should not be stigmatized. A Hamilton mother who gave birth to twins affected by thalidomide declared that she would raise the babies at home. Likewise, an unnamed mother in Winnipeg said she intended to keep her baby.[114] Mrs Marilyn Bamber, of Victoria, while still in hospital, declared her armless newborn "cute." Perhaps to emphasize her acceptance of the child, Mrs Bamber described his resemblance to his father, as any new mother might. Mr Bamber added that the baby was a "beautiful little fellow. We'll try to treat him as if nothing was wrong." Though their first inclination was to place the baby in an institution, Mr Bamber reported, "[W]e changed our minds. You can't send somebody to a home and wonder for the rest of your life where he is and how he is. . . . I told Marilyn I wanted to keep him and she said the same thing. I think she was much happier." Mrs Bamber agreed, saying, "I don't want to shut him off in a back room—he has to live his own life. . . . We will have to face each little crisis as it comes. We may have to send him away to a special school. He's cute, and I like him."[115]

The other parents cited above who initially considered institutionalization also changed their minds. After meeting a 15-year-old girl born without legs but assisted through surgery to live a normal life, Mr Case explained, "We didn't know whether we should keep our son or place him in an institution. . . . But after seeing that girl, we know we would be crazy to give him up."[116] Almost a year later, as they welcomed their second child, the Cases reported that they had turned down a recent offer of a spot in an institution for their son.[117] Mr and Mrs Beeston also had a quick change of heart. Mrs Beeston stated, "I don't want Kim to go to an institution. She is not mentally retarded, she is as bright as a button. I think they belong in a home where they are loved and cared for."[118] In another article, Mrs Beeston reiterated her disapproval of institutionalization. Painting a rather grim picture, she asserted, "Unless they are mentally retarded, I don't see why they should be locked up. I won't put mine in any institution."[119] A third couple, William and Mary Thompson, also grappled with placing their limbless son, Brian, in an institution. They worried about their older son's reaction to his baby brother and whether they would be able to afford the care Brian would require. In the end, "We decided Brian would have more will to learn his lessons and how to use his artificial limbs if he has a family to come home to." For other parents of thalidomide children, William and Mary urged, "Don't worry about what other people think—consider yourself first. If bringing your baby home would upset you too much, then don't. The baby would suffer as much as you would."[120] As these examples demonstrate, many thalidomide parents decided to keep their children at home, in this way expressing their commitment to including their thalidomide-scarred children in their family life. However, the fact that they even had the discussion about institutionalization among themselves and in the media indicates that it was seen as a socially permissible option. Further, it suggests that the acceptance of these children by their parents was by no means instantaneous and, in fact, was a process that often began with rejection because of their physical deformities. Thus, once again, the debate about whether or not to institutionalize these children highlights the emphasis placed on the conventional body as a requirement for entry into the Canadian family. It also suggests that many Canadians may have agreed with eugenicists who wished to accept only optimum levels of both physical and mental health in the next generation.

Indeed, even after a consensus emerged that a supportive family life would be best for the thalidomide babies, experts continued to assert that institutional care must remain an option for parents unable to cope. They insisted that this choice did not make the parents reprehensible. This continuing discourse suggests great sympathy and admiration for thalidomide parents who struggled to integrate physically damaged children into a society that was clearly not comfortable with them. An article reprinted in *The Globe and Mail* from the British medical journal *The Lancet* stated that home was the best place for thalidomide babies, but that "[e]ven good parents may be so overwhelmed by the deformities that they will feel quite unable to cope with their child. . . . In these cases, long-term or permanent institutional care will be required."[121] Also in the summer of 1962, Dr A.L. Chute, chief of pediatrics at the Hospital for Sick Children in Toronto, agreed that children should be cared for at home, but that institutions had to remain an option since some parents could not manage.[122] In May 1963, Montreal psychiatrist Dr Denis Lazure reflected on his experience with thalidomide mothers. He noted, "Most parents in Canada wanted to keep the child in the home, but where parents were psychologically unable to cope with the child they should not be made to feel that they are perverted parents if they choose to place it in an institution."[123] That parents who chose institutional care for their thalidomide babies were regarded with such compassion reflects perhaps a deep uncertainty about absorbing their children into the wider society.

Help for the Thalidomide Babies? Artificial Limbs

Despite discourses advocating abortion, mercy killing, or institutionalization, others in Canada promoted the use of artificial limbs. According to Trent Stephens and Rock Brynner's book on thalidomide's impact, artificial limbs were favoured even though they weren't very functional. The authors note, "The artificial limbs were among the greatest sources of misery for almost all the victims, and consumed much of their young lives while remaining, for all but a few, completely useless." It was very difficult for thalidomide victims to use prosthetics since the basic nerve pathways between the brain and limbs were never established. Additionally, many of their existing limbs, though malformed, might have proved useful to the children. Instead, in many countries, surgeons removed any limbs so the children could be fitted for prosthetics. In Canada especially, the government promoted artificial limbs and provided them to thalidomide children. Stephens and Brynner argue that "although some of the families remained destitute, almost every one of Canada's 115 victims who were limb-deprived had to be fitted with these utterly ineffective prosthetics."[124] The willingness of Canadian doctors to amputate the existing limbs of thalidomide babies may reflect a eugenic impulse to discard their malformed bodies and rebuild them as normal, healthy children.

Contemporary Canadian newspaper stories that discuss the treatment and rehabilitation of thalidomide babies reflect this emphasis on surgery and prosthetics. Many stories report that the thalidomide victims were either undergoing or expected to undergo surgeries.[125] Government aid, when it was forthcoming, particularly focused on paying for the costs of surgeries, prosthetics, and training.[126] In this activity, government officials may have been acting on the advice of the medical profession. Doctors seemed to have felt that the best treatment course for thalidomide victims lay in prosthetics. In August 1962, Dr John T. Law, director of Toronto's Hospital for Sick Children, asserted, "There's not a great deal we can do [for thalidomide victims], except see about artificial arms and limbs."[127] Many

thalidomide victims in Canada were treated at the Rehabilitation Institute of Montreal under the care of Dr Gustave Gingras. Here, "the children are taught what Dr. Gingras calls the double life. At home, they find it easier to do things, such as writing or picking up objects, with their toes, but in public they can use their artificial arms and hands."[128] This statement begs the question: if it was easier for the thalidomide children to use their toes, why were they pressured to use artificial limbs in public? Was this "double life" intended to help the children or ease the discomfort of a society not prepared to witness their physical differences? The article goes on to report that limbs were fitted very early so the child could become accustomed to them.

Dr Henry H. Kessler, the medical director of the Kessler Institute for Rehabilitation in New Jersey, was also quick to reassure parents that, with artificial limbs, thalidomide children could lead useful lives. Dr L.W. Davidson, medical director of the Ontario Crippled Children's Centre, agreed that, with prosthetics, thalidomide children could learn to walk, dress, and feed themselves.[129] However, some medical authorities expressed awareness that thalidomide children might have difficulty using artificial limbs. Dr Kessler, for example, said that limbs must be fitted early "to enable that part of the brain which handles the work of the arm to be aware that there is work to be done, and that an artificial limb is part of the body."[130] A November 1962 article in *Chatelaine* likewise cautioned that thalidomide babies must receive medical treatment very soon as "it is feared that the parts of the brain that normally control arm and leg movements may deteriorate unless these limbs can be made useful, or unless artificial limbs are properly substituted."[131] Thus, doctors in the early 1960s did seem to be aware of the potential difficulties in fitting prosthetics for infants who had never had limbs. However, they persisted in doing so. Was it because it was the best bet for the children or because artificial limbs gave the appearance of normalcy? Margaret McQueen, the coordinating assistant at the Crippled Children's Centre in Toronto, confirmed the connection between prosthetics and normalcy in the thalidomide cases, stating, "Often it is the child who convinces his parents that he needs a prosthesis. . . . How else is he going to learn to walk, eat, clothe himself and even play football?"[132]

Most Canadians seemed to accept that artificial limbs represented the best chance for thalidomide babies to have a "normal" life and, though it was not stated explicitly, to become "fit." An editorial from July 1962 reported, "Present information is that many of the victims can be helped to live something approaching a normal 'life,' but this will require specially designed limbs and a long course of training in their use."[133] Another *Toronto Star* editorial, written six months later, urged the government to provide facilities for the rehabilitation of the thalidomide children. The writer said the children "can be equipped to lead reasonably normal lives but it will require a great deal of patient, intensive, highly-specialized training and supervision."[134] In May 1963, Leonard Bertin affirmed in a *Toronto Star* article that artificial limbs could reduce the possibility of a child being a burden on his or her family.[135]

The parents of the thalidomide children likewise invested a great deal of hope in prosthetics to secure a normal life and a fit body for their physically damaged children. Mr and Mrs Case, discussed above, decided to keep their son at home after meeting a 15-year-old girl helped by Toronto plastic surgeon Dr William K. Lindsay. They were also reassured by their meeting with the doctor. The father reported, "I came out of the doctor's office with more hope than when I went in."[136] In August 1962, Mr Case stated that his son would undergo surgery in the fall. The plan was to "amputate, and then fit artificial limbs and train him to walk. When he comes home (in two years' time), if everything's successful, he'll be walking."[137] The parents of the Hamilton thalidomide twins also hoped their boys could be helped by corrective surgeries.[138] Perhaps the most revealing example of how much parents relied on surgeries and artificial limbs for their children is found in the testimony of Belgian mother Mrs Vandeput. As detailed earlier, Mrs Vandeput killed her eight-day-old daughter who was born without arms because of thalidomide exposure. At her trial, "Mrs Vandeput said she and the other women defendants searched for some assurance that armless baby Corinne could get arms, even if they had to be artificial." According to Mrs Vandeput, it was only after she was told prosthetics were not possible that she decided there was no other choice but to kill Corinne.[139] Ultimately, then, even the treatment of the thalidomide babies was geared towards repackaging them as physically normal. If they could not be eliminated through abortion or euthanasia or born physically whole in the first place, as eugenicists and others would have tried to ensure, they could at least be made to appear it.

Conclusion

"Useless," "a burden to society," "pathetic creatures." These were only some of the words and phrases used to describe thalidomide babies, born without limbs due to a drug ingested by their mothers during pregnancy. While other Canadians took issue with these characterizations, the rhetoric demonstrates that, even during a period in which psychology was increasingly prominent in society, the conventional physical body remained deeply important as a prerequisite for a happy, useful life. If the success of antibiotics and vaccines in combatting disease in the preceding decade had encouraged doctors and child-rearing experts to focus more on psychological development, this did not mean that the physical body became insignificant. Rather, the case of the thalidomide babies shows that, though parents may have started to take the physical health of their children for granted, they never for one moment felt that a flawed body was anything but a huge obstacle to success and happiness. Newspaper coverage reveals a society deeply divided over the merits of incorporating so-called malformed children into the post-war family. The nuclear family was idealized in this period and, to integrate the physically imperfect into this unit would, according to some, have a destabilizing effect.

Those Canadians who felt this way argued for abortions, mercy killing, and institutionalization. Whether aware of it or not, in doing so, they were drawing on a eugenic discourse. In the interwar decades, eugenicists in North America and Europe called for the optimization of humanity through selective breeding and the sterilization of the unfit. German eugenicists during the Third Reich practised both euthanasia and eugenic abortions in an attempt to control their population. While Canadians arguing for the destruction or removal of thalidomide babies would not have been happy with the comparison, they did share with eugenicists an interest in managing the population and eliminating the "unfit."

Notes

1. Mary Louise Adams, *The Trouble with Normal: Postwar Youth and the Making of Heterosexuality* (Toronto: University of Toronto Press, 1997), 20.

2. Mona Gleason, *Normalizing the Ideal: Psychology, Schooling, and the Family in Postwar Canada* (Toronto: University of Toronto Press, 1999), 7. Gleason points out that Canadians in this period were in fact deeply troubled by concerns over women's work, juvenile delinquency, the rising divorce rates and, most seriously, the threat of nuclear war.

3. Katherine Arnup, *Education for Motherhood: Advice for Mothers in Twentieth-Century Canada* (Toronto: University of Toronto Press, 1994), 10. In her book on Canadian child-rearing advice, Arnup argues that "During the post-war economic boom, as national health improved with increased knowledge and enhanced nutrition, psychological concerns began to emerge as central issues on the child-rearing agenda."

4. Ibid.

5. Francis Galton, *Inquiries into Human Faculty and Its Development* (New York: Dutton, 1907), 17n. Quoted in Angus McLaren, *Our Own Master Race: Eugenics in Canada, 1885–1945* (Toronto: McClelland & Stewart, 1990), 15.

6. Wendy Kline, *Building a Better Race: Gender, Sexuality and Eugenics from the Turn of the Twentieth Century to the Baby Boom* (Berkeley: University of California Press, 2001), 2.

7. McLaren, 41 and 109; Nancy Ordover, *American Eugenics: Race, Queer Anatomy, and the Science of Nationalism* (Minneapolis: University of Minnesota Press, 2003), 195–8. In her book on American eugenics, Ordover argues that eugenicists clamoured to prevent the reproduction of both physically and developmentally disabled women.

8. Linda Revie, "More Than Just Boots! The Eugenic and Commercial Concerns behind A.R. Kaufman's Birth Controlling Activities," *Canadian Bulletin of Medical History* 23, 1 (2006): 125; Cicely Devereux, *Growing a Race: Nellie McClung and the Fiction of Eugenic Feminism* (Montreal and Kingston: McGill-Queen's University Press, 2006), 86–7.

9. McLaren, 9, 55 and 147. In Germany, Canada, Britain and the United States, "fitness" was often tied to race, class and ethnicity. Emphasis varied by country.

10. Ibid., 90–1 and 100.

11. Gleason, 23-4.

12. For more on eugenic principles at work in contemporary prenatal medicine see Carol H. Browner and Nancy Ann Press, "The Normalization of Prenatal Diagnostic Screening," in *Conceiving the New World Order: The Global Politics of Reproduction*, edited by Faye D. Ginsburg and Rayna Rapp (Berkeley: University of California Press, 1995).

13. Diane Paul, "From Eugenics to Genetics," *Journal of Policy History* 9, 1 (1997), 104.

14. Alexandra Stern, *Eugenic Nation: Faults and Frontiers of Better Breeding in Modern America* (Berkeley: University of California Press, 2005), 155 and 167.

15. Kline, 148 and 156.

16. Angus McLaren, *A History of Contraception: From Antiquity to the Present Day* (Cambridge: Basil Blackwell, 1990), 241.

17. Barbara Clow, "'An Illness of Nine Months' Duration:' Pregnancy and Thalidomide Use in Canada and the United States," in *Women, Health, and Nation: Canada and the United States Since 1945*, edited by Georgina Feldberg, Molly Ladd-Taylor, Alison Li and Kathryn McPherson (Kingston: McGill-Queen's University Press, 2003).

18. Ibid., 52–3.

19. Joel Lexchin, *The Real Pushers: A Critical Analysis of the Canadian Drug Industry* (Vancouver: New Star Books, 1984), 191–2. Specifically, Lexchin claims that the thalidomide case shows the resistance of the Canadian government to recall any drug once it is for sale. Additionally, according to Lexchin, had the government enforced a 1954 law prohibiting false advertising, the thalidomide tragedy could also have been prevented.

20. The Insight Team of *The Sunday Times*, *Suffer the Children: The Story of Thalidomide* (London: André Deutsch Limited, 1979), 23, 35, 206–223, 171–3, 226, 234–8. That this book was not published until 1979 seems to be related to censorship and confidentiality laws in Britain. According to the authors, they were prohibited from publishing any material that might prejudice ongoing court cases against Distillers Company Limited, the firm which marketed thalidomide in Britain. In addition, in 1974, Distillers successfully argued in court that company documents obtained by reporters from *The Sunday Times*, through the lawyer of the parents of British thalidomide victims, were confidential. *The Times* launched several legal challenges against these rulings, culminating in a favourable decision by the European Commission of Human Rights in 1977, and it was finally able to publish an article detailing Distillers' role in 1977, by which time almost all of the thalidomide cases had been settled.

21. Ibid., 134.

22. Trent Stephens and Rock Brynner, *Dark Remedy: The*

Impact of Thalidomide and Its Revival as a Vital Measure (Cambridge: Perseus Publishing, 2001), 9 and 25–6.

23. Stephens and Brynner, 12; Insight Team of *The Sunday Times*, 3 and 48–9.

24. Insight Team of *The Sunday Times*, 46–51.

25. Insight Team of *The Sunday Times*, 23 and 29–30.

26. Stephens and Brynner, 16.

27. Ibid., 20–21.

28. Insight Team of *The Sunday Times*, 35.

29. Clow, 47.

30. Ibid., 96–100.

31. Stephens and Brynner, 33–34.

32. "Thalidomide History," *The Globe and Mail*, August 1, 1962, p. 9.

33. Eric Dowd, "Withdraw Drug after 3 Months of Investigation," *The Globe and Mail*, March 31, 1962, p. 3.

34. Hyman Soloman, "Drug Ban Delayed by Firms' Plea—Ottawa," *Toronto Star*, August 3, 1962, p. 1. Insight Team of *The Sunday Times*, 104. Morrell does not clarify what he means by "bad publicity," but presumably he was referring to increasing reports of side effects. According to the team at *The Sunday Times*, Grünenthal similarly blamed the withdrawal of thalidomide in West Germany on what it termed sensational media coverage linking the drug to birth defects.

35. Hyman Solomon, "Ottawa Has No Power to Bar Dangerous Drug," *Toronto Star*, August 2, 1962, pp. 1 and 2. "Minister Given Power to Ban New Drug Sales," *The Globe and Mail*, October 29, 1963, p. B-2. As a result of the thalidomide tragedy, these laws were changed in October 1963 to give the health minister the power to block the sale of drugs and to get more experimental data from companies on a new drug before it could be approved.

36. Clow, 49.

37. Stephens and Brynner, 164.

38. Insight Team of *The Sunday Times*, 1, 113 and 134. For the Canadian numbers, see Jean F. Webb, "Canadian Thalidomide Experience," *Canadian Medical Association Journal* 89, 19 (November 9, 1963), pp. 989–990.

39. Harold Weir, "Hysteria Has Been Overdone," *The Vancouver Sun*, August 7, 1962, p. 4.

40. Research and Statistics Division, Department of National Health and Welfare, *Rehabilitation Services in Canada: Part 1—General Review* (Ottawa, 1960), pp. 105, 22, 113, and 109.

41. "Famous Canadian Physicians," www.collectionscanada.gc.ca/physicians/030002-2200-e.html

42. Mary Tremblay, "Going Back to Main Street: The Development and Impact of Casualty Rehabilitation for Veterans with Disabilities, 1945–1948," in *The Veterans Charter and Post-World War Two Canada*, edited by Peter Neary and J.L. Granatstein (Montreal and Kingston: McGill-Queen's University Press, 1998), pp. 172–3.

43. *Rehabilitation Services in Canada*, pp. 110 and 109.

44. *Rehabilitation Services in Canada*, pp. 110, 114, and 23.

45. *Rehabilitation Services in Canada*, p. 23.

46. Dennis Guest, *The Emergence of Social Security in Canada*, 3rd Edition (Vancouver: UBC Press, 1997), p. 138; James J. Rice and Michael J. Prince, *Changing Politics of Canadian Social Policy* (Toronto: University of Toronto Press, 2000), p. 72; *Rehabilitation Services in Canada*, pp. 65–66.

47. Rice and Prince, pp. 72–3. For more on the development of disability policy in Canada in general, see Jerome E. Bickenbach, *Physical Disability and Social Policy* (Toronto: University of Toronto Press, 1993). Disability history also exists as a distinct international field. See particularly *The Disability Studies Reader*, 2nd edition, edited by Lennard J. Davis (New York: Routledge, 2006); Paul K. Longmore and David Goldberger, "The League of the Physically Handicapped and the Great Depression: A Case Study in the New Disability History," *The Journal of American History* 87, 3 (December 2000): 888–922; Catherine J. Kudlick, "Disability History: Why We Need Another 'Other,'" *The American Historical Review* 108, 3 (June 2003): 763–793.

48. Stanley Westall, "Knowles Charges Negligence, Calls Government Responsible," *The Globe and Mail*, July 31, 1962, p. 1; Val Sears, "Demand Ottawa Pay Full Cost of Deformed Babies," *Toronto Star*, July 31, 1962, pp. 1 and 8.

49. For further reaction to the federal government's initial position, see Editorial, "No Federal Responsibility?" *Toronto Star*, July 31, 1962, p. 6; Editorial, "A Government Responsibility," *The Globe and Mail*, July 31, 1962, p. 6; "Ottawa Called Tardy Over Thalidomide," *The Globe and Mail*, August 1, 1962, p. 9; "Thompson, Douglas Demand Baby Aid," *Toronto Star*, August 1, 1962, p. 9. On the government's subsequent offer of aid, see "Ottawa Offering Aid for Victims of Drug," *The Globe and Mail*, August 2, 1962, p. 1 and "Thalidomide May Be Lever to More Help for Disabled," *The Globe and Mail*, August 18, 1962, pp. 1 and 9.

50. McLaren, *A History of Contraception*, 241; Johanna Schoen, *Choice and Coercion: Birth Control, Sterilization, and Abortion in Public Health and Welfare* (Chapel Hill, NC: The University of North Carolina Press, 2005), 180. In the United States, Johanna Schoen argues that "In 1962, the Sherri Finkbine case raised public awareness of the dangers of thalidomide and inaugurated a nationwide debate about the use of abortion to avoid birth defects. The debate not only altered the national consciousness concerning abortion but also played a crucial role in emerging reform efforts." Finkbine was an American woman who feared that her child would be born deformed because she took thalidomide early in the pregnancy. She sought a legal abortion in Arizona. Her case will be discussed in more detail later.

51. F.L. Morton, *Morgentaler v. Borowski: Abortion, the Charter, and the Courts* (Toronto: McClelland & Stewart Inc., 1992), pp. 17–18.

52. Angus McLaren and Arlene Tigar McLaren, *The Bedroom and the State: The Changing Practices and Politics of*

Contraception and Abortion in Canada, 1880–1980 (Toronto: McClelland & Stewart, 1986), 133–136.

53. Schoen, 143 and 286, n. 7.

54. Ian Dowbiggin, *A Concise History of Euthanasia: Life, Death, God, and Medicine* (Oxford: Rowman & Littlefield Publishers, Inc., 2005), 113–114; Jocelyn Downie, *Dying Justice: A Case for Decriminalizing Euthanasia and Assisted Suicide in Canada* (Toronto: University of Toronto Press, 2004), 37; *Martin's Annual Criminal Code* (Toronto: Canada Law Books Company Ltd., 1963), 201. Ian Dowbiggin is one of the few to make a connection between the euthanasia movement and thalidomide. In his book, he notes that the thalidomide tragedy legitimated the discussion of euthanasia in the 1960s.

55. Dowbiggin, p. 73; Martin S. Pernick, *The Black Stork: Eugenics and the Death of "Defective" Babies in American Medicine and Motion Pictures Since 1915* (Oxford: Oxford University Press, 1996), pp. 4–6, 159, 73, and 76.

56. Dowbiggin, p. 113. Dowbiggin accurately notes that "[thalidomide] rapidly became a horror story that raised many of the same issues as Harry Haiselden's decision in 1915 not to provide surgery that would prolong the life of a baby born deformed or with serious medical complications."

57. Pernick, p. 159; Dowbiggin, p. 152.

58. McLaren, *Our Own Master Race*, 147.

59. "Abortion Plan Changed by Arizona Hospital," *The Globe and Mail*, July 25, 1962, p. 20.

60. Ibid.

61. "Finkbines Await Swede Abortion O.K.," *Toronto Star*, August 7, 1962, p. 3; "Mother's Abortion Plea Meets Delay in Sweden," *The Globe and Mail*, August 7, 1962, p. 4. According to *The Globe and Mail*, Swedish law permitted abortion if continuing the pregnancy represented a threat to the woman's mental health or if the child might be deformed.

62. "Belgian Woman Goes on Trial for Slaying of Thalidomide Baby," *The Globe and Mail*, November 5, 1962, p. 34; "Killing Only Solution for Armless Infant, Belgian Mother Says," *The Globe and Mail*, November 6, 1962, p. 1.

63. "Court Frees Thalidomide Baby Doctor—Colleagues Order Professional Trial," *Ottawa Citizen*, November 12, 1962, p. 24.

64. McLaren, *Our Own Master Race*, 8; Schoen, 143.

65. Dowbiggin, p. 113. More generally, commentators worldwide shared Mrs. Vandeput's skepticism about the quality of life these children could expect.

66. "Twins in Hamilton among More Than 40 Canadian Drug Babies," *The Globe and Mail*, July 30, 1962, p. 4; Ian Dowbiggin, *A Merciful End: The Euthanasia Movement in Modern America* (Oxford: Oxford University Press, 2003), 214–5. Dr Chisholm (1896–971), a Canadian, was elected the first director general of the World Health Organization in 1948. He served in this post until 1952. For more on this controversial Canadian doctor see Allan Irving, *Brock Chisholm: Doctor to the World* (Associated Medical Services Incorporated, 1998).

67. "Human Tests Needed, MDs Say," *The Globe and Mail*, August 7, 1962, p. 4.

68. "Ask Canada Study Mercy Death," *Toronto Star*, July 30, 1962, p 2.

69. "Born Handicapped," letter by Anonymous, *Toronto Star*, August 9, 1962, p. 6.

70. Quoted in "Deformed Babies: Should We Legalize Abortions?" *Toronto Star*, July 27, 1962, p. 6

71. "Deformed Babies Show Need for Legal Abortions," letter by David G.R. Wilkinson, *Toronto Star*, July 31, 1962, p. 6.

72. "Law Archaic," letter by Ralph H. Braux, *Toronto Star*, August 3, 1962, p. 6

73. "A Pity Men Don't Bear Children," letter by A Mother, *The Vancouver Sun*, August 1, 1962, p. 4

74. "Let Unfit Die," letter by Harold P. Koehler, *Toronto Star*, August 7, 1962, p. 6.

75. "It's Cruel to Permit Birth of Deformed Children," letter by K. Rutherford, *Toronto Star*, August 3, 1962, p. 6.

76. "Change Abortion Law," letter by D.G.P., *Toronto Star*, August 3, 1962, p. 6.

77. "Money Bar," letter by Mrs. May Buchard, *Toronto Star*, August 9, 1962, p. 6.

78. "Form Association to Fight for Aid, Drug Baby's Father Urges Parents," *The Globe and Mail*, July 31, 1962, p. 1.

79. "Should Let Deformed Baby Die—Mother," *Toronto Star*, July 30, 1962, p. 1

80. "Thalidomide Tragedy," letter by Gordon Arthurs, *The Globe and Mail*, November 16, 1962, p. 6.

81. "Deformed Baby," letter by Mostyn Paull, *Ottawa Citizen*, November 10, 1962, p. 6

82. "Parents Face Terrible Decisions," letter from F.L.M., *The Globe and Mail*, November 19, 1962, 18.

83. Pernick, p. 94. According to Pernick, American supporters of Dr. Haiselden who, in the 1910, promoted eugenic euthanasia, used almost the same arguments. They "focused on those cases in which euthanasia might end individual suffering, enhance personal freedom, and cut social costs at the same time, rather than trying to choose among these goals in cases where they conflicted."

84. "Mercy Killing Horrific," letter by Rita Larense, *Toronto Star*, August 3, 1962, p. 6.

85. "Disabled Baby," letter by Philip L. Copper, *Ottawa Citizen*, November 21, 1962, p. 6.

86. W. Gunther Plaut, "Morality and Baby Killing," *The Globe and Mail*, December 1, 1962, p. 12.

87. "Jury Condoned Wanton Murder," letter by Robert F. DuMont, *The Vancouver Sun*, November 19, 1962, p. 4.

88. "God's Children," letter by J. McKay, *Toronto Star*, August 3, 1962, p. 6.

89. "Our Child Born Crippled But We're Grateful to Have Her," letter by Nora Ludlow, *Toronto Star*, August 2, 1962, p. 6.

90. "The Whole Man," editorial, *The Globe and Mail*, November 13, 1962, p. 6.

91. Gary Miedema, *For Canada's Sake: Public Religion, Centennial Celebrations, and the Re-Making of Canada*

(Kingston: McGill-Queen's University Press, 2005), 16 and 203.

92. Pernick, p. 76. As mentioned above, Pernick finds strikingly similar arguments in his survey of public reaction to Dr Haiselden's crusade in the 1910s. He concludes likewise that "[t]o point out that many defectives made useful contributions to society did not necessarily contradict anti-utilitarian claims for the equal value of all human souls."

93. "A Revolting Proposal," Editorial, *Toronto Star*, August 1, 1962, p. 6.

94. "No Mercy Deaths," letter by Mrs. B. Sullivan, *Toronto Star*, August 2, 1962, p. 6.

95. Martha Robinson, "Clerics Disagree on Abortion Issue," *The Vancouver Sun*, August 4, 1962, p. 14.

96. "Worth of the Deformed," letter by Peter Morris, *Ottawa Citizen*, August 22, 1962, p. 6.

97. Mrs. Allan McPhail, "Deformed Babies," *Ottawa Citizen*, November 17, 1962, p. 6.

98. Robert DuMont, "Jury Condoned Wanton Murder," *The Vancouver Sun*, November 19, 1962, p. 4.

99. Gary Doyl Gottlieb, "Judaism Prohibits," *Toronto Star*, November 16, 1962, p. 6.

100. Veronica Strong-Boag, "'Children of Adversity': Disabilities and Child Welfare in Canada from the Nineteenth to the Twenty-First Century," *Journal of Family History* 32, 4 (2007): 424.

101. Michael J. Dear and Jennifer R. Wolch, *Landscapes of Despair: From Deinstitutionalization to Homelessness* (Oxford: Polity Press, 1987), 3.

102. Ibid., 16.

103. "Deformed Baby Is Placed in Home to Spare Mother Mental Anguish," *The Globe and Mail*, July 20, 1962, p. 1 and "Armless Baby Made Children's Aid Ward," *Toronto Star*, July 20, 1962, p. 1.

104. "Deformed Baby Made a Ward," *Ottawa Citizen*, July 20, 1962, p. 5.

105. "Deformed Baby Is Placed in Home to Spare Mother Mental Anguish," *The Globe and Mail*, July 20, 1962, p. 1. As a sad postscript to this story, a November 1962 story in *The Globe and Mail* records that this baby died in hospital.

106. "Society Is Responsible," editorial, *The Globe and Mail*, July 21, 1962, p. 6.

107. Marvin Schiff, "Health Welfare Workers Divided on Institutions for Deformed," *The Globe and Mail*, August 1, 1962, p. 9.

108. Leonard Bertin, "Need Special Deformed Baby Institutions," *Toronto Star*, July 31, 1962, p. 1.

109. Dinah Kerr, "Mother 'Wept All Day' For Armless, Legless Baby," *Toronto Star*, July 26, 1962, pp. 1 and 2 and "Toronto MD to Study Deformed Sarnia Baby," *The Globe and Mail*, July 26, 1962, p. 1. In these initial articles, the couple's names were withheld at their request and they were referred to as Mr and Mrs C. According to their child's grandmother, quoted in the 26 July article in

The Globe, they wanted to discourage inquisitive people. However, a 28 July article in *The Globe and Mail* identified them as Mr and Mrs Daniel Case.

110. Catherine Sinclair, "What Future for Thalidomide Babies?" *Chatelaine*, November, 1962, 35, no. 11, p. 110.

111. "'Our Baby Will Face World,' Vow Thalidomide Parents," *The Vancouver Sun*, November 15, 1962, p. 2.

112. Marvin Schiff, "Health Welfare Workers Divided on Institutions for Deformed," *The Globe and Mail*, August 1, 1962, p. 9.

113. Catherine Sinclair, "What Future for Thalidomide Babies?" *Chatelaine*, November, 1962, 35, no. 11, p. 110.

114. "5 More Deformed Babies Include Hamilton Twins," *Toronto Star*, July 28, 1962, p. 2 and "Deny London Baby Thalidomide Victim," *Toronto Star*, July 28, 1962, p. 2.

115. "'Our Baby Will Face World,' Vow Thalidomide Parents," *The Vancouver Sun*, November 15, 1962, pp. 1 and 2.

116. "Father Hopes Doctor Can Assist Child," *The Globe and Mail*, July 27, 1962, p. 4.

117. "Thalidomide Couple Have Normal Child," *The Globe and Mail*, April 9, 1963, p. 15.

118. "Form Association to Fight For Aid, Drug Baby's Father Urges Parents," *The Globe and Mail*, July 31, 1962, p. 1.

119. "Robarts Promises Help to Thalidomide Babies," *Toronto Star*, August 1, 1962, p. 8.

120. Carol Gregory, "Teenage Parents Will Keep Their Thalidomide Baby," *Toronto Star*, October 18, 1962, p. 21.

121. "Perils in the Wake of Thalidomide," *The Globe and Mail*, August 20, 1962, p. 7.

122 "Treat All Babies Alike," *Toronto Star*, July 31, 1962, p. 2.

123. "Mothers of Deformed Suffer Guilt Feelings," *The Globe and Mail*, May 16, 1963, p. 16.

124. Stephens and Brynner, 112–114.

125. "Should Let Deformed Baby Die—Mother," *Toronto Star*, July 30, 1962, p. 2; "Deformed Baby's Father Fired from Chatham Job," *Toronto Star*, August 1, 1962, p. 2; "Operate on Deformed Babies," *The Globe and Mail*, July 9, 1963, p. 14; Catherine Sinclair, "What Future for Thalidomide Babies?" *Chatelaine*, November, 1962, 35, no. 11, p. 110.

126. "Split-Cost Plan for Drug Babies Held Favoured," *The Globe and Mail*, September 22, 1962, p. 9.

127. "Deformed Twins Raise Drug Toll to 40 in Canada," *Ottawa Citizen*, July 30, 1962, p. 3.

128. Joan Hollobon, "More Deformed Children Seen in Past 2 Years: MD," *The Globe and Mail*, June 16, 1965, p. 1.

129. Carol Gregory, "Teach Handicapped Children How to Live Normal Lives," *Toronto Star*, August 1, 1962, p. 33 and 37.

130. "Should Let Deformed Baby Die—Mother," *Toronto Star*, July 30, 1962, p. 2.

131. Catherine Sinclair, "What Future for Thalidomide Babies?" *Chatelaine*, November, 1962, 35, no. 11, p. 110.

132. Betty Schill, "Where There's Youth, There's Hope," *Toronto Star*, March 4, 1964, p. 51.

133. Editorial, "No Federal Responsibility?" *Toronto Star*, July 31, 1962, p. 6.

134. Editorial, "A Centre for Deformed Babies," *Toronto Star*, January 30, 1963, p. 6.

135. Leonard Bertin, "Anguished Mother Learns to Love Armless Child," *Toronto Star*, May, 7, 1963, p. 42.

136. "Deformed Baby Has 'Flicker of Hope,'" *Toronto Star*, July 28, 1962, p. 2.

137. "Deformed Baby's Father Fired from Chatham Job," *Toronto Star*, August 1, 1962, p. 2.

138. "Birth of Deformed Twins Linked to Now-Banned Drug," *The Vancouver Sun*, July 28, 1962, p. 19.

139. "2nd Deformed Birth Shocks Court," *Toronto Star*, November 6, 1962, p. 1.

PRIMARY DOCUMENT

"Demands Right to Abortion," *Toronto Daily Star*, 26 July 1962

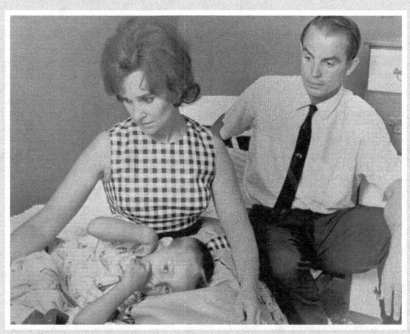

DEMANDS RIGHT TO ABORTION

Phoenix, Ariz., television personality Mrs. Robert Finkbine yesterday filed suit aimed at clearing the way for a legal abortion. She says she inadvertently took a drug blamed for the birth of malformed babies and does not want to risk the birth of such a child. Here she and her husband tuck Stevie, 4, one of their four healthy children, into bed. Story on Page 21.

Source: *Toronto Daily Star*, 26 July 1962, p. 1.

Study Questions

1. The essays by Gleason and Haynes in this chapter explore how children's health and physical embodiment shaped what they experienced. How did medical experts define who and what was considered "normal" earlier in the twentieth century? In our contemporary times, who or what has the power to define normalcy?

2. Mona Gleason argues that age and size are useful categories of historical analysis, in conjunction with categories such as race, class, gender, and sexuality. How and why do attitudes toward age and size change over time?

3. Like the work of Magda Fahrni and Jane Nicholas, Jessica Haynes's research confronts difficult ethical questions. Is historical research that explores the experiences of young people with disabilities, with differences, or as victims of tragedy problematic? Why or why not?

Selected Bibliography

Articles

Barman, Jean, "Encounters with Sexuality: The Management of Inappropriate Body Behaviour in Late-Nineteenth-Century BC Schools," *Historical Studies in Education/Revue d'histoire de l'éducation* 16 (Spring 2004): 85–114.

Cale, Michelle, "Girls and the Perception of Sexual Danger in the Victorian Reformatory System," *History* 78 (1993): 201–17.

Gleason, Mona, "Disciplining the Student Body: Schooling and the Construction of Canadian Children's Bodies, 1930 to 1960," *History of Education Quarterly* 41 (Spring 2001): 189–215.

Gleason, Mona, "Embodied Negotiations: Children's Bodies and Historical Change in Canada, 1930–1960," *Journal of Canadian Studies,* 34 (Spring 1999): 112–38.

Gleason, Mona, "From 'Disgraceful Carelessness' to 'Intelligent Precaution': Accidents and the Public Child in English Canada, 1900–1950," *Journal of Family History* 30, 2 (Spring 2005): 230–41.

Gleason, Mona, "Navigating the Pedagogy of Failure: Medicine, Education and the Disabled Child in English Canada, 1900 to 1945," in Graham Allan and Nathaniel Lauster, eds, *The End of Children? Changing Trends in Childbearing and Childhood.* Vancouver: UBC Press: 140–60.

Kelm, Mary Ellen, "'A Scandalous Procession': Residential Schooling and the Shaping of Aboriginal Bodies," *Native Studies Review* 11, 2 (1996): 51–81.

Levine, David, and Julie Savoie, "A Riddle Wrapped in a Mystery Inside an Enigma: Bi-modal Fertility Dynamics and Family Life in French-Canadian Quebec," *Social History/Historie sociale* 38, 76 (2005): 307–37.

Minnett, Valerie, and Mary Anne Poutanen, "Swatting Flies for Health: Children and Tuberculosis in Early Twentieth-Century Montreal," *Urban History Review/Revue d'histoire urbaine,* 36 (Fall 2007): 32–44.

Myers, Tamara, "Embodying Delinquency: Boys' Bodies, Sexuality, and Juvenile Justice History in Early-Twentieth-Century Quebec," *Journal of the History of Sexuality* 14 (2005): 383–414.

Neff, Charlotte, "Ontario Government Funding and Supervision of Infants' Homes 1875–1893," *Journal of Family History* 38, 1 (January 2013): 17–54.

Rutherdale, Myra, "Ordering the Bath: Children, Health and Hygiene in Northern Canadian Communities, 1900–1970," in Krasnick Warsh and Veronica Cheryl Strong-Boag, eds, *Children's Health Issues in Historical Perspective.* Waterloo, ON: Wilfrid Laurier University Press, 2005.

Sangster, Joan, "Masking and Unmasking the Sexual Abuse of Children: Perceptions of Violence Against Children in "the Badlands" of Ontario, 1916–1930," *Journal of Family History* 25, 4 (October 2000): 504–26.

Books

Comacchio, Cynthia, *Nations Are Built of Babies: Saving Ontario's Mothers and Children, 1900--1940.* Montreal and Kingston: McGill-Queen's University Press, 1993.

Gleason, Mona, *Normalizing the Ideal: Psychology, Schooling and the Family in Postwar Canada.* Toronto: University of Toronto Press, 1999.

Gleason, Mona, *Small Matters: Canadian Children in Sickness and Health, 1900–1940*. Montreal and Kingston: McGill-Queen's University Press, 2013.

Kelm, Mary-Ellen, *Colonizing Bodies: Aboriginal Health and Healing in British Columbia, 1900–50*. Vancouver: University of British Columbia Press, 1998.

Korinek, Valerie J., *Roughing It in the Suburbs: Reading Chatelaine Magazine in the Fifties and Sixties*. Toronto: University of Toronto Press, 2000.

8 Challenging "Normal"

Editors' Introduction

From the late-nineteenth to the mid-twentieth century, Canada embraced child saving and fostered a growing appreciation for childhood as a special and protected phase of life. The words of social reformers and policy-makers from that time suggest that Canada was a new nation that was child-centric and child-loving. And yet, as this chapter shows, the rise in the value of children was a complex process involving the inclusion of some young people at the exclusion of others. This meant that not all children fit the definition of deserving or "normal," and that many were denied access to society's protection during this life stage.[1]

Nic Clarke's and Jane Nicholas's essays in this chapter highlight why critical attention to the changing definitions of "child" and "youth" over time matters. By foregrounding the attitudes toward, and the treatment of, children labelled with physical and cognitive differences and disabilities, the authors challenge fundamental assertions regarding children's social, emotional, and economic value.[2] Viviana Zelizer argued in her classic study that children in the West in the late nineteenth and early twentieth centuries, regardless of class, were reconceptualized as emotionally important, indeed precious, at the same time their economic contributions to their families were declining.[3] Clarke and Nicholas urge us to pay close attention to which particular children were considered precious throughout history and which children—particularly those labelled with physical and cognitive differences and disabilities—were not.

In its scrutiny of the attitudes of medical and educational professionals toward young people declared "mentally deficient" in British Columbia at the turn of the twentieth century, Nic Clarke's essay marks one of the first explorations of the history in Canada of children labelled with disabilities.[4] The primary document accompanying Clarke's essay, an excerpt from Helen MacMurchy's *The Feebleminded in Ontario, Eighth Report for the Year 1913*, reports on the "clearinghouse" approach to "mental defectives" used in places such as New York and advocated for use in Canada. Such an approach, the excerpt makes clear, relied heavily on labelling and then weeding out those judged "abnormal." Clarke convincingly argues that these children were seen primarily as economic threats to the province and were treated that way in both social and economic policy. He is also careful to discern both marked and subtle differences in professionals' conceptualization of "mentally deficient" children as burdensome. Some doctors and social workers dismissed these children as hopeless drains on the public purse, as well as objects of scorn and shame to family members. Other professionals, and many parents, emphasized the opposite view. While securing adequate support was challenging, some children labelled with disabilities were loved and valued as important and contributing family and community members.

In her article on the structural and cultural violence done to children considered "different," Jane Nicholas draws our attention to a particular kind of representation of childhood in the early twentieth century. She argues that the rush to construct a definition of a "normal childhood" sometimes endangered those on the margins. Attempts to "affirm, regulate, and promote the dominant conceptions of health, beauty and normalcy" put children who did not live up to these conceptions at risk. One such boy, Ernie, referred to as "The World's Strangest Living Boy," spent his childhood on the circus sideshow with society's other "freaks." The act of exploiting children as spectacle, she notes, was most famously committed against the Dionne quintuplets in the 1930s.

A photograph of the sideshow where Ernie appeared is included with Nicholas's essay. In it, we can see how his performance was sold to audiences such as the children standing in the foreground, and how he was placed on a continuum of freakishness with the Dionne quints. Nicholas helps us to think through the historically contingent nature of disability and of childhood in the early-twentieth-century sideshow. Importantly, she goes further by confronting the difficult ethical subject of historians' using photos of children, a use that has the potential to further exploit those children.[5]

Although Clarke and Nicholas focus on children in different contexts, they share an interpretive strategy that foregrounds the children and families who were pushed beyond the closely policed boundaries of "normal." They challenge us to consider what consequences befell these families and children, and whether and how those boundaries have expanded in contemporary culture.

Notes

1. Perry Nodelman and Mavis Reimer, "Common Assumptions about Childhood," in *The Pleasures of Children's Literature* (Boston: Allyn and Bacon, 2002), pp. 86–95.

2. On the history of children labelled with disabilities in Canadian schools, see Gerald Thomson, "Through No Fault of Their Own: Josphine Dauphinee and the 'Subnormal' Pupils of the Vancouver School System, 1911–1941," *Historical Studies in Education—Revue d'histoire de l'éducation* 18, 1 (Spring, 2006): 51–73; Jason Ellis, "'All Methods—and Wedded to None: The Deaf Education Methods Debate and Progressive Educational Reform in Toronto, Canada, 1922–1945," *Paedagogica Historica* 50, 3 (2014): 371–89; Karen Yoshida, Fady Shanouda, and Jason Ellis, "An Education and Negotiation of Differences: The 'Schooling' Experiences of English-Speaking Canadian Children Growing Up with Polio during the 1940s and 1950s." *Disability & Society*, 29, 3 (March 2014): 345–58; Jason Ellis. "'Inequalities of Children in Original Endowment': How Intelligence Testing Transformed Early Special Education in a North American City School System." *History of Education Quarterly* 53, 4

(November 2013): 401–29.

3. Viviana Zelizer, *Pricing the Priceless Child: The Changing Social Value of Children* (Princeton: Princeton University Press, 1985).

4. Clarke's attention to disability as an important category of analysis for historians of children and youth in Canada was influential for subsequent work, such as Mona Gleason, "Navigating the Pedagogy of Failure: Medicine, Education and the Disabled Child in English Canada, 1900 to 1945" and Graham Allan and Nathaniel Lauster, eds., *The End of Children? Changing Trends in Childbearing and Childhood* (Vancouver: UBC Press, 2012), pp. 140–60.

5. As Sherry Farrell Racette demonstrates in "Haunted: First Nations Children in Residential School Photography," the purpose for which documentary sources such as photographs are used can change over time. They can, for example, be reclaimed as tools for personal recovery and restitution, as they were for adults who survived the incarceration and assimilation efforts of the residential schools. See Racette in Loren Lerner, ed., *Depicting Canada's Children* (Waterloo: Wilfrid University Press, 2009), pp. 49–84.

Sacred Daemons: Exploring British Columbian Society's Perceptions of "Mentally Deficient" Children, 1870–1930

NIC CLARKE

In the October 1919 issue of the *Canadian Journal of Mental Hygiene,* Dr Helen MacMurchy, a leading figure in Canada's child-saving movement, published a short article entitled "The Parents' Plea."[1] In this article MacMurchy stated that it was sadder for parents to "bear, to rear and find that the son or daughter of many hopes and prayers will never grow up, but is, and always will be mentally deficient . . . than to lose a child."[2] With these words MacMurchy identified how many Canadian (and, indeed, Western) medical and educational professionals differentiated between "mentally deficient" children and "normal" children.[3] Rather than a bundle of joy offering proud parents the promise of a bright and happy future, a mentally deficient child presented the prospect of suffering, pain, and angst on a level so immense that it exceeded the grief parents experienced with the death of a normal child. Indeed, in many cases the death of a mentally deficient child was seen by medical professionals as a loss that one should rejoice over rather than lament. As Dr G.H. Manchester, the acting medical superintendent of British Columbia's Public Hospital for the Insane (PHI),[4] stated in a letter to Albert Green[5] on the death of Green's daughter, Marigold, in 1901:

> [Marigold] passed away at 7pm . . . and I made an examination of the brain. It showed that the left half of the brain was very deficient, in fact almost wanting entirely and its place taken by water which filled out the membranes like a sack. With such a brain as this it is not hard to understand the fact of her being as she was a cripple physically and

mentally. . . . It is well that it is all over with her as she was a very great care and would never have had the slightest chance to be anything but an idiot.[6]

Dr. Manchester's letter of commiseration to Green is interesting, in particular, because it indicates why Marigold's death should be seen as a "blessed" event. It was "well that it [was] all over" not because Marigold was suffering but, rather, because she was "a very great care [who] would never have had the slightest chance to be anything but an idiot." Dr. Manchester did not see his patient's death as fortunate because she had escaped the (very real) torments of her mortal coil but, rather, because it meant that both her father and PHI's staff would no longer bear the burden of caring for an individual who would never amount to anything or fulfil a "useful" position within society.[7] In other words, Marigold's death was a blessing because she was no longer an emotional and economic encumbrance to her family and the province of British Columbia.

The fact that Dr. Manchester chose in his letter of "condolence" to regale Albert Green with the details of Marigold's autopsy results further supports this interpretation. By describing to Green the neuroanatomical deficiencies of his daughter's brain, Dr. Manchester underlined the fact that Marigold was a mental and physical "cripple" and, thereby, added weight to his assertion that it was "well" that she was dead. Indeed, it seems clear that, in the superintendent's mind, Marigold was little more than an animal incapable of any form of human emotion or understanding. For example, when discussing the death of Marigold's mother, Manchester coldly

Source: From *BC Studies* 144 (Winter 2004/05): 61–89.

stated that Marigold would "never know the difference."[8] Manchester's construction of Marigold as less than human is also evidenced by the lack of respect he showed her corpse, which he treated more like an interesting laboratory specimen than the mortal remains of a recently deceased child. The autopsy he conducted on Marigold's body immediately after her death, and which he described in detail to her father, was less focused on discovering the cause of her death than on allowing the medical superintendent to conduct a detailed examination of her "deficient" brain.

Dr. MacMurchy's comments about the pain that parents suffered with the birth of a mentally deficient child, along with Dr. Manchester's treatment of the severely disabled Marigold, demonstrate the dangers of historians omitting children labelled as mentally deficient from their explorations of Western societies' changing constructions of children and childhood in the late nineteenth and early twentieth centuries.[9] Recent scholarship on the history of children and childhood has identified the period from 1870 to 1930 as a time when many Western societies dramatically changed their economic and sentimental valuations of children from "objects of utility" to "exclusively emotional and affective assets."[10] Children became economically "worthless" but emotionally "priceless" figures infused with strong "sentimental or religious meaning."[11] However, while many children may have enjoyed "sacralization,"[12] the above stories indicate that, far from becoming "exclusively emotional and affective assets," children like Marigold were viewed by many health professionals as burdens both to their families and to the societies in which they lived. In fact, it would seem that, in many circumstances, the identity of mentally deficient children as "children" was overshadowed by their classification as "defectives." In other words, not only were mentally deficient children not considered "priceless" but the authorities did not see, or indeed regulate, them as children. This last statement requires some clarification because it is central to understanding the way in which mentally deficient children were perceived and treated in both late-nineteenth- and early-twentieth-century British Columbia.

In her 1992 study of the Dionne Quintuplets,[13] Mariana Valverde argued that the girls were victims of what she calls "fractures in social regulation," a phrase she uses to describe the processes by which social issues and problems are shifted from their expected regulatory category (such as race) to another (such as gender), depending on time, circumstance, and individual points of view.[14] Rather than constructing and regulating the Quints as children, Valverde argued, the Ontario provincial government defined them as an economic entity and, more specifically, as a resource that was to be administered to ensure the best possible revenue returns for the province.[15] While the Quintuplets—Annette, Cécile, Yvonne, Emilie, and Marie—were portrayed for an adoring public as "models of childhood," in the eyes of the authorities they were "no more 'children' . . . than Mickey Mouse is a mouse."[16]

Valverde's observations apply equally well to the way many in the BC government saw mentally deficient children. For, as with the Quintuplets, within the bodies of mentally deficient children, the boundaries between economic policy and social policy were often blurred. However, rather than being viewed as positive economic resources, mentally deficient children were often seen as "monsters" who threatened the very survival of British Columbian society—biologically, morally, and economically. Rather than enjoying "sacralization," the majority of mentally deficient children in BC society were subjected to "daemonization."[17]

However, although the BC government increasingly "daemonized" mentally deficient children, it would be wrong to believe that they were totally dehumanized or that all members of BC society, professional or lay, agreed with and supported the authorities' views and treatment of these children. Indeed, as is shown below, many mentally deficient children were dearly loved by their parents and protected by their communities. In a number of cases, individual parents and whole communities were willing to go to great lengths and expense to ensure the well-being and freedom of their mentally deficient members. Equally, some doctors and school board officials openly questioned both the growing public hysteria, fuelled by the rise of eugenics, relating to the supposed threat mentally defective children presented to society and the provincial government's policies designed to combat this "peril." In fact, some officials argued that these children did not present an imminent threat to society and that, wherever possible, they should enjoy the same rights as did normal children. In other words, while many individuals, especially in the BC government, attempted to daemonize children defined as mentally deficient, many others sacralized them.

***

In Western societies of the late nineteenth and early twentieth centuries, the mentally deficient were, in the eyes of many, a menace. Seen as socially and economically incompetent deviants who, if not properly controlled, threatened the economic, social, physical, and moral well-being of their families and communities, the mentally deficient were linked by large tracts of Western society not only with chronic dependency, poverty, vagrancy, prostitution, crime, and a myriad of other forms of "immoral" and "antisocial" behaviours but also with the biological degeneration of the human race. Although treating economic and social incompetence as indicators of mental deficiency and linking mental deficiency with social deviancy was not new, the focus on mental deficiency as a "threat" to society that required a response increased substantially during the nineteenth and early twentieth centuries.[18] This was largely due to the rise of eugenics. A wide variety of studies from this period argued that mental defectives were "throwbacks" to an older, or "lesser," form of humanity and that these conditions were hereditary and could be directly linked with anti-social behaviour and racial degeneration.[19] Not only did many of these studies stress the financial and social burden that mentally defective individuals and families had placed on their communities and states, but they also purported to demonstrate that the mental defectives, "the unfit," breed at a much faster rate than the "fit."[20] When coupled with the fact that most Western countries were experiencing a steady but noticeable decline in the birth rates of their "best" classes, the "exponential" procreation of the unfit presented for many an obvious threat: the stagnation and collapse of civilized society. Thus, if "race suicide" was

to be avoided, steps had to be taken to encourage the procreation of the fit (positive eugenics) while limiting that of the unfit (negative eugenics).[21]

In Canada, eugenics spread like wildfire.[22] Numerous pressure groups, such as the National Council of Women of Canada, the United Farm Workers Association, and the Canadian National Committee for Mental Hygiene,[23] as well as individual medical and educational professionals and legislators, actively involved themselves in promoting the cause. This promotional campaign took a number of forms. One was the education of the public through the use of public lectures and the publication of pro-eugenics periodicals, such as the *Canadian Journal of Mental Hygiene* which focused on the dangers that "mental defectives" posed to Canada.[24] Another was the lobbying of governments at the federal and provincial levels for passage of legislation designed to both control and limit, through segregation and/ or sterilization, the propagation of the unfit. Many eugenicists also demanded tighter immigration policies to stem the "huge flood" of defectives they believed to be entering Canada every year from other countries.[25] The growing influence of the "mental hygiene" movement is perhaps best expressed in the fact that, by the 1920s, mental hygienists had placed themselves and their values at the centre of the child welfare movement. Indeed, in 1920 one of Canada's strongest proponents of mental hygiene and eugenics, the aforementioned Dr. Helen MacMurchy,[26] was appointed the first chief of the Child Welfare Division of the federal Department of Health, an acknowledgment of her work in both mental hygiene and infant health.[27]

Even before MacMurchy had taken this position, eugenics ideologies had found fertile soil in British Columbia—especially among provincial authorities. For example, Bertha Winn, head of Victoria's special schools, stated the following in an address to the friends and members of the Women's Canadian Club at Victoria's Empress Hotel in 1917:

the histories of thousands of these cases [of mental deficiency] reveal the tragic and pitiable fact that unless special provision is made for their custodianship earlier in life they will find their respective ways into . . . crime, pauperism, vagrancy, prostitution and general indecency. . . . All mentally defective persons are antisocial in the sense that their presence in the community means disruption, disorder and dependency. They are the running wounds of society, infecting it and weakening its vitality, placing a blight upon each succeeding generation. There is only one way to deal with this stupendous evil, and that is in checking it at its source— segregating all cases of mental defectiveness from the normal population.[28]

Winn's message was clear: through their economic, social, and biological deviancy, the mentally deficient presented a danger to British Columbia that could not and should not be ignored. And it was not. In 1919 the provincial secretary, Dr J.D. Maclean, following the lead of Manitoba, requested that the Canadian National Committee for Mental Hygiene conduct a survey of the province's mental hygiene programs and offer advice for better combating mental deficiency in the province.[29] Moreover, in 1925 the Legislative Assembly appointed the Royal Commission on Mental Hygiene to examine ways to combat the perceived increase in the number of mentally deficient individuals in the province. The recommendations of this body were one of the major factors that ultimately led to the passing of British Columbia's Sexual Sterilization Act in 1933.

One of the first responsibilities the commissioners faced was defining what the term "mental deficiency" meant. While definitions of mental deficiency had existed in English law since the Middle Ages and had been further developed by the work of a number of eugenicists, this task was far from easy.[30] From the mid-nineteenth century, medical and educational professionals (not to mention laypeople and legislators) had "invoked a myriad of different terms to identify people as intellectually below average."[31] Moreover, the way in which such terminologies were employed was anything but exact. The term "feebleminded," for example, was at once used to refer to the entire class of people who would today be categorized as intellectually disabled as well as

to "high grade mental deficients."[32] In fact, authorities differed considerably in their understanding of what characteristics defined mental deficiency. Thus an individual defined by one professional as mentally deficient was often not mentally deficient according to another.[33] Indeed, even though differences between mental deficiency and mental illness had been recognized since the medieval period,[34] the commissioners noted that it was "desirable *again* to stress the necessity *of making a clear distinction* between the two broad classes of mentally abnormal person," (emphasis mine),[35] thereby indicating that there was still, in many peoples' minds, considerable crossover between the two categories.[36] The commissioners differentiated between insanity and mental deficiency by stressing that insanity was a curable disease of a "normally developed mind," while mental deficiency was an intractable condition of "arrested mental development" whose victims' mental capacity never progressed beyond that of a child.[37] The commissioners then proceeded to describe the levels of graduation within mental deficiency, again stressing that mentally deficient individuals had the minds of children: "According to general practice, the term 'idiot' is used to denote mental deficients with a 'mental age' of 3 years or less; 'imbecile' is used to indicate individuals with a mental age of 3 to 7; while the terms 'moron' and 'feeble-minded' are applied to those whose mental ages are from 7 to 11 years."[38] Echoing the words of Bertha Winn and a myriad of eugenicists, they also stated that: "Neglect of mental deficients leaves them free to cause grave social evils by their delinquencies and depredations. . . . Under proper treatment and by continuous care and training, it is possible to make them acceptable, happy, and to some extent useful members of society."[39]

These passages indicate not only the influence of eugenics ideologies among British Columbia's authorities but also the factors that led mentally deficient children in British Columbia to become the victims of both daemonization and "fractures in social regulation." Medical and educational professionals constructed the "affliction" of mental deficiency in such a way that individuals so labelled, no matter what their age, appeared as children in the eyes of the authorities. Like normal children, such individuals required care and protection both to ensure their safety and comfort in an often hostile world and to further their development into useful citizens. However, while normal children would grow out of this need for care and guidance as they reached adulthood and gained the skills necessary to become successful and constructive members of society, mentally deficient children, because of their arrested mental development, would never grow out of their need for supervision and assistance. The state would always have to watch over them. Moreover, as well as requiring government assistance throughout their lives so that they might become "acceptable, happy, and to some extent useful members of society," the commissioners believed that, unless controlled, mentally deficient children's "delinquencies and depredations" threatened the well-being of British Columbian society. Indeed, specialized schooling was required if they were to develop any measure of economic and social competency. This view was reinforced by the belief that placing mentally deficient children in regular schools only exacerbated their condition and, thereby, the threat they presented to society. As the Royal Commission on Mental Hygiene stated: "In school they [mentally deficient children] are from two to four years behind other children of the same age. Shamed by their failure to progress with their fellows, they eventually drop out of school and go into the world unequipped to meet the demands placed on them as citizens . . . and it is, therefore, not strange that they often find themselves in the gaols, reformatories, and houses of refuge."[40]

Although the City of Vancouver had maintained two special classes for "low grade defectives" (idiots and imbeciles) between 1911 and 1917, it was not until the provincial government provided custodial care for these children in 1918 that civic authorities attempted to segregate the majority of mentally deficient pupils from the "normal" student body. In 1918–19 Vancouver's school board began, through the use of psychological testing, actively to hunt out "high grade defectives" from among the student population. Once these children had been discovered, they were placed in special classes. By the end of 1920, the board had placed 205 "subnormal" pupils in 15 special classes across the city. Similar classes were established in Victoria.[41] Recognizing the "diminished" intellectual capabilities of their students, special classes placed an emphasis on teaching employment skills rather than the three "Rs" (reading, 'riting, and 'rithmetic).[42] Although it is possible to see these classes as havens where "mentally deficient" children could learn skills that would allow them to take their place in society, and although the classes were certainly presented as such by some educationalists and reporters,[43] authorities were ultimately less concerned with developing these children's self-esteem and dignity than with making certain that they became less of a burden to society. Indeed, in advocating training schools for the mentally deficient, writers stressed the economic advantages that the province would receive rather than the benefits "defective" individuals would obtain. That these classes were seen as industrial training centres is demonstrated by the way they were visually promoted to the public. Promotional photographs depicted students from special classes employed gardening, sitting at workbenches, or learning a myriad of other "useful" skills.[44]

In a similar vein, after the First World War it became a tradition for Vancouver's special classes to display student crafts to the public at the Vancouver Exhibition (now called the Pacific National Exhibition).[45] Equally, Josephine Dauphinee, director of Vancouver's special schools from 1911 to 1941,[46] defended their (considerable) cost: "We feel . . . the cost of the work is small, when viewed in dollars and cents, [as it is] a preventative of pauperism, vagrancy and crime."[47] However, perhaps the most telling indicator that special classes were run for reasons of economic utility rather than concern for "bettering" the children is the fact that such classes were designed only for "high grade defectives." "Imbeciles" and "idiots" were not included. While this ban can be viewed as recognition of the fact that some children were unable to participate actively in vocational training due to the severity of their intellectual impairment, it also demonstrates that authorities were unwilling to "waste" educational resources on children they considered "uneducable."[48]

Eugenicists believed that mentally deficient children not only injured themselves by attending normal schools but also impeded the education of their "normal" classmates by hindering classroom efficiency. As J.S. Gordon, inspector of Vancouver schools, noted in 1921: "It has been found that the removal of special class children from ordinary classes makes it possible to increase the size of the latter and to do better work than could be done in smaller classes handicapped by the presence of sub-normal pupils."[49] Moreover, many BC educational-ists believed that, as well as detrimentally affecting classroom efficiency, mentally deficient children would also negatively affect any normal children with whom they came in contact.[50] Some even im-plied that mental defect was physically contagious.[51] In other words, mentally deficient children were painted as a direct threat not only to the education of normal children but also to their mental health.[52]

When examined in its entirety, the treatment of mentally deficient children by British Colum-bia's educationalists indicates a number of ways in which eugenics ideologies informed the treatment and perception of mentally deficient children. First, while normal children were coming to be seen less as economic units, the defective child was still be-ing judged in economic terms. While education for normal children aimed to provide the educational and social tools that they would need to operate successfully in society, education for the mentally deficient child was designed simply to stop him/her from becoming a burden to the state. Second, the segregation of mentally deficient children from normal children meant that the former were seldom offered opportunities for mixing with their peers and, thereby, making social contacts within the greater community. Equally, and more important, it also differentiated them from normal children geo-graphically, visually, and educationally. Indeed, it pathologized them by presenting them as a "threat," which, like cancer, needed to be removed in order to ensure the health of society as a whole.

***

With the above in mind it is not surprising that some BC schools refused to admit "defective" children into their classes. In 1920, after the administrations of schools at Grand Forks and Cascade had refused to enrol a 13-year-old girl named Ruth, who was described as having a "brain that has not properly developed," her anxious mother wrote to the super-intendent of neglected children to ask that he provide her with information as to where she could place her daughter so that she might receive an education.[53] Declaring that Ruth was "willing [and] bright but oh it is such a trouble to [watch] over her," the woman further stated that, as both she and her husband were "only working people [. . . we] could not afford to pay much [for any specialist education the superintendent might recommend]."[54] This concerned mother's com-ments are indicative both of the trouble some parents faced in finding adequate schooling for their mentally deficient children and of the very real problems that many families faced when trying to raise mentally de-ficient children. Ruth's parents were worried not only about finding their daughter some form of schooling but also about the cost of said schooling and the fact that she had to be watched constantly.[55]

It was situations such as Ruth's that caused au-thorities to conclude that parents were ill equipped to provide the guidance that the mentally deficient required and that mentally deficient individuals threatened the mental and physical health of their parents and siblings. In fact, the commissioners stated in their report that "[The] care [of idiots and imbeciles] in the average home is too great a burden and too often results in break-down of other mem-bers of the family."[56] Either way, some authorities argued that it was better for the province to take control of these children, even against their parents' wishes.[57]

The belief that mentally deficient individuals placed families under huge strain was not without factual basis. The economic realities of life in British Columbia during the period under consideration, especially in rural communities, often meant that parents were unable to provide the care and supervi-sion that their "defective" children required without adversely affecting the family's economic produc-tiveness. Indeed, the Provincial Asylum's admis-sions records for 1894 contain the pitiful account of a single mother who had been driven to destitution by her "defective" son's need for constant supervision, which had left her unable to work.[58] Another single parent, Robert Garfield, stated that work commitments meant that he was unable to provide his eleven-year-old son Michael—who would wander away if left unsupervised—with "the proper care and attention." As a result, he was forced to tie Michael up at home. Robert acknowledged that binding his son was "a cruelty" but defended his actions by stating that he had to do so or Michael "would . . . get lost. . . if he got away he would be liable to fall into the river or get killed in other ways by falling over precipices." The doctors who admitted Michael into institutional care also noted that he would destroy property if he was left unsupervised for any length of time.[59]

However, while there is no doubt that many mentally defective children did place a huge strain on family economies, the point should not be overstressed. An examination of asylum records also reveals that some mentally defective individuals were involved in productive labour before their institutionalization. A prime example of such an individual is Joseph McCray, an inhabitant of one of British Columbia's smaller Gulf Islands. Although Joseph's entry in the PHI's admissions book states that he had no occupation, his brother-in-law noted on the form he filed with the local magistrate requesting Joseph's committal that "he will work when he takes the notion."[60] While Joseph's work may not have generated income for his family, the fact that his brother-in-law—who had little else good to say about Joseph other than "he don't drink"—chose to mention this would seem to indicate that Joseph did usefully contribute to his family's economic survival.[61] Nor is Joseph the only example of a mentally deficient individual to be found in PHI's case files who provided economically productive labour for his/her family. Under the heading of occupation in Melody Smith's record of admittance, one finds the word "housework" recorded. Angus Jonstone said his son Richard "sometimes worked like a Trojan," while Alfie Rowan's mother complained that it was "hard to teach [him] *new* chores or tasks around the house" (my emphasis).[62] While this last statement might seem to indicate that Alfie did not help his

mother with the successful running of their home, reconsideration of her statement hints otherwise. Rather than stating that Alfie did nothing around the home, she told doctors that it was hard to teach him *new chores*. This would seem to indicate that Alfie did know how to do *some* chores. Moreover, while his mother stated that it was *hard* to teach Alfie new chores, she did not say it was *impossible*. Taken together, it is highly likely that Alfie did usefully contribute, albeit in a limited way, to his family's economic survival and that he could have, with some hardship, been taught new ways of contributing if the need had arisen.

Considerable evidence also exists to suggest that some mentally deficient British Columbians held wage-earning positions before their institutionalization.[63] Given these individuals' ages at the time of admittance, usually early to mid-twenties, this information is important for a number of reasons. First, it demonstrates that some mentally deficient individuals were capable of successfully navigating the cash-nexus of BC society. This fact in itself questions the claims of eugenicists that the mentally deficient needed special training in special schools/institutions since many had obviously gained needed skills already. Second, it demonstrates that many mentally defective individuals avoided institutionalization well past childhood. Joseph McCray, for example, was 33 years old at the time of his incarceration in 1900.[64] These observations present two possibilities: first, that these people's disabilities manifested themselves in later life due to illness or accident[65] or, second, that they had in fact been intellectually disabled from birth, or very early age, and had been employed and protected by their parents until the latter were no longer able to care for them. While both possibilities found expression in a number of instances, in others they did not. Some of the admittance records make no mention of family or friends at all.[66] In other words, it seems that these individuals had found employment and accommodation for themselves. Admittedly this is only speculation, as on occasion admitting doctors were less than clear in their comments when referring to a patient's employment history or the employment status of his/her father or guardian, but the number of individuals admitted to PHI who were described as being employed, and for whom no mention of guardians of any sort was given, should not be ignored. Moreover, the fact that, across the Western world, only relatively small numbers of mental deficients, compared to the estimated total population,[67] were incarcerated in institutions would further suggest that at least some mentally deficient individuals were capable of successfully navigating their way through the reefs and shoals of society.

Colonial British Columbia's economic and geographic characteristics probably played more than just a supporting role in mentally deficient people's long-term institutional avoidance. It would be reasonable, for example, to expect that individuals with a slight intellectual impairment would have found work as labourers in British Columbia's many primary resource communities, where economic necessity and local conditions privileged physical strength over intellectual prowess. Furthermore, British Columbia's geography, consisting of many small, isolated communities severely restricted the government's attempts to identify the mentally defective within its population.[68]

This problem was especially evident in relation to schools. Neil Sutherland has shown that Canadian schools—through standardized testing and health checks—played a major part in bringing to the attention of educational authorities those children considered to be mentally deficient.[69] Given that a number of British Columbia's smaller and more isolated communities had no schools, it is reasonable to believe that many children who would have been classified as "mentally defective" in Vancouver or Victoria would not have been designated as such in rural areas. Indeed, even if such a community did have a school, such children may have gone unnoticed, or at least unreported, because, as Mona Gleason has shown, a significant minority of these education facilities did not receive regular visits from health inspectors, and some may not have received any at all.[70]

While this evidence suggests that some mentally deficient individuals could have functioned to some extent in BC society, it is also obvious that many parents worried about the dangers society presented to their mentally defective children. In the case of boys, parents generally worried that criminals would prey on their sons' gullibility and draw them into illegal endeavours. Records indicate that these fears were well founded. A gang of thieves in Victoria recruited the 11-year-old "idiot" Henry Blain to help them break into houses and commit other acts of theft.[71] As well as worrying that their daughters would be unwittingly drawn into a life of crime, parents of mentally deficient girls also faced the very real fear that their daughters would be taken advantage of sexually, especially since mentally deficient women were considered to be hyper-sexual.[72] These fears were expressed by A. Miller, inspector of schools for Revelstoke, in a letter to the Provincial Secretary's Office asking for the institutionalization of a 14-year-old girl whose recently widowed mother could no longer control her:[73] "As the girl is now adolescent physically, but only a child mentally, the situation is rather disturbing, particularly as there is a logging camp [nearby] with all kinds of rough men [who] would have no scruples about taking advantage of such a girl. . . . [The girl should be placed] in a proper institution . . . at the earliest possible moment as . . . serious trouble may develop any day."[74]

Government officials held the same fears, albeit for slightly different reasons. For while the authorities recognized that both the "leadability" of "subnormal" children and their inability to differentiate between "right" and "wrong" made them vulnerable, the authorities equally stressed the danger these children presented to society. Indeed, although many activists who argued for the segregation of the mentally deficient from mainstream society did so in order to fulfil the state's "obligation" to guard the "subnormal child" from the very real perils of society, a close reading of these activists' arguments indicates that they were more concerned with the dangers the mentally deficient presented to society than vice versa.[75]

Despite the realization that society presented very real dangers to the mentally deficient, authorities sometimes ignored evidence of abuse when reported by the mentally deficient themselves. For example, a report to Vancouver's Juvenile Court in 1923 by one of the court's investigators stated that a 13-year-old "subnormal" girl had "made some unpleasant suggestions" with regard to her stepfather's behaviour towards her but that the child was "really so mentally defective" it was "hard to understand her, let alone believe her."[76] The court accepted the investigator's analysis of the girl's "unpleasant suggestions," which implied she was being sexually abused by her stepfather, and made no attempt to investigate the veracity of the girl's story. Given that authorities were quick to employ sexually suggestive language by "subnormal girls" as justification for incarcerating them,[77] the investigator's lack of respect for this girl's comments not only indicates that the authorities took little stock in the cognitive abilities of mentally defective children or of their ability to tell the "truth" but also that they were much more focused on finding fault in these children than in seeing them as victims. In fact, it is fair to say that mentally deficient children were treated in much the same way as were children labelled "delinquent."[78]

If some families worried that they could not adequately provide for the care of their mentally deficient members, others worried about the physical danger these individuals presented to themselves or other people. Charles Wick, for example, was committed to PHI in September 1906 at the age of 15 because of the increasing danger he was seen to present to his family. In the few months before his incarceration, Charles had not only viciously attacked his mother but had also repeatedly threatened to kill his younger brother.[79]

Some parents were equally concerned about the impact that their mentally deficient children would have on their social standing. A number of factors explain this anxiety. First, a mentally deficient child's lack of social competency could lead the child to perform acts—such as screaming, "gibbering," or soiling themselves—that were outside social norms and that might embarrass their parents, especially if the behaviour occurred in a public place. If a child's acts were potentially dangerous, either physically or morally, then his or her parents could have faced ostracism in their communities and, perhaps, the unwelcome attention of the authorities.[80]

Second, in the case of those mental conditions that were accompanied by noticeable physical "defects," such as microcephaly or macrocephaly, parents faced the very real stigma of having children who not only acted "funny" but who also looked "unusual." This embarrassment may have been reinforced by the increased "visibility" of mental deficiency during the period between 1870 and 1930 due to freak shows (which, at this time, reached the height of their popularity in North America) and the rise of photography. In many freak shows, individuals who suffered from intellectual and physical defects were paraded in front of crowds under the less than complimentary labels of "wild men," "missing links," and "pinheads."[81]

At the same time as freak shows were reaching the zenith of their popularity, the use of photography to identify the mentally deficient was also becoming common. As Mark Jackson has noted, photographs allowed mental defectives to be seen, identified, and thereby tracked by society to an extent never before possible. They also, allowed their classification into readily identifiable groups. Thus, whereas before the rise of photography a child with a physically identifiable intellectual condition, such as Down's Syndrome, might simply have been seen as "different" or "strange," now that child could be readily labelled as "defective."[82] Indeed, a perusal of PHI's records reveals a number of occasions where doctors based or supported their diagnosis of mental deficiency by referring to an individual's "defective" physical characteristics. The aforementioned Michael Garfield, for example, was described as "small for his age, except [for his] head which is oversized." Another patient's appearance was characterized in the following manner: "microcephalic head, very flat and slanting occipital, low unintelligent forehead, illshapen [sic] ears . . . teeth very irregular particularly those of the lower jaw . . . infantile genitalia."[83]

Third, a number of parents may have been embarrassed by their mentally defective children because of what the latter's condition implied about the former. Many professionals in education and medicine, not to mention laypeople, believed that mental deficiency could be directly linked either to bad parenting[84] or as discussed above, to hereditary defect.

In light of both the embarrassment and social stigma that a mentally deficient child could cause his or her parents, it is not surprising that some parents chose to hide these children from prying eyes. Peter Cox's mother, for example, placed him in PHI in 1903 when he was approximately six years of age[85] and paid for his upkeep through an intermediary—G.J. Smith, superintendent of the Children's Aid Society—until her death in 1919. On reporting her death to the medical authorities, Smith stated that he had "kept her secret religiously all these years."[86]

It is highly likely that other children were hidden from view by their parents in less than favourable circumstances (e.g., being imprisoned within the family home). Admittedly, finding these children is an almost impossible task for the historian. Unless they were discovered by the authorities, or mentioned in family or community memoirs, one is unlikely to find any evidence that they existed at all. This is especially the case for children who lived in isolated rural areas where there was little state supervision. That said, evidence from other countries with political and social characteristics similar to those of British Columbia strongly argues for the existence of these "ghost children" and offers some insight into the experiences they may have faced. One such example comes from the Patient Casebook of the Sunnyside Asylum, in Christchurch, New Zealand. In 1890 police officers acting on a tip discovered a 25-year-old mentally deficient man locked in a room in his father's house. The police estimated that, at the time of his discovery, the man—who was naked, covered in his own feces, and unable to communicate in any fashion—had been imprisoned by his father for at least six years. They could find no information of his life before this time.[87]

Although this is an extreme case, discoveries of children in more recent times,[88] and the common literary convention of the "crazy sibling" locked away out of sight, perhaps indicate that this practice, although uncommon, was not unknown. Therefore, historians should be prepared to entertain the possibility that some BC families imprisoned their mentally defective members in order to keep them out of sight. This argument is given further weight by the fact that there is considerable evidence, alluded to

above, of parents restraining their mentally deficient children. One such child was reported to have been kept "secluded by his friends for fifteen years."[89]

However, while many families obviously suffered hardships caused by their mentally deficient members, eugenicists often faced considerable difficulty in persuading the parents of mentally deficient children and the public at large of the worthiness of their policies. The author of one article in the *Canadian Journal of Mental Hygiene* even went so far as to reject calls by eugenicists for sterilization as a method for combating feeblemindedness because they had not taken into account "the long period of preparation and education the public will need to support it."[90] The author further noted that, while the segregation and incarceration of the "feebleminded" was far more practical than sterilization, it also suffered from a number of "public relations"-based problems.[91]

Indeed, in many cases eugenicists and provincial legislators pursuing eugenics agendas faced significant opposition from powerful institutions. The Roman Catholic Church, for example, actively campaigned against the passing of British Columbia's 1933 Sexual Sterilization Bill, and, when it failed to prevent the bill's passing, strongly condemned the act.[92] Even within governmental and educational circles, eugenics did not hold complete sway. For example, while the Royal Commission on Mental Hygiene stressed the danger that mental deficients presented to British Columbia, the commissioners also noted that, "in the field of mental deficiency[, . . .] in recent years there has been, among experts in all parts of the world, a definite trend away from the alarmist attitude common around the opening of the present century. The percentage of the general population afflicted by mental deficiency is not increasing."[93]

These views echoed a report presented to the Victoria School Board in 1923 by its medical officer, Dr David Donald. In his report Donald asserted that the idea that Victoria schools were being overrun by mentally defective pupils was absurd; in a school population of 6,000, he had been able to find only 11 children suffering from mental defect.[94] The point made by Donald and the mental hygiene commissioners was clear: Canada, and, more specifically, British Columbia, was not in danger of being swamped by mental deficients.

As well as questioning the supposed size of British Columbia's mentally deficient population, some members of British Columbia's governing elite even questioned the need for special classes for "high grade defectives" at all. When Bertha Winn delivered a report to the Victoria School Board in 1921 arguing for the expansion of the special schools program and the removal of all "retarded" children from normal classes, her ideas were strongly attacked by provincial school inspector W.H. May, who believed that these children should not be segregated: "If there is any spark of intelligence in the children they [. . . should] stay with their classmates. If [. . . they are placed in special schools] the stigma will remain for life."[95] The fact that a school inspector would so publicly challenge the segregation of mentally deficient children demonstrates that it would be incorrect to believe that British Columbia's education system was a bastion of support for eugenics, as often, at first, appears to have been the case.

***

While some authorities and powerful institutions such as the Roman Catholic Church questioned the eugenicist treatment and depictions of the mentally deficient, it is clear that resistance to the "daemonization" of mentally deficient children came primarily from their families. Indeed, despite Dr MacMurchy's claims that it was sadder for parents to rear a mentally deficient child than to experience the death of a normal child, many parents dearly loved their mentally deficient children and were devastated by their deaths. What is more, many were also prepared to fight to keep their children out of institutions.

Angus Johnstone's short letters to asylum staff about his son Richard, who had been institutionalized in November 1904 at 14 years of age, are a prime example of the devastation that the loss of a mentally deficient child could wreak on a loving parent.[96] An itinerant miner, Johnstone repeatedly sent letters—often little more than "scraps" of paper—to medical authorities requesting that they send him "[A] few lines about my son" and notifying them of his change of address.[97] This correspondence not only reflects Johnstone's love for his "idiot" child but also demonstrates that he thought about Richard frequently and cared about his continued well-being. However, perhaps the strongest expression of Johnstone's attachment and concern for his son can be seen in the letters he wrote in November 1918 about Richard's serious, and ultimately unsuccessful, battle with influenza. Severely ill with influenza himself, Johnstone was under no illusion as to the probable outcome of Richard's illness. In a letter dated 7 November 1918, he explained that he was unable to travel to be with his son because of his own ill health, and he then went on to request that, if Richard were to die, he be given "the best possible last service under existing circumstances."[98] Hearing of Richard's death from pneumonia eleven days later, Angus Johnstone wrote to A.G. Greaves, acting medical superintendent, lamenting the fact that his own illness had rendered him "unable to take a last look at him [Richard] before he passed away."[99]

Nor is Angus Johnstone the only example of a loving parent to be found in PHI's records. On 24 June 1912, four days after the death of his 12-year-old daughter Hannah, François Ben wrote the following note to the medical superintendent and staff of the hospital, thanking them for the care that his "little girl" had received: "Now the remains of our little girl . . . have been laid to rest I am penning these few words . . . to express . . . gratitude for the kind treatment our little girl received. . . . the little girl's well kept body spoke volumes for the care bestowed upon her."[100]

While the fathers of both Richard Johnstone and Hannah Ben demonstrated love for their children through their letters, the parents of Henry and Oscar Fraser expressed their love for their sons by going to great financial lengths to resist the attempts by authorities to institutionalize their "defective" children. Described as "idiots," Henry and Oscar were admitted to PHI on 20 December 1904 after repeated run-ins with the Vancouver police for throwing stones at streetcars and people.[101] Their stay was to be very short. Five days later the medical superintendent, Dr Manchester, released the boys on probation into their parents' care after their father had made a formal promise, in writing, to the medical authorities that he would remodel the family home on Vancouver's Howe Street in order "to prevent them from running at large to the annoyance of others and to the public danger."[102] The boys' loving relationship with their parents is further underlined by the letter Manchester wrote to Vancouver's chief of police explaining his decision to release them. In it he stated, with more than a hint of mystified exasperation, "The sending in of the two [Fraser] boys seems to have been a severe blow to the mother who is apparently greatly attached to them."[103] Manchester further went on to stress that he would be inspecting the renovations made to the Fraser home and that, if he found them to be less than adequate or if the boys got into further trouble, he would readmit them. Both the renovations to the Fraser house and the subsequent behaviour of Henry and Oscar obviously passed muster, for on 25 July 1905 both boys were given a full discharge from PHI. Henry was never to be readmitted, while Oscar was well into his fifties the next time he became an inmate.[104]

The case of Henry and Oscar Fraser was not the only one where a medical superintendent wrote to the police to notify them that parents had removed a patient from custodial care. In 1906 PHI's new medical superintendent, Dr Charles Doherty, wrote to Nanaimo's chief of police, James Crossan, informing him that the family of the "imbecile" Paul Manning had removed him from PHI against all medical advice. Doherty explained that he feared that, without hospital discipline, Paul would "develop vicious habits and even might become a criminal." In light of this possibility, Doherty requested that Crossan and his men "keep an eye on him, as there is a strong possibility of him becoming a nuisance."[105] It seems Dr Doherty's fears were unfounded as, like Henry Fraser, Paul Manning never returned to PHI.

These stories are compelling because they graphically indicate the dual world that mentally deficient children and youths inhabited in late-nineteenth- and early-twentieth-century British Columbia. Paul, Henry, and Oscar were at once dearly loved by their parents and daemonized by the authorities

who constructed them—and thereby attempted to regulate them—as threats to society rather than as children.

***

In examining the way in which mentally deficient children were perceived and treated in late-nineteenth- and early-twentieth-century British Columbia, it becomes clear that the belief that, between 1870 and 1930, children enjoyed a "dramatic change in economic and sentimental value" requires some careful qualification. For, while many child savers were trying to better the lives of normal children, they were also demanding the incarceration and sterilization of mentally deficient children. In fact, if the results of their actions had not often led to negative consequences for children designated as mentally deficient and for their families, then one might be forced to smile at the irony that, in trying to "rescue" one group of children, British Columbia's child savers actually injured another.

This study also reveals the "special" position that mentally deficient children held within the classification systems of many people and, in doing so, shows how these children, like the Dionne Quintuplets, were victims of a "fracture in social regulation." All mentally deficient individuals, as a result of their arrested mental development, were constructed by medical and educational professionals as children, no matter what their age, thereby justifying the authorities' claims that mentally deficient individuals would require the government's supervision and control throughout their lives. Yet, equally, the fact that mental deficient were seen to threaten BC society morally, biologically, and economically meant that mentally deficient children were often denied their "rights" as children. Indeed, rather than being regulated as children, more often than not mentally deficient children were regulated on the basis of the threats they were believed to present to society. This fact is highlighted in the sphere of education in three ways. First, attempts were made to segregate mentally deficient children from their "normal" peers in order to prevent them from "infecting" the "fit" with their "defective" characteristics. Second, education programs for the "defective" were designed to ensure that they were not burdens to society rather than to make them "well-rounded" adults. Third, the segregation of mentally deficient children into separate classes allowed for their control and supervision.

However, while many, especially in the medical and educational professions, both daemonized mentally deficient children as threats to society and continued to see them in utilitarian terms, many mentally deficient children were loved and supported by their families. The comments of Dr Manchester to Vancouver's chief of police after the discharge of Henry and Oscar Fraser from PHI, and the heartbroken letters of Angus Johnstone and François Ben, are indicative of the fact that many parents invested their mentally deficient children with the same sentimental value that, according to many historians of childhood, parents increasingly projected onto their normal children in the period between 1870 and 1930. Moreover, the resistance of many parents to attempts by government officials and medical and educational professionals to enact eugenics policies further indicates the emotional attachment between parents and their mentally deficient children.

Finally, the eugenicists' depictions of the role that mentally deficient individuals (both as children and adults) played in society, including their relationships with their families and communities, were not always correct. Despite the very real struggles mentally deficient individuals faced in what was often a hostile world, and the very negative portrait that eugenicists painted of them, they often exercised considerable agency in shaping their own lives. This is not to romanticize the lives of individuals outside of institutions but, rather, to point to the dangers of focusing solely on institutions and authorities when examining the history of disability in British Columbia. Indeed, the history of people with disabilities has long been trapped within the walls of institutions built in the late nineteenth and early twentieth centuries—institutions built to segregate these individuals from, and make them invisible to, "normal" society. Although the closure of Woodlands (1996–97)[106] and other facilities in British Columbia may promise an end to the practice of segregating the disabled from the greater community, by concentrating on institutions and medical and educational ideologies, scholars have continued to relegate the disabled to non-speaking, supporting roles that tell us little about either their lives or the lives of their families. This has left the disabled without a voice and, more important, without a recognized place in the history of British Columbia. These individuals can only be given a place if historians are willing to step beyond the bounds of the institution, as I have attempted (in a limited way) to do in this study, and engage with the lives of the disabled and their families.

Notes

1. On MacMurchy's involvement in the Canadian child saving movement, see Cynthia Comacchio, *Nations Are Built of Babies: Saving Ontario's Mothers and Children, 1900–1940* (Montreal: McGill-Queen's University Press, 1993), 70–9, 95–6; and Neil Sutherland, *Children in English-Canadian Society: Framing the Twentieth-Century Consensus* (Waterloo: Wilfrid Laurier University Press, 2000), 62–3, 229–30.
2. H. MacMurchy, "The Parents' Plea," *Canadian Journal of Mental Hygiene* 1, 3 (1919): 211.
3. Throughout this paper I use "normal" to designate an individual who is seen to rest within the constructed "norms" (physical, psychological, and sociological) of the society in which he or she lives. It is not intended as a value judgment. Equally, because disability is a social construct that varies widely depending on historical, cultural, and geographic context, I have chosen to use the nomenclature of the period under consideration ("mental defective," "mental deficient," "idiot," "imbecile," "feeble-minded," and "moron") to describe the subjects of this article. While many of these words are considered highly offensive in contemporary Western society and, in a number of cases, have become insults, they reveal the sensibilities of the people who used them, the meanings people attached to intellectual impairment, and the way in which mainstream society judged those it deemed intellectually impaired. In other words, terminology reflects the nature of the discourse surrounding intellectual impairment in the late nineteenth and early twentieth centuries. Indeed, to resort to the use of today's terminologies when discussing the historical experiences of children judged by their societies to be intellectually impaired would be to assert anachronistic understandings and constructions of intellectual impairment that simply did not exist at the

time, and it would be to deny past societies their own dia-
logue on the subject. See James Trent, *Inventing the Feeble
Mind: A History of Mental Retardation in the United States*
(Berkeley: University of California Press, 1994), 5; T.
Bedirhan Ustùn, ed., *Disability and Culture: Universalism
and Diversity* (Seattle: Hogrefe and Huber, 2001); Sandra
Lane, Blanche I. Mikhail , Alice Reizian, Paul Courtright,
Rani Marx, and Chandler R. Dawson, "Sociocultural
Aspects of Blindness in an Egyptian Delta Hamlet: Visual
Impairment vs. Visual Disability," *Medical Anthropology*
15, 3 (1993): 245–60; E. Peter Volpe, "Is Down Syndrome
a Modern Disease?" *Perspectives in Biology and Medicine*
29, 3 (1986): 423–36. I am also grateful to Keith T.
Carlson of the University of Saskatchewan for his enlight-
ening comments regarding concepts of disability among
the Coast Salish peoples of British Columbia.

4. Dr G.H. Manchester was appointed assistant medical su-
    perintendent of PHI on 1 March 1899. He had previously
    worked with mentally ill patients at Verdun Protestant
    Hospital in Montreal and became medical superinten-
    dent in 1901 on the resignation of the then superinten-
    dent Dr George Fowler Bodington. Dr Bodington, who
    was seventy-three at the time of his resignation, had been
    medical superintendent since 1895. See Val Adolph, *In
    the Context of Its Time: A History of Woodlands* (Victoria:
    Ministry of Social Services, Government of British
    Columbia, 1996), 54–5, 57, 64–5.

5. In the following examples, all names of patients and their
    families have been changed in accordance with the priva-
    cy laws of Canada and New Zealand.

6. Letter from Dr G.H. Manchester, Acting Medical
    Superintendent, to Mr A. Green, 20 December 1901,
    British Columbia, Mental Health Services Patient Case
    Files 1872–1942, GR-2880, box 9, file 1174, British
    Columbia Archives and Records Services (hereafter cited
    as MHS).

7. As well as being intellectually disabled, Marigold was also
    severely physically disabled. Her admission file describes
    her as "physically helpless" (although it notes she was cap-
    able of feeding herself), and in at least one of his letters
    to Dr Manchester, Marigold's father calls her a "cripple."
    Mr A. Green, 14 November 1901, Dr G.H. Manchester,
    16 November 1901, 20 December 1901, MHS, box 9, file
    1174.

8. Letter from Dr G.H. Manchester to Mr Green, 16
    November 1901, MHS, box 9, file 1174.

9. Indeed, this omission is indicative of the problems caused
    when historians fail to include in their thinking and
    writing both the issue of disability and experiences of in-
    dividuals labelled as disabled. See Catherine J. Kudlick,
    "Disability History: Why We Need Another 'Other,'"
    American Historical Review 108, 3 (2003): 763–93; Paul K.
    Longmore and Lauri Umansky, "Disability History: From
    the Margins to the Mainstream," in *The New Disability
    History American Perspectives*, ed. Paul K. Longmore and

Lauri Umansky (New York: New York University Press,
2001), 1–32.

10. Viviana Zelizer, *Pricing the Priceless Child: The Changing
    Social Value of Children* (Princeton: Princeton University
    Press, 1994), 11. See also Roger Cooter, ed., *In the Name
    of the Child: Health and Welfare, 1880–1940* (London:
    Routledge, 1992); and Hugh Cunningham, *Children
    and Childhood in Western Society since 1500* (Harrow:
    Longman, 1995), 134–85. In relation to Canada see
    Comacchio, *Nations Are Built of Babies;* and Sutherland,
    Children in English-Canadian Society.

11. Zelizer, *Pricing the Priceless Child,* 11.

12. Ibid.

13. Mariana Valverde, "Representing Childhood: The
    Multiple Fathers of the Dionne Quintuplets," in
    *Regulating Womanhood: Historical Essays on Motherhood
    and Sexuality,* ed. Carol Smart (London: Routledge,
    1992), 119–46.

14. Sonya Rose, Kathleen Canning, Anna Clark, Mariana
    Valverde, and Marcia Sawyer, "Gender History/Women's
    History: Is Feminist Scholarship Losing Its Critical
    Edge?" *Journal of Women's History* 5, 1 (1993): 123–4.

15. And, one might add, political returns for the then ruling
    Liberal government.

16. Valverde, "Representing Childhood," 119.

17. My use of the term "daemonization" is meant to infer
    that mentally deficient children were constructed as
    figures that threatened and tormented the general pop-
    ulace. My use of this term is heavily influenced by Victor
    Frankenstein's use of the word "daemon" to describe his
    creation in Mary Shelley's *Frankenstein; Or The Modern
    Prometheus,* because, as with the Monster, mentally de-
    ficient children's positive traits were often overshadowed
    by negative—socially constructed—first impressions.
    Mary Shelley, *Frankenstein: The Original 1818 Text,* ed.
    D.L. Macdonald and Kathleen Scherf (Peterborough:
    Broadview Press, 2001).

18. Indeed, in England the legal definitions of madness and
    idiocy changed little between the reign of Edward II and
    the mid-nineteenth century. See R. Neugebauer, "Mental
    Handicap in Medieval and Early Modern England:
    Criteria, Measurement and Care," in *From Idiocy to
    Mental Deficiency: Historical Perspectives on People with
    Learning Disabilities,* ed. David Wright and Anne Digby
    (London: Routledge, 1997), 22–43.

19. Some of the "classics" in the field are John Langdon
    Heydon Down's "Observations on an Ethnic Classification
    of Idiots," *London Hospital Reports,* 3, (1866), 259–62;
    Sir Francis Galton's *Hereditary Genius: An Inquiry Into
    Its Laws and Consequences* (London: Macmillan, 1869);
    Richard Dugdale's *The Jukes: A Study in Crime, Pauperism,
    Disease and Heredity* (New York: Putnam, 1875); Gina
    Lombroso-Ferrero's, *Criminal Man, According to the
    Classification of Cesare Lombroso,* (New York: Putnam,
    1911); and Henry Goddard's *The Kallikak Family: A Study*

in Heredity of Feeble-Mindedness (New York: Macmillan, 1913). By the early twentieth century, Down's ethnic degeneracy model for explaining mental defect was being questioned by a number of academics, including his son, Reginald Langdon Down. See Edgar Millar, "Idiocy in the Nineteenth Century," in *History of Psychiatry*, ed. German E. Barrios and Roy Porter (London: Alpha Academic, 1996), 367–8. On Galton, see Angus McLaren, *Our Own Master Race: Eugenics in Canada, 1885–1945* (Toronto: McClelland & Stewart, 1990), 14. On Lombroso, see Stephen J. Gould, *The Mismeasure of Man*, rev. ed. (New York: W.W. Norton, 1996), 151–77. It should be noted that, while many of these academics stressed that the propensity towards antisocial behaviour was hereditary, most also recognized that sociological and environmental factors could also play their part. See, for example, Carolyn Steedman, "Bodies, Figures and Physiology: Margaret McMillan and the Late Nineteenth-Century Remaking of Working-Class Childhood," in *In the Name of the Child: Health and Welfare, 1880–1940*, ed. Roger Cooter (London: Routledge, 1992), 24–6.

20. Arthur Eastbrook, for example, in his follow-up study of the Jukes, calculated that, by 1915, the family had cost the state of New York $2,093,685. See Arthur Eastbrook, *The Jukes in 1915* (Washington: Carnegie Institution, 1916), 78. In 1919 C.M. Hincks, the associate medical director and secretary of the Canadian National Committee for Mental Hygiene, stated that mental defectives cost Canada $26 million per year. See C.M. Hincks, "The Scope and Aims of the Mental Hygiene Movement in Canada," *Canadian Journal of Mental Hygiene* 1, 1 (1919): 23.

21. McLaren, *Our Own Master Race*, 13–27.

22. For the best discussion of the eugenics movement in Canada, see McLaren, *Our Own Master Race*.

23. The Canadian National Committee for Mental Hygiene had been founded in 1918 by Dr C.K. Clarke, Dean of Medicine at the University of Toronto, and it included a number of famous Canadian medical pioneers and eugenicists (including Dr Helen MacMurchy) in its membership. See Ian Dowbiggen, *Keeping America Sane: Psychiatry and Eugenics in the United States and Canada, 1880–1940* (Ithaca: Cornell University Press, 1997), 133–90.

24. The *Canadian Journal of Mental Hygiene*, first published in 1919, was the mouthpiece for the Canadian National Committee for Mental Hygiene. Intended for both a lay and professional readership, the journal published "non-technical" articles written by eugenicists from across Canada, the United States, and Europe. It also republished "noteworthy contributions which have added to our knowledge of mental disorders . . . which would otherwise not be within the reach of the general public." The journal's aim was simple: "To interest the general public, as well as the medical profession, in all the mental problems confronting the community, in their bearing upon the welfare of the individual and of society, and in the work which is being done towards their clearer definition and more adequate solution." See "Foreword," *Canadian Journal of Mental Hygiene* 1, 1 (1919): 3; Dowbiggen, *Keeping America Sane*, 133–90; and Theresa H. Richardson, *The Century of the Child: The Mental Hygiene Movement and Social Policy in the United States and Canada* (Albany: State University of New York Press, 1989), 59–74.

25. In relation to immigration, see the following primary and secondary sources: J. Halpenny, "One Phase of the Foreign Invasion of Canada," *Canadian Journal of Mental Hygiene* 1, 3 (1919): 224–6; Government of the Province of British Columbia, Royal Commission on Mental Hygiene, *Immigration* (Report of the Royal Commission on Mental Hygiene) (Victoria: King's Printer, 1927), CC29–CC31, CC43–CC46; McLaren, *Our Own Master Race*, 46–67; Barbara Roberts, *Whence They Came: Deportation from Canada, 1900–1935* (Ottawa: University of Ottawa Press, 1988); Patrick Dunae, "Waifs: The Fairbridge Society In British Columbia, 1931–1951," *Historie Sociale/Social History* 42 (1988): 225–50.

26. For discussions of MacMurchy's work in eugenics, see Dowbiggen, *Keeping America Sane*, 162–7; and McLaren, *Our Own Master Race*, 30–45.

27. Sutherland, *Children in English Canadian Society*, 76–7.

28. "[Bertha Winn] Discusses Problem of Mental Defectives," *Daily Colonist*, 21 March 1917, 7. Winn's comments were echoed by the Royal Commission on Mental Hygiene: "We have no hesitation in reaching the conclusion that mental deficiency creates a great burden on the community, and that it contributes largely to dependency, delinquency, crime, prostitution, illegitimacy, vagrancy, and destitution." See British Columbia, Royal Commission on Mental Hygiene, *Mental Deficiency: Care and Treatment of Subnormal Children* (Report of the Royal Commission on Mental Hygiene) (Victoria: Charles F. Banfield, 1927), CC21–23.

29. Canadian National Committee for Mental Hygiene, "Mental Hygiene Survey of the Province of British Columbia, *Canadian Journal of Mental Hygiene* 2, 1 (1920): 3–59.

30. Neugebauer, "Mental Handicap in Medieval and Early Modern England," 22–4. See, for example, Anthony Highmore, *A treatise on the law of idiocy and lunacy: to which is subjoined an appendix, containing the practice of the Court of Chancery on this subject, and some useful practical forms,* (London: Butterworth, 1807); George Dale Collinson, *A Treatise on the Law Concerning Idiots, Lunatics and Other Persons Non Compos Mentis* (London: W. Read, 1812).

31. Steven Noll, *Feebleminded in Our Midst: Institutions for the Mentally Retarded in the South, 1900–1940* (Chapel Hill: University of North Carolina Press, 1995), 1.

32. Noll, *Feebleminded in Our Midst*, 1–2. See also British Columbia, Royal Commission on Mental Hygiene, *Final Report of the Royal Commission on Mental Hygiene* (Victoria: Charles F. Banfield, 1928), G4.

33. Meghan Burn, for example, was classified alternately as an imbecile, an idiot, and as not suffering from mental deficiency at all. Abigail Hunt was classified as an idiot, the lowest category of mental deficiency, despite doctors describing her as "intelligent and well educated." Albert McGrew was described as insane by one of his admitting doctors and as an imbecile by the other (MHS, box 5, file 761; box 20, file 1975; box 23, file 2329).

34. Neugebauer, "Mental Handicap in Medieval and Early Modern England," 34–5.

35. British Columbia, *Final Report of the Royal Commission on Mental Hygiene*, G4.

36. The admission records include numerous examples of individuals diagnosed as mentally deficient who seem to be suffering psychiatric problems rather than innate intellectual "defects." Indeed, in some cases patients' admittance files were altered at a later date from a term for mental deficiency (usually "idiot") to a descriptor for a mental illness (such as "schizophrenia"). In another case, a man classified as insane by Vancouver's Saint Paul's Hospital was later diagnosed as being mentally deficient (MHS, box 9, file 1136; box 17, file 1975; box 17, file 1823; box 20, file 2066; and British Columbia, Essondale Provincial Mental Hospital Admission Registers, GR-1754, vol. 1, Registration Numbers 2494, 2535, British Columbia Archives and Record Services [hereafter cited as EPM]).

37. British Columbia, *Final Report of the Royal Commission on Mental Hygiene*, G4. See also British Columbia, *Mental Deficiency*, CC21.

38. British Columbia, *Final Report of the Royal Commission on Mental Hygiene*, G5.

39. Ibid, G4.

40. Ibid., G5.

41. Sutherland, *Children in English Canadian Society*, 76; Gerald E. Thomson, "Remove from Our Midst These Unfortunates: A Historical Inquiry into the Influence of Eugenics, Educational Efficiency as well as Mental Hygiene upon the Vancouver School System and Its Special Classes, 1910–1969" (Ph.D. diss., University of British Columbia, 1999), 158.

42. MacMurchy advised teachers not to waste their time on attempting to teach their defective students difficult things such as reading, writing, and arithmetic but, rather, to focus on occupational training. Equally, in a report given to the Toronto Board of Education after inspecting a number of classes for the mentally deficient in the United States, W.E. Groves quoted one of the teachers she interviewed as saying that teachers often only gave defective children enough academic work as a "sop to [their] parents." These ideologies echoed the special needs education policies of New Zealand, Australia, and Great Britain during the same time period. See Thomson, "Remove from Our Midst These Unfortunates," 180–1; E.W. Fuller, "General Role of an Institution for Mental Deficients," in British Columbia, *Final Report of the Royal Commission on Mental Hygiene* (Victoria: Charles F. Banfield, 1928), GII; W.E. Groves, "Special Auxiliary Classes: Report Given to the Toronto Board of Education after Visiting a Number of Auxiliary Classes in the United States," *Canadian Journal of Mental Hygiene* 1, 2 (1919): 186; Charles Kinnaird Mackellar, *The Treatment of Neglected and Delinquent Children in Great Britain, Europe, and America, with recommendations as to amendment of administration and law in New South Wales*, (Sydney, W.A. Gullick, 1913) 93, 96; MacMurchy; "Letter to Inspectors, Principals and Teachers," *Canadian Journal of Mental Hygiene* 1, 3 (1919): 269–77; and Trent, *Inventing the Feeble Mind*, 107.

43. "Miss Winn and Her Pupils," *Daily Colonist*, 9 March 1919, 12.

44. Thomson, "Remove from Our Midst These Unfortunates," 163a.

45. Special classes work was also displayed in the offices of the Vancouver School Board. See Thomson, "Remove from Our Midst These Unfortunates," 174a, 177a.

46. For an excellent short biography of Dauphinee, see Thomson, "Remove from Our Midst These Unfortunates," 150–1.

47. Thomson, "Remove from Our Midst These Unfortunates," 181.

48. Dauphinee argued that any attempt to teach idiots and imbeciles even the simplest forms of unskilled menial labour was a futile task and that these children would only be "safe and happy" under permanent custodial care. The Royal Commission of Mental Hygiene echoed her views. Evidence also shows that both Great Britain and New Zealand authorities banned "low grade defectives" from training institutions because they were deemed to be a waste of resources. Indeed, the unwillingness to waste resources on "uneducable idiots" can be seen as the major reason behind the resignation of George Benstead, the first principal of New Zealand's Otekaike Special School for Boys, in 1917. Benstead was forced to resign after he was accused of allowing the school to become a dumping ground for "low grade custodial cases." See "Urge Appointment of Psychiatrist," *Daily Colonist*, 3 March 1922, 8; "State Should Guard Subnormal Child," *Daily Colonist*, 12 October 1922, 6; Thomson, "Remove from Our Midst These Unfortunates," 158; British Columbia, *Mental Deficiency*, CC21; David Gladstone, "The Changing Dynamic of Institutional Care: The Western Countries Idiots Asylum, 1864–1914," in *From Idiocy to Mental Deficiency: Historical Perspectives on People with Learning Disabilities*, ed. David Wright and Anne Digby (London: Routledge, 1997), 157; and Stephen Bardsley, "The Functions of an Institution: The Otekaike Special

School for Boys," (BA thesis, Otago University, 1991), 7.

49. J.S. Gordon, quoted in Thomson, "Remove from Our Midst These Unfortunates," 175. See also Thomson, "Remove from Our Midst These Unfortunates," 85, 160, 172.

50. The Subnormal Child Is Considered," *Daily Colonist*, 19 April 1922, 1; and Thomson, "Remove from Our Midst These Unfortunates," 226.

51. Thomson, "Remove from Our Midst These Unfortunates," 303.

52. Ibid., 160.

53. Letter from Mrs. Albert to Dr E.S.H. MacLean, Provincial Secretary, 4 August 1920, British Columbia, Provincial Secretary Correspondence 1918-26, re: New Building on Colony Farm for Defectives, GR-0344, box 1, file 5, British Columbia Archives and Records Service (hereafter cited as PS). A subsequent letter from the MPP for Grand Forks, Mr. E.C. Henniger, to the minister of education stated that Ruth was an incurable epileptic who was "deficient both mentally and phisically [sic]." See letter from E.C. Henniger, MPP, to the Minister of Education, 22 August 1920, PS, box 1, file 5.

54. Letter from Mrs. Albert, PS, box 1, file 5.

55. Ruth's parents' endeavours to have her placed in a school and her mother's request to the superintendent of neglected children for aid could be constructed as a limited form of what David Wright has called "strategic confinement." See David Wright, "Families' Strategies and the Institutional Confinement of 'Idiot' Children in Victorian England," *Journal of Family History* 23, 2 (1998): 190–208. See also M. Friedberger, "The Decision to Institutionalize: Families with Exceptional Children in 1900," *Journal of Family History* 6, 4 (1981): 396–406.

56. British Columbia, *Mental Deficiency*, CC21. This statement echoed similar comments made in both the United Kingdom and the United States. For example, in 1909 Mrs Hume Pinsent, the Chairperson of the Birmingham Special Schools Committee, noted that "the great majority [of mental defectives] are still without the care and control they so aptly need. This is not only deplorable for them, but means wearing out the overburdened mother, and often spoiling the lives and chances of normal brothers and sisters." While in 1931 the superintendent of South Carolina's State Training school, Benjamin O. Whitten, stated, "Many families are completely disorganized because of their inability to properly care for their defective child." Mrs. Hume Pinsent, quoted by Dr George Benstead, principal of New Zealand's Otekaike Special School for Boys, in his annual report. See "Education: Special Schools and Infant Life Protection," *Appendix to Journal of the House of Representatives* (Wellington: Government Publisher, 1910), 13; Benjamin O. Whitten, quoted by Noll, *Feebleminded in Our Midst*, 135. See also Noll, *Feebleminded in Our Midst*, 134.

57. "Legislature Deals with Various Bills," *Daily Colonist*, 27 February 1920, 12.

58. MHS, box 3, file 555.

59. MHS, box 19, file 1925.

60. MHS, box 8, file 1028.

61. It is evident from Joseph's admittance records that his brother-in-law had very little time for him. It is also evident that the dislike was mutual; Joseph is recorded as having attempted to brain his brother-in-law with an axe in the month before his committal to PHI (MHS, box 8, file 1028).

62. EPM, vol. 1, registration nos. 2701; MHS, box 14, file 1527; MHS box 27, file 2762.

63. Included in these positions were charwoman, delivery boy, domestic, labourer, laundry worker, and fisherman (EPM, vols. 1 and 2, registration nos. 30, 646, 1339, 1572, 3351, 3433, 3943, 3962, 4173, 4257, 4535, 4788, 4833)

64. MHS, box 8, file 1028.

65. EPM, vol. 1, registration nos. 989, 3277.

66. See, for example, MHS, box 1, file 30; MHS box 18, file 1793.

67. The American special education theorist Philip Ferguson argues that, even at the height of the eugenics era in the United States, "less than 10 percent of the identified population of mentally retarded people was actually confined in large, public institutions." He acknowledges that his population calculations are open to criticism on a number of different levels but argues that his general point—that at the height of the asylum era, the large majority of intellectually disabled individuals did not reside in institutions—is a valid one. I am inclined to agree with Ferguson as there is considerable independent evidence to support his contention. See Philip Ferguson, *Abandoned to Their Fate: Social Policy and Practice toward Severely Retarded People in America, 1820-1920* (Philadelphia: Temple University Press, 1994), 167; and Ferguson, correspondence with the author. See also Peter Bartlett and David Wright, "Community Care and Its Antecedents," in *Outside the Walls of the Asylum: The History of Care in the Community, 1750-2000*, ed. Peter Bartlett and David Wright (London: Athlone Press, 1999), 1–18; Philip Reilly, *The Surgical Solution: A History of Involuntary Sterilization in the United States* (Baltimore: Johns Hopkins University Press, 1991), 13; and Jessie Taft, "Supervision of the Feebleminded in the Community," *Canadian Journal of Mental Hygiene* 1, 2 (1919): 164–71.

68. My own unpublished research on admissions into Seaview and Sunnyside asylums in New Zealand between 1854 and 1912 has unearthed similar examples of long-term institutional avoidance. The New Zealand government attempted to alleviate this problem with the passing of the *Education Amendment Act 1914*, which made it obligatory for parents, teachers, police constables, and other public servants to report mentally defective children to the Department of Education. The fact that this act was passed seven years after the Education Amendment Act, 1907, which had first made education compulsory for

defective or epileptic children between the ages of 6 and 21, and that it stipulated significant fines for those who failed in their duty to report mentally defective children, would seem to indicate that many of these children were eluding the institutional net. See New Zealand, Seaview Register of Patients 1869-1912, CH 22/73, patient nos. 222, 442, 453, 522, Archives New Zealand Te Whare Tohu Tuhituhinga o Aotearoa (hereafter SRP); New Zealand, Sunnyside Lunatic Asylum Registers of Admission 1854-1890, CH 388 /1-4, patient nos. 14, 34, 45, 53, 96, 100, 297, 301, 356, 372, 392, 393, 570, 1289, 1321, Archives New Zealand Te Whare Tohu Tuhituhinga o Aotearoa, (here after SLA); New Zealand Education Amendment Act, 1907 s. 15; and New Zealand Education Amendment Act, 1914, s. 129.

69. Sutherland, *Children in English Canadian Society,* 71-81; and McLaren, *Our Own Master Race,* 38, 91-2. Ian Copeland, *The Making of the Backward Pupil in Education in England, 1870-1914* (London: Woburn Press, 1999), examines the role that schooling played in identifying mentally defective children in Great Britain.

70. Mona Gleason, "Race, Class, and Health: School Medical Inspection and 'Healthy' Children in British Columbia, 1890-1930," *Canadian Bulletin of Medical History* 19 (2002): 99, 102-3, 107.

71. MHS, box 1, file 140.

72. Noll, *Feebleminded in Our Midst,* 40-1,113-15; and Peter Taylor, "Denied the Power to Choose the Good: Sexuality and Mental Defect in American Medical Practice, 1850-1920," *Journal of Social History* 10 (1977): 472-89. Some experts questioned the "over-development" of the sex element in the mental and physical makeup of mentally deficient girls. See, for example, Fuller, "General Role of an Institution for Mental Deficients," GII.

73. Since her father's death, the girl was reported to have attacked her mother and to have become so unmanageable that she required physical restraint. See letter from the Office of the Inspector of Schools (Revelstoke) to Dr E.S.H. MacLean, Provincial Secretary, 20 December 1920; and letter from C.F. Nelson, Druggist and Stationer, to Dr E.S. MacLean, Provincial Secretary, 29 December 1920, Provincial Secretary Correspondence 1918-1926, PS, box 1, file 4.

74. Letter from the Office of the Inspector of Schools (Revelstoke) to Dr. E.S.H. MacLean, Provincial Secretary, 20 December 1920, PS, box 1, file 4.

75. "[Bertha Winn] Discusses Problem of Mental Defectives," *Daily Colonist,* 21 March 1917, 7; and "State Should Guard Subnormal Child," *Daily Colonist,* 12 October 1922, 6.

76. Report of E.D. LeSuear to Vancouver Juvenile Court, 23 February 1923, PS, box 1, file 8.

77. For example, one of the major factors leading to Sarah Thomas's admittance to PHI in 1895 was her "insane sexual desire," which—according to both Sarah's mother and the admitting doctors—was evidenced by Sarah's repeated use of lewd language and her saying that she wanted to become a prostitute in order to earn money to buy clothes (MHS, box 4, file 646). See also Noll, *Feebleminded in Our Midst,* 113-14.

78. For studies of the treatment of delinquent children in Canada, see Franca Iacovetta, "Gossip, Contest, and Power in the Making of Suburban Bad Girls: Toronto, 1945-60," *Canadian Historical Review* 80, 4 (1999): 585-623; Tamara Myers, "The Voluntary Delinquent: Parents, Daughters, and the Montreal Delinquents' Court in 1918," *Canadian Historical Review* 80, 2 (1999): 242-68; and Joan Sangster, "'She Is Hostile to Our Ways': First Nations Girls Sentenced to the Ontario Training School for Girls, 1933-1960," *Law and History Review,* 20, 1 (2002): 59-96.

79. MHS, box 17, file 1818.

80. See, for example, the case of Henry and Oscar Fraser below.

81. R. Adams, *Sideshow USA: Freaks and the American Cultural Imagination* (Chicago: Chicago University Press: 2001).

82. M. Jackson, "Images of Deviance: Visual Representations of Mental Defectives in Twentieth Century Medical Texts," *British Journal for the History of Science* 28 (1995): 319-37. See also Martin S. Pernick, *The Black Stork: Eugenics and the Death of "Defective" Babies in American Medicine and Motion Pictures Since 1915* (New York: Oxford University Press, 1996); and Volpe, "Is Down Syndrome a Modern Disease?"

83. MHS, box 19, file 1925; and MHS, box 30, file 3027.

84. "Some Children are Reared in Chaos Here," *Daily Colonist,* 21 February 1920, 9.

85. Peter's records do not provide exact age. At the time of his death in 1924 he was stated to be "about thirty" (MHS, box 13, file 1459).

86. Given that there is no mention of Peter's having a father in any of his records, Superintendent Smith might also have been keeping the identity of Peter's mother a secret because the boy was "illegitimate."

87. SLA, CH 388/18, patient no. 29.

88. The most famous recent case is that of Genie, who was discovered in Los Angles in 1970. See Linda Garmon, *The Secret of the Wild Child* (Boston, MA: WGBH, 1994), video; and Russ Rymer, *Genie: An Abused Child's Flight from Silence* (New York: HarperCollins, 1993).

89. Admittedly, in all these cases the community was aware of the existence of these individuals. See MHS, box 12, file 1294; and MHS box 19, file 1925. See also letter from C.R. Nelson, Druggist and Stationer, to Dr E.S. MacLean, Provincial Secretary, 29 December 1920, PS, box 1, file 4.

90. Taft, "Supervision of the Feebleminded," 166.

91. Ibid. See also "Subnormal Cases Require Provision," *Victoria Daily Times,* 27 February 1920, 15.

92. Indeed, Angus McLaren has argued that the only reason that the Alberta and BC governments were able to pass

their respective sterilization acts in 1928 and 1933 was because the Roman Catholic minority in each of these provinces was too small to offer effective opposition. In Ontario and Manitoba, on the other hand, Roman Catholics, while still in the minority, made up a large enough percentage of the population to successfully defeat attempts to pass similar acts. With this in mind, it should come as no surprise that eugenics ideologies were at their weakest in Quebec. See McLaren, *Our Own Master Race*, 104, 122–3, 125–6, 149–54.

93. Royal Commission on Mental Hygiene, "Report of the Commission on Mental Hygiene," G4.

94. "Mental Cases in Schools Are Few," *Daily Colonist*, 24 August 1923, 12.

95. "School Board Hears Opposing Views," *Daily Colonist*, 31 May 1921, 13.

96. MHS, box 14, file 1527.

97. Johnstone was not the only parent who corresponded with asylum staff requesting updates about their children. That these progress reports were important to some inmates' parents is not only evidenced by those, such as Johnstone, who religiously reported their change of address but also by those who wrote letters criticizing asylum staff for not keeping them informed on a regular basis. Marge Flanders, in a letter requesting information about her son, Ned, pointedly noted that "I have not heard concerning him for a long time." See MHS, box 17, file 1818. See also MHS, box 17, file 1772; MHS box 18, file

1879; MHS box 23, file 2329; and MHS, box 30, file 3027.

98. A. Johnstone, Letter, 7 November 1918, MHS, box 14, file 1527.

99. A. Johnstone, Letter, 19 November 1918, MHS, box 14, file 1527.

100. F. Ben, Letter, 24 June 1912, MHS, box 20, file 2069.

101. MHS, box 14, file 1580; MHS, box 14, file 1581.

102. MHS, box 14, file 1580.

103. Letter from Dr G.H. Manchester to the Chief of Police, Vancouver, 25 December 1904, MHS, box 14, file 1580.

104. Oscar was readmitted in 1943. See MHS, box 14, file 1581.

105. Letter from Dr. C. Doherty to James Crossan, Esq., 22 September 1906, MHS, box 17, file 1776.

106. Woodlands School, New Westminster, was the site of British Columbia's first permanent asylum for the mentally afflicted. Simply called the Provincial Asylum at the time of its opening in 1878, its name was officially changed to the Public Hospital for the Insane (PHI) in 1897. With the reorganization of the Mental Hospitals of British Columbia into Provincial Mental Health Services in 1950, PHI—which had become the chief educational and training facility in the British Columbian Mental Health system—was renamed Woodlands School. By the 1960s, Woodlands had become designated as British Columbia's training school for intellectually disabled children. For an excellent overview of the history of this institution see Adolph, *In the Context of Its Time*.

PRIMARY DOCUMENT

Helen MacMurchy, *The Feeble-Minded in Ontario, Eighth Report for the Year 1913*

20   REPORT OF THE

A Clearing House for the Mentally-Defective.

In New York the Commissioner of Charities, Michael J. Drummond, established in 1913 a " Clearing House for Mental-Defectives " which is held at the Post-Graduate Hospital. It is stated that children are sent to this Clearing House from 147 different sources in the City, such as Courts, Churches, Schools and Church Settlements. Dr. Max G. Schlapp is in charge, and is assisted by seven Assistant Neurologists and three Psychologists. Every help that medicine and surgery can give is made available for the children at the clinic. About 2,800 such examinations have been made. In October moving pictures at the Metropolitan Insurance Building showed the work of the " Clearing House," and a free exhibit with lectures took place during the whole of October. Valuable information and help is thus given to the public in an easily understood form.

A great many new cases have been sent to the Clearing House for help since the Exhibit opened, and the attendance at the latter has been sometimes over 2,000 per day.

The outline sketches below from *The Survey* show the places where different grades of Mentally-Defective persons stop and can go no farther.

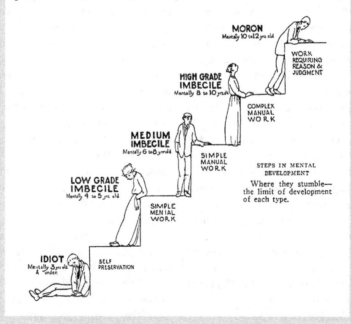

Source: Helen MacMurchy, *The Feeble-Minded in Ontario, Eighth Report for the Year 1913*. Toronto: King's Printer, 1914, 20.

Child Freak Performers in Early-to Mid-Twentieth-Century Canada

JANE NICHOLAS

In May 1934, Yvonne, Annette, Cecile, Émilie, and Marie were born to Elzire and Oliva Dionne. The extraordinary birth of these children, better known as the Dionne quintuplets, caused a national and international furor. Five living identical girls in 1934, when infant mortality rates for all children remained high, was certainly unusual.[1] The Dionnes, a French-Canadian, working-class, Catholic family living in Ontario, a province defined by Anglo, middle-class, Protestant hegemony, already had five children; and surviving as a family in the Great Depression, as the welfare state was only beginning to emerge, was a struggle for many. In the historical literature on the sisters, much attention has been focused on the medical community involved in their care; the role of the government in claiming custody of the children; the regulation of motherhood and the creation of a specific ideal of modern, scientific parenting; and the commodification of the girls' images to sell goods as well as spark tourism.[2] A particular detail in their history has, however, been largely left unexplored: that Oliva Dionne initially arranged to have the girls shown by Chicago fair promoter Ivan Spear. It was this arrangement that provided the excuse, if not the impetus, for the Ontario government to step in and claim guardianship of the children. Quite simply, this move was an extraordinary measure of state interference into the sanctity of the patriarchal family—long seen as the bedrock of the nation-state itself. In this essay, I will utilize this detail to explore a different context for the display of the Dionne quintuplets: the appearance of children in sideshows from the 1920s to the 1940s.

If the procurement of the quints on behalf of the showman caused alarm in the Ontario

government in 1934, this was only one reaction toward what was otherwise a routine way for show promoters to find new acts. The profits of the side-shows were based on a wider cultural investment in the freak show, and showmen and -women pursued news of extraordinary births because they knew they could build or tap into existing audiences hungry for seeing something new and different.[3] One case occurred in Canada in the early 1930s. Ernie Defort was born in 1931 in Winnipeg to parents Emma and Frank Defort, identified in one newspaper article as Polish immigrants. Ernie was born with an asymmetrical conjoined twin, frequently referred to as a parasitic twin, which he reportedly called Lester.[4] The twin (publicly known as Len in the Ernie-Len exhibits) had a fully formed lower body (including pelvis, liver, and kidneys, although the latter were removed in an operation when Ernie was two years old) and arms and hands.[5] After entertaining a number of offers from sideshows, the Deforts placed Ernie with the Conklin shows run by Patty Conklin. Reportedly, his mother travelled with him, although all promotional materials include only references to medical professionals present at his birth. Ernie-Len appeared as a baby and child on the sideshow circuits, travelling across the country as Conklin's feature attraction in the 1930s and early 1940s until he had "corrective" surgery to remove the twin. On the sideshow, Ernie-Len was billed as "The World's Strangest Living Boy" and as "Two Living Brothers with Only One Head."[6] One of the custom-made show fronts declared: "Rarer Than the Dionne Quintuplets."[7] The parents had received a number of offers from sideshows (as had the Dionnes), but they trusted Patty Conklin, even though he could offer less money.[8] By the 1930s, Conklin had become a significant commercial force in the travelling carnival business, securing the premier carnival circuits in western Canada and, by 1937, the permanent, annual contract for the lucrative Canadian National Exhibition (CNE) in Toronto.[9]

While the Dionnes' story was and is extraordinary, the contracting of children to the sideshow in mid-twentieth century North America was not. Perhaps what was extraordinary in this case was the public nature of the agreement and the intervention by the government. As Mariana Valverde has argued, the government did not intervene to give the girls a chance to be "normal" children, but rather "the Dionne quintuplets figured as capital, mainly tourist-industry capital."[10] If the Dionnes represented childhood for many consumers in the 1930s, they were not conceived of as "children."[11] Child performers on sideshows represented neither of these categories, but, like the Dionnes, they were often seen through a quasi-medical or educational gaze, which rendered their bodies suitable for public consumption. Both the Dionne quints and sideshow performers, illustrated here through the case of Ernie Defort, were displayed because of their physical differences in what amounted to a sideshow. As fair and exhibition directors well knew, sideshows were profitable, if not lucrative.[12] Using the history of the Dionnes as a starting point to explore other children's histories as child performers on the sideshows provides an opportunity to understand how the category of childhood was mobilized in twentieth-century consumer culture as part of structural and cultural violence that devalued the bodies of different or disabled children while simultaneously rendering them profitable in commercial displays.[13] The Dionnes became fetishized figures of childhood, and Ernie-Len's[14] small but different body was used as an example of freakishness and abnormality.

Structural and cultural violence are about disparities in power and the construction, maintenance, and experiences of the consequences of those power imbalances. Structural violence encapsulates how discourses of gender, race, class, ability, and age work simultaneously to increase the risk of harm for certain people. The result of increased risk of harm is violence: not necessarily personal violence (although that is also possible) but the wider violence of dehumanization wherein basic necessities of life and culturally sanctioned expectations of care and protection are withheld. Structural violence draws attention to the limits on agency without erasing its possibility, and implicates social and cultural values in the production of inequities. Cultural violence, in particular, refers to the cultural discourses that normalize particular types of violence as natural and appropriate. As Johan Galtung argues, "[C]ulture preaches, teaches, admonishes, eggs on, and dulls us into seeing exploitation and/or repression as normal and natural, or into not seeing them (particularly exploitation) at all."[15] Importantly, structural and cultural violence also implicate witnesses, in the sense that who gets their suffering noticed and addressed becomes an important part of the maintenance, reduction, or perpetuation of violence.[16]

Childhood may have been a cultural expectation in mid-twentieth-century Canada, but as Nic Clarke's essay on children with intellectual disabilities reveals (see earlier in this chapter), significant gaps existed within the dominant category of the protected child. These gaps meant that children deemed to be intellectually unfit were often seen in economic as opposed to sentimental terms by teachers, doctors, and administrators of institutions.[17] Their value—literally and metaphorically—was deemed to be lesser than that of children who were "fit." While the particular cases of the Dionnes and Ernie do not involve children with intellectual disabilities, they do reveal that the gaps in constructions of sentimental childhood extended also to those with so-called extraordinary bodies.[18] As sideshows and showmen and -women became the scapegoats for exploitation, such accusations erased the wider structures that kept the shows popular with audiences across Canada. Moreover, depicting the sideshow exclusively as exploitative erases the social and cultural processes that made the extraordinary bodies of certain children available as spectacles of public consumption—a process that was ultimately based on the structural and cultural violence of power inequities of poverty and socially constructed ideas of age and corporeal difference.

It also erases any assertion of agency by families or children performing as freaks.

Evidence from freak shows in the twentieth century suggests that many performers started their careers as children, including Emmitt Bejano, Percilla Lauther, Daisy and Violet Hilton, Yvonne and Yvette Jones, and Frieda Pushnik, to name a few of the most famous examples. The historiography on freak performers, however, has yet to consider the age of performers or the participation of children as performers.[19] The number of children working on the sideshows was certainly small, but these children are historically significant for at least two reasons. One is their continuing appeal as commercial amusements to which adults and children were drawn to gaze and gawk. As such, their piecemeal histories confirm that spectacle was indeed an important element of commercial culture and one in which children figure as important workers and consumers. And the other is that juxtaposing the history of the Dionnes and the history of child sideshow performer Ernie Defort brings into relief the limits of the category of the child with regard to disability.

This essay is part of a wider project on the history of the freak show in twentieth-century Canada, and I have wrestled with the ethics of conducting this study.[20] Much of the archival material consists of photographs, and I was startled in beginning my research to find so many images of children working as performers. As many historians of children and childhood have noted, the available evidence is usually made by, about, and for adults.[21] The situation here is not different. I am working largely from representations of children in newspapers, archival documents, and photographs. The voices of actual children, especially children in the sideshow whose lives and careers were made of ballyhoo, are incredibly difficult to access, but records of the sideshows, and of other places where children were exhibited, do exist, albeit in scattered form. This piecemeal quality is in part due to the transitory nature and the transnational patterns of twentieth-century sideshows. In Canada, there were a number of sideshows touring with travelling shows, carnivals, and circuses, including Conklin, Sam Alexander Shows,

Rubin and Cherry, and Royal American. I have consulted collections held at the North American Carnival Museum and Archives, Circus World Museum, and smaller collections on sideshow history at the New York Public Library and the University of Santa Barbara, as well as the collections on the Dionnes held at the Archives of Ontario, the Library and Archives of Canada, and the City of North Bay Dionne Quintuplet Digitalization Project. Rich, if frustratingly imprecise and contradictory accounts of sideshows and performers can be found in various Canadian newspapers as well as in trade magazines for circuses and carnivals. Given the connection to medicine, I have also consulted major Canadian, American, and British medical journals of the period. As such, this essay is very much about representations of childhood, and although I am discussing "real" children, they are only present in the historical records I am using in very limited ways. They neither manufactured nor controlled the representations of their lives or bodies and still do not here. I have tried to piece together the information about their lives using "empathetic inference," being sensitive to wider processes that brought their lives into the realms of sideshow history.[22]

The Dionnes' Sideshow History

After a less-than-enthusiastic initial response to the births, the Dionne quintuplets soon excited the Canadian public and the press. As word of the extraordinary births was publicized, Chicago-based showman Ivan Spear, among others, expressed a desire to exhibit the girls. Spear had success. Reports on the Dionnes and the contract with Spear in the *Globe* changed dramatically in a matter of weeks. In a rather bland article on 1 June 1934, the paper reported on negotiations happening in Orillia, Ontario, that included Oliva Dionne, the parish priest Father Daniel Routhier, and two Chicago-based promoters. About six weeks later, on 27 July 1934, an article on the front page of the *Globe* began by stating, "An exploitation scheme 'which meant certain death to one or more of the quintuplets' was circumvented by the Ontario Attorney-General's Department when it broke the contract for exhibiting the Dionne babies at the Chicago

Century of Progress Exposition, it was announced last night by Hon. Arthur W. Roebuck."[23] By early 1935, the Ontario government had decided on more permanent guardianship and passed a bill through the provincial legislature to make the girls wards of the Crown.[24] Again, the spectre of sideshows and commercial culture were given as reasons in the public debates. Oliva and Elzire Dionne had been working vaudeville circuits as the parents of the famous girls, and the original showmen who had contracted the family to be exhibited in Chicago were now threatening a million-dollar lawsuit for breach of contract.[25] In response to both the threat of legal action and the parents' vaudeville performances, Ontario's premier, Mitchell Hepburn, spoke out, as quoted in the *Border Cities Star*:

"If there is any action that the Ontario Legislature can take to protect these babes from profit-seeking promoters, that action will be taken. Any action that can protect them against these chiselers (sic) will be taken. And I deprecate to the fullest extent the degrading spectacle of the parents going on the vaudeville stage. It is a disgrace and it's cheap. The parents are of no value as anything but parents. We are going to try to save the children from such exploitation if at all possible. . . . It is revolting, disgusting and cheap and it reflects on the people of Canada as a whole. But regardless of this, we are going to protect the children."

Mr. Hepburn did not attempt to hide his anger about the situation. He contended that the Dionne parents haven't any accomplishments which would fit them for the stage and that it was just an exploitation of the freak of nature which had sent them five babes at one time. . . . "And they are not because of their previous environment, of the type who protect themselves from the exploiting promoters."[26]

About one month later, Minister of Public Welfare David Croll was quoted as saying, "We are trying to treat the children as human beings and not as freaks. We want them to be home under the care of their mother and father, rather than exhibited between a sword-swallower and a bearded woman on a Chicago midway."[27] Hepburn's and Croll's passionate comments on keeping the children private is fascinating in that other children had been displayed in Toronto at the CNE. Children like Ernie performed in public, were reported on in newspapers, and had photographs of them circulating freely in the *cartes de visites* consumers could buy.

Hepburn's statements on protecting the Dionne children meshed with the wider discourses of child welfare in the period. Child welfare strategies grew alongside a wider strategy by scientists, physicians, educators, social workers, and other experts to reframe the category and construction of childhood. Influenced by the experiences of the First World War, the recognition of the poor health of Canadians, high infant mortality rates, and initiatives to produce sound, healthy citizens, widespread campaigns emerged focusing on improving children's health and welfare. The development of these campaigns both reflected a shift in the dominant conceptions of childhood and helped to reshape them. Mothers, who were deemed responsible for children's health and their general care, came under increasing pressure to raise children using modern, scientific strategies put forth by experts.[28] Children themselves were targeted at schools through a health curriculum that was guided by public health campaigns.[29] These campaigns and the men and women at their helms were often influenced by the pseudo-science of eugenics and the desire to produce a "fitter" race of peoples by eliminating those deemed to be feeble-minded or otherwise defective.[30]

These wider social and cultural shifts help to explain the impetus for the radical intervention into the Dionne family and the subsequent display of the children. In early 1935, the Dionne quintuplets were named wards of the Crown until they came of age. The legislation taking control of the children named four male guardians, including Oliva Dionne and Dr Allan Dafoe. Dafoe was a country doctor who had assisted the local midwives with the birth of the girls, but he quickly became the public paternal face of the modern, scientific practices meant to ensure their health and welfare. Following the initial judicial order that took the girls from their parents' custody in 1934, the quints were moved from the family home and placed in a new, custom-built hospital (the Dafoe Hospital) where they were to be raised according to the best child-rearing practices known to modern scientific medicine.[31] Yet, when initially contacted by the showmen, Oliva Dionne had consulted with his parish priest and Dafoe, and both men consented to the deal, provided the girls were well enough to travel. The contract would have included a 7 percent cut of the profits for Routhier, the parish priest, and would have required Dafoe's consent to move the girls.[32]

The contract would have placed the family on display at the Chicago Century of Progress Exposition. Forty years earlier in Chicago, the Chicago World's Columbian Exposition had given birth to the Midway Plaisance. By the 1930s, however, the midway had been moved from the centre to a peripheral spot on the fairgrounds. This push to the periphery was not only geographic but also symbolic of cultural shifts, and similar moves occurred in fairgrounds like those of the CNE.[33] Once the height of middle-class entertainment, by the end of the nineteenth century, freak shows and the lust for "deformitomania" had soured to the point that sideshows were, at best, culturally low.[34] By the 1920s, communities across Ontario led by voluntary associations, boards of trade, and municipal councils actively protested such shows as being American, commercial, an affront to good taste, promoting bad habits, and simply being detrimental to impressionable Canadian youth. The Sault Ste. Marie Board of Trade passed a resolution similar to those of other groups, which called for the premier, the attorney general, and the Ontario Provincial Police to "take the necessary action to forbid the showing in Ontario of questionable amusement orgies and carnivals of inanity and vice, of which Ontario had a surfeit during the Summer of 1920 and which made for weeks of immense pollutive influence from the United States being focused upon and intensified in Canadian communities." In 1921, members of the Brantford, Ontario, Chamber of Commerce held a referendum on carnivals, which

included commentary from citizens. Some commentators wrote that carnivals were a "degrading and a worn out class of entertainment," and "a positive danger to our young people."[35] By the 1930s, even circus owners engaged in transatlantic travelling shows expressed serious concerns that respectable circuses were being too closely associated with the "fairground business," which they deemed too "commercial."[36]

Three important points must be made. First, the outcry never succeeded in banning the freak show, despite attempts made by various groups across the country to influence municipal, provincial, and federal authorities.[37] Indeed, by the 1930s, even World's Fairs deemed a midway with sideshows essential to their financial success.[38] Their commercial value speaks to widespread if silent support in the form of audience popularity. Second, none of the opposition was directed toward actual children working and performing on the sideshow. Their "freakery" seemed to keep them beyond the purview of middle-class concern about the influence over audiences, especially children and youth. The lack of attention paid to the child workers of freak shows is especially interesting given the rising importance of youth as consumers of the shows in the period, and the need to protect them from certain detrimental elements of popular culture.[39] Third, while informal adoption gave the gloss of formal family bonds to children procured by showmen as infants or toddlers (lending the appearance that the children were simply exhibited as part of the family business), only in the case of the Dionnes was the government willing to breach those family bonds and sideshow contracts.

In the early days of their lives, no one believed the quints could or would survive. When it became clear that they would, the contract was broken and the government and the media publicly painted the parents, along with the showmen, in a negative light. The parents were deemed to be provincial and gullible, while the showmen were degraded as "American," which meant commercial, vulgar, and cheap. In English-language newspapers, the government was depicted as benevolent in taking control of the girls and building their own hospital replete with viewing grounds for tourists. Although the girls did not travel, they were shown twice a day in a facility designed for their exhibition to mass audiences—the parking lot at the hospital, for example, had one thousand spots. As Valverde reports, "[B]y 1936, Quintland equalled Niagara Falls as Canada's leading tourist attraction."[40] Visitors were amused by the ordinariness of the quints, who were viewed through one-way glass but who noted later in their lives that they were aware of being watched.[41] In sideshows, exhibitors used ordinary, everyday settings to highlight the extraordinariness of freak performers.[42] In the case of the quints, the well-designed rustic Northern Ontario scene fit within the romanticized anti-modern sentiments of the period, and the combination of modern hospital and domestic play highlighted five beautiful little girls made extraordinary only by their multiplicity.[43] Ironically, the girls were removed from their parents on the grounds that they would be exploited by showmen in Chicago, only to end up as part of a permanent spectacle wherein they performed as infants, toddlers, and young girls for paying audiences.

In some ways, the girls' display echoed earlier spectacles like baby shows, held from the mid-nineteenth century onwards. Historian Susan J. Pearson argues that mid- to late-nineteenth-century American baby shows, while being slightly controversial, achieved widespread support because they "introduced a new form of exhibition: the objectification of normal human beings and of normalcy, coded as domesticity itself."[44] Like the freak show and the beauty contest, the baby show had connections to P.T. Barnum's American Museum in New York City. As early as the 1850s, Barnum had included baby shows in the same venue where he displayed freaks.[45] By the time of the Dionnes' exhibition, however, baby contests themselves had changed from being "prideful, subjective, and sentimental" to "objective, scientific, and educative."[46] Beginning in the 1920s, baby contest organizers desired to find the best and healthiest specimens of childhood, who met hegemonic standards of health and attractiveness, while freak shows highlighted the margins of those categories. Baby contests, more than either freak shows or beauty contests, achieved legitimacy because of

their sponsorship ties, and the judges were often closely associated with eugenics, child welfare campaigns, scientific mothering, medical professionals and other health experts, and groups like women's councils. All of them, however—the baby contest, the beauty contest, and the freak show—did similar cultural work in trying to affirm, regulate, and promote dominant conceptions of health, beauty, and normalcy.[47] At the CNE, as in other locales, baby contests allowed doctors and nurses the chance to weigh, measure, and examine large numbers of children in line with health and welfare campaigns.[48] The canvases and pamphlets used to promote Ernie-Len's shows used appeals to modern medicine. The doctors and nurses present at his birth were named and he was identified as a "Living Thoracopagus Parasiticus"—at best, a partially correct medical diagnosis.[49] Ernie-Len was also described as "the talk of the medical profession"; consumers were told to "ask their doctors" and that profits from the sale of pamphlets would go to educate "the boy."[50] He was, then, a medical mystery to be solved by paying audiences, who may have been convinced that their gawking did some good in supporting his education.

The offer from the showmen would have resulted in the display of the Dionne family. However, critics raised the concern that such exhibitions, especially when they showcased multiple births, simply showcased good breeders. The concern is particularly apt given the criticisms, inspired by eugenics, that the French-Catholic Dionnes faced.[51] The Dafoe Hospital worked to create a literal and representative distance from the parents and the spectre of breeding, but the hospital's permanence and the repetition of the display crossed the line from baby show to sideshow. The girls performed their childhood in a carefully controlled clinical setting where they could be seen in any number of staged performances of normal childhood, set apart from the "messiness" of procreative parents or degraded, unscientific domesticity. The combination of the modern hospital and the rustic, romanticized Northern Ontario setting brought together seemingly contradictory impulses to make modern changes seem safe, familiar, and natural. Its imagery was simply part of the staging.

If the government had ever intended to avoid the cheap consumer culture of the sideshows, by 1937 this ruse was more difficult to maintain. By this time, Keith Munro had been named as the quints' full-time business manager, and the name and image of the girls was under a federal trademark. In almost three years, the girls' trust fund held about a half a million dollars. Their pictures appeared on all sorts of commercial products and they made appearances on radio and film. Criticism of the spectre of the sideshow haunted the quints' exhibition and some of the individuals in charge of it, in part because the entire enterprise smacked of commercialism. On 28 September 1937, in one of her many letters home to her mother in Sweden, Louise de Kiriline, who nursed the Dionne girls through their first year, wrote, "Dr Dafoe has lost all his prestige among medical men in Toronto. He is called the showman, which is not very flattering."[52]

Two years later, when the New York World's Fair reportedly offered one million dollars to exhibit the girls in a specially built exact replica of the Dafoe Hospital, Canadians and Dafoe were incredulous. As one *New York Times* reporter in Ottawa noted, many Canadians were more interested in the Dionnes' participation in the fair than they were in the war.[53] The self-contradictory public response from Dr Dafoe was telling, however, in how it crossed the lines of spectacle, freak show, profits, and health. At the time, Dafoe was in New York for a radio interview, and reporters implied that this might have been an opportunity to work out the deal with the fair. The *Globe* quoted him as saying, "'Why, we have our own World's Fair right in Callander, [Ontario]' he beamed proudly, 'Don't you think that the kiddies are a fair in themselves? . . . Suppose you were their father. Would you want them on perpetual exhibition as dolls in a store window? The health of the children is paramount, and I feel that the continual exploitation would retard their normal development. They are not freaks.'"[54] At play here was a convoluted mix of medical concern and commercialism, and clearly some confusion around the purpose of the exhibition of the girls in Ontario.

The tensions in the girls' display were real. In August 1939, *The Globe and Mail* frankly reported, "Callander is reconciled to their commercial exploitation as a necessary evil, but resents having them considered mere freaks in a circus sideshow."[55] Yet, despite Dafoe's recently accepted honorary degree of "Doctor of Litters," bestowed in New York by the Circus Saints and Sinners Club in 1939, which he accepted in person, the participation in an actual fair with a real sideshow seemed to trouble him, the press, politicians, and some members of the public.[56] While the girls were never displayed in a true travelling freak show, their actual display in the Dafoe Hospital was, at least, not free from the criticism that it was its own sideshow.

In 1941, the girls were returned to their parents. Their parents had never accepted the removal of the girls from their custody, and the quints' return was the result of their cumulative efforts in combination with pressure from the Catholic Church and the francophone community in Ontario and Quebec.[57] Other potent reasons for their return were "the girls' loss of baby cuteness"; their media overexposure, which meant diminishing media and tourist interest (and a related decline in revenue); and a need to modernize their appearance.[58] In short, by the early 1940s, the quints were rapidly losing commercial value, and a return to their parents quelled some of the rising debate over the government's custody.[59]

The girls' increasing age was a factor. The appropriate display of children for middle-class audiences in the 1930s used "cuteness"—a category also shaped by race and class—to compel a maternal response. Gazing upon five beautiful babies or small children had sentimental value for audience members and could be deemed to be a wholesome and innocent activity. The purity and innocence associated with the tender years was something that could be shared through watching. As Lori Merish argues, "The cute child, unlike the Victorian sacred child, is pure spectacle, pure display. What is lost in this idealization of the cute is sexuality and the dangers of its powers."[60] Gazing upon older children heading into adolescence was another matter. Adolescence is a time of rapid physiological change, and staring at five young women smacked of licentiousness. The display of adolescent women for the public's visual consumption had been a point of public debate in Canada.[61]

While the experience of being gazed upon as "pure spectacle" was something the Dionnes and sideshow performers shared—along with their ability to garner profits—for other children, like Ernie Defort, there was little to no public debate on their precise situation. But in neither case did child welfare organizations become involved.[62] Certainly by the early to mid-twentieth century, there were objections to the degrading influence of sideshows; yet the ongoing popularity of the shows and the significant profits from them reveal the reason for their continuing existence. Moreover, despite the existence of a child welfare movement with growing power, and the very public displays of these children, debate about the appropriateness of sideshows did not focus on children as exploited workers. However, when faced with a rare criticism of the sideshows' interest in "unusual" children, show people had a ready response: sideshows, they argued, offered acceptance, a sense of family, and most importantly, paid work.[63] Both sides of the debate positioned pity and economic need as determining factors, although it must be noted that not all children and parents would have seen their situation as pitiful. Neither pity nor economic desperation is a natural reaction to, or outcome for, people with differences. A close look at the case of Ernie Defort reveals the wider social and cultural structures that made sideshows more complicated sites of work and cultural violence than either side of the debate represented.

Sideshows, Childhood, Work, and Agency

For much of the first half of the twentieth century, exhibitions, fairs, and circuses (all of which carried freak shows) represented childhood fun and the abandonment of both social propriety and the daily grind of life, work, community, and church. Travelling in and out of towns for short periods of time during warm months, the shows represented a life of freedom and escape.[64] Sideshows billed themselves as places of fun for adults and children, but with the rising dominance of youth culture, itself firmly embedded in commercial culture, show promoters began to appeal more directly to children from the 1920s onwards.[65] Special children's days and discounted pricing for admission, or sometimes even no fees for admission to the show, along with reduced rates for rides, were common. In August 1924, a *Globe* article announced, "New Record Reached as 203,000 Children Throng Great Fair." The article on the CNE noted, "The amusements of the Exhibition, and they are so many that for the average visitor one day seems but a moment, suffered a similar fate. Fat people and midgets, clowns and ponies, freaks and houses of mystery—for them was a gala day indeed. But the entire Exhibition lent a free hand and Young Canada underwent no restrictions. Free admission came from the officials of the Exhibition, while from the Midway people the sum of five cents admitted even to the most costly of the main attractions."[66] Despite an outbreak of polio in 1937, the CNE refused to cancel Children's Day that year. While attendance on Children's Day was reduced by 78,000 and the CNE's overall admissions were lower by 300,000, one of the showmen noted that he still managed to break even.[67]

Sideshow promoters seemed especially interested in newsboys; working-class children engaged in low-paying, often late-night, work; and orphans. In 1941, the Shriners and the CNE teamed up to bring 2,000 orphans to the "Ex." According to a newspaper account and accompanying photograph, the children were entertained by Conklin's sideshow and its performers, who would have included Ernie-Len.[68] Appealing to newsboys and orphans allowed the sideshows to stake a claim to working- and middle-class respectability by illustrating a sense of care for local hardworking or vulnerable populations of children. Show managers were also adept at harnessing and exploiting notions of deserving children and pity. In the shifting context of the construction of child welfare, such an appeal was politically, culturally, and commercially savvy. For children who did not live up to the ideal construction of childhood—for example, working children and orphans—the fairgrounds could be a place to reclaim the sense of fun, abandon, and wonder belonging to "normal" childhood. The photographic evidence is telling in its juxtaposition. Children at play on the midway stood outside of Ernie-Len's show-front and saw his body as a representation of difference and entertainment value. Behind the canvas, he would have been working.

Working-class newsboys and orphans, along with the other children who attended, got a break at the fair, but for other children, sideshows were not entertainment but work. Either on or off stage (and almost regardless of economic need), transient work on the sideshows existed beyond the constructions of either respectable work or dominant middle-class visions of childhood. Children's labour had long been an important resource for Canadian families, especially working ones, but during the Depression, even middle-class children were expected to contribute in both formal and informal ways to the family economy.[69] With the Depression, children's paid employment took on deeper significance for family survival, and children, sometimes willingly and sometimes grudgingly, helped their families survive by leaving school to bring in an income. Others balanced school and paid labour, took on unwaged work in the home or on the farm, or engaged in informal, illegal activities like stealing. Conflicts with the police, educational authorities, child welfare authorities, and even within families regarding the proper activities for children were common.[70] Children's labour was often about survival, so breaking the law, working at night, leaving school, and turning over portions or the whole of pay packets were about need and often resulted from parental unemployment.[71] For many families, an alternative such as "relief," a limited welfare strategy, was difficult to attain, wrapped in shame, and inadequate.[72] While sideshow performances were not often seen as respectable work, they continued to be a good draw of people and money. Even in the heart of the Depression, sideshows continued to make money, and the persistence of the smaller companies certainly speaks to their popularity, if not their ability to turn a profit. Ernie-Len was reported to have made $14,000 in the seven years he worked only summer circuits.[73]

Economic necessity would have certainly shaped the decision of Ernie Defort's family to exhibit him, as well as Oliva Dionne's decision to enter into a contract with Spear. Ernie's mother recalled, "My husband was out of work then and I thought the travelling would build up my boy's health."[74] As with many biographies of sideshow child performers, however, the actual negotiations that brought Ernie-Len to show remain largely undocumented. But the wider context of the care of children with disabilities may be illuminating. In Depression-era Winnipeg, a child with a so-called parasitic twin, and who might need substantial medical attention, could have been seen as a social and economic burden to the family. Work as a spectacle on the sideshow might have been rationalized as a means of off-setting potentially expensive medical care and treatment and/or decreasing dependency on other family members. In 1937, Ernie and his parents travelled to Europe to consult with doctors on the possibility of separating the twins. They were told such surgery would lead to death.[75] The possibility of receiving medical care and of making a living might have made freak work appealing. Unlike some other sideshow child performers, Ernie was not fully removed from his parents' care by means of an informal adoption.[76] Nonetheless, Ernie's work as a freak provided the chance for some semblance of "normal" childhood during the off-season when he was not performing, and it seems to have ultimately provided the financial means for his decision in the early 1940s to undergo surgery to remove Lester. Sideshow life promised financial reward.

The birth of a child, while potentially joyful, was also a time of increased vulnerability, especially economically, for many families. Such vulnerability is apparent in the offers both made and received by the New York World's Fair. In 1939 and 1940, New York hosted a World's Fair, and from 1938 onward organizers had attempted to secure the Dionne quints as an exhibit. While multiple attempts failed, news of the offer to the family caused North American parents, along with at least one teacher, one newspaper editor, and one doctor, among others, to write to the Fair offering children with a range of disabilities for exhibition. This collection of letters is extraordinary in that it documents parents' and other adults' reasons for offering children as freaks. Importantly, the letters also reveal that it was not just showmen's search for freaks that brought children to the sideshows as paid performers.

The rumour of a one-million-dollar offer to the Dionne quints certainly helped motivate the letter writing. A Mrs Orbeck from Lloydminster, Alberta, for example, offered her two albino sons, aged 18 and 9, writing, "The government wanted to take them but I would not agree to that. People have come from far to see these boys, nobody has ever seen any body like them. Everybody says that I should put them in a side show. Everybody seen in the paper about taking the Dionne Quintriplets. They say why not haves my sons there too as they are just as odd as them."[77] Two large French-Canadian families—the Masse family of Exeter, Ontario, and the Bourassa family of Saint-Barnabé, Quebec—offered themselves for exhibition based solely on their size.[78] The letters reveal that economic necessity was a compelling reason for the offers. With the exception of people writing about children who were not their own, none of the letters was without a sense of care for the child. Some parents took pride in their children's differences and talents, some were deeply embarrassed, and some saw their child's existence as pitiful and unfortunate but as having special value in teaching others that not all children were "normal." Many parents of infants were clearly coming to terms with the lack of options available to them and saw the sideshow as a legitimate, if not preferable, one for their child.

The letters from the New York World's Fair files reveal the mix of economic desperation, disappointment, and embarrassment in having an extraordinary child, but they also convey care and concern. One letter by an American father reveals the complexities:

> Just a few words. I am sorry to write to you about my baby boy, that is so deformed, at birth, May 6, 1939.
>
> He has no arms, and has but one leg. But his is a normal baby from what the doctors say, and there is no cure for him. We tried so not to bring him home, But they said that they couldn't place the baby in an institution, because it was to young.

> We are poor people and are on Home Relieve and me and the Mres thought that we would like to put the baby on exhibition at the Worlds Fair, so that other people can see that every baby can't be normal. We have another baby girl 3 years old, which is alright, and very bright. This baby is going to be a burden on us if it lives the rest of our lives. The doctor at the Hospital said that he had never seen or heard of anything like this before as long as he has been a doctor, and the people I speak to say the same. They never seen anything like it before if you can not put it on exhibition at the World's Fair, please write me and tell me what to do. Maybe there is a place to send him to, You see it isn't so bad now. But when it grows up it will be an awful burden as is. So please do what you can for us, every body else turns us down.[79]

Poverty and disability merged to bring certain children to the sideshow or, at least, provided the context for their being offered.

One letter from an American physician to the New York's World Fair, about a child with missing limbs, expressed regret that it seemed the disabled child would live. As research on American history reveals, the birth of a child with disabilities in the period sometimes led to passive or active euthanizing.[80] From the perspective of many doctors, institutionalization was a good strategy. Yet, the decision was complicated by a host of factors including economic means, location, and levels of care. While physicians might have expressed regret regarding a child's life or recommended institutionalization, parents need not have always shared those ideas.[81] The surrender of a child—temporarily or permanently—was hardly a decision made lightly.[82] By the 1920s, provincial institutions were overwhelmed with less "desirable" children. By the end of the decade—before the massive economic crisis of the Depression—one staff member of the Canadian Council of Child Welfare reported on the deplorable state of "disabled" and "undesirable" children already in institutions. As Strong-Boag concludes, "abnormality stigmatized countless children and helped ensure that they would be hard put to find supporters or function with confidence."[83]

Sideshow owners and employees repeatedly defended their exhibits and way of life as being more humane for those labelled "freaks," and given the wider social, cultural, and economic context of the period, this cannot be simply dismissed as a crass effort to defend against exploitation. As British Columbian carnival agent and promoter Hazel Elves explained,

> Many people who do not fit into every day life find their way into the carnival grounds: people with physical disabilities or those condemned by nature to be different from the so called norm. Freaks you call them, side show entertainers we call them; human beings with feelings and desires as all people have. They fit in, on the carnival, as most carnies see people for what they are. They are able to work with each other performing the many hazards which constitute carnival life. Here they are all safe and if people wish to stare at least they must pay for the privilege, affording these special people a chance to work and maintain themselves.[84]

Other sideshow performers, like Celesta Geyer, who worked from the 1920s to the 1950s, recalled the limited but still important power they had in being able to speak back to audience members or at least make them pay for the privilege of staring.[85] Significantly, however, these were adult performers. Part of the lure of the child, especially the infant, was the restrictions on their ability to speak back or control the nature of their own display. They were the least confrontational performers, although as the case of the Dionnes reveals, they could still cry, act obnoxiously, and as toddlers and children, refuse to perform "properly."[86]

Freak shows have been rightfully questioned for their role in upholding and perpetuating stereotypes of corporeal difference, and they were no doubt difficult and complicated sites of work. Scholars have more recently challenged the simplistic dichotomy between disability and the ability to find meaningful work that underscores Elves's perspective on the acceptance of "freaks."[87] Yet in the context of the very limited opportunities available during the middle decades of the twentieth century, this perspective reflects the perpetuation of structures of violence that reduced choices for parents and children and rested inequalities on the bodies of children who were cast as different. The sideshow was framed as a safe place for children who would otherwise experience pain, ridicule, and mistreatment in a parallel way that the Ontario government argued the Dionnes must be protected from "ignorant" parents and their suspicious deals with showmen. The quints and Ernie-Len are related examples of the way structural violence made the privilege of "protected" childhood disappear in dehumanizing commercial spectacles that shored up stigmas about disabled people, reaffirmed the culturally produced line between normality and abnormality, and perpetuated cultural violence.[88] Given the options and strategies available to parents at the time, sideshows can be seen as having been a means to assert some agency, to find paid work, and perhaps to gain some acceptance and care. Work as a "freak" on the sideshow may have been a strategy of securing care born out of necessity for some children with intellectual or physical differences. For Ernie, the situation was even more atypical, as sideshow work provided funds for the radical surgery to "norm" his body.

Norming the Disabled Child Body

The 1920s witnessed an intensification of defining normal children, normal families, and normal childhood. Constructing and mobilizing categories of "normal" as well as "childhood" created a hierarchy of classifications for children and their families.[89] By the 1930s, discourses structuring normalcy and child welfare had solidified to the point that provincial governments—led by Ontario—had developed complex systems of regulation of and intervention into families that fell outside the norm.[90] Being outside the realm of "normal" meant that these children would never mature into "normal" adulthood, and dominant medical discourse argued for early identification, intervention, and containment of "the disabled child."[91]

From school-based surveillance and intervention to more institutional and community-based strategies designed to house and care for orphaned, abandoned, surrendered, and otherwise vulnerable children, such seemingly well-intentioned efforts upheld white, middle-class ideologies (with the presumption that "ability" was natural and permanent) and often exacerbated vulnerabilities.[92] Childhood as a hegemonic construct provided for measures of protection for certain children and formed part of structural violence. Children such as sideshow freaks and the Dionne quints were not children for all that they were merely meant to represent childhood and were not deemed worthy of privacy.[93]

In the early 1940s, Ernie made the decision to undergo surgery to remove his twin at the Mayo Clinic, and as with the Dionne quintuplets, his performances, which required nudity or semi-nudity, ended as he entered into adolescence. After the successful surgery by Dr Henry W. Meyerding, the doctor reported that the twin "had sapped much of the strength of the boy [Ernie] before its removal."[94] When interviewed post-surgery by a reporter from the *Winnipeg Tribune* in 1944, Ernie provided a fascinatingly oblique response to the question "Why did you decide to have this operation?" He is quoted having said, "I made up my mind to have it done and that was all there was to it. I didn't want to keep on the way I was, and an operation was the only answer."[95] It is unclear from the documentary record whether Ernie was referring to living with the conjoined asymmetrical twin or to working as a sideshow performer. In newspaper reports, Dr Meyerding suggested, "Ernie was depressed at the thought of losing the twin body."[96] The surgery was heralded as a success and widely reported in newspapers across North America for making Ernie a "normal" boy. Although Patty Conklin continued to discuss Ernie-Len in interviews and press releases, Ernie did not return to the sideshows as a performer after the surgery.[97]

Sideshow owners and promoters like Conklin were not immune to shifts in child welfare discourses that were rooted in wider social and cultural shifts, and beginning in the 1920s the billing of freak performers changed to tap into both medical discourses and new standards of care and education. Pamphlets and *cartes de visites* sold at the show, along with other promotional material, reveal the changes, as owners appealed to audiences' sense of charity or duty by emphasizing that profits would go to the education of the child.[98] In the presentation of the extraordinariness of Ernie-Len's body, Conklin appealed to ideals of "normal" middle-class experiences such as schooling, the celebration of birthdays, and interest in particular hobbies. In 1943, the *Fort William Daily Times Journal* reported, "Questioned regarding Ernie Defort, the two-bodied boy from Winnipeg, who was with him for seven years, Mr Conklin stated that the boy's operation performed at Rochester [the Mayo Clinic] on October 17, 1943, was a success and Ernie is coming along fine, although he still has to have another operation. He said that it is Ernie's ambition to become a music composer. 'Ernie is musically inclined and while in Winnipeg last week I purchased him a violin so he could study music,' said Mr. Conklin. He added that he plans to send him to Rochester this summer to undergo his final operation."[99] Conklin's statement revealed the potential benevolence of a sideshow owner and could have reassured audience members that their gawking had done well in contributing to the norming of an "abnormal" child. It may have also presented a compelling argument for desperate parents in search of some means of economic relief and care. In an era where medical treatment was expensive, the sideshow could offer a means of securing money for any available treatment.

In the celebratory articles on the surgery that removed the parasitic twin from Ernie Defort, reporters, physicians, and other commentators on Ernie's body repeatedly highlighted the norming of his body through surgery. A few mentioned the sense of grief and loss Ernie experienced in being separated from his brother, but the overall sense was that Ernie had been saved from abnormality.[100] The surgery to "norm" Ernie's body by removing Lester's was based on particular ideas of what counted as normalcy. One of the cultural functions of the sideshow was to reaffirm the normal bodies of audience members by showing them what they were not. In doing so, freak shows were engaged in cultural violence.

Treatment such as that of Ernie-Len's body was and remains complicated, potentially life-threatening, and painful. In early to mid-twentieth century Canada, the cultural push and policing of the category of "normal" and the dominant need to contain the disabled body of children could be a powerful form of cultural violence.

Conclusion

One article reported Ernie's response to his work on the sideshows: "I'm through with all that—forever. But it might have been worse."[101] Ernie's comment is telling, as it suggests a sense of discomfort with his sideshow past. Real material needs shaped relationships between the sideshows and those they displayed, but these relationships cannot be simply conceived of as exploitative, as though the problem rested with the sideshow itself. Structures of poverty, as well as paying audiences with an interest in the usual, the spectacular, and the extraordinary must also be considered factors. Sideshows included not just a fringe group but a much wider swathe of people who, as consumers, participated in the maintenance of the freak show. As *Protecting the Dionnes*, a pamphlet written by and to advertise Lysol cleaner, aptly stated, "The world has marvelled at the blooming health and vitality of the five babies. . . . "[102] If Ernie-Len's experience as a sideshow performer fell well beyond the idealized hegemonic construction of childhood through his spectacularization as a freak, his "corrective" surgery allowed him to disappear from the public's gaze, an option never afforded to the Dionnes. Given contemporary prejudices against disability and difference, sideshow life may have provided some measure of economic security among a host of other limited options, but it was not a bulwark against a cruel world—it was part of it. If not able to find a place within the category of childhood (and the protection that deserving children received), in the sideshow one could perhaps find comfort in being a child who had carved out some place of significance with some measure of material comfort. Perhaps one of the greatest tragedies of the Dionnes is that they could not find such comfort. In one of the sideshow canvases for Ernie-Len, he was described as "Canada's Problem Boy," and the persistent problem seems to be our collective inability to challenge the structures that produce child poverty and the (not unrelated) cultural assumption of a singular normal, able body.

Overall, the continued existence of freak shows and their popularity into the 1970s certainly reflects a massive social and cultural failure to address small, different bodies in meaningful, humane ways. In short, it is structural and cultural violence rendered in and through the social construction of the category of childhood that put the Dionne quintuplets and Ernie Defort in harm's way. They were seen almost exclusively as different—and that difference was irreconcilable with the category of childhood that would have seen them deemed children deserving of a certain type of protection and care. The shame remains that finding a place for such children in early to mid-twentieth-century Canada meant perpetuating the cultural violence inherent in definitions of absolute difference and freakery. But that shame lies with the society and the culture, not with the individual.

Acknowledgments

Research funding came from the Social Sciences and Humanities Research Council of Canada. Special thanks to Jennifer Walker of the North American Carnival Museum and Archives, and to research assistants Whitney Wood, Sabrina del Ben, Jamilee Baroud, and Ulysses Patola.

Notes

1. Cynthia Comacchio, *Nations are Built of Babies: Saving Ontario's Mothers and Children* (Montreal and Kingston: McGill-Queen's University Press, 1993), 213–216.
2. See, for example, Pierre Berton, *The Dionne Years: A Thirties Melodrama* (Toronto: McClelland & Stewart, 1977); Veronica Strong-Boag, "Intruders in the Nursery: Childcare Professionals Reshape the Years One to Five, 1920–1940" in *Childhood and Family in Canadian History* edited by Joy Parr (Toronto: McClelland & Stewart, 1982), 160–178; Mariana Valverde, "Representing Childhood:

The Multiple Fathers of the Dionne Quintuplets," in *Regulating Womanhood: Historical Essays on Marriage, Motherhood and Sexuality* edited by Carol Smart (New York and London: Routledge, 1993), 119–146; and the Winter 1994 issue of the *Journal of Canadian Studies* on the Dionnes.

3. For an example from the Ringling Bros.–Barnum & Bailey Combined Shows, the largest touring North American spectacle in the period, see, University of California Santa Barbara [hereafter UCSB], Toole-Stott collection Clyde Ingalls, newspaper clipping, box 42, "Strange Loves and Ambitions of Circus Freaks" and "Hidden Tragedies of the People of Never-Never Land."

4. North American Carnival Museum and Archives [hereafter NACMA], Conklin Scrapbooks 1940s, newspaper clipping.

5. "Miracle Operation Proves Successful," *Winnipeg Free Press* 10 February 1944, 1.

6. NACMA, Conklin Scrapbook, pamphlet.

7. NACMA, Conklin Scrapbook, photograph.

8. William Good, "Surgery Makes Him One," *Winnipeg Tribune*, 10 February 1944, 1, 11. Patty Conklin's ongoing presence may have influenced this particular version of Ernie's history with the sideshow. According to Pierre Berton, the Dionne quintuplets were of interest to more than one sideshow promoter. Berton, *The Dionne Years*, 59.

9. Joe McKennon, *A Pictorial History of the American Carnival: Volumes I and II* (Sarasota, FL: Carnival Publishers, 1972), 160.

10. Valverde, "Representing Childhood," 122. See also her "Families, Private Property and the State," *Journal of Canadian Studies*, 29, no. 4 (Winter 1994), 15–35.

11. Valverde, "Representing Childhood," 119.

12. Published sources that support this conclusion include Stanley Appelbaum, *The Chicago World's Fair of 1893: A Photographic Record* (New York: Dover, 1980), 95; Kenneth Coates and McGuiness, *Pride of the Land: An Affectionate History of Brandon's Agricultural Exhibitions* (Winnipeg: Peguis Publishers, 1985); David C. Jones, *Midways, Judges, and Smooth-Tongued Fakirs: The Illustrated Story of Country Fairs in the Prairie West* (Saskatoon: Western Producer Prairie Books, 1983); H.W. Waters, *History of Fairs and Expositions: Their Classification, Functions and Values* (London, ON: Reid Bros. & Co. Limited, 1939), 127; McKenzie Porter, "Queen of the Midway," *Maclean's* 1 October 149, 60. It is also supported by archival evidence from Vancouver's PNE and Toronto's CNE.

13. See Paul Farmer, "On Suffering and Structural Violence: A View from Below," *Daedalus* 125, no. 1 (Winter 1996): 261–283.

14. I have chosen to refer to the twins as Ernie. I have used Ernie-Len only when referring to performances.

15. Johan Galtung, "Cultural Violence," *Journal of Peace Research* 27 (1990): 295.

16. Paul Farmer, *Pathologies of Power: Health, Human Rights, and the New War on the Poor* (Berkeley: University of California Press, 2003), 50.

17. Nic Clarke, "Sacred Daemons: Exploring British Columbian Society's Perceptions of 'Mentally Deficient' Children, 1870–1930," *BC Studies* 144 (Winter 2004/2005): 63–64. [See also earlier in this chapter.]

18. Clarke, "Sacred Daemons," 65, note 17 and Rosemary Garland Thomson, *Extraordinary Bodies: Figuring Physical Disability in American Culture and Literature* (New York: Columbia University Press, 1997).

19. Major works on the history of the freak show in the twentieth century include Robert Bogdan, *Freak Show: Presenting Human Oddities for Amusement and Profit* (Chicago: University of Chicago Press, 1988); Rosemarie Garland Thomson, Ed. *Freakery: Cultural Spectacles of the Extraordinary Body*, (New York: New York University Press, 1996); Garland Thomson, *Extraordinary Bodies*; Rachel Adams, *Sideshow U.S.A.* (Chicago: University of Chicago Press, 2001); and Nadja Durbach, *Spectacles of Deformity: Freak Shows and Modern British Culture* (Berkeley: University of California Press, 2010).

20. Jane Nicholas, "A Debt to the Dead? Ethics, Photography, History and the Study of Freakery," *Histoire sociale/Social History* 47, no. 93 (May 2014) 139–55.

21. Mary Jo Maynes, "Age as a Category of Historical Analysis: History, Agency, and Narratives of Childhood," *Journal of the History of Childhood and Youth* 1, no. 1 (Winter 2008): 114–124 and Kristine Alexander, "Can the Girl Guide Speak?" *Jeunesse: Young Peoples, Texts, Cultures*, 4, no.1 (2012): 132. [See also Chapter 4 of this volume.]

22. Gleason's concept of "empathetic inference" is quoted in Alexander, "Can the Girl Guide Speak?," 142.

23. "Change of Diet Is Beneficial to Quintuplets," *Globe* 1 June 1934 and "Order Obtained for Guardians of Dionne Babes," *Globe* 27 July 1934.

24. For an overview see Valverde, "Representing Childhood," 123–124.

25. The suit, filed in Chicago, was dismissed. Newspapers covered the proceedings. See AO, RG 3 Premier Mitchell F. Hepburn, Press Clippings, Dionne Case. 1 September 1938-30 April 1939, Dept. of Welfare.

26. Archives of Ontario [hereafter AO], Premier Mitchell F. Hepburn Press Clippings, Dionne Case, 1934–36, "Dionnes Irk Mr. Hepburn" *Border Cities Star* 9 February 1935.

27. "Dionne Bill" *Globe* 12 March 1935, p. 2.

28. Comacchio, *Nations Are Built of Babies*, 13. Comacchio notes that, despite the intensity of the message, women ignored, discounted, or modified such advice and continued to rely on the advice of family and community members. See also Denyse Baillargeon, *Babies for the Nation: The Medicalization of Motherhood in Quebec, 1910-1970*.

29. Mona Gleason, "Race, Class and Health: School Inspection and 'Healthy' Children in British Columbia,

1890–1930," *Canadian Bulletin of Medical History* 19, no. 1 (2002): 95–112.

30. Angus McLaren, *Our Own Master Race: Eugenics in Canada, 1885–1945* (Toronto: McClelland & Stewart, 1990). Of note here were the official and unofficial programs of sterilization of those adults and children deemed "unfit."

31. Kathryn Arnup, *Education for Motherhood: Advice for Mothers in Twentieth-Century Canada* (Toronto: University of Toronto Press, 1994), 97, 132.

32. Berton, *The Dionne Years*, 11.

33. On the Canadian National Exhibition see Keith Walden, *Becoming Modern in Toronto: The Industrial Exhibition and the Shaping of a Late Victorian Culture* (Toronto: University of Toronto Press, 1997), 287–288.

34. "Deformitomania" is quoted from the British newspaper *Punch* in Erin O'Connor, *Raw Material: Producing Pathology in Victorian Culture* (Durham, NC: Duke University Press, 2000), 148.

35. AO, Attorney General's Files, Travelling Sideshows and Circuses; AO, Attorney General's Files, Office of the Attorney General, RG 4-32, File 1636; AO, Attorney General's Files, Circuses and Travelling Shows, 1919–1921, RG 23-26-20, File # 1.57; AO, Attorney General's Files, Circuses and Travelling Shows, 1919–1921, RG 23-26-20.

36. UCSB Toole-Stott Collection, Box 2, File "Correspondence," Letter from Cyril B. Mills to Toole-Stott, 7 June 1934.

37. The evidence is voluminous. For example see, City of Saskatoon Archives, 1069-1062 (3) Licensing, 1931 letter to Frank Miley from City Clerk 29 July 1931; Library and Archives Canada [hereafter LAC], RG 76, Volume 594, File 841690, Part 3, letter from Minister of Immigration and Colonization to Rev. J.H. Edmison, 20 June 1921; AO, Attorney General's Files, Circuses and Travelling Shows, 1919–1921, RG 23-26-20, File # 1.57, and City of Vancouver Archives, S-10-2 Box 524 C-6 folder 1 Bulletins 1913–1924, Vancouver Exhibition—Bulletin No. 8, no. 8, p. 51 and Jones, *Midways, Judges, and Smooth-Tongued Fakirs*, 51–53.

38. Stanley Appelbaum, *The Chicago World's Fair of 1893: A Photographic Record* (New York: Dover, 1980), 95; Robert Rydell, *World of Fairs: The Century-of-Progress Expositions* (Chicago: University of Chicago Press, 1993); and Elspeth Heaman, *Inglorious Arts of Peace: Exhibitions in Canadian Society during the Nineteenth Century* (Toronto: University of Toronto Press, 1999), 250.

39. Cynthia Comacchio, *The Dominion of Youth: Adolescence and the Making of Modern Canada, 1920–1950* (Waterloo: Wilfrid Laurier University Press, 2006), chapter 6.

40. Valverde, "Representing Childhood," 129.

41. Berton, *The Dionne Years*, 158.

42. Bogdan, *Freak Show*. Rosemarie Garland Thomson also notes the importance of the spiel given by an "expert," the related promotion material like pamphlets, the costuming

and theatrics of the display, and the photographs in the making of sideshow exhibits. See her "Introduction: From Wonder to Error—A Genealogy of Freak Discourse in Modernity" in *Freakery*, 7.

43. Patricia Jasen, *Wild Things: Nature, Culture, and Tourism in Ontario, 1790–1914* (Toronto: University of Toronto Press, 1995), chapter 5 and Sharon Wall, *The Nature of Nurture: Childhood, Antimodernism, and Ontario Summer Camps, 1920–55* (Vancouver: University of British Columbia Press, 2010). On the quints, see Valverde, "Families, Private Property, and the State."

44. Susan J. Pearson, "'Infantile Specimens': Showing Babies in Nineteenth-Century America," *Journal of Social History* Winter 2008: 346.

45. Lois Banner, *American Beauty* (New York: Alfred A. Knopf, 1983), 250–257.

46. Pearson, "'Infantile Specimens,'" 362.

47. Interestingly, all also owe a debt to P.T. Barnum's career. On the baby contests see Susan J. Pearson, "'Infantile Specimens,'" 341–370 and, for twentieth-century Canada see, Gerald E. Thomson, "'A Baby Show Means Work in the Hardest Sense': The Better Baby Contests of the Vancouver and New Westminster Local Councils of Women, 1913–1939," *BC Studies* 128 (Winter 2000–2001): 5–36; on freak shows and the construction of normalcy, see Bogdan, *Freak Show*.

48. "Walter Wicks Wins at Boys' Baby Show" *Toronto Daily Star* 19 September 1927, p. 26; "Baby Contest Will Attract Many Entries" *Vancouver Sun* 4 June 1927, p. 2; AO 17-1 Original Newspaper Collection, *News Mirror* 31 May 1924, pp. 15 and 22 and 14 June 1924, p. 23; "Babies Purr and Gurgle with Delight," *The Globe* 7 September 1920, p. 5; "Roma Holland Prize Baby, Quickly Stars in Movies," *Evening Telegram* 6 September 1927, p. 24 and *Hamilton Spectator* 6 September 1927, p. 1.

49. They were not joined at the thorax.

50. NACMA, Conklin Scrapbooks, 1930s, pamphlets and photos.

51. Berton, *The Dionne Years*, 68, Pearson, "'Infantile Specimens.'"

52. LAC, MG 31 J18, Louise de Kiriline fonds, Letters to Hillevid de Flach, 28 September 1937.

53. AO, RG 3, Hepburn Pressing Clippings, 1 September 1938–30 April 1939, and Berton, *The Dionne Years*, 186.

54. "Retirement of Quints Predicted by Dafoe," *Globe and Mail* 6 December 1938, p. 1.

55. "Artistic Career Seen for Quints," *Globe and Mail* 1 August 1939.

56. "Club Initiates Dafoe as 'Doctor of Litters,'" *Globe* 13 April 1939.

57. Denyse Baillargeon, *Babies for the Nation: The Medicalization of Motherhood in Quebec, 1910–1970*, transl. W. Donald Wilson (Waterloo, ON: Wilfrid Laurier University Press, 2009), 63.

58. Valverde, "Representing Childhood." See also Cynthia

Comacchio, *The Infinite Bonds of Family: Domesticity in Canada, 1850–1940* (Toronto: University of Toronto Press, 1999), 137. The quints' reintegration with their birth family was difficult, and decades later, the three surviving quints wrote a book accusing their father of sexual abuse. See *Family Secrets: The Dionne Quintuplets' Own Story* (New York: Berkley, 1997).

59. AO, RG 3-14, B 308107—Premier Mitchell F. Hepburn Press Clippings, Box 407 Mitchell F. Hepburn Press Clippings, Dionne Case.

60. Lori Merish, "Cuteness and Commodity Aesthetics: Tom Thumb and Shirley Temple" in *Freakery and the Extraordinary Body*, 188.

61. Comacchio, *The Dominion of Youth*. Beauty contests are a good example of the debate. See Jane Nicholas, *The Modern Girl: Feminine Modernities, Commodities, and the Body in the 1920s* (Toronto: University of Toronto Press, 2014) chapter 4.

62. On the Dionnes see, Valverde, "Family, Private Property and the State." I have been unable to find records of child welfare involvement with child freak performers.

63. For an example from each side of the debate, see the article by noted British physician John Bland-Sutton, "A Lecture on the Psychology of Conjoined Twins: A Study of Monsterhood" *British Medical Journal* 1, no. 3548 (5 January 1929): 1–4, and William Lindsay Gresham, *Monster Midway: An Uninhibited Look at the Glittering World of the Carny* (New York and Toronto: Rinehart and Company Inc., 1953), 101.

64. See, for example, accounts of visiting the freak show in Neil Sutherland, *Growing Up: Childhood in English Canada from the Great War to the Age of Television* (Toronto: University of Toronto Press, 1997), 176–177 and Jones, *Midways, Fairs, and Smooth-Tongued Fakirs*, Grant MacEwan, *Between the Red and the Rockies* (Toronto: University of Toronto Press, 1952).

65. Comacchio, *The Dominion of Youth*.

66. "New Record Reached as 203,000 Children Throng Great Fair," *Globe* 27 August 1924.

67. On the 1937 polio epidemic and the CNE see, Christopher J. Rutty, "The Middle Class Plague: Epidemic Polio and the Canadian State," *Canadian Bulletin of Medical History* 13, no. 2 (1996): 289–291; Lewiston, *Freak Show Man*, 218.

68. For examples of these types of appeals to children, see Canadian National Exhibition Archives, CNE catalogues from the 1920s to 1960s. Young Canada Day became Children's Day in 1935. See also *Fort William Daily Times Journal* 28 August 1923, 18 August 1930, 3 August 1940, 2 August 1952, and 9 August 1962. On newsboys' work during the Great Depression, see Lara Campbell, *Respectable Citizens: Gender, Family and Unemployment in Ontario's Great Depression* (Toronto: University of Toronto Press, 2009), 93–94. On the orphans see NACMA, Conklin Scrapbook 1941, newspaper clippings.

69. Sutherland, *Growing Up*, 114.

70. Campbell, *Respectable Citizens*, chapter 3.

71. Gender differences are important to note here. See Campbell, *Respectable Citizens*, 95.

72. James Struthers, *The Limits of Affluence: Welfare in Ontario, 1920–1970* (Toronto: University of Toronto Press, 1994); and Campbell, *Respectable Citizens*.

73. Reportedly, once school aged, he worked only during the summer. NACMA, Conklin Scrapbook Newspaper Clipping.

74. "Miracle Operation Proves Successful," *Winnipeg Free Press* 10 February 1944, 1.

75. NACMA, Conklin Scrapbook, newspaper clippings.

76. On informal adoption in the sideshows from a largely uncritical perspective see Joe Nickell, *Secrets of the Sideshows* (Lexington: University of Kentucky Press, 2005), chapter 6 and Ward Hall, *Struggles and Triumphs of a Modern Day Showman: An Autobiography* (Sarasota, FL: Carnival Publishers of Sarasota, 1981). On adoption and children with disabilities see Veronica Strong-Boag, *Fostering Nation? Canada Confronts Its History of Childhood Disadvantage* (Waterloo: Wilfrid Laurier University Press, 2011).

77. New York Public Library (NYPL) Manuscripts and Archives Division New York World's Fair 1939/40 Central Files, P1 630, Box 540, File 3, letter from Mrs Ed Orbeck dated 9 February 1939.

78. NYPL, New York World's Fair 1939/1940 Central Files, File 9.

79. NYPL, New York World's Fair 1939/40 Central Files, File 9 "P1 637 Freaks A–K (1939).

80. Martin S. Pernick, *The Black Stork: Eugenics and the Death of "Defective" Babies in American Medicine and Motion Pictures Since 1915* (New York: Oxford University Press, 1996).

81. Jessa Chupik and Donald Wright, "Treating the 'Idiot' Child in Early 20th-Century Ontario" *Disability and Society* 21, no. 1 (2006): 87.

82. Strong-Boag, *Fostering Nation?* chapter 5; Clarke, "Sacred Daemons," and Chupik and Wright, "Treating the 'Idiot' Child in Early 20th-Century Ontario."

83. Strong-Boag, *Fostering Nation?* The Canadian Council for Child Welfare staffer is quoted on pages 56–57. Strong-Boag's conclusion can be found on page 57.

84. Hazel Elves, *It's All Done with Mirrors: A Story of Canadian Carnival Life* (Victoria: Sono Nis Press, 1977), 19.

85. See, for example, Celesta "Dolly Dimples" Geyer with Samuel Roen, *Diet or Die: The Dolly Dimples Weight Reducing Plan* (New York: F. Fell, 1968), 115.

86. For example, "Yvonne Goes 'On Strike' Can't See Pups, Won't Act" *Toronto Star* 8 June 1938.

87. Brigham A. Fordham, "Dangerous Bodies: Freaks Shows, Expression, Exploitation," *UCLA Entertainment Law Review* 14, no. 207 (2007).

88. Ernie-Len's performances required nudity, which added a significant layer to other vulnerabilities.

89. Mona Gleason, *Normalizing the Ideal: Psychology, Schooling and the Family in Postwar Canada* (Toronto: University of Toronto Press, 1999).

90. As Valverde notes, Ontario was influential in developing welfare and social services because of its size and financial resources. Valverde, "Representing Childhood," 120.

91. Mona Gleason, *Small Matters: Canadian Children in Sickness and Health, 1900–1940* (Montreal and Kingston: McGill-Queen's University Press), 120–121.

92. See Strong-Boag, *Fostering Nation?* and Mona Gleason, *Small Matters.*

93. Valverde's "Representing Childhood" argues that the Dionnes were also not children.

94. NACMA Conklin Scrapbook, newspaper clipping, "Surgeon Removes 'Parasitic Twin,' Boy Now Normal."

95. William Good, "Surgery Makes Him One" *Winnipeg Tribune*, 10 February 1944, 1, 11.

96. The quotation appears in a number of newspapers using reporting from the Associated Press (AP). These include "Parasitic Twin Cut from Youth: Clinic Performs Operation Formerly Held Fatal," *The Deseret News* 11 February, 1944; "'Siamese Twin' Cut from Boy," *Eugene Register-Guard* 11 February 1944; and "Boy Normal After Partial Twin Removed From Body," *The Free Lance-Star* 11 February 1944.

97. A.W. Stencell reports that Ernie worked behind the scenes at various shows in the 1950s before becoming a banker. See A.W. Stencell, *Circus and Carnival Ballyhoo: Sideshow Freaks, Jaggers, and Blade Box Queens* (Toronto: ECW Press, 2010), 272.

98. NACMA, Conklin Scrapbook 1935, *carte-de-visite.*

99. "'Patty' Conklin Urges Paved Midway at Fair," *Fort William Daily Times Journal* 8 August 1944. In all quotes, the errors in spelling or grammar are true to the original. I have not included "(sic)" after each error as I find it obnoxious.

100. See, for example, "Parasitic Twin Severed from Body of Boy, 12: Extra Arms, Legs, and Liver Removed; Winnipeg Youth Now Reported Normal," *Pittsburgh Post-Gazette* 11 February 1944; "Knife Gives Normal Life to Partial Twin," *The Palm Beach Post* 11 February 1944; "Boy Normal After Partial Twin Removed from Body," *The Free-Lance Star* 11 February 1944; and "Surgery Makes Him One: Through with Sideshows Now, Young Defort Is Happy at School," *Winnipeg Tribune*, 10 February 1944.

101. NACMA, Conklin Scrapbook, newspaper clippings.

102. AO, F1322, B253341, MU 7486-1137, Joseph Sedgwick Fonds, Dionne Quintuplets Correspondence and Guardianship, "Protecting the Dionnes."

PRIMARY DOCUMENT

Ernie-Len Promotion, c. 1935

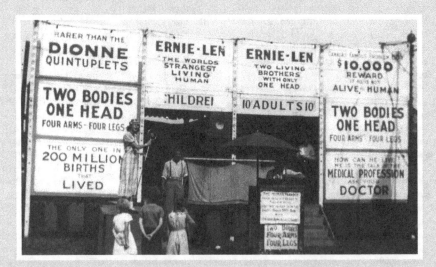

Source: Ernie and Len Single-O front, c. 1935. Courtesy of The Carnival Museum, F01-AC2014002.

Study Questions

1. Consider the role of experts in deciding definitions of "normal" children and childhoods in Clarke's essay in this chapter. How did families respond to the power of experts? What do their responses tell us about the ability of families to shape their children's experiences?
2. Note that the primary sources that accompany Clarke's and Nicholas's essays in this chapter trade on strong emotions: fear, sadness, shock, and anxiety, for example. Is emotional investment particularly important in the histories explored in this chapter? Why?
3. What difference do race, class, age, and gender make to the histories explored in Clarke's and Nicholas's essays? Do the authors do an adequate job of exploring these important categories of historical analysis?

Selected Bibliography

Articles

Barmaki, Reza, "The Bourgeois Order and the "Normal" Child: The Case of Ontario, 1867–1900," *International Journal of Mental Health and Addiction* 5, 3 (May 2007): 263–76.

Bullen, John, "Orphans, Idiots, Lunatics, and Historians: Recent Approaches to the History of Child Welfare in Canada," *Social history/Historie sociale* 18, 35 (May 1985): 133–145.

Dickinson, Harley D., "Scientific Parenthood: The Mental Hygiene Movement and the Reform of Canadian Families, 1925–1950," *Journal of Comparative Family Studies* 24 (Autumn 1993): 387–402.

Ellis, Jason, "'All Methods—and Wedded to None: The Deaf Education Methods Debate and Progressive Educational Reform in Toronto, Canada, 1922–1945," *Paedagogica Historica* 50, 3 (2014): 371–89.

Ellis, Jason, "'Backward and Brilliant Children': A Social and Policy History of Disability, Childhood, and Education in Toronto's Special Education Classes, 1910 to 1945," Ph.D. dissertation, York University, 2011.

Ellis, Jason, "'Inequalities of Children in Original Endowment': How Intelligence Testing Transformed Early Special Education in a North American City School System," *History of Education Quarterly* 53, 4 (November 2013): 401–29.

Gleason, Mona, "Disciplining Children, Disciplining Parents: The Nature and Meaning of Psychological Advice to Canadian Parents, 1948–1955," *Social History/Historie sociale* 29, 57 (1996): 187–209.

Gleason, Mona, "Navigating the Pedagogy of Failure: Medicine, Education and the Disabled Child in English Canada, 1900 to 1945," in Graham Allan and Nathaniel Lauster, eds., *The End of Children? Changing Trends in Childbearing and Childhood.* Vancouver: UBC Press, 2012: 140–60.

Gleason, Mona, "Psychology and the Construction of the 'Normal' Family in Post-war Canada, 1945–1960," *Canadian Historical Review* 78, 3 (1997): 442–77.

Jasen, Patricia, "Student Activism, Mental Health, and English-Canadian Universities in the 1960s," *The Canadian Historical Review* 92, 3 (September 2011): 455–80.

Revie, Linda, "More Than Just Boots! The Eugenic and Commercial Concerns behind A.R. Kaufman's Birth Controlling Activities," *Canadian Bulletin of Medical History* 23, 1 (2006): 119–43.

Strong-Boag, Veronica, "'Children of Adversity': Disabilities and Child Welfare in Canada from the Nineteenth to the Twenty-First Century," *Journal of Family History* 32, 4 (October 2007): 413–32.

Thomson, Gerald E., "'Not an Attempt to Coddle Children': Dr Charles Hegler Gundry and the Mental Hygiene Division of the Vancouver School Board, 1939–1969," *Historical Studies in Education/ Revue d'histoire de l'éducation* 14, 2 (Fall 2002): 247–78.

Thomson, Gerald, "'Through No Fault of Their Own': Josephine Dauphinee and the 'Subnormal' Pupils of the Vancouver School System, 1911–1941," *Historical Studies in Education/Revue d'histoire de l'éducation* 18, 1 (Spring 2006): 51–73.

Yoshida, Karen, Fady Shanouda, and Jason Ellis, "An Education and Negotiation of Differences: The 'Schooling' Experiences of English-speaking Canadian Children Growing Up with Polio during the 1940s and 1950s," *Disability & Society*, 29, 3 (March 2014): 345–58.

Books

Adams, Mary Louise, *The Trouble with Normal: Postwar Youth and the Making of Heterosexuality*. Toronto: University of Toronto Press, 1997.

Arnup, Katherine, *Education for Motherhood: Advice for Mothers in Twentieth-Century Canada*. Toronto: University of Toronto Press, 1994.

Gleason, Mona, *Normalizing the Ideal: Psychology, Schooling, and the Family in Postwar Canada*. Toronto: University of Toronto Press, 1999.

Kline, Wendy, *Building a Better Race: Gender, Sexuality and Eugenics from the Turn of the Twentieth Century to the Baby Boom*. Berkeley: University of California Press, 2001.

9 Residential Schooling Reconsidered

Editors' Introduction

By the end of the nineteenth century, Canadian childhood was increasingly spent in schools. Some children, however, had a much more prolonged relationship with state institutions. For this reason, foundational texts on the history of Canadian young people have focused on orphanages, asylums, and various custodial "schools." Since the publication of Neil Sutherland's classic study *Children in English-Canadian Society: Framing the Twentieth Century Consensus*, scholars have concentrated on progressive reformers' attempts, starting in the nineteenth century, to ensure the moral and physical well-being of young people.[1] The impulses toward institutionalizing and reforming particular children, however, were predicated on white, middle-class, patriarchal, and ableist assumptions about proper families and childhoods. For example, the hospitalization of "mentally deficient" children, as Nic Clarke argues in the previous chapter, allowed nineteenth- and twentieth-century reformers to separate the "normal" from the "abnormal." Likewise, juvenile delinquency reform often policed gender norms and class affiliation as much as it did legal transgressions such as theft or assault.[2] And the residential school system, a particularly insidious form of state control disguised as child rescue, formed a central piece in the colonizing mission directed at Indigenous youth.[3]

The essays by Sarah de Leeuw and Ian Mosby in this chapter engage with histories of the residential schools in new ways. They emphasize that the state and its representatives used violence, neglect, and starvation as deliberate and sanctioned strategies of control and domination, and as a key component of colonization efforts. While the historical mistreatment that young Aboriginal people faced in institutional settings has not escaped the attention of scholars and the popular media,[4] de Leeuw and Mosby remind us how deliberate that mistreatment was and how those in positions of power justified it.

Sarah de Leeuw points out that colonial officials maintained that Aboriginal adults were "childlike" and needed much guidance and surveillance, an attitude that helped justify removing their children from their homes and placing them in residential schools. A historical geographer, de Leeuw pays close attention to physical space as an important factor in how Aboriginal people experienced the effects of such colonizing actions. They were trapped, she deftly shows, by colonial attitudes that painted them as children and incapable of looking after their own affairs. They were also literally trapped in the schools themselves. The physical isolation and incarceration of Aboriginal children in institutions was deliberately intended to sever familial

and cultural ties and to thereby destroy Aboriginal culture. However, the accompanying photographs taken by de Leeuw of art objects produced by girls in two residential schools in British
Columbia show that this goal was ultimately elusive. The images speak back loudly against the
colonizers' attempts to extinguish Aboriginal culture.

Ian Mosby's essay reveals the previously unexplored history of biomedical experimentation
in Aboriginal communities and residential schools in the period following the Second World
War. The withholding of adequate food supplies for the purposes of nutritional experimentation, Mosby found, was perpetuated without the consent, and often without the knowledge, of
Aboriginal adults and children. The deliberate nature of the abuse renders this episode in an
already dark history of colonization in Canada even more egregious. Mosby demonstrates how
racism, unethical scientific practice, and government policy dovetailed to make such experimentation possible and, at the time, unremarkable. The primary source accompanying this
essay is a letter sent by Russell (Russ) Copeland Moses, a survivor of the Mohawk Institute
Residential School, to a meeting of residential school principals that took place in Elliot Lake
Ontario in 1966. During the late 1960s and early 1970s, Moses served as a special assistant to
the then minister of Indian affairs and northern development, Jean Chrétien (who would serve
as Canadian prime minister from 1993 to 2003). While he confirms that inadequate food, along
with many other shameful conditions, were routine at the residential school, Moses includes
suggestions that he believed would enable First Nations students and their families to thrive.
We might ask ourselves, as we read Moses's letter, whether he was listened to then and whether
we are listening now.

Both essays in this chapter remind us that in nineteenth- and twentieth-century Canada,
the state's impulse to save Aboriginal children from poverty, neglect, abuse, and immorality
was never far from its impulse to colonize, to sequester, and to nullify challenges to the hegemonic social order. They also remind us that Aboriginal people resisted these efforts.

Notes

1. Neil Sutherland, *Children in English-Canadian Society: Framing the Twentieth Century Consensus* (Toronto: University of Toronto Press, 1976).

2. See Tamara Myers, *Caught: Montreal's Modern Girls and the Law, 1869–1945* (Toronto: University of Toronto, 2006).

3. See, for example, Basil H. Johnston, *Indian School Days* (Toronto: Key Porter Books, 1988); Robert Carney, "Aboriginal Residential Schools Before Confederation: The Early Experience," *Historical Studies: Canadian Catholic Historical Association* 61 (1995): 13–40; J.R. Miller, *Shingwauk's Vision: A History of Native Residential Schools* (Toronto: University of Toronto Press, 1996); John S. Milloy, *A National Crime: The Canadian Government and the Residential School System, 1879 to 1986* (Winnipeg: University of Manitoba Press, 1999).

4. See note 2 above as well as Law Commission of Canada's report entitled *Dignity Restored: Responding to Child Abuse in Canadian Institutions* (Ministry of Public Works and Government Services, March 2000). The report incorporated historical information of abuse of children at res-idential schools as well as reform schools such as the Grandview Training School for Girls, formerly the Ontario Training School for Girls—Galt (pri-or to 1967). Under the Conservative government of Stephen Harper, the Law Commission had its budget cut in 2006 and was closed down shortly thereafter. For details on the closure, see Voices-Voix website at http://voices-voix.ca/en/facts/profile/law-commission-canada; Wayne K. Spears, "Canada Still Lacks the Political Will to Curb Sexual Abuse," *National Post*, March 21, 2012, http://news.nationalpost.com/full-comment/wayne-k-spear-canada-still-lacks-the-political-will-to-curb-sexual-abuse (Retrieved on September 2, 2014).

"If Anything Is to Be Done with the Indian, We Must Catch Him Very Young": Colonial Constructions of Aboriginal Children and the Geographies of Indian Residential Schooling in British Columbia, Canada

SARAH DE LEEUW

Introduction

Stephen Harper, the [then] prime minister of Canada, offered in June 2008 an official apology for the country's Indian[1] residential schooling system. Residential schooling, Harper stated, was designed to

> remove and isolate [Aboriginal] children from the influence of their homes, families, traditions and cultures, and to assimilate them into the dominant culture. [It was] based on the assumption that aboriginal cultures and spiritual beliefs were inferior and unequal. Indeed . . . it was infamously said "to kill the Indian in the child." First Nations, Inuit and Métis languages and cultural practices were prohibited in these schools. Tragically, some of these children died while attending residential schools and others never returned home. (Harper 2008)

With wording about the removal of children from one place and their relocation to another, about school spaces regulating and curtailing behaviours, and about the emplacement of children into spaces built with the express purpose of assimilating Indigenous peoples into a colonial society, Harper's apology acknowledges the inherency of geography and the power of place in Canadian colonial projects. The apology

Source: From *Children's Geographies* 7, 2 (May 2009): 123–40. Reprinted by permission of the publisher (Taylor & Francis Ltd, www.tandfonline.com).

also highlights colonial efforts to kill Indianness as it was embodied by Indigenous children, thus illustrating colonialism's preoccupation with childhood and the centrality and importance of the child in colonial projects.

This paper focuses on the centrality of Indigenous children and related concepts of childhood to colonial projects in Canada and, more specifically, in Canada's most westerly province of British Columbia. This centrality, I argue, manifested both discursively and materially. As outlined in the next section of this essay, various discourses carefully constructed Aboriginal peoples as children, thus providing ideological cornerstones to governmental and ecumenical strategies seeking legitimations to expand territory and manage Indigenous peoples' cultures, bodies, minds, and spirits. Successive settler-colonial structures constructed Indigenous peoples as childlike in order to produce the idea of a group in need of protection and management. This leads me to section three, where I discuss contemporary theorizations about childhood and children's geographies. Here I suggest children's geographies can be expanded upon by addressing considerations of Indigenous children and questions about colonialism. Following this, I move beyond discursivities to focus on material sites and grounded realms. In the fourth section of the paper, I argue Indigenous children were understood as eminently concrete embodiments of a culture that the Eurowestern colonial project was intent on aggressively circumscribing, if not expunging, from a newly emerging Canada.

As embodiments of extant Indigeneity, Indigenous children were threats to settler-colonial imaginations. So something had to be done with Aboriginal children. That something occurred through residential schools and imprinted itself on the bodies of children.

I am interested, then, in demonstrating linkages between the discursive formations of Indigenous subjects produced by Canadian hegemonic elites and the lived realities of Indigenous children within colonially constructed school spaces. To make these arguments, I work with examples from somewhat disparate times and spaces, including government policy documents, records about residential schools, and memories and narratives produced by former students of the schools. Many of the examples cited draw from only a handful of schools in British Columbia about which exists a strong archival record.[2] Much of this paper focuses on the early and mid-twentieth century, when residential schooling reached an apex in Canada (Titley 1986, Miller 1997, Milloy 1999). Examples from these time periods, however, are framed by broader temporal and spatial references in order to illustrate Canadian colonialism's persistent focus on Aboriginal children. The governance of Indigenous peoples in Canada was a complex and fragmented project, undertaken by multiple interests (Carney 1995, Borrows 2002, Fletcher 2002). It is my contention, though, that commonalities can be found across broad geographies, particularly with reference to themes pertaining to children and childhood.

An eclectic array of theories forms the foundation from which I contemplate the role of children and childhood to the colonial project in Canada. The majority of my argument is informed by (post) colonial theorists and the burgeoning literature relating directly to children's geographies. By focusing on children and their small scale geographies, I am interested in corroborating Ann-Laura Stoler's eloquent observation that tender microcosms comprise the marrow of imperial projects (2006). Ultimately, I propose that in the Canadian colonial contest high stakes were placed on the small, arguably tender, bodies of Indigenous children.

"To Produce Indians": Theorizing Colonial Discourses and Aboriginal Peoples

While discourses operate in the realms of semantics and semiotics, their power lies in the production of that which they name and represent. As Michel Foucault reminds us, discourses are anything but immaterial; they are more than "groups of signs . . . but . . . [are] practices that systematically form the objects of which they speak" (1972, p. 49). In (post)colonial studies, government policies and legal frameworks are understood as powerful discursive structures that function to marginalize certain subjects in order to legitimate the rights of others to social and spatial supremacy (McClintock 1995, Spivak 1996, Razack 2002, Lawrence 2003). The discourses produced by colonialists in reference to colonized or Indigenous subjects are particularly encoded with struggles to attain and maintain power over bodies and territory (Bhabha 1994, Said 1994, Harris 2004, Li 2007). Indeed, as Edward Said so compelling demonstrates, the violence of (re)territorializing people and their lands requires a careful thinking-through of the process, a thinking-through that involves producing socio-cultural products that legitimate colonial desires:

> At some very basic level, imperialism means thinking about, settling on, [and] controlling land that you do not possess, that is distant, that is lived on and owned by others. That struggle is complex and interesting because it is not only about soldiers and cannons but also about ideas, about forms, about images and imaginings. For all kinds of reasons it attracts some people and often involves untold misery for others. . . . Just as none of us is outside or beyond geography, none of us is completely free from the struggle over geography. (1994, p. 7)

In British Columbia, a geography simultaneously at the "edge of empire" (Harris 2004) yet central to the way that Canada was articulated as a nation in relationship to the metropole of Britain, texts, signifiers, and semiotic structures were inextricable from the material and grounded efforts of colonial impositions. Indeed, despite a significant skepticism about geography's cultural turn and the ensuing ramifications for how colonization in British Columbia is understood within the discipline, the province's leading historical geographer on Native issues concedes that imaginaries about Aboriginal peoples as uncivilized and disappearing savages were propagated by cultural products and "pervaded thought[s] about native people in the Colonial Office, in political, administrative, legal, and missionary circles in British Columbia, and in the settler mind" (Harris 2004, p. 170). Material and grounded violences toward Indigenous peoples in British Columbia, in many respects, turned on the work of rhetoric and semantics: discourses provided the "legitimation of and moral justification for" (p. 165) Eurocolonial dispossession of territory from First Nations.

Despite the pivotal nature of colonial discourses in forming a foundation for material and territorial interventions into the geographies of Aboriginal peoples, the discourses themselves (and the subjects responsible for producing and disseminating them) were heterogeneous, contradictory, and often fractious. As the contours of Canada solidified through the eighteenth and nineteenth century, the nature of "The Indian Question" shifted. Indigenous peoples were, at different times, by different interests, and in different spaces, understood and positioned as allies of the state, as economic opportunities, as noble, as savage, as salvageable, as beyond redemption, as viscous, as vanishing, and as an ever-present force to be reckoned with, particularly in the realm of land acquisition and expansion (Clayton 1992, Raibmon 2006). Strategies to manage Indians shifted accordingly, from focuses on Indians as facilitators of trade and resource extraction to ideals of enculturation and then assimilation. Colonialism in Canada and British Columbia was not unique in this regard: it is impossible, when looking at the workings of colonialism anywhere in the world, to extrapolate universality or consistency (Scott 1990, Thomas 1994). Additional levels of complexity are realized when relationships between colonists and Indigenous subjects are understood to constitute social relations and to encompass everyday spaces and times as well

as administrative or governmental scales. As Cindi Katz powerfully observes of other social relations, the nature of colonial relationships between Indigenous and non-Indigenous subjects would most certainly have been comprised of "fleshy, messy, and indeterminate stuff" that precludes fixed, stable, or concretely-bounded understandings (Katz 2001, p. 711). Such an understanding of colonial discourses is in accordance with Mary Louise Pratt's (1991a, 1991b) observation that contact zones of the colonial encounter are socio-cultural spaces in which "disparate cultures meet, clash and grapple with each other in highly asymmetrical relations of domination and subordination" (p. 4).

Discourse produced about Indigenous peoples by settler-colonial interests in Canada adjusted and shifted as various subjects grappled and clashed with each other. There was, as others have suggested, always a dialectical nature to the discourses that defined, and consequently formed, Indigenous subjects across Canada and British Columbia (Tennant 1990, Schouls 2003). The muddled and disordered characteristic of social productions, including discourses, does not however diminish their power to perpetuate and produce hegemonic ideologies and socio-cultural imbalances. Indeed, the power of colonial discourses to form Indigenous peoples, and other "othered" peoples, likely lays in the amorphous nature of discourses. While always managing to position non-colonial subjects as deficient, the nature of how and why those subjects were deficient shifted to match the desires of the colonial powers producing the discourses. As Catherine Nash observes, discursive changeability is eminently strategic:

> Colonial discourses were effective precisely because they were enormously flexible and adaptable. The tensions and ambiguities of colonial representation speak of a less monolithic but no less problematic colonial project characterized by unequal exchanges and partial understanding. (2002, p. 221)

Such, then, are the theories through which I contemplate questions about discursivities concerning

Aboriginal children, Indian residential schooling, and the colonial project in Canada and British Columbia.

During the nineteenth century, and into the early twentieth century, as the Canadian government struggled to assert Canada's nationhood, efforts were focused and concentrated upon displacing and assimilating Indigenous peoples. Similarly, as British Columbia made effort to assert itself within the confederation and secure territory for its settler population, discourses produced at the provincial level turned on addressing how best to deal with Indians to allow for settler colonial expansion (Harris 2004). Certainly, as outlined just previously, these efforts shifted, adjusted, and even explicitly contradicted their own logic but, as it had from onset of confederation, the "Indian Problem" remained a paramount concern to the both the federal and provincial governments. Like colonial incursions into lands around the world, settler occupation of Canada relied heavily on discourses of a terra nullius, an empty untamed frontier occupied by no one and, consequently, freely available for non-Indigenous occupation. This construction permeates most Canadian colonial government literatures and policies, including those concerning early formalization of the country's boundaries and regions, land usage and governance strategies, and treaty and compensation agreements between Indigenous and colonial subjects (see for instance Government of Canada 1869, Government of Canada 1879, Rawson et al. 1845). Representations of territory, particularly maps, were important tools by which discourses of terra nullius were produced and circulated amongst settler-colonial interests (Brealey 1995, Sparke 1998, Harris 2002). Government policies and legal frameworks were also concerned with documenting an empty territory, thereby establishing legal rights over lands (Fletcher 2005). When evaluated carefully, many of the discursivities and policies about the authenticity of a terra nullius, and how to achieve and maintain it for settler occupation, were infused with considerations about Aboriginal children and childhood.

In 1845, one of the first documents to comprehensively address the Indian question in what became Canada was presented to the Legislative Assembly of the then Province of Canada. *The Report on the Affairs of Indians in Canada*, known as *The Bagot Report*, was a summary of existing British imperial thought and practices about Indians in the Province of Canada. The report's purpose was to "inquire into the Affairs of the Indians in Canada and the application of the annual grant of money made by the Imperial Parliament for the benefit of that Race" (Canada, Province of, 1845, p. 1). The document provides insight into colonial views of Indigenous peoples following the 1763 Royal Proclamation and leading up to 1867 Confederation and the signing of the 1876 Indian Act, particularly as those views pertained to schooling and Indigenous children as they fit within the colonial project. At base, the government could neither fully trust nor entirely ignore Indians, often because of their child-like—and thus unpredictable—characteristics. Indians embodied the possibility of a noble subject, the threat of unrelenting and uncontrollable violence, and a natural tendency toward laziness and ineptitude:

> The history of this period afforded abundant evidence of their [Aboriginal peoples'] enterprise and prowess as warriors, with many remarkable instances of heroism and magnanimity, and no less striking examples of bloody revenge, and savage cruelty. . . . To these [negative characteristics] must be added the natural indolence of the Indian temperament, which, in the absence of the excitement of savage life, keeps many of his race in a state of inertness, destructive alike to the energy and health of body and mind. In his native state the Indian is simple-minded, generous, proud and energetic; his craftiness is exhibited chiefly in the chase and in war. He is generally docile, and possesses a lively and happy disposition. (Canada, Province of, 1845, pp. 3–15)

The commissionaires further argued that a defining aspect of Indigenous peoples, namely their savagery, was predicated on a close connection with nature. These innate characteristics of Indigenous peoples were linked directly with an unmediated proximity to wild and unsettled land. Consequently, and not unlike the duty of a parent to monitor a child's propensity to indulge in things not in his/her best interest, the role of colonial powers was to manage Indians' access to what ailed them: wild or unmanaged land, territory, nature. Fortuitously for colonial powers, then, Indian assimilation, the childlike qualities of Indian subjects, colonial desire for land, and concerns about territorial expansion were all intertwined.

Troubling to the commissionaires, however, were the long-standing tensions that existed between government land policies and Aboriginal peoples' acquiescence to policies concerning land and territory. Authors of *The Bagot Report* noted the Royal Proclamation of 1763 "furnished [Aboriginal peoples] with a fresh guarantee for the possession of their hunting grounds and the protection of the Crown" (p. 4). The commissionaires observed Aboriginal peoples took such promises seriously: "This document [the Royal Proclamation], the Indians look upon as their Charter. They have preserved a copy of it, to the present time, and have referred to it on several occasions in their representation to the Government" (p. 4). Further, "... dispossess[ing] the Indians of their lands" required "rendering some compensation" (p. 5). The difficulty, however, was that compensation was costly and sometimes Indians were loath to leave their lands, even with compensation. The government thus sought just cause and moral legitimacy to justify dispossession of Indians from their territories. Justification was found by constructing Indians as childlike and in need of colonial subjects to act on their behalf:

> [Land] transactions have been made the subject of reproach to the Government, and ground for subsequent claims on behalf of the Indians[, so] it may be proper here to offer a few remarks on the subject. It has been alleged that these agreements were unjust, as dispossessing the natives of their ancient territories, and extortionate, as rendering a very inadequate compensation for the lands surrendered. If, however, the

Government had not made arrangement for the voluntary surrender of the lands, the white settlers would gradually have taken possession of them, without offering any compensations whatsoever; it would, at that time, have been impossible to resist the natural laws of society, and to guard the Indian Territory against the encroachment of the Whites. . . . The Government, therefore, adopted the most humane and the most just course, in inducing the Indians, by offers of compensation, to remove quietly to more distant hunting grounds, or to confine themselves within more limited reserves. . . . (p. 5)

In order to explain colonial agendas of territory expansion and the subsequent confinement of Indians onto small parcels of land, the commissionaires turned to "the natural laws of society," according to which the savage yet childlike Aboriginals would lose their land to heartless settlers unless the government first dispossessed them. The commissionaires employed a for-their-own-good argument to justify expropriation. For the authors of early federal government considerations about Indians, then, discursive constructions of the Indian as childlike wards of the state were intrinsically linked to more material and grounded practices of territorial expansion.

The Bagot Report also linked colonial education of Aboriginal children to the dispossession of Aboriginal peoples from their lands. The government, the commissionaires argued, had a moral and protectionist duty to ensure Aboriginal peoples become acclimatized to Eurocolonial expectations of civilization, including agricultural proficiency and settlement on delineated, privately owned properties. These obligations could most efficiently be achieved through education of the Indian. It was the commissionaires' sense that land was an important component of transformation Aboriginal peoples and that education was the most efficient means of inscribing traits of civility upon Indians. The commissionaires lauded the logic of an 1828 report that had been prepared by Sir John Kemp for the government of the Province of Canada:

It appears that the most effectual means of ameliorating the condition of the Indians, of promoting their religious improvement and education, and of eventually relieving His Majesty's Government from the expense of the Indian Department are: 1st to collect the Indians in considerable numbers, and to settle them in villages, with a due portion of land for the cultivation and support. 2nd. To make such provision for their religious improvement, education, and instruction in husbandry as circumstances may from time to time require. . . . (Kemp 1828 quoted in Report of the Affairs, 1845, p. 7)

Moral imperatives concerning the betterment of a childlike people thus formed an integral component of colonial logics about lessening governmental costs associated with managing Indians. Education became central to these concerns (Furniss 1992). It was understood as a system to ameliorate the childlike qualities of Indigenous subjects, which in turn would result in a civilized (grown-up) Indigenous population who would both cost the government less and, due to adult sedentaryness, not stand in the way of colonial land acquisition and settlement. These discourses carried forth in other areas of Indian management considerations in Canada.

As a single entity, The 1876 Indian Act was perhaps the most comprehensive and impactful piece of legislation enacted by the federal government in reference to Indigenous peoples in Canada (Government of Canada 1996). The Indian Act's principal aim was "to consolidate the several laws relating to Indians now on the statute books of the Dominion and the old Provinces of Upper and Lower Canada" (Liard 1876 quoted in Leslie and Maguire 1978, p. 61). The Act focused specifically on: defining the Indian; recognizing, protecting, managing, and arranging for sale of reserves and associated lands; payments of monies to support and benefit Indians (including monies to support schools attended primarily by Indians); elections of chiefs and Band Councils; taxation and debt issues surrounding Indians; control of intoxicants; and ongoing considerations of enfranchising Indians (Leslie and Maguire 1978, Armitage

1995). The Indian Act was anchored in discourses set forth by its predecessor, the 1869 Act for the Gradual Enfranchisement of Indians.[3] The purpose of the Enfranchisement Act was to standardize how Aboriginal people could legally possess land and territory, either on or off a reserve, to which they would have full claim and ownership separate from claims granted by Indian reserve lands. Claim to territory was inextricably linked to Aboriginal identity. Imbedded within the rhetoric of the Enfranchisement Act, and thus found in the Indian Act, were colonial assumptions about Indigenous peoples' childlike nature and their potential for "growing up" into a more elevated state of non-Indigenousness through the attainment of identity characteristics deemed suitable by Eurocolonial subjects:

> The Governor General of Council may, on the report of the Superintendent General of Indian Affairs, order the issue of Letters of Patent granting to any Indian *who from the degree of civilization to which he has attained, and the character for integrity and sobriety which he bears, appears to be a safe and suitable person to become a proprietor of land*, a life estate in the land which has been or may be allotted to him . . . [and from this time] . . . any Indian, his wife or minor children as aforesaid, [will] so declared to be enfranchised, *[and] shall no longer be deemed Indians within the meaning of the laws relating to Indians*. . . . (Government of Canada, Act for the Gradual Enfranchisement of Indians, CAP VI: 1869, my emphasis)

Colonial rhetoric about Aboriginal peoples, then, turned on tacit assumptions of Aboriginal childlikeness and, correspondingly, Aboriginal peoples were constructed as subjects who would grow up into a state of adulthood that corresponded to non-Aboriginalness and Eurocolonial whiteness. Both the Indian Act and Enfranchisement Act's focus on Indian identity, and corresponding links between character, territory, and claim to land, had direct implications for the guiding principals behind policies about colonial education for Aboriginal children.

In January 1879, three years after the passing of the 1876 Indian Act and in part to develop education models to assimilate and civilize Aboriginal peoples, Nicholas Flood Davin was commissioned by John A. Macdonald to investigate schooling methods for Indians in the United States. *The Davin Report* offers insight into the development of nineteenth-century colonial anxieties about Aboriginal peoples, about colonial imaginaries concerning Aboriginal peoples, and about how these anxieties and imaginaries translated into policy imperatives concerning Indian education in Canada, particularly the merits of day versus boarding schools. Davin was convinced that residential schools, as opposed to day schools, could best civilize Indigenous peoples. He argued that the primary hindrance to civilization was the "call of the wigwam," the influence of other Indigenous peoples, and consequently argued that

> Little can be done with [the adult Indian]. He can be taught to do a little farming and at stock-raising and to dress in a more civilized manner but that is all. The child, again, who goes to a day school learns little, and what little he learns is soon forgotten when his tastes are trained at home, and his inherited aversion to toil is in no way combated. . . . If anything is to be done with the Indian we must catch him very young. The children must be kept constantly in the circle of civilized conditions. . . . (Davin 1879, p. 2)

Davin's vision of Indian assimilation, not unlike the visions that predated his work, was spatialized. He anchored his rhetoric in place and envisioned a child's personality as shaped by proximity to adverse forces of family and community. Consequently, he suggested that the only solution was a complete immersion within a new and civilized environment: "The plan now is to take young children, give them the care of a mother, and have them constantly in hand. Such care must go pari passu with religious training" (p. 12).

By 1879 in Canada, then, the federal government had in hand a report arguing that the state, through colonial education and by way of the child, should break cultural and biological bonds among Aboriginal peoples. Davin argued against earlier rhetoric, some of which *The Bagot Report* encapsulated, that allowed for a simple (re)settlement of Indians, on their own lands and often separate from white-colonial society. Instead, he promoted cultural rupture premised on a material and spatialized set of practices that would disaggregate Aboriginal peoples from one another and sever generational and genealogical links to Aboriginality. Residential schools, as spaces to contain children, were understood and promoted by Davin as physical interventions into the family and community structures of Indigenous people.

Perhaps the most aggressive period of colonial intervention into Aboriginal children's lives through residential schooling occurred during the latter years of the eighteenth century into the mid-nineteenth century, under the tenure of Department of Indian Affairs (DIA) official Duncan Campbell Scott. Scott's time with the Department of Indian Affairs corresponds with the tabling of Davin's report and substantive amendments to the Indian Act made throughout the early twentieth century to strengthen the federal government's control on Indian education. Scott's approach to the Indian problem was anchored in stern and unchanging sentiments about the negative biological and cultural character of Indians. His writings demonstrate an unwavering sense that Aboriginals were inevitably dying out and that their remnants ought to be fully assimilated and enfranchised within the Dominion of Canada.[4]

By 1920, with Scott's input, the Indian Act was amended to criminalize failing to send an Aboriginal child to school (Titley 1986, Armitage 1995). This policy was specific to Aboriginal peoples—no such criminalization was applied to non-Aboriginal Canadians. In 1927, the Act was once more amended, again tightening the language concerning compulsory attendance at schools and vesting the governor-in-council with the ability to establish schools on band and reserve land, even without the approval of the local chief and council. By 1927, then, the Act stated

> Every Indian child between the ages of seven and fifteen who is physically able shall

attend such day, industrial or boarding school as may be designated by the Superintendent General for the full periods which such a school is open each year . . . Any parent, guardian or person with whom an Indian child is residing who fails to cause such child, being between the ages aforesaid, to attend school . . . [is] libel on summary conviction before a justice of the peace or Indian agent to a fine of not more than two dollars and costs, or imprisonment for a period not exceeding ten days or both, and such a child may be attested without a warrant and conveyed to school by the truant officer. . . . The Governor-in-Council may take the land of an Indian held under location ticket or otherwise, for school purposes, upon payment to such Indian of the compensation agreed upon, or in case of disagreement . . . in such manner as the Superintendent General may direct. (Indian Act 1927, Chapter 98)

In the latter years of the nineteenth century and into the early years of the twentieth century, then, regulations became increasingly stringent with reference to Aboriginal children and colonial education. Parents were criminalized for failing to send their children to school. Children could be arrested without warrant and returned to the confines of a school. Land and territory could be procured in order to establish educational facilities, a policy that once again underscored linkages between Indian education and land appropriation. The federal government's agenda of colonial education reached into every aspect of Indigenous peoples' lives, including their children, families, and communities, their cultures and their lands.

Of such importance was schooling children in Scott's vision of civilizing Aboriginal peoples that, in his final reports prior to retirement in 1932, he made specific mention of his educational efforts, noting that between 1912 and 1932 Indian student enrolment in schools had increased by 51 per cent. These increases were particularly dramatic for students attending residential schools. Residential school enrolment increased from just over 3,000 students to over 8,000, an increase of 110 per cent,

during Scott's final years with the Department of Indian Affairs (Titley 1986).

Colonial education, which transpired within residential schools and through the pedagogies delivered in the schools, was motivated by a highly embodied and child-focused goal: the (re)production of Indians starting at childhood. The production of Indians rested on a fundamental assumption that children could be moulded and transformed from one state of being to another, namely from a colonially undesirable Indian to one who conformed to colonial expectations (Thorton 1944). The assumptions did not abate with time. In 1947, the Honourable J.A. Glen of Indian Affairs circulated through the *Indian School Bulletin* (I.S.B.)[5] his departmental objectives concerning Indian education in Canada. Minister Glen's opined that it was the duty of the Canadian government to ensure Indians were "capable of meeting the exacting demands of modern society, with all it complexities":

> *To produce Indians* of such capacity is not an easy task. It may mean 100 or 200 years of the keenest kind of insight and understanding. *Education of every type must be utilized.* This should include schools, community groups, the press, the radio and all available forces, both positive and negative. (*Indian School Bulletin*, February 1947, n.p. my emphasis)

Glen's objectives were prophetic of future colonial pedagogic goals in which education was conceptualized as a colonial "force." In 1952 the cover page of the *ISB* reminded residential schools teachers that their teaching pedagogy was also a force to transform Indigenous children and thus "should think in terms of the whole child, body and soul, intellect and will, sense, imagination, and emotions" (n.p.). Such sentiments were also mirrored by ecumenical representatives. Father André Renaud, who by 1962 was the vice-president of the Indian Eskimo Association and the director general of the Indian Eskimo Commission of the Oblate Fathers, was deeply invested in questions of Indian residential schooling. His writings were emblematic of broad colonial considerations about Aboriginal children. In 1958, he authored "Indian Education Today" and, that same year, contributed to a document prepared by the Indian and Eskimo Welfare Commission of the Oblate Fathers in Canada entitled *Residential Education for Indian Acculturation*. Renaud's writings display a remarkable faithfulness to historic conceptions of Indian education and the need to break Indian cultural identity through modern colonial and Catholic educational practices.

Renaud's vision of breaking Indianness was fundamentally anchored in ideas about intervening into children's bodies, spirits, minds, and lives. His intervention goals were infused with spatial and geographic considerations, replete with tactics that could only unfold within and through material sites. His discourses employed pseudo-scientific, objective, and anthropological evidence that by the mid-twentieth century had become dominant paradigms by which to consider socio-cultural questions (Fabian 1983). They also dialogued with broader medical and pedagogical discursivities concerning how to educate Indians and the potential for educational interventions to fully transform them:

> [In] acculturating Indian children, the following prescriptions appear necessary for success and thoroughness: isolate the child as much as possible from his native background, ideally twenty four hours a day and twelve months of the year, to prevent "exposure" to Indian culture; upon graduation, integrate the young trans-cultured Indian in a non-Indian community, following him through till he or she is permanently settled away from his community of origin. The purpose of such prescriptions, particularly of removing the child permanently from his original environment, is to provide him with a unified experience and thus prevent a later disorganization in his personality. (Renaud in *Residential Education for Indian Acculturation*, 1958, p. 34)

Much of Renaud's thinking about Indian education, particularly residential schooling and educational practices premised on severing children from their communities and families, was located in considerations of nationalism and citizenship:

> Now that Canada is maturing into a nation, her citizens more and more think of themselves as Canadians, first and foremost. . . . This is not true as yet of most Indians. Psychologically as well as historically, they are Indians first and Canadians afterwards. Or to put it differently, their way of being Canadians is to be Indians (Renaud 1958, p. 31).

For Renaud, the ultimate question with regard to Indian education in the mid-twentieth century was: "Will they [Indians] keep rearing their children in a truncated cultural tradition or will they eventually give their children basically the same kind of home-background as non-Indians? There is only one way to prevent the former and insure the latter: . . . education" (Renaud 1958, p. 45). The discursive construction of Aboriginal children as aberrant to the norms valued by colonial subjects and structures provided the rationale for colonial education and, ultimately, for the construction of residential schools.

Children's Geographies and Aboriginal Children

If the goal of residential schooling was the (re)production of Indians (when they were children) through eminently spatialized and material means, it is worthwhile to review some considerations about the concepts of children and childhood, a topic of increasing interest to geographers (James 1990, Mathews 2003, Kraftl 2006, Ansell and Smith 2006, Aitken et al. 2007). Although, at first glance, childhood may appear as an unproblematic marker of human development preceding adulthood, an increasing number of geographers realize that (like gender, race, sexuality and other markers of humanity that are often taken for granted as naturalized) childhood is socially constructed with spatialized and historicized roots (Holloway and Valentine 2000; Prout 2000). Childhood is infused with aspects of invention that considered the child either as "devil-like" and in need of subordination or as "angel-like," the archetype of social innocence in need of protection and sanction. Furthermore, children tended to be (and still are) seen as "human becomings rather than human beings" (Holloway and Valentine 2000, p. 5). Historically, however, and not unlike the construction of Indigenous peoples across the Americas as primitives and savages whom imperialism sought to transform (Gagen 2007), Aboriginal peoples of all ages in Canada were constructed as (often barbarous devil-like) children with reference to non-Aboriginal peoples (Raibmon 2005). The Indian Act, even in its more recent late-twentieth-century incarnations, insisted that "Indians were like children to a very great extent . . . and required a great deal more protection than white men" and that "[Indians] must either be treated as minors or as white men" (Leslie and Maguire 1975, p. 61). Residential schooling policy was informed by a belief that "the [Indian] race is in its childhood. . . . There is in the adult [Indian] the helplessness of a child; there is too a child's want of perspective. . . ." (Davin 1879, n.p.).

With reference to Aboriginal children, then, the discussion becomes complex. All Aboriginal people within the purview of colonial imperatives were not really fully grown human beings given their Indigenousness. They needed to become fully human/adult (i.e., non-Aboriginal/preferably white) by the educational forces of the Indian Affairs Branch of the Government of Canada. Associatively, the social construction of Aboriginal children by non-Aboriginal powers was markedly different from the social construction of (their own) white children. Certainly white children, consistent with conceptualizing children as requiring shaping and development by adults in order to become adults, would have been schooled, tutored, and shaped in both the family setting and within institutions, including schools (Gleason 1999, Gagen 2004). The process of white children becoming white adults, however, was premised on the possibility of developing an extant set of characteristics, including whiteness, which necessarily led to a white adulthood. Aboriginal children within residential schools were not schooled by people who recognized in the children basic qualities of their white colonial selves, qualities that simply required

appropriate nurturing in order to mature. Instead, childness in the Aboriginal person could be understood as having been viewed, by white educators and policy-makers in the context of Indian schools, as much more particularly *Indian childness*; thus it was not something merely to shape into adulthood, because that would assume Indian adulthood, but rather something to do away with entirely, thus preventing the child from maturing into an Indigenous adult (who in turn were seen as children themselves) (see for instance Churchill 2004 and Harper 2008 who write on the adage "killing the Indian child to save the Man").

For both Aboriginal and non-Aboriginal children, the socio-cultural moulting out of childhood and into adulthood is spatially influenced and, in turn, affects space. The contribution of geography to studies of childhood illustrated the importance of place and space and, additionally, adds detail and texture to broad-brush analyses of childhood constructions (Holloway and Valentine 2000). Like other topics understood geographically, when children and childhood are conceptualized spatially, and when place and space are understood as active actors in the lives of children, the locations where children's lives unfold can be theorized as agents unto themselves (Massey 1993, 2005, Malpas 1999). Furthermore, when everyday places of childhood (the home, the school, and the community) are accounted for as influential agents in the production of children and childhood, the sites themselves can serve to illustrate social attitudes towards the children who occupy them. Unfortunately, much of the existing literature neither theorizes children and their spaces historically (Gagen 2007) nor theorizes children's spaces wherein children are doubly othered, both as child and racialized child (racialized with reference to the adult who is tasked with the child's construction). There are gaps therefore with reference to Aboriginal children and childhood, particularly in an historic context.

In essence, then, students in residential school were more than just children. They were Aboriginal children, fundamentally othered within a context of residential schools created, operated, and directed by non-Aboriginal adults. The school-places where efforts were made to transform Aboriginal children into adults, or, more specifically into non-Aboriginal adults, were, as I will discuss in the next section, of white colonial design constructed with the express purpose of producing de-Indigenized Aboriginal citizens of Canada.

Building Colonial Imaginations: Aboriginal Children and Residential Schooling in British Columbia

Colonial discourses about Indigenous peoples circulated in semiotic and rhetoric realms and at policy levels in government and ecumenical forums. In these realms, as I have outlined, they formed the Indigenous subjects upon which they focused. Discourses also materialized as physical sites and touched down as corporeal violences upon the bodies and minds of Indigenous children. Discursivities about colonial education and Indigenous children, then, were not innocent or devoid of physical consequence. Indeed, in the case of many residential schools in British Columbia,[6] the very grounds upon which schools were constructed underwent powerful colonial narrations prior to a single brick being laid or a single child attending an institution. Histories written by missionaries and teachers at the Kitimat School for Girls emphasize battles over place between Indigenous peoples and settler colonialists, the outcome of which were high-ranking Haisla chiefs transforming into Christians who came to believe residential schooling was in the best interest of their Haisla children. In this colonial tale, land was then handed over, with the blessing and support of First Nations, so that a school could be built.[7] Histories written about the residential school in Metlakatla are almost identical, replete with Indian Chiefs who, upon transforming from brutal savages to Christian advocates of residential schooling, sign over land to the missionaries for a residential school (Touch and Blackett ca. 1886). *The Coqualeetza Story: 1886–1956*, written by teachers from the school to celebrate Coqualeetza's seventieth anniversary, (re)historicized the site as hallowed education ground. The publication linked the idea of "cleansing" with civilizing and educational imperatives:

Like most old stories, this one began "Long, long ago." [B]efore the white man came to the Fraser Valley . . . the Indians knew Coqualeetza as the "place of cleansing" [where blanket washing occurred]. It was symbolic of discarding the old and beginning anew. This idea of exchanging old ideas for new has been developed through the story of Coqualeetza. When the white man came, bringing with him, we must admit, much that was bad, but also more that was good, gradually the superstitions were replaced by education. (in Edmeston, Editor ca. 1956)

In each of these cases, moral discourses about transforming children and the value of residential school education are linked to colonial land acquisition for the construction of material sites in which to contain and transform Indigenous subjects.

Residential schools were built to mirror the discursive constructions and pedagogic intents that colonial subjects had toward Aboriginal peoples: material space and colonial discursivities were mutually constitutive and served to reproduce each other. Place and spatiality may be understood as active and compelling agents of, in this case, colonial social undertakings (Massey 2005) and might be added to the list of forces required to (re)produce Indians. As other geographers have argued, places constructed at the behest of those who hold social power are often concretized realizations of that power (Ploszajska 1994, Philo 1997). That four of British Columbia's Indian residential schools remain standing is perhaps testament to the immense material power of the institutions. Even among the twenty-first-century landscapes of the province, they are imposing architectures. They are architectures that, like Kamloops, St Mary's, Lejac, St Eugene's, and Kuper Island Indian Residential Schools, tended to be multi-storeyed, duo-winged, brick or cement-block buildings with façades dominated by a steep staircase leading up to tall double doors. The schools' bifurcated design reflected colonial efforts to separate children by gender, something which was at odds with the more interwoven lives children would have experienced at home (Fournier and Crey 1997). Reflective of discourses about the need to quarantine and cordon off Indigenous peoples from non-Indigenous peoples, the rooms around the entry stairway tended to be the domain of educators and school staff and included the school office and staff rooms. In layouts reflective of panoptical surveillance, long straight hallways and large open areas ensured students were always within the supervisory gaze of school staffs. Dorm rooms were heavily monitored spaces in which children of the same family where prohibited from speaking with each other. Interior spaces were expressly designed to impart colonial norms of hygiene, of order, and of certain behaviours. Classrooms were structured around nationalistic and Christian symbols including photos of the queen of England, the crucifix, and the Canadian flag.

As material entities, then, the schools enforced certain conducts upon the Aboriginal children who attended them. The schools were surrounded by farm and agricultural land, key spaces in efforts to break the perceived nomadic, hunter-gatherer predilections of Aboriginal peoples (Milloy 1999). Family structures were shattered when children could not communicate across spatial divisions based on gender and language and cultural retention evaporated in large open spaces where behaviour was constantly monitored and community practices were forbidden. In efforts to intercede into the lives of children in disorienting ways, the schools were successful. The Nuu-chah-nulth Tribal Council (1996) attested that residential schools which Nuu-chah-nulth people attended were

> often laid out on or near the top of a hill, giving them an imposing, looming, even scary appearance in the eyes of young Nuu-chah-nulth children new to such places. The comparatively huge residential school buildings implied an importance above and beyond that of any local traditional authority, including that of the highest ranked Chief. On their first day at Indian Residential Schools, along with the trauma of being separated from their parents, Nuu-chah-nulth students new to the schools faced the realization that physical conditions, at those

institutions, were very different than those they were used to in their home villages. (pp. 27–28)

Residential schools attended by Nuu-chah-nulth students were not unique in materializing colonial ideals about intervening into the lives of Aboriginal peoples.

In 1924, Coqualeetza Residential Schools' longest-serving principal (Reverend George Raley) oversaw the expansion of the institution, a process which offered him the opportunity to directly link the materiality of buildings with the transformation of Aboriginal children. The school, in keeping with the spatial narratives circulated about it, operated under the school motto "Vestigia Nulla Retrorsum" (No Step Backwards). The buildings of Coqualeetza were personified as a living spirit, modifiable like a student under educational alteration. In his 1924 writings about the construction of the third building (to replace and expand upon the 1894 complex), principal Raley wrote:

> [T]he old building [will] fit into the main part of the new building, leaving the new wings projecting on the sides. The old school will soon be demolished, probably during the holidays. There will be many ways in which Old Coqualeetza will live—its influence will be felt and its spirit will be reflected from one generation to another and so on until, ultimately the Old and New Coqualeetza become blended into the ideals for which the Institute stands. (Raley June 30th, 924, n.p.)

The 1894 school building was fully replaced in 1924 by "a monument to the advancing policy of the Department of Indian Affairs" (Raley 1924, n.p.). Duncan Campbell Scott, deputy superintendent-general of Indian Affairs Canada at the time, laid the first brick at "an imposing ceremony," thereby materially marking, and spatially demarcating, discursive imperatives of the educational project:

> [That first brick marked] an epoch in the education of the Indian of British Columbia.

Every effort will be made to impress the native mind that the occasion [of the school building's completion] is one when the standard of ideas is raised to a higher plane than ever before. (Raley 1924, n.p.)

Students experienced these carefully imagined and discursively formed schools as material articulations of assimilationist violence and an agenda of eliminating Indigenousness from British Columbia. The experiential nature of residential schools, particularly as it was expressed in situ by children, is difficult to access. The history has not been preserved in the formal record. Adult testimonies about childhood times in schools offer the most comprehensive record about school experiences (see for instance, Secwepemc Cultural Education Society 2000). Working with a memory record about childhood experiences poses some challenges (see Jones 2003 and Philo 2003), and it seems important to note than many of the memories cited here involve traumatic emotional relationships with space. There are, however, some documentation of children's experiences, produced during their time in schools: these tend to corroborate adult's memories. In a 1968 school newsletter published at St Michael's Residential School in Alert Bay, a 10-year-old child juxtaposes the profound loneliness of residential schooling against an alternative vision of connectedness to family and community:

I am ten now. I have been here ever since I was five. I have lots of friends. I didn't think I would meet so many friends before when my sisters were here, but they left for grade 8. My brother and I have been here so long we're getting tired now.... I miss my sisters. I haven't seen them for a long time. I hope they will write and think about us, but I am sure they will. My mother died when I was a baby. My father died when I was eight, but we've got sisters to look after us. I like it here and I don't at the same time. I'm a big girl now and can look after myself better than when I was five. And I hope soon we will not come back [to] this school any more. (1968, p. 14)

Experientially, then, St Michael's Residential School materialized the discourses of separating Indigenous children from their families and communities. The schools were unhappy spaces that produced feelings of alienation, loneliness, isolation, and a desire to flee. If the discourses produced by colonial powers sought to deindigenize the lands that came to be known as British Columbia, residential schools were their material embodiments, spaces that slowly broke the Indigenous children who attended them.

Colonial discourses about the desirability of assimilation imprinted themselves onto other children's bodies. For one girl, who attended St Mary's Indian Residential School from 1946 to 1957, the shower stalls in the bathrooms of the schools were places through which the colonial ideal of whiteness was imposed. As an adult, she testifies that

There were five showers, but there was no curtain dividing one from another, and when I was in lower grades we would have a senior girl in the shower and they would put us in and the senior would scrub us down. Then the nun was standing at the door . . . and she would check to see if we were clean, and with me, I am naturally dark, so I would always get sent back. I always got sent back because to her I was, not that I was dirty, it is just because I was naturally dark. So I would get sent back and they would scrub the heck out of me and that had a really, really bad effect on me, and through the years, even up to now, I would feel myself washing and washing and never feeling clean. It had a lifelong effect on me. (quoted in Glavin 2002, p. 47)

Space, materially and literally, was violently transformative of First Nations children, inscribing upon them both a sense of inferiority and sense that they would never achieve the (white) ideals demanded of them by colonial educators. Space became an agent of colonial ideology. The disciplinary possibilities of schools rested in the space of the school, or put another way, the spaces of Indian schools were disciplinary.

When Lloyde Baptiste was a child, St Eugene's

Indian Residential School left an indelible physical mark on him. Baptiste, a member of the Osoyoos First Nation in south-eastern British Columbia, Canada, attended the institution between 1956 and 1957 and again from 1964 to 1965. So powerfully affecting were the material spaces of St Eugene's that Baptiste walks with a permanent limp. When he speaks of his time at the school, his recollections of childhood nearly bring him to tears. He recalls how, at the age of eight, for an infraction of school regulations, he was made to scrub St Eugene's long corridors. On the day of his punishment, as his scrubbing brought him closer to the stairs at the far right-hand end of the building, Baptiste recalls an Oblate (Catholic) teaching Brother walking down the corridor to conduct an inspection of the work. What happened next is permanently etched into Baptiste's memory and body.

The Brother found fault in the way the floor was washed and, according to Baptiste, lost his temper, lashing out at the child with fists and feet and sending the eight-year-old hurtling down the school stairs: "When I hit the floor something in my leg cracked. I never received medical treatment, so I crippled up and now it is getting worse. My right leg is two-and-a-half inches shorter than the other" (quoted in Johnson 2002, p. 1). Lloyde Baptiste is adamant that the school building itself, its surfaces, layout, and concrete presence, is an integral part of his memory about colonial education. He speaks of the pedagogical and curricular lessons endured within the school and of the built environment of St Eugene's: the long hallways, the walls in the schools, the feel of the bricks against their hands, the desk alignment in the classrooms, the ordering of the beds in the dorm rooms.

Notwithstanding the tactile reality of St Eugene's for Lloyde Baptiste, the materiality of school was also symbolic. As an articulation of nineteenth-century colonial discourse in which First Nations people were childlike, savage, and perishing: a relative of Lloyde Baptiste's insists there was, and remains, a symbolic power of the structure that extended beyond the school's walls and grounds. "The Kootenay kids had to see the building every day, they were never able to get away from it. I think this contributed to the high incidence of early deaths and suicides due to accidents, drinking and drug abuse and other factors. . . . We didn't need to be saved" (quoted in Johnson 1999, p. 2). Virg Baptiste believes "the fact that 90 per cent of [our] classmates lie in the graveyard nearby is mute confirmation of the far-reaching impact the mission school had on the native children who attended" (quoted in Johnson 1999, p. 2). That graveyard is still there, a reminder that residential schools were (and are) spatialized expressions of colonial discourses in British Columbia and Canada.

Conclusions

This essay sought to document the centrality of children, and concepts of childhood, to colonial projects in Canada and, more specifically, in British Columbia. I was interested in making tangible and clear the linkages between discursive colonial formations about Indigenous children and the related construction of material spaces designed to propagate colonial ideals by intervening into Indigenous children's bodies. I do not, however, want to conclude this paper on a note that privileges colonial power. Despite the relative newness of research about children's geographies, particularly in reference to colonialism, a powerful message from the growing literature is a reminder that children have agency, that they effect change in their surroundings, that they influence as well as reflect their environments (Katz 2004). This premise can be coupled with nuanced geographic understandings of place, including ideas of nested place (Malpas 1999) that insist place is narrated by subjects who occupy and make sense of it, thereby constructing it. Children can thus be theorized as actively producing place, through their experience and narration of it. Following from this is the possibility that children can re-narrate colonial places by experiencing them, can alter the contours of places by living them. As much as residential schools were imagined and designed by colonial minds, they were also lived and experienced by those whom the schools were structured to transform and produce: Aboriginal children.

Ten years prior to Prime Minister Harper's apology for residential schooling, the grand chief of the Assembly of First Nations, Phil Fontaine, made another statement about residential schooling and government apologies concerning colonial education in Canada:

> The days of First Nations citizens as victims are over. We are a strong, resilient people and we are confident that we can move forward and forge a new future for ourselves. . . . Our lands were taken, our children brutalized, and our languages, governments, religions, and ways of living stifled. But miraculously, we survived and here we are today, standing before you, strong and determined to reclaim our birthright in the Canadian Confederation. . . . While today we are celebrating a new beginning, it is appropriate to remember those who were victims of the colonization experience, in particular, the many survivors of the residential school system. . . . We as First Nations, say, "Let us go forward together." (Fontaine 1998, pp. 1–2)

Fontaine's statement came almost eight years (to the day) after his disclosure of abuse within Fort Alexander Residential School. His statement raises intriguing questions, particularly in reference to the assimilative aim of residential schooling and the consequent victimization of Indigenous children within the institutions. Fontaine's focus on strength, resilience, and survival is compelling because it suggests Indigenous children, who lived through the abuses, stood up to and fought colonial violences. In doing so, they secured the survival of First Nations peoples. That survival tells a story of Aboriginal peoples' immense strength and resilience, particularly of Aboriginal children.

Notes

1. The term *Indian* is well recognized as highly problematic. Offensive and dated, it legitimizes and formalizes the conflation and homogenization of peoples on the basis of exclusion from the category European and/or white. Some First Nations and Aboriginal communities are deliberately and strategically reclaiming the term. My use is not intended to appropriate or mimic this strategy. Instead, and as others like Prime Minister Harper do, I use the term throughout this paper to accurately reflect the languages that circulated and continue to circulate with reference to residential schools. I also use the term to highlight the socio-cultural assumptions about the peoples the term names and to signal a set of assumptions that circulated and continue to circulate about "Indians." I suspect the term may be uncomfortable for some to read, as it should be given the continuing pain caused by the schools and the colonial practices and mentalities they embodied. I also use the terms *First Nations*, *Aboriginal*, and *Indigenous* to denote Canada's First Peoples. The terms *Aboriginal* and *Indigenous* are used to inclusively denote First Nations, Inuit, and Métis people and to reflect the ongoing research and contemporary shifts in colonial languages toward more accurate and respectful descriptors of the territory's First Peoples. The term First Nations is used with reference to Nations, in the case of this research usually in British Columbia. Where possible I use the names of specific First Nations (e.g., Haisla).

2. Residential schooling is a contentious subject in Canada that makes accessing historical records about the schools difficult. Litigation, compensation, healing interventions, and multiple and fractious debates about the practice abound across the country. Ecumenical organizations have centralized their collections and protect them carefully. Government archives rarely capture students' experience of the schools and are heavily censored so as to protect the anonymity of anyone whom the record names.

3. Enfranchisement of Indigenous peoples in Canada meant significantly more than the federal government bestowing upon Indians the right to vote (which was not granted universally to Indigenous peoples across Canada until the mid-twentieth century). To be enfranchised meant renouncing any right to be recognized as "Indian" by the federal or provincial governments in Canada. Becoming enfranchised meant relinquishing any claims settled between Indigenous peoples and the British Crown and not being entitled to the (albeit very small) rights established for Indigenous peoples under the Indian Act. Enfranchisement was, until the late twentieth century, imposed upon all Indigenous women (and their children) who married non-Aboriginal men.

4. Scott was also a poet. His creative writings also illustrate his sentiments concerning the dying savage: his 1926 poem "Indian Place Names" is insightful.

5. For over a decade between the early 1940s and mid-1950s, during some of the peak periods of residential schooling in Canada, the logics and justifications of the Indian education project were circulated to teachers and others on the front lines via *The Indian School Bulletin* (ISB). The ISB

was the only nationally distributed publication, produced by the federal government's Department of Indian Affairs, dedicated entirely and specifically to disseminating pedagogical and curricular advice to those involved in the country's Indian education project.

6. Eighteen residential schools were built in British Columbia, operating for over 120 years in the province. The longest-running institution, St Mary's Indian Residential School in Mission, operated between 1861 and 1984. Like St Mary's, eight other residential schools in

British Columbia were operated in partnerships between the Catholic Church and the Government of Canada: the remaining nine schools were operated, respectively, in federal government partnership with the Methodist, Anglican, and Presbyterian churches.

7. See for instance *Na-Na-Kwa; or Dawn of the Northwest Coast*. Compiled by George Henry Raley. Kitimat, British Columbia April 1898–May 1907. Personal collections, original held by The Kitimat Community Museum Archives and Collections, no accession numbers.

References

Primary Sources (Including Newspapers and Government Documents)

Davin, N.F., March 14th, 1879. *Report on industrial schools for Indians and half-breeds*. Report presented to the Government of Canada: Ottawa.

Edmeston, H., ca. 1956. *The Coqualeetza story: 1886–1956*. Sardis, British Columbia: Coqualeetza Indian Residential School and Hospital. Chilliwack Community Archives.

Fontaine, P., March 1998. A new beginning: National Chief's remarks on the government's RCAP response. *In: Residential school update*. Ottawa: The Assembly of First Nations Secretariat.

Government of Canada, Department of Indian Affairs, 1869. *An Act for the Gradual Enfranchisement of Indians*. Ottawa, Ontario.

Government of Canada, Department of Indian Affairs. *The Indian Act*, 1876. Amendments to the Indian Act, 1910, 1911, 1927, 1951, 1970, & 1981. Ottawa, Ontario.

Government of Canada, Department of Indian Affairs Branch; Department of Mines and Resources and Department of Citizenship and Immigration, 1946-1956. *The Indian School Bulletin*, Volumes 1–9. Les Archives Deschatelets.

Government of Canada, Indian and Northern Affairs Canada, 1996. The Royal Commission on Aboriginal Peoples. Ottawa, Ontario. Available from: www.ainc-inac.gc.ca/ch/rcap/sg/cg_e.html [Accessed November 2007].

Harper, S., 2008. *Prime Minister Harper offers full apology on behalf of Canadians for the Indian Residential Schools System*. Ottawa, Ontario: Office of the Prime Minister.

Available from: http://pm.gc.ca/eng/media.asp?id=2149 [Accessed April 2009].

Johnson, W., 1999. Memories of residential school recalled on video by OIB member. *The Oliver Chronicle*. Available from: www.oliverchronicle.com/1999_3.htm [Accessed 2 October 2006. n.p].

Johnson, W., 2002. Residential school victims fight time. *The Oliver Chronicle*. Available from: www.oliverchronicle.com/2002_33.htm [Accessed 2 October 2006. n.p].

Raley, G.H., (1924, June 30th). *Coqualeetza Institute Commencement Exercises*. Sardis, British Columbia: Coqualeetza School. Chilliwack Community Archives.

Rawson, W.R., Davidson, J. and Hepburn, W., March 20th, 1845. *Report on the affairs of the Indians in Canada*. Report submitted by Charles Bagot to The Legislative Assembly, the Province of Canada at Kingston, Ontario.

Renaud, A., 1958. *Indian education today. Excerpt from* Anthropologica. Le Centre de Recherches D'Anthropolgie Amerindienne. WD Jordan Special Collections–Lorne Pierce, Queen's University.

Renaud, A., 1962. The future of the Indians as an ethnic group. *Citizenship Items: Canadian Citizenship Council*, XV (1), 2–4, Port Alberni Historical Society.

Thorton, M.V., 1944. Education buries the Tomahawk: typical Indian schools. *The Vancouver Sun*, 7.

Touch, J.G., and Blackett, W.R., ca. 1886. *Report of the deputation to Metlakatla*. London: The Church Missionary Society.

Secondary Sources

Aitken, S.C., Lund, R., and Kjorholt, A.T., 2007. Why children, why now? *Children's Geographies*, 5 (1–2), 3–14.

Ansell, N., and Smith, F., 2006. Emerging issues in children's geographies. *Children's Geographies*, 4 (3), 255–257.

Armitage, A., 1995. *Comparing the policy of Aboriginal assimilation in Canada*, Australia and New Zealand. Vancouver: UBC Press.

Baptiste, V. (Director), 1999. *Survivors of the red brick school*. Osoyoos, British Columbia: Osoyoos Indian Band.

Bhabha, H.K., 1994. *The location of culture*. New York: Routledge.

Brealey, K., 1995. Mapping them "out": Euro-Canadian cartography and the appropriation of the Nuxalk and Ts'ilhqot'in First Nations' territories, 1793–1916. *Canadian Geographer*, 39 (2),140– 168.

Borrows, J., 2005. Contemporary and comparative perspective on the rights of indigenous peoples: indigenous legal traditions in Canada. *The Washington Journal of Law and Policy*, 19 (273), 168–311.

Carney, R., 1995. Aboriginal residential schools before confederation: the early experience. *Historical Studies*, 61, 13–40.

Churchill, W., 2004. *Kill the Indian, save the child: the genocidal impact of American Indian residential schools.* San Francisco, CA: City Lights Publishing.

Clayton, D.W., 1992. Geographies of the lower Skeena. *BC Studies*, 94, 29–58.

Fabian, J., 1983. *Time and the Other: how Anthropology makes its object.* New York: Columbia University Press.

Fletcher, M.L.M., 2005. Contemporary and comparative perspective on the rights of indigenous peoples: the insidious colonialism of the conqueror—the Federal Government in Modern Tribal Affairs. *The Washington Journal of Law and Policy*, 19 (273), 271–311.

Foucault, M., 1972. *The archaeology of knowledge.* Translation A.M. Sheridan. New York: Pantheon Books.

Fournier, S., and Crey, E., 1997. *Stolen from our embrace: the abduction of first nations children and the restoration of Aboriginal communities.* Vancouver: Douglas & McIntyre.

Furniss, E., 1992. *Victims of benevolence: discipline and death at the Williams Lake Indian Residential School, 1891–1920.* Williams Lake, BC: The Cariboo Tribal Council.

Gagen, E., 2004. Making America flesh: physicality and nationhood in early twentieth century physical education reform. *Cultural Geographies*, 11, 417–442.

Gagen, E., 2007. Reflections of primitivism: development, progress and civilization in imperial America, 1898–1914. *Children's Geographies*, 5 (1–2), 15–28.

Glavin, T., and Former Students of St Mary's, 2002. *Amongst God's own: the enduring legacy of St Mary's Mission.* Mission, BC: Longhouse Publishing.

Harris, C., 2002. *Making native space: colonialism, resistance, and reserves in British Columbia.* Vancouver: UBC Press.

Harris, C., 2004. How did colonialism dispossess? Comments from an edge of Empire. *Annals of the Association of American Geographers*, 94 (1), 165–182.

Holloway, S.L., and Valentine, G., 2000. Children's geographies and the new social studies of childhood. In: S.L. Holloway and G. Valentine, eds. *Children's geographies: playing, living, learning.* New York: Routledge, 1–26.

James, S., 1990. Is there a place for children in geography? *Area*, 22, 378–383.

Katz, C., 2001. Vagabond capitalism and the necessity of social reproduction. *Antipode*, 33 (4), 709–728.

Katz, C., 2004. *Growing up global: economic restructuring and children's everyday lives.* Minneapolis, MN: University of Minnesota Press.

Lawrence, B., 2003. Gender, race, and the regulation of native identity in Canada and the United States: an overview. *Hypatia*, 18 (2), 3–31.

Leslie, J., and Maguire, R., 1978. *The historical development of the Indian Act.* Ottawa, Ontario: Treaties and Historical Research Centre, Research Branch, Corporate Policy, Indian and Northern Affairs Canada.

Li, T.M., 2007. *The will to improve: governmentality, development and the practice of politics.* London: Duke University Press.

Malpas, J., 1999. *Place and experience: a philosophical topography.* New York: Cambridge University Press.

Massey, D., 1993. Politics and space/time. In: M. Keith and S. Pile, eds. *Place and the politics of identity.* New York: Routledge Press.

Massey, D., 2005. *For space.* London: Sage Publications.

McClintock, A., 1995. *Imperial leather: race, gender and sexuality in the colonial contest.* New York: Routledge.

Miller, J.R., 1997. *Shingwauk's vision: a history of native residential schools.* Toronto: University of Toronto Press.

Milloy, J., 1999. *A national crime: the Canadian government and the residential school system, 1879–1986.* Winnipeg: University of Manitoba Press.

Nuu-chah-nulth Tribal Council, 1996. *Indian residential schools: the Nuu-chah-nulth experience*, Printed in Canada.

Jones, O., 2003. "Endlessly revisited and forever gone": on memory, reverie and emotional imagination in doing children's geographies. An "addendum" to "to go back up the side hill": memories, imaginations and reveries of childhood" by Chris Philo. *Children's Geographies*, 1 (1), 25–36.

Philo, C., 2003. "To go back up the side hill": memories, imaginations and reveries of childhood. *Children's Geographies*, 1 (1), 7–23.

Ploszajska, T., 1994. Moral landscapes and manipulated spaces: gender, class and space in Victorian reformatory schools. *Journal of Historical Geography*, 20 (4), 413–429.

Pratt, M.L., 1991a. *Imperial eyes: travel writing and transculturation.* New York: Routledge.

Pratt, M.L., 1991b. Arts of the contact zone. In: *Profession 91.* New York: Modern Language Association.

Prout, A., ed., 2000. *Childhood bodies: construction, agency and hybridity, the body, childhood and society.* New York: St Martin's Press, 1–18.

Raibmon, P., 2005. *Authentic Indians: episodes of encounter from the late nineteenth-century northwest coast.* Durham and London: Duke University Press.

Razack, S., 2002. When place becomes race: introduction. In: S. Razack, ed. *Race, space and the law: unmapping a white settler society.* Toronto: Between the Lines.

Said, E., 1994. *Culture and Imperialism.* New York: Vintage Books.

Schouls, T., 2003. *Shifting boundaries: Aboriginal identity, pluralist theory, and the politics of self-government.* Vancouver: UBC Press.

Scott, D.C., 1926. *The poems of Duncan Campbell Scott.* Toronto: McClelland Press.

Scott, J.C., 1990. *Domination and the arts of resistance: hidden transcripts.* New Haven: Yale University Press.

Secwepemc Cultural Education Society, 2000. *Behind closed doors: stories from the Kamloops Indian residential school.* Penticton, BC: Theytus Books.

Sparke, M., 1998. "A map that roared and an original atlas: Canada, cartography, and the narration of nation." *Annals of the Association of American Geographers*, 88 (3), 463–495.

Spivak, G.C., 1996. Subaltern talk: interview with the Editors, 29 October 1993. In: D. Landry and G. Maclean, eds. *The Spivak reader*. New York: Routledge.

Stoler, A.L., 2006. Tense and tender ties: the politics of comparison in North American history and (post)colonial studies. In: A. Laura Stoler, ed. *Haunted by Empire; geographies of intimacy in North American history*. Durham: Duke University Press.

Tennant, P., 1990. *Aboriginal peoples and politics: the Indian Land Question in British Columbia, 1849–1989*. Vancouver: UBC Press.

Thomas, N., 1994. *Colonialism's culture: anthropology, travel and the Government*. Princeton, NJ: Princeton University Press.

Titley, B.E., 1986. *A narrow vision: Duncan Campbell Scott and the Administration of Indian Affairs in Canada*. Vancouver: UBC Press.

Haida Mountain Goat Pillow Case and Glass Ball

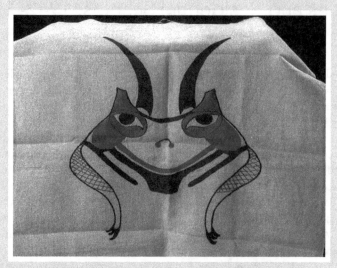

Source: Image15471, courtesy of the Royal BC Museum
and Archives. Photo by Sarah de Leeuw.

Source: Image13696, courtesy of the Royal BC
Museum and Archives. Photo by Sarah de Leeuw.

Administering Colonial Science: Nutrition Research and Human Biomedical Experimentation in Aboriginal Communities and Residential Schools, 1942–1952

IAN MOSBY

In March 1942, and after months of planning, a group of scientific and medical researchers travelled by bush plane and dog sled to the Cree communities of Norway House, Cross Lake, God's Lake Mine, Rossville, and The Pas in Northern Manitoba. The trip was jointly sponsored by Indian Affairs, the New York–based Milbank Memorial Fund, the Royal Canadian Air Force (RCAF) and the Hudson's Bay Company but had been spearheaded by Indian Affairs Branch Superintendent of Medical Services Dr. Percy Moore and RCAF Wing Commander Dr. Frederick Tisdall—Canada's leading nutrition expert and the co-inventor of the infant food Pablum. The goal was to "study the state of nutrition of the Indian by newly developed medical procedures," which meant that—in addition to collecting information on local subsistence patterns—the research team conducted detailed physical examinations, blood tests, and x-rays on nearly 400 Aboriginal residents of these communities.[1] But even before they began to administer their battery of medical tests, the researchers were immediately struck by the frightening toll that malnutrition and hunger appeared to be taking. At both Norway House and Cross Lake, they reported that "while most of the people were going about trying to make a living, they were really sick enough to be in bed under treatment and that if they were white people, they would be in bed and demanding care and medical attention." Following a visit to the homes of some of the elderly residents of Norway House at the request of the Chief and Council, moreover, researchers found that "conditions were

deplorable where the old people were almost starved and were plainly not getting enough food to enable them to much more than keep alive."[2]

In their official reports, the researchers drew explicit connections between the hunger and malnutrition they had witnessed and the broader health problems facing these northern Cree communities which, they noted, included a tuberculosis death rate of 1,400 per 100,000 (compared to 27.1 for the non-Aboriginal population of Manitoba), an infant mortality rate eight times that of the rest of Canada, and a crude mortality rate almost five times that of Manitoba as a whole.[3] At the same time, the research team also sought to situate the findings within a broader popular understanding of Canada's so-called "Indian Problem."[4] In a preliminary report on their study in March 1942, they concluded:

> It is not unlikely that many characteristics, such as shiftlessness, indolence, improvidence and inertia, so long regarded as inherent or hereditary traits in the Indian race may, at the root, be really the manifestations of malnutrition. Furthermore, it is highly probable that their great susceptibility to many diseases, paramount amongst which is tuberculosis, may be directly attributable to their high degree of malnutrition arising from lack of proper foods.[5]

To test this hypothesis fully, they proposed that an intensive one- to two-year study be conducted "on a limited number of Indians" to demonstrate the effects of nutritional interventions into the diet of an already malnourished population. This central study

Source: From *Histoire sociale/Social History*, 46, 91 (May 2013): 145–72. Reprinted with permission.

would then be complemented with an "[e]nquiry into the agricultural economy of the Indian," a "study of the foods supplied by traders and the food subsidy for the destitute and aged in light of modern nutritional knowledge," and an examination of the effectiveness of "teaching of domestic science and dietary knowledge in the schools." They then added, by way of conclusion: "It is our belief that the Indian can become an economic asset to the nation."[6]

The result, over the next decade, was not just a single examination of these communities in Northern Manitoba, but instead an unprecedented series of nutritional studies of First Nations communities and Indian residential schools by some of Canada's leading nutrition experts in co-operation with Indian Affairs and, after 1945, with the Indian Health Services Branch of the Department of National Health and Welfare. The most ambitious and perhaps best known of these was the 1947–1948 James Bay Survey under the leadership of Tisdall, Moore, and University of Toronto anthropologist G. Gordon Brown.[7] Less well known—to the extent that they appear to have received virtually no attention from historians—were two separate long-term studies that went so far as to include controlled experiments conducted, apparently without the subjects' informed consent or knowledge, on malnourished Aboriginal populations in Northern Manitoba and, later, in six Indian residential schools.[8]

This article explores these particular nutritional studies conducted between 1942 and 1952, in part simply to provide a narrative record of a largely unexamined episode of exploitation and neglect by the Canadian government while also contributing to a broader international literature on nutrition research and colonial science.[9] At the same time, however, it also seeks to situate these studies within the context of broader federal policies governing the lives of Aboriginal peoples, a shifting Canadian consensus concerning the science of nutrition, and changing attitudes towards the ethics of biomedical experimentation on human beings during a period that encompassed, among other things, the establishment of the Nuremberg Code of experimental research ethics. In doing so, this article argues that—during the war and early post-war period—bureaucrats, doctors, and scientists recognized the problems of hunger and malnutrition, yet increasingly came to view Aboriginal bodies as "experimental materials" and residential schools and Aboriginal communities as kinds of "laboratories" that they could use to pursue a number of different political and professional interests. Nutrition experts, for their part, were provided with the rare opportunity to observe the effects of nutritional interventions (and non-interventions, as it turned out) on human subjects while, for Moore and others within the Indian Affairs and Indian Health Services bureaucracy, nutrition offered a new explanation for—and novel solutions to—the so-called "Indian Problems" of susceptibility to disease and economic dependency. In the end, these studies did little to alter the structural conditions that led to malnutrition and hunger in the first place and, as a result, did more to bolster the career ambitions of the researchers than to improve the health of those identified as being malnourished.

Nutrition in the North

Although it was only during the 1940s that nutrition experts and Indian Affairs officials alike began to make serious, sustained inquiries into the prevalence of malnutrition in remote Aboriginal communities or in residential schools, there had been warnings of widespread hunger in both for decades.[10] Well before the first systematic studies of food in residential schools were conducted by the Nutrition Services Division during the mid- to late 1940s, for instance, reports from Aboriginal children, their parents, and even Indian Affairs employees had indicated that students were underfed and, in many cases, severely malnourished. As John Milloy's extensive study of the residential school system shows in considerable detail, hunger was a "continual and systemic problem," and food shortages in schools were a persistent issue during the interwar years.[11] Mary Ellen Kelm and J.R. Miller have also both shown that hunger and the frequently inedible food that children were forced to eat often dominates the memories of survivors of residential schools. These conditions in all likelihood contributed to the appalling death rates of children either during their residency or immediately upon discharge from these institutions, which in some cases exceeded 50 per cent of pupils.[12]

Hunger and malnutrition also extended well beyond the doors of the country's residential schools, particularly during the 1930s. The communities in the central subarctic region that were the subjects of these major nutrition studies during the 1940s had been hit disproportionately hard by the economic collapse of the Great Depression. To a certain extent this was because incomes within the fur trade had plummeted, dropping by 66 per cent in the Prairies between 1924 and 1935 and by 38 per cent in Northern Ontario between 1925 and 1935. To make matters worse, many areas had seen steadily declining populations of fur-bearing and food animals during the interwar years, in no small part due to over-hunting by unscrupulous non-Aboriginal trappers throughout the preceding decades.[13] Hunger in these communities was not simply a product of declining incomes and disappearing fur-bearing animals, however. The 1930s also saw Indian Affairs actually cut back on its provision of unemployment relief. Between 1922 and 1934, the government's total relief payments fell by 32 per cent, from $242,000 to $164,000. As Hugh Shewell has shown, much of this was done through orders prohibiting relief payments to able-bodied men, reducing sick relief rations, and other forms of so-called "austerity" and "restraint" within Indian Affairs. These cuts meant that, throughout the Depression, per capita expenditures on relief were consistently between two and three times higher for non-Aboriginal Canadians than they were for Aboriginal peoples. The onset of war did little to change the economic circumstances for the Cree First Nations in Northern Manitoba and the James Bay region. The collapse of export markets meant that fur prices remained low, few on-reserve job opportunities became available, and relief policies were, according to Shewell, "harsher even than those of the interwar years."[14]

It was in this context that, in 1942, Tisdall, Moore, and the rest of their research team—which included Millbank Memorial Fund associate director and leading international nutrition expert Dr H.D. Kruse—began the study of malnutrition among the Cree First Nations of Northern Manitoba. As Chief Andrew Crate Sr of the Norway House First Nation told the research team, the causes of poor health among his people were clear:

> A lot of us are living in the bush, trying to live off the country, but, for the scarcity of fur and eatable animals, we sometimes have a very hard time to supply our families with food. If it wasn't for the patience and kindness of the Hudson's Bay Company, a lot of us would have nothing to day. . . . The Indian Agent has told us, that the Indian Department has asked him not to give any able-bodied man any relief, and the only way we can help ourselves was by getting a treaty debt from the Indian Agent. . . . The Band feel that if the taking away of the treaty rations will help in winning the war, then we are satisfied, but may hope to have the rations given to us again after the war.[15]

Chief Spence Ross of the Cross Lake First Nation similarly acknowledged that, because of the war, Canada was "carrying a heavy burden, so heavy that I cannot bring myself to ask for any extension of services among us at the present time." He lamented, however, that his band was running out of treaty money and that from May to October, when the muskrat trapping season was over, they were likely to face six months of no earnings and little food. He added: "At that time we will be thinking of the Government at Ottawa. I hope the Government at Ottawa will be thinking of us."[16]

Representatives of the various First Nations visited by the research team proposed a number of practical suggestions for ending the hunger and malnutrition in their communities. In addition to more generous relief during times of extreme hardship, these included increased rations for the old and destitute, timber reserves to be set aside for the building and repairing of houses, and additional fur conservation efforts by the federal government, as well as a request that they be given fishing reserves "so that they could get fish both for themselves and for dog feed, free from competition with the large commercial fisheries."[17] The primary response of the researchers, however, was a familiar one. As Moore would tell a House of Commons Special Committee in May 1944, "As a result of the survey one of the first steps considered necessary in any program to improve the health of the Indian through better nutrition was to demonstrate whether provision of some of the food substances or food factors found to be lacking in their diet would result in an improvement in their health."[18] Moore and the rest of the research team therefore almost immediately set about organizing a scientific experiment on the effectiveness of vitamin supplements conducted primarily by the resident physician for the Indian Affairs Branch at Rossville, Dr Cameron Corrigan.

The experiment began in 1942, shortly after Corrigan returned from a post-graduate course in medicine in New York City under the supervision of Kruse. Of a group of 300 malnourished Aboriginal test subjects, 125 were provided with riboflavin, thiamine, or ascorbic acid supplements—or a combination of these—while the rest acted as a "control" group. The local nurse, Miss Wilson, regularly visited those involved in the study to ensure that they were taking the vitamin therapy and to remove "unreliable" people from study. The goal was to see whether the physical manifestations of disease could be treated using vitamin supplements alone. To this end, over the course of two years, detailed medical examinations were conducted on both groups and colour photos taken of eyes, gums, and tongues. Part of the study therefore included additional visits by Tisdall and Moore as well as ophthalmological examinations by members of the British Oxford Nutrition Survey and the RCAF.[19]

From the perspective of Tisdall, Kruse, and the other nutrition experts involved in the study, it was clear that the levels of malnutrition witnessed at Norway House, Cross Lake, and other communities visited in 1942 were a tragedy, but also an unprecedented research opportunity. This was because, even as late as the 1940s, nutrition was still a relatively young area of scientific inquiry. Scientists only really began to understand the function of vitamins and minerals during the interwar period, and most experts readily admitted that much of their understanding of human nutrition was based upon animal studies and had not been put to the test on human subjects in any rigorous or controlled manner.[20] The late 1930s and early 1940s were also the formative period for Canada's nutrition professions. The Canadian Council on Nutrition (CCN), an advisory body made up of the nation's leading nutrition experts, was formed in 1938, and the Nutrition Services Division of the Department of Pensions and National Health was created in 1941 under the leadership of biochemist and medical doctor Lionel Bradley Pett, largely in response to public warnings by the CCN that upwards of 60 per cent of Canadians were suffering from some form of vitamin or mineral deficiency. While such dramatic claims brought nutrition experts into the public spotlight during the war, scientists readily admitted—to one another, at least—that they still knew very little about the relative effectiveness of vitamin and mineral supplements on malnourished populations, let alone the precise vitamin and mineral requirements of human beings. Debates over this latter issue, in particular, would lead to major internal divisions within the profession by the late 1940s and meant that experts like Tisdall and Pett were eager to test their theories on actual human subjects.[21]

There are a number of indications that these kinds of scientific questions, more than humanitarian concerns, played a key role in defining the response to the nutritional deficiencies in Aboriginal populations encountered by the researchers. Based on the research team's own published findings, for instance, the vitamin deficiencies being experienced by the Norway House and Cross Lake First Nations constituted just one among many nutritional problems. Hunger seems to have been the most serious of these. According to their own calculations, the average diet in these communities provided only 1,470 calories per person during much of the year.[22] This suggests that the Aboriginal peoples who were the objects of these studies were surviving on a diet comparable to the 1,570 calories per day being used to induce starvation among the 36 volunteer conscientious objectors who took part in Ancel Keys's ground-breaking University of Minnesota starvation experiment between 1944 and 1946.[23] Clearly the research team was well aware that these vitamin supplements only addressed a small part of the problem and that, if they really wanted to deal with the immediate problem of malnutrition and hunger, emergency food relief that met all of the nutritional needs of the community was badly needed.

The experiment therefore seems to have been driven, at least in part, by the nutrition experts' desire to test their theories on a ready-made "laboratory" populated with already malnourished human "experimental subjects." It also reflected some of Moore's larger ambitions for what would eventually become, under his leadership, the Indian Health Services Branch of the Department of National Health and Welfare. During the interwar period—and the Depression, in particular—the Medical Branch of the Department of Indian Affairs languished: it was perennially under-funded, minimally staffed, and wholly inadequate to the task it had been assigned. As the superintendent of Medical Services for Indian Affairs and, after 1945, as director of the newly created Indian Health Services Branch, Moore sought to increase the scope of his division's work by continually reiterating the message that poor health—and malnutrition in particular—were at the heart of the so-called "Indian Problem" of "dependency" and, therefore, that the provision of modern, scientific medical care needed to become one of the core missions of any modern Indian administration.[24]

For Moore and others, addressing the problems of poor health and malnutrition in Aboriginal communities was not only essential to protecting the white population from Indian "reservoirs" and "vectors" of diseases like tuberculosis—language that became a central justification of the work of Indian Health Services. It was also necessary to fulfil the longer-term goal of integrating and assimilating Aboriginal peoples into the Canadian population. The preferred solution was intervention by non-Aboriginal experts like doctors, dieticians, and social workers. As Shewell has argued, Moore "represented the new, professional voice of the bureaucracy." He believed that Indian Affairs administrators had failed, not because their assimilationist policies were wrong, but "because they had been insufficiently guided and informed, and as a result they did

not fully understand the difficulties facing Indians in their adjustment to civilization." They therefore needed "a base of scientific knowledge on which to build successful programs for Indian integration."[25] Studying malnutrition in First Nations such as Norway House and Cross Lake provided a key first step in this direction and was therefore viewed by Moore as a crucial element in his broader programme of "modernizing" Canada's Indian administration.

The James Bay Survey

The 1947–1948 James Bay Survey, as it came to be known, was perhaps the most complete articulation of Moore's vision regarding the role of nutrition in dealing with the so-called "Indian Problem." The study—which once again included Tisdall and Moore as two of the primary researchers—expanded significantly upon the work done in Northern Manitoba to the extent that it included a team of twelve researchers: six physicians, a dentist, an x-ray technician, a photographer, and three anthropologists. The goals of the two studies were nonetheless similar in that both sought to explore the connection between nutrition and health in the North. To this end, residents of the Attawapiskat and Rupert's House Cree First Nations were ultimately chosen as subjects because of the "pronounced dependence on relief" in the area—which made the residents "typical of the Canadian Bush Indians"—and also because, by way of contrast, the economic conditions in Attawapiskat were much worse than at Rupert's House, where the HBC had been operating a successful beaver conservation programme for nearly a decade.[26] Funding for the study once again drew upon a range of both public and private sources, including the Department of National Health and Welfare, the Department of Mines and Resources, and the Canadian Life Insurance Officers Association. Research contributions were similarly diverse and included researchers from a number of federal departments and Canadian universities as well as from the United States Public Health Service.[27]

One of the primary stated goals of the study was, from the outset, to explore "possible methods for augmenting or improving the food supplies of the Bush Indians" as well as to conduct a study of the "practical means for increasing their supplies of wild foods, of the chances of really interesting the Indians in raising gardens, and of the possibility of improving the nutritional value of the food purchased at the posts." The anthropologists would play a major role in the latter part of the project, particularly inasmuch as they would shine a light on "how the Indian thinks and on how he could best be helped to improve his living conditions."[28] As Tisdall told a parliamentary committee in 1947:

> We do not know as much as we should as to what motivates the Indian. We have to find out what incentive we can place in front of him. The Indian is very different from us. We have to find out how the Indian can be encouraged, how his work can be diversified, his efforts diversified, so he can make himself self-supporting, so he can obtain the food he needs.[29]

The James Bay Survey, in other words, was not simply a study of the nutritional status of the Attawapiskat and Rupert's House First Nations but was also intended to elucidate the connection between food, nutrition, and the "Indian Problem" more generally.

In part, this approach reflected one of the key conclusions that Moore, Tisdall, and others had taken away from their earlier study: that levels of malnutrition had been, in no small part, due to the increasing dependence of Aboriginal peoples on "store foods"—which was the common term used for imported goods from the south—and their movement away from the more nutritious "country foods" like fish, game, and berries. Not only had the Norway House and Cross Lake First Nations been consuming an almost wholly inadequate diet, they argued, but "no less than 1,258 [calories], or 85% of the total, were supplied by white flour, lard, sugar and jam."[30] As a 1948 press release from Indian Affairs promoting Moore's nutrition efforts among "bush Indians" argued, "Canada's northern Indians have lost the art of eating."

> They have abandoned the native eating habits of their forefathers and adopted a semi-civilized, semi native diet which lacks essential food values, brings them to malnutrition and leaves them prey to tuberculosis and other disease. The white man, who unintentionally is responsible for the Indians' changed eating habits, now is trying to salvage the red man by directing him towards proper food channels.[31]

This theory that the partial adoption of non-Aboriginal foodways had led to a decline in the health of Aboriginal peoples was not new and had been put forward during the 1930s by Weston A. Price and others.[32] Moore, however, sought to address the problem directly by adopting a range of decidedly experimental strategies designed to promote the purchase of more nutritious store foods and, where they were plentiful, to encourage greater consumption of country foods. These strategies ranged from education to coercion, and they provide some important insight into motivations behind the James Bay study.

One of Moore's key strategies was to introduce vitamin supplements and fortified foods into the diet of Aboriginal peoples through relief allotments and residential schools. In fact, even before the results of the vitamin supplement experiments in Cross Lake and Norway House had been completed, Moore began work developing a number of novel nutritional supplements including a special "carrot" biscuit containing large quantities of vitamin A and a "Blood Sausage" product containing a long list of ingredients, including beef blood; pork scalps, rinds, snouts, and ears; beef lungs; beef, pork, veal, sheep, and lamb spleens; beef or pork brains; hog stomach; beef tripe; cooked pork carcass bones; cooked pigs' feet; oatmeal flour; and seasoning. While the biscuit was ultimately distributed to northern communities, the blood sausage—along with a similarly "nutritious" "Meat Spread"—was rejected by the Department of Agriculture because it contravened the *Food and Drugs Act* provisions governing food adulterants like bone meal.[33]

Perhaps the policy that had the greatest impact on the diets of Aboriginal peoples in the North—at least until the many "experimental" relocations of Inuit communities that would begin during the

1950s[34]—was the regulation put in place by Moore and others that limited the kinds of goods that could be purchased with Family Allowances. These universal monthly payments of between $5 for children under 6 and $8 for children between 13 and 16 came into effect in 1945 and had a profound impact on the diets of Aboriginal peoples throughout the Canadian subarctic. It was estimated by John J. Honigmann, one of the James Bay Survey's anthropologists, that Family Allowances saw the per capita income in the Attawapiskat Cree First Nation—where he lived doing field research for nearly a year—increase by 52 per cent in 1946–1947 and by 38 per cent in 1947–1948. He also suggested that, in 1949–1950, they accounted for an astonishing 54 per cent of per capita income among the Great Whale River Inuit community in Northern Quebec.[35]

Moore sought to harness the profound economic and nutritional potential of Family Allowances by preventing indigenous families in the North from collecting them as cash, as all other Canadians were entitled to do, and instead establishing a separate, in-kind system of payment for so-called "Bush Indians" and "Eskimos." Purchases were therefore limited to certain items of clothing and "foods of high nutritive value over and above their basic subsistence requirements."[36] These included canned tomatoes (or grapefruit juice), rolled oats, Pablum, pork luncheon meat (such as Spork, Klick, or Prem), dried prunes or apricots, and cheese or canned butter.[37] In some cases, moreover, it seems that Indian Affairs officials went so far as to experiment with preventing some families from using Family Allowances to purchase flour—despite the fact that it had long been a key dietary staple—as part of a broader effort both to encourage them to increase their consumption of country food and to discourage families from returning to the local HBC post too often. In Great Whale River, the consequence of this policy during late 1949 and early 1950 was that many Inuit families were forced to go on their annual winter hunt with insufficient flour to last for the entire season. Within a few months, some went hungry and were forced to resort to eating their sled dogs and boiled seal skin.[38]

In many ways, then, the James Bay Survey was viewed by Moore and others as an opportunity—not just to examine the nutritional status of the James Bay Cree, but also to provide some kind of expert guidance for developing new policies and programmes in Canada's North that not only would reduce rates of malnutrition, but would combat the ever-present threat of so-called "dependency." The findings and recommendations therefore followed a familiar pattern. On the one hand, both Attawapiskat and Rupert's House First Nations were found to be doing considerably better, nutritionally, than the communities in Northern Manitoba visited by Tisdall and Moore between 1942 and 1944—attributed, in large part, to the recent introduction of Family Allowances.[39] On the other hand, however, clinical examinations appeared to show that members of both First Nations showed an "inadequate state of nutrition" and, to this end, the researchers noted that they "were impressed by the general apathy, slowness and inertia of the group as a whole as well as by the evidence of premature ageing."[40] The researchers attributed these perceived conditions, of course, not to the economic realities in the two communities, but instead to the need for residents to be educated in "the elementary rules of sanitation and health, and the need for better preservation, preparation, and choice of food." They even went so far as to suggest that raising the economic level in Attawapiskat or Rupert's House would "accomplish little without accompanying health and nutrition programs."[41]

While the researchers involved in the study often proposed different solutions to these perceived nutritional problems, they nonetheless agreed that the solution would only come about through expert intervention. Honigmann, for his part, argued that any future efforts at "community rehabilitation" should be assigned to someone "who has some anthropological sophistication" given the "problems to be faced in working with an alien culture."[42] Moore, Tisdall, and the other medical researchers instead suggested that the communities should be strongly encouraged to use more locally available foods—whether through hunting, trapping, fishing, or gardening—but that, in addition, it would "be desirable to improve the vitamin and mineral value of the staple foods which the Indians must purchase." "It is entirely feasible," they noted, "to do this by incorporating thiamine, riboflavin, niacin, vitamin D, calcium and iron into the flour. Studies should be carried out to determine the practicability of incorporating vitamin A in the lard and vitamin C in the powdered milk."[43] If First Nations were not willing to give up their "dependence" on store foods, in other words, the solution was to persuade them—through either education or official edict—to use novel food technologies designed to ease their dietary transition to "modernity."

Nutrition Experiments in Residential Schools, 1948–1952

The "discovery" of widespread hunger and malnutrition in Canada's Indian residential schools in the early post-war period prompted a similarly paternalistic and opportunistic response by both the federal government and nutrition experts. Although Aboriginal parents had been warning of widespread hunger in the schools for decades, it was only following a series of "official" investigations during the mid-1940s that Indian Affairs officials themselves began to admit to the systemic nature of the problem. According to Milloy, Moore had instigated the first investigations of the food service after being "troubled by what he observed during the war and by reports that reached his desk."[44] He quickly found an ally in federal Nutrition Services Division director Lionel Pett who, as it turned out, was eager to expand his small department's mandate.

The first investigations began in 1944 with the assistance of the Nutrition Services Division of the Canadian Red Cross Society, but these studies were later expanded in the years following the war. Most were conducted by trained dieticians working for either the Red Cross or the federal Nutrition Division, and schools were typically notified in advance of inspections. Over the course of a few hours or an entire day, the investigator would interview staff and examine everything from the menus being served to the food purchase ledgers, the conditions of kitchen and food storage facilities, the food service area, and, where they existed, agricultural production

facilities. When possible, the investigator would also eat with the students to obtain their assessment of the quality of the food actually being served. Occasionally, inspectors would also visit nearby reserves to talk with parents about food and nutrition. Clinical exams were not usually a component of these early investigations, but visible signs of illness among the students were sometimes recorded in reports. Most importantly, the reports assessed the daily value of the students' meals against the recommendations found in Canada's Food Rules or other widely accepted sets of recommended daily nutritional requirements.[45]

There were, of course, major problems with this method of investigating food services. Basil H. Johnson, a survivor of the Spanish Residential School in Northern Ontario, distinctly remembered the visits by nutrition inspectors as well as the ways in which school administrators tried to alter the results in their own favour. Upon the arrival of the investigators, he recalled, "instead of lard, there were pats of butter on a tin plate, and the soup was thicker than usual, with more meat and vegetables—almost like a stew." Despite attempts by some of the boys to make the investigators aware that their usual menu consisted of broth, bread, lard, and tea, nothing ultimately came of the investigations, and the boys saw the return of their typical diet of "just enough food to blunt the sharp edge of hunger for three or four hours."[46] Whether inspectors recognized that they were intentionally being misled is unclear, but they did quickly realize that their inspections were causing problems within the schools. One inspector was told by an Indian Affairs official that the work was "making it more difficult for the principals, sister superiors and cooks to operate the schools because the Indian children realize that we are there to try to improve the food services." She added that First Nations had "been agitating for betterment in the food served, and this makes it very hard for the principal."[47]

Despite the tendency of inspectors to see better food service than was typically being provided, their investigations nonetheless showed overwhelmingly poor conditions in the schools. The food provided typically failed to meet the government's own stated basic nutritional requirements. In many schools, items such as meat, milk, fruits, and vegetables were rare; schools often lacked a trained cooking staff; and many lacked even rudimentary appliances, refrigeration, or basic standards of sanitation. Even when kitchens were well equipped, there were rarely sufficient funds to purchase the kinds of daily menus outlined in the Food Rules.[48] It quickly became clear to investigators that this latter issue, in particular, was the heart of the problem. As was the case with relief rates in Aboriginal communities, the Depression and the war saw significant cutbacks in per capita grants provided to schools to the extent that, by 1947, Pett estimated that the per capita grant provided for food in most schools was often half that required to maintain a balanced diet.[49] Once again, however, the official response was not to increase these grants immediately, but instead to launch further investigations.

In September 1946, the federal Nutrition Division, in co-operation with Indian Affairs, created a staff position for the sole purpose of investigating schools and, where possible, implementing a food services training program for both staff and students responsible for cooking. A large part of this task meant following up with previously investigated schools to see whether any recommendations had actually been implemented. The results were, to say the least, disappointing. The lead investigator for the project, Alice McCready, at one point reported that she was "utterly disgusted" by the lack of improvements at revisited schools and wondered: "How can a report on each one of these schools be effective if it is to be a repetition of the first report?"[50] Training, she argued, was often wasted on kitchen staff who—because of the low pay and often very poor working conditions—were subject to extremely high turnover. The religious orders operating the schools blamed the federal government for the lack of funding, while Indian Affairs placed the onus on the churches. Pett, for his part, lamented that the administration of residential schools seemed to "drift aimlessly on a sea of uncertainty, tossed about by winds of quandary and gales of ignorance."[51] In the process, however, little was done to address the poor diets of the Aboriginal children caught in the middle.

It was in this context that, starting in 1947, Pett began planning an ambitious research project using Aboriginal students as experimental subjects. Before he became the director of the Nutrition Services Division in 1941, Pett was already a well-respected scientific researcher and was the co-author of a pioneering nutritional survey of low-income families in Edmonton. He was therefore not simply aware of the divisive post-war debates among Canada's leading nutrition experts and scientists concerning human nutritional requirements but was, in fact, a key player in these debates.[52] To this end, the seemingly intractable situation in Canada's residential schools provided Pett with an unprecedented scientific and professional opportunity. Without necessary changes to the per capita funding formula for the schools, there was little likelihood that the students' nutritional status would improve in any meaningful way. This meant that the schools had become, through decades of neglect by Indian Affairs, a possible laboratory for studying human requirements for a range of nutrients as well as the effects of dietary interventions on a group of malnourished children.

Pett argued that his long-term study would be "designed to investigate certain questions already raised regarding Indians." These included:

(1) Are conditions observed in Northern Manitoba found elsewhere in Canada?
(2) What type of food service in residential schools will economically provide the best maintenance of health *and* carry over desirable food habits to the reserve?
(3) Will foods fortified with vitamins and minerals provide demonstrable results over the course of 5 years?
(4) Can health educational methods be introduced effectively in these schools? etc.[53]

In other words, as did researchers in the James Bay Survey, Pett sought to examine the effects of malnutrition firsthand and, at the same time, to assess the adaptability of a diet that was making its supposedly inevitable transition from "traditional" to "modern." He was quickly able to gain the support of both the

Department of Indian Affairs and Indian Health Services for his proposal and, in the fall of 1948, Pett began a series of five-year experiments on the effects of different nutritional interventions into the diets of close to 1,000 Aboriginal students at six residential schools across the country. These included the Alberni school in Port Alberni, British Columbia; the St Mary's and Cecilia Jeffrey schools in Kenora, Ontario; the Shubenacadie school in Shubenacadie, Nova Scotia; and the St Paul's and Blood schools in Southern Alberta near Lethbridge.

Like the Northern Manitoba and James Bay Surveys before them, the investigations employed a variety of different experts, ranging from nutrition professionals, doctors, and nurses to dentists, photographers, and lab technicians. Research included medical and dental examinations, blood tests, and intelligence and aptitude tests, as well as collection of menu and dietary records from each of the schools. The particular schools chosen had all previously been investigated by McCready and, while they differed in specifics, were found to be lacking in a number of areas. This information, in combination with clinical examinations of the students conducted by the larger research team in the fall of 1948, was subsequently used to assess which experimental interventions would be assigned to each school.

At Alberni, early investigations found not only an inexperienced staff and out-of-date, run-down kitchen facilities but that the diets of the children were lacking in vitamins A, B, and C and iodine because they were not being provided with enough foods like milk, fruit, vegetables, eggs, cheese, and iodized salt. Partly because clinical examinations showed that students in Alberni had the highest incidence of riboflavin deficiency of all the experimental schools, Pett chose to use this particular school to test the effects of tripling the children's milk consumption from its existing serving of 8 ounces per day—less than half of the quantity recommended in Canada's Food Rules—to 24 ounces. First, however, the 8-ounce ration was maintained for two years to provide a "base line" that could be used to assess the later results.[54] At Schubenacadie, Pett designed an even more ambitious experiment. McCready's initial investigation identified a similarly deficient diet

in that it was lacking in the intake of vitamins A, B, and C, iron, and iodine. Clinical investigators also noticed a "[c]onsiderable increase during the winter in the number of children showing low blood levels of ascorbic acid, and in the amount of gingivitis." They therefore designed a double-blind, randomized study that would "compare the effect on gums and on haemoglobin, of ascorbic acid (vitamin C) supplements in the form of tablets." To do this, the children were "divided into experimental and control groups which received 100 mg. ascorbic acid tablets or placebos daily."[55]

The experiments chosen for the other schools followed a similar pattern. At the Blood school, the possibility of thiamine deficiency saw the children's diet, after a two-year "base-line" period, supplemented with Canada Approved Vitamin B Flour—a product introduced by government nutrition experts during the early years of the war, which, due to an alternative milling technique, maintained more of the wheat's nutritional value than other white flours. At St Mary's school, on the other hand, the high incidence of riboflavin deficiency led to the introduction of "Newfoundland Flour Mix"—a product that could not be legally sold outside of Newfoundland under Canada's laws against food adulteration because it contained added thiamine, riboflavin, niacin, and bone meal. At the Cecilia Jeffrey school, children were supplied with the option of consuming whole wheat bread, combined with an educational program for staff and children, so as to "study the effects of educational procedures on choice of foods and nutrition status in a residential school." Finally, the St Paul's school was chosen as a "control"—meaning that no changes were made to its menus during the course of the study, despite the fact that the initial investigation had found that students were being fed poor quality, unappetizing food that provided inadequate intakes of vitamins A, B, and C as well as iron and iodine.[56]

J.R. Miller has argued that the early architects of Canada's residential school system saw the schools as "social laboratories in which people's beliefs and ways could be refashioned."[57] But as these experiments made clear, the systematic neglect and mistreatment of students in these schools also made them into ideal scientific laboratories. For Pett and his research team, in particular, the malnourished Aboriginal subjects of these experiments provided the means to weigh in on a number of scientific controversies, including ongoing disagreements over the effectiveness of dental interventions like fluoride treatment versus nutritional supplementation for maintaining an individual's oral health. Indeed, when researchers learned that Indian Health Services dentists had visited the Alberni, St Mary's, and Cecilia Jeffrey schools in the early years of the study, the research team quickly sent off telegrams and letters insisting that, for the duration of the study, "no specialized, over-all type of dental service should be provided [to the students], such as the use of sodium fluoride, dental prophylaxis or even urea compounds." It was argued that, because dental caries and gingivitis were both "important factors in assessing nutritional status," any significant dental interventions would interfere with the results of the study.[58] Students in the experimental schools, in other words, were denied treatment that other students would have had access to during the five year study period.

It is also clear that, from both Pett's and Moore's perspective, the experiments also provided a means to investigate the effectiveness of the kinds of nutritionally fortified foods that Moore had long been proposing be incorporated into Aboriginal diets. While Pett had been somewhat sceptical of Moore's "sausage" and "meat pastes" schemes, he eventually began to agree that nutritionally fortified foods and vitamin supplements could, if properly implemented by nutrition experts, be effective. To test whether such products would succeed on the reserve, as well as in the school, Pett therefore also began a number of concurrent investigations into the connection between Aboriginal eating habits at home and the dietary practices learned in schools. These included, among other projects, a series of nationwide poster and placemat drawing contests among residential school pupils that were designed, in part at least, to find out what kinds of foods were being consumed on reserves and in schools. The result of such investigations, according to Pett, would be a rough psychological and culinary portrait of the "typical" Indian diet.[59]

While the stated goal of these particular experiments was, in the long term, to improve the nutrition in residential schools around the country, they were clearly also designed to offer a range of possible solutions to the "Indian Problem" more generally. Alberni school principal A.E. Caldwell, for his part, felt that the goal of the experiment was consistent with what he viewed as the goals of residential schooling. "Constructive teaching in the residential school," he wrote,

> will lead the Indian people away from indolent habits inherent in the race because of their hitherto easy means of sustenance by hunting anf [sic] fishing, teaching them habits of consistent industry necesxary [sic] to compete inan [sic] industrial age, and will furthermore dispel the almost universal Indian opinion of "white" antagonism that makes the Indian people so difficult to negotiate with.[60]

While Pett and others involved with the study saw nutrition as an alternative explanation for the so-called inherent "racial traits" of Aboriginal peoples, their studies were nonetheless grounded in the related set of racialized assumptions that seemed to form the starting point for all investigations of Aboriginal nutrition conducted during this period—namely, that malnutrition was the cause of many of the perceived racial characteristics that had typically been used to define the scope of the so-called "Indian Problem" more generally, and that the observed levels of malnutrition tended to be a consequence of an inevitable transition from "traditional" to "modern" foods. As Pett argued in 1951 in a paper presented to the Panel on Indian Research of the Indian Affairs Branch,

> Indians seem to be caught in a transition state nutritionally, between the fully adequate native diet, and an adequate white man's diet. Even for white people nutritional adequacy is not easily achieved by *purchase* of foods alone, yet that is what the Indian is expected to do. He has neither the background nor the opportunity for the step

forward to solutions like self-production of food, nor have the social and educational policies for Indians developed to the point of considering this nutritional predicament and working towards a solution. The result is malnutrition with its toll of listlessness and diseases like tuberculosis.[61]

The solution, of course, was once again more expert intervention—whether through education or the kinds of nutritional technologies being tested at the six residential schools involved in these experiments.

Biomedical Research Ethics and Human Experimentation

In 1952, Pett presented a paper to the American Institute of Nutrition entitled "Development of Anemia on Newfoundland Enriched Flour." After outlining his five-year study of the effects of a vitamin- and mineral-fortified flour fed to children at an unnamed "boarding school"—along with the analysis done at another unnamed "control" school—Pett described a set of unfortunate results. Rather than an improvement in nutritional status, the students at the experimental school saw their blood haemoglobin levels decline, while at the control school haemoglobin levels actually improved. Whether or not the flour itself was the cause of the increased levels of anemia found at the school, Pett noted that "the fact remains that no beneficial effect was observed from the iron in enriched flour." For Pett, however, the most important finding to be taken away from the experiment was that more such studies were clearly necessary. "Proof of theoretical benefits or probable safety of the food to which chemicals have been specifically added," Pett argued, "requires tedious physiological studies." Such studies, however, "are often omitted or are confined to certain animal experiments rather than to humans." He added that "the benefits or hazards of adding chemicals to foods cannot, in the present state of knowledge, be judged on theoretical grounds or on limited animal experimentation, but need physiological testing on humans."[62]

Pett, of course, neglected to mention that his study was largely made possible because of his access to a population of chronically malnourished and vulnerable children who, as wards of the state, had little say in whether or not they participated in the study. Nor did he mention that the success of the study depended on so-called "controls" and experimental subjects alike being fed, for anywhere between two and five years, diets known to be nutritionally inadequate or, for that matter, that they were being actively denied certain types of dental care for the duration of the study. The anemia that developed among students at St Mary's, moreover, seems to have simply highlighted one of the main barriers to the kinds of human experiments being advocated by Pett—when confronted with the possible risks, few would consciously choose to allow themselves or their children to take part in such a study.

In May 2000, when a 90-year-old Pett was confronted about the experiments by David Napier, a journalist with the *Anglican Journal*, Pett maintained that the experiments had been ethical and argued that "the findings of the study were made readily available to the schools and communities involved so that nutrition could be improved."[63] By contemporary standards of medical research ethics, of course, such an experiment would never have been approved. Neither the parents nor the children themselves were given an opportunity to provide their informed consent.[64] There also seems to be little evidence that details of the experiment were explained to the subjects in the Norway House and Cross Lake studies. Moore, for his part, observed in a 1941 article that, because "the Indian" often has the "psychology of a child," researchers should avoid alarming him "by speaking within his hearing of procedures that he does not understand."[65] Although the Manitoba study likely required a greater degree of consent than the residential school studies—as was evidenced by the fact that the researchers had trouble getting the "experimental subjects" to continue taking their supplements and seem to have eventually abandoned the project because of increasing rates of non-participation and inconclusive results—there is little evidence to indicate that the participants were aware that they were the subjects of a controlled scientific experiment.[66]

While these experiments were, without a doubt, ethically dubious by current standards, the reality during the 1940s was that few written rules governed the ethics of medical research, and there was no legal requirement that research subjects give their informed consent to take part in a medical study. Although it is often assumed that the revelation of the atrocities committed by Nazi doctors and scientists during the Nuremberg Doctors Trials led to an immediate rethinking of how scientific research on human beings was conducted, recent research in the North American context has shown that, in fact, the Nuremberg Doctors Trials—which ended in 1947 and whose verdict included the 10 principles that would later become known as the Nuremberg Code—received little coverage in the popular press and seem to have had little effect on mainstream medical research practices. As Jay Katz has shown, moreover, even scientists who were aware of the Nuremberg Code tended to view it "as a code for barbarians and not for civilized physician investigators."[67]

As a number of historians have argued in recent years, the reality in the United States and other Western industrialized nations was that non-therapeutic experimentation on humans actually increased after the Second World War. As Harvard Medical School Professor Henry Beecher exposed in a groundbreaking 1966 article, during the 1940s, 1950s, and 1960s, prominent medical and scientific journals had proven more than willing to publish the results of experiments that put the life and health of human research subjects at risk without their consent or knowledge. Beecher's revelations were soon followed by even more high-profile cases, including the notorious Tuskegee Syphilis Experiment which, between 1932 and 1972, tracked the effects of untreated syphilis on impoverished African American men—well after the development of effective antibiotics to treat the condition in the 1940s.[68]

It was only amidst the public outcry over these and other instances of medical malpractice during the 1960s and 1970s that a series of both voluntary and legally binding statements on the ethical limits of medical research were put into place in most Western nations. This started with the 1964 Helsinki Declaration by the World Medical Association which, over the next two decades, would be followed by the United States Federal Regulations for the Protection of Subjects of Research and, in Canada, the Social Sciences and Humanities Research Council Guidelines and the Medical Research Council Guidelines on Research Involving Human Subjects. Throughout much of the early post-war period, however, medical research on humans was largely unregulated by legal or institutional constraints on ethical practice. Instead, as David J. Rothman argues, the autonomy of researchers conducting human experiments was limited "only by their individual consciences, not by their colleagues, their funders, their universities, or any other private or public body."[69]

Like the Canadian nutrition experiments, many of the ethically dubious human experiments conducted in the middle decades of the twentieth century tended disproportionately to use institutionalized, racialized, and otherwise vulnerable populations as research subjects. Jordan Goodman, Anthony McElligott, and Lara Marks have suggested that this was, in part, a reflection of the ways in which such research was often explicitly connected to larger national goals and interests. Starting in the 1930s, they argue, "the modern state increasingly used its prerogative to lay claim to the individual body for its own needs, whether social, economic, or military."[70] Not only were many of the groups chosen—whether they were orphans, the mentally ill, the poor, the elderly, or Indigenous peoples—often simply incapable of giving informed consent, but, more often than not, they also tended to be seen by the majority as public burdens. "Through medical experimentation," these authors therefore argue, "use*less* bodies were rendered use*ful* by being made us*able* in the national project of regeneration, thus gaining a utility they were believed otherwise to lack."[71] That the state was often a key player in such experiments simply highlights the ways in which this kind of research was often made possible by the existence of larger legal and political structures of—usually racial—inequality and oppression.

As the profound international backlash following Beecher's exposé or the revelations surrounding the Tuskegee Syphilis Study suggested, however, while such practices might have been considered normal within the research community, they were often not considered to be so by the general population. Susan Lederer's work on human experimentation prior to the Second World War shows that there have long been concerns about the ethics of research on human beings and, from the late nineteenth century, antivivisectionists and others launched wide-ranging campaigns to protect both animal and human experimental subjects from the dangers of non-therapeutic research. And, well before 1939, public revelations of medical experiments on orphans, prisoners, and other institutionalized groups had often led to considerable public backlash. Lederer argues that such incidents suggest that, despite the lack of formal legal or institutional constraints on non-consensual and non-therapeutic human experimentation, such practices were not necessarily considered ethical—there was simply an expectation that researchers themselves would govern the moral and ethical boundaries of their own research.[72]

There is little evidence in the documentary record as to whether Pett, Tisdall, Moore, or any of the other researchers involved in the Canadian nutrition studies discussed the ethical implications of their work. When interviewed in May 2000 about the fact that dental treatments were withheld from children in certain residential schools, Pett distinguished between his experiment and one that would be considered unethical by arguing that it "was not a deliberate attempt to leave children to develop caries except for a limited time or place or purpose, and only then to study the effects of Vitamin C or fluoride."[73] In the case of the residential school experiments, the limitations of existing documentary sources means there is no way to know how much these ethical considerations—or the fact that children known to be malnourished would be used as controls—played into the design of the experiment or were explicitly discussed by the researchers.

Whether these studies met the ethical standards of the time or not, it is clear that they did little to address the underlying causes of malnutrition in residential schools. For many students, moreover, it seems that the regular physical examinations that went along with the experiments could be confusing, painful, and potentially traumatic. The dozens of photographs taken of the experiments tend to hide this element, showing laughing children and smiling researchers. Yet the looks of fear and confusion in some photos—particularly those showing blood extraction and dental work—betray another story.[74] A series of letters sent by pupils at the Alberni residential school to Nutrition Services in 1952 suggest that fear, confusion, and compulsion may have been common. The letters all follow a similar format and were likely spurred by a set of specific instructions from the teacher. For instance, each letter thanks the researchers for their work and, in addition, provides a list of all the foods that were not available in the residential school but that the children were looking forward to eating when they got home. These latter sections of the letters were likely part of Pett's larger project of investigating the diets of children both in schools and their home communities. These lists typically include a range of both "store" and "country" foods, including a number of common items like dried fish, homemade bread, pancakes, fish eggs, seaweed, seagull eggs, herring, fruit, corn, pie, duck soup, cherries, and alphabet soup.[75]

The rest of the letters range from simple statements like "Thank you for the medical you gave us" to the more revealing "Tell the nurse I said thank you for the pokes she gave me." Many letter writers complained that the nurses wrote down the wrong age on their charts and that they were upset that the nurses would not change them. One child who complained of having the wrong age recorded also added that she "didn't understand the words that Doctor Brown was saying. I was listening very carefully too." Another student attempted to remember the "funny words" spoken by the dentist "like this downer light 6 missing, downer right 2 missing. Something like that. And the nurses put them on pieces of paper what the dentist says."[76]

Another common—and far more troubling—theme of the letters was that many children wanted to reassure the doctors that their tests had not hurt. One child, for instance, wrote to thank them for showing educational movies and added that "The pokes that I got didn't hurt me very much" and that "I got a couple of my teeth out by the dentist but it didn't hurt very much when he pulled them out." Another student wrote, "Thank you for all the pricks you gave us. I hope we are all going to be healthy all through the year, and not to take so many teeth out. We will all try not to get sick." The fear involved in the clinical interaction between doctors and students was perhaps best captured by a student who wrote, "When the nurse pricked me it did not hurt me at all but a little part of it is showing yet. I hope I am O.K." Perhaps tellingly, the same student's letter also included a correction in which the original statement thanking the doctors and nurses "for what they have done to us all" was changed to "for what they have done for us." Although many of the students thanked the research team for "coming here to help us be well strong and healthy," it was clear by the end of the study that its benefits were disproportionately skewed towards the professional interests of Pett and the other researchers. For children like those who developed anemia during the course of the study, moreover, the risks to their own health often far outweighed any possible benefits they might have received.[77]

Conclusion

Ultimately, it seems that none of these experiments and studies conducted between 1942 and 1952 had much in the way of long-term positive effects on the lives of those being studied. There is little evidence, for instance, that the experiment started in Northern Manitoba was ever actually finished but, even if it was, the results do not appear to have been published in a scientific journal. Some of the results of the other experiments in residential schools were presented at conferences or workshops or were published in journals, but they too seem to have had little effect on the operation of food services in residential schools beyond those that took part in the study.[78] Nor was the effect in the schools being examined always positive. In 1952, Pett actually initiated plans to repeat the failed Newfoundland Flour experiment at the Shubenacadie school, even though it was found that

consumption of the flour correlated with increased levels of anemia at St Mary's.[79] Reports also continued to come in regarding the poor food service in schools not included in the experiments. In 1953, for instance, Indian Health Services received reports from carpenters working on the Brandon residential school in Manitoba that the children "are not being fed properly to the extent that they are garbaging around in the barns for food that should only be fed to the Barn occupants"—a situation largely confirmed by a subsequent surprise inspection.[80] In the end, it was only in 1957 that the largely inadequate per capita grant system that had governed federal funding of residential schools since 1892 was replaced by a more consistent "controlled cost" system. This new system gave Ottawa the power to audit the schools it was funding and, for the first time, the federal government had some direct say in the quality of food being served in the institutions through a system of formal standards and inspections. Yet, as Milloy has argued, even the new system was "far from effective" and allowed the persistence of both neglect and abuse of students.[81]

Nearly a decade of experiments and studies of Aboriginal foodways and malnutrition appears to have similarly done little to alter the pre-existing assumptions held by federal policy makers and bureaucrats like Pett and Moore. Both continued to push for expert-driven, technological solutions as a means of easing the so-called transition from "traditional" to "modern" foodways. In the mid-1950s, they also jointly opposed introduction of a cash relief system, instead lobbying for continuation of an "in-kind" system of relief and family allowances as well as for the introduction of a nutritionally improved "bannock mix" to be distributed as part of these federally administered social welfare programs.[82] In many ways, such attitudes simply fit within the technocratic and paternalistic ethos of Canada's administration of Aboriginal peoples during this period. The 1950s, after all, saw the Department of Northern Affairs and Natural Resources (DNANR) attempt to socially engineer a solution to the so-called "Eskimo Problem" of hunger and "dependency" in a number of Inuit communities by "experimentally" relocating them without their informed consent to unfamiliar, and often unforgiving, new Arctic settlements.

As has since been well documented, the result was not only profound social and cultural dislocation but—in the tragic case of the Ahiarmiut of Ennadai Lake—hunger, starvation, and misery. The decision to engage in such attempts at brazen social engineering, of course, came from the same mindset that drove Moore, Tisdall, and Pett to conduct their own scientific experiments. As DNANR executive officer Robert Phillips wrote to the Deputy Minister in 1955, it was useful for the Department to "think of 9,000 Eskimos as a laboratory experiment and give the imagination full rein on what might be done to improve the culture."[83] Aboriginal peoples, in other words, continued to be seen as "experimental materials" and their communities as "laboratories" for both scientific and social experimentation well after the experiments of Pett, Moore, and Tisdall had ended.

Perhaps the most significant legacy of these studies of Aboriginal nutrition during the 1940s and 1950s is that they provide us with a unique and disturbing window into the ways in which—under the guise of benevolent administration and even charity—bureaucrats, scientists, and a whole range of experts exploited their "discovery" of malnutrition in Aboriginal communities and residential schools to further their own professional and political interests rather than to address the root causes of these problems or, for that matter, the Canadian government's complicity in them. This was made possible in large part due to the persistence of the false perception that First Nations had somehow been left behind by modernity and were therefore in need of the benevolent hand of settler scientists, experts, and professionals.[84] As Paulette Regan, the director of research for the Truth and Reconciliation Commission of Canada, has forcefully argued, real truth and reconciliation can only occur when settlers genuinely begin to understand and take responsibility for the legacy of systematic violence and oppression that characterized the residential school system and Indigenous settler relations in Canada more generally.[85] These experiments therefore must be remembered and recognized for what they truly were: one among many examples of a larger institutionalized and, ultimately, dehumanizing colonialist racial ideology that has governed Canada's policies towards and treatment of Aboriginal peoples throughout the twentieth century.

Notes

1. See P.E. Moore, H.D. Kruse, and F.F. Tisdall, "Nutrition in the North: A Study of the State of Nutrition of the Canadian Bush Indian," *The Beaver*, 273 (March 1943), pp. 21–23, and the final report on the study, P.E. Moore, H.D. Kruse, F.F. Tisdall, and R.S.C. Corrigan, "Medical Survey of Nutrition Among the Northern Manitoba Indians," *Canadian Medical Association Journal*, vol. 54 (March 1946), pp. 223–233.

2. Library and Archives Canada [hereafter LAC], RG 29, Vol. 936, File 386-6-10, Report by P.E. Moore, March 26, 1942.

3. Moore et al., "Medical Survey of Nutrition," p. 226.

4. On the shifting perception of the so-called "Indian Problem" during this period and the place of Tisdall's and Moore's conclusions within a broader national discussion of the place of Aboriginal peoples in Canada's post-war future, see R. Scott Sheffield, *The Red Man's on the Warpath: The Image of the "Indian" and the Second World War* (Vancouver: University of British Columbia Press, 2004), pp. 162–163; Hugh Shewell, "'What Makes the Indian Tick?' The Influence of Social Sciences on Canada's Indian Policy, 1947–1964," *Histoire sociale/ Social History*, vol. 34, no. 67 (May 2001), pp. 133–167.

5. LAC, RG 29, Vol. 936, File 386-6-10, F.F. Tisdall and H.D. Kruse, "Summary of Findings From a Nutritional Survey of Approximately Three Hundred Indians," March 15, 1942. Also see their final report, Moore et al., "Medical Survey of Nutrition," p. 233.

6. Tisdall and Kruse, "Summary of Findings."

7. For a good account of the James Bay study, see Shewell, "'What Makes the Indian Tick?'"

8. With the exception of a short article written in the *Anglican Journal* in May 2000, little has been written about these experiments. See David Napier, "Ottawa Experimented on Native Kids," *Anglican Journal*, vol. 126, no. 5 (May 2000).

9. See, for instance, Deborah Neill, "Finding the 'Ideal Diet': Nutrition, Culture and Dietary Practices in France and French Equatorial Africa, c. 1890s to 1920s," *Food and Foodways*, vol. 17, no. 1 (2009), pp. 1–28; James Vernon, *Hunger: A Modern History* (Cambridge: Harvard University Press, 2007); Nick Cullather, "The Foreign Policy of the Calorie," *American Historical Review*, vol. 112, no. 2 (2007), pp. 1–60; Marilyn Little, "Imperialism, Colonialism and the New Science of Nutrition: The Tanganyika Experience, 1925–1945," *Social Science & Medicine*, vol. 32, no. 1 (1991), pp. 11–14; Michael

Worboys, "The Discovery of Malnutrition Between the Wars" in D. Arnold ed., *Imperial Medicine and Indigenous Societies* (Manchester: Manchester University Press, 1988).

10. See Walter J. Vanast, "'Hastening the Day of Extinction': Canada, Quebec, and the Medical Care of Ungava's Inuit, 1867–1967," *Etudes Inuit Studies*, vol. 15, no. 2 (1991), pp. 50–51; Constance Backhouse, *Colour-Coded: A Legal History of Racism in Canada, 1900–1950* (Toronto: University of Toronto Press, 1999), pp. 33–34.

11. See John Sheridan Milloy, *A National Crime: The Canadian Government and the Residential School System, 1879 to 1986* (Winnipeg: University of Manitoba Press, 1999), pp. 109–127.

12. See Mary Ellen Kelm, "'A Scandalous Procession': Residential Schooling and the Shaping of Aboriginal Bodies," *Native Studies Review*, vol. 11, no. 2 (1996), pp. 51–81; J.R. Miller, *Shingwauk's Vision: A History of Native Residential Schools* (Toronto: University of Toronto Press, 1996), p. 290.

13. See Hugh Shewell, *"Enough to Keep Them Alive": Indian Social Welfare in Canada, 1873–1965* (Toronto: University of Toronto Press, 2004), p. 124; Vanast, "'Hastening the Day of Extinction,'" pp. 50–51; Mary Ellen Kelm, *Colonizing Bodies: Aboriginal Health and Healing in British Columbia, 1900–50* (Vancouver: University of British Columbia Press, 1998), pp. 28–29; Naomi Adelson, *"Being Alive Well": Health and the Politics of Cree Well-Being* (Toronto: University of Toronto Press, 2004), pp. 43–45.

14. Shewell, *"Enough to Keep Them Alive,"* pp. 123–126. On the broader context of the government policies that led to hunger and malnutrition in Aboriginal communities, see, for instance, Sarah Carter, *Lost Harvests: Prairie Indian Reserve Farmers and Government Policy* (Montreal and Kingston: McGill-Queen's University Press, 1990); Kelm, *Colonizing Bodies*; Maureen Lux, *Medicine That Walks: Disease, Medicine and Canadian Plains Native People, 1880–1940* (Toronto: University of Toronto Press, 2001); Douglas C. Harris, *Landing Native Fisheries: Indian Reserves and Fishing Rights in British Columbia, 1849–1925* (Vancouver: University of British Columbia Press, 2008); John Sandlos, *Hunters at the Margin: Native People and Wildlife Conservation in the Northwest Territories* (Vancouver: University of British Columbia Press, 2007).

15. LAC, RG 29, Vol. 936, File 386-6-10, Chief Andrew Crate Sr., Norway House, to P.E. Moore, March 11, 1942.

16. LAC, RG 29, Vol. 936, File 386-6-10, Address Made by Chief Spence Ross of Cross Lake Band to P.E. Moore, March 10, 1942.

17. LAC, RG 29, Vol. 936, File 386-6-10, Report by P.E. Moore, March 26, 1942.

18. LAC, RG 10, Vol. 8585, File 1/1-2-17, House of Commons Special Committee, *Minutes of Proceedings and Evidence*, May 24, 1944. As Kelm has argued, deciding to "study the problem first and then determine the correct course

of action" was a "time-honoured Canadian tradition" (*Colonizing Bodies*, p. 119).

19. Moore, Kruse, and Tisdall, "Nutrition in the North," pp. 21–23; LAC, RG 29, Vol. 2986, File 851-6-1, P.E. Moore to R.S.C. Corrigan, September 14, 1943, and "Minutes of Meeting of Indians and Doctors, Norway House, Manitoba," March 20, 1944; LAC, RG 10, Vol. 8585, File 1/1-2-17, House of Commons Special Committee, *Minutes of Proceedings and Evidence*, May 24, 1944; J.V.V. Nicholls, "Ophthalmic Status of Cree Indians," *Canadian Medical Association Journal*, vol. 54, no. 4 (April 1946), pp. 344–348.

20. For a good background, see Vernon, *Hunger*; Rima Apple, *Vitamania: Vitamins in American Culture* (New Brunswick, NJ: Rutgers University Press, 1996); Harvey Levenstein, *Revolution at the Table: The Transformation of the American Diet* (Berkeley: University of California Press, 1988).

21. For a comprehensive background to these issues, see chapters 1 and 5 in Ian Mosby, "Food Will Win the War: The Politics and Culture of Food and Nutrition During the Second World War" (Ph.D. thesis, York University, 2011).

22. Moore et al., "Medical Survey of Nutrition," p. 228.

23. See Todd Tucker, *The Great Starvation Experiment: Ancel Keys and the Men Who Starved for Science* (Minneapolis: University of Minnesota Press, 2008), pp. 96–98.

24. See Kelm, *Colonizing Bodies*, p. 100, and "Diagnosing the Discursive Indian: Medicine, Gender, and the Dying Race," *Ethnohistory*, vol. 52, no. 2 (2005), pp. 371–406; T. Kue Young, "Indian Health Services in Canada: A Sociohistorical Perspective," *Social Science & Medicine*, vol. 18, no. 3 (1984), pp. 257–264, and *Health Care and Cultural Change: The Indian Experience in the Central Subarctic* (Toronto: University of Toronto Press, 1988); as well as Lux, *Medicine That Walks*.

25. Shewell, *"Enough to Keep Them Alive,"* pp. 155–156.

26. John J. Honigmann, "The Logic of the James Bay Survey," *The Dalhousie Review*, vol. 30, no. 4 (January 1951), p. 380; R.P. Vivian et al., "The Nutrition and Health of the James Bay Indian," *Canadian Medical Association Journal*, vol. 59, no. 6 (December 1948), p. 506. On the history of the Rupert's House beaver conservation programme, see Tina Loo, *States of Nature: Conserving Canada's Wildlife in the Twentieth Century* (Vancouver: University of British Columbia Press, 2006), pp. 102–111.

27. Vivian et al., "The Nutrition and Health of the James Bay Indian," p. 505.

28. Ibid., pp. 505–506.

29. Tidsall cited in John J. Honigmann, *Foodways in a Muskeg Community: An Anthropological Report on the Attawapiskat Indians, 1948* (Ottawa: Department of Northern Affairs and Natural Resources, 1961), pp. 1–2.

30. Moore et al., "Medical Survey of Nutrition," p. 228.

31. LAC, RG 29, Vol. 2986, File 851-6-1, "Indians in North

Forsake Health-Giving Native Diet," January 14, 1948.

32. See, for instance, Weston A. Price, *Nutrition and Physical Degeneration: A Comparison of Primitive and Modern Diets and Their Effects* (New York: P.B. Hoeber, Inc., 1940); I.M. Rabinowitch, "Clinical and Other Observations on Canadian Eskimos in the Eastern Arctic," *Canadian Medical Association Journal*, vol. 34, no. 5 (May 1936), pp. 487–501. Also see Mary Jane McCallum, "This Last Frontier: Isolation and Aboriginal Health," *Canadian Bulletin of Medical History*, vol. 22, no. 1 (2005), p. 108.

33. The Department argued that "they would not be on very good ground in allowing products for sale to the Indians in Canada, that they would not be prepared to release for the benefit of the White People" (LAC, RG 29, Vol. 961, File 387-9-1, Part 21, P.E. Moore to E.W. McHenry, September 5, 1945).

34. See Alan R. Marcus, *Relocating Eden: The Image and Politics of Inuit Exile in the Canadian Arctic* (Hanover: University Press of New England, 1995); Frank J. Tester and Peter Keith Kulchyski, *Tammarniit (mistakes): Inuit Relocation in the Eastern Arctic, 1939–63* (Vancouver: University of British Columbia Press, 1994); Shelagh D. Grant, "A Case of Compounded Error: The Inuit Resettlement Project, 1953, and the Government Response, 1990," *Northern Perspectives*, vol. 19, no. 1 (Spring 1991).

35. Honigmann, *Foodways in a Muskeg Community* and "An Episode in the Administration of the Great Whale River Eskimo," *Human Organization*, vol. 10, no. 2 (Summer 1951), pp. 5–14. In Rupert's House, family allowances became a source of income "second only to beaver." See A.J. Kerr, *Subsistence and Social Organization in a Fur Trade Community: Anthropological Report on the Ruperts* [sic] *House Indians* (Ottawa: National Committee for Community Health Studies, 1950), p. 176. For an excellent account of the social and economic effects of family allowances in non-Aboriginal communities, see Dominique Marshall, *The Social Origins of the Welfare State: Quebec Families, Compulsory Education, and Family Allowances, 1940–1955* (Waterloo, ON: Wilfrid Laurier University Press, 2006).

36. S.J. Bailey, "By Canoe to the Arctic," *Canada's Health and Welfare*, vol. 3, no. 4 (January 1947), pp. 2–3. On the provision of in-kind family allowances in the North more generally, see Marshall, *The Social Origins of the Welfare State*, p. 76; Shelagh D. Grant, *Sovereignty or Security: Government Policy in the Canadian North, 1936–1950* (Vancouver: University of British Columbia Press, 1988), p. 163.

37. LAC, RG 29, Vol. 973, File 388-6-1, "Indian Affairs List of Special Food and Clothing, Family Allowances Act," October 27, 1945. Also see Kerr, "Subsistence and Social Organization," pp. 221–223.

38. Honigmann, "An Episode in the Administration of the Great Whale River Eskimo," pp. 5–14. On the experience of the Great Whale River Cree, see Adelson, *"Being Alive Well."*

39. See Vivian et al., "The Nutrition and Health of the James Bay Indian," p. 516; Honigmann, "The Logic of the James Bay Survey," p. 383, and *Foodways in a Muskeg Community*, p. 208; as well as Kerr, *Subsistence and Social Organization*, pp. 224–225.

40. Vivian et al., "The Nutrition and Health of the James Bay Indian," p. 516.

41. Ibid., p. 518.

42. Honigmann, *Foodways in a Muskeg Community*, p. 208.

43. Vivian et al., "The Nutrition and Health of the James Bay Indian," pp. 517–518.

44. Milloy, *A National Crime*, p. 263.

45. See LAC, RG 29, Vol. 941, File 387-2-1 and Vol. 973, File 388-6-1, reports and correspondence of Mrs. Allan (Rosamond) Stevenson, National Director of Nutrition Services for the Canadian Red Cross Society.

46. Basil H. Johnson, *Indian School Days* (Toronto: Key Porter, 1998), pp. 40, 141.

47. LAC, RG 29, Vol. 973, File 388-6-1, Margaret Lock to L.B. Pett, October 9, 1947.

48. See, for instance, LAC, RG 29, Vol. 973, File 388-6-1, "Health Aspects in Relation to Food Service, Indian Residential Schools—Nutrition Division, Dept. of National Health and Welfare, November 1946."

49. LAC, RG 29, Vol. 974, File 388-6-3, L.B. Pett to B.F. Neary, August 22, 1947, and E.L. Stone to P.E. Moore [March 1947]. On the cutbacks to the per capita grant system during the 1930s and 1940s, see Miller, *Shingwauk's Vision*, pp. 318, 384–385.

50. LAC, RG 29, Vol. 973, File 388-6-1, McCready Report, December 4, 1947; L.B. Pett to B.F. Henry, July 9, 1947; and L.B. Pett to P.E. Moore, December 8, 1947.

51. LAC, RG 29, Vol. 973, File 388-6-1, L.B. Pett to Alice McCready, October 20, 1947.

52. George Hunter and L.B. Pett, "A Dietary Survey in Edmonton," *Canadian Public Health Journal*, vol. 32, no. 5 (May 1941), pp. 259–265; L.B. Pett, C.A. Morrell, and F.W. Hanley, "The Development of Dietary Standards," *Canadian Public Health Journal*, vol. 36 (June 1945), p. 234; L.B. Pett, "The Use and Abuse of Vitamins," *Canadian Medical Association Journal*, vol. 52 (1945), pp. 488–491, and "Errors in Applying Nutrient Allowances to Dietary Surveys or Food Policies," *Canadian Public Health Journal*, vol. 36, no. 2 (1945), pp. 67–73. For the broader context, see chapters 1 and 5 in Mosby, "Food Will Win the War."

53. LAC, RG 29, Vol. 2989, File 851-6-4 part 1, L.B. Pett to G.D.W. Cameron, October 18, 1948.

54. L.B. Pett, "Values from Tripling the Milk Used, in an Institution," *Federation Proceedings*, vol. 12 (1953), p. 426; LAC, RG 29, Vol. 2989, File 851-6-4 part 1, L.B. Pett to P. E. Moore and B.F. Neary, July 21, 1949; and Alice McCready, "Report on Inspection of Food Service, Alberni Indian Residential School, Port Alberni, BC, June 17 and 18, 1948."

55. The "experimental" group received up to four times the daily intake of the "control" group. See G.F. Oglivie

and L.B, Pett, "A Long Term Study on Ascorbic Acid Supplementation," *Canadian Services Medical Journal*, vol. 10, no. 3 (October 1954), pp. 191–197; LAC, RG 29, Vol. 2989, File 851-6-4, L.B. Pett to P.E. Moore and B.F. Neary, July 21, 1949; and Alice McCready, "Report on Inspection of Food Service, Shubenacadie Indian Residential School, Shubenacadie, NS, May 18 to 19, 1948."

56. See LAC, RG 29 Vol. 974, File 388-6-4, "Indian Residential Schools Nutrition Project—Diet Changes to Be Started in September, 1949" and "Outline of Nutrition Study in Indian Residential Schools—April 1948."5

57. Miller, *Shingwauk's Vision*, p. 119.

58. LAC, RG 29, Vol. 974, File 388-6-4, H.K. Brown to P.S. Tennent, October 3, 1949; H.K. Brown to W.J. Wood, September 26, 1949; and H.K. Brown to H.M. McCaffery, April 7, 1948.

59. LAC, RG 29, Vol. 974, File 388-6-1, "Food Contest—For pupils 9 year[s] and over"; and L.B. Pett to E.L. Stone, March 14, 1947. Also see LAC, RG 29, Vol. 974, File 388-6-2, P. Jegard, "Analysis of Indian Food Posters" [n.d.].

60. LAC, RG 29, Vol. 974, File 388-6-4, A.E. Caldwell to R.A. Hoey, May 8, 1948.

61. LAC, RG 29, Vol. 923, File 385-7-2, L.B. Pett, "Nutrition Research for Indians and Eskimos in Canada," November 1951.

62. LAC, RG 29, Vol. 974, File 388-6-4, L.B. Pett, "Development of Anemia on Newfoundland Enriched Flour," April 1952.

63. Napier, "Ottawa Experimented on Native Kids," pp. 1–4.

64. At most, it seems that the children were told that the scientists were "carrying on what we call a nutrition study in your school to find out if there are any particular foods which you need to improve your health" and, further, that the study was "being done to help you and the school." See LAC, RG 29 Vol. 974, File 388-6-4, "Outline of Talk to Children in Indian Schools Prior to Taking Dietary Records in Autumn, 1948."

65. P.E. Moore, "Tuberculosis Control in the Indian Population of Canada," *Canadian Public Health Journal*, vol. 32, no. 1 (January 1941), pp. 16–17. The closest we have to an account of what the research subjects were told about the study is a transcript of speeches given at Norway House in March 1944, nearly two years into the study. Tisdall and the other researchers focused on encouraging the research subjects to continue to take the vitamin pills by highlighting the improvements that they were having on their health and the importance of the research. Little in the way of specific detail about the nature of the study seems to have been provided (LAC, RG 29, Vol. 2986, File 851-6-1, Pt. 1, Minutes of Meeting of Indians and Doctors, Norway House, Manitoba, March 20, 1944).

66. The documentary record is decidedly spotty in this regard, but the fact that the supplement study was ultimately not included in the 1946 report on the project seems to indicate its failure (Moore et al., "Medical Survey of Nutrition"). The lead researcher on the experiment,

Cameron Corrigan, also argued in a 1946 article that he did "not believe that an Indian can be treated for any sickness unless he is hospitalized, as he cannot be trusted to take medicine intelligently"—suggesting that he may very well have had difficulties ensuring that his research subjects took their vitamin capsules as directed. See Cameron Corrigan, "Medical Practice Among Bush Indians," *Canadian Medical Association Journal*, vol. 54, no. 3 (March 1946), pp. 220–223. But even as late as April 1948, a report on the residential schools experiment noted that the results of Corrigan's experiments at Norway House—which the report erroneously suggested started in 1945—"have not yet been clear enough to publish" (LAC, RG 29, Vol. 974, File 388-6-4, "Outline of Nutrition Study in Indian Residential Schools—April 1948").

67. Jay Katz, "The Nuremberg Code and the Nuremberg Trial: A Reappraisal," *Journal of the American Medical Association*, vol. 276, no. 20 (November 27, 1996), p. 1663. In the American context, see R.R. Faden, S.E. Lederer, and J.D. Moreno, "US Medical Researchers, the Nuremberg Doctors Trial, and the Nuremberg Code: A Review of Findings of the Advisory Committee on Human Radiation Experiments," *Journal of the American Medical Association*, vol. 276, no. 20 (November 27, 1996), pp. 1667–1671; Ruth R. Faden, Tom L. Beauchamp, and Nancy M.P. King, *A History and Theory of Informed Consent* (Oxford: Oxford University Press, 1986), pp. 153–156; Susan Reverby, *Examining Tuskegee: The Infamous Syphilis Study and its Legacy* (Chapel Hill: University of North Carolina Press, 2009), p. 66; Rebecca Skloot, *The Immortal Life of Henrietta Lacks* (New York: Crown, 2010), pp. 131–132. My own analysis of the *Toronto Star's* coverage confirms these conclusions and shows not only that was there no mention of the Nuremberg Code, but that the Doctors Trial itself received little attention.

68. For the best works on human experimentation, see Susan E. Lederer, *Subjected to Science: Human Experimentation in America Before the Second World War* (Baltimore: Johns Hopkins University Press, 1997); Jordan Goodman, Anthony McElligott, and Lara Marks, eds. *Useful Bodies: Humans in the Service of Medical Science in the Twentieth Century* (Baltimore: Johns Hopkins University Press, 2003); David J. Rothman, *Strangers at the Bedside: A History of How Law and Bioethics Transformed Medical Decision Making* (New York: Basic Books, 1992); Faden, Beauchamp, and King, *A History and Theory of Informed Consent*. On Tuskegee, see James H. Jones, *Bad Blood: The Tuskegee Syphilis Experiment*, rev. ed. (New York: Free Press, 1992) as well as Reverby's *Examining Tuskegee* and *Tuskegee's Truths: Rethinking the Tuskegee Syphilis Study* (New York: Scholarly Book Services Inc., 2002).

69. Rothman, *Strangers at the Bedside*, p. 69. For the Canadian context, see Carol Collier and Rachel Haliburton, *Bioethics in Canada: A Philosophical Introduction* (Toronto: Canadian Scholars' Press, 2011).

70. Goodman, McElligott, and Marks, *Useful Bodies*, p. 2.

71. Ibid., p. 12.

72. Lederer, *Subjected to Science*.

73. Napier, "Ottawa Experimented on Native Kids," pp. 1–4.

74. See the photos in LAC, National Film Board of Canada, Fiche 589-602, Box 2000813467.

75. These letters can be found in LAC, RG 29, Vol. 974, File 388-6-4.

76. LAC, RG 29, Vol. 974, File 388-6-4.

77. Ibid.

78. Oglivie and Pett, "A Long Term Study on Ascorbic Acid Supplementation," pp. 191–197; Pett, "Values from Tripling the Milk Used," p. 426; LAC, RG 29, Vol. 923 File 385-7-2, L.B. Pett, "Nutrition Research For Indians and Eskimos in Canada," November 1951; LAC, RG 29, Vol. 906, File 440-1-9, Pett, Brown, Gibbard, Bynoe and Naubert with assistance from Miss W.A. Warren, "A Study of the Relationship of Oral Lactobacillus Counts to Dental Caries Activity" [n.d.].

79. See LAC, RG 29, Vol. 923, File 385-7-2, L.B. Pett to J.B. Mackey, May 23 and July 17, 1952; LAC, RG 29, Vol. 2989, File 851-6-4, L.B. Pett to P.E. Moore, April 21, 1952.

80. LAC, RG 29, Vol. 2989, File 851-6-4, J.W. Breakey to P.E. Moore, September 16, 1953; and Nan Tupper Chapman, "Dietician's Report on Brandon Indian School" [October, 1953].

81. Milloy, *A National Crime*, p. 260; Miller, *Shingwauk's Vision*, p. 393.

82. Shewell, *"Enough to Keep Them Alive,"* pp. 245–251.

83. LAC, RG 22, 310/40-2-20/4, R.A.J. Phillips, Eastern Arctic Patrol 1955, Montreal to Resolute, cited in Marcus, *Relocating Eden*, p. 33. Also see Tester and Kulchyski, *Tammarniit*; Grant, "A Case of Compounded Error"; Frédéric Laugrand et al., "'The Saddest Time of My Life': Relocating the Ahiarmiut from Ennadai Lake (1950–1958)," *Polar Record*, vol. 46, no. 2 (2010), pp. 113–135.

84. These assumptions similarly guided the design of the Nutrition Canada surveys conducted between 1964 and 1975, which continued to single out so-called "Indians" and "Eskimos" as being uniquely at risk for malnutrition. See Krista Walters, "'A National Priority': Nutrition Canada's *Survey* and the Disciplining of Aboriginal Bodies, 1964–75" in Franca Iacovetta, Marlene Epp and Valerie Korinek, eds., *Edible Histories, Cultural Politics: Towards a Canadian Food History* (Toronto: University of Toronto Press, 2012), 433–451.

85. Paulette Regan, *Unsettling the Settler Within: Indian Residential Schools, Truth Telling, and Reconciliation in Canada* (Vancouver: University of British Columbia Press, 2010).

PRIMARY DOCUMENT

Russell Moses's 1965 Residential School Memoir

INDIAN AFFAIRS BRANCH		DIRECTION DES AFFAIRES INDIENNES
DEPARTMENT OF CITIZENSHIP AND IMMIGRATION	CANADA	MINISTÈRE DE LA CITOYENNETÉ ET DE L'IMMIGRATION

Ottawa 2, December 10, 1965.

OUR FILE NO. 1/25-20-1 (E.24)
Notre dossier n°

Mr. Russ Moses,
Information Section,
Room 425,
Bourque Building,
Ottawa, Ontario.

Dear Mr. Moses:

During the week beginning with January 10, 1966, the Residential School Principals from all regions will be meeting at Elliot Lake, Ontario, to discuss various aspects of residential schools.

In order to bring as many view points as possible to these deliberations, a selected number of Indians have been invited to submit their views and you are one of the persons who has been selected.

We would be most grateful to you if you would put your thoughts regarding residential schools down on paper and send this to me by the end of December. Please feel free to express your views candidly. We want to benefit both from your experience and your insights and frankness will be appreciated.

All the best to you and yours during the Yuletide Season and I will very much appreciate hearing from you at your earliest convenience.

Yours sincerely,

G. Jampolsky,
Chief Superintendent of
Vocational Training and
Special Services.

WILL SUBMIT VIEWS. R.M. 13/12/65 DONE 28/12/65

MOHAWK INSTITUTE - 1942-47

First, a bit of what it was like in the "good old days".

In August 1942, shortly before my 9th birthday a series of unfortunate family circumstances made it necessary that I along with my 7 year old sister and an older brother, be placed in the Mohawk Institute at Brantford, Ontario.

Our home life prior to going to the "Mohawk" was considerably better than many of the other Indian children who were to be my friends in the following five years. At the "mushole" (this was the name applied to the school by the Indians for many years) I found to my surprise that one of the main tasks for a new arrival was to engage in physical combat with a series of opponents, this was done by the students, so that you knew exactly where you stood in the social structure that existed.

The food at the Institute was disgraceful. The normal diet was as follows:

Breakfast – two slices of bread with either jam or honey as the dressing, oatmeal with worms or corn meal porridge which was minimal in quantity and appalling in quality. The beverage consisted of skim milk and when one stops to consider that we were milking from twenty to thirty head of pure bred Holstein cattle, it seems odd that we did not <u>ever</u> receive whole milk and in my five years at the Institute we <u>never</u> received butter once.

This is very strange, for on entering the Institute our ration books for sugar and butter were turned in to the management – we never received sugar other than Christmas morning when we had a yearly feast of one shreaded wheat with a sprinkling of brown sugar.

Lunch - At the Institute this consisted of water as the beverage, if you were a senior boy or girl you received (Grace V or above) one and a half slices of <u>dry</u> bread and the main course consisted of "rotten soup" (local terminology) (i.e. scraps of beef, vegetables some in a state of decay.) Desert would be restricted to nothing on some days and a type of tapioca pudding (fish eyes) or a crudely prepared custard, the taste of which I can taste to this

continued

- 2 -

day. Children under Grade V level received <u>one</u> slice of dry bread
– incidentally we were not weight watchers.

Supper -   This consisted of two slices of bread and jam, fried potatoes, <u>NO
            MEAT</u>, a bun baked by the girls (common terminology – "horse
            buns") and every other night a piece of cake or possibly an apple
            in the summer months.

The manner in which the food was prepared did not encourage overeat-
ing. The diet remained constant, hunger was never absent. I would say here
that 90% of the children were suffering from diet deficiency and this was
evident by the number of boils, warts and general malaise that existed within
the school population.

I have seen Indian children eating from the swill barrel, picking out
soggy bits of food that was intended for the pigs.

At the "mushole" we had several hundred laying hens (white leghorn).
We received a yearly ration of <u>one</u> egg a piece – this was on Easter Sunday
morning, the Easter Bunny apparently influenced this.

The whole milk was separated in the barn and the cream was then
sold to a local dairy firm, "the Mohawk Creamery", which I believe is still in
business. All eggs were sold as well as the chickens at the end of their laying
life – we never had chicken – except on several occasions when we stole one or
two and roasted them on a well concealed fire in the bush – half raw chicken
is not too bad eating!

The policy of the Mohawk Institute was that both girls and boys would attend school for half days and work the other half. This was Monday to Friday
inclusive. No school on Saturday but generally we worked.

The normal work method was that the children under Grade V level
worked in the market garden in which every type of vegetable was grown
and in the main sold – the only vegetables which were stored for our use
were potatoes, beans, turnips of the animal fodder variety. The work was
supervised by white people who were employed by the Institute and beatings
were administered at the slightest pretext. We were not treated as human
beings – we were the Indian who had to become shining examples of Anglican
Christianity.

I have seen Indian children having their faces rubbed in human excre-
ment, this was done by a gentleman who has now gone to his just reward.

– 3 –

The normal punishment for bed wetters (usually one of the smaller boys) was to have his face rubbed in his own urine.

The senior boys worked on the farm – and I mean worked, we were underfed, ill clad and out in all types of weather – there is certainly something to be said for Indian stamina. At harvest times, such as potatoe harvest, corn harvest for cattle fodder – we older boys would at times not attend school until well on into fall as we were needed to help with the harvest.

We arose at 6:00 a.m. each morning and went to the barn to do "chores". This included milking the cattle, feeding and then using curry comb and brush to keep them in good mental and physical condition.

After our usual sumptuous breakfast we returned to the barn to do "second chores" 8:00 to 9:00 a.m. – this included cleaning the stables, watering the young stock and getting hay down out of mow, as well as carrying encilage from the silo to the main barn.

We also had some forty to eighty pigs depending on the time of year – we never received pork or bacon of any kind except at Christmas when a single slice of pork along with mashed potatoes and gravy made up our Christmas dinner. A few rock candies along with an orange and Christmas pudding which was referred to as "dog shit" made up our Christmas celebrations. The I.O.D.E. sent us books as gifts.

Religion was pumped into us at a fast rate, chapel every evening, church on Sundays (twice). For some years after leaving the Institute, I was under the impression that my tribal affiliation was "Anglican" rather than Delaware.

Our formal education was sadly neglected, when a child is tired, hungry, lice infested and treated as sub-human, how in heavens name do you expect to make a decent citizen out of him or her, when the formal school curriculum is the most disregarded aspect of his whole background. I speak of lice, this was an accepted part of "being Indian" at the Mohawk – heads were shaved in late spring. We had no tooth brushes, no underwear was issued in summer, no socks in the summer. Our clothing was a disgrace to this country. Our so called "Sunday clothes" were cut down first world war army uniforms. Cold showers were provided summer and winter in which we were herded en masse by some of the bigger boys and if you did not keep under the shower you would be struck with a brass studded belt.

continued

- 4 -

The soap for performing our ablutions was the green liquid variety which would just about take the hide off you.

Bullying by larger boys was terrible, younger boys were "slaves" to these fellows and were required to act as such – there were also cases of homosexual contact, but this is not strange when you consider that the boys were not even allowed to talk to the girls – even their own sisters, except for 15 minutes once a month when you met each other in the "visiting room" and you then spoke in hushed tones.

Any mail coming to any student or mail being sent was opened and read before ever getting to the addressee or to the Indian child – money was removed and held in "trust" for the child.

It was our practise at the "Mohawk" to go begging at various homes throughout Brantford. There were certain homes that we knew that the people were good to us, we would rap on the door and our question was: "Anything extra", whereupon if we were lucky, we would be rewarded with scraps from the household – survival of the fittest.

Many children tried to run away from the Institute and nearly all were caught and brought back to face the music – we had a form of running the gauntlet in which the offender had to go through the line, that is on his hands and knees, through widespread legs of all the boys and he would be struck with anything that was at hand – all this done under the fatherly supervision of the boys' master. I have seen boys after going through a line of fifty to seventy boys lay crying in the most abject human misery and pain with not a soul to care – the dignity of man!!

As I sit writing this paper, things that have been dormant in my mind for years come to the fore – we will sing Hymn No. 128!!

This situation divides the shame amongst the Churches, the Indian Affairs Branch and the Canadian public.

I could write on and on – and some day I will tell of how things used to be – sadness, pain and misery were my legacy as an Indian.

The staff at the Mohawk lived very well, separate dining room where they were waited on by our Indian girls – the food I am told, was excellent.

When I was asked to do this paper I had some misgivings, for if I were to be honest, I must tell of things as they were and really this is not my story, but yours.

– 5 –

There were and are some decent honourable people employed by the residential schools, but they were not sufficient in number to change things.

SUGGESTED IMPROVEMENTS FOR RESIDENTIAL SCHOOLS
1. Religion should not be the basic curriculum, therefore it is my feeling that non-denominational residential schools should be established. (dreamer)
2. More people of Indian ancestry should be encouraged to work in residential schools as they have a much better understanding of the Indian "personality" and would also be more apt to be trusted and respected by students.
3. Indian residential schools should be integrated – the residential school should be a "home" rather than an Institute.
4. Salaries paid to the staff members should be on par with industrie – otherwise you tend to attract only social misfits and religious zealots.
5. The Indian students should have a certain amount of work (physical) to do – overwork is no good and no work is even worse. I believe that a limited amount of work gives responsibility to the individual and helps him or her to develop a well-balanced personality.
6. Parents of Indian children should be made to contribute to the financial upkeep of their children – I realise that this would be difficult, but it at least bears looking into.
7. Each child should be given individual attention – get to know him or her – encourage leadership, this could be accomplished by giving awards for certain achievements.
8. Last, but most important, solicit ideas from the students, we adults do not know all the answers.

SUMMATION – The years that an Indian child spends in an Indian residential school has a very great deal to do with his or her future outlook on life and in my own case it showed me that Indian are "different", simply because you made us different and so gentlemen I say to you, take pains in molding, not the Indian of to-morrow, but the Canadian citizen of to-morrow. FOR "As ye sow, so shall ye reap".

Russell Moses,
Former Student, Mohawk Institute

continued

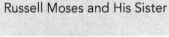

Russell Moses and His Sister

Source: Russell Moses' 1965 residential school memoir and photo provided to the editors by his son, John Moses, and used with permission of the Moses family.

Study Questions

1. Read over the primary source that accompanies Ian Mosby's article. On page 6 of his letter, Russ Moses offered "Suggested Improvements for Residential Schools." What do his suggestions aim to improve and protect? Do his suggestions continue to have importance even in contemporary times?

2. The two photographs that accompany Sarah de Leew's essay are of remarkable art objects produced by girls in two of British Columbia's Indian residential schools. One photo captures a pillow case, cross-stitched around 1936 by Haida girls attending St Michael's Indian Residential School in Port Alberni. The second photo is of a glass ball, a weight from one of the Japanese fishing nets found often on the west coast of BC. It was beautifully beaded around 1971 by two 12-year-old Nuu-chah-nulth children attending Kuper Island Indian Residential School and presented to the then lieutenant governor of British Columbia, John Robert Nicholson. What comes to your mind when you see these objects? What can historians learn about young First Nations people by looking at these objects?

Selected Bibliography

Articles

Alfred, Taiaiake, "What is Radical Imagination? Indigenous Struggles in Canada," *Affinities: A Journal of Radical Theory, Culture, and Action* 4, 2 (Fall 2010): 1–4.

Barman, Jean, "Schooled for Inequality: The Education of British Columbia Aboriginal Children," in Jean Barman and Mona Gleason, eds., *Children, Teachers, and Schools in the History of British Columbia*, 2nd Edition. Calgary: Detselig Press, 2002: 57–80.

Jones, Alison, and Kuni Jenkins, "Disciplining the Native Body: Handwriting and Its Civilizing Practices," *History of Education Review* 29, 2 (2000): 34–46.

Carstairs, Catherine, and Rachel Elder. "Expertise, Health, and Popular Opinion: Debating Water Fluoridation, 1945–1980." *Canadian Historical Review* 89, 3 (September 2008): 345–71.

Featherstone, Lisa, "Doctors, Mothers, and the Feeding of Children in Australia, 1880–1910," in Cheryl Krasnick Warsh and Veronica Strong-Boag, eds. *Children's Health Issues in Historical Perspective*. Waterloo: Wilfrid University Press, 2005: 131–61.

Gidney, Catherine. "'Less Inefficiency, More Milk': The Politics of Food on the University Campus, 190–1950," in Franca Iacovetta, Valerie Korinek, Marlene Epp, eds., *Edible Histories, Cultural Politics: Towards a Canadian Food History*. Toronto: University of Toronto Press, 2012: 286–304.

Gleason, Mona, "Race, Class, and Health: School Medical Inspection and 'Healthy' Children in British Columbia, 1890 to 1930." *Canadian Bulletin of Medical History* 19 (2002): 95–112.

Henry, Carol J., Derek G. Allison, and Alicia C. Garcia, "Child Nutrition Programs in Canada and the United States: Comparisons and Contrasts," *Journal of School Health* 73 2 (February, 2003): 83–5.

Moffat, Tina, and Ann Herring, "The Historical Roots of High Rates of Infant Death in Aboriginal Communities in Canada in the Early Twentieth Century: The Case of Fisher River, Manitoba." *Social Science and Medicine* 48 (1999): 1821–32.

Ostry, Alec, "The Early Development of Nutrition Policy in Canada," Cheryl Krasnick Warsh and Veronica Strong-Boag, eds. *Children's Health Issues in Historical Perspective*. Waterloo: Wilfrid University Press, 2005: 191–209.

Sangster, Joan, "'She Is Hostile to Our Ways': First Nations Girls Sentenced to the Ontario Training School for Girls, 1933–1960," *Law and History Review* 20, 1 (2002): 59–96.

Sealander, Judith, "Diet, Health, and America's Young in the Twentieth Century," in Cheryl Krasnick Warsh and Veronica Strong-Boag, eds. *Children's Health Issues in Historical Perspective*. Waterloo: Wilfrid University Press, 2005: 161–91.

Books

Chunn, Dorothy E., *From Punishment to Doing Good: Family Courts and Socialized Justice in Ontario, 1880–1940*. Toronto: University of Toronto Press, 1992.

Fournier, S., and E. Crey, *Stolen from Our Embrace: The Abduction of First Nations Children and the Restoration of Aboriginal Communities*. Vancouver: Douglas & McIntyre, 1997.

Iacovetta, Valerie Korinek, and Marlene Epp, eds., *Edible Histories: Towards a Canadian Food History*. Toronto: University of Toronto, 2012.

Johnston, Basil. *Indian School Days*. Toronto: Key Porter Books, 1988.

Miller, J.R., *Shingwauk's Vision: A History of Native Residential Schools*. Toronto: University of Toronto Press, 1996.

Mosby, Ian, *Food Will Win the War: The Politics, Culture and Science of Food on Canada's Homefront*. Vancouver: UBC Press, 2014.

10 Local and Global Citizenship

Editors' Introduction

In the twentieth century, children and youth participated in a rich associational life that was created both for and by them. Canadian young people could be found in Girl Guides, Boy Scouts, Canadian Girls in Training, the 4-H Clubs, and the Junior Red Cross, while also comprising the throngs required to raise money for a variety of causes, from overseas packages for the armed forces during wartime to world hunger to disease research. Youth organizations served adult desires to instill in children a sense of patriotism, citizenship, and global awareness, and, in many cases, Judeo-Christian duty. Recent scholarship, including the essays in this chapter by Tarah Brookfield and Tamara Myers, reveals how local belonging had a global reach. For example, children participating in a rite of twentieth-century childhood—fundraising for UNICEF on Halloween—served Canada's Cold War commitment to internationalism and foreign relief programs. Both essays are excellent studies of young people's place within more broadly connected histories; both situate seemingly local stories of youthful engagement within a wider global context.

Fundraising in the Cold War era compelled young people to imagine and engage with worlds beyond their own. Brookfield uses the lens of children's foreign relief activities to shed light on the relationship between empowered children in Canada and the so-called needy children of the Global South. She demonstrates how post-war internationalism was presented to schoolchildren as a path to citizenship that could be achieved by participating in raising money for foreign "friends" or sponsoring foster children. Brookfield shows how Aboriginal children—themselves survivors of colonialism and in many cases perceived as in need and at times "foreign"—also took up the cause of global neediness.

Fundraising in the mid-twentieth century both targeted children and exploited their images. Although often sentimental and nostalgic, the iconography of childhood is far from simplistic or neutral. Beyond their use in art and advertising, images of children have been deployed for political, ideological, social, and erotic purposes, and so it is not surprising that historians of children and youth have turned to visual representations of children to help explain the past.[1] Tamara Myers provides an example of how children became what Loren Lerner calls "projections of society's fondest desires and evidence of its worst failures" through visual representations.[2] Analyzing the pictorial archive of child and youth participation at the Miles for Millions annual fundraising march, Myers shows how children were deployed to represent a young, peaceful, and humanitarian nation in a world erupting in crises. Canadian children adorned newspaper and magazine pages as symbols of able-bodiedness and a bright future, particularly when contrasted with the targets of that fundraising effort, the stereotypical starving and abandoned waifs of the Global South. Beyond examining the ideological work that images of children are employed to do, Myers suggests that carefully unpacking the pictorial legacy of the Miles for Millions campaign can lead to revelations about childhood and its wider representation in the late 1960s.

Post-war child welfare foreign relief programs generated volumes of text instructing young people to take action. The Unitarian Service Committee Public Service announcements from the 1960s and '70s, included with Brookfield's essay, implore children and adults to assume the role of global do-gooder and to see the protection of the health of children around the world as their personal responsibility. The Miles for Millions Declaration circulated widely in the late 1960s, giving language to the children's physical feat on Walk Day. It appeared on a poster and on postcards to be sent to the federal government, in both forms encouraging children to be active participants in politics.

Notes

1. Patricia Holland, *Picturing Childhood: The Myth of the Child in Popular Imagery* (London: I.B. Tauris and Co., 2004)

2. Loren Lerner, ed., *Depicting Canada's Children* (Waterloo: Wilfrid Laurier Press, 2009), xviii.

Children as "Seeds of Destiny": Nation, Race, and Citizenship in Post-war Foreign Relief Programs

TARAH BROOKFIELD

Costumes, candy, and coins. For over 50 years, this triumvirate was a Halloween ritual mixing childhood fantasy and indulgence with the ideals of charity and global citizenship. Beginning in 1955, Canadian children dressed as ghosts, princesses, and pirates knocked on their neighbours' doors, calling out "Trick or Treat," returning home later with pillowcases full of candy and cardboard boxes heavy with donated coins. Afterwards, the coins were handed over to teachers and youth group leaders to be sorted, rolled, and sent to the United Nations International Children's Emergency Fund (UNICEF). On the first Halloween campaign Canadian children raised $15,000—enough money, according to UNICEF promotional material,

to purchase 7.5 million glasses of milk for underfed children.[1] By 1969 close to 600,000 Canadian children participated, and by 1975 donations approached $1 million.[2] "A gift" from "thousands of children across Canada who shared their treats with children all over the world" was how Mimi Macdonald, a 12-year-old girl from Gander, Newfoundland, characterized this nationwide movement."[3] While the UNICEF Halloween campaign became entrenched in children's culture it was only one of several popular foreign relief programs active in the post-war period to mobilize Canadian youth in international charitable efforts.[4] While the purpose of these organizations was to build healthy bodies and minds of children living in developing nations and war zones, the programs also strove to inaugurate young Canadians into the nation's new

Source: Reprinted with permission from the author.

post-war commitment to internationalism and teach them to be generous, co-operative, responsible, and globally aware citizens. Children on both sides of the foreign relief equation, the young donors and the young recipients, were portrayed by the foreign relief agencies as "seeds of destiny"—future leaders who, if nurtured properly in terms of nutrition, health, education, and democracy, would grow up to be peaceful and productive citizens.[5]

While Canadian and non-Canadian children may have been seen as sharing an intertwined destiny, they were not portrayed as equal or alike in foreign relief discourse. Rather, they were on opposing sides of a problem–solution binary steeped in foreign policy priorities and complicated by constructions of nation, race, and class. As Laura Briggs has argued, the image of the anonymous "rail-thin waif, maybe with an empty rice bowl" has been the standard representation of need in the developing world for Western audiences since the post-war period.[6] In general, the young recipients of foreign relief were conceived as weak, vulnerable, and in desperate need of Canadian attention, love, and financial contributions. Yet not all needy children were considered equally deserving; children living in nations allied with Canada or nations where political or economic influence was desired received the bulk of attention and aid. Given these considerations, the most dreaded outcome was not that these unfortunate children could die but that, should they be ignored by Canada, they might grow up to become a destructive force and a threat to global peace.

Frequently a "waif's" salvation was suggested to be in the hands of the white heterosexual Western family, portrayed as "fundamentally caring and committed to the well being of local non-white and working class children, as well as infants, youth and families around the globe."[7] Whether this image was invoked in the context of UNICEF donations, foster parent plan sponsorships, or in the most extreme circumstances, international adoption, Western families were typically positioned as the benevolent rescuers. Tamara Myers's research emphasizes the special role that Western children played in this construction of need and salvation. As young

donors and volunteers, Canadian children were presented as being blessed with health and wealth, and were shown to be enthusiastic in their quest to assist their underprivileged counterparts. In particular for the Canadian context, Myers argues that "As cultural objects," images of young Canadian school children in "robust health" with "a go-getter mentality" transmitted "compelling messages about the country's present and future and were used to mobilize adults around Canada's relatively new role in international development."[8]

Although Canadian children of all backgrounds were encouraged to participate in foreign relief projects, their efforts were contextualized differently based on their perceived economic and social status within Canadian society. In particular, the contributions of Indigenous children were singled out as exceptional because these children were considered by many Canadians to be somewhat foreign and needy themselves. Therefore, heartwarming tales about the generosity of residential school students and First Nations families were used in promotional material to encourage donations from middle-class Canadians of European background and to silence critics who felt Canadians should focus on assisting children within their own borders. These stories also represent the intense focus on "Canadianizing" Indigenous youth in this era, where the "seeds of destiny" model was imbued not only in Cold War internationalism but in Canada's ongoing colonial policies and projects.

Save the Children, Save the World: Ideology and the Origins of Post-war Foreign Relief

After the Second World War, the Canadian government invested a considerable amount of money and resources in foreign relief. It donated more than two billion dollars to European reconstruction, much of which was channelled through the United Nations Relief and Rehabilitation Administration (UNRRA). Under Prime Minister Louis St Laurent's administration, Canada expanded its foreign aid focus from Europe to include Asia, starting with an annual commitment of $850,000 to assist with the development of the decolonized British Commonwealth nations, particularly India.[9] The reasons for this spending were threefold. As with the United States's Marshall Plan, this aid was a continuation of the financial assistance made during the war and was viewed as a necessary step to preserve what Canada and its allies had fought six years to achieve. It also represented a renewed commitment to internationalism, the policy that encouraged political and economic co-operation among nations, specifically via the United Nations (UN), and was deemed just as important to continue in peacetime. For a middle power country like Canada, this was one area of international relations in which the government believed Canadians could assert influence.[10] Most importantly, the gifts of cash, wheat, food products, and technology were viewed as a critical part of Canada's national defence plan, especially when tensions between the Soviet Union and United States escalated in the late 1940s. Pouring resources into unstable overseas regions was a way to build Cold War alliances and reduce the chances of an overseas conflict affecting Canada.[11]

Although the Canadian government focused on large-scale development projects, the majority of non-governmental organizations, usually funded by government grants and private donations, were often dedicated to children's health and safety. In addition to the already mentioned UNICEF, Canadian branches of CARE, Save the Children, World Vision, Oxfam, and Foster Parents Plan International (FPPI), as well as the Canadian-founded relief organization the Unitarian Service Committee (USC), developed fundraising programs centred on providing basic needs—food, clothing, shelter, medicine, and education—to children living in war-affected communities or developing nations. Several of these organizations also had a foster parent plan that facilitated Canadian individuals, families, or groups in sponsoring and sending letters to an orphaned or impoverished child. Many non-governmental agencies focused their efforts on assisting children because it was a cause that had a wide, seemingly apolitical appeal. Although the projects were promoted by the agencies as humanitarian missions, there were several political aims embedded within the goals and delivery methods.

Certainly the consequences of war, poverty, and natural disaster particularly affected "the little ones," the term frequently used by the USC, making children the natural recipients of relief projects.[12] Throughout the 1940s, there was growing awareness of the specific vulnerabilities children faced during war and shock over how many children had been affected by the Second World War in particular. In 1943, Dr Anna Freud and Dr Dorothy Burlingham published *War and Children*, the first academic study of the effects of war on the young, based on the doctors' work with European child evacuees in Britain. They concluded that child development could be severely stunted by war, noting, "Adults can live under emergency conditions and, if necessary, on emergency rations. But the situation in the decisive years of bodily and mental development is entirely different."[13] Freud and Burlingham listed the physical and psychological malformations of children under severe wartime stress and recommended ways to minimize the impact of war on children, most notably by ensuring that normal routines such as attending school were kept up, and that attentive adults were made available to care for displaced children. The theories articulated in *War and Children* would become a guide for the foreign relief agencies operating in post-war Europe and Asia, whose programs promised to intervene when parents and communities were unable to offer a secure and stable environment on their own. By 1945, it was clear what an enormous task this would be. At the war's end, over 13 million children had been classified as orphaned, separated, or abandoned by their parents. Additionally, thousands of children suffered from malnutrition and disease, others had been crippled and maimed, and more had been traumatized by living through invasions, bombings, and genocide.[14] Canadians were greatly moved by the plight of these young victims of war and generously offered their financial support.

In addition to being deemed so vulnerable, children were also considered to be worthy of protection because of their supposed blamelessness. The association of innocence, held so dear in the Western conceit of childhood, meant that "a child can be the bearer of suffering with no responsibility for its causes."[15] Dominique Marshall argues that since the First World War "the fate of children in times of war has provoked spontaneous movements of sympathy for their rights, across borders and across enemy lines."[16] This sentiment evolved into serious discussions about the importance of child rights that began in the interwar period. In 1924, the League of Nations produced the *Declaration of the Rights of the Child*, written by Eglantyne Jebb, the founder of Save the Children, which began by stating that "mankind owes to the child the best that it has to give" and justifies this by explaining "the child, because of his physical and mental immaturity, needs special safeguards and care."[17] Marshall argues that support for saving the children—all children, regardless of race, religion, or nation— was particularly popular during the Cold War era because issues surrounding child rights and child welfare were ones that countries on both sides of the Iron Curtain could usually find popular support for at home.[18] Therefore, UNICEF became one of the few UN agencies to avoid being a site of Cold War–driven power struggles. This was helped by UNICEF's policy that funds be sent and received by both communist and capitalist nations. In spite of rumours circulating in the early 1960s that most UNICEF money was going to communist nations because most UNICEF volunteers were socialists, UNICEF managed for the most part to avoid controversy.[19] In the words of Kathleen Bowlby, the national secretary of Canada's United Nations Association, UNICEF was the "United Nations organ for which everyone has the highest praise and which has a universal appeal. One of the world body's most cherished agencies."[20]

Despite UNICEF's reputation and intentions, children have never been politically neutral subjects, and most foreign relief programs devoted to child welfare were ripe for politicizing. As Briggs argues, child saving has long been an exceedingly popular form of foreign policy because it presents such an easy yet narrow vision of need. This has been used to mobilize "ideologies of rescue" that appeal to the public on a moral basis while ignoring the "structural explanations for famine, poverty or other disasters, including international, political, military and economic causes."[21] It has also been used

by powerful countries to avoid accountability for the causes of hunger or war or poverty because their "only role was to rescue the unfortunate victims of such events."[22] Although serious cause-and-effect arguments were never explicit, the rhetoric and imagery found in foreign relief agencies' promotional material usually blamed someone or something for the state of a child's suffering. Naturally this blame was filtered through perceptions about donor and recipient nations' history and politics or a culture's strengths and weaknesses. In the aftermath of the Second World War, the Axis powers were commonly named as the reason behind the devastation to children's bodies and families, while the UN was positioned as the saviour.[23] During the Cold War, the heroes and villains shifted, and the most dominant dialogue in Canada blamed communist regimes' governing and war-mongering for dismal child welfare conditions in Eastern Europe, North Korea, and China. By sharing its wealth through foreign relief, Canada could demonstrate the benefits of capitalism and the generosity of democratic states. If ever asked to take sides, it was hoped that recipients of Canadian aid would choose their long-distance benefactors.[24]

Meanwhile, Canadian donors were encouraged to participate in relief efforts so they could "fight a little cold war of our own." These were the very words FPPI used to recruit the prime minister's wife, Olive Diefenbaker, who became the foster mother to Huizhong, a Chinese girl living in Hong Kong, referred to as a refugee from communism.[25] As Christine Klein has argued, making a donation to a foreign relief agency like FPPI was a way for the average citizen to play a role in the nation's foreign policy.[26] Therefore it is not surprising that the majority of child welfare agencies active in Canada spent their aid money in sites of pivotal Cold War conflict, most notably Germany, Greece, Hungary, South Korea, Hong Kong, and South Vietnam. Despite having significant development needs, Africa and Latin America were barely on the Canadian foreign relief radar in the 1950s and 1960s. Unsurprisingly, the needs of young people in communist nations were deliberately ignored up until critiques over American intervention in Vietnam sparked the creation of at least two relief agencies in Canada collecting money and goods to assist civilians living in North Vietnam in the late 1960s.[27]

Before the anti–Vietnam War movement changed the politics of relief, Cold War politicization led to foreign children, even in allied nations, regularly being conceived as potential security threats. Should the children be left poor, hungry, uneducated, and disenchanted, they could succumb to communist influence or resort to civil disobedience, scenarios that could affect global security and Canada's own well-being. FPPI's foster parent advertisements hinted at these aims, telling prospective sponsors that "By aiding these children you are working for the greatest aim of all—peace."[28] One recurring magazine and newspaper ad featured Yolanda, a Greek girl who was already a veteran of two wars; orphaned during the Second World War, she later lost an eye when hit by a mortar shell during the civil conflict in Greece and needed an operation so she could be fitted with a glass eye.[29] Subsequent ads featured the healed Yolanda with the new Americanized name Annie, expressing her thanks to FPPI and her Canadian donors for helping her get well and allowing her to pursue her dream of becoming a nurse or a hairdresser.[30] FPPI strived to show that their children were productive, happy, and grateful. Their information director aimed to emphasize

> that Plan children probably have a better-than-average chance of becoming leaders in their countries tomorrow . . . [and] it is far better that these brighter children be helped through maturity through western aid, than through communist aid . . . that the friendships and understanding established through these children today can have a life-and-death difference to our world tomorrow.[31]

This attitude made foreign aid an important tool in neutralizing threats and winning allies. Therefore, it was critical to avoid the "ruin, doubt, defeatism and despair [that] will breed Fascism, more Hitlers, more Togos . . ." and instead to encourage the development of "Einsteins, Toscaninis, Manuel Quezons, Madame Curies, and Sun Yat Sens."[32]

The quotation above is a centrepiece of *Seeds of Destiny*, a documentary made by the U.S. Army on behalf of UNRRA. The film depicted horrific images of homeless and maimed European and Asian children attempting to survive alone in the aftermath of the Second World War. This imagery was followed by shots of the untouched suburban homes and schoolyards of North America.[33] Undoubtedly these startling contrasts were meant to provoke pity, anger, guilt, sadness, and responsibility in North American viewers. Private screenings of the film (deemed too graphic to be shown in public theatres) at service clubs, church groups, women's clubs, unions, and parent–teacher associations between 1946 and 1948 generated $11 million in private donations to UNRRA in North America.[34] It was assumed that Canadian money and attention could heal the war wounds or rather ensure that the "seeds of destiny" were planted, fertilized, and harvested appropriately.

The connection that *Seeds of Destiny* made between unsettling images of war-scarred children and the untouched childhoods of Canadian children was also meant to suggest that foreign aid would help prevent Canadian children from ever experiencing war first-hand. Armed with tools such as *Dr Spock's Guide to Baby and Child Care* and an expanded welfare system, many parents were told it was scientifically and socially possible to nurture Canadian children through infancy, childhood, and adolescence.[35] In some ways the ideals behind foreign relief paralleled the ones in Canada's expanding welfare state, particularly the 1945 family allowance program, which gave a monthly benefit to all children in Canada. While orphaned, neglected, and sick children had always been the recipients of charity in Canada, the new family allowance was offered to all Canadian children, regardless of their family's income. The universal allowance was seen as a good investment in building active citizens who would grow up to be Canada's next generation of workers, soldiers, mothers, and leaders.[36] In the case of foreign relief, it was hoped that if the basic needs of children overseas were met, these children would become friendly, productive adults. Thus, foreign relief would act like a secondary welfare system to keep Canadian children safe and healthy. As Lotta Hitschmanova, the founder of the USC, explained to donors, helping children in Europe and Asia "is not only our humanitarian duty, but it is also a very wise move for the future to help your own Canadian children ten or fifteen years from now."[37]

"Friends" in Need: The Canadian Child as Philanthropist

In the mid-1950s, a segment of foreign relief programs developed around the idea of children helping children. This was not an entirely new phenomenon. Acts of charity had long been part of children's moral and religious instruction, and foreign relief had been a staple in Sunday schools and youth clubs in particular since the late nineteenth century. The French Catholic St Enfance Association in Quebec had been asking school children to save their pennies to redeem and educate children in "unfaithful" countries since 1843.[38] What was new about these post-war initiatives was how they fit into Canada's grander commitment to internationalism, a largely secularized ideal. There were also more children in Canada than ever before. Doug Owram calculated that the annual "number of babies born [in Canada] went up from just over 300,000 at the war's end to 372,000 by 1947, and to more than 400,000 by 1952. It would be 1966 before the number of children born fell below 400,000 again."[39] Family sizes increased as couples wed younger and improved nutrition and prenatal care lowered rates of maternal and infant mortality. The upsurge in births was attributed to the celebratory zeal following the end of the Second World War, when economic prosperity and peace encouraged marriages and children the same way years of economic depression and war had discouraged them.[40] The youth-oriented nature of the Canadian population made children more visible in this period, which meant that they became included in more aspects of public life, particularly as consumers.[41]

While allowances and wages undoubtedly went to their own needs and wants, Canadian youth were also encouraged to share their good fortune with their "friends," the term often used by the relief agencies to describe their foreign counterparts, even if they would most likely never meet or even communicate. This language was useful to bridge the geographic, linguistic, cultural, economic, and situational distance between the lives of Canadian children living in relative harmony and the children living in war zones and impoverished regions. Helping "friends" also made charity feel less like a financial or emotional burden and inspired good will and warm feelings. It was also a good starting point, especially for young children who would be unlikely to refute the notion of helping out a friend in need. To establish this bond, often the financial aid element was de-emphasized and the emotional side of the relationship was played up. In one USC appeal to the schoolchildren of British Columbia, Hitschmanova explained that South Korean orphans would not only be thrilled to get enough money to build a new school, "they would have the most priceless gift of all, the knowledge that their young school friends in Canada are doing their share to help them."[42] As sweet as this sentiment of friendship and gratitude was, it was also disingenuous as it did not acknowledge the imbalance in power between giver and receiver or the political reasons for ensuring that South Korean boys and girls were educated appropriately. Of course, referring to the fundraising effort as a way to give "their share" did make the act seem more than a simple gift between friends and established the normalcy of responsibility held by a Canadian child to his or her "friends."

From the perspective of a non-governmental organization, it was also practical to involve Canadian children as canvassers and donors. With many local, national, and international charities competing for the philanthropy of Canadians, being able to tap into a consistent, if not personally well endowed, pool of participants was a boon.[43] Once children were registered with the school system, relief agencies knew when and where to find their labour pool. Unlike adult donors who could be fickle in their commitment, the children were often obliged to participate as part of their curriculum and could not opt out without risking a bad grade or stigmatization for lack of participation. It was also hoped that support for foreign aid would become a habit, one that would follow the children into adulthood. But recruiting Canadian youth was not just an issue of expanding the donor pool. As with the young recipients of this aid, the child-led foreign relief programs were seen as a good opportunity to indoctrinate Canadian youth. Interweaving foreign relief projects into the school day or making it an extracurricular activity gave children several spaces to learn about the world through an internationalist lens. Ideally this would convince boys and girls about the important role Canada had to play in the world. Just as the programs were designed to improve the minds, bodies, and characters of the foreign youth, Canadian youth were considered "seeds of destiny" as well, ready to be shaped into responsible national and global citizens.

Child welfare foreign relief programs became enshrined as a part of children's school and leisure time in the 1950s, 1960s, and 1970s. In addition to the annual UNICEF Halloween campaigns, young people contributed to localized and nationwide milk, shoe, clothing, and diaper drives by collecting money and goods. Young people also flocked to participate in walkathons, dance-a-thons, and famine awareness events, where the funds raised to alleviate global hunger and poverty were symbolically matched by the physical exertion and emotional drama of walking great distances or temporarily going without food. In high schools, a charitable project often grew out of a social studies, geography, or history class. Many of these projects seemed to be initiated by the students themselves, born out of critically thinking about Canada's role in the world. In a letter to the USC, one grade 10 social studies teacher in Calgary explained that his students had decided to donate 10 per cent of their weekly allowances to the USC "after a discussion on whether or not affluent Canadians should take responsibility for the welfare of those less fortunate throughout the world."[44] The class raised $124, and the teacher made a point of emphasizing that the school was in a working-class area of the city and that the students had therefore done "an excellent job of accumulating the amount they did."[45] Student councils

and clubs often took on the sponsorship of a foster child, with the responsibility for writing letters to the child falling to the student secretary or divided among the entire membership. One student council in Vancouver sponsored five children from France, South Korea, and India over 18 years. The students in this school took their responsibility seriously, frequently asking for more details about their foster children and explaining how happy it made them to help "the needy children of our world," even when their own community faced high unemployment.[46] That these activities frequently took place in schools makes it clear they were deemed to have an educational value, teaching students about the world around them and how, as Canadians, they could make a difference. Since payments had to be made in a timely manner, the activities also built budgeting, organizational, and time management skills, equally relevant aspects of the good citizen. Considering that letter-writing was often part of a project, spelling and handwriting were related competencies being taught.

Participation was simpler and smaller in elementary schools, and was structured around lessons in sharing and civic engagement. An example of how teachers presented their projects to younger students and how the students internalized them can be seen in the results of one classroom project. In 1968, 25 grade 2 students from Regina raised money to buy blankets for Palestinian babies living in refugee camps in Jordan in the chaotic aftermath of the Six Day War with Israel. To commemorate their efforts, the class made a picture book of illustrations detailing how they each earned their portion of the $23.73 collected.[47] An analysis of the images and language on display can be used to theorize the level of engagement the children had in the project and the assignment's overall goals. The book was filled with sketches depicting what tasks the students performed to earn their contribution. Underneath the crayon-coloured drawings were explanations such as, "I am selling popcorn" and "I am making my bed." Eighteen children were shown doing chores around the house or farm, which may or may not have already been part of their regular responsibilities. It is impossible to know if they went out of their way to help out or if their parents just gave them money for everyday tasks. Six children are shown doing something specific to earn money: four sold drinks or snacks to earn their contributions, while two helped their neighbours. Only two of the children withdrew money from their bank account or piggy bank. In the artwork the children are mostly smiling as they go about their work. In four of the illustrations made by boys, planes and paratroopers dominate the scene, with the actual task being squeezed into one corner of the page. These students' apparent passion for aviation could be interpreted as a lack of interest in the actual assignment, perhaps because they did not care about the class project or simply because they were seven years old and had planes on the brain. There is not enough information to link the planes to militarism or to show that the children made any connection between war and their money for Jordan. In fact none of the pictures indicate what the money is being raised for, which could suggest that the main object of the lesson was singling out the importance of good behaviour, as sons and daughters at home and as well-behaved children in the community, rather than as global citizens like their high school peers. Nonetheless, projects like the Jordan blanket fundraiser established schoolchildren's familiarity with the concept of giving, which would become more informed and nuanced as the children grew up.

Often it was mothers and fathers, not teachers, who organized their children's participation. The donations were often contextualized as pride on behalf of parents who witnessed what they deemed as a sign of their children's kindness, such as in the case of Marie Labelle, a mother from Hull, Quebec. Labelle mailed in a cheque for $1.38, a donation organized by neighbourhood children ranging in age from 2 to 10 years old, including her own daughter Claire, who raised 42 cents. Labelle explained that the money was to go to children in South Korea, the hotspot for aid in 1953, and added, "C'est bien peu, mais c'est de bon coeur."[48] It was common for donors, especially those who sent in the typically smaller amounts collected on the behalf of children, to apologize for the low sums being given. Other parents claimed their child's donation was

an example of their family's values being practised, even if the act was performed under duress rather than as an expression of a "bon coeur." Such is the case of Mrs Cope from Oak Lake, Manitoba, who punished her children by charging them money for not respecting the good fortune they had in Canada. She enclosed a donation of four dollars to the USC, stating, "We are pleased to send you this collection which the children have made since last year. When they did not thoroughly clean their plates at table they were reminded to put several pennies away for the children who have no or very little food to eat, and so are sending you their support."[49] In response, the USC wrote back saying that they planned to advertise Cope's system in their next newsletter. This highly praised idea is a reminder of the value placed on using foreign relief to mould Canadian children's characters and habits.

Even if written under the direction of their teachers or parents, the letters penned by the children themselves often show a special kinship with the recipient of the aid. If they did not see them as "friends," they were able to relate to them on some level, sometimes quite candidly. One seven-year-old child's letter is amusingly frank about her thoughts (and taste buds) regarding the plan to send the boy sponsored by her class a case of powdered milk. She wrote, "King Edward School adopted a little Indin [sic] boy. We are senting [sic] some milk. I do not think he will like it, but we are still sending it. Love from Marissa Jones."[50] For the Chan brothers, their familiarity perhaps stemmed from a shared heritage. In 1974, the three brothers from Calgary earned the large sum of 50 dollars house-sitting for their neighbours, and they sent their earnings to the USC with a written request: "Please forward this entire cheque to some needy child in any of the Asian countries."[51] It is possible that these Chinese Canadian boys felt particularly close to a child from Asia, or maybe they just associated the region with greater need. The agency wrote back advising that the money had gone as a one-time gift to Huang Han, a nine-year-old boy in Hong Kong who had tuberculosis and epilepsy. In another case, two brothers from Maklin, Saskatchewan, kept their thoughts succinct when they decided to send their family allowance money to the USC with a handwritten note that read, "I hope it helps some other little boy."[52] In this case, a shared gender was the boys' only stipulation. Interestingly, these brothers were among the few donors who did not underline their designation with the adjective, "needy."

Whether they were instructed by teachers or parents or individually inspired, boys and girls from across the country, from rural and urban areas, and from different economic situations and ethnic backgrounds were considered to be key players in child welfare foreign relief. They participated because it was expected or because it was fun or because they truly thought caring for their foreign "friends" was important. Despite this phenomenon appearing to be a common experience for Canadian children from coast to coast in the post-war period, one group of Canadian children's contributions were continually singled out as exceptional in terms of their participation and identity as donors, not recipients, of this aid.

Indigenous Children as "Seeds of Destiny"

In the post-war period, First Nations, Métis, and Inuit communities were still viewed by the Canadian government and the majority of the public as having a tenuous claim to Canadian citizenship. This was one of the reasons for moving Indian Affairs, originally located in the Department of Mines and Resources, to the Department of Citizenship and Immigration, where the training of Indigenous people was heavily modelled after the citizenship campaigns being developed for newcomers to Canada.[53] Furthermore, for almost a century the federal government had used its extensive residential and industrial school system to "save" Indigenous youths from their ancestry by removing the "Indian" from the young people and assimilating them into Euro-Canadian and Christian society.[54] As Sherry Farrell Racette argues, "Government attention consistently focused on the children, viewing them as mute bodies to be emptied and erased, and upon that blankness, an appropriate text of modest knowledge inscribed."[55] The state saw

residential schools as one method to guarantee a superior and more sustainable future for these vulnerable youths, who were viewed as comparable to the foreign children needing Canadian financial support. In other words, Indigenous children had their own "seeds of destiny" mythos. The Canadianizing process was very much alive in the post-war period; however, it is important not to generalize the experience of all First Nations, Métis, and Inuit children in this era as levels of integration and exposure to mainstream Canadian society and claims to Indigenous identity varied by region, nation, and status, as did economic opportunities for individual families living on and off reserves.

Statistics Canada documented noticeable trends regarding the health and welfare of First Nations, Métis, and Inuit families in the post-war period. One significant and well-publicized marker was that the overall life expectancy of Indigenous people in Canada was measured as significantly lower than that of non-Indigenous people, and eight times as many Indigenous children died before the age of two as non-Indigenous children in the same category.[56] There were also much higher rates of communicable diseases on reserves, as well as health problems stemming from an irregular diet and high rates of alcohol and drug use. The poor quality of health was particularly high in northern communities, where First Nations and Inuit were being exposed to germs carried by Canadians and Americans involved in the construction of the Alaska Highway and radar stations in the Arctic, and where there was a lack of access to affordable fresh food and vitamins.[57] It was also during this period that the proportion of Indigenous children in state protective custody was 34 per cent higher than that of other children. The gap was due to concerns from child and family services agencies about the living conditions of Indigenous children. Rather than address the legacies of colonialism that contributed to the economic and social challenges facing Indigenous families, the welfare solutions (foster homes, adoption, and residential schools) usually removed Indigenous children from their families, communities, and cultures.[58]

Ironically, despite brutal attempts at forced adaptation to white values and lifestyles, the

Indigenous population did not disappear. By the 1950s the First Nations population was actually growing at a rate 5 per cent higher than the rest of the population, a figure related to advances in curbing the spread of tuberculosis. This offered optimism amid concerns over Indigenous people's health and welfare.[59] Yet as Daniel Francis notes in his book *The Imaginary Indian*, the stereotype of the disappearing Indian still persisted. Unlike in earlier periods, many liberals lamented this idea and wanted to protect Indigenous cultures from extinction, but they still often promoted assimilation into white culture as the best method for survival.

The romantic image of the vanishing Indian, combined with evidence that life was difficult and dangerous for many Indigenous children in Canada, became a problem for foreign relief agencies focusing on the vulnerability of children oceans away. Organization like FPPI and the USC were sometimes besieged with questions about why Canadians should send money to help poor people overseas when there were so many people who could use their help at home. This understanding was expressed in one of many letters of critique kept on file by the USC. In an anonymous letter signed "Disgusted" the writer complained that the USC's charitable ventures in India were sickening because "thousands of Canadians need food and financial help." The writer continued with a strong rebuke: "your appeal makes me sick to my stomach, and if you really want to do something constructive, take a walk around our slums, or start on our Indians."[60] The use of the term "our Indians" implied a paternalistic attitude toward a group who needed care, attention, and financial support; it was also a nod to the oft-spoken proverb that charity should begin at home. Presumably, before we help "those Indians," the letter-writer felt Canadian money should be spent on "our Indians." The witty juxtaposition of the nation of India and the "Indians" in Canada was rhetorical device commonly used by foreign aid critics and supporters alike.

A different spin on this sentiment was expressed in a letter from a confused grade 2 student in Edmonton, whose school had raised money for the sponsorship of Mukul, a seven-year-old boy in India. The girl's class had been set the task of contributing money toward the purchase of powdered milk for the orphanage where Mukul lived. In a letter to the representative of the charity, the student wrote,

> We are very fortunate because we have homes and even a big school. When our family went to the farm I saw many Indians and they had old boards and tents to live in. They are poor too. My mother almost cried when she saw how poor dressed they were. In Edmonton the trees are all most all green. Everything is so nice in Edmonton. I hope everything is all right in India. I hope Mukul is fine. We are all fine and learning well. Are the poor people any better now? Annabelle brought 25 for powdered milk. She is the only one to bring that much. . . . I am sad that they cannot put clothing in boxes and send them. The Indian people that I saw on the way to the farm only had patches for clothes.[61]

It is interesting that this young student compared the First Nations people she saw near Edmonton with the boy she was helping in India. Whether she had no idea a separate country of India existed or was in fact correlating a group of people sharing the moniker "Indian," the student made a strong connection between the people she had observed and designated as poor in her own city and those she was asked to help on another continent.

To combat these common criticisms and confusions, foreign relief agencies used two different strategies. First, they offered explanations about why their programs were aimed at non-Canadian children rather than those at home. They did not deny that "our Indians" needed attention; instead, they emphasized the extremely harsh circumstances in nations like war-torn South Korea or refugee-overwhelmed Hong Kong, where populations had been uprooted by war and where economic or political circumstances rendered governments and other local institutions unable to care for their own populations.[62] Meanwhile, Canada, they pointed out, had a growing welfare state that provided resources that were supposed to provide for all Canadian children's basic needs, in the form of family allowances, widows' pensions, free schooling, and public health care. In a brochure explaining why they did not service First Nations and Inuit children, FPPI explained that it would be unaffordable to run a comparable relief program at home, where the Canadian dollar could only go so far. In 1972, it only cost $17 a month to sponsor a child in South Vietnam, but to do the same for a Canadian child would cost much more, and presumably this charitable act would be too expensive for the average Canadian donor.[63] It was never mentioned that helping "our Indians" was not as politically expedient as assisting children in sites of Cold War conflict.

A second method of fighting the "charity begins at home" critique was to raise the profile of Indigenous donors in relief agencies' promotional material. This was done to demonstrate that "our Indians" were not as badly off as their Asian Indian counterparts and other foreigners in need, based on the fact they could afford to put aside money for charitable ventures. UNICEF's annual report for 1964–5 proudly noted that for the first time the Halloween campaign reached into the Northwest Territories, where "10 Eskimo children, 2 Indians and 5 white children collected $2.00 for UNICEF."[64] Meanwhile, the USC in its annual reports and newsletters frequently featured human interest stories of giving on the part of Indigenous people in Canada. One story described how an Inuit woman from Sachs Harbour, Northwest Territories, sent in the $20 she earned sewing with a note that read, "Thank God that my own children are not stricken like those you are trying to help."[65] Anecdotes such as these, whether real or invented, were used to provoke guilt in middle-class non-Indigenous Canadians who had yet to donate, and they reinforced another common stereotype: that of the helpful noble Indian. Yet an unpublicized letter from a different Inuit mother presents a more challenging image. "I'm sorry that I haven't given any money to the USC," writes Mae from Baker Lake, Northwest Territories (now located in Nunavut), in a letter written in Inuktitut. "I haven't been working for a long time now. The only way I can get money is by making

carvings. . . . I have had 11 children, 4 of them are dead. I used to be really hungry and really starved for food. . . . Now other people help me but the only thing I need is a job."[66] Mae does not offer to help the USC or ask them for any type of assistance for her family; rather, her letter seems to be a means of explaining why she cannot help, as she had previously written to inquire if donations need to be paid on a monthly basis. Neither of Mae's letters were made public, probably as they revealed need within Canada.

Young Indigenous people were often singled out as special donors. In the three decades after the Second World War, the formal education of most Indigenous children was administered by the federal government, with children attending residential schools, reserve schools, and occasionally integrated provincial schools. This is where many young people would have encountered appeals made by both religious and secular charities recruiting them to become involved in philanthropic endeavours. These projects would have been viewed as another way to assimilate the young people into Euro-Canadian and Christian traditions, and into the new internationalism of the post-war era. Stories of Indigenous children's generosity helped to defuse concerns about the rumoured poor conditions at the residential schools and to emphasize that these children had a bright future ahead of them because they were learning to be good Canadians and global citizens. For example, the principal of Beauval Residential School in northern Saskatchewan notified the USC of his pupils' donation of $13.25 in 1967. After sharing the amount raised, he made sure the USC was aware that

> The children of the school are of Indian background. Poverty is very real here too, but the children nevertheless wish to make a contribution. It is a small one, granted, but the spirit in which it is given is heart-warming. Perhaps next year we can increase the sum of the donation.[67]

USC founder Lotta Hitschmanova's comments following a visit to one of the largest residential schools in Alberni, Manitoba, display similar hyperbole:

You should have seen these small and older Indian boys and girls, they were just as much impressed by [me] . . . as I was from by [*sic*] their black straight hair and their piercing round eyes. But we soon became excellent friends, and now they are packing a "big box" for their little friends in Czechoslovakia.[68]

In this passage, Hitschmanova emphasizes the visual differences between herself and the children but erases the distance between them by suggesting they were "excellent friends" and had a common goal of helping their "friends" in post-war Europe. This type of anecdote made for good public relations because it celebrated the success of foreign relief in reaching the hearts and minds of all Canadians. Singling out the young donors' ethnicity also demonstrated that even those considered to be living on the geographic, cultural, and economic margins of Canada found the means to care about children living on the other side of the world. There was never any acknowledgment that residential school students had no choice but to participate in the relief efforts.

Conclusions

Post-war representations of young recipients and donors in foreign relief literature offer varied and contradictory images of children. The non–North American children are usually portrayed as being alone and unable to be cared for properly by their families or states. They always appear to be eternally grateful for care shown to them by their Canadian "friends." Their youth, size, and status designate them as vulnerable and innocent; yet while they may be helpless now, they are also seen as potentially dangerous. Their very circumstances challenge faith in the stability of family, government, and society. But worse, it is often implied that their isolated and unstructured childhoods could turn them into deadly threats: future dictators, anarchists, communists, or simply a drain on society. Being presented as "seeds of destiny" makes them prizes to be won in the global game of geopolitics. They have unbridled potential to become useful economic and political allies—or at the very least, to

be harmless—as adults. So they are to be wooed and won over with the offerings of new shoes, vitamins, and loving letters from Canadian foster parents. They are also silent, and their true wants and needs are mediated by the foreign relief agencies, which use their images and existences to create a portrait of suffering and a need for rescue—problems to be addressed with a Canadian solution.

On the other side of this binary are Canadian children, who, in post-war representations, become the deliverers of this solution. They are meant to participate in foreign relief as part of a national mobilization and as a means to improve their own characters. They are to share their own fortune and be grateful for what they have as a result of living in a country like Canada. They are to practise service and charitable giving as children so they will bring these characteristics, fully developed, into adulthood. Their future has been doubly secured by doing what they can to ensure the needs of their foreign "friends" are alleviated so that these friends do not become enemies as a result of poverty, hunger, ignorance, or anger. The representations specifically relating to Indigenous children in Canada are obvious reminders of the important role of race and nationality in informing post-war opinions about service and charity, and in shaping the construction of the capable donor and the needy child. While there was a popular consensus that Indigenous children were at risk in the post-war period, this was weighed and contrasted against the projected destinies of the symbolic foreign waif. As a result, young Indigenous people were characterized by two images. On the one hand, they were shown as children whose health and welfare were at risk and who therefore needed attention to be paid to their care and education. But on the other hand they were portrayed as having big enough hearts and deep enough pockets to share what they had with their more downtrodden counterparts overseas. Despite the intentions of the relief agencies to present all children as united by their young age and their shared future as leaders of their nations, conceptions about the children's nationality and race determined the different roles, spaces, and representations they would occupy within the rhetoric of foreign relief.

Notes

1. City of Edmonton Archives (CEA), Bertha Lawrence Fonds, MSS 688, box 3, UNA in Canada, Hallowe'en for UNICEF for children everywhere—Planning Manual Produced by the National UNICEF Committee, Toronto, 1960.
2. In total, $988,521 was raised in 1975.
3. CEA, Bertha Lawrence Fonds, MSS 688, box 3, UNA in Canada Report of the exec secretary for the UNA's National UNICEF Comm. by Mary P. Carter, June 1960. Please note that the names of all adults (except for staff and board members) and children identified in the promotional material of UNICEF, FPPI, and the USC are pseudonyms.
4. It should be noted that the Trick or Treat program was changed to other forms of fundraising in 2006 when the processing of coins was deemed to be counterproductive.
5. *Seeds of Destiny*, Defense Department, United States Army War Department, 1946.
6. Laura Briggs, "Mother, Child, Race, Nation: The Visual Iconography of Rescue and the Politics of Transnational and Transracial Adoption," *Gender & History* 15 (2003), 179 and 182.
7. Ibid, 182.
8. Tamara Myers, "Blistered and Bleeding, Tired and Determined: Visual Representations of Children and Youth in the Miles for Millions Walkathon," *Journal of the Canadian Historical Association* 22 (2011), 248, 247.
9. David Morrison, *Aid and Ebb Tide: A History of CIDA and Canadian Development Assistance* (Waterloo: Wilfrid Laurier University Press, 1998), 28–30.
10. Adam Chapnick, *The Middle Power Project: Canada and the Founding of the United Nations* (Vancouver: UBC Press, 2005).
11. Louis St Laurent, "Consequences of the Cold War for Canada," speech to the Canadian Club in Toronto, 27 March 1950, www.collectionscanada.ca/primeministers/h4-4015-e.html.
12. Library and Archives Canada (LAC), Unitarian Service Committee (USC) Fonds, MG28, I322, vol. 384, file 44, Annual Reports and Annual Audited Reports of the Unitarian Service Committee, 196, Annual Report—1961, Year End Review, 1.
13. Anna Freud and Dorothy Tiffany Burlingham, *War and Children* (New York: Medical War Books, 1943), 11.
14. Everett M. Ressler, Neil Boothby and Daniel J. Steinbock, *Unaccompanied Children: Care and Protection in Wars, Natural Disasters, and Refugee Movements* (New York: Oxford University Press, 1988), 12.
15. Patricia Holland, *Picturing Childhood: The Myth of the Child in Popular Imagery* (New York: I.B. Taurus, 2004), 156.
16. Dominique Marshall, "Humanitarian Sympathy for Children in Times of War and the History of Children's Rights 1919-1959," *Children and War: A Historical Anthology*, ed. James Marten (New York: New York University Press, 2002), 196.
17. United Nations, "Declaration on the Rights of the Child," 1959.
18. Marshall, "The Cold War, Canada, and the United Nations," 185.
19. UCO, UNICEF Canada, Annual Report, 1961–1962, Report of Executive Director—Mrs Gordon Richards.
20. CEA, Bertha Lawrence Fonds, MSS 688, Box 1, UNA in Canada, Letter from Kathleen E. Bowlby, National Secretary, National office to all Branch Presidents and Secretaries, 8 May 1952.
21. Briggs, 180.
22. Ibid, 198.
23. See for example the heroes and villains positioned in the film *Seeds of Destiny*, Defense Department, United States Army War Department, 1946.
24. Marshall, "The Cold War, Canada, and the United Nations," 214.
25. University of Rhode Island Archives (URIA), Foster Parents Plan International (FPPI) Records, series X—donors countries 117, box 96, file 51, Canada: Correspondence, 1961–63. Letter from Tam Deachman, Information Director, Industrial Advertising Agency, to Gloria Matthews, FPP New York, 17 June 1963.
26. Christina Klein, "Family Ties and Political Obligation: The Discourse of Adoption and the Cold War Commitment to Asia," *Cold War Constructions: The Political Culture of United States Imperialism, 1945-1964*, ed. Christian Appy. (Amherst: University of Massachusetts Press, 2000): 35–66.
27. Tarah Brookfield, *Cold War Comforts: Canadian Women, Child Safety, and Global Insecurity* (Waterloo: Wilfrid Laurier University Press, 2012): 181–8.
28. URIA, FPPI Records, series X—donor countries 117, box 96, file 51, Canada: Correspondence, 1949–52. "I want a blue eye," Advertisement from an unidentified Canadian newspaper, 1949.
29. Ibid.
30. URIA, FPPI Records, series X—donor countries 117, box 96, file 51, Canada: Correspondence, 1949–52. Letter from Constance Gurd Rykert, Director Public Relations, 1 May 1950.
31. URIA, FPP Records, series X—donors countries 117, box 96, file 51, Canada: Correspondence, 1961–63. Letter from Tam Deachman, Information Director, Industrial Advertising Agency, to Gloria Matthews, FPP New York, 17 June 1963.
32. *Seeds of Destiny*, Defense Department, United States Army War Department, 1946.
33. Ibid.
34. Irene Kahn Atkins, "Seeds of Destiny: A Case History," *Film and History* 250 (1981, March), 31.

35. For more information on this subject, see Mona Gleason, *Normalizing the Ideal: Psychology, Schooling, and the Family in Postwar Canada* (Toronto: University of Toronto Press, 1999) and Mary Louise Adams, *The Trouble With Normal: Postwar Youth and the Construction of Sexuality* (University of Toronto, 1997).

36. Marshall, "The Language of Children's Rights, the Formation of the Welfare State and the Democratic Experience of Poor Families in Quebec, 1940–1955," *Canadian Historical Review* 78 (1997): 261–83.

37. LAC, USC Fonds, MG28, I322, vol. 235, DLH Speeches—1947, Speech to Hamilton Synagogue, 7 February 1947.

38. Alain Larocque, "Losing Our Chinese—The St Enfance Movement," Working Paper 49, Joint Centre for Asia Pacific Studies (June 1987), 6.

39. Doug Owram, *Born at the Right Time: A History of the Baby Boom Generation*. (Toronto: University of Toronto Press, 1996), 4.

40. Veronica Strong-Boag, "Home Dreams: Canadian Women and the Suburban Experience, 1945–60," *Canadian Historical Review* 72, 4 (December 1991): 473–4.

41. Cynthia Comacchio, *The Dominion of Youth: Adolescence and the Making of Modern Canada, 1920 to 1950* (Waterloo: Wilfrid Laurier Press 2006), 185–7.

42. LAC, USC Fonds, MG28, I322, Vol 52, Test of DLH "Morning Visit" Broadcast—appeal for help from BC schools, 3 October 1955.

43. For more information on the history of modern fundraising in Canada see Shirley Tillotson, *Contributing Citizens: Modern Charitable Fundraising and the Making of the Welfare State, 1920–66* (Vancouver: UBC Press, 2008).

44. LAC, USC Fonds, MG28, I322, Vol 52, Alberta Schools, Bowness School, 26 June, 1972

45. Ibid.

46. LAC, USC Fonds, MG28, I322, Vol 52, British Columbia, Britannia School, 1957–75.

47. LAC, MG28, I322, Vol 250, Drawings from WC School in Sask. For project for Blankets for Jordon.

48. LAC, USC Fonds, MG28, I322, Vol 52, Radio and Television, 8 October 1953.

49. LAC, USC Fonds, MG28, I322, Vol 228, Human interest 1955–9, DLH, personal and Misc. 28 Sept. 1959.

50. Ibid.

51. LAC, USC Fonds, MG28, I322, Vol 304, Alberta Files, 15 August 1974.

52. LAC, USC Fonds, MG28, I322, Vol 228, Human interest 1955–9, DLH, personal and Misc.

53. Heidi Bohaker and Franca Iacovetta, "Making Aboriginal People 'Immigrants Too': A Comparison of Citizenship Programs for Newcomers and Indigenous Peoples in Postwar Canada, 1940s–1960s," *The Canadian Historical Review* 90 (2009): 427–61.

54. For a general history of the effects of colonialism of First Nations communities see J.R. Miller, *Skyscrapers Hide the Heavens: A History of Indian–White Relations in Canada* (Toronto: University of Toronto Press, 1991). There are dozens of excellent sources written by historians and former students on residential school. Two these are Isabelle Knockwood, *Out of the Depths: The Experiences of Mi'kmaw Children at the Indian Residential School in Shubenacadie, Nova Scotia* (Lockeport, NS: Roseway, 2002) and Jean Barman, "Schooled for Inequality: The Education of British Columbia Aboriginal Children," *Children, Teachers and Schools in the History of British Columbia*, ed. J. Barman et al. (Calgary: Detselig, 1995): 57–80.

55. Sherry Farrell Racette, "Haunted: First Nations Children in Residential School Photography," *Depicting Canada's Children*, ed. Loren Lerner (Waterloo: Wilfrid Laurier University Press, 2009), 51.

56. Alice Prentice et al., *Canadian Women: A History* (Toronto: Nelson/Thompson Learning, 2006), 382.

57. Miller, 250.

58. Wendy Crichlow, "Western Colonization as Disease: Native Adoption and Cultural Genocide," *Canadian Social Work* 5 (2003): 88–107. Statistic about foster care is from R. Douglas Francis, et al., *Destinies: Canadian History Since Confederation* (Toronto: Nelson Education, 2008), 422.

59. Daniel Francis, *The Imaginary Indian: The Image of the Indian in Canadian Culture* (Toronto: Arsenal Press, 2000), 58.

60. LAC, USC Fonds, MG28, I322, Vol. 250, Letters of Criticism 1956–67.

61. LAC, USC Fonds, MG28, I322, Vol. 228, Human interest 1955–9, DLH, personal and Misc.

62. URIA, FPP Records, series X—donor countries 117, box 99, file 76 Canada: Minor Halliday and Associates Ltd. Conference report, Oct. 1972–Feb 1973, "Facts about Foster Parent Plan."

63. Ibid.

64. UNICEF *Annual Report 1964–1965*, 33.

65. LAC, USC Fonds, MG28, I322, Vol. 384, file 46, Annual Reports and Annual Audited Reports of the Unitarian Service Committee, 1963, Annual Reports, Year End Review—December 1963, 3; Vol. 235, DLH Speeches—1946, Untitled speech given by Hitschmanova, Winnipeg, 15 December 1946.

66. LAC, USC Fonds, MG28, I322, Vol. 445, NWT and Yukon records, 10 July 1979.

67. LAC, USC Fonds, MG28, I322, Vol. 384, file 50, Annual Reports and Annual Audited Reports of the Unitarian Service Committee, 1967.

68. LAC, USC Fonds, MG28, I322, Vol. 235, DLH Speeches—1946, 15 December 1946.

Unitarian Service Committee Public Service Announcements from the 1960s and 1970s: A Selection

"Is there a little fellow sick in your house today? With simple, uncomplicated care he'll soon be back at school. But thousands of mothers in other countries lack the basic necessities of warm housing and good food to make their children well again. One dollar will give a child a warm bowl of nourishing barley or 16 days. Will you help this Christmas by sending a contribution to the Unitarian Service Committee?"

"Money makes miracles. One cent buys one cup of milk, helps a child to live another day."

"This is Lotta Hitschmanova of the Unitarian Service Committee. The child that starves in a distant land isn't your child and you aren't concerned. And yet, if it were your child, and you were helpless in the face of catastrophe, wouldn't you hope that someone would care. Please help through the USC, 56 Sparks Street, Ottawa 4."

"This is Lotta Hitschmanova of the Unitarian Service Committee. Charity begins at home. Indeed it does. And then it goes on to embrace next door neighbours and all those who need help. So start by caring for those near you and then give a thought, and if you can a dollar, to the children far away, who have no hope without your help. One dollar buys 100 cups of milk through the USC, 56 Sparks Street, Ottawa 4."

Blistered and Bleeding, Tired and Determined: Visual Representations of Children and Youth in the Miles for Millions Walkathon[1]

TAMARA MYERS

A photographer frames a group of marching children against spring's clear blue sky, capturing them mid-stride, not in lockstep but with a sense of common

Source: From the *Journal of the Canadian Historical Association*, 22.1 (2011): 245–75. Reprinted with permission.

venture or cause. The picture's subject (young people) and setting (spring-time and out of doors) presuppose a lighthearted moment of childhood activity, play, and innocence. Yet walking briskly the marchers seem to be performing determination more than joy. Their collective gaze is fixed on the ground in front of them; they seem unaware of the camera, except one

Figure 1. Kids on the Move: Miles for Millions Walkathon, 1969

Source: Courtesy of Clive Webster

boy who glances up, his eyes meeting, momentarily at least, those observing him. He does not appear distracted by the photographer or by being recorded: he, too, is focused on the task at hand.[2]

The image of marching young people (see Figure 1) introduces a 1969 *Maclean's* magazine story on the Miles for Millions walkathon, a wildly popular charity event whose origins lie in Canada's Centennial celebrations. The "Walk," as it came to be known, drew thousands of young people across Canada into the streets, where they attempted to cover 30 miles in one day in an effort to raise money for the developing world. Although the Miles for Millions was not exclusively a children's fundraiser, young people predominated among the participants and were featured in both the promotional materials for the event and the photo stories produced in its wake. That representations of children and youth are ubiquitous in the visual archive—and arguably the historical memory—of this nation-wide event, reinforces the importance of both the event to late 1960s and 1970s childhood and of young people to

national identity.[3] Together images of young "milers" advanced the vibrant and determined spirit of a nation that had just celebrated its centennial birthday.

This essay examines the use of children and childhood in the visual culture associated with the Miles for Millions walkathons in the late 1960s and early 1970s. It argues that adults (organizers, supporters, and the media) asserted a particular ideological message about the nation and international development through visual materials—especially photographs—featuring children. As cultural objects, images of children delivered compelling messages about the country's present and future and were used to mobilize adults around Canada's relatively new role in international development. The trope of the marching child spoke to a complex combination of the nation's strengths: its robust health, its pluck and go-getter mentality, and most obviously its youth. Using children to promote and celebrate the Miles for Millions also did the work of reassuring the nation that Canadian youth were all right in an era when youthful demonstrations and reactions to them around the globe spoke to an unsettled and violent moment; as the text accompanying the above photograph indicates, this particular youth-oriented walk was not "like most marches these days, manifestations of something else that has gone wrong with the world," but a sign that "maybe things are finally going right."⁴ Juxtaposing these positive images of Canada's youth with the suffering developing-world child similarly reinforced the conceit that the nation was thoroughly immersed in its benevolent role in resolving the world's humanitarian crises. Canada's young generation then came to signify those Canadian attributes that image makers insisted on in the late 1960s and 1970s: Canada as a peaceful, peacekeeping, and non-violent nation, as well as a doer of "deeds of global goodness."⁵ While focused on the semiotics of the Miles for Millions pictorial, this essay also explores the possibility of reading the images of youth for what they can tell us about the social history of the event—particularly the embodied experience of the walkathon that has remained a prominent memory of childhood for many.

The history of children and youth is increasingly benefiting from the analytic richness of visual culture studies.⁶ As Loren Lerner's recent edited collection, *Depicting Canada's Children*, testifies, analyses of visual representations of youth can help deepen our understanding of how children in both symbolic and material ways contributed to our past. Studying the changing imagery of childhood over time and the work it was employed to do serves to complicate the place of children in history and move beyond seeing photographs "simply as illustrations of a verifiable external reality."⁷ Historians of visual culture insist that the "history [photographs] show is inseparable from the history they enact."⁸ Miles for Millions photographs were produced at a particular moment when image making was ubiquitous and when conventions around photography had shifted toward a documentary or eyewitness style, as Image 1 conveys.⁹ While it is very tempting to treat the photo as a "privileged conveyor of information," or as transmitting an historic truth, students of visual culture have for decades challenged this approach.¹⁰

Methodologically, this means the historian should, and this essay will, treat them critically: as "artifacts that provoke a construction of history," and in relationship to the world that produced them.¹¹

To explore the pictorial history of the Miles for Millions walkathons, this paper relies on a range of images produced for different but related purposes, such as to enlist people to the cause as donors and participants or because an event's scale made it newsworthy. Like other contemporary humanitarian agencies, the Miles for Millions organizers created a wealth of promotional materials that included graphic images that often spoke directly to the global issues—hunger especially—that the fundraiser targeted. They also employed familiar images of starvation to prompt sympathy and spark high participation rates. In addition to highlighting the global problems to be resolved by the fundraising at home, the organizers took advantage of pictures of children from past successful marches. Photographers captured the spirit of Walk Days; their work appeared in a wide range of media, from local newspapers to national magazines, from glossy promotional materials to crudely reproduced fliers. This essay makes particular use of one photographer's collection, privately held, and only partly published. Toronto photographer Joan Latchford shot nearly 1,000 images of walks around the country in 1968 and 1969.

The Walk

The Canadian Miles for Millions phenomenon was modelled on the Oxfam Walk, a British fundraising event that had begun more than 40 years before.¹² A long walk for which participants gathered pledges based on distances covered became one of the most successful and popular activities in that humanitarian organization's history: the first walk in 1967 raised £7,000 for famine relief in India. Without hesitation, Oxfam Canada—known as the "jewel" of the Oxfam international family¹³—embraced the idea of a walk to alleviate Third World hunger and poverty. The fundraiser captured the imagination of the Centennial International Development Program organizers, who turned it into Canada's birthday gift to the developing world.[14] The rising interest in international develop-ment,[15] alongside the jubilance surrounding the cen-tennial moment, resulted in the Canadian effort far outdoing its British counterpart both in terms of par-ticipants and money raised: that year 100,000 walkers in 22 communities raised $1.2 million.[16] Within two years the participation quadrupled.

The Canadian version of the Oxfam walk was renamed the Miles for Millions in English and Rallye Tiers Monde in French Canada. Although its centrality in the Miles for Millions walkathon is undisputed, Oxfam Canada helped organize it alongside many other foreign aid organizations, such as the Canadian Hunger Foundation, Save the Children Fund, the Canadian UNICEF Committee, Canadian University Service Overseas, World Uni-versity Service of Canada, and Canadian Crossroads International, among others. Together these organi-zations sought a vehicle for educating the Canad-ian public about the developing world and Canada's potential role in international development.[17] This unprecedented co-operation and the Miles for Mil-lions National Committee effort communicated to Canadians that their role in the "Global Village" of necessity involved international development and that the time had come to tackle the urgent issue of world poverty, which "represent[ed] the greatest threat to mankind's survival."[18]

Between 1967 and 1980, hundreds of thousands of men, women, and children participated in the an-nual Miles for Millions walkathon to raise money for development projects. "Milers" ostensibly walked for the purpose of "helping the hungry," although monies raised went to diverse causes, from crisis re-lief work to family planning clinics in Asia, Africa, Latin America, and also to First Nations reserves in Canada. Part of a growing international practice of hunger walks, this one-day event incorporated daunting distances—from 26 to 40 miles.[19] Each par-ticipant canvassed for per-mile pledges in prepar-ation for the gruelling walk. Part parade, part pil-grimage, it was a celebration of collective action on the part of the nation, where political leaders walked heroic distances alongside citizens as an embodied commitment to end poverty around the world; it inevitably involved a measure of suffering—often

in the form of dehydration, exhaustion, bleeding and blistered feet—designed to awaken empathy for the starving bodies the fundraiser sought to help. The Miles for Millions' huge success—earning over 20 million dollars in the first five years—eventual-ly led to its downfall: by the late 1970s, most cities had hundreds of copycat walkathons, bikeathons, and danceathons, and the Miles for Millions simply could not replicate the numbers and fundraising of its early years. Yet in its heyday of the late 1960s and early 1970s, the Miles for Millions became what its organizers had hoped: a vehicle for raising aware-ness about crises around the globe and the potential for international development, and a momentous occasion that brought Canadians into the streets in a gesture of solidarity with people of the Third World.[20]

Perhaps most remarkable was the Walk's over-whelmingly youthful face.[21] At least superficially, the event appeared inclusive of gender, was repre-sentative of the ethnic and racial communities in which it was held, and included the working class as well as the very privileged.[22] A range of inten-tions was also evident as it drew those politically committed to addressing global injustices as well as those politically oblivious. The vast majority of walkers were elementary and high school students: in the first years Oxfam claimed that 80 per cent of participants were high school students.[23] The 1969 Surrey-Delta, B.C., Walk comprised roughly 90 per cent children and teenagers, according to chairper-son Ted Deadman, which included two six-year-old students who completed the 24-mile walk, one in 11 hours and one 12 hours.[24] In Metropolitan To-ronto, apparently, "every school" was represented and in some cases entire classes walked. In what the Toronto Star dubbed the "teenage takeover," youth made up 40,000 of the 55,000 walkers and 8,000 of the 12,000 who finished the 32.2 miles in that city in 1969.[25] Many late baby boomers were swept up in the campaigns to raise money for emerging crises in the Third World, as Canadian schools endorsed the Miles for Millions event and Oxfam education programs that gave meaning to the 1960s notion of a global village and the new responsibility with which it was imbued.[26] The Walk became an important vehicle for education and activism among youth on global poverty.[27]

Miles for Millions and the Visual Iconography of Need and Help

Like many public demonstrations of the 1960s, the Miles for Millions Walkathon was a highly visual medium of communication. Powerful symbols and a familiar, contemporary vernacular adorned the posters, pamphlets, and educational materials used to recruit participants and generate pledges for the annual walkathons. The Miles for Millions visual materials referenced both the local physical event—the walkathon—and the global issues targeted by the fundraiser, as a 1968 graphic indicates. Three figures walking at an apparently robust pace superimposed on the globe demonstrated that Canadians of all sizes could participate in this event, and insisted that this collective local action was of global significance. Another 1968 graphic used as a poster, entitled simply "The Walk," also invoked the globe to indicate the

magnitude of the problem addressed by the Miles for Millions while four disembodied hands represent the "hungry half" of the world (see Figure 2).[28]

Like 1968 protest movement iconography, which used a similar black, white, and red colour scheme, the walkathon imagery contained a quality of urgency and righteousness and elevated the event to international if not universal importance. Yet in place of the iconic clenched fist of 1960s movement culture—seen in women's liberation, black power, workers' rights, and Paris '68 posters—was the outstretched hand of the Third World apparently awaiting deliverance by the West.[29] Not coincidentally, the walkathon's historic moment overlapped with an era in which street protests and marches were widespread and seemingly global.[30] The Walk itself was constitutive of a discourse in which Canada was promoted as having, in the words of Barbara Heron, "a national calling" to "alleviat[e] the woes of the poor global Others," by taking to the streets.[31]

As popular as images of the globe were, much of the imagery in newspapers and promotional materials emphasized youthful participants and used

Figure 2. Metro Toronto Miles for Millions, 1968, Information Brochure

Source: LAC, Oxfam Fonds, MG 28, I 270, vol. 4, file 4-2

childhood to symbolize the ideological and social space of international development and Canada's "helping imperative."[32] Even without the globe dichotomizing the South as "in need" and the North as powerful, healthy, and benevolent, a binary of imagery is striking. This was particularly evident in the use of the child in Miles for Millions publicity in which brown barely-clothed children represented the crises of the Third World and healthy, vigorous children represented Canada and the solution. A good example of this dichotomy in play is a 1968 pamphlet featuring an undernourished child holding an empty bowl beside the question "What's on *Your* Plate Today?" Perhaps it was the most resonant image of the child associated with the Miles for Millions: the emblematic child represents the problems of developing nations and is deployed purposefully as a generic symbol, never identified or associated with a particular famine, war, or country. Here, the pamphlet mentions crises in Sierra Leone, Haiti, India, South America, and Africa, but does not situate the child as a victim or survivor of a particular historic event nor as belonging to a family, community, or nation. This lone child of the Third World implores the Canadian viewer to examine, and act on, the wastefulness of the developed world and the want of its underdeveloped global neighbour while making generic and nondescript the particular peoples in need and masking the economic and social forces causing such hardship.

In representing humanitarian agencies (Oxfam, UNICEF, and Save the Children, among others), the Miles for Millions organization used the visual trope of the needy Third World child that by the late 1960s and 1970s was undoubtedly familiar to Canadians. By this time, photos of emaciated, apparently orphaned developing-world children had been mobilizing pity among Western adults for decades. The wide circulation of early-twentieth-century atrocity photographs depicting the brutality of colonialism in the Congo, for example, helped produce a human rights discourse, which itself was "bound to a particular kind of aesthetic encounter."[33]

Laura Briggs's genealogy of the visual iconography of rescue and the "representation of need" shows how the photograph of the orphan waif with sunken eyes and skeletal frame became commonplace. In 1950s publicity for international aid organizations and news reports, these photographs helped to "organize [. . .] cultural knowledge of the Third World and its needs," as well as American understanding of "poverty and race" at home.[34] These images, as Stanley Cohen writes, persisted through the twentieth century and became more extreme in reaction to "compassion fatigue," the neutralizing of emotions in response to endless exposure to graphic, disturbing human suffering. This in turn gave rise to what Patricia Holland calls "aid pornography" in which images of children moments from death were deployed to evoke action.[35]

In asking "What's on your plate today?" and in representing developing-world famine as a malnourished child, the 1968 campaign achieved two goals. Most directly, it hit a nerve with many Canadian children and youth who had plenty to eat and could be made to feel guilty about it. The use of symbolic children in this way was highly instrumental: modifying John Berger's assertion that "men act and women appear," Karen Dubinsky has recently argued that "children appear so that adults can act."[36] The Miles for Millions is an example of how children and youth were *also* mobilized by those images, although much less is known about the relationship of children and youth in Western countries to this visual "iconography of rescue." We do know that school children in Canada were fed static images—ones evoking tragedy but without revealing a news story—that were specific enough to elicit compassion but so general as to be broadly applicable to the changing geography of human suffering. In the late 1960s and 1970s, the image of the abandoned, malnourished infant oversimplified the problem and the solution: a child's hunger could be relieved with dollars for food aid. Directed at school children in Canada, this visual message implored them to "do something" to help these other(ed) children. The child that appeared to represent Third World suffering in Miles for Millions literature therefore necessarily also embodied hope: the message being that if Canadians would act now, that child's dinner plate could be filled. "$1 will give a child a school meal for a month in Haiti," a Miles for Millions pamphlet promised. Another promotional pamphlet featured 20 photos, 5 of which portrayed Third World children. Two photographs could be called the before shots—children holding empty bowls—while three signalled that the needy had been helped—one of a child eating and two of cheerful children in what appears to be a classroom.[37] The meaning was clear: once well nourished, these children might have lives more closely resembling Canadians'—a nuclear family in which to grow and a school in which to learn. This equation neglected the complexity of poverty and suffering and the specificity of war and famine. They were nevertheless powerful messages to children and youth and likely motivated many of them to act.[38] Whether gratuitous images of starving children were pragmatically "worth it"—that is, instrumental in prompting action (through donation of money and time; pursuing knowledge about global issues; or on a political level) from Canadians of all ages—requires further examination; the imagery does, however, run counter to the stated outrage of the Miles for Millions organization that human dignity is denied in "a world divided between the rich and the poor."[39]

The second effect of deploying the starving waif image in Miles for Millions promotional materials was that it, in the words of Laura Briggs, "constructed its counterpart."[40] A dualism emerged in which Third World children were depicted as "dependent and passive," while Canadian children were enabled as "active and autonomous."[41] Critics of such representations in the 1970s argued that images of children caught in the midst of tragedy (famine, disease, war) promulgated the notion that the developing-world child was submissive and clearly not of able body; exploiting its suffering "secure[s] our sense of First World comfort by assuring us that we have the power to help."[42]

Exhortations and catch-phrases for the Miles for Millions reinforced the dichotomy between the passive other and the able-bodied Canadian, and contributed to the same discourse we find in the photographs. For example, in 1967: "You walked—that others may live." Slogans such as "Sole Power" and "Feet against Famine," along with copious shoe and foot graphics, also underscored the physical ability that Canadian children and youth could exploit to end global famines, not to mention the implicit suggestion that the Third World child-in-need did not have the ability to walk much less the necessary footwear to do so. News stories about, and photos of, milers with physical challenges—represented by crutches and wheelchairs—functioned to reinforce the dichotomy and reassure the reader and viewer that Canadians' hardships were surmountable, especially by the "rising generation."[43]

Picturing Canadian Children

It is not happenstance, therefore, that the Miles for Millions was not a simple charity event but a test of endurance, a performance of able-bodiedness, and a spectacle of Canadian financial, moral, and physical fortitude. In promotional materials and the press coverage following Walk Days, photographs of children promoted these messages, celebrating the nation's global responsibility through local action. They therefore shared some features with the suffering child images—being highly symbolic, even propagandistic. Yet the pictorial archive of the Miles for Millions was shaped by contemporary conventions of filmmaking and photography, especially an observational documentary style, the ostensible purpose of which was to present children in their spontaneous, unmediated worlds.[44] Furthermore, the visual representations of children in this era tended to emphasize what art historians have called the "knowing child," which replaced the long-standing "romantic child," that ultimate trope of innocence.[45] Unlike the romantic child, "knowing children have bodies and passions of their own," writes Anne Higonnet; and, for our purposes here, are indications of a paradigm shift toward children being seen and portrayed as historical actors.[46]

Photo series of the Miles for Millions were quite popular in the aftermath of Walk Days, appearing in newspapers, magazines, and the like, functioning as promotional and celebratory material, some of them recycled in brochures by the National Walk Committee for the following year's campaign. Newspaper photographers, such as Clive Webster of *Maclean's* and Frank Chalmers of the *Winnipeg Tribune*, joined freelance professionals such as

Toronto's Joan Latchford, in capturing the scale, energy, and symbolism of the Walk. Frank Chalmers's photo-story of the 1969 Mother's Day Miles for Millions Walk in Winnipeg comprised a stand-alone section in the *Winnipeg Tribune*.[47] Joan Latchford's photographs appeared in Miles for Millions promotional brochures and on an episode of CBC's *Take 30*.[48] Unlike many other photographers working for local newspapers who focused on one city, Latchford conducted a tour of five Canadian cities in 1968 and 1969: Toronto, Vancouver, Calgary, London, and Quebec City. She designed this photo assignment and sought Canada Council funding. She was also apparently the first female photographer to receive a Canada Council grant.[49]

The Walk lent itself to a style of photography that had recently come into fashion. In her work on the image of the child in the National Film Board of Canada's Still Photography Division, Carol Payne points to a mid-1960s watershed moment in the history of the visual representation of children. In the 1950s and early 1960s NFB images of children tended to be "instructional and formalized" and did not represent childhood so much as they sent a message about "an idealized citizenry" and a paternalistic state.[50] Symbolically, children's obedience and innocence were key to the successful message that whatever social problem needed fixing, the government—never directly represented—had matters in hand. Many of the NFB's photo stories using children's images located them in adult institutions (schools and hospitals, for example), whereas by the mid-1960s children appear to have been liberated from these confines. Using Higonnet's idea of the "knowing child," Payne shows how photographs of children started to emphasize children's agency and autonomy from the adult world;[51] the replacement of the "god's eye view" with "vantage points that implicate the viewer . . . through the use of the gaze," helped to facilitate this shift.[52]

Clive Webster's photograph (see Figure 1) demonstrates these developments. The children and youth are captured in a spontaneous moment outside, unencumbered by adult authority; there is no obvious instructional message; the shot appears not to be posed but rather spontaneous; and, one boy gazes at the camera, acknowledging the viewer. Other photographers incorporated these elements into their work. For his part, Frank Chalmers, an award-winning photographer and head of the photography department at the *Winnipeg Tribune* for many years, is remembered for his ability to "captur[e] emotion."[53] Joan Latchford took pictures of children (and adults) engaged in outdoor activities in the 1960s and after: of youth at the first Caribana festivals, then of the migration of young people across the country, and later of Toronto street kids.[54]

Latchford drew inspiration from the 1950s photography exhibit organized by the Museum of Modern Art in New York City, Edward Steichen's "The Family of Man." This exhibit, which featured well-known photographers such as Henri Cartier Bresson and Dorothea Lange, broke attendance records at the MOMA and enjoyed an extended tour to many other countries.[55] At the same time that humanitarian organizations were helping to normalize images of hunger using the Third World child, this exhibit proposed an elimination of difference—preferring the universal themes of commonality, humanity, and peace. In the exhibit's section that focused on children, youth from around the world were shown at play—devoid of adult worries and conflicts—deployed as representative of "global reconciliation."[56] Many of the exhibit's works representing children had an observational documentary quality that rejected sentimentality, not unlike what Payne found in the mid-1960s NFB stills involving children. Latchford was compelled by a desire to create "sincere" images that revealed an individual's humanity. Her former life as a nun and life-long commitment to social justice can be seen as foundational for this perspective.[57] It is this attempt to reveal an essence of humanity in a gesture, an emotion, a moment, which we can see in the Walk's visual archive.

Confirming that the Miles for Millions was youth's moment, the images of Walk Day feature throngs of children and youth. Although physically active politicians made good newspaper copy,[58] images of thousands of cheering young people starting out on the Walk predominated, helping to create an image of an able-bodied, activist, and purposeful citizenry. Typically, these photos were taken from the sidelines or in front of the milers and at some elevation, giving the viewer a sense of the momentum and sheer mass of humanity.[59] Frank Chalmers used the elevation of Marion Street, an expansive corridor in St Boniface, to his advantage, capturing the young milers as they walked toward him waving and smiling. Latchford's collection contains many similar photos of hordes of beaming young people in motion. These images made for a compelling message, telling the story of the crowded and giddy atmosphere characteristic of the walkathons across the country, congratulating those who walked, and encouraging those who did not, to consider it next year. In Quebec City, she documented groups of young people singing as they walked on a rainy day; in Vancouver, they waved to her while crossing the Burrard Street Bridge. The start of Toronto's 1969 Walk Day—involving 55,000 people—was captured by the *Globe and Mail* photographers who stood high above the crowd that moved away from the camera, giving visual confirmation of the dramatic size of the effort.[60] The images that expose the magnitude of participation and the convivial atmosphere are, in a number of forms, markers of success. Clive Webster's plucky kids stood in for the financial achievement of the Walk: the accompanying caption read, "This is a picture of $4,500,000 on the march."[61] Beyond representing the monetary importance of the fundraiser, the voluminous youthful crowd signified the size of the nation's commitment to work collectively; its determination to make a difference and sacrifice, if necessary; and a nation quite literally on the move. The message was clear, these children and youth were figuratively and literally walking into the future.[62]

The connection between groups of Canadian young people walking, performing their own able-bodiedness, and the country's potential to resolve global crises was central to the early mission of the Miles for Millions. As Prime Minister Lester B. Pearson noted: "If we can get the youth of Canada to stir up opinion, to point out that we have these obligations to our fellowmen who are not as well off as we, if we do that, then we will have made our contribution to the development of peace and security in the world.[63]

One Oxfam Canada education committee worker also made the connection in 1970:

> Those who are young today will be at the peak of their influence between 1985 and the year 2000 when they will range in age from the mid 30s to the early 50s. In involving young people today we are really involving future politicians and businessmen [*sic*] [on whose shoulders] the major decisions involving world development will rest. If they become concerned today they will make the right decisions tomorrow.[64]

Interestingly, the adult manipulation of youth lies outside the frame of the Miles for Millions visual record. In fact, adults seem to occupy peripheral roles in the visual culture of the Walk: as administers of first aid, providers of refreshments, and as parents picking up miler children.

Media reports alongside visual representations confirmed that the Miles for Millions was an unthreatening performance of youth activism. Calling it a "groovy way to spend a Saturday" and a "swinging, youth-oriented" event helped to construct a positive discourse about autonomous, knowing youth.[65] But it would be incorrect to deny that for some children and youth the Walk became an expression of political awakening and conviction about global inequities, especially around food and hunger.[66] They carried placards that acknowledged their own privilege relative to others. In a Calgary-based photograph by Latchford, young people hold a "Biafra–Canada" sign that juxtaposes a chubby Canadian child holding a hot dog with a crudely-drawn Biafran child, a victim of a devastating civil war in Nigeria in the wake of decolonization, who has nothing. Another placard read "Food, Not Tears for Biafra." In Quebec City, a more general "Paix" sign visually confirmed the anti-war message of its carrier.[67] The visual record of the Miles for Millions participated in this counter-discourse about the nature of youth activism and protest.

In an age of protest, the joyous atmosphere, sheer scale, and involved commitment of this outdoor performance conveyed the message that the kids were all right. Discursively, young people emerge in this era as either too radical or on the road to self-indulgent excess. Students themselves remarked on the political commitment and drive that characterized the participation in the Miles for Millions walkathon. One student wrote to the newspaper that the efforts of his cohort on Walk Day proved that "kids today" were neither "apathetic" nor "mindless" in their protesting.[68] Even those who may not have walked for global humanitarian reasons embodied a kind of citizenship that made for images that helped construct an opposing discourse around young people who were often visually connected to the student protests of 1968 and beyond. Frank Chalmers's souvenir photos from the Winnipeg walk included images of kids walking into the night, demonstrating perseverance, and also kids sweeping up the mess left behind by 30,000 milers, demonstrating civic duty.

A Joan Latchford photo from the 1968 Toronto Miles for Millions Walk similarly evoked an optimistic interpretation about today's youth, although with a different and even more powerful message (see Figure 3). Taken at Toronto's City Hall, in Nathan Phillips Square, this image comprises a group shot of Vaughan Road Collegiate students. At first it appears to be a simple portrayal of school spirit with multiple placards identifying the students' purpose: "Vaughan Walks Miles for Millions."

Several students are captured waving and smiling, or just looking at the camera, held by Latchford just above them. Her vantage point provides her with a good window on the physical proximity, even physical intimacy of the Walk, showing the students cheek by jowl. What's important is that no image of Walk Day represents the multicultural fact of Canada more than this one. With these students calling the shots on Walk Day, the viewer is reassured about

Figure 3. Toronto Miles for Millions, May 1968

Source: © Joan Latchford

the future of cultural diversity in Canada, a similar message Payne found with the NFB's 1964 "Nation's Future Belongs to Them," a photo-story that juxtaposed groups of cheerful children of different races.[69] Notably, the NFB publication contained separate, distinct photographs of children of different races; the only racial mixing occurred with the collaging of images on the printed page. In the Miles for Millions image the students of various races and ethnicities overlapped, their bodies seemingly contiguous with one another.

In addition to signifying the triumph of diversity at home, this image was also used to signify the importance of Canadian humanitarian efforts overseas with its "there is but one race—humanity" message.[70] An image very similar to this one appeared in a Miles for Millions/Rallye Tiers Monde brochure, alongside the before and after shots of developing-world children described above, implicating Canada's success at peaceful diversity with the struggle for global justice. Latchford likely did not intend to be celebratory about the state of race relations; indeed, the penetrating stare of the black female student near the centre of the image, which makes the photograph so compelling, can be read as a direct communication with the viewer, urging that we acknowledge what she and others have accomplished collectively while at the same time asking, "What can we say for ourselves?"[71]

The Latchford Collection as Social History

Having access to Joan Latchford's complete photographic collection of the Walks provides a useful contrast to the published Walk pictorial.[72] Containing almost 1,000 photographs taken as she herself completed the Walks, the collection provides insight into her own aesthetic while detailing the significant visual and textual information about the Miles for Millions. Overall her collection confirms the theme of autonomous and independent children and youth. She virtually never sentimentalizes young people. In fact, in addition to her many photos of jubilant youth, there are spontaneous shots that are

neither flattering nor, frankly, advertisements for the fundraiser.

The social historian is drawn to a variety of mundane quotidian details in her collection that contains a compelling commentary on youth consumption and waste. Her photos capture young people eating and smoking along the way. We see children and youth eating in corner stores en route, eating and walking, and stopping at checkpoints to gulp lemonade and other drinks offered by sponsors. The images also reveal the incredible mess left behind by the milers—paper cups and garbage strewn along the walk's path. Perhaps telling of the difference that 40 years of anti-smoking campaigns have made, the near ubiquity of the smoking teenager seems shocking and utterly at odds with the healthful spirit of the day. Teenagers candidly lit up on the walkathon and appeared to relax with a cigarette when they paused for a break and comforted themselves with a smoke when they could go no further.

Latchford's photographs offer a powerful and striking message that the walk was an unmarked, unregulated, and only modestly overseen 26- to 40-mile corridor. Children and youth walked with their hand-drawn maps and met up with adult organizers and volunteers at checkpoints along the way, but it was largely up to them to find their way and take care of each other. Even children who knew well their own areas of the city walked far outside familiar neighbourhoods, parks, and beaches. This was not designated children's space, this was city space, and while their presence on Walk Day disrupted the idea that children and youth were not constituent parts of urban life, the collocation of childhood with heavy traffic and in areas of questionable safety deserve note. Her photos show the walk route high atop a hillside in Calgary—and young people choosing to slide down the grassy escarpment, apparently at some speed, that abuts a major roadway; in another, two adolescents look into the camera as they sit on a curb near the busy intersection of Burrard and 4th Street in Vancouver, their legs jutting into traffic. Latchford also illustrates that as the throngs thinned out over the marathon distance, young children were found walking alone or in the company of one other young miler. It is impossible to tell whether an adult or older sibling was outside of the frame, but the frequency with which she photographed pre-adolescent children alone or in pairs speaks to her own sense of what was remarkable. Newspaper reports similarly commented on this feature of the annual walkathon: for example, in Vancouver girls as young as 10 years old set out alone on the 1970 walk.[73] As it took many hours to finish, at least some children were walking in the dark until late at night. Latchford documents these juxtapositions without being alarmist or intending a panic over children's safety; her role as a participant-observer provides us with one view of the milers' experiences along the way.

This aspect of the Walk and the construction of young people speak to a specific—if fading—moment in the history of children and youth. The walkathon took place on the eve of the great decline in unstructured play beyond the home, especially among middle-class youth. During the late 1960s and continuing for several years of the 1970s, children and youth retained the "freedom to investigate and master their home turf," in what Steven Mintz, an historian of childhood, suggests was a "rehearsal for the real world."[74] The walkathon also predates the radical elimination—"annihilation" according to certain geographers of childhood—of "free space" by development and privatization.[75] It is worth remembering that the walk emerged in the years prior to the notion that children should be confined to fenced-in, childproofed playgrounds and safe zones while outdoors.[76] It is not to argue that this earlier era of children's history was simpler or better than what followed; rather, it is worth understanding how dramatic changes in attitudes toward children and youth produced very different practices on a quotidian basis—such as children trick or treating, or walking 30 miles in one day without much adult supervision.[77] On the walk, children and youth appeared to be free to experience psychological and physical challenges—that is, learn through that experience, outside the confines of the modern school and beyond adult supervision and constraint. To the middle-class sensibility of today, the images of young children walking such distances are surprising and even alarming, as are some of the images of

physical challenges they faced. The Latchford images are reminders of an era different from our own when children were considered to have a measure of competence, independence, and agency at a younger age.

Latchford's visual narrative of the Miles for Millions was not always an advertisement for the event. The multiple difficult moments faced in walking a long distance in one day refute the simplistic imagery of Canadian youth and its able-bodiedness. Photographs capture the moments when the milers gave up and when they needed assistance from the St John's Ambulance service. The walk was ultimately an endurance test for which young people did not train. It is worth noting that the walkathon emerged prior to the jogging and aerobics crazes that developed in the late 1970s.[78] Certainly, schools encouraged children to walk these great distances, but they did little to train or prepare them. Those engaged in the walk therefore faced tests of will and stamina and wore it on their bodies and faces—personal and communally shared epics that Latchford captured masterfully.

Narratives of their experiences—visual, textual, and oral—are dramatic. In a Vancouver photo, Latchford presents a teenage girl sitting alone, far from others, her body bent over outstretched legs, her hands holding her head. The girl does not know the photographer, or the viewer, are witnessing this desperate moment. In a single image Latchford powerfully represents the solitary nature of the walk, and the mental, emotional, and physical toll it took on some milers. *The Globe and Mail* described the Toronto City Hall final checkpoint scene late in the evening of Walk Day, with "children and teenagers collapsed everywhere" and parents carrying their children.[79] Many of these young people gravitated to the walkathon compelled by the idea of testing their physical limits. While it is true that many of them finished what they set out to accomplish, the visual message from the Latchford collection indicates they did it accruing blisters and bloody feet (many discarded their shoes along the way), and that the Walk involved sacrifice, pain, and personal disappointment.

The challenge of the Walk was represented in both the visual and the textual archives in highly

Figure 4. Quebec City Miles for Millions, May 1969

Source: © Joan Latchford

gendered ways. Put a different way, images and stories of milers in distress, even tears, were given the most power of poignancy in the female form. Certainly, boys were featured applying bandages and attended by St John's Ambulance workers, but girls seemed to make better emotional gauges of the day's demands. This fits with contemporary notions of heteronormativity and gender difference, with vulnerability and sensitivity, especially when expressed publicly, being associated with the feminine.[80] Latchford presents three teenage girls in Quebec City standing together, arms folded against the cold, none looking directly into the camera (see Figure 4).

Although not alone, there is no boisterous crowd around them and their expressions seem to indicate an emotional, if not physical, solitude. A cold and rainy day appears to have depleted them, and their expressions reveal any number of disheartening thoughts about their journey. On a metaphoric level, two of the three appear to be looking uneasily into the distance or the future. The viewer cannot be sure why they have stopped or what the matter is, although matted hair and their general discomfort and uncertainty seem plausible. Contrast these teenage girls in their frozen state with Figure 1, portraying kids on the move. Both contain central tropes associated with youth. The latter is an inspiring display of youthful fortitude representing an optimistic future, while the former is an emotional portrait of three teenagers seemingly contemplating—perhaps weighed down—by what is past and what lies ahead.

Conclusion

In the late 1960s and early 1970s, thousands of young people tackled the gruelling Miles for Millions walkathons, many finishing "pained [and] triumphant."[81] Images of these children and adolescents form the centrepiece of the Miles for Millions visual archive.

Walk promoters and print media used representations of youthful milers in symbolic ways: to point to the good health and vigorous spirit of a nation heading toward a bright future and as a powerful reminder that collectively Canada took seriously the need to do its part to end world hunger. The nation's youth became potent markers of able-bodiedness, playing the role of counterpart to the sentimentalized needy Third World child. Visual representations of Canadian children on the Walk also challenged prevalent contemporary discourses about youth as unreliable, radical, and apathetic. This generation, captured in the photographs of the walk, was "all right": committed to a worthy cause and able to literally go the distance in its support.

Miles for Millions photographs are excellent examples of the popularity of the observational documentary style and confirm the arrival of the "knowing child." The visual archive of the event comprises images of young people that open up ideas about childhood and assert the historical agency of children.

Joan Latchford's photographs of the Miles for Millions are an especially rich collection that contains powerfully symbolic images that use children to mark important social and political change. At the same time they can be read for what they contribute to social history that goes beyond clamorous beginnings and heroic finish-line moments. Her published and unpublished photographs together can be read for their symbolic messages that both use and are about children. By capturing young people in the moment, her collection presents us with the blistered and the bleeding, the tired and the determined. It also contributes to a discourse that merged the nation's rhetoric on multiculturalism with the ambition of the Miles for Millions—to accept humanity as one race—as seen in Figure 3. Her unpublished photographs hint at the experiences of children as performing subjects, as well as a more complex symbolism involving the child as object. Figure 4, of three teenage girls, illustrates how youth, as an index for the future, could point to a future of uncertainty. The many images of girls suffering quietly along the Walk route underscore both how physical limits were tested and how suffering itself was gendered. Social historians can engage the Miles for Millions pictorial record for its hints at contemporary assumptions about childhood and competence; while not windows on events, the images can help deepen our thinking about the changing meanings and experiences of 1960s and 1970s childhood.

Notes

1. The author wishes to acknowledge the generous financial support for this project from the University of British Columbia's Hampton Fund, as well as the wonderfully constructive guidance from two anonymous reviewers, and Karen Dubinsky and John Pettegrew.

2. This image, taken by Toronto photographer Clive Webster, accompanied a Douglas Marshall article, "This is the Picture of $4,500,000 on the move," *Maclean's* (August 1969): 44–5. Webster was best known for work on home interiors. See City of Toronto Archives, Clive Webster Collection Fonds 11.

3. On children as markers of national identity, see Carol Payne, "A Land of Youth: Nationhood and the Image of the Child in the National Film Board of Canada's Still Photography Division," in *Depicting Canada's Children*, ed. Loren Lerner (Waterloo, Ont.: Wilfrid Laurier Press, 2009), 85–107. The importance of children to the future of the nation is a well-worn trope of Canadian history. See Neil Sutherland, *Children in English-Canadian Society: Framing the 20th-Century Consensus* (Waterloo, Ont.: Wilfrid Laurier Press, 2000); Cynthia Comacchio, *The Dominion of Youth: Adolescence and the Making of Modern Canada* (Waterloo, Ont.: Wilfrid Laurier Press, 2006). For a transnational treatment of the national child, see Karen Dubinsky, *Babies without Borders: Adoption and Migration across the Americas* (New York: New York University Press, 2010).

4. Marshall, 46.

5. Scott Rutherford, Sean Mills, and David Austin make this point in "Editorial," *Race and Class* 52, 1(2010): 2; J.L. Granatstein, "Canada and Peacekeeping: Image and Reality," in *Canadian Foreign Policy: Historical Readings*, ed. J.L. Granatstein (Toronto: Copp Clark Pitman, 1986).

6. For example, see Jessica Evans and Stuart Hall, eds., *Visual Culture: The Reader* (London: Sage Publications, 1999); Nicholas Mirzoeff, ed., *The Visual Culture Reader*, 2nd ed. (London: Routledge, 2002); and the *Journal of Visual Culture*.

7. Lerner, "Introduction," *Depicting Canada's Children*, xvi.

8. Alan Trachtenberg, *Reading American Photographs: Images as History, Mathew Brady to Walker Evans* (New

York: Hill and Wang, 1989), xvi. See also Peter Burke, *Eyewitnessing: The Uses of Images as Historical Evidence* (Ithaca, NY: Cornell University Press, 2001).

9. See Lynn Hunt and Vanessa R. Schwartz, "Capturing the Moment: Images and Eyewitnessing in History," *Journal of Visual Culture* 9 (2010): 259–71.

10. Hunt and Schwartz, 260.

11. Sharon Sliwinski, "The Childhood of Human Rights: The Kodak on the Congo," *Journal of Visual Culture* 5 (2006): 354.

12. David Cutting, Cecilia Horlick, George Kent, and Carrie Travers, *Celebrating 40 years of the Oxfam Walk* (Cambridge, UK: Cambridge Oxfam Walk Group, 2007).

13. Dominique Marshall, "The Beginning of Oxfam in Canada, from 1942–1971: A Study in the History of the Political Culture of Humanitarianism," Paper presented to the Canadian Historical Association Meeting, Carleton University, 25 May 2009. The Canadian Oxfam organization was the most successful in terms of participation and fundraising.

14. The first Oxfam walk might have had a more modest start had it not benefited from the federal money put into centennial projects. A Centennial International Development Program, for example, was created to generate awareness of and fundraise for international development. This organization helped to set up the initial 1967 walk, with Oxfam and other humanitarian aid organizations coming together in subsequent years to form the National Walk Committee. Library and Archives Canada (hereafter LAC), Oxfam Canada Fonds (hereafter OCF), MG 28, I 270, vol. 4, file 42, National Walk General Publications, Information re: walks, 1968, "Miles for Millions: Idea of a March," 1.

15. The emergence of the hunger march coincides with the creation of the Canadian International Development Agency (CIDA), as well as the secularization of foreign aid work. See David R. Morrison, *Aid and Ebb Tide: A History of CIDA and Canadian Development Assistance* (Ottawa: North-South Institute, 1998).

16. "Those Walks," *The Blister* [Miles for Millions] 1 (April, 1970): 2.

17. LAC, OCF, MG 28, I 270, vol. 4, file 1, National Walk General Correspondence with Committees, "Proposal for a Nation Wide March to Assist International Development," 6 December 1967, 1.

18. Ibid., Ottawa Miles for Millions Fonds (hereafter OMMF), I 299, vol. 4, Correspondence—General, 1969, 1974, T.L. Mooney, "Why—An Education Committee," 20 May 1970.

19. In 1968, Fargo, North Dakota, and Moorhead, Minnesota, hosted American Freedom from Hunger Foundation "Walks for Development" which entailed walking 33 miles. These would spread in subsequent years. www.mealsformillions.org (viewed 20 May 2011).

20. The Miles for Millions organizers recognized the walkathon played a small part in resolving the world's crises. "We have participated in a walk as a gesture of our concern; we are aware that this is not adequate," formed part of the Miles for Millions Declaration, a postcard-petition campaign directed at the federal government insisting on the transfer of the equivalent of one percent of gross national product be sent to developing nations. Reprinted in *The Blister* 1 (April 1970).

21. The press emphasized this characteristic. For example, "Youthful Tone to March," *The Victoria Daily Times* (15 November 1969), 1.

22. These are generalizations based on press coverage, oral interviews, photographs (from the press and the Joan Latchford Collection, and Miles for Millions archival materials). Impressionistically, the walks seem to have been very inclusive and at least superficially free of the sexist stereotypes around physical activity that had recently been challenged by feminists. The press also noted that students with disabilities participated when they could.

23. LAC, OCF, MG 28, I 270, vol. 4, file 4–2, National Walk General Publications, "Miles for Millions: Idea of a March," 3. Perception of media commentators followed this line, too. Richard J. Needham, "What the Kids want Is Blisters," *The Globe and Mail* (26 April 1968).

24. "2 Six-Year-Olds Star in Surrey-Delta Walk," *The Vancouver Sun* (5 May 1969), 16.

25. *Toronto Star* (4 May 1969), 4; "12,000 marchers cross finish line in gruelling Miles for Millions," *The Globe and Mail* (5 May 1969), 1.

26. Although 1960s commentators noted that only a small percentage of students were involved in youth groups beyond their schools, although such organizations had been popular beginning in World War I and continuing through World War II. Building productive, obedient, and healthy citizens attuned to a democratic society unified organizations such as Girl Guides, 4-H, and Boy Scouts. Engaged voluntarism and citizenship training were common goals. Charity work on behalf of distressed peoples around the world had long been part of youth organizations. Cynthia Comacchio, *The Dominion of Youth: Adolescence and the Making of Modern Canada, 1920 to 1950* (Waterloo, Ont.: Wilfrid Laurier University Press, 2006), chap. 7; Louise Bienvenue, *Quand la jeunesse entre en scène: l'Action catholique avant la révolution tranquille* (Montréal: Boreal, 2003). It is not surprising, then, that many youth found their way to the Miles for Millions through church and other groups. The centennial march in Scarborough, Ont. (a suburb of Toronto), was organized by the Mid-Scarboro Youth Club. "Ontario on March to Aid Humanity," *The Globe and Mail* (6 November 1967), 19.

27. Activism among high school students during the 1960s is a relatively new area of historical scholarship and one that my larger research project seeks to address. See Gael Graham, *Young Activists: American High School Students in the Age of Protest* (DeKalb: Northern Illinois University

Press, 2006); Rebecca de Schweinitz, *If We Could Change the World: Young People and America's Long Struggle for Racial Equality* (Chapel Hill: University of North Carolina Press, 2009).

28. For a discussion on the globe as iconography, see Benjamin Lazier, "Earth Rise; Or, the Globalization of the World Picture," *American Historical Review* 116, 3 (June 2011): 602–30.

29. This ideological placement of power and need was resoundingly critiqued beginning in the 1970s.

30. See Jeremi Suri, *Power and Protest: Global Revolution and the Rise of Détente* (Cambridge, MA: Harvard University Press, 2003), chap. 5.

31. Barbara Heron, *Desire for Development: Whiteness, Gender, and the Helping Imperative* (Waterloo, Ont.: Wilfrid Laurier Press, 2007), 5. The "social spaces" of international development include educational campaigns in schools and organized events such as the Miles for Millions or the UNICEF Halloween box fundraiser.

32. Ibid.

33. Sliwinski, 334. Sliwinski argues that the Congo Reform Association was the first humanitarian organization to use atrocity photographs to rouse public opinion and action against the brutality of empire. She argues that "human rights discourse serves principally as a response to the witnessing of traumatic violence," 334–5.

34. Laura Briggs, "Mother, Child, Race, Nation: The Visual Iconography of Rescue and the Politics of Transnational and Transracial Adoption," *Gender and History* 15, 2 (August 2003): 181–2.

35. Stanley Cohen, "Images of Suffering" (chap. 7), *States of Denial: Knowing about Atrocities and Suffering* (Cambridge, UK: Polity Press, 2001), 168; Patricia Holland, *Picturing Childhood: The Myth of the Child in Popular Imagery* (London and New York: L.B. Tauris, 2004), 154. Susan Sontag explored how the shocking and ubiquitous images of atrocity dulled the viewers' empathy for victims of war in *On Photography* (New York: Picador, 1977), a position she revisits in *Regarding the Pain of Others* (New York: Farrar, Straus and Giroux, 2003).

36. Karen Dubinsky, "Children, Ideology, and Iconography: How Babies Rule the World," *Journal of the History of Childhood and Youth* 5, 1 (Winter 2012): 7–13, at 8. John Berger, *Ways of Seeing* (London: British Broadcasting Corporation, 1972), 47.

37. Miles for Millions/Rallye Tiers Monde brochure, n.p., n.d., but it refers to 1969 as "The year of the walk."

38. Why children and youth enrolled in the Miles for Millions is the question asked by the larger research project. Oral histories and testimonies taken at the time go some distance in answering the question and getting at the impact of the visual imagery.

39. "Miles for Millions Declaration," printed in *The Blister* 1 (April 1970). In this declaration the Miles for Millions organization calls for a partnership in development: "Only such a partnership does justice to our shared humanity," and calls for action "out of a sense of outrage at a world which denies Man dignity."

40. Briggs, 184.

41. Briggs, 184 and 198.

42. Cohen, quoting Holland's 1992 *What Is a Child?*, 178.

43. "Surrey Youth Grinds out 25 Miles in Wheelchair," *Vancouver Sun* (5 May 1969), 16.

44. Payne, 98 and 102.

45. Anne Higonnet, *Pictures of Innocence: The History and Crisis of Ideal Childhood* (London: Thames and Hudson, 1998), chap. 9, "Knowing Childhood."

46. Higonnet, 207; Jayne, 100; Lerner, xvi.

47. Frank Chalmers, photographs, "Miles for Millions, 1969 Souvenir Edition," LAC, OCF, MG 28, I 270, vol.4, file 4-2, "National Walks General Publications," 1969.

48. Joan Latchford, interview by author, Toronto, 9 December 2010.

49. "Former Nun to Focus Camera on Rochdale," *The Globe and Mail* (13 March 1969), W10. In the late 1960s, Latchford was in her early forties, a mother of eight children, and an experienced photographer.

50. Payne, 87.

51. Ibid., 101.

52. Ibid., 102.

53. See his obituary in the *Winnipeg Free Press* online, "Passages" (4 February 2006). http://passages.winnipegfreepress.com/passage-details/id-105040/name-Frank-Chalmers. Accessed January 15, 2012.

54. Joan Latchford interview.

55. Linda Gordon, *Dorothea Lange: A Life Beyond Limits* (New York: W.W. Norton, 2009), 360. This exhibit remains on display in Luxembourg, www.family-of-man.public.lu. Accessed January 15, 2012

56. Holland, 95. This theme of "youth as reconciliation" is also made by Richard Ivan Jobs, who examines how Western European countries emphasized post-war mobility of youth as a means of fostering "international understanding." He writes, "Young people were increasingly viewing the world in international terms and participating in it in transnational ways." Richard Ivan Jobs, "Youth Movements: Travel, Protest, and Europe in 1968," *American Historical Review* 114, 2 (April 2009): 378.

57. "Former Nun," and Joan Latchford, email interview by author, 11 May 2011, which was follow up to 9 December 2010 interview.

58. Politicians were also a feature of the visual archive of the walk.

59. In 1969, Winnipeg's Miles for Millions walk drew 30,000 people; 8,000 completed the 35 miles. "1969 Souvenir Edition," n.p.

60. "Walk Raises $500,000 and Blisters," *The Globe and Mail* (5 May 1969), 2nd section. Franz Maier and John McNeill, photographers.

61. Marshall, 44–5, 46.

62. Youth as a bellwether for the future is a common trope. See Comacchio and Mary Louise Adams, *The Trouble with Normal* (Toronto: University of Toronto Press, 1997), as examples.

63. LAC, OCF, MG 28, I 270, vol. 4, file 4–2, National Walk General Publications, "Miles for Millions: Idea of a March," 1.

64. Ibid., I 299, vol. 4, Correspondence—General, 1969, 1974, T.L. Mooney, "Why—An Education Committee." 20 May 1970.

65. Marshall, 45, 46.

66. Gael Graham's *Young Activists* is an important intervention into the history of children and activism in high schools.

67. Joan Latchford, Miles for Millions private collection, Quebec City, 10 May 1969.

68. Bruce West, "The Readers Say" *The Globe and Mail* (13 August 1969), 23.

69. Payne, 87.

70. This slogan was used in Oxfam of Canada literature in the late 1960s. LAC, OCF, MG 28, I 270, vol. 4, File 4–1, "National Walk, General Correspondence with Committees," Oxfam of Canada solicitation copy, n.d.

71. Latchford herself remarked recently about her long-standing interest in social justice, with race being a central component of this. In the 1970s, she attended Howard University, an important African-American institution, and she and her husband adopted several mixed race and black children. As she notes, the two events are directly connected. Latchford, letter to author, 29 January 2012.

72. Latchford. Miles for Millions private collection.

73. *B.C. Express* (5 May 1970), 4.

74. In his history of American childhood, Steven Mintz argues that 1980s and 1990s saw a retrenchment of freedom for children, linking it to smaller families, working parents, panic over child molesters, and the general endangerment of children. Steven Mintz, *Huck's Raft: A History of American Childhood* (Cambridge, MA: Harvard University Press, 2004), 347–8.

75. Ibid., 348; Tracey Skelton and Gill Valentine, eds., "Introduction," *Cool Places: Geographies of Youth Cultures* (London: Routledge, 1998), 7; Stuart C. Aitken, *Geographies of Young People: The Morally Contested Spaces of Identity* (London: Routledge, 2001).

76. Child safe zones comprise designated areas free of threats to children or where there is a monitoring system in place to keep track of allegedly vulnerable kids. See www.childsafezones.co.uk. Accessed May 6, 2011. These zones go hand in hand with the privatization and commercialization of public space, processes which entail the hiring of security guards, the use of curfews, and close-circuit television monitoring to keep youth away. See Skelton and Valentine and Aitken on spatial justice for young people.

77. Not all children experienced these broad changes in the same way. Neighbourhood, class, race, and gender affected parental attitudes toward children. There certainly were detractors of the walk who saw the physical and psychological challenges as unsuitable for children of a certain age.

78. Kenneth H. Cooper's *Aerobics* was published in 1968, though the jogging and aerobics crazes would take some time to catch on. ParticipAction was created in 1971.

79. Letters to the editor, *The Globe and Mail* (6 May 1971).

80. Despite the emergence of the feminist movements at the time and challenges to expectations around gendered personality characteristics, these remained quite traditional.

81. "12,000 marchers cross finish line in gruelling Miles for Millions," *The Globe and Mail* (5 May 1969), 1; Peter Whelan, "Pained, triumphant, 32,000 go distance in miles for millions," *The Globe and Mail* (8 May 1972), 1.

PRIMARY DOCUMENT

Miles for Millions Declaration Poster, c. 1968

MILES FOR MILLIONS DECLARATION

We see the world divided between the rich and the poor; we consider this division immoral.

We see the rich through political and economic decisions ensuring their wealth and increasing the disparity; we find this inexcusable.

We see our rich country spending six times more for implements of war than for implements of peace; we are appalled at our folly.

We have talked and written about poverty but we have failed to act; we condemn this inaction.

We have participated in a walk as a gesture of our concern; we are aware that this is not adequate.

Today, with a sense of urgency and frustration, we ask you as our elected representative, to press for the following:

1. Our Government listen to and act upon the needs of the developing nations as they are defined by these nations;

2. A true transfer of material resources equivalent to 1% of our Gross National Product (of which .70 should be official aid) take place no later than 1975;

3. Major changes in our unfair trade policies with the developing countries be enacted immediately.

We make these demands out of a sense of outrage at a world which denies Man dignity. We recognize that we have talked of rich and poor in purely economic terms. But who is really rich? Who is really poor? We seek a partnership in development — social, economic, and cultural. Only such a partnership does justice to our shared humanity.

We have said little, but perhaps we have said too much.

Truth is action done.

Source: Miles for Millions Declaration, c1968

Study Questions

1. In what ways did citizenship training in twentieth-century Canada demand a global outlook? How do the authors of the two essays in this chapter suggest such training was limited? How did service announcements make it an imperative?

2. What did it mean to be a "seed of destiny" as a child in the post-war world? How were Aboriginal children included in or excluded from this designation?

3. Read the Miles for Millions Declaration. Summarize the declaration and explain why this message appealed to children and youth in the late 1960s. How is this source different from the Unitarian service announcement?

Selected Bibliography

Articles

Briggs, Laura, "Mother, Child, Race, Nation: The Visual Iconography of Rescue and the Politics of Transnational and Transracial Adoption," *Gender & History* 15 (2003): 179–200.

Lerner, Loren, "Adolescent Girls, Adult Women: Coming of Age Images by Five Canadian Women Artists," *Girlhood Studies* 1, 2 (Winter 2008): 1–28.

Lerner, Loren, "Photographs of the Child in Canadian Pictorial from 1906 to 1916: A Reflection of the Ideas and Values of English Canadians about Themselves and 'Other' Canadians," *The Journal of the History of Childhood and Youth* 3, 2 (Spring 2010): 233–63.

Norris Nicholson, Heather, "'At the centre of it all are the children': Aboriginal Childhoods and the National Film Board," *London Journal of Canadian Studies* 17 (2001): 73–100.

Payne, Carol, "A Land of Youth: Nationhood and the Image of the Child in the National Film Board of Canada's Still Photography Division," in Loren Lerner, ed., *Depicting Canada's Children*. Waterloo, ON: Wilfrid Laurier Press, 2009: 85–107.

Payne, Carol, "'The Materials of Citizenship': Documentary and the Image of Childhood in NFB Still Photography," in *The Official Picture: The National Film Board of Canada's Still Photography Division and the Image of Canada, 1941–1971*. Montreal and Kingston: McGill-Queen's University Press, 2013: 53–78.

Racette, Sherry Farrell, "Haunted: First Nations Children in Residential School Photography," in Loren Lerner, ed., *Depicting Canada's Children*. Waterloo, ON: Wilfrid Laurier University Press, 2009: 49–84.

Spike, Sara, "Picturing Rural Education: School Photographs and Contested Reform in Early Twentieth-Century Rural Nova Scotia," *Historical Studies in Education/Revue d'histoire de l'éducation* Special Issue (Spring 2012): 49–71.

Books

Lerner, Loren, ed., *Depicting Canada's Children*. Waterloo: Wilfrid Laurier Press, 2009.

Low, Brian J., *NFB Kids: Portrayals of Children by the National Film Board of Canada 1939–89*. Waterloo, ON: Wilfred Laurier University Press, 2002.

Miller, Mary Jane, *Outside Looking In: Viewing First Nations Peoples in Canadian Dramatic Television Series*. Montreal and Kingston: McGill-Queen's University Press, 2008.

11 Making Youth Culture

Editors' Introduction

Many of the essays in this volume consider children and adolescents within well-defined, recognizable, albeit historically specific, age categories. In this chapter, both essays discuss youth cultures created after the adolescent or teenage years. Between the turn of the twentieth century and the 1970s, cohorts of students and hitchhikers, respectively, embraced youth as an important part of their identity within rapidly changing societies. Common to both groups was the formation of an identity in opposition to adult authority as represented by parents, professors, university administrators, the Establishment, and police and other legal authorities. These groups felt they had the power and the right to forge a life-stage-based identity and subculture; the authors here show how youthful identity and subcultures were expressed and perpetuated.

Through an analysis of visual and textual materials produced by and for early-twentieth-century university students, E. Lisa Panayotidis and Paul Stortz explore how these students made sense of their world. The authors point to an intricate hierarchy of students based on the stages of the four-year undergraduate degree and often extending to encompass gender, and illustrate how satire was used to police and reinforce this hierarchy. The university environment during this period emphasized the importance of age in identity formation. As one valedictorian noted, "The tie that will bind us to our university will be one of the purest since it will also unite us with our youth." The accompanying satirical article, "The True and Modest History of the Noble Class of Arts '20," from the yearbook of UBC's 1920 graduating class, reveals how privileged young people saw themselves as an entity apart from the rest of society because of their age, and how they claimed the university as an institution of their own. This elite group of mostly male students embraced the extension of their youth through the higher education experience. Panayotidis and Stortz's essay confirms what Karine Hébert suggests about student identity in Montreal from the late nineteenth century to the 1960s: that it shifted from the self-conscious shaping of an elite social group to the wielding of a more broad-based powerful social force.[1]

Linda Mahood shows how teenagers and twenty-somethings in the late 1960s and 1970s popularized a trend in mobility, turning hitchhiking into a craze and simultaneously helping to define a romantic subculture. Mahood explores the meanings of, and reactions to, "thumbing a ride," through both an investigation of the volumes written about this youth behaviour and a series of interviews mostly with former hitchhikers. She uncovers the complexity of the pursuit of freedom, especially in terms of the contemporary hierarchies of gender, ethnicity, class, and region. The accompanying excerpt from the Canadian Welfare Council's *Transient Youth: Report of an Inquiry in the Summer of 1969* points to how anxious policy-makers, and adults in general, became about this development in youth culture.

This chapter's essays confirm that youth subcultures emerged and transformed over the twentieth century, and that even those individuals we might consider young adults found youth a powerful identity around which to act and (re)invent themselves. Such research into young people living beyond the supervision of their parents but not yet responsible for their own households and families provides an interesting window into the contingency of youth as a cultural construct.

Note

1. Karine Hébert, *Impatient d'être soi-même. Les étudiants montréalais, 1895–1960* (Québec: Presses de l'Université du Québec, 2008)

Visual Interpretations, Cartoons, and Caricatures of Student and Youth Cultures in University Yearbooks, 1898–1930[1]

E. LISA PANAYOTIDIS AND PAUL STORTZ

Apart from beds of intellectual inquiry and institutes of advanced research, universities in Canada have long been social institutions characterized by shifting interpersonal politics, diverse cultures, discourses, and allegiances. Students were the integral historical agents on campus who inhabited academic spaces for three or four years before moving on to other endeavours, almost all of which were off campus, and into life-long occupations and careers. As part of this passage, students produced annual yearbooks as repositories of memories of their experiences and perspectives on campus. The yearbooks were intended as "souvenir remembrances." More than pseudo-official institutional texts, yearbooks re-inscribed normative definitions and specific understandings about youth

and in some cases "family." Through the intermingling of textual and visual production that interpreted the students' progress from childhood to adulthood—signalled by achieving the goal of a university degree—the yearbooks helped shape how students ultimately valued their undergraduate years. Although mainly the province of the graduating class (Seniors), yearbooks provided all students with possibilities to imagine new identities other than those they already held or were assigned by others.

Yearbooks were not static, nor could they be considered merely encyclopedic. Their content was historically significant, revealing subtly or explicitly the social relations among young people aspiring to personal and professional advancement. The yearbooks were replete with humorous poetic odes, rhymes, short stories, and skits, as well as condescending images of Freshman (and "Freshettes"), Sophomores, Juniors, and occasionally even

Source: Article with images originally published in the *Journal of the Canadian Historical Association*, 19, 1 (2008): 195–227. Reprinted with permission.

self-serving Seniors. Initiation rhymes, such as: "The Seniors were born for great things; [t]he Sophs were born for small; But it has never been recorded / Why the Freshmen were born at all,"[2] indicated the tone of students' discursive social relations and practices over the four years of their undergraduate degree. Specific satirical literary representational strategies, made acutely resonant by visual images, were used to distinguish and order the various years. Descriptions of the years, including that of the Senior class, were inextricably intertwined with notions of academic progress, cognitive learning, and social and intellectual growth. These understandings, intertextually supported through campus newspapers and journals, were also manifest in Freshman initiations, hazing, and other competitive and elite practices, enacted to keep educational and social margins in place.

In this paper, we draw on *Torontonensis*, the University of Toronto's yearbook (1898–1966), the University of Alberta's *Evergreen & Gold* (1921–1971), and the University of British Columbia's *The Annual* (1915–1925), later renamed Totem (1926–1966),[3] between the years 1898–1930, to examine how fourth-year Senior students—the group of students largely entrusted with the production of the yearbook in their graduating year—visually represented and textually narrated their place and that of their less-advanced peers in the university.[4] We focus on the key features of these representations, specifically highlighting how self-identities of the graduating class were woven into the fabric of official memory, and especially the intransigence of fixed divisions and characterizations of the different academic years as they were ordered and legitimated by a select number of mostly upper-level students. Critically analyzing how visual texts were subject to contextual, institutional, and cultural variables,[5] we illustrate some of the constructed understandings of their producers and the readers/viewers within the framework of early twentieth-century higher education student experiences.

We also seek to understand how yearbooks highlighted the shift of ideas about an educational life cycle metaphorically expressed as childhood/ first-year student; adulthood/upper level student.

Multiple and shifting subjectivities, identities, and the politics of student cultures are vital to any study of yearbooks. We are interested in understanding how identities arose and visual images are forged to construct categories of students who were said to exhibit particular social and intellectual traits, behaviours, and knowledge in keeping with their assigned educational rank.[6]

The yearbook images provide a fruitful forum for critical study of student cultures and the way contemporary agents interpreted their place in the academy, and indeed that of others. Each university yearbook we examined, from its inception in the late nineteenth century to 1930—the year chosen to end this study because of a shift in meaning and aesthetic representation brought on by the emergence of documentary photography—was uniquely evocative. A material artifact in its own right, yearbooks boasted their own organizational logic and aesthetic layout, educational values, and perspectives. Visually, supported by textual caption and reference, with some contextual and idiosyncratic variances, we noticed that the volatile and gendered relations and experiences among students in diverse undergraduate years as depicted in the yearbooks of all three universities were starkly similar. Despite their regional differences and their year of establishment (in chronological order: Toronto, 1898; University of British Columbia, 1915; and Alberta, 1921), we were struck by shared discourses among all the yearbooks about how students envisioned university life. The continual repetition of educational themes, debates, and aesthetic tropes suggested the powerfully sustainable potency of these conventional images. Although changes over time within and among the yearbooks encompassed items such as the inclusion of new faculties, organization of sections, style of the front and end matter, advertisements, content of student biographies, presentation of student club and faculty listings, and the cartoonists themselves,[7] the surprising resemblances and consistency of student satire drew our attention.

The genre of literary texts reveals undercurrents of irony and ambiguity, allusions, metaphors, symbols, innuendo, parody, and analogies. In the yearbooks, these shaped the ideological and social contexts of educational life cycles as a student proceeded from one year to the next. As important and elucidatory components of the yearbook, cartoon captions were a bridge that spanned the written word and the image: the textual described while the visual expanded. The caption embellished the image as effectively as the image placed the textual. In attending to the visual, we situate our work within the interdisciplinary field of visual culture's broader debates around visuality and vision and questions about the inextricable relationship between text and image. We are interested in the complex and contextual historical network of relations from which images arise, to what they are responding, and their ultimate effects. Visuality was a mode of seeing and looking that was neither innocent nor fixed but organized around the reader's/viewer's interpretive understandings.

Contemporary theories of pictorial representation and visual culture are grounded in the premise that, similar to language, images, artifacts, and spatial environments are powerful in shaping attitudes, prejudices, and identities. Visual culture is not a reflective and transparent backdrop to our experiences; rather it is crucially theorized as an active mode of learning about the world.[8] Visual texts, as in the case of cartoons and drawings in the historic yearbook, did not embody essential meanings, but were informed by the interests and desires of the reader/viewer and by the social relations between the perceiver and the perceived. Yearbooks functioned as "iconotexts" or "imagetexts" in a rich interplay—"a dialectic of language and vision"[9]—between the visual and the textual.

The visual, specifically cartoons and caricature, uncovered and interrupted seemingly innocuous official remembrances and allowed us to question the yearbooks' manifold shifting subjectivities, the intentions of their content, and their constructions of students' social and academic understandings. As Gillian Rose has suggested, strict appeals to definitive authorial and artistic intent were not always possible or desirable: "Since the image is always . . . seen in relation to other images, this wider visual context is more significant for what the image means than what the artist thought they were

doing."[10] Viewers become powerful. They are not a tabula rasa; rather memory and experience shape the way one views images.[11] In this sense, texts and cartoons in the yearbooks did not merely iterate prevailing values and ideologies, but they continually mediated competing beliefs, often bringing forth new issues and debates. Students consciously and subconsciously, explicitly and subtly, created and interpreted text and images in diverse ways based on their class and academic year, social and cultural backgrounds, gender, age, religion, personal and political aspirations, and intellectual and philosophical predispositions and interests. Whether the editors and editorial boards knew the extent of each cartoon's impact, however, is debatable.[12]

As part of the wider historiography on universities and students, research has uncovered shifting cultures of intense and capricious relationships on campus. Ideas and practices of "youth" in the university forged the evolving nature of historical academic cultures. Students spoke in particular ways to their intellectual worlds, many of which were affected temporally and spatially with difference and power.[13] We are contributing to this scholarly literature by looking at how students were "seen" through self-renderings of character and appearance. Using an interdisciplinary "critical practice around the use of visual imagery [as] a source material," we see the rich, multifaceted visual cultures of universities conveying ways of seeing and understanding the world. New theoretical possibilities arise from what Antonio Novoa called "a historiographical renewal," by illustrating how images "reshape the remembering imagining."[14]

As pieces of material history, as well as from its content, the university yearbook between 1898 and 1930 is instrumental in offering new and detailed interpretations of student cultures. Yearbooks were striking in their visual commentaries on student comportment. Through ubiquitous use of satire and parody, the yearbooks reflected a gendered and "youth" dynamic on campus that diminished students in the lower academic years as well as women, generally. Elaborate rites and initiations, also referred to as "hazing," were related to this inequality in power and authority. Some studies have focused on the problematic competitive and ex-clusionary nature of the late-nineteenth- and ear-ly-twentieth-century North American university in relation to its links to athletic rivalries and the rise of fraternities and attendant rituals on campus.[15] Hank Newer noted that historical (and contempor-ary) studies of initiations "reveal the destructive patterns of organizational life . . . [and] how they socialize new members."[16] Indoctrinating students, albeit harshly, into unfamiliar cultures was essen-tial in the initiations, even in light of their formal and overtly constructed ritualistic and marginaliz-ing practices. Paul Axelrod noted for the end of the nineteenth century and early twentieth century that "initiations . . . introduced new, frequently insecure students to campus culture and taught the impor-tance of fraternity, hierarchy, and conformity."[17]

Performances such as hazing illustrated how relations among students, the imposition of place and belonging, and acceptance were established and reproduced. Keith Walden paints a picture of the culture of student initiations as having a deeper pur-pose of reflection and anxiety about what transpired

and what awaits after graduation. The university years were an unsettling and unusual time for stu-dents. "Initiations, for most students, were brief episodes of frivolity, but they were also important social dramas that marked the attainment of matur-ity, delineated the structure of campus life, and dis-played concerns about past and future prospects."[18] Walden's examination of the University of Toronto between 1880 and 1925 exposed underlying political and social forces in the sometimes acrimonious stu-dent cultures.[19] We add to the studies about student rituals and initiations, and student socio-political cultures, by contending that the historical vicissi-tudes, relationships, quality, and character, as well as codes of behaviour, language, and appearance, of student life were front and centre and unabashedly exposed in the creative visual expression of the most obvious and wide-spread student media of the time.

Representations of Campus Life

It is the special mission of Torontonensis
to lessen the pain of parting. In the days to

A SENIOR ON THE "SCHOOL" STEPS

Figure 1. A Senior on the "School" Steps, *Torontonensis*, 1907

come [the yearbook] . . . will speak to us like the voice of an old College friend, reminding us that . . . though scattered, our family is unbroken; that we are not . . . forgotten by our brothers . . . nor by our Alma Mater.[20]

Mawkish assertions aside, the yearbook was an interpretive window on campus life. The images in the yearbooks focused on professors, buildings, and, to a lesser extent, administrative personnel; but they were heavy on self-depiction. On the surface, perspectives on the harmonious nature of student life and culture seemed to enjoy an uneasy consensus. In appearance, behaviour, and speech, Seniors were drawn as more worldly, wise, and mature—indeed, in comparison to students in the lower academic years, more akin to the professoriate itself. Although the Senior class strove to represent itself as dignified, solemn, and reverential, their members were clearly not adverse to inter-class ribbing. Figure 1 shows a "typical" day in the life of a male Senior at the University of Toronto. While the image may have evoked the stereotypical figure of a student idling the day away, it may also have symbolized the advanced Senior who had earned for himself some necessary leisure from the heavy demands of his scholarly work.[21]

Visual images of Seniors often showed them as optimistic and confident graduates, as represented in a *Torontonensis* image, Figure 2. Against the backdrop of these images framed by conventional, recognizable symbols (the posture and accoutrements—the pipe, the robes—of a professorial graduate of distinguished intellectual acumen, for example), students' maudlin allusions to, and affection for, their alma mater took on a notable resonance. The yearbook constructed what appeared to some as an educational Valhalla, a nostalgic take on four years of challenging intellectual work. Valedictory addresses and "class histories" waxed poetic on the "glorious" time as an undergraduate. "The tie that will bind us to our university," noted University of Alberta valedictorian George Bryan, "will be one of the purest since it will also unite us with our youth."[22] With varying degrees of success, such remembrances emotively tried to sanitize past struggles. Not everyone was partial, however, to these overly romantic

constructions of university life. In his 1903 valedictory address, student and future University of Toronto professor Maurice Hutton bemoaned "traditional" and "conventional thinking," instead viewing commencement as "an ending and not a beginning."[23] In his honorary valedictory address in 1904, English Professor W.J. Alexander echoed Hutton's questioning of how students sought to narrate the past in the present, noting that "we dwell on the past to gather its lessons, not to see ourselves in sentimental regrets. . . . It is a shallow view that represents our earlier years as the best or happiest part of our lives." Having said that, Alexander partook of the conceptualization of the university as a place and a time in which (male) students were "carried . . . from youth to manhood" and where "childish illusions [are] finally abandoned."[24]

Despite their official purpose, valedictory addresses were at times incendiary events, revealing an underlying tension that was reflected in images. Once published prominently in the yearbooks for a wide readership, they became sites of contention. Perhaps, surprisingly, instead of reminiscences on educational hurdles breached, they could be

Figure 2. Senior, *Torontonensis*, 1903

biting attacks and accusations against the university and its practices, curriculum, and particularly its professors. Valedictory addresses and the yearbook itself provided Senior students with the power and opportunity to comment harshly on existing conditions and official institutional discourses, practices, and policies. Fervently eschewing romantic and emotional appeals to varsity life and alma mater, University of Alberta valedictorian Walter B. Herbert, for example, shattered conventional platitudes about leaving the university by delivering an acerbic indictment of its professors.

> It is foolish for us to try to believe, at this late date, that all our lectures and "labs" and essays have been delightful, thought inspiring things . . . [as well as] that we have been deeply impressed by the learning of our teachers, by their idealism and culture and their profound anxiety to help us increase in wisdom and stature and in favour of God and man. We have all had our views regarding professors and their lectures, and have frequently discussed them in no uncertain terms. It is a pity that our outpourings could not have been heard by ears that would have profited most of them.

Without mentioning names, but with enough detail to make clear to whom he was referring, Herbert followed with specific examples of various professors with their annoying and unprofessional characteristics and foibles. In assuming this critical position, Herbert illustrated a common perspective of the Senior class which experienced "well-defined places in that somewhat complete and care-free little world," of varsity, and raised a direct challenge to the professoriate and their questionable pedagogy and curricular offerings.[25]

While some disagreement was expressed over sentimentalizing the university experience, the yearbooks concur, with few critical disputations by the student body and reader/viewership, that graduation was at once an august yet intimidating event. In the University of Alberta's *Evergreen and Gold*, students were shown sailing in hot-air balloons or

in ships on the high seas.[26] Turbulent waves on a seemingly endless sea were an interesting metaphor for a university situated in the prairies, signifying the turmoil and unpredictability of the virtual unknown outside of the university. Students in academic robes traversed the rough water in ships or balloons, perhaps in imagining their educational capital and privileges afforded them by a university degree. The university as a matriarchal caretaker was implied in many of the images. In his valedictory speech in *Evergreen and Gold*, J.M. Cassels orated: "Playing, ourselves, on the seashore of truth under the watchful eye of our kind 'foster mother,' we have come, during the past four years, through a great period of transition in our lives. Growing from youth towards maturity we have developed inquiring dispositions which urge us on in the quest of greater knowledge. We have heard the call of the sea."[27] Clichéd images of educational learning as a "voyage," "adventure," or "heroic quest" signified by migration from the cosseted enclave of the university to the harsh realities of the "outside world" highlighted the grand scope of the students' vision of their lives in the hopes of a successful and satisfying career and life. The degree in the form of parchment, grasped by the graduate, was prominent as a compass or a symbol for a ticket of passage. In one image, the degree was as fundamental as the sail with which to fly over "The Sea of Life" and breach the walls of "Success" (Figure 3).

Several images also suggested a sense of trepidation. By depicting risky technologies of travel over stormy seascapes, the drawings may be suggesting the vulnerability of graduating students to the unpredictable nature of the winds and waters of life. An image from *Torontonensis* showed a male student in academic robes aboard a pirate ship clutching his degree, being forcefully ushered onto the gang plank. A certain apprehension on the student's face might have indicated that the joy and accomplishment of graduation is mixed equally with unease, fear, and anxiety. Upon successfully negotiating the transition out of university life, where did the students arrive? A 1925–1926 image (Figure 4) from *Evergreen and Gold* entitled "Glimpses into the Future" lampooned the feelings of uncertainty of future aspirations and

Figure 3. Another Lindbergh? *Evergreen and Gold*, 1928–1929

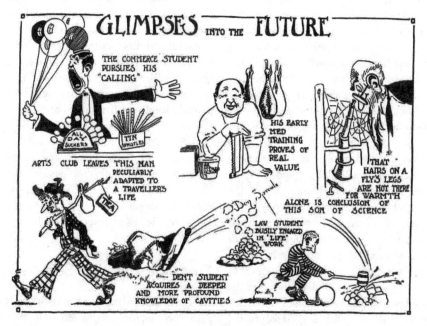

Figure 4. Glimpses Into the Future, *Evergreen and Gold*, 1925–1926

career prospects. The practice of satire was applied by the yearbook to non-academic life, yet still related to the efficacy of the degree and "treasured" experiences on campus. Almost as a last act of bravado, the students targeted their possible future choice of profession as easily as the university itself.

The Perceived Authority to Construct

"*Torontonensis*," noted a 1903 yearbook "Greeting," "is the peculiar property of 'our' graduating class . . . our life together during the four short years [has] indeed been pleasant . . . [e]ach year has drawn us closer together, made us more like a single family."[28] This "pleasant" educational experience enjoyed by all was overly roseate. From their inception, university yearbooks from all three universities were fraught with conflict and contestation about how students were represented and how their higher education experiences were made, and not made, meaningful. Individual and collective interpretations of the yearbook gave rise to vociferous debates that fractured the smooth recounting of memory, bringing into question who was allowed to "speak" on behalf of whom and what was acceptable to "say." How might one be portrayed relative to their undergraduate peers and what were the implications of those depictions? Students on the yearbooks' editorial boards traditionally authorized such representations with a dubious right—from the perspective of some other students not affiliated with the publication—to articulate the meaning of a university education.

In Toronto in the early years of the twentieth century, accusations of self-interest and self-promotion on the part of the yearbook's editors, the membership of which was elected exclusively by the Senior executive of the graduating class, spawned a protracted debate over who had legitimate control over the content of the yearbook. While some rumblings were felt among the Toronto Seniors as to editorial control,[29] as early as 1904, editorials in the campus newspapers questioned the lack of participation of lower classmen. They acknowledged the vastly dissimilar experiences of students at different times in their university careers and the paucity of alternative student voices over collective self-representations and class histories. The fundamental issue was control over the reins of the official printed memories: Who should construct and disseminate interpretations of experiences on behalf of the entire student body? Appealing to precedents already set at McGill and Yale Universities where only Juniors, not Seniors, were responsible for the production of the yearbook, students outside of the select group of imminent graduates vociferously agitated for more direct editorial involvement, so that "the book, as a record of the year, would appeal to all the classes in the University, to Freshmen as strongly as to Seniors."[30]

The editorial boards at both the University of Alberta and University of British Columbia were clearly more "democratic," if student representation was taken into account. Both universities included students from lower years in addition to members of the Senior year, but Junior, Sophomore, and, particularly Freshmen editorial members were in the minority and carried less decision making power—for example, as advertising assistants—in comparison to the Seniors. The Seniors ultimately held editorial imperium, directing the yearbook to segregate Freshmen, Sophomores, Juniors, and Seniors into remarkably similar satirical portrayals regardless of the university. Most editorial members of the yearbooks saw themselves as veterans distinct from a cohort of the less experienced among the student body and felt deeply entitled to authoritatively depict the student cultures they claimed to have known so well. Emboldened by a sense of privilege, the legitimacy and educational purpose of a student was only realized once the student was ensconced as a Senior. The ultimate reward of the Senior class was the prerogative to define one's peers—and those peers were often regarded as undeserving of charitable expression in the yearbook.

From Freshmen to Seniors

As sanctioned in the yearbooks, students were expected to unquestioningly adhere to the social and academic values and expectations within predictable and immutable stages of student experience. A 1898 "Greeting" in *Torontonensis*, for example, spoke about the "the fondness of a last sweet embrace to the quiet life . . . [that Seniors] . . . have known and loved for the four years," while heralding "those who are passing through the middle stage of their metamorphosis in their junior year; to the Sophomores just awakening to the joys, the delights, the beauties, the charm of college life and to the Freshmen, the most fortunate of the most fortunate company."[31] In the *Evergreen and Gold*, Valedictorian Cassels noted that "each stage in our metamorphosis from Freshman to Seniors . . . [has] its characteristic colour tone."[32] The tone, however, was

wildly interpretive according to a relatively small group of students. A yearbook image presented a socio-academic classification: "The Evolution of the Student" from *Torontonensis* (Figure 5) designated the "typical" student in each year. A series of student types are shown as participating in social and academic life, accompanied by humorous rhymes that revealed specific characteristics of each group. From "[t]he Freshmen, fearful and fatuous," to "[t]he Senior, sage and sapient. The pride of all college," these depictions conflated individual identities and differences, reducing them to stereotypes (note that the Senior in the bottom right panel is holding the key of knowledge).

The Evolution
of a Student

By

GEORGE F. SCOTT.

Illustrated by

N. McCONNELL.

The Freshman, fearful, fatuous,
   Freed from his native stubble,
Soon learns to find, in every wind,
   Some trouble—trouble—trouble!

The Junior, jimp and jocular,
   A downy moustache groweth;
For ladies lives, and freely gives
   His heart to all he knoweth.

The Sophomore so strenuous,
   Holds liberal opinions;
And happy feels, when by the heels,
   He drags his luckless minions.

The Senior, sage and sapient,
   The pride of all the college;
Sought formerly another key
   Besides the Key of Knowledge.

—30—

Figure 5. The Evolution of a Student, *Torontonensis*, 1904

In Figure 6, a more stylized approach was used to illustrate the seemingly fixed intellectual and social disposition of members of each year. Through the physiognomy of facial expression, the Freshman is shown with his head down in a subservient pose while the Senior is imagined as an unapproachable elite with his nose contemptuously in the air. The Sophomore has a hesitantly curled grin, perhaps indicating an incipient confidence in his academic work and growing social place on campus; the Junior's frown is diametrically opposite, perhaps suggesting an empty confidence after all—an anxiety toward university life. Might it also indicate a creeping cynicism with academics brought on by classroom and fraternity experiences? This simple visual image forcefully registered the spectrum of educational types and the "cycle of regeneration" as envisioned by students, and indeed might represent a self-parody of the graduating class.[33]

As encapsulated by the vision of the editorial boards, the yearbooks gave the Seniors considerable leeway to label student "subordinates." A 1903 *Torontonensis* class history noted:

> At the beginning of each academic year an increasing large number of freshmen gather for the first-time in the halls of Varsity. They come from farm, from rural village, from country town. With how great anxiety are their first few days at college fraught. . . . They are awed by the arrogance of the sophomore, wounded by the studied neglect of the juniors, humbled by the condescending gravity of the seniors.[34]

The "metamorphosis" that formed a dominant theme in the yearbook of the journey from Freshman to Senior was seen as a transformation not only of intellect and academic attainment but of personal maturity. From infant to adulthood in four short years, students in lower years were delineated in terms of "growing up," of leaving the carelessness and naïveté of childhood to be later transformed into the relative wisdom of the independent and responsible citizen. The group most visualized and sardonically ill-treated in the yearbook was the first-year class. A quote from University of British Columbia's *The Annual* paints the freshmen as ignorant and oblivious to their fate as undergraduate students:

> Alas regardless of their doom
> The little victims play;
> No care have they of ills to come,
> Nor care beyond today[35]

The Freshmen were drawn as a group of "newbies" hopelessly lost in the big league world of the complex campus. As campus newspaper *The Ubyssey* curtly noted: "It is an ancient University tradition that the Freshman is a fair target for ridicule. Everybody accepts his ignorance as inevitable—the professors do it, so do the other students, sometimes even a Freshman with more humility recognizes the fact."[36] Freshmen (and "Freshettes" as the women were called) were consistently described and visually cast as "babies" or "small children" with all the accessories of early childhood: sun bonnets, sand and milk pails, and strollers. In one image, they are portrayed as lost or powerless in the face of the university. The structured and imposing order of campus was beyond them across a desolate field (Figure 7). Freshmen are shown crying (Figure 8),[37] needy, simple, playful, and, patronizingly depicted, curious but hopelessly clueless babies or "diminutive little freshies." Figure 9 shows a little girl struggling to grasp a book—signifying knowledge—just out of her reach.

Figure 6. Editorial. *Evergreen and Gold*, 1922

Figure 7. *The Annual*, 1916

Figure 8. *The Annual*, 1917

"FRESHIES, YOU ARE VERY
LITTLE!"

Figure 9. *The Ubyssey*, 16 October 1919

Following the lead of *The Annual*, *The Ubyssey* seemed to relish reporting on the humiliating rituals that welcomed Freshmen every year, demonstrating a common campus culture of demeaning newly enrolled students. Designed to intimidate and embarrass, to single out who was academically immature and needed to be put firmly in a social place, Freshmen were subjected to rituals that were physically and emotionally demanding. For example, in acknowledgment of the term used to denote a neophyte—"greenhorn"—early University of British Columbia students were forced to wear a green ribbons and ties in their first Freshmen term.[38] From its inception in 1918, the weekly *The Ubyssey* gleefully chronicled such initiation activities on campus. To further the metaphor of Freshmen as children, according to *The Ubyssey*, the University of British Columbia hosted what they called "kiddie parties," where first-year students were given "peanuts . . . [played] hopscotch, hide-and-seek, ring-around-a-rosy [and finished off by ample servings of] . . . molasses candy . . . ice-cream and doughnuts."[39]

Mocking poems and rhymes likened first-year students to a bemused and entertaining pet or an irritating younger sibling. One 1919 verse (note that the Freshmen were reduced to an inanimate "it") read:

> I have a little Freshie that goes in and out
>   with me;
> And what can be the use of it is more than
>   I can see.
> It is very loud and noisy from its heels up
>   to its head,
> And at noon it runs before me, in a hurry
>   to be fed.
> The funniest thing about it is the way it likes
>   to go
> Along with other Freshies, all walking very
>   slow,
> In large and compact masses, segregated in
>   the hall,
> Until there's hardly room for me, squeezed
>   up against the wall.[40]

The Freshmen were not always personated as infants. They were openly susceptible to the debasing gaze of the Seniors even when satirized as adults. In an interesting reversal, *Torontonensis* depicted a first-year male student as an older, somewhat dishevelled country bumpkin wearing ill-fitting clothes, a rube to the sophisticated ways of the campus. In Figure 10, the Freshman's father is shown holding hands with his innocent son, asking for the "Head Teacher." They seemed to be wholly out of their element.[41] "Self-conscious rustics" or "farmer lad," as one yearbook "Class History" referred to them, were "transformed" into "the glass of fashion and the mould of form."[42] The newness of the helpless infant converged with the senility of the aged. This eccentric image is also striking for its comment on the rural–urban divide in Canada, which at the turn of the last century tended to separate country and city into drastically different social, political, and economic worlds. From the city, the country could be imagined as backward and simple; indeed, the image may also have reflected an intrinsic elitism of the university as an advanced institution of learning and culture, at least as seen by ambitious,

Figure 10. *Torontonensis*, 1903

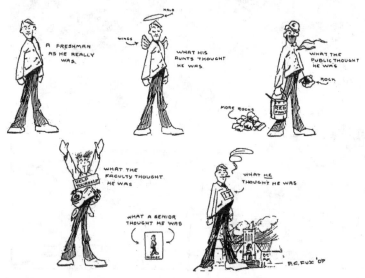

Figure 11. *Torontonensis*, 1904

upwardly mobile students. For those students who had come from the country, the yearbook creators were perhaps actively shedding ". . . unwanted parts of their background and identities." In a self-parody (Figure 11), the Freshmen were interpreted from the perspective of various constituents as self-important, in one panel, and delusional, as a "big man on campus" (lower right) in another. Here, the student is initially (and unusually) seen as confident; the various interpretations were intended to belittle him, indeed literally in the eyes of Seniors (middle panel, lower row).

In the yearbooks, the success of Freshmen in navigating the rigorous intellectual and social requirements of the university was obviously underestimated. A common theme among the yearbooks in relation to first-year students was failure. Freshmen were faced with a Sisyphean struggle during their first few months on campus. The "Short Course at College for Freshies" was the typical length of time the Freshmen spent at the university (Figure 12). He (the protagonist would almost always be male) would be expelled by Christmas for failing to meet the stringent challenges of a university education

by irresponsibly concentrating too much on extracurricular activities. Amid complaints of excessive hazing at the University of British Columbia in 1919, *The Ubyssey* raised the possibility of a new category of student: "Some difficulty is experienced in finding a suitable title for those students who are repeating their first year. They are obviously not Sophomores, yet one would not insult them with the term Freshmen. It is suggested that a compromise might be effected in the expressive world 'Freshmore.'"[43]

With each year completed, students assumed a new academic position, elevating their status and at least a modicum of esteem from Senior peers. On their new perch, they now became the Freshmen's antagonists. The newly minted Sophomores finally had a subaltern. In Figure 13, a Sophomore is seen disciplining a Freshmen, notably authoritative in both space and gender. The towering father figure is lecturing—note the aggressive posture—to what seems to be a confused and frightened little girl. From the image, the unequal and dichotomized gendered relations (masculine: strong; feminine: dependent) among the Freshmen and Sophomore class could be extrapolated.

Figure 12. *Evergreen & Gold*, 1930

Figure 13. *The Annual*, 1918

Having survived the hustles, hazing, and visual and literary insults and humiliations of the year before, and finally ascending to a more respectful "rank" of student, the Sophomores were still open to satire. Some yearbook commentaries and images equated the second-year students to first-year students, but slightly higher up in the educational evolutionary ladder. Sophomores were routinely depicted as indolent, cheeky, brash, and, as seen in Figure 14, lazy. The Sophomores were defined by rest, not work. They were also described as a chimera, or more scientifically, a Darwinian development. For 1921 University of Alberta class historian Margaret Villy, the "freshmen tadpole with monstrous head" gave way to the "sophomore tadpole just

Figure 14. *Torontonensis*, 1902

beginning 'to get his feet.'" She added: "In the junior stage, having now a head of normal size, our friend the tadpole judiciously strikes out with his four feet into the enticing waters and mysterious depths of knowledge, to emerge from the pond next year, a serious-minded, fully developed, google-eyed frog."[44]

The features of campus life of the Sophomore were laid out in an instructive image from the 1930 *Evergreen and Gold* (Figure 15). The collage included a rather explicit depiction of a hazing ("Ardent Sophs Preparing Their Big Reception For The Frosh"), while what appeared to be a Senior nonchalantly walking by blissfully ignoring the event. Sophomores are also seen in an intimate embrace, an exploding thermometer between them that likely represented the heat of undergraduate sexual passion. Included as well in *The Annual* and *Torontonensis*, depictions of women, often as sexual beings, suggested young romantic or sexual interests at the expense of academic study. Sophomore women were undoubtedly objectified. In this figure, while a cultured, pipesmoking Sophomore seems to be supervising, and possibly approving the derisive cartoon, the cartoon's space is anchored by an elegant co-ed, an unapproachable debutante "in a class by herself." If not the centre of attention, women were literally appendages. They were a conscious distraction to their male colleagues and serious-minded professors (lower centre). Academic ranks could be imbued with contempt, where Sophomores were essentially the devil incarnate (left centre). A morbid panel was also part of the image. When Sophomores "hang together," it was perhaps in reference to educational suicide or death of that cohort of students who were inadequate to the considerable task of academic achievement.

While Freshmen and Sophomores experienced their share of ridicule, the Juniors were not impervious to derision, although they were far less skewered than students in their first two years. They were often depicted as pseudo-serious scholars, progressing from the incompetent to the barely capable, still overwhelmed by conventional grown-up responsibilities. The Junior class was sketched as struggling under the burden of academic pressures and crushed by the heavy weight of knowledge

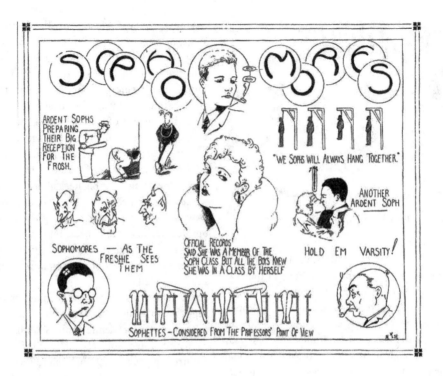

Figure 15. *Evergreen & Gold*, 1930

(Figure 16). Due to their relatively advanced stage of higher education, however, they were offered one of their first measures of respect as the recurring visual trope used to represent them was the studious owl. In going from Sophomores to Juniors, class historian Minnie J. Wershof wrote in the 1922 *Evergreen and Gold*: "[G]one were the care free days, and more serious thoughts and matters claimed attention."[45]

Figure 16. *Torontonensis*, 1902

Gender, and its attendant notions of femininity and masculinity, was unambiguously ordered in all three yearbooks. Men occupied the lion's share of space in most of the illustrations of students. The quintessential student was the infant, child, young rube, or bumpkin who woefully lacked knowledge and experience, the majority of whom were male or constructions of masculine character. Women were the "other." Apart from the stereotype of a desirable sexual object of the young male student, similar to men, they were often embodied in caricatures as young children or infants. In Figure 17, for example, in a banner that introduces the biographies of first-year women students, a young girl with a doll safely tucked under her arm heads to bed promptly at "9 p.m." possibly after a study session. The feminized vision of the child is embellished by the adjacent panel of a bouquet of flowers, something that would very likely not be present if the image were of a male Freshman.

Where women were included in the cartoons, the finely wrought delineation of the various grades in

Figure 17. *The Annual*, 1916

part vanishes. Women were more cohesively rendered as a gendered category as opposed to an academic one. Gendered humour and allusions to sexual innuendo were dissymmetrical between men and women. Socially produced, masculinities and femininities were forged and regulated through a continual series of repetitive viewing(s). Contemporary historiographical writing about female voice in the university has offered elucidating accounts of how women's identities were historically created on campus and how they were variously represented by themselves and by male students.[46] These representations were inextricably linked to debates about coeducation and access of women to higher education.[47] Echoing the overarching semiotic descriptions of the various academic years that categorized students into phases of biological and emotional growth, women students were dictated through caricature by their desire to marry, a sign of social, not intellectual, advancement and success. Higher education for women was trivialized in the patriarchal world of male students. Figure 18, for example, was a *Torontonensis* take on co-eds, whose primary purpose at the university was not to support each other academically but to come together as a sorority devoted to finding husbands. The stereotype, undoubtedly driven by wider prescribed social roles of women off campus, was naturalized through the yearbook satire.

Rites of Passage and the "Joking Relationship"

Despite attempts by the Senior class and a select group of other students to impose its vision of the educational world on others, students who were portrayed in unflattering ways might have been somewhat complicit in their own making. Through repetition and socially accepted regulation, the circulation of cartoon images was persistent. The victims of the parodies were never deserving of their satirized fate, but the continued acceptance of initiation practices that replicated social borders between students was powerfully driven by traditional agendas. Humorous remembrances were imagined within the consensual structure of behavioural expectations and academic programmes inhabited by all students. The images in the yearbook could be seen as a self-parody, an integral element of the creator's identities and experiences at the university, as well as a penetrating commentary on the unsophisticated and immature mindset of the undergraduate dividing his time between learning the ways of campus/the world and his leisure and love lives. Particular expectations were attached to students in each year, and the members of each cohort were constrained to act in specific ways to successfully graduate from one status level to the next—a practice agreed upon as part of student life and culture. An educational cycle of intellectual and emotional growth was created by students as much as it was imposed on them.

As demonstrated in the yearbook, proceeding through the undergraduate years was considered by upper-level students as a "rite of passage." This rite, which could be connected to initiation and hazing, was interpreted for a wide readership. As early as 1909, in his seminal book of the same name, French ethnographer and anthropologist Arnold van Gennep (1873–1957) coined the term "rites of passage." Van Gennep's theory was based

Figure 18. The Ring, *Torontonensis*, 1915

on change: "A person passes through a series of . . . clearly defined positions . . . and ritual is the primary means of safely navigating the rapids."[48] Van Gennep used a three-stage model to explain all rites of passage: separation, transition, and incorporation (originally, he used the terms preliminal, liminal, postliminal). As applied to undergraduate students in Vancouver, Edmonton, and Toronto, the student cohort was clearly separated through course and program registration; in transition, graduating from one year to the next was equated with the crib to maturity; and incorporation finally took place once the student entered his final year and graduated. These "rites" were ubiquitous in the yearbook visual and textual images.

The rites of passage in the academy as analogous to the life experiences of youth was intended not only as biting critique, but was also, at its base, meant to be humorous. The use of humour had deep implications. "Like other aspects of language, humour is a way in which people how their allegiance [or disapproval of] to a group."[49] British social anthropologist Alfred Radcliffe-Brown (1881–1955) defined "joking relationships" as when "one is by custom permitted, and in some instances required,

to tease or make fun of the other, who in turn is required to take no offence . . . which in any other social context . . . would express and arouse hostility." He continued that such relationships "enter the social structure at points of stress . . . where some aspect of the relationship involves both disjunction and conjunction by the participants."[50] In our study, the communication practices between years of students were part of complex group dynamics, situated on a continuum of "friendship and hostility" with "non-optional" status; in large part, students were beholden to their surroundings and cultures populated by various political and social agendas. Yearbook humour not only illustrated the tenuous and tension-filled social relations among students, but also explained how such wholesale images and textual references can become mainstream for many students.[51]

Humour was seen, either explicitly or implicitly, as an obligatory part of student culture. In its multiple expressions, yearbook humour provided propitious occasions for joking relationships to categorize the "self"—the producers of the images—and the "other"—the subject and viewers of the yearbooks, and especially women. Such relations and practices were not homogeneous nor collectively generalizable to all students at all times. As *Torontonensis*'s valedictorian Blanche Ketcheson noted in 1905: "[T]he students of the various colleges and departments cannot share very much in one another's life." She implied that competition among the different years was "natural," being, according to academic attainment from one year to the next, simply an "exercise of one's moral and intellectual faculties."[52] The yearbook images and associated captions and poems were notable but, to contemporaries, not surprising.

Conclusion

Yearbooks were more than mirthful nostalgic souvenir remembrances. They were potent vestiges of unequal and gendered social relations on campus. Although attempting to control the meaning of a university education, Senior students unwittingly forged yearbooks as ongoing sites of struggle for authority to interpret. The university was seen as a life cycle, a "natural," "acceptable," or even a "desirous" metamorphosis, where students within the three universities and four years of undergraduate work were slotted into categories based on perceived experience, skill, understandings, and expectations. This perception revealed an ageist culture, where simply being "too young," as the first year students were deemed, was an exclusionary stamp of naïveté. Only when the student advanced in academic years could he or she be seen as growing older and wiser in the ways of the world.

While these satirical images and texts had the potential to amuse, they more importantly raised intriguing historical questions about social relations, academic and personal identities, educational hierarchies, the meanings of "progress" of working towards a degree, and, in the main, deeply contested student cultures based on power and knowledge. In the yearbooks, representational boundaries of academic attainment and personal status were solidified—they both constructed and reflected stereotypical appearances and behaviours. Overt strategies of marginalization were practised, as, for example, seen in the yearbook quotation of an upper-classman at the University of Alberta reflecting

on his earlier years: "How green we were, and how the Sophs' mouths watered at the sight of us."[53] These cultures of difference had considerable power to label and separate. A rhyme in the 1918 *The Annual* showed unyielding prescribed identities according to year:

> Freshman—Freddie
> Sophomore—Fred Law
> Junior—Frederick Law
> Senior—Frederick Law Esq . . . [54]

The upper-level students esteemed themselves through the satirical subordination of others. They prejudicially slotted students younger than themselves into a homogeneous whole. This seemed to be the case among all three universities despite their geographical location, the provincial jurisdictions in which they were funded and served, the local communities in which they resided, and the composition of the editorial boards and the year in which the yearbooks were produced.

A study of yearbook representations integrally provokes debates over the co-ed experience, and how women were marginalized and objectified. The universities in Canada at the turn of the twentieth century (with echoes up to the present) were patriarchal in terms of administrative policy, demographics, authority of the professoriate, and the liberty of behaviour enjoyed by male students vis-à-vis the far more strict regulations applied to co-eds.[55] The yearbooks maintained a sanctimonious perspective toward women, making co-eds more of a prize or siren than a colleague. Sexist renditions were rife, as seen in one class history: "The blue-stocking can talk as eloquently with her eyes as with her tongue."[56] Student cultures in the first decades of the twentieth century were very much a masculine world. A *Torontonensis* "Greeting" remarked that a "college course, the firm foundation of the Temple of Culture[, made possible] the moulding of a common life . . . full in hope and rich in the possibilities of opening manhood."[57]

Part of this gendered structure was contingent on the social expectations of men. Depending on the student, males went to university for intellectual fulfillment—"knowledge for knowledge sake"—but also to gather credentials as someone with potential to secure a stable income and living. Much was at stake. The disparagement of feminine and youthful identities was tantamount to an academic subjugation; self-aggrandizement was helpful in a competitive capitalistic workforce. From the heady times of pre-World War I, through the war, to the unsettled post-war reconstruction (and arguably re-entrenchment) of a mostly "conservative" society, this overriding pursuit of a profession by many male students went unabated (Figure 19).[58]

In many media, late-nineteenth- and early-twentieth-century visual images served as vital forms of education and popular entertainment.[59] Yearbook cartoons can be similarly classified, but the caricatures served multiple professional and personal agendas based on individual and collective interpretative practices. Students knew that it was the time of their lives where they, in most cases, as young adults felt for the first time a sense of independence to express personal ideologies and visions couched in promises of a successful graduation and life beyond campus. In the yearbooks, Seniors took advantage of this liberty in imagining their auspicious destinies while adjudicating other, relatively less favourable horizons of the students in the years below them.

Student cultures and identities, and the social development of youth, were inextricably linked. Yearbook images had the power to subjectively transform how students and readers/viewers made sense of themselves and the world around them. Narratives, such as those of Freshmen and -women, were often trivialized. As articulated in the yearbooks, other perspectives became dominant. Depictions in the yearbooks deepen our understandings about the historical and cultural links among material practices, visuality, the contingent and contextual use of language, and the unequal and unequivocal purveyance of power among historical agents in higher education. Looking at the yearbook also introduces challenges to the ideas of a "golden era" of universities, of the romantic and idealized form of advanced education that was predicated on apparently harmonious student relations. The production of the yearbooks could provoke conflict among students within and between years, and this formed a culture that was in perpetual and contested change. In the end, the argument that university

Time to Change!

Figure 19. *The Ubyssey,* 1922

Figure 20. *Torontonensis*, 1906

education was a good thing was far from consensual. Academic advancement could indeed lead to intellectual devolution, as expressed dramatically in Figure 20. A Freshman learns too much as he progresses through the academic ranks to an unfortunate conclusion. Visions of student cultures in the yearbook were myriad and complex, and, as rendered through satire, were tumultuous, cynical, and undeniably farcical.

Notes

1. We would like to thank the Alma Mater Society of the University of British Columbia for permission to cite from *The Annual* (later the *Totem*) and *The Ubyssey* student newspaper. As well, we gratefully acknowledge our research assistant Georgia Gaden and the research support of the Social Sciences and Humanities Research Council of Canada.

2. "Freshette Initiation Highly Successful," *The Ubyssey* II, no. 1 (9 October 1919), 1.

3. The University of Alberta's *Evergreen and Gold* evolved from "magazine" editions of the *Annual Graduation Gateway* of the student newspaper, *The Gateway*. With increasing costs and the possibility of non-publication of this special issue, the Senior class undertook to "follow the custom of other universities by producing an elaborate and distinctive Year Book." *The Gateway*, XI, no. 8 (22 November 1920), 2. The University of British Columbia's premier issue in 1915 was presented as the "official record of student activities . . . faithfully and adequately present[ing] student life." "Editorials," *Annual* (1915,) 7. On the origins of *Torontonensis* and its founding, see E. Lisa Panayotidis, "Constructing 'Intellectual Icebergs': Visual Caricature of the Professoriate and Academic Culture at the University of Toronto, 1898–1915," in *Historical Identities: The Professoriate in Canada*, eds. Paul Stortz and E. Lisa Panayotidis (Toronto: University of Toronto Press, 2006), 299–331.

4. The universities discussed in this paper were selected for their regional diversity: the University of Toronto was in a large central urban centre, University of Alberta was situated in a relatively large prairie city, while the University of British Columbia was established in a growing port city. As part of a broader ongoing study, University of Saskatchewan, Queen's University, and Dalhousie University will be brought in for further comparative analysis.

5. Concurring with Dónal O Donoghue and other scholars, we conceive of "all learning [as] . . . emplaced . . . and embodied." See Dónal O Donoghue, "'James Always Hangs out Here': Making Space for Place in Studying Masculinities at School," *Visual Studies* 22, no. 1 (April 2007): 62–73. See also Elizabeth Kenworthy Teather, *Embodied Geographies: Spaces, Bodies and Rites of Passage* (London, New York: Routledge, 1999), and E. Lisa Panayotidis and Paul Stortz, "Intellectual Space, Image, and Identities in the Historical Campus: Helen Kemp's Map of the University of Toronto, 1932," *Journal of the Canadian Historical Association*, New Series, 15 (2004): 123–52.

6. The contemporary notion of identities as in flux and in a state of *becoming* seems an apt way to conceive of how students in different years might have experienced their university education. See Jane Danielewicz, *Teaching Selves: Identity, Pedagogy, and Teacher Education* (New York: State University of New York, 2001), xii.

7. For an expanded discussion on the use of cartoons as a particular mode of expression and the student and professional artists who were enlisted to provide caricatures for *Torontonensis* in the early decades of the twentieth century, see Panayotidis, "Constructing 'Intellectual Icebergs.'" Unfortunately, substantial source material that would uncover backgrounds and biographies of cartoonists for the University of British Columbia and University of Alberta has been scarce. As well, for these two universities,

documentary evidence is elusive as to how exactly cartoonists were chosen by the yearbook staff.

8. Some of the more compelling work in the expansive field of visual culture studies include: Jonathan Crary, *Techniques of the Observer on Vision and Modernity in the Nineteenth Century* (Cambridge: Massachusetts Institute of Technology Press, 1992) and *Suspensions of Perception: Attention, Spectacle, and Modern Culture* (Cambridge: Massachusetts Institute of Technology Press, 2001); Martin Jay, *Downcast Eyes: The Denigration of Vision in Twentieth- Century French Thought* (Berkeley: University of California Press, 1993); Hal Foster, ed. *Vision and Visuality* (New York: New Press, 1998); Mieke Bal and Norman Bryson, *Looking In: The Art of Viewing* (London: Routledge, 2001); Mieke Bal, Jonathan Crewe, Leo Spitzer, eds., *Acts of Memory: Cultural Recall in the Present* (Hanover, NH: Dartmouth College: University Press of New England, 1999); and Teresa Brennan and Martin Jay, eds. *Vision in Context: Historical and Contemporary Perspectives on Sight* (New York: Routledge, 1996).

9. See Peter Wagner, *Reading Iconotexts: From Swift to the French Revolution* (Chicago: Reaktion Books, 1997) and W.J.T. Mitchell, *Picture Theory* (Chicago: University of Chicago Press, 1995), 70.

10. Gillian Rose, *Visual Methodologies: An Introduction to the Interpretation of Visual Materials* (London: Sage, 2007), 23.

11. Richard Leppert, *Art and the Committed Eye: The Cultural Functions of Imagery* (Boulder, CO: Westview Press, 1996), 7.

12. Little if any information exists from early editorial boards indicating their specific understandings about and the intent of visual communication. By the 1940s, however, *Torontonensis*'s editorial board minutes demonstrated a conscious and deliberate use of visuality in the yearbook. See E. Lisa Panayotidis, "'Picture-Prose Panoramas': Visuality and the Work of Memory in Historical University Yearbooks." Paper given at 15th Biennial Meeting of the Canadian History of Education Association, Sudbury, Ont., October 2008.

13. Work on the mostly English-Canadian history of student cultures in higher education include Catherine Gidney, *A Long Eclipse: The Liberal Protestant Establishment and the Canadian University, 1920–1970* (Montreal and Kingston: McGill-Queen's University Press, 2004), Charles M. Levi, *Comings and Goings: University Students in Canadian Society, 1854–1973* (Montreal and Kingston: McGill-Queen's University Press, 2003), and A.B. McKillop, *Matters of Mind: The University in Ontario, 1791–1951* (Toronto: University of Toronto Press, 1994). Two books on how student cultures related to youth in Canadian society are Paul Axelrod, *Making a Middle Class: Student Life in English Canada During the Thirties* (Toronto: University of Toronto Press, 1990) and Paul Axelrod and John Reid, eds., *Youth, University, and Canadian Society:*

Essays in the Social History of Higher Education (Montreal and Kingston: McGill-Queen's University Press, 1989). For French Canada, see Karine Hébert's *Impatient d'être soi-même: les étudiants montréalais, 1895-1960* (Montreal: PUQ, 2008), which looks at the ongoing negotiation of student experiences at McGill University and Université du Québec à Montréal. Studies of student cultures can be found in most university histories, although they vary widely in terms of analytical depth. For the University of Toronto, see Martin Friedland, *The University of Toronto: A History* (Toronto: University of Toronto Press, 2002), especially chaps. 15, 17, 22, 23, and 25. For the University of Alberta, see Walter H. Johns, *A History of the University of Alberta: 1908-1969* (Edmonton: University of Alberta Press, 1981), chaps. 1–10. The University of British Columbia has yet to have a social history completed on its cultural and institutional growth, but useful discussions can be found in Lee Stewart, *It's Up to You: Women at UBC in the Early Years* (Vancouver: University of British Columbia Press for the UBC Academic Women's Association, 1990), Patricia Vertinsky and Sherry McKay, eds., *Disciplining Bodies in the Gymnasium: Memory, Monument, Modernism* (London: Routledge, 2004), and Peter B. Waite, *Lord of Point Grey: Larry MacKenzie of U.B.C.* (Vancouver: University of British Columbia Press, 1987).

14. Antonio Novoa, "Ways of Saying, Ways of Seeing Public Images of Teachers (19th–20th Centuries)," in "The Challenge of the Visual in the History of Education," *Pedagogica Historica* 36, no. 1 (2000): 21.

15. For example, see Winton U. Solberg, *The University of Illinois, 1894-1905: The Shaping of the University* (Urbana: University of Illinois Press, 2000), Hank Nuwer, *The Hazing Reader* (Bloomington: Indiana University Press, 2004), and Jay Mechling, "Paddling and the Repression of the Feminine in Male Hazing," *Thymos: Journal of Boyhood Studies* 2, no. 1 (2008): 60–75. Mechling's psychoanalytic methodology is based on Freud's 1919 essay "A Child Is Being Beaten."

16. Hank Nuwer, *Wrongs of Passage: Fraternities, Sororities, Hazing and Binge Drinking* (Bloomington and Indianapolis: Indiana University Press, 1999), xiii.

17. Axelrod, *Making a Middle Class*, 17–18.

18. Keith Walden, "Hazes, Hustles, Scraps and Stunts: Initiations at the University of Toronto, 1880–1925" in Axelrod and Reid, eds., 116.

19. See also Keith Walden, "Male Toronto College Students Celebrate Hallowe'en, 1884–1910," *Canadian Historical Review* 68 (1987): 1–34.

20. "To all Friends of 'Varsity', Torontonensis gives Greeting," *Torontonensis* (1903).

21. At the University of Alberta, "student watching" was recorded as a popular past time, where students would passively observe and critique their counterparts with particular attention to diverse types and differences

among them. "University Types—A Study of Differences," *The Gateway*, XI, no. 13 (2 February 1921), 3.

22. George Bryan, "University of Alberta Valedictory 1925," *Evergreen and Gold* (1924–1925), 62. University of Alberta Archives, accession # 84-25.

23. Maurice Hutton, "Valedictory," *Torontonensis* (1903), 284–5.

24. W.J. Alexander, "Valedictory," *Torontonensis* (1904), 299.

25. Walter B Herbert, "Valedictory 1926," *Evergreen and Gold* (1925–1926), 70–71.

26. In the early years, the image of an eighteenth-century schooner was a leitmotif at the University of Alberta. It was repeatedly shown on the decorative banner (the flag replaced by the year of the graduating class), announcing the valedictory address. In the University of British Columbia's *The Annual* in 1925, a less grand single-manned sailboat was shown sailing away from a crying female personification of alma mater, who is dressed in an eighteenth-century garment (p. 43).

27. J.M. Cassels, "Valedictory," *Evergreen and Gold* (1923–1924), 52.

28. "To all Friends of 'Varsity.'"

29. For a closer examination of the lingering and bitter controversies that centred around *Torontonensis*, in particular intra-class fighting over who should have ultimate control over its narrations, see E. Lisa Panayotidis and Paul Stortz, "Contestation and Conflict: The University of Toronto Student Yearbook *Torontonensis* as an 'Appalling Sahara,' 1898–1910," *History of Education* (UK) iFirst (7 November 2008): 1–18. http://pdfserve.informaworld.com.ezproxy.lib.ucalgary.ca/693397_770885140_905135144.pdf.

30. Critic, "To the Editor of the *Varsity*," *The Varsity* XXIV, no. 5 (10 November 1904), 76.

31. "Greeting," *Torontonensis* (1898), 6.

32. Cassels, 51.

33. The "cycle of regeneration" is discussed in the introduction of Kenworthy Teather, 13.

34. "History of the Class of 06," *Torontonensis* (1903).

35. Verse attributed to Gray, *The Annual* (1918), 61. University of British Columbia Archives, catalogue #LE3 85 T6.

36. "Our Infant Protégés," *The Ubyssey* V, no. 15 (15 February 1923), 4.

37. This image of the "crying baby" seems to have been a "stock" image of Freshmen as it also appears in University of Alberta's *Evergreen and Gold*.

38. On the debates concerning the wearing of green ribbons and ties as a "distinguishing mark" by first year male and female students at the University of British Columbia, see "Thursday and Friday Big Days for Freshmen," *The Ubyssey* VII, no. 1 (2 October, 1924), 1; "The Wearing of Green," *The Ubyssey* VIII, no. 3 (16 October 1924), 4; "Regulations for Conduct of Freshmen Class Outlined," *The Ubyssey*, special issue, Freshman Number VIII, no. 3 (6 October 1925), 1; and "Green Bands," *The Ubyssey* VIII, no. 27, (12 February 1926), 2.

39. "Arts '23 Holds Class Party: Feverish Frolics of the Frivolous Frosh," *Ubyssey* II, no. 18 (26 February 1920), 1. The *Ubyssey*'s inaugural issue ran an article entitled "Freshman Reception: 'Frosh' have the Privilege of Shaking Hands with Important Personages" I, no. 1 (17 October 1918), 1, 3. The article suggested: "Now that initiation rites are over, and the Freshies really belong to the college, we thought that we could afford to spend a few hours . . . being nice to them and trying to get them to be nice to each other," 1.

40. "A Freshie's Garden of Verse," *The Ubyssey* II, no. 1 (19 October 1919), 2.

41. See *Torontonensis* (1903), 50.

42. W.E.B. Moore, "Class History," *Torontonensis* (1905), 32.

43. "Here is a Good One," *The Ubyssey* II, no. 3 (23 October 1919), 1.

44. Margaret Villy, "Junior History," *Evergreen and Gold* (1921), 97.

45. Minnie J. Wershof, "The History of the Class of 22," *Evergreen and Gold* (1922), 60.

46. For example, see S.J. Aiston, "'A Woman's Place . . .': Male Representations of University Women in the Student Press of the University of Liverpool, 1944–1979," *Women's History Review* 15, no. 1 (March 2006): 3–34.

47. The University of Toronto had a particularly vociferous debate over coeducation. See Sara Z. Burke, "Women of Newfangle: Co-Education, Racial Discrimination and Women's Rights in Victorian Society," *Historical Studies in Education / Revue d'histoire de l'éducation* 19, no. 1 (Spring 2007): 111–34; and "'Being unlike Man': Challenges to Co-Education at the University of Toronto, 1884–1909," *Ontario History* 93, no. 1 (Spring 2001): 11–31. See also Anne Rochon Ford, *Path Not Strewn with Roses: One Hundred Years of Women at the University of Toronto, 1884–1984* (Toronto: Women's Centenary Committee, University of Toronto, 1985). For discussions about the academic conditions of women students in the 1920s in Vancouver, see Stewart, *It's Up to You*.

48. Ronald L. Grimes, *Deeply into the Bone: Re-Inventing Rites of Passage* (Berkeley: University of California Press, 2000), 103. Arnold Van Gennep, *The Rites of Passage*, trans. M.B. Vizedom and G.L. Caffee (London: Routledge and Kegan Paul, 1960 [*Les Rites de Passage* (Paris: Noury, 1909)], Nicole Belmont, *Arnold Van Gennep: The Creator of French Ethnography*, trans. Derek Coltman (Chicago: University of Chicago Press, 1979), Thomas A. Leemon, *The Rites of Passage in a Student Culture: A Study of the Dynamics of Transition* (New York: Teachers' College Press, 1972), Steven Zeitlin, "The Life Cycle: Folk Customs of Passage," Rites of Passage in America: A Traveling Exhibition Organized by The Balch Institute for Ethnic Studies, 22 June 1992–2 January 1995. www2.hsp.org/exhibits/Balch%20exhibits/rites/lifecycle.html.

49. Alison Ross, *The Language of Humour* (London: Routledge, 1998). Contemporary social historians have

also made an important link between humour as enacted through language and visual images, social protest, and the formation of collective identities. For example, see Marjolein 't Hart and Dennis Bos, eds., *Humour and Social Protest*, vol. 52, supplement 15 (Amsterdam, 2007), and Joseph Boskin, *The Humour Prism in 20th Century America* (Detroit: Wayne State University Press, 1997).

50. Alfred R. Radcliffe-Brown, "On Joking Relationships" in *Structure and Function in Primitive Society* (New York and London: Cohen/West, 1965 [1940]), 90–104. For an expanded discussion of Radcliffe-Brown's work, see Jerry Palmer, *Taking Humour Seriously* (London: Routledge, 1994).

51. Palmer, 15.

52. Blanche Ketcheson, "Valedictory," *Torontonensis* (1905), 386.

53. "History of 25," *Evergreen and Gold*, 1924–1925, 64.

54. *The Annual* (1918), 116.

55. For example, see Sara Z. Burke, "New Women and Old Romans: Co-Education at the University of Toronto, 1884–95," *The Canadian Historical Review* 80, no. 2 (June 1999): 219–41; and Gidney, chap. 2, "'Training for Freedom': Moral Regulations in the University from the 1920s to the 1960s."

56. Moore, 32.

57. "Greeting," *Torontonensis* (1904). See also Paul Deslandes, *Oxbridge Men: British Masculinity and the Undergraduate Experience, 1850–1920* (Bloomington: Indiana University Press, 2005).

58. Axelrod discusses the impact of the rise of professions in Canadian society and higher education in *Making a Middle Class*. See especially chap. 4, "Professional Culture."

59. See Vanessa Toumlin and Simon Popple, eds., *Visual Delights—Two: Exhibition and Reception* (Eastleigh, UK: John Libbey Publishing, 2005).

PRIMARY DOCUMENT

The True and Modest History of the Noble Class of Arts '20,
The Annual, 1920

The True and Modest History of the Noble Class of Arts '20

In the year of our Lord, nineteen hundred and sixteen, there enters the portals of the University of British Columbia the greenest and most refractory Freshman class that institution had yet beheld. Naught knew they of the college tradition, and they endeavored to conceal their ignorance by forming traditions of their own. Intrigued by the sarcasms of a certain member of the faculty, they won for themselves lasting notoriety by a calm and studied resistance to all authority. The members of the three upper years regarded them rather as a necessary evil, and made the fact obvious at every opportunity—and thus, out of the fiery furnace of their trials, in Twenty was born a class spirit which has lasted through their undergraduate career. Great as has always been the friction between several individual members of Arts '20, the class has always presented a united front to the world in the matter of outside hostile criticism.

In the Sophomore year of this unique class a gentleman from Boston became permanent honorary president. Probably because of this fact there was a great influx of new members. Several of the Arts '20's most notorious characters entered the class in the second year, and at this time the aforementioned class spirit of Twenty became so obnoxious to some of the Upper Years that they labelled "upstarts." Nothing daunted, however, Arts '20 continued its self-imposed task of molding public opinion. Deprived of the innocent love of a class banquet by an unfeeling students' council, they retaliated by having a dance at Killarney in addition to the usual yearly functions, and, in revenge, put up Twentyites for all the big positions in the University. This was against all precedent, and great was the consternation and wrath of Arts '19. It availed nothing, however; Twenty voted solidly in support of their candidates, and put them in. Thus ended their second year.

In their third year, Arts '20 settled down to work pretty steadily. They were kept so busy writing essays for English, 7, that there was not much time for frivolity. It must be confessed, however, that they established a record for not handing in essays on time. As usual the class party was a marvellous success (due to the fact that certain Twentyites had taught on the prairies the summer before and discovered the "medley"). Some of the songs the men sang deserve to be handed down to posterity. The most popular of all was "Profs:"

"In old U.B.C. there are Profs of each degree;
Every kind is met with there; we have them all, you see—
Small ones, tall ones, too
Mild ones, wild ones, old and new—
They love us and we love them
As you now will see.

Chorus:

"There are Profs that make us sorry
That our work we have not done,
There are Profs that fill our lives with misery,
Make us want to see a Lewis gun.
There are Profs that give us each a feeling
That we haven't met the worst ones yet,
But the Profs that fill our lives with sunshine
Are the Profs we've never met."

As usual, this year the members of '20 again had their fingers in the electioneering pie, and, as a grand finale, they managed to get five of their members on the Students' Council.

It was in their Senior Year, however, that the peculiar characteristics of Arts '20 were most prominently displayed. As Seniors they endeavored to comport themselves with becoming dignity. They resolved early in the year that all must wear gowns, and promptly ordered them. After four months delay they arrived and the Seniors blossomed forth, their dignity surprisingly enhanced. At first there were some slight casualties, but, after a little

continued

practice, they all learned to walk the length of the reading-room without upsetting any of the furniture.

A second innovation as the publication of a class paper, "Spasms," a rabid and scurrilous publication wherein the various vices and virtues of the different members of the class were exhibited to the public gaze.

It has long been the privilege of the Senior Year in U.B.C. to have the freedom of the Stack Room. Arts '20 made the Stack Room particularly their own. They descended upon it in a body, and so persisted in placing their feet upon the bookshelves that, to save his cherished volumes, Mr. Ridington was forced to install most convenient little tables (such as they have in Stanford!), and to Arts '20 be all the credit.

The Senior class parties were surprisingly original, even in a year noted for the excellence of its entertainments. The first took the form of a masquerade at a private home, where everyone was given an opportunity to distinguish himself or herself, and all took advantage of the opportunity.

The second affair was a Leap Year party, help in North Vancouver. Space forbids us to relate the joys of that memorable event. What chiefly remains in our mind were the expressions of some of the girls as they requested the pleasure of dances with rather embarrassed-looking gentlemen. Before the party a "lottery" was held where the girls had the inestimable privilege of drawing for their escorts. (Smelling salts were provided and proved most useful.) It then became the duty of each maiden to write a little note of invitation to her victim. Most of these letters were truly remarkable. (We speak whereof we know, for we all read them.) Even more remarkable were some of the letters of acceptance. New Westminster, Burnaby and Central Park were given as places of residence, and the girls were requested to call for their escorts. It is not too much to say that for a week the whole College was demoralized as the result of the Arts '20 voluminous correspondence. The girls proved ideal escorts. They sent their gentlemen valentines and bouquets on the proper occasions with due devotion. It was certainly fitting that Arts '20 should wind up their career with such an original festivity.

Epilogue

As a class we have always claimed to be "original." Is the claim justifiable? We think so. It was not we who gave ourselves the name. We went contrary to custom in electing Mr. Wood as honorary president for three years in succession, and finally choosing him as our permanent honorary president.

We always knew what we wanted, and let no considerations stand in the way of our getting it. Our main policy has always been to demolish precedent in every walk of college life, and we have carried it out pretty well. We *have* been different in everything we did. We didn't do things better than any other year, but we at least did them differently. And, moreover, we have been a class with a real class spirit. Everybody was interested in the affairs of the class. Our class meetings were a continual joy, for everybody used to turn out to them, and express their opinions freely. Usually the remarks grew somewhat personal, but that only made them the more interesting. We should like to take this opportunity to thank our honorary president for all the kind things he has done for us during the three years we have known him. NO class could be prouder of their president that we are of "Freddy," for he has been a good friend to us all, under all circumstances. Three cheers for Freddy! We give them with hearty good will.

Arts '20 has not confined its attention to matters exclusively pertaining to the class. In 1917, 1919, and 1920 Arts '20 students have carried off the gold medal in the oratorical contest. Twice the inter-class essay prize has been won by a Twentyite. The men of the class originated the idea of challenging all the other years to an eight-mile relay race, and practically all the other years accepted. The race was most interesting. As a class we have shown a marked fondness for wild nature, and at various times have explored Whytecliff, Indian River, Crescent, Bowen Island, and Pitt Lake. We even went so far as to climb Grouse Mountain in a snow storm. Yes, we were an original lot. We lay no claim to being exceptionally brilliant, we have on record no exceptionally great achievements, but it is our proud boast that Arts '20, as a class, is "One and Indivisible." We leave old U.B.C. with regret, and with many happy memories of the days when we played at "being different."

Permanent Executive

Honorary President..............................Prof. F.G.C. Wood
President...Mr. A Swencisky
First Vice-President..................................Miss. J. Gilley
Second Vice-President..............................Mr. W. Coates
Secretary...Miss. E. Abernethy
Treasurer.. . . .Mr. A. Peebles

Source: *The Annual* (The Alma Mater Society, UBC), 1920, 20–1.
Courtesy of AMS Archives, University of British Columbia.

Hitchin' a Ride in the 1970s: Canadian Youth Culture and the Romance with Mobility

LINDA MAHOOD

Travel always occurs within a social and historical context.[1] Today, a "gap year" is regarded as an excellent opportunity for the next generation of "pillars of society" to take short vacations "from affluence" and travel for their own personal growth and self-fulfilment.[2] The expectation is that, in the process, young travellers will accumulate cultural capital for future careers in the global marketplace. However, a couple of generations ago, social workers, teachers, and parents believed that dropping out of school or work and drifting around were the actions of alienated young people with crazy hippie ideas. In 1969, Canadian adults were so anxious about "transient youth" and the "new style" of vagrancy that the Trudeau government struck a task force to investigate why thousands of middle-class teenagers and university students were seen hitchhiking along the Trans-Canada Highway.[3] At the time, many communities across Canada viewed the "summer army" of hitchhikers as "going nowhere in search of adventure."[4]

Academic interest in alternative forms of travel such as hostelling and backpacking is growing; however, very little is known about the hitchhikers of the late baby-boom cohort, who were the "pioneers of alternative tourism."[5] Given that civil society depends upon charity, trust, diversity, and tolerance, we have much to learn from the intimacy and risk-taking that hitchhiking implies.[6] This research stands at the junction of several scholarly approaches to youth subculture, mobility, and social problems. It is indebted to Erving Goffman's (1959) dramaturgical sociology, Stanley Cohen's (1972) and Mike Brake's (1977) pioneering studies of comparative youth subculture, and John Urry's work on

automobility and the tourist gaze, which emphasizes the sensual, visual, and bodily nature of the tourist performance.[7] Looking at the federal government's reaction to the "transient youth" subculture, this article examines what hitchhiking meant to restless teenagers and twenty-somethings and how they made sense of the liminal moments in late adolescence when travel was part of their subcultural identity.[8] The links between the public spectacle of hitchhiking, the performance of youth subculture, and the construction of a social problem lie in Erik Cohen's assertion that "the drifters" of the 1970s were true rebels of the tourist establishment.[9] Their road stories highlight more than the monotonous and carnivalesque moments of alternative travel; they can reveal key biographical moments when, as tourism research on youth travel has shown, understandings of national identity and citizenship are formed.

In the early twentieth century, due to the expansion of the automobile industry, highway construction, the "democratization" of car ownership, and the association of automobility with "the good life," social status became connected to "road status."[10] While car ownership made various modes of private and public travel possible, hitchhiking afforded the carless thumb-traveller an extraordinary opportunity for physical and social encounters along the motorscape. From the perspective of the tourist gaze, hitchhiking and backpacking were romantic, individual, social, and collective forms of travel.[11] To many impressionable teenagers, a hitchhiking trip was not unlike an hallucinogenic drug trip. Both experiences offered new realms of consciousness and an exotic and authentic experience.[12] The embodied performance of hitchhiking required the presence of other people, too. It was collective

Source: *Histoire sociale/Social History*, 47, 93 (May 2014): 205–27. Reprinted with permission.

and akin to being present at a "happening." Or in the language of the sixties' counterculture, "making the scene."[13] From the perspective of host communities, or the "local gaze," the public spectacle of youth hitchhiking was a social problem.[14] One dominant truth at the time about youth hitchhiking was that it was naive, misguided, and inviting trouble to expect to get something for nothing.[15]

The most informative primary sources on the topic of youth hitchhiking are contemporary newspaper accounts, the reports by the Canadian Welfare Council's *Transient Youth Inquiry*,[16] and oral history narratives from people who took long and short trips during the late 1960s and the 1970s. Travel narratives are an essential part of tourism and, more generally, part of the pleasures of leisure travel. Chandra Mukerji argues that "road talk" is a special kind of oral travel story because the pleasure of telling a hitchhiking story is as important to

the narrator as the content of the story. For Mukerji, therefore, road stories sit somewhere between "road reality," a "fish-story," and "scary bullshit."[17] More succinctly, Chaim Noy's work on Israeli backpackers suggests that post-trip travel adventure narratives illuminate hegemonic gender expectations and the ways in which young travellers resist, improvise, and subvert normative discourses.[18]

The data for this paper consist of written accounts and open-ended interviews with 100 women and men of the late baby-boom generation who participated in the "transient youth" movement.[19] A snowball sample was created in three ways. First, to capture the romantic and collective travel gazes, I enlisted the assistance of friends who had been hitchhikers or knew hitchhikers. Second, I used Google to locate travellers and youth workers who were quoted in contemporary newspaper reportage about youth hostels. Finally, following

Hitchhikers on the Trans-Canadian Highway

Source: University of Manitoba Archives & Special Collections, Winnipeg Tribune Fonds, 1972 , PC 18 (A.81-12), Box 44, Folder 3518, Item 15

public talks and press interviews, many people contacted me to offer their stories about hitchhiking and hostelling in the late 1960s and the 1970s.[20] To capture the full public reaction to hitchhiking, I compared interviewees' travel accounts with media coverage, the reports of social welfare and voluntary agencies, and government records on transient youth. The challenge of travel narratives is how to interpret the way people recreate tales over time. In this research, the tellers-as-responsible-adults were asked to reflect upon their "self-imposed" rite of passage and the reactions of significant others to their adolescent risk-taking.[21] Long after the crisis of adolescence had passed, interviewees' travel memories captured the emotion and imagination of travel.[22] No doubt, in the construction of this generation's coming-of-age story, some details about "back in the day" when "everyone" was hitchhiking were exaggerated, romanticized, manipulated, or omitted.

By the middle of the twentieth century, "the triumph of the automobile in everyday life was undeniable."[23] In the 1920s, there were approximately one million automobiles in Canada. According to the Motor Vehicle Registry, automobile ownership doubled between 1945 and 1962 and doubled again by 1964. Fifty per cent of householders owned a car in 1953, and by 1960, two-thirds had a motor vehicle.[24] Automobile hitchhiking began in the 1920s with girls and boys looking for rides to the beach or the ball diamond or simply seeking the novel experience of riding in a car.[25] College students in letterman sweaters thumbed to campus, and universities had hitchhiking clubs and contests. During the Second World War, servicemen and women in uniform hitchhiked to the military base.[26] Entire families were on the road during the Depression, thumbing toward greener pastures.[27] In Canada, hitchhiking was a violation of various sections of the Highway Traffic Act of the 1930s. However, the law was rarely enforced because the purpose was to protect drivers from harassment by "road beggars" and, by extension, from feeling guilty about passing someone in need. The police usually issued warnings to troublesome "knights of the highway" rather than fine them or put them in jail.[28] From the pre-1970s

perspective of the double-sided mutual tourist gaze, picking up a hitchhiker could be variously regarded as an act of charity, patriotism, paternalism, or chivalry and a real or imagined danger.[29]

Following World War II, Cold War paranoia generated a suspicion of strangers, and motorists were cautioned against picking up unfamiliar hitchhikers. In 1950, *Reader's Digest* magazine depicted a wave of American road crime by hitchhikers, and crime fiction, cinema noir, and urban legends of vanishing hitchhikers dramatized the violence perpetrated upon innocent motorists by hitchhiking ex-cons, wayward women, and teenaged gangs.[30] By the late 1960s, hitchhiking was associated with "drifters, deviants and escapees," and sociological theories regarded it as a quasi-deviant mode of escape for runaways, particularly teenage girls.[31] Nevertheless, oral history interviews show that Canadian girls and boys hitchhiked a lot. For many, it "seemed like the right way to travel."[32] An Ontario boy said hitchhiking "was not scary back then."[33] A girl from Edmonton said, "it was fun to see who might pick you up."[34] By the summer of 1967, the sight of thousands of young Canadians thumbing rides on the "summer roads" led many motorists to conclude that hitchhiking was a "craze" stemming from youth's performance of the 1960s counterculture that rejected middle-class values and lifestyles.[35]

In 1969, the Trudeau government responded to a barrage of complaints about "dropouts" and the drugs, dirtiness, and sexual diseases that "The Establishment" associated with the transient lifestyle by commissioning the *Transient Youth Inquiry*. The final draft of this Canadian Welfare Council report included submissions from a transatlantic network of professionals, semi-professionals, grassroots youth workers, and volunteers with social service agencies, urban planning councils, city hospitals, and charities. Notably represented were the Canadian Mental Health Association, Department of Youth and Education, Jewish Child and Family Services, Travelers' Aid Society, Canadian Youth Hostel Association, Children's Aid Society, RCMP, Catholic Family and Children's Services, University Settlement, Student Christian Movement, Parks and

Recreation, Manpower Department, and the YMCA and YWCA. Youth experts' impressions of the transient youth problem were varied and contradictory. The most open-minded viewpoint was that young people on the road were "motivated by the wish to 'see and to know Canada' and hitchhiking afforded the opportunity."[36] The most conservative assessment was that transient youth were "social misfits" who had dropped out of society and "into a private world of rootlessness, drink, drugs and madness."[37] Intertwined within the general concern about the "new-style" of vagrancy was the "special problem" facing young women whose "whole chance of happiness" was being "destroyed."[38] To address the most pressing problems that young people on the road posed to the community, the task force recommended developing a temporary youth hostel program that would ease the transition of transient youth back into mainstream society.

Youth mobility and travel patterns had long been a concern of civil society. In the eighteenth century, young aristocrats misbehaved on their Grand Tours of Europe; at the other end of the social spectrum, travelling apprentices clashed with the law over public drunkenness, lewd behaviour, and street brawling. In the nineteenth century, missionaries and social reformers described youth restlessness as wanderlust. They worried that an "addiction to travel" could cause juvenile delinquency.[39] In the post-WWII period, youth experts also used the concept of wanderlust to explain why teenagers asserted a restless desire for independence and an intense yearning to get way from home and family and to be on their own or with peers.[40]

In the 1960s, a number of global, social, and demographic factors influenced the late-baby-boom hitchhiking subculture. Canadian youth graduated from high school in unprecedented numbers, and new universities and colleges opened. Subsidized tuition and student loans gave young people from diverse backgrounds unparalleled opportunities for post-secondary education, which delayed their transition from school to full-time work and other adult responsibilities and wreaked havoc in the summer job market. The resulting youth movement expanded the generational consciousness of young people beyond that of their parents' generation and motivated them to seek "authentic experiences" such as travel and to "run" their own lives without schedules and obligations.[41] These social changes created an environment in which many radical and rebellious youth subcultures in Britain, Europe, and North America thrived.[42] In many ways, the transient youth subculture flourished among white middle-class youth the way other subcultures did: by borrowing values from the dominant culture and other subcultures and creating a unique constellation of symbolic behaviours and rituals that attracted new recruits.[43]

In North America, leisure activities, holidays, and travel were constructed through discourses of rest and relaxation following a period of hard work and discipline. For many impressionable teenagers, a hitchhiking trip promised freedom and personal growth and, in the dialect of the subculture, it was "cool."[44] Due to their middle-class status, liberal education, and dependence upon technology and consumer goods, notably automobiles and backpacks, hitchhikers shared many progressive middle-class tastes and values. Interviewees stated that, by the time they had reached adolescence, many had taken long-distance car trips with their families and internalized from their neighbourhoods and the media the link between automobility and the good life. A Peterborough teenager got the idea to hitchhike to Vancouver from some "hippie people" she met when she was twelve years old. They had "backpacks on their backs" and she "fell in love with the way they looked." She plastered her bedroom with the pictures she drew of them dressed in their "bellbottoms and sandals, and long hair and beards and guitars and stuff. . . . It looked cool." She told her mother, "These are all the people I am going to meet when I go to Vancouver."[45] A seventeen-year-old Guelph girl "loved the hippies" too. She wanted to buy a pair of Huarache sandals, head to the West Coast, and "be cool."[46] A 15-year old boy thought it would be "cool" to hitchhike across the country like his older brothers.[47] A Vancouver Island teenager said everyone she "wanted to be like, was hitchhiking."[48] For them, hitchhiking was not like a traditional family vacation. In the jargon of the subculture, it was a "trip": a social status and a style of life motivated by the desire for an authentic experience.[49]

In addition to the desire to be cool, hitchhikers were motivated to travel for a variety of other reasons. For many, it marked a milestone such as completing a semester or graduating. Many "left for cross country trips the morning following graduation."[50] A college student thought that "hitchhiking from Colorado to Santa Fe" would be "a real adventure" and a well-deserved "break" from studying for her undergraduate degree.[51] A Vancouver tire plant employee saw his hitchhiking trip as an alternative form of labour. In 1967, he was 21-years-old and "the hippie thing was starting . . . and there was a lot of questioning going on. . . . Middle-age men" at the factory were "getting divorced" and he did not "want to become like them." His travelling friend told him "great stories" about hitchhiking. "One day [he] decided, that's it, I quit!"[52] Others saw travel as a solution to a personal crisis. One Ontarian said he "was doing poorly at school from having too much fun" and there were "difficulties with his parents and a girlfriend." He decided to thumb to Florida and "just hang out for a while."[53] These young people were not rejecting school, work, or responsibility, but embracing alternative learning experiences, personal growth, and self-fulfillment.

Hitchhiking personified the romantic tourist gaze and the desire for collective fun and adventure.[54] It was also a fully embodied gender performance. Subcultural style, fashion, and demeanour, whether punk, preppy, or hippie, advertise a constructed gender identity that conveys a subliminal intellectual and emotional message about the wearer's personality, values, and lifestyle.[55] To become hitchhikers, interviewees recalled self-consciously altering the symbolic elements of their dress and demeanour to achieve a more immediate and authentic experience. Some adopted the artistic style of the bohemians, the illegal drug use of the delinquents, the "cool" of the beatniks, and a mode of automobility (albeit alternative mobility) like the bikers and hot rodders.[56] One teenager wore a pair of "John Lennon glasses and a belt made from beer can flip tops."[57] Another young man bought a coat like Leonard Cohen's and wore a flower in his hair, "just

for something to do."[58] A teenage girl said, "I wore my hair in braids and had grannies glasses. . . . I was ready to fit in with the hippies as soon as I found them."[59] Some travellers became "back-to-the-landers" and prepared their bodies for a more natural experience by shunning commercial soaps, shampoos, and deodorants.[60] One traveller explained the relationship between natural bodies and the back-to-the-landers. She said, "It was just the way they felt they could be."[61] Such choices of fashion and demeanour enabled thumb-travellers to exchange the trapping of gendered social-class status for a new independent road status.

In 1969, the *Transient Youth Inquiry* showed that the majority of hitchhikers were young men. The case was the same in the United States. Mukerji observed that the male hitchhikers she interviewed in 1971 and 1972 were just "sowing their wild oats" and delighted in identifying themselves as "bums." They had abandoned their homes and were exploring "possibilities that were beyond their horizons in childhood."[62] The men interviewed in this research were aware that they were violating hegemonic notions of masculine respectability. Their post–Protestant ethic dress, hippie hair, and unemployed status transgressed traditional codes of successful manhood, including owning key material possessions such as a car. The son of a college vice-principal and a homemaker-bookkeeper always travelled with a knapsack and a "hammock so [he] wouldn't get picked up as a vagrant," even though technically he was one.[63] A British Columbian traveller said he never hitchhiked without money, because he was not really "a Dharma Bum."[64] A hitchhiker from Edmonton knew that a man who did not drive his own car fell short of normative masculine expectations. As a hitchhiker, he nevertheless did not want to be perceived as "a guy who did not have it together enough to own a car." He asserted his middle-class status through his body language. He explained, "I don't wear a hat, you can't see the face. . . . You don't stand with your hands in your pockets. Always use the thumb . . . stand straight up."[65] Some travellers used social-class-inflected gimmicks, like the hitchhiker who "always wore a tweed jacket with blue jeans; kind of my uniform." Motorists told him that he looked "more interesting."[66] A Winnipeg hitchhiker wore a "striped shirt and tie" and smoked a "pretentious looking pipe . . . to overcome the deficit of a beard and lots of hair."[67] Other travellers subverted hegemonic gender ideals through the use of humour to conceal anxiety about how they looked. To counter the dirty hippie stereotype, a Montreal teenager carried a sign that said, "I Just Took a Bath."[68]

The material artifact of the travelling identity that male and female interviewees remembered most clearly was the backpack. The physical and social affordance of the backpack enabled thumb-travellers to display their true selves and magically transcend mundane daily life and rigid class-gender expectations.[69] In the 1920s and 1930s, hitchhiking was called road begging; it was the mode of transportation for vagrants, hobos, and the down-and-out. By the 1970s, hitchhiking was largely a white-middle-class activity. Similar to the "mundane technology" of a hiking boot, the backpack, rucksack, or haversack was the equipment of respectable patriotic occupations such as mountaineer, explorer, and soldier. For men, the backpack symbolized a rugged masculine individualist and not the "square" travelling salesmen who picked them up. Hitchhikers hoped their backpacks would afford them direct and meaningful encounters, but, in many cases, a backpack did not help them pass the formal legitimacy test of nomadic status. When an American customs officer at Detroit interrogated a Canadian hitchhiker "wearing a ski jacket, long curly hair and a scruffy beard," neither the hiker's nomadic image nor the "cans of food, plenty of matches, and a big hunting knife and sleeping bag he was packing" impressed the border guard. He told the hitchhiker that, if he did not "come back with a round-trip bus ticket, he would be put in jail."[70]

Women hitchhikers were fewer in number than their male counterparts. From a feminist perspective, the very notion of "nomadism" reveals the ambiguous place that women have on the road.[71] However, interviewees revealed that they were also seeking identities outside school, work, and domesticity. A Guelph hitcher put it clearly: she did not want to "go to university, and get married and be miserable like everybody else." When she left for Vancouver, she only packed her "hippie clothes."[72] The "coolest thing about hitchhiking," women travellers said, "was that total sense of freedom . . . you could literally just walk onto the road and get yourself anywhere in North America that you wanted to go."[73]

By the late 1960s, the women's liberation movement offered emancipation to women who wanted to defy patriarchal rules. To broadcast their rejection of patriarchal baggage, female thumb-travellers bought backpacks, clothing, and jewellery to assert an emancipated identity.[74] "I had long straight hair," a Saskatchewan traveller recalled. Some women wore "beads, amulets and crosses and stuff." She preferred a bohemian style and wore "flowery, colourful clothes, and sewed inserts into [her] jeans to flare them out big and wide."[75] Adopting the style of the flower child or women's libber entailed rejecting conventional makeup and beauty products, and some women went braless. A Montreal hitchhiker described her "long dark hair . . . elephant pants and probably a see-through shirt or little cotton gauzy top, a backpack, and a bag of weed to share."[76] One hitchhiker said her travelling companion got them many rides because she was "voluptuous and a real hippie."[77] A nursing student did not wear a bra, but she "still covered up . . . relatively modestly" and did not let herself get "really dirty" when she was on the road.[78]

Women travellers expected their backpacks, demeanour, and wardrobes to symbolize their resistance to a number of sexist stereotypes about women and mobility, including *Barbie* with her pink plastic luggage, the sexually submissive stewardesses in the *Coffee, Tea, or Me* (1969) books, and the hetero-privileged upward mobility of the *Stepford Wives* (1972). However, the reality of hitchhiking for women was that their bodies were a form of currency on the patriarchal highways. Even women who dressed androgynously, like the 20-year-olds who bought "overalls and T-shirts" or the Moose Jaw woman who wore "unisex" kibbutz pants and jacket, discovered that some motorists assumed that giving a woman a lift was proxy for consent to sex.[79] In a rare contemporary study of hitchhiking, sociologists J.P. Greeley and D.G. Rice argued that feminism was responsible for a reduction in the fear of rape among contemporary female undergraduates and high school girls. They argued that Kate Millet's *Sexual Politics* (1971) led "younger liberated co-eds" to believe that they had the same prerogatives as men, namely, "the right to take a walk at night, to thumb a ride, to have freedom of access and movement at any time and in any place." Greeley and Rice concluded that the more positive hitchhiking experiences a female traveller had, the more strongly she believed that she could handle a dangerous situation.[80]

Following Urry and Foucault, Darya Maoz constructs the tourist gaze as a two-sided picture wherein hosts and visitors see each other as "the mad behind bars."[81] This kaleidoscopic gaze embodies a mental perception comprising stereotypes and assumptions about modes of travel, and it shapes how hosts treat alternative tourists, especially hitchhikers, who generally contribute nothing to the local economy and are therefore less welcome than wealthy tourists.[82] Historically, youth cultures that became social problems were the ones that appeared to be hedonistic, irresponsible, and threatening to collectively shared social values.[83] Due to the tune-in-turn-on values of rock music lyrics, which seemed to denounce "The Establishment" and promote drug experimentation and sexual freedom, it was difficult for many older Canadians to understand where fashion trends stopped and true rebellion began. Some adults could not see "any difference between the long-haired lazy and rebellious bums who live[d] off welfare and the sincere travelling student intent upon seeing Canada."[84] Unlike the unemployed people who took to the open road or the rails in search of work during the dark days of the Depression, these "kids set out only to enjoy themselves."[85] Conservative youth also took the view that drifting around was "reckless." An Ontario teenager said, "Grandparents had not allowed moms and dads to 'race off to Toronto.'" He pointed out that "young people have obligations like adults. . . . We have school to attend, jobs in the summer, friends, a place in the community. . . . Drifters are frowned upon everywhere; a person is considered to be of good character if he goes to church regularly, holds a job in the community, or

gets high marks in school or is an athlete."[86] To flesh out what hitchhiking meant to the restless teenagers and twenty-somethings, we must focus on how the transient youth subculture was perceived in the community.

On the individual level, the values of church, conformity, and community were at the heart of traditional family life following World War II, and the announcement of the hitchhiking trip meant a tough negotiation between would-be thumb-travellers and their anxious parents. Adolescent psychologists and Dr. Benjamin Spock told parents that adolescence was a time of storm and stress, so a little restlessness, impulsiveness, and grumpiness was normal. However, media reports of youth unrest in the United States, France, and Britain alerted many Canadian parents to the troublesome consequences of too many idle and defiant youth hanging around street corners.[87] Early signs of teenage rebellion such as goofing off or drifting around, as well as the trend toward permissive parenting in the post-war period, could cause failure in adulthood.[88] Naturally, parental reaction to transient youth ranged from worry, to expressions of disappointment, to anger. In 1969, a 15-year-old boy said his parents would not give him permission to hitchhike from Banff to Vancouver. He complained: "They wouldn't even let me go on the train."[89] A university student said, "You'd have thought somebody died, in my Jewish family, quitting school was a big deal."[90] After graduation, a Toronto teenager and his 16-year-old girlfriend decided to hitchhike out west for the summer. He said, "We lied through our teeth. . . . We said we're taking the bus and . . . [I had] relatives to stay with."[91] A Saskatoon teenager got his mother's permission to go to Victoria after grade 11 by promising to register with local branches of the RCMP along the way, but "of course we didn't."[92] Two women from northern British Columbia wanted to thumb in Quebec because India "was too expensive." One said: "I didn't tell my mother. . . . It was just our generation . . . you kept your mouth shut."[93] Four 16-year-olds from Winnipeg decided to hitchhike to Vancouver together. One said,

> We bolted . . . I can't remember whose idea was. . . . We were safe in the sense that we

had the boys with us. . . . We snuck out early. I lived in a very creaky house. I went down the stairs really slowly. It did not take them long to realize that we were together. They called the police. In fact, we were in Saskatchewan and the police stopped the car because the person was driving too fast. He looked in the car and saw these young people and started getting suspicious and got us out.[94]

She confessed that she had a hard time hurting her parents, but she was "just tired of being controlled by a strict Catholic family."[95] A traveller from Vancouver Island said, "I don't think I negotiated with my parents." She just "announced" that she was hitchhiking to the Maritimes. "They were just so glad I was leaving." She qualified this by saying that she was almost twenty and "so obnoxious . . . they thought, at least she'll smarten up. . . . They were at their wit's end."[96]

It must be noted that, since the late 1960s, family norms in the middle class were changing; some parents saw the value of "doing your own thing" and encouraged their children to take chances.[97] A traveller from a large family remembered his mother driving his older brothers "to the edge of town to hitch a ride to a faraway destination."[98] In 1966, the mother of a 17-year-old boy confessed that she was upset when her son went hitchhiking and was robbed, but she decided "it was a valuable educational experience for him."[99] A Vancouver girl suspected that her "Dad wanted to be a hippie, but he was a dentist so he used to pick up a lot of hippies and squeeze them into our car with the whole family. . . . Part of him really related to it."[100]

There is no way of knowing how many young people hitchhiked across North America. In the summer months from 1970 to 1975, media sources claimed that between 50,000 and 100,000 hitchhikers would pass through Winnipeg every summer. Readers of Canadian national and local newspapers were kept aware of the "Summer Army of Hitchhikers" marching "Across this Land."[101] Under the headline, "Canada's Great Trek: 40,000 Transients Will Walk this Summer," the *Vancouver Province* proclaimed, "Hitchhiking has become a National

Phenomenon."[102] The *Globe and Mail* predicted, "The roads will look like a re-enactment of the Children's Crusade."[103] In 1970, the *Montreal Gazette* said, "Thousands of youngsters will be on the road this summer."[104] In 1971, the *Vancouver Sun* announced, "50,000 transients only the beginning."[105] The *Calgary Herald* told "taxpayers" to brace for transients because 50,000 hitchhikers "passed through in '71."[106] In June 1972, *The Globe and Mail* claimed that an "Army of Hitch-Hikers [was] Already on the March."[107] Many diverse segments of the Canadian adult establishment began to wonder what was wrong with Canadian young people.

Trudeaumania played a role in the transient youth movement.[108] Prime Minister Pierre Elliot Trudeau was cognizant of how to appeal to young people with his gunslinger style and rhetoric, and he spoke of his own hitchhiking travels in Europe and the Middle East. In 1968, he dropped in at the opening of a youth hostel in Jasper National Park and encouraged the hostellers to follow in his footsteps and learn about "Canada and the world," through national and international travel.[109] The *Transient Youth Inquiry* was a small part of the Liberals' attempt to maintain their pre-election appeal to youth, as well as adult voters. In response to public complaints about hitchhikers' panhandling, shoplifting, sleeping in parks and ditches, rock music, venereal disease, drug trafficking, and indecent sexual activity, and with an eye on American youth unrest in the summer of 1968, the federal government adopted a subcultural approach to the problem of youth in Canada. The expert opinion cited in the *Transient Youth Inquiry* concluded that the transient lifestyle was a form of deviance sustained by the media and peer pressure from weekend hippies, teenyboppers, draft dodgers, black leather jacket types, and student radicals.[110] However, the majority of hitchhikers were harmless high school and university students and young workers on a "carefree holiday."[111] It was easier to see hitchhiking as a rite of passage for restless young men than for girls, who appeared to have transgressed further from respectable feminine behaviours. A social worker stated, "boys, when they wish to do so, can return to a settled and ordinary life but in many cases a girl's whole chance of happiness is destroyed."[112]

The *Transient Youth Inquiry*'s solution to the gendered youth problem was not prohibition, but practical surveillance by way of a network of sex-segregated youth hostels that would be chaste, clean, and cheap. In June of 1970, federal secretary of state Gerard Pelletier committed $200,000 to fund a temporary hostel program and ordered that 11 armouries across Canada be converted as temporary summer youth hostels. The following summer the Secretary of State's Opportunities for Youth program was established, and funds were channelled directly to local community groups so that they could set up their own youth hostels.[113] These hostels were run by a new breed of long-haired civil servants and hip youth workers who could refer hostellers to job banks, education programmes, family counselling, VD clinics, psychiatric centres, and the police. By the summer of 1973, 120 youth hostels were funded through the Secretary of State's hostel program. The ultimate goal of these "receiving centres" was to ease the transition of "all youth" back into society when they were ready to leave the road.[114]

The Liberal government's temporary hostel program was baffling to many older Canadians, who regarded holidays, relaxation, and leisure as rewards for hard work. Penticton residents were "Up in Arms about Ottawa's idea."[115] A crowd of 200 onlookers watched a group of Charlottetown women put up a blockade to prevent the federal government from establishing a hostel in East Royalty.[116] *The New York Times* ran the baffling headline: "Canadian Youths Take to the Road with Government's Blessing."[117] A skeptical youth delegate of the *Transient Youth Inquiry* was afraid "that a lot of the 'older' participants left with the impression that a few hostels across the country would . . . keep the kids quiet." The hostel program reminded him of "the way the average North American father attempts to solve a conflict with his son by offering the car or tuition for yet another year of university."[118] In 1972, a Calgary youth worker agreed that perhaps "society" had gone "overboard helping out the kids on the road because everyone thought the kids must be screwed up."[119]

Trudeau faced his critics with the argument that "national unity is a product of national understanding and national pride. . . . Never in our history has there been the same opportunity for mobility for young people as now exists. With or without help, young people will be travelling. . . . We should help make their experiences worthwhile."[120] In 1972, the Department of National Health and Welfare produced a 32-page "colourfully" illustrated guide called "On the Road." The pamphlet, with maps to hostels and VD clinics, nutrition advice, and a summary of Canada's narcotics laws, explained how to hitchhike across the country. Critics called the pamphlet "the apple . . . [and] Ottawa has handed out almost a million of them."[121] A full-blown moral panic was pre-empted, however, because many long-haired young journalists and freelancers hitched along with the kids and filed articles in national newspapers, assuring readers that hitchhikers were not roving gangs of hippie anarchists and sex fiends. For example, after a long day of "Singin' the Espanola Blues," Martin Dorrell, a 24-year-old journalist for *The Globe and Mail* described the "good feeling" among the hitchhikers at the YMCA. "English talk to French, guys from the United States talk to Canadian girls about everything. Drugs, sex, the state of the world, card games, hitchhiking techniques. You name it. The noise drops to a murmur and then only the hissing of the oil heater disturbs the silence of total exhaustion."[122]

In contrast with today, when civil society regards a gap year, alternative travel, and international volunteering as a "secular rite of passage" that assists youth in developing a global consciousness and self-enhancement through personal growth,[123] in the 1970s, many civil society groups worried that transient youth were deliberately ruining their futures. With hindsight, we can see that the youth transition theories of the 1960s and 1970s that predicted which young people were "at-risk" reveal more about the "taken-for-granted prerequisites for adult achievement" and how a successful "imaginary adult" should behave than about the real lived experience of adolescence. Rather than the negative youth-at-risk discourse, Peter Kelly uses the concept "the entrepreneurial self," which is a productive, positive way for youth workers to see how young people participate in their own socialization and identity construction.[124] The road narratives used in this research demonstrate how, at the time of their travels, hitchhikers did not see themselves as dropping out of society; rather, they saw themselves as opting in—by embracing experience, personal growth, and self-awareness. For them, hitchhiking was not a deviant career, but an optimistic participatory physical experience that would improve the unity of mind and body and create a union of peers across the country.

In the 1970s, and today, more romanticism than rebellion features in the vivid descriptions interviewees gave of the people and places they encountered across North America. Their road stories contain similar tropes and accounts of sleeping in ditches, fields, and "Trudeau-hostels," which some said were "like jails" but others described as "great if you weren't looking for the Taj Mahal."[125] On the road, travellers performed the rituals of traditional Canadian tourism with a new twist.[126] Some hitchhikers were "not attracted to drugs,"[127] while others smoked pot and panned for gold in the Fraser River Valley, ate magic mushrooms in Pacific Rim National Park, and dropped LSD on the Plains of Abraham. A female hitchhiker said, "We never worried about taking stuff from a stranger. We just thought WOW! A new friend."[128]

These road stories reveal how thumb-travellers made sense of regions and landscapes within the framework of their own social class, regional, and cultural gazes. Maoz's mutual gaze is illustrated by hitchhiker's use of 1960s and 1970s hegemonic and derogatory language to describe hosts and host communities. Many interviewees used terms such as *Newfie, Redneck, Indians, freak-haters, drunks, pill-poppers, truckers, bikers, weirdoes, creepy guys,* and *perverts* and commented on cowboy hats, slimy teeth, and BO, but they also appreciated the generosity of the waitresses at the Husky truck-stops who gave them chips and gravy for free. The hitchhikers' travel gaze reflected the post–World War II cultural prejudices of class, gender, and generation, but the gaze also reveals their resistance to prejudice and stereotypes through their keenness to embrace intimate cross-class encounters.

Today, interviewees believe that, by travelling at this time in their lives, they became more confident, trusting, and tolerant adults. They remembered how they taught each other the code of the road. For example, one day on Route 66, a motorist let a British Columbian hitchhiker out on a roundabout. There were already about 60 hitchers standing there, and he thought, "We're in trouble, here man!... [N]obody's got water or anything.... I held a meeting of hitchhikers and I made sure everybody came. We've got to get more people off this corner. If somebody stops, ask them, 'Can you take another person?' So, in about three hours we had the corner cleared.... I thought organizing the hitchhikers was a good job for that day."[129]

The first hitchhiking experience for two southern Ontario teenage girls was in the Alberta Rockies, around Maligne Lake, and they were nervous until they met Gus. He drove them to a former WWII internment camp that had become the Jasper Free Camp. It was "this giant hippie camp" and Gus was "like the mayor." He introduced them around, helped them set up their tent, and showed them how to clap sticks together to frighten away bears.[130] During their transnational roadside encounters hitchhikers told each other where to go, what to see, and where to stay. The psychological experience of "dwelling in mobility"[131] enabled hitchhikers to feel at home in strange towns and cities, with motorists in cars, and among the strangers with whom they shared tents, beds and ditches, musical instruments for busking and rations from panhandling, details about good and bad drug trips, sex, and love.

Being young backpackers enabled them to cross over geographical barriers and enter communities outside the "tourism bubble."[132] Doug Owram says the early baby-boomers grew up in the shadow of "*Barbie* and the World Series."[133] Indeed, all across Canada, the influence of American popular culture was strong. "California was the nexus for all that was happening in our little world," a prairie teenager said. He and a friend "wanted to go down and check it out."[134] Quebec teenagers were also listening to pop songs like "California Dreamin'" by The Mamas & the Papas, which inspired two sisters from Montreal to hitchhike the California coastline. One said, "We spoke zero English . . . we don't know so much about the world at that time . . . but we know the song about 'California Dreams,' so we went to see if you can dream a lot in that place."[135]

Owram argues that late boomers were more sensitive to the deterioration of the image of the United States than early boom cohorts.[136] A Toronto teenager on his way to Florida ended up in Fort Lauderdale. At one point in Florida, he said,

> . . . [he] walked out to where the highway starts and there's a circular ramp to get onto it. Above it there's this huge billboard with a picture of a guy all slumped over in his car and there's a hoodlum running off in the distance. Underneath it says: "Don't Pick Up Hitchhikers." I'm looking at the sign wondering if I'm ever going to get a ride. . . . This in a place were people have guns in the back of their trucks and bumper stickers that say: "God, Guns and Guts made America Free. Keep all three and Free we'll be."[137]

In 1979, two young women from Edmonton made it all the way to the Haight Ashbury neighbourhood of San Francisco before they realized that the hippie heyday had ended there in the 1960s.

> We got there and it's really depressing, windows boarded up and everything. We were really naive. . . . We had cameras and were taking pictures . . . in an area that is all blacks and pretty rough and then this little girl comes up and looks us right in the eye and says, "White Motherfuckas." She couldn't have been more than 10. . . . We just kept walking. She really freaked us out and we realized how stupid we were.[138]

While the intention of hitchhiking was to celebrate anti-materialism and independence, the apparent freedom had its own frightening constraints. The sexual politics of hitchhiking meant that would-be thumb-travellers encountered unequal power relations, ambiguous gazes, conflicting stereotypes,

physical obstacles, and danger. There was a dark side to hitchhiking for young men and women. The open road was a contested spatial and temporal terrain where hitchhiking bodies were paraded before drivers. From the perspective of guest-host relations, the reaction to young men with long hair reveals that lifestyle choice can lead to conflict. Hitchhiking with long hair in the United States, especially after the Vietnam draft, was dangerous for Canadian men who were mistaken for "draft-dodgers." Some tried sewing Canadian flags onto their backpacks, but it did not prevent them from being harassed.[139]

Hitchhikers ride on the contradiction between the freedom of the road and the confinement of a car, specifically a stranger's car. Male and female interviewees were aware that their bodies on the patriarchal state's motorway were a form of currency and therefore at risk. On the road, hitchhikers learned that fear is as natural a part of travel as broadening one's horizons.[140] An Albertan said he was "stuck" in Kamloops: "it was cold out, then this trucker stopped, I was really tired. . . . He was drinking Scotch and popping [Benzedrine]. . . . Anyway, I kept nodding off and every time I did, he'd jerk the steering wheel. He said, 'I didn't pick you up so you could sleep; I picked you up so you could keep me company.'"[141] When a northern British Columbian hitchhiker thumbed alone, she tried to make it clear that she did not want to "screw around . . . I babbled like a little brook. . . . My brother this and my brother that. Maybe you know him?" She thought that "it was good to let them know that someone knew me, so don't try anything. . . . There will be retaliation."[142]

All hitchhikers reported the false assumption made by some drivers that, by consenting to a ride, the hitchers would not strongly object to a sexual encounter. A man said, "You have to keep an eye on the conversation. They wait to see what your interest in sex is . . . you can tell him you aren't interested, but they still keep feeling you out."[143] A woman from northern British Columbia said that a "young guy in a red car" drove her to a bridge near some railway tracks, parked, and then got out. "I remember sitting frozen, knowing that my life was in his hands." She never hitchhiked again after that.[144] Hegemonic patriarchy and sexism influenced how the cult of heteronormativity constructed relations between riders and drivers on the road.[145] One dominant truth of hitchhiking was that the safest and fastest way to travel was in small groups and with other hitchhikers. On busy highways, boys hid in ditches while girls thumbed the ride. Once, two boys from Edmonton and three girls from Cold Lake made it all the way to Kenora as a group of five, but their luck ran out at 2:00 a.m. at a truck stop. "This was the plan, we put all the bags in the ditch and my buddy and I would lay in the ditch while the girls hitched."[146] A teenager from Ottawa confirmed that it helped to have a gimmick, "but it still isn't as good as being a girl . . . they are the ones that always seem to get the rides."[147] All interviewees talked openly about "bad rides." Some victims of assault reported the motorist to the police, but others kept silent, blaming their poor hitchhiking radar. According to one: "We thought we were invincible . . . a guy was supposed to be able to take care of himself."[148] Years after a Montreal woman gave up hitchhiking, she took a Women's Studies course at Simon Fraser University, and it dawned upon her that "there had been a double standard."[149] Thinking back on their rides nearly four decades later, three women described the pleasures and dangers of hitchhiking: "You never knew what ever sort of vehicle or driver was going to drive up. It could be some beater truck, or a hot car, or Mercedes, or it could be some bloody pervert. . . . Hmmmm [in chorus] . . . You just never knew!"[150]

On the road, hitchhikers learned that each new ride was an encounter with a new person. Their ride stories, both good and bad, reveal the excitement many felt when they first discovered unfamiliar regions of North America.[151] Two sisters travelled together the "summer when there were youth hostels running all across the country, and you could get a bed for 50 cents and maybe breakfast or supper for free or another 50 cents." The interviewee said, "The best parts were the times we walked between rides along the Trans-Canada Highway."[152] Somewhere between the Alberta and Saskatchewan border, a traveller from Surrey witnessed the "magic" of prairie thunderstorms. He said, "We were stuck on the edge of town and I remember the bald prairie. There were

seven or eight of us. We sent up our tents . . . no one wanted to sleep. . . . You could smell the rain coming."[153] Hitchhikers told "horror stories" about being marooned in Wawa, Ontario, and an urban legend about a guy who was stuck there for so long he married a local girl.[154] Young travellers discovered what they had in common with people from other provinces. A dairy farmer's daughter hitchhiked around Newfoundland. She "loved being by the ocean in Conche . . . and came to respect the fishermen," who were just like the farmers in Ontario, "generally honest, hard-working and quiet natured."[155] One Christmas Eve in Brockville, two hitchhikers went to the "County Jail and asked for a place to sleep. . . . The cops put us in the women's section . . . we spent the night reading the lipstick messages."[156] Interviewees recall that most rides were with "decent folks, just trying to help someone out." They could tell that adult motorists were "worried about young kids hitchhiking, so they'd stop."[157] One night in Deep River, Ontario, 30 or 40 hitchhikers were preparing for a night in the ditch with the black flies.

> Suddenly, a long row of cars came rolling out of the town of Deep River to where we were situated on the Trans-Canada Highway. We, of course, had visions of *Easy Rider* in our minds and weren't sure what was coming. Well, much to our surprise, the convoy of cars was filled with townspeople . . . they'd come out to see if we needed a place to sleep and a hot meal. . . . I asked a guy why they would pick up such a scruffy, dirty bunch of longhaired kids. He said, "We have kids of our own out on the road . . . and we'd like to know that someone's treating them decently as well."[158]

Hitchhiking was a rite of passage for many restless teenagers and twenty-somethings who thumbed along the Trans-Canada Highway to points unknown. Youth cultures tend to be temporary solutions to issues that develop when adolescents encounter "gaps" between what is happening in their lives and "what they have been led to believe would happen."[159] While on the road, hitchhikers took pride in the unpredictability and risks; however, once they were ready to leave the road, the temporal gaze and spatial topography became less clear. After a year on the road, a teenager later remembered this dissonant moment clearly. "It was the Thursday before Thanksgiving. . . . We were sitting on the curb in Gastown, reading *Jonathan Livingston Seagull* and getting really inspired by the book. I started thinking how nice it would be back in Ontario. . . . All the kids got together up at the cottage for Thanksgiving weekend. . . . I said: 'Why don't we just go home?'" His tourist gaze shifted from the romance and freedom he coveted back to the "familiar, convenience and guidance" of family and friends.[160]

Canada's youth hitchhiking "craze" declined in the mid-1970s because anti-hitchhiking groups put pressure on the police and RCMP to levy fines and enforce restrictions on highways, and some local municipalities succeeded in enacting by-laws banning hitchhiking in towns and cities. The media publicized the link between hitchhiking and a number of murders. The commercial tourism sector increased the number of cheap alternatives for young passengers through student discounts and stand-by tickets on Greyhound coaches, CN/VIA railway, and airlines. In the early 1970s, funding and monitoring the activities in youth hostels, especially in the aftermath of the FLQ kidnappings, was an opportunity for the federal government to maintain their popularity with young people and keep the student movement under surveillance. In 1977, the secretary of state established Katimavik, which offered youth the opportunity to travel and volunteer in different parts of the country. Under the supervision of bilingual group leaders, Katimavik's original three rules were no sex, no drugs, and no hitchhiking.[161]

In the 1970s, thousands of young Canadians became tourists, drifters, and wanderers in their own regions and provinces as well as across the continent. By resisting, subverting, and improvising hegemonic class and gender expectations, they put a new twist on the rituals associated with traditional Canadian tourism. Then as now, their road stories highlight biographical moments when their understandings of landscapes and citizenship were formed. By self-consciously adorning themselves with beads, feathers, Canada flags, and long bushy hair, or by flipping a peace sign to oncoming traffic, they performed embodied rituals of a romantic subculture. In 1967, a Wawa boy and a neighbour girl hitchhiked all the way to Montreal for Expo '67, but did not go in because they "didn't give a damn!"[162] It was the trip, not the destination, that defined the experience.

Notes

1. Christopher Howard, "Speeding Up and Slowing Down: Pilgrimage and Slow Travel Through Time," in Simone Fullagar, Kevin Markwell, and Erica Wilson, eds., *Slow Tourism: Experiences and Mobilities* (Bristol: Channel View Publications, 2012), p. 11.

2. Anders Sørenson, "Backpacker Ethnography," *Annals of Tourism Research*, vol. 30, no. 4 (2003), p. 849; Greg Richards and Julie Wilson, "Drifting Towards the Global Nomad" in Richards and Wilson, eds., *The Global Nomad: Backpacker Travel in Theory and Practice* (Clevedon: Channel View Publications, 2004), p. 6; Kate Simpson, "Dropping Out or Signing Up? The Professionalization of Youth Travel," *Antipode*, vol. 37, no. 3 (June 2005), p. 448.

3. The term "transient youth" was coined during the St-Adele Consultation. Canadian Welfare Council, *Transient Youth: Report of an Inquiry in the Summer of 1969* (Ottawa: Canadian Welfare Council, 1970), pp. 5, 9–10; John A. Byles, *Alienation, Deviance and Social Control: A Study of Adolescents in Metropolitan Toronto* (Toronto: Interim Research Project on Unreached Youth, 1969), pp. 7–10, 77–78.

4. "Youth Going Nowhere in Search of Adventure," *Globe and Mail*, July 18, 1970.

5. Greg Richards and Julie Wilson, "Widening Perspectives in Backpacker Research," in Richards and Wilson, eds., *The Global Nomad*, p. 265; Jo-Anne Hecht and David Martin, "Backpacking and Hostel-Picking: An Analysis from Canada," *International Journal of Contemporary Hospitality Management*, vol. 18, no. 1 (2006), pp. 70–71; Marg Tiyce and Erica Wilson, "Wandering Australia: Independent Travelers and Slow Journeys Through Time and Space" in Fullagar, Markwell, and Wilson, eds., *Slow Tourism*, pp. 115, 117; Stephen Wearing, Deborah Stevenson, and Tamara Young, *Tourist Cultures: Identity, Place and the Traveller* (London: Sage Publications, 2012), p. 47; Sørenson, "Backpacker Ethnography," p. 852. For Canada, see Lawrence Aronsen, *City of Love and Revolution: Vancouver in the Sixties* (Vancouver: New Start Books, 2010), p. 18; Doug Owram, *Born at the Right Time: A History of the Baby-Boom Generation* (Toronto: University of Toronto Press, 1996), p. 206; Crystal Luxmore, "Vice, Vagabonds, and VD: The Skyrocketing

Popularity of Hitchhiking During the Sixties and Seventies Led to a Generation of 'Modern Nomads,'" *The Walrus*, July 2008, accessed March 22, 2011.

6. Graeme Chesters and David Smith, "The Neglected Art of Hitch-Hiking: Risk, Trust and Sustainability," *Sociological Research Online*, vol. 6, no. 3 (2001), section 1.2; Erik Cohen, "Nomads from Affluence: Notes on the Phenomenon of Drifter-Tourism," *International Journal of Comparative Studies*, vol. 14, nos. 1–2 (March 1973), p. 90.

7. John Urry, *The Tourist Gaze: Leisure and Travel in Contemporary Societies* (London: Sage, 2002). The individual solitary gaze is the romantic gaze and the collective gaze is levelled at sights and events where crowds of fellow-gazers add to the experience. See also Erving Goffman, *Presentation of Self in Everyday Life* (New York: Doubleday, 1961); Stanley Cohen, *Folk Devils and Moral Panics* (London: Routledge, 2002); Mike Brake, *Comparative Youth Culture: The Sociology of Youth Cultures and Youth Subcultures in America, Britain, and Canada* (New York: Routledge, 1985).

8. Chandra Mukerji sees hitchhiking as a "voluntary role." Hitchhikers may "spend only a few months or summers on the road, never committing themselves to the road in the way that a worker may become committed to their jobs, but they can develop stakes in making life on the road a stable, if not long-term, source of identity." See Chandra Mukerji, "Bullshitting: Road Lore among Hitchhikers," *Social Problems*, vol. 25, no. 3 (February 1978), pp. 246–247.

9. Erik Cohen, "Toward a Sociology of International Tourism," *Social Research*, vol. 39, no. 1 (Spring 1972), p. 177.

10. Mimi Sheller and John Urry, "The City and the Car," *International Journal of Urban and Regional Research*, vol. 24, no. 4 (December 2000), pp. 737, 749.

11. Irena Ateljevic and Stephen Doorne, "Theoretical Encounters: A Review of Backpacker Literature" in Richards and Wilson, eds., *The Global Nomad*, p. 62; Torun Elsrud, "Risk Creation in Traveling: Backpacker Adventure Narration," *Annals of Tourism Research*, vol. 38, no. 3 (January 2001), p. 600; Chiam Noy, "Traveling for Masculinity: The Construction of Bodies/Spaces in Israeli Backpackers' Narratives" in A. Prichard, N. Morgan, I Atelijevic, and C. Harris, eds., *Tourism and Gender: Embodiment, Sensuality and Experience* (Oxford: CAB International, 2007), p. 48.

12. Cohen, "Towards a Sociology," pp. 89–90; Jay Vogt, "Wandering: Youth and Travel Behavior," *Annals of Tourism Research*, vol. 4, no. 1 (September/October 1976), p. 33; Phil Macnaughton and John Urry, eds., *Bodies of Nature* (London: Sage in association with Theory, Culture, and Society, 2001), p. 2.

13. Luke Desforges, "Traveling the World, Identity and Travel Biography," *Annals of Tourism Research*, vol. 27, no. 4 (2000), pp. 10–11.

14. Darya Maoz, "The Mutual Gaze," *Annals of Tourism Research*, vol. 33, no. 1 (2005), pp. 221–239, and "The Conquerors and the Settlers: Two Groups of Young Israeli Backpackers in India" in Richards and Wilson, eds., *The Global Nomad*, pp. 115–116.

15. Jeremy Packer, *Mobility without Mayhem: Safety, Cars and Citizenship* (Durham, NC: Duke University Press, 2008), p. 91.

16. In 1970, the Canadian Welfare Council was reconfigured and renamed the Canadian Council of Social Development. See Canadian Welfare Council, *Transient Youth;* Canadian Welfare Council, *More About Transient Youth* (Ottawa: Canadian Welfare Council, 1970); Canadian Council of Social Development, *Transient Youth, 70–71: Report of an Inquiry about Programs in 1970, and Plans for 1971* (Ottawa: Department of National Health and Welfare, 1970); Canadian Council of Social Development, *Youth, '71* (Ottawa: Department of National Health and Welfare, 1972).

17. One traveller warned Mukerji that hitchhikers like to bullshit. By this he meant they told great stories that may not be entirely true, but were valuable nonetheless. Like Georg Simmel, Mukerji sees "bullshitting as a form of sociability" ("Bullshitting," pp. 241, 244).

18. Noy, "Traveling for Masculinity," p. 67.

19. Reginald Bibby defines the baby boomers as born between 1945 and 1965 in *The Boomer Factor* (Bastion: Toronto, 2006), p. 3; Doug Owram says that "if you were born in 1960 you are more likely a Generation X-er in outlook and experience, what ever the demographers say" (*Born at the Right Time,* introduction). See also Lesley Andres and Johanna Wyn, *The Making of a Generation: The Children of the 1970s in Adulthood* (Toronto: University of Toronto Press, 2010), p. 33.

20. Interview with Mark Forsythe, "Hitchhiking in 1971," *BC Almanac* (CBC, Vancouver, June 10, 2011), https://gpodder.net/podcast/bc-almanac-from-cbc-radio-british-columbia/ hitchhiking-in-1971/; Interview with Anna Maria Tremonti, "Hitch-Hiking Eco-Friendly Transportation or Risky Ride," *The Current* (CBC, Toronto, March 13, 2013), www.cbc.ca/thecurrent/episode/2013/03/13/hitch-hiking-ecofriendly-transportation-or-risky-ride.

21. Sørenson, "Backpacker Ethnography," p. 853.

22. Wearing, Stevenson, and Young, *Tourist Cultures*, p. 47.

23. Steve Penfold, *The Donut: A Canadian History* (Toronto: University of Toronto Press, 2008), p. 54.

24. *Ibid.*; Owram, *Born at the Right Time,* p. 181.

25. John T. Schlebecker, "An Informal History of Hitchhiking," *Historian*, vol. 20, no. 3 (May 1958), p. 311; "Just Kids' Safety: Here's Where We Meet," *Globe and Mail*, July 9, 1932; "Along Boy Scout Trails; Discourage Hitch-Hiking," *Globe and Mail*, December 10, 1932; "Along Boy Scout Trails; Hitch-Hiking Taboo," *Globe and Mail*, June 3, 1933; Robert Sellow, Juliana Shellow, Elliot Liebow, and Elizabeth Unger, "Suburban

Runaways of the 1960," *Monograph for the Society of Research in Child Development*, vol. 42, no. 3 (1967), pp. 29, 31.

26. Schlebecker, "An Informal History of Hitchhiking," p. 311; "A Canadian's Journey: Hitch-hiking round the World," *The Scotsman*, September 14, 1928; "Any Mode of Travel Welcome as Youths Head for Congress," *Globe and Mail*, June 22, 1939; "Two Students Hitch-hike 600 Miles to Spend Week-end at Home," *Globe and Mail*, November 12, 1938; "Young Hitch-Hikers Have Bennett's Blessing," *Globe and Mail*, July 27, 1934; "He Thumbed His Way Through College," *The Reader's Digest*, May 1941, pp. 77–78; "Grows With Hitch-Hiking Among Students," *Globe and Mail*, December 12, 1935; "Emily Post Gives Nod to Hitch-hiking and Frames Rules for 'Defense Debutants,'" *New York Times*, December 23, 1942.

27. "Hitch-hikes across Huron to Save Farm," *Globe and Mail*, January 30, 1935; A photograph of the River Family from Vankoughnet, Ontario, includes three women, two girls and an eight-month old baby under headline: "Hitch-Hikers—Even the Baby," *Globe and Mail*, August 1, 1938.

28. Section 39, Section 1 of the *Highway Traffic Act* provided a fine from $5 to $25 for "soliciting a ride from any motor vehicle on the traveled portion of the public highway." See also "Hitch-Hiking Pass Jobs on Farms, Say Police," *Globe and Mail*, July 10, 1935.

29. Maoz, "The Mutual Gaze," pp. 221–239; Schlebecker, "An Informal History of Hitchhiking," pp. 306, 314; Sheller and Urry, "The City and the Car," pp. 741, 748.

30. Don Wharton, "Thumbs Down on Hitchhikers! Too Many Rob and Kill," *Reader's Digest*, April 1950, pp. 21–25; *The Violent Years*, directed by William Morgan (Alpha Video, 1956, 2003); *The Night Holds Terror*, directed by Andrew Stone (Columbia Pictures, 1955). See Schlebecker, "An Informal History of Hitchhiking," pp. 315–316; Tim Cresswell, "Embodiment, Power and the Politics of Mobility: The Case of Female Tramps and Hobos," *Transactions of the Institute of British Geographers*, vol. 24, no. 2 (1999), pp. 179–181; Richard K. Beardsley and Rosalie Hankey, "A History of the Vanishing Hitchhiker," *California Folklore Quarterly*, vol. 2, no. 1 (January 1943), pp. 19–22; Ernest W. Baughman, "The Hitchhiking Ghost," *Hoosier Folklore*, vol. 6, no. 2 (June 1947), pp. 77–78; Packer, *Mobility without Mayhem*, pp. 84–87.

31. Chesters and Smith, "The Neglected Art of Hitch-Hiking," p. 4.1; Sørenson, "Backpacker Ethnography," p. 852.

32. Personal correspondence with #48, January 19, 2011.

33. Personal correspondence with #31, June 20, 2011.

34. Interview with #91, June 22, 2011.

35. Aronsen, *City of Love*, p. 18.

36. Canadian Welfare Council, *Transient Youth*, p iii.

37. Ibid., pp. 9–10.

38. Ibid., p. 9.

39. Judith Adler, "Youth on the Road: Reflections on the History of Tramping," *Annals of Tourism Research*, vol. 12 (1985), pp. 341, 342.

40. Rolf E. Muuss, *Theories of Adolescence* (New York: Random House, 1964), pp. 56–57.

41. Andres and Wyn, *The Making of a Generation*, p. 33. Stuart Henderson, *Making the Scene: Yorkville and Hip Toronto in the 1960s* (Toronto: University of Toronto Press, 2011), argues that some late baby boomers turned away from materialism and the conformity of suburban imagery (p. 9). Abigail J. Stewart and Cynthia M. Torges, "Social, Historical and Developmental Influences on the Psychology of the Baby Boomer at Midlife" in Susan Krauss Whitbourne and Sherry L. Willis, eds., *The Baby Boomers Grow Up: Contemporary Perspectives in Midlife* (Mahwah, NJ: Lawrence Erlbaum, 2006), say that late baby boomers were engaged and concerned observers of the Vietnam War and the civil rights movement, but they were too young to have been active or mobilized like the early boomers (p. 32).

42. Brake, *Comparative Youth Culture*, p. 152.

43. Cohen, "Nomads from Affluence," p. 93; Wearing, Stevenson, and Young, *Tourist Cultures*, p. 103; Brake, *Comparative Youth Culture*, p. 18.

44. Julie Wilson and Greg Richards, "Backpacker Icons: Influential Literary 'Nomads' in the Formation of Backpacker Identities" in Richards and Wilson, eds., *The Global Nomad*, pp. 123–125.

45. Interview with #87, June 15, 2011.

46. Interview with #80, June 27, 2011.

47. Interview with #82, March 1, 2012.

48. Interview with #22, June 22, 2011.

49. Andres and Wyn, *The Making of a Generation*, p. 33. Henderson says that this generation turned away from materialism and the conformity of suburban imagery by "seeking out an authentic experience after growing up in cookie cutter post-war suburbs" (*Making the Scene*, p. 9).

50. Personal correspondence with #45, January 1, 2012.

51. Interview with #56, June 23, 2011.

52. Interview with #63, February 23, 2012.

53. Personal correspondence with #25, January 19, 2012.

54. John Urry, "The Tourist Gaze 'Revisited,'" *American Behavioral Scientist*, vol. 36, no. 2 (November 1992), p. 172.

55. Brake, *Comparative Youth Culture*, pp. 14, 18.

56. Ibid., pp. 12–16.

57. Interview with #77, June 28, 2011.

58. Interview with #31, October 11, 2012.

59. Interview with #80, June 27, 2011

60. Macnaughton and Urry, eds., *Bodies of Nature*, p. 3.

61. Interview with #83, March 8, 2012.

62. Mukerji, "Bullshitting," p. 243.

63. Interview with #11, June 22, 2011.

64. Interview with #92, June 22, 2011.

65. Interview with #85, June 29, 2011.

66. Interview with #92, June 22, 2011.

67. Interview with former *Winnipeg Free Press* journalist Duncan McMongle, Winnipeg, August 24, 2012.

68. Press interview with 15-year-old Montreal boy on his way to Niagara Falls, *Montreal Gazette*, August 7, 1971.

69. On a hitchhiking trip, backpacks, hippie clothes, physical demeanour and argot are affordances. The concept of "affordance" is used in tourism research to animate the role that material objects and artefacts play in transforming the "places and landscapes" the traveller encounters. According to Michael Haldrup and Jonas Larsen, *Tourism, Performance and the Everyday: Consuming the Orient* (London: Routledge, 2009), "a variety of prosthetic objects and technologies...afford increased bodily capabilities, and as such, they expand the affordances that nature permits the otherwise 'pure' [naked] body" (p. 6); Ateljevic and Doorne, "Theoretical Encounters," p. 60; Tiyce and Wilson, "Wandering Australia," p. 117.

70. Personal correspondence with #25, January 19, 2012.

71. Ateljevic and Doorne, "Theoretical Encounters," p. 72. Feminist studies of women on the road include Carol Sanger, "Girls and the Getaway: Cars, Culture, and the Predicament of Gendered Space," *University of Pennsylvania Law Review*, vol. 144, no. 2 (December 1995); Alexandra Ganser, "On the Asphalt Frontier: American Women's Road Narratives, Spatiality, and Transgression," *Journal of International Women's Studies*, vol. 7, no. 4 (May 2006).

72. Interview with #80, June 27, 2011. The Canadian Welfare Council noted that the young women they surveyed were ambivalent about marriage (*Transient Youth*, p. 105).

73. Interview with #81a and #81b, June 23, 2011.

74. James R. Greenley and David G. Rice, "Female Hitchhiking: Strain, Control, and Subcultural Approaches," *Sociological Focus*, vol. 7, no. 1 (Winter 1973-1974), p. 98. Typical non-feminist studies are Robert W. Johnson and James H. Johnson, "A Cross Validation of the *Sn* Scale on the Psychological Screening Inventory with Female Hitchhikers," *Journal of Clinical Psychology*, vol. 34, no. 2 (April 1978), p. 366-367; Nicholas Guéguen, "Bust Size and Hitchhiking: A Field Study," *Perceptual and Motor Skills*, vol. 105, no. 3 (December 2007), p. 1295.

75. Interview with #83, March 8, 2012.

76. Interview with #96, June 22, 2011.

77. Interview with # 48.

78. Interview with #83, March 8, 2012.

79. Interview with #91, June 22, 2011; Interview with #76, June 29, 2011. Analysis of the role of cars in rape cases suggests the "law assumes that a woman who gets into a man's car or gives him a lift in her's also gives a proxy for consent to sex." (Sanger, "Girls and the Getaway," p. 711).

80. Greenley and Rice, "Female Hitchhiking," p. 99.

81. Maoz, "The Mutual Gaze," pp. 222, 225.

82. Ibid.

83. Brake, *Comparative Youth Culture*, p. 18.

84. Glenbow Museum, Canadian Youth Hostel Association, news clipping from *Penticton Herald*, May 21, 1971.

85. For many, the Mecca of their journey was "Canada's Los Angeles, the almost always sunny city of Vancouver" (*Globe and Mail*, August 10, 1970).

86. Press interview with teenager from Aurora, Ontario, Richard Needham, "Something to Do, Nothing to Do," *Globe and Mail*, September 13, 1966.

87. Muuss, *Theories of Adolescence*, pp. 16–17; Canadian Welfare Council, *Transient Youth*, p. 1; Cynthia Comacchio, *The Dominion of Youth: Adolescence and the Making of Modern Canada, 1920 to 1950* (Waterloo, ON: Wilfrid Laurier University Press, 2006), pp. 20, 31.

88. Canadian Welfare Council, *Transient Youth*, p. 67; Owram, *Born at the Right Time*, p. 141.

89. Interview with #92, June 22, 2011.

90. Interview with #56, June 23, 2011.

91. Interview with #82, March 1, 2012.

92. Interview with #82a and #82b, February 22, 2012.

93. Interview with #81a and #81b, June 23, 2011.

94. Interview with #86, March 4, 2012.

95. Ibid.

96. Interview with #48.

97. Parents are also caught in the social trends that regulate parenting practices. In the early 1970s, American popular culture mocked the "square" family man and the oppressed housewife. Naomi Wolf argues that the rising divorce rate eroded the emotional family-centric "contract" between parents and children. Parents were doing "their own thing" too, and the "modern 'kid,' whom no one paid attention to was born." Naomi Wolf, *Promiscuities: The Secret Struggle for Womanhood* (New York: Random House, 1997), pp. 21–22.

98. Personal correspondence with #45, January 1, 2012.

99. Richard Needham, "Something to Do, Nothing to Do," *Globe and Mail*, September 13, 1966.

100. Interview with #78, June 27, 2011.

101. "Youth Going Nowhere in Search of Adventure," *Globe and Mail*, July 18, 1970.

102. Glenbow Museum, Canadian Youth Hostel Association Archive, "Canada's Great Trek: 40,000 Transients Will Walk this Summer," *Vancouver Province*, April 6, 1971.

103. Martin Dorrell, "Going Down the Road: A Really Big Bedroom," *Globe and Mail*, June 14, 1971.

104. "Thousands of Youngsters Will be on the Road this Summer," *Montreal Gazette*, August 25, 1970.

105. "50,000 Transients Only the Beginning," *Vancouver Sun*, February 5, 1971.

106. Glenbow Museum, Canadian Youth Hostel Association Archives, "City Braced for Transients," *Calgary Herald*, May 17, 1972.

107. "Army of Hitch-Hikers Already on the March," *Globe and Mail*, June 22, 1972.

108. Liberal leadership convention polls showed that young Canadians overwhelmingly preferred Trudeau. A youth

said, Trudeau was "the most exciting single thing that could happen to this country" (Owram, *Born at the Right Time*, p. 201).

109. Glenbow Museum, Canadian Youth Hostel Association Archives, Letter from Pierre Elliot Trudeau to Members of the Canadian Youth Hostel Association, *Pathfinder*, September 1968; Canadian Youth Hostel Association 1986-1969 Annual Report.

110. The taskforce report includes a scholarly bibliography that is 12 pages long. Canadian Welfare Council, *Transient Youth*, pp. 5–7; Greeley and Rice, "Female Hitchhikers," p. 98.

111. Contemporary sociologists argued that youth alienation and deviance increased as social class increased. Most hippies were middle class and became deviant as a consequence of their alienation from social institutions (religion, school, or work), whereas working class delinquents became alienated (isolated and stigmatized) as a consequence of their law-breaking behaviour. Byles, *Alienation, Deviance and Social Control*, p. 11; Canadian Welfare Council, *Transient Youth*, p. 60.

112. Canadian Welfare Council, *Transient Youth*, pp. 9, 105.

113. "Military Building Opened for Hitchhiking Youths," *Globe and Mail*, July 9, 1970.

114. Canadian Welfare Council, *Transient Youth*, pp. 5, 9–10.

115. Glenbow Museum, Canadian Youth Hostel Association Archive, Clipping File, *Penticton Herald*, June 8, 1971, and *Calgary Herald*, May 10, 1971.

116. Glenbow Museum, Canadian Youth Hostel Association Archive, Prince Edward Island Association Photo Album, "Women Hold Position Along Hostel Barrier," *The Guardian* [Charlottetown], June 8, 1971.

117. "A Communal Pilgrimage—Along Canada's Highways," *New York Times*, June 20, 1971; "They Use Their Thumbs to Roam the Land," *New York Times*, August 8, 1971; "Youth in Canada: Drifting Around with the Government's Blessing," *New York Times*, April 22, 1973.

118. Canadian Welfare Council, *More About Transient Youth*, p. 31.

119. Glenbow Museum, Canadian Youth Hostel Association Archive, Clipping File, "Poll Changes Transient 'Pauper Image'," *Calgary Herald*, September 6, 1972; "Hitchers On the Road a Blind Alley Withdrawn," *Montreal Gazette*, June 20, 1972.

120. "Youth in Canada: Drifting Around with the Government's Blessing," *New York Times*, April 22, 1973.

121. 600,000 copies were printed. See Michael Moore, "The New Ottawa Booklet That's Bound to Lead Youth Astray," *Globe and Mail*, June 17, 1972.

122. Martin Dorrell, "Going Down the Road: Singin' the Espanola Blues," *Globe and Mail*, June 10, 1971.

123. Ateljevic and Doorne, "Theoretical Encounters," p. 64.

124. Peter Kelly, "The Entrepreneurial Self, and 'Youth-At-Risk': Exploring the Horizons of Identity in the Twenty-first Century," *Journal of Youth Studies*, vol. 9, no. 1 (February 2006), p. 17; Johanna Wyn and Peter Dwyer, "New Directions in Research on Youth in Transition," *Journal of Youth Studies*, vol. 2, no. 1 (1999), pp. 9, 16. Adolescence is an historical construct but it is very real to the individual experiencing it. See Comacchio, *The Dominion of Youth*, pp. viii, 216.

125. Interview with #63, February 23, 2012; Interview with #29, March 23, 2013; Interview with Patrick Esmonde White, National Coordinator of Temporary Youth, Hostel Task Force (1970), December 5, 2012.

126. Crouch and Desforges, "The Sensuous in the Tourist Encounter," p. 6.

127. Interviews with #80, June 27, 2011, and with #63, February 23, 2012.

128. Interview with #81a and #81b, June 23, 2011.

129. Interview with #83, March 8, 2012.

130. Interview with #80, June 27, 2011; Annalee Grant, "History of the Point: The Jasper Internment Camp, *The Fitzhugh: Jasper's Independent Newspaper*, February 3, 2011.

131. "Dwelling in mobility" is a psychological process that enables travellers to feel at home in environments that are transient, unfamiliar and strange. David Crouch and Luke Desforges, "The Sensuous in the Tourist Encounter," *Tourist Studies*, vol. 3, no. 1 (April 2003), p. 9.

132. Ibid., p. 18.

133. Owram, *Born at the Right Time*, p. 14; "Canadian Seek to Spur National Consciousness, *New York Times*, May 11, 1975.

134. Personal correspondence with #11.

135. Personal correspondence with #27, June 28, 2011.

136. Owram, *Born at the Right Time*, p. 14; "Canadian Seek to Spur National Consciousness," *New York Times*, May 11, 1975.

137. Interview with #79, June 22, 2011.

138. Interview with #91, June 22, 2011

139. Interview with #63, February 23, 2012.

140. Cresswell, "Embodiment, Power and the Politics of Mobility," p. 186; Ganser, "On the Asphalt Frontier," pp. 160-161; Sanger, "Girls and the Getaway," pp. 715, 737–734. Macnaughton and Urry argue, "Affordances do not cause behavior, but constrain it along certain possibilities" (*Bodies of Nature*, pp. 2, 9).

141. Interview with #85, June 29, 2011

142. Interview with #81a and #81b, June 23, 2011.

143. Interview with #89, June 22, 2011.

144. Interview with #49, June 25, 2011.

145. Tim Cresswell and Tanu Priya Uteng, "Gendered Mobilities: Towards an Holistic Understanding" in Cresswell and Priya Uteng, eds., *Gendered Mobilities* (Aldershot: Ashgate, 2008) pp. 3, 5.

146. Interview with #85, June 29, 2011.

147. His sign said, "Keep B.C. Clean, Take Me to Seattle." See "Gimmick," *Winnipeg Free Press*, August 1, 1973.

148. Interview with #88, June 22, 2011.

149. Interview with #96, June 23, 2011.

150. Interview with #81a, #81b and #90, June 22, 2011.

151. Mitch Rose, "Landscapes and Labyrinths," *Geoforum*, vol. 33, no. 4 (November 2002), argues that landscapes become significant within a network of meanings and relations. Its "ongoing presence in the world is contingent upon what it initiates, activates and inspires elsewhere" (pp. 456–457).

152. Personal correspondence with #18, December 21, 2011.

153. Interview with #63, February 23, 2012.

154. Interview with #30, October 11, 2012; Interview with Duff Sigurdson, Peachland, BC, August 22, 2012.

155. Personal communication with #16, January 26, 2012.

156. Personal communication with #25. January 19, 2012.

157. *Ibid.*

158. Personal communication with #48, January 19, 2012.

159. Brake, *Comparative Youth Culture*, p. 21.

160. Desforges, "Traveling the World," p. 938; Vogt, "Wandering," p. 39; Cohen, "Toward a Sociology," pp. 176-177.

161. Michael Sherraden and Donald J. Eberly, "Reflection on Katimavik, an Innovative Canadian Youth Program," *Children and Youth Services Review*, vol. 8, no. 4 (1986), p. 290.

162. Interview with #30.

PRIMARY DOCUMENT

Canadian Welfare Council, "Transient Youth: Report of an Inquiry in the Summer of 1969," excerpt

Early in 1969, the Canadian Welfare Council came to the conclusion that there should be an inquiry into a situation that is obvious to everyone who travels by car: the presence of large numbers of young people travelling on the summer roads. In itself, the situation might appear to be simply a feature of the pleasant freedom of summer after the rigours of work and winter. For many young people, and for the drivers who give them lifts, it's no more than that. Why then an inquiry?

First, the increasing number of young people who travel has created problems of shelter and of health to such a degree that some communities have organized their resource to cope with the problems. [. . .]

Second, youth on the roads may serve to remind people of the widespread rebellion of youth in the 1960s that has become stereotyped as "alienation." Opinion is divided as to the merits of the rebellion.

Third, communities are anxious about the apparent increase among young people of theft, disease, and drug misuse. Here too, public opinion s divided. It is divided between those who find the picture alarming and those who believe that the picture has been blown up by people who are apt to over-dramatize every social problem. [. . .]

[. . .] It is naive to lump transient youth together and call them hippies. [. . .] In the youth culture, which parallels what might be called the mainstream culture, there are groupings that are discernable but they are not discrete, they are not stable groupings either, since people move in and out of them because of changes in their interests, geographic mobility and, alas, the implacable process of ageing even in the teens and twenties. The following are discernable groups:

continued

Most observers think that the largest group of transient youth consists of young people, usually students, on a carefree holiday. They are personally well-organized and are able to handle their situations well. The report of the YMCA hostel in Sault Ste Marie states that "the great majority claimed that their reason for travelling was to see Canada." We believe this reason would be dominant everywhere. [. . .]

People to have adopted the hippie value system are present in the total group of transients. They are probably not numerous and everywhere people seem to believe that their numbers are decreasing. However, their influence is felt, especially through their gentleness toward the very young, the sick and disturbed.

There are weekenders and teeny-boppers who take a break from affluence and stability. They come from stable homes and like to drop into the youth milieu downtown out of curiosity or because their own neighbours are unattractive and boring or they are looking for boyfriends. Their average age may be 17 years, with a good many who are younger.

Youth often moves from economically poor areas into the big cities with the idea, which may be vague or definite, of bettering their conditions. They are often poorly educated and poorly equipped for the labour market. [. . .] Young persons of Indian background, literally moving from the Canadian bush to the metropolis, have many problems besides lack of employment and skills, not the least of which are the hang-ups of the dominant white culture.

Again, there are the black-leather jacket types who generally have dropped out of school and employment, may have delinquent characteristics, and who are on the move most of the year. As a rule they are somewhat older than other transients. Particular concern is often expressed about the very young girls who are associated with these groups or organized gangs. [. . .]

Source: Excerpt from Canadian Welfare Council,
"Transient Youth: Report of an Inquiry in the Summer of 1969," Ottawa, 1970, pp. 1–6

Study Questions

1. What did it mean to be a youth in the early twentieth century?
2. These essays show university-age students establishing sites where youth subcultures flourished. Compare and contrast these loci of identity formation. Think about these sites in relation to the world of adults and authority—were they truly separate from this world? What role did notions of risk and danger play in these sites' popularity?
3. Examine the primary sources included here. How do the textual and visual sources help us to understand the category of "youth" at different times and spaces? What role does self-presentation play in identity formation?

Selected Bibliography

Articles

Axelrod, Paul, "Spying on the Young in Depression and War: Students, Youth Groups and the RCMP, 1935–1942" *Labour / Le Travail* 35 (Spring, 1995): 43–63.

Chenier, Elise, "Class, Gender, and the Social Standard: The Montreal Junior League, 1912–1939," *The Canadian Historical Review* 90, 4 (December 2009): 671–710.

Comacchio, Cynthia, "Inventing the Extracurriculum: High School Culture in Interwar Ontario" *Ontario History* 2001 93(1): 33–56.

Levi, Charles, "Sex, Drugs, Rock & Roll, and the University College Lit: The University of Toronto Festivals, 1965–69," *Historical Studies in Education/Revue d'histoire de l'éducation* 18, 2 (2006): 163–90.

Martel, Marcel, "'They smell bad, have diseases and are lazy'": RCMP Officers Reporting on Hippies in the Late Sixties," *The Canadian Historical Review* 90, 2 (June 2009): 215–45.

Myers, Tamara, and Joan Sangster, "Retorts, Runaways and Riots: Patterns of Resistance in Canadian Reform Schools for Girls, 1930–60" *Journal of Social History* 34, 3 (Spring, 2001): 669–97.

Sethna, Christabelle, "The University of Toronto Health Service, Oral Contraception, and Student Demand for Birth Control, 1960–1970," *Historical Studies in Education/Revue d'histoire de l'éducation* 17, 2 (2005): 265–92.

Walden, Keith, "Male Toronto College Students Celebrate Hallowe'en, 1884–1910," *Canadian Historical Review* 68 (1987): 1–34.

Books

Adams, Mary Louise, *The Trouble with Normal: Postwar Youth and the Making of Heterosexuality* (Toronto: University of Toronto Press, 1997).

Bienvenue, Louise, *Quand la jeunesse entre en scène: l'action catholique avant la révolution tranquille* (Montreal: Boréal, 2003).

Comacchio, Cynthia, *Dominion of Youth: Adolescence and the Making of Modern Canada, 1920 to 1950* (Waterloo: Wilfrid Laurier University Press, 2006).

Gidney, Catherine, *Tending the Student Body: Youth, Health, and the Modern University* (Toronto: University of Toronto Press, 2015).

Hebert, Karine, *Impatient d'être soi-même: les étudiants montrealais, 1895–1960* (Montreal: Les Presses de l'Université du Québec: 2008).

Henderson, Stuart, *Making the Scene: Toronto and Hip Culture in the 1960s* (Toronto: University of Toronto Press, 2011).

Wall, Sharon, *The Nurture of Nature: Childhood, Antimodernism and Ontario Summer Camps, 1920–1955* (Vancouver: UBC Press, 2009).

INDEX